INDIA SINCE INDEPENDENCE

MAKING SENSE OF INDIAN POLITICS

V. KRISHNA ANANTH

Pearson

PHOTO CREDITS

All photographs used in this book are courtesy *The New Indian Express*

The views and opinions expressed in this book are those of the author, and the facts are as reported by him; they do not necessarily represent the official position or the views of the publisher.

ISBN 978-81-317-3465-0

First Impression

Published by Pearson India Education Services Pvt. Ltd, CIN: U72200TN2005PTC057128

Head Office: 1st Floor, Berger Tower, Plot No. C-001A/2, Sector 16B, Noida – 201 301,Uttar Pradesh, India.

Registered Office: Featherlite, 'The Address' 5th Floor, Survey No 203/10B, 200 Ft MMRD Road,Zamin Pallavaram, Chennai - 600044
Website: in.pearson.com; Email:companysecretary.india@pearson.com

Digitally printed in India by Trinity Academy for Corporate Training Ltd, New Delhi in the year of 2025.

Indian politics is a riveting drama of interesting personalities, ideas in conflict, intrigues, serious policy-making and more. But there are few books that offer a comprehensive view of what has transpired in the name of politics in India in the last 60 years. *India Since Independence* is a work of political history shorn of academic jargon and rich in details.

The Crest Edition—The Times of India, 3 April 2010

A sound and exhaustive narrative of 'high politics' in Independent India, ... this book is useful for students and general readers alike. Two things about the organisation of the book and writing style of the author are noteworthy. The subject has been chronologically, not thematically, treated. This has its own advantage. Someone interested in knowing just what happened on June 25, 1975, may turn to the pages on Emergency and be done with it, without much ado.

Bhupendra Yadav, *The Hindu,* 10 November 2009

The book also takes into account some of the most challenging and testing times faced by the country like the unrest in Assam, Punjab, and Jammu and Kashmir and the political upheaval created by the Bofors scandal, the Ayodhya issue and the implementation of the Mandal Commission ... the analysis as detailed in the book gives a new vantage point to observe these scenarios which ... almost threatened to balkanise the country .... If history is about facts and journalism is about storytelling, [this] is what you get when both of these combine. V. Krishna Ananth's book is simply unputdownable.

Santosh Kr Singh, *The Tribune,* 18 April 2010

A strictly factual narrative [which can] help in an informed debate on the Emergency along with allied issues and meet the need of those trying to find and fathom the event's extra-party-political significance .... For [many], Ananth's story brings back a slew of memories.

J. Sri Raman, *The Herald of India,* October 2009

Krishna Ananth has succeeded in providing an account that would stand historical and literary scrutiny and would help the readers, not necessarily students, obtain a proper understanding of post-Independence Indian history. It is no mean achievement for a historian to steer clear of political bias in writing a book of this nature, particularly when he too had played a small role, either as a reporter or as a political commentator.

A. J. Philip, *Economic and Political Weekly,* 17 April 2010

If Ramachandra Guha, in his sweeping *India After Gandhi*, approached political events shaping modern India (1948–1989) from a historian's point of view, Ananth's take is political, thick with details. There is plenty of material for researchers looking for a snapshot view of politics.

The Indian Express, 28 November 2009

In a succinct account suitably peppered with anecdotes, V. Krishna Ananth's book is an attempt to fill an important space—a journalistic, non-academic pedagogical narrative for students who wish to explore the contours of the evolution of politics in independent India.

Hormazd Mehta, *Combat Law*

To my parents

Contents

Acknowledgements

It was in the course of formulating and teaching a module on political reporting at the Asian College of Journalism, Chennai, that I felt the need for a book of this kind. The module was intended to equip the aspiring journalists with a sense of history while they looked into the contemporary political events. However, I found in them a sense of remoteness whenever I lectured to them about an event that I felt was contemporary. It then occurred to me that even the national Emergency of June 1975–March 1977 belonged to the distant past to them. The book was conceived in that context.

The training that I received from Professor Sabyasachi Bhattacharya, my supervisor at the Centre for Historical Studies, Jawaharlal Nehru University, New Delhi, equipped me to cull out facts from the past. Bappa, for all of us who had the privilege to work under his supervision, was a task master. He taught me to respect facts in history. That made the difference.

The immediate provocation, however, came from V. P. Singh. In one of my casual interactions with him, he felt that it was time I began working on a book. I began thinking of a break from active journalism. I had, by then, gained immensely from my association with *The Hindu*. N. Ravi and Malini Parthasarathy of *The Hindu* were liberal in letting me travel across the hinterlands and explore the political terrain across the country and accumulate information. K. K. Katyal, Chief of the Bureau then at *The Hindu* in New Delhi, was a constant source of guidance.

The long interactive sessions I had with Madhu Limaye helped me gain insights into our political history. Interactions with George Fernandes, Jaipal Reddy, Surendra Mohan, Sharad Yadav, Nitish Kumar and Ramakrishna Hegde helped me make sense of some of the critical events in our short political history. M. S. Appa Rao, freedom fighter, human rights activist and above all a man who loved books, was a source of inspiration.

My parents groomed me into becoming a follower of political events. My father, K. Vaidyanathan, initiated me into the world of political history; and my mother, P. A. Lakshmi, a stoic woman with strong views, infused the confidence in me to chart my own course. E. K. Santha, my best friend and partner, has been a trenchant critique and honest with her comments. Her reviews, at various stages, helped me make this book into what it is. My son, Chinku, still in his teens, did not mind my tantrums and mood swings, during the several months, when I was engrossed in this work. He believed that his father was doing something useful!

My friend, C. Ram Manohar Reddy, stood by me in times of crises. His polite but stern reprimands helped me tide over bad times. M. V. R. Menon, with whom I had long and spirited debates, forced me muster a lot of facts for the making of this book. I acknowledge K. P. R. Nair for his guidance and help in this project from its inception to the end. T. Sigamani shared a lot of documents from his collection and discussions with him were of immense help.

Subhashini Dinesh, my friend, went through the draft of this book and came up with a lot of suggestions. Ruhi Tewari, who happened to be my student for a while, was prompt whenever I asked her for specific information on the events covered in this book.

The librarians at *The Hindu* and *India Today* facilitated access to the back volumes of the publications for reference. Aditya Sinha, Editor-in-Chief, *The New Indian Express,* Chennai, permitted the use of the photographs from their archives. Bala Murali Krishna, P. Nataraj and Rajagopal at *The New Indian Express* culled out the necessary pictures from the archives.

I thank Yegammai Subramanian for having made the index; and Alpana Williams, Preeta Priyamvada and Gaurav Jain at Pearson Education for putting the manuscript together in this form.

V. Krishna Ananth

Prologue

In the first couple of decades after independence, the political discourse in India was guided, by and large, by the legacy of the freedom movement. The reorganisation of states in 1956, for instance, marked the culmination of a political principle that the Indian National Congress had internalised. Congress provincial committees were constituted on linguistic principles rather than on the basis of the administrative divisions evolved by the colonial rulers. A separate committee of the Congress was set up for the Andhra circle to function within the Madras Provincial Congress Committee in 1918 and, over the years, more Congress committees were formed on linguistic basis across the nation.

Similarly, the dynamics of the freedom struggle served as the basis for the evolution of a *national popular culture* that was essentially pluralist in its core and a commitment to democracy was an expression of this at the political level. The Indian National Congress session at Karachi (March 1931) was, in a sense, the culmination of a project to define *swaraj* that began in the early twentieth century; its rudiments were manifest in the spirit of *swadeshi* since 1905. The resolution at the Karachi session was indeed a statement that defined Indian nationalism as an inclusive concept and as rooted in secular and democratic principles. The core of the Republican Constitution adopted after independence was derived from the resolution at the Karachi session of the Indian National Congress.

There have been instances, during the 60 years after independence, when some of these founding principles were threatened. The mobilisation of forces in Assam, Punjab and Kashmir in the early 1980s led the articulate sections in the polity to demand a strong and authoritarian state even if it meant curbing civil rights and curtailing freedom. Over the years, the Indian polity has been led to a situation where the idea of pluralism (whether religious, ethnic or linguistic) is sought to be condemned and even described as divisive. This has been on the rise since the 1980s. The media as well as other platforms for political discussion have reflected this perception in a big way and ended up lending legitimacy to measures that curb democratic rights and freedom. Such enactments as the TADA and POTA were illustrations of these. That these measures failed to prevent the increasing alienation of the democratic state from its people is evident.

The majority of the Indian people, denied as they are of an opportunity to participate in these debates and discussions, have been making use of the elections to express themselves. Meanwhile, members belonging to the articulate classes (constituting the intelligentsia), despite being a minority, have managed to position themselves in critical areas of the democratic edifice. By virtue of this, they play an important role in assisting and guiding the political leadership of the country. The events that have dominated the political arena of independent India reflect the dynamics of this reality. These political events should be seen as part of a historical process, rather than be treated as isolated events.

Such an exercise could lead us to explain the unrest in Punjab and Assam during the 1980s as movements that successfully resisted attempts to destroy the federal principles of the Constitution and as rooted in the dynamics of the freedom struggle. This and many other events that determined the course of India's political discourse can be seen as part of a process. This will necessitate a voyage, back in time and space, to the making of India as a nation and will be of use to navigate the complex mosaic that contemporary Indian politics is made of. For instance, the caste structure and its importance in the political discourse cannot be understood and placed in perspective without discussing the socio-economic structure in the countryside and revealing the important role that caste, as a category, plays in the political discourse.

A discussion of this nature could help us understand the affiliation of the various caste groups with different parties. For instance, the social base of the Congress party (constituted by an alliance of the land-owning upper castes, the landless Dalits and the minorities), in the couple of decades after independence, cannot be explained without discussing the social groups that positioned themselves to guide the course of the Congress party around the time when India won freedom. This, in turn, will explain the character of the independent Indian state and also the nature of the opposition to the Congress at that time.

The results of the two general elections (1952 and 1957) and the landslide win registered by the Congress party can be explained as a reflection of a combination of these factors as well as the ability of the Congress, under Jawaharlal Nehru, to construct a *national political* culture that was essentially modernist and egalitarian, the two core principles of the nationalist struggle. It is imperative for any such discussion then to dwell, at length, into the dynamics of the freedom struggle and focus on the changing face of the Indian National Congress in a historical context.

This discussion, in turn, could lead us to evaluate the character of the political platforms (at that time) that opposed the Congress. The Socialist Party, for instance, was one such platform that led the opposition at that stage. Its legitimate claim to the legacy of the freedom struggle was that its leaders had influenced the radical surge by the Indian National Congress at the Karachi session. The socialists, however, could hardly emerge as the dominant force after independence. An explanation to this could be found in the fact that the Congress party, under Jawaharlal Nehru, could present its own idea of economic development as representing the spirit of independence against the Socialist party's programme of Gandhian Socialism.

Yet another aspect that comes out clearly in this context is that, in the decade and a half after independence, the contest in the political realm was essentially between two distinct approaches to nationalism that evolved from within the Indian National Congress. Both were integral parts of the mainstream national movement and committed to the egalitarian, secular and democratic agenda that was concretised within the Indian National Congress at its Karachi session. In other words, the contest for political power was restricted between the Congress party wedded to Nehru's socialist scheme and the Socialist party committed to Gandhian principles of economic development. Socialism, indeed, was central to both the approaches. The Bharatiya Jan Sangh, formed by leaders who belonged to the Hindu Maha Sabha in 1951 (to which the Rashtriya Swayamsevak Sangh [RSS] lent its cadres as well as ideological basis), was to remain on the fringes of the political discourse. This was the reality for at least a decade after the first general elections.

Similarly, it took at least a decade and a half after independence, before this 'consensus' was questioned in the public sphere. This change was manifest in the formation of the Swatantra Party, whose leaders, including some from the Congress stable, were overtly committed to the idea of free enterprise. It is of significance that the inspiration for the Swatantra Party came from the resolution passed at the Nagpur session of the Congress party (in 1959) committing itself to the idea of land reforms and cooperative farming. In the 1962 general elections, the Swatantra Party polled over 10 million votes and won as many as 18 seats in the Lok Sabha. As for the Jan Sangh, its tally went up from only four seats in the second Lok Sabha (1957–62) to 14 in the 1962 general elections. The Jan Sangh also won in 116 assembly constituencies (in various states in the elections to the assemblies held simultaneously with the Lok Sabha polls) against the 1957 tally of only 49.

This was also the phase that marked the beginning of the decline of the Congress party. It also reflected the beginning of a process when the idea of socialism (whether Nehruvian or Gandhian) was no longer the dominant feature of the *national political* culture. All this took place when Jawaharlal Nehru was still at the helm of the Congress party. This is also the period when the Congress party's claims as the natural inheritor of the *national political* culture came under challenge. While the discourse within the Congress by this time was marked by an intense debate over the need to rethink on the socialistic model, the discourse outside the Congress party too underwent a transformation with the Socialist Party leadership finding it prudent to make common cause with those in the Swatantra bandwagon. In other words, the foundations were laid for the grand unity against the Congress that finally matured before the 1967 general elections.

Thus, it is possible to look at the outcome of the 1967 elections as the fallout of a number of factors such as the failure or the inadequacy of the Nehruvian socialist model to tackle poverty; the monsoons failing in successive years between 1963 and 1965; the demise of Nehru and the tussle within the Congress party; and the emergence of Indira Gandhi at the helm, even while the provincial leadership of the Congress was in the hands of leaders to whom the socialistic pattern of development was a mere rhetoric. In other words, the shape of things, as they unfolded in 1967, could not have been as they were if any one of these events or factors had not taken place in the manner and at the time they took place. This, in turn, will lend the basis to analysing the split in the Congress (in 1969) and the emergence of Indira Gandhi, and the nationalisation of banks and other such measures. Similarly, the Emergency, declared on 25 June 1975 can be seen as part of a process wherein the weak links in the Nehruvian socialist framework were beginning to snap.

This book is an attempt to look at the developments in the political arena after independence from a historical perspective and present as much information as is possible and necessary so that the narrative becomes useful to the reader. It is a conscious decision, hence, to resist the temptation to load the text with a long list of references and footnotes. An extensive list of readings at the end of the book should serve some purpose. The facts presented here are drawn from published sources such as books, government reports and also from newspapers and news magazines of the period.

However, some aspects of India's short political history, such as the genesis of the communist movement, the Dravidian movement or the Shiv Sena and the various trends in the Dalit assertion across the country—distinct in their own way and specific to the region and the long history of the politico-social reforms agenda in those regions—have not been dealt with in this book. An explanation to this omission is that this book is an account of the events as they occurred in history, and is not an attempt to look at the undercurrents and construct a theory. This is not, in any sense, to undermine the relevance of such works. While dealing with a huge canvas as this, in both time and space, it is not possible to propose a theory and be able to do justice to the project.

I have taken care to avoid two concepts – *If* and *But* – in this book and chosen to narrate the events as they happened. In doing so, I was guided by one notion: 'If. Cleopatra's nose was longer or shorter than what it was, even by a fraction of an inch, the history of the world would have been different'. Well, Cleopatra's nose was what it was and hence history moved in a particular way. And that is true of our own short history as a nation and a nation state.

If Sardar Patel had not died in 1950, Jawaharlal Nehru would not have been the natural choice for the prime minister's job in 1952. If Nehru had not marginalised Morarji Desai in 1963, Lal Bahadur Shastri would not have become India's prime minister in 1964; if Indira Gandhi was not Jawaharlal Nehru's daughter, the Congress leaders would not have behaved in the way they did and made her the prime minister in 1966; if Indira Gandhi and Jayaprakash Narayan had reconciled their differences, the Emergency would not have been imposed; if Rajiv Gandhi had realised the importance of the Mandal Commission recommendations, the Congress (I) would not have lost its position of pre-eminence; if Rajiv Gandhi had not spoken out of turn on the Bofors issue, it would not have cost him an electoral defeat; if V. P. Singh had not set out to implement the Mandal report, he could have remained in power for a longer time; and if the Congress (I) had not played its cynical games over the Ayodhya issue, the BJP would not have raised the pitch on the issue.

But then, India's political history moved in a direction, as it did, because all those things happened. The book is intended to record, in context, the events that shaped the political discourse in the course of the half-century after independence. The long narrative accounts stop at June 1991. The events from then, and until Manmohan Singh was sworn in as prime minister in May 2004, are dealt with in as brief a manner as it is possible. They are too recent to warrant as elaborate a treatment as the remote past that the book deals with.

The Interim Cabinet as on 15 October 1946

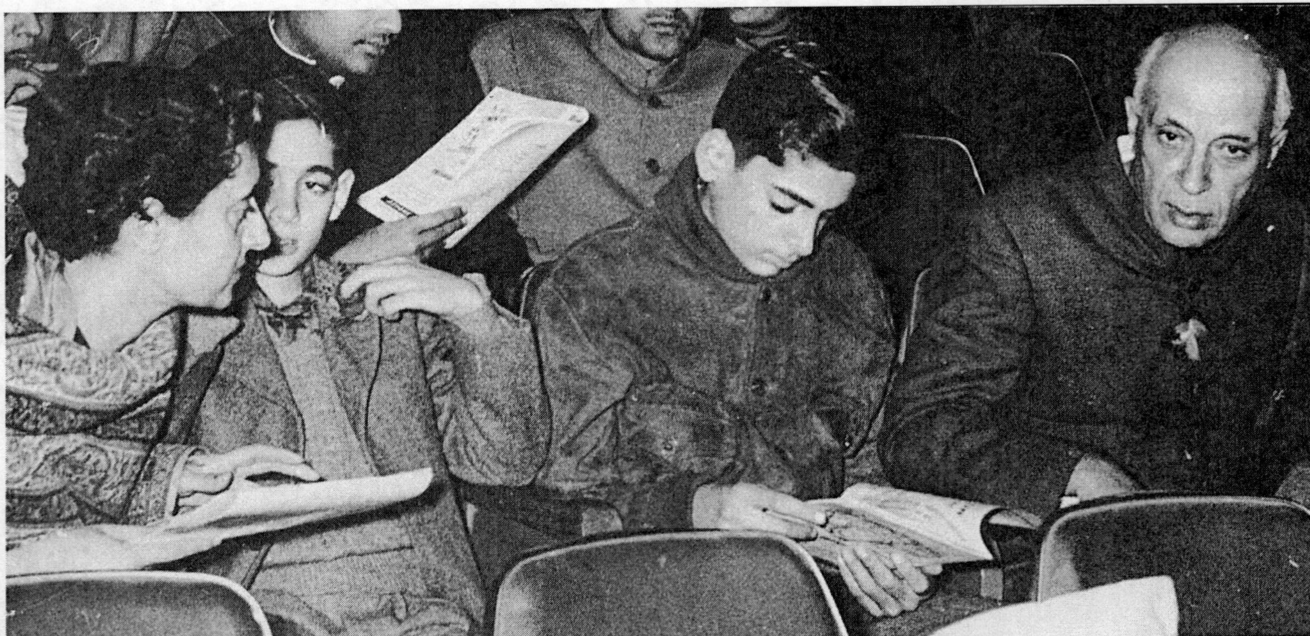

Indira Gandhi, Sanjay Gandhi, Rajiv Gandhi and Jawaharlal Nehru

Morarji Desai, Indira Gandhi and D. R. Gadgil at a meeting of the Planning Commission in 1968, when they were the Finance Minister, Prime Minister and Deputy Chairman of the Planning Commission, respectively

Indira Gandhi addressing the nation from the ramparts of the Red Fort on Independence Day

Jayaprakash Narayan

Sanjay Gandhi

V. P. Singh, Chandra Shekar and Ramakrishna Hegde at the foundation of the Janata Dal in October 1988

Justice H. R. Khanna

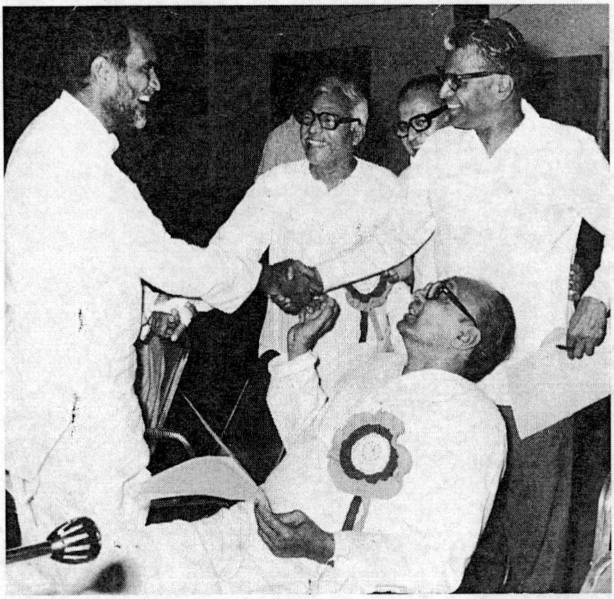

Chandra Shekar, Karpoori Thakur, S. R. Bommai, George Fernandes and Biju Pattnaik (sitting), all leaders of the Janata Party before the disintegration of the Janata Party in 1979

V. P. Singh, Rajiv Gandhi and Arun Singh, when they were the Defence Minister, Prime Minister and the Minister of State for Defence, respectively

I

Nineteenth-Century Intellectuals and the Emergence of Nationalist Thought

> It was in England ... that the bourgeoisie developed out of Indian gold, the unlimited profits of the Indian trade and, later, Indian wars. The profits of Spain ... only strengthened reaction ... and moribund feudalism; Portugal hardly fared better from its Eastern trade ... The Dutch did progress, but the pressure of Spain and France by land and England by sea was fatal. France was a hundred years too late with its bourgeois revolution. In England alone were the necessary conditions satisfied.
>
> —D. D. Kosambi, *An Introduction to the Study of Indian History*

The conclusion of the Battle of Plassey and the series of treaties that led to the various native rulers ceding territory to the East India Company in exchange for large purses and perks to themselves set in motion a process that culminated in the making of the Indian nation. While the birth of the nation had to wait until 15 August 1947, the factors that influenced the making of the Indian nation and the play of forces therein had an impact on the manner in which the political history of independent India unfolded. It is also true that these very factors continue to influence the political discourse today. Hence, it is imperative that the historical roots of Indian nationalism are discussed in brief.

After the fall of the Mughal Empire—the last of the medieval enterprises whose command and revenue system constituted the law in most parts of the subcontinent—the agents and the servants of the English East India Company put in place an administrative structure that was distinct from the past. The East India Company, in this course, imported the theory of law (jurisprudence) that was in vogue in England at that time. This was distinct, in its basics, from the system that prevailed across the subcontinent until then. Its striking feature was the concept of right, as it evolved in the context of the French Revolution and the larger concept of rule of the law. The days of the empire and the emperor were thus brought to an end, marking the birth of a distinct framework on which collectives could be constructed. A notion that was modern and based on the ideas of liberty, equality and fraternity and the principle of equality before the law came to determine public policy and this made the British rule in India distinct from all previous invasions and the empires that were built.

The inevitable fallout of this enterprise was the setting up the law courts and an elaborate machinery for collection of land revenue and other taxes. The agents of the company and their officers were also under the illusion of permanence; they presumed that the British Empire was there to stay. Hence, they went about creating in India a set of men who would look after the administration of the Company's affairs. They found it convenient to recruit the 'natives' into positions in the administration. This was what Lord Macaulay outlined in his minutes.

History, however, does not progress merely on the lines prescribed by those who were involved in crafting the present. History, in India and all over the world, was made not exactly in the manner that the rulers liked it to move. The unintended consequence, in the case of India, was the emergence of a class of people who, by virtue of their exposure to concepts such as liberty, equality and fraternity, began dreaming of constructing in India a mirror image of the society and the socio-economic set-up that prevailed in the West in their times. The rise of the new order in Europe on the ruins of the feudal set-up and the notions of modernity influenced the thought process of the English-educated intelligentsia in India at that time. Foremost among them was Raja Rammohun Roy, who wrote in 1828:

> I regret to say that the present system of religion adhered to by the Hindus is not well calculated to promote their political interest. The distinctions of castes introducing innumerable divisions and sub-divisions among them has [*sic*] entirely deprived them of patriotic feeling, and the multitude of religious rites and ceremonies and laws of purification have totally disqualified them from undertaking any difficult enterprise. It is, I think necessary that some change should take place in their religion at least for the sake of their political advantage and social comfort.

Rammohun Roy was not alone. Ishwar Chandra Vidyasagar and Akshay Kumar Dutt in Bengal, the Aligarh movement of which Sir Syed Ahmed Khan was a leading light, the powerful tradition of social reforms pioneered by Mahadev Govind Ranade in Maharashtra were all part of this process. The ground laid by Ranade was developed into a powerful tradition by Jyotibha Phule whose trenchant criticism of the scriptures and codes that legitimised the oppressive caste system took the reforms tradition a few steps forward. In southern India, there was Sri Narayanaguru whose campaign for reforms among the Ezhava community (among the backward castes in Kerala society) laid the foundations for substantive changes in the socio-economic set-up that prevailed among the Malayalam-speaking people.

All these reformers had a sense of purpose. The social relations and the customs that guided the social life at that time, in their perception, were bound to impede the progress of India. But then, their vision for progress was guided by the perception that the East India Company officers were committed to carve out in India a mirror image of the society in England. This led them to look at the Company's officers as potential collaborators. Such a perception was not off the mark completely. In the legislation to abolish *sati,* Rammohun Roy found much more than a mere collaborator in Lord William Bentinck and Vidyasagar found tremendous support from the establishment in his campaign against child marriage. These were instances where the commitment of the rulers to effect changes in the social set-up in India was evident. This, however, led to a reaction from within the intelligentsia. Bankim Chandra Chatterjee, for instance, was among those who found in the reformist zeal a threat to the tradition and the cultural life in India. The challenge to the traditional social set-up, after all, did not come from the Indian intelligentsia alone. The activities indulged in by the young Derozians (Henry Derozio was an English teacher whose students went about throwing pieces of bones on the premises of the orthodox Brahmin households) in Calcutta (now Kolkata) and similar campaigns were seen as threats to the Hindu way of life.

It was not as if the nineteenth-century reformers were anti-religion. Rammohun Roy, for instance, was not contemptuous of religion as such. His approach was that religious practices based on the scriptures and rituals were a hindrance to progress. Vidyasagar, similarly, based his campaign on the premise that there was nothing in the scriptures that legitimised child marriage. Syed Ahmed Khan, again, stressed the need to modernise Islamic tenets rather than rejecting Islam as such. Khan was also of the view that if Islam did not keep pace with the changing times, it would get fossilised. In other words, the force behind the nineteenth-century reformers was that of universalism. They were iconoclasts and their campaigns targeted the rituals that vested the priestly class with privileges.

This strand of the reform movement was picked up and further developed in the campaigns spearheaded by Sri Narayanaguru and his disciple Sahodaran Ayyappan in Malabar (and in the princely states of Travancore and Cochin) leading to the rejection of the Brahmanical order in a substantive sense. A similar movement was witnessed in the Marathi-speaking regions in Western India. After Ranade's pioneering effort, the social reform movement in Maharashtra took a radical turn under Jyothiba Phule. These movements too tended to look at the British rulers as collaborators for progress and social change in the same way as the early reformers did. The perception, hence, was that it was possible to construct a social set-up similar to the one that came into existence in Europe after the industrial revolution.

There was, indeed, resistance to all these ideas. There were attempts, most of them localised, to invent virtues within the Hindu way of life, which manifested in campaigns against the British policies, particularly where they involved the religious and cultural dimensions of life.

The Arya Samaj movement in Punjab and the Anand Math set up by Bankim Chandra Chatterjee sought to revive the traditional values while attempting to incorporate egalitarian values without having to collaborate with the rulers and their agents. The theosophical society that came up in Madras (now Chennai) could also be placed in this category. These attempts, in a sense, did lay the foundations towards an assertion of Indian nationalist identity from a cultural framework. This aspect could also be traced in the several localised campaigns against the Western system of medicine and against English education. These campaigns, however, lacked a systemic critique of the economic order. In other words, even if these campaigns were distinctly anti-British and revolved around the idea of self-rule, its leaders did not develop a systemic critique of the colonial order.

An Economic Critique of Colonialism

Unlike the social reformers of the earlier period who perceived British rule in India as an opportunity to lead the society into modernity and hence supported the Company and its officers, the intellectuals who emerged on the scene towards the end of the nineteenth century were able to place self-rule as a precondition for India's passage to modernity. In their perception, the march to modernity was not just a social agenda. They were clear that the transition in the social sense would be possible only in the event of a transformation in the economic sense. They considered India's development into a capitalist society as a necessary precondition to the building of a liberal social order. This, indeed, laid the foundation for the emergence of nationalist thought in India.

The experience of industrial development in India during the 100 years after the Battle of Plassey was the force behind the process of disillusionment with the British rule. The development of the railways to ensure that the ports were connected with the mineral-rich interiors and the regions cultivating raw material so that that they could be transported to the metropolis and the nature of industries that came up were sufficient to convince the intelligentsia that India was certainly not evolving as a spit image of the metropolis. This led to a quest among them, laying the basis for Indian nationalist thought.

Among the founding fathers of the Indian nationalist thought was Dadabhai Naoroji, who devoted his time and intellect to understand and explain how the national wealth was being drained out of the country to finance the industrial enterprise in England. Naoroji's theory of 'Drain of Wealth' and his trenchant indictment of the British policies in India through his work *Poverty and Un-British Rule of the British in India* (1901) served the basis for the emergence of Indian nationalist thought. Dadabhai Naoroji launched a relentless campaign through the press and pamphlets driving hard his thesis that 'the Indian is starving, he is dying off at the slightest touch, living on insufficient food'. The early nationalists refused to treat poverty and the consequent suffering as inherent and unavoidable. They were also clear that the suffering was not the consequence of any divine curse. Instead, they were able to see it as a fallout of the British policy in India.

Another nationalist in this context was Romesh Chandra Dutt, who went on to publish *The Economic History of India in the Victorian Age* (1903), in which he exposed the plunder indulged in by the rulers on behalf of the East India Company (during the 100 years after the Battle of Plassey) and the half-century after 1858, when the dispensation was brought directly under the Crown. Similarly, R. C. Dutt could convince a whole generation of educated Indians that poverty in India would have to be seen in the context of the operation of economic causes rather than anything inherent to the traditional Indian economy. Dutt and his contemporaries could come to this realisation on the basis of their observations of the manner in which the traditional economic structure, in which the rural artisan played a prominent role, was destroyed with the advent of the British. Heartrending stories of poverty and starvation among the artisans in Bengal and similar experiences elsewhere in the subcontinent could not have escaped the attention of the intelligentsia, particularly those who were exposed to the thoughts of the libertarian thinkers of the era from the West.

The most striking aspect of the nationalist thought process in this context was the clarity with which the early nationalists could draw a blueprint for India's economic development. Ranade, for instance, could convince an entire generation of educated Indians, of the virtues of modern industrial development. In other words, the early nationalists were categorical against celebrating the old socio-economic order, inspired as they were, by the progress made in the West. This indeed was the basis on which the first slogan of the Indian independence movement—*swadeshi*—was built.

It must be noted that the Indian National Congress, founded around the same time, was beginning to emerge into a platform from where the demand for self-rule was being raised. These voices, however, were weak and it was only after several years that they matured into a mass movement. In fact, the last few decades of the nineteenth century was the period when Indian nationalism was taking concrete shape and the Indian National Congress was becoming the platform from where these ideas were echoed. *The Hindu,* among the newspapers that came into existence in the late nineteenth century as part of the nationalist campaign, wrote in September 1889:

> Where foreign capital has been sunk in a country, the administration of that country becomes at once the concern of the bondholders. If the influence of foreign capitalists in the land is allowed to increase, then adieu to all chances of success of the Indian National Congress whose voice will be drowned in the tremendous uproar of "the empire in danger" that will surely be raised by the foreign capitalists.

A more illustrative example of the linkage between the Indian National Congress and the incipient Indian capitalists, who had begun carving out a space for themselves in the context of industrial development in India, was found in the strong views that were expressed in Surendranath Banerjee's newspaper, *Bengalee* (in January 1902):

> The agitation for political rights may bind the various nationalities of India together for a time. The community of interests may cease when these rights are achieved. But the commercial union of the various Indian nationalities, once established, will never cease to exist. Commercial and industrial activity is, therefore, a bond of very strong union and is, therefore, a mighty factor in the formation of a great Indian nation.

Thus, it is clear that the early Indian nationalist thought was rooted firmly in two distinct premises: (i) That the making of the Indian nation shall have to be on the basis of a modernist notion of development and not on a shared or perceived notion of unity based on denominational identities rooted in tradition and culture. (ii) Flowing out of this, the early nationalists were also categorical that the potential for such a development could be realised only when Indian capital itself initiated and developed the process of industrialisation. *Swadeshi,* thus, was not a slogan rooted in notions of tradition or culture. It was, instead, a concept that evolved at a time when the national bourgeoisie began to emerge and assert itself.

The partition of Bengal in 1905, a decision that sent ripples among the people of the undivided Bengal presidency, was grabbed by this new class—the incipient Indian bourgeoisie—to give concrete shape to Indian nationalism. The orchestration of this was evident in the call for boycott of foreign goods, particularly clothes manufactured in Britain. The policies of the British Indian government all the while, particularly in the context of regulating the conditions of labour in Indian industries (the Indian Factories Act, 1881), had convinced the incipient bourgeois class that the objective of the British rule in India was to reduce the subcontinent to a colony of the metropolis rather than facilitate capitalist enterprise. The call for *swadeshi,* as it evolved and spread across the towns in the presidencies, turned out to be the beginning of a movement, which was rooted firmly in the idea of building India into a modern industrial society on the lines of the modern West. The idea of India as a nation was also rooted in this.

In other words, the making of the Indian nation was based on the same principle of modernity that had led to the evolution of nationalism and nation states in Europe a couple of centuries earlier. The distinction, however, was that while in Europe, the nation states were built on the ruins of the feudal estates (whose destruction was finally achieved by the march of industrial capitalism), the Indian nation was built on the ruins of the colonial order. If the battle cry in Europe was liberty, equality and fraternity, the battle cry that dominated the course in the making of the Indian nation was *swadeshi*.

II

The Emergence of Gandhi and the Nationalist Struggle

> No matter to what part of the world one might go, one would find numberless people who look upon Gandhiji as the world's greatest symbols of resistance to oppression and injustice and even solace in suffering, suffering that may have nothing to do with government and laws, suffering that may result out of the very fact of living.
>
> — Ram Manohar Lohia, *Marx, Gandhi and Socialism*

The decision to partition Bengal was effected at a time when the Indian nationalist thought was already maturing into a concrete idea. The intelligentsia, as discussed in the previous chapter, was convinced by this time that the British rule was a stumbling block in the course of India's development as a modern nation. The partition, hence, turned out to be the conjuncture that precipitated a crisis of legitimacy for the British Indian administration. This sparked off a movement.

The events between December 1903 (when the proposal to partition Bengal was mooted) and 1908, by which time almost all the leaders involved in the movement were convicted for long prison terms, brought out the potential for a mass movement against the colonial order in India. The idea of *swaraj* was born in this period and the resistance, from now on, was no longer based on simple perceptions of identity. The *swadeshi* struggle marked the beginning of a process that would define freedom as a quest for an egalitarian order in the social as much as in the economic sense of the term. The four decades after 1908 also witnessed a course when the different social and economic groups would contest and negotiate their demands from within the Indian National Congress. This indeed determined the dynamics of the Indian National Movement. We shall deal with, as briefly as possible, the dynamics of this phase and the movement in this chapter. This is necessary in order to make sense of the complex mosaic that constitutes the national political discourse as it evolved after 15 August 1947 and into the present.

The Spirit of *Swadeshi*

The initial opposition to the partition proposals was in the form of petitions and public meetings. These were restricted to the various towns in the undivided Bengal presidency. The objective behind these actions was to turn public opinion, both in

India and England, against the partition. The leaders, however, realised very soon that such actions alone were not leading them to success. The colonial administration announced on 19 July 1905 that the partition of Bengal will be effected from 16 October 1905. Meanwhile, those who assembled at public meetings against the partition proposal in the small towns of Bengal were raising slogans seeking boycott of foreign goods. In this context, a formal call for boycott of foreign goods was given in a meeting at the town hall in Calcutta on 7 August 1905. Thus, the *swadeshi* spirit that was building up and even gathering strength was now integrated with the anti-British sentiment provoked by the partition proposal. Most parts of the Bengal presidency witnessed the beginnings of a nationalist upsurge by this time. The value of British goods sold in some of the towns in Bengal, according to some accounts, fell from five to 15 times during the period.

The partition of Bengal, thus, turned out to provoke a combination of forces. The slogan of *swadeshi* raised in Bengal, to begin with, was taken to Maharashtra. Lokmanya Tilak could orchestrate the spirit across Western India. Bombay (now Mumbai) turned out to be a centre for the boycott movement. Scenes of people making a bonfire of British manufactured cloth on the streets were witnessed in Bombay almost by the day. While shocking the rulers, these images also inspired similar campaigns in other presidencies. Ajit Singh and Lala Lajpat Rai carried the torch in Punjab and elsewhere in northern India while V. O. Chidambaram Pillai carried the *swadeshi* spirit further by setting up a steam navigation company in the port town of Tuticorin in the Madras presidency. Thus, the idea of economic independence—*swaraj* and *swadeshi*—began to overshadow the campaign against the partition of Bengal. In other words, the core demand of the movement when it began—against partition of Bengal—was blitzed by the idea of *swadeshi* (an expression of economic nationalism) and the demand for independence from British rule within a couple of years. The campaign, by this time, was no longer restricted to the Bengal presidency.

The annual session of the Indian National Congress in 1906 (in Calcutta), presided over by Dadabhai Naoroji, was a watershed in this regard. Naoroji, the Grand Old Man of Indian Nationalism, declared in his presidential address the goal of the Indian National Congress to be 'self-government or *swaraj* like that of the United Kingdom or the Colonies'. It is important to note here that by colonies, Naoroji was referring to the United States of America, by then a nation in its own right and not a conglomeration of colonies as in the metropolis-colonies framework.

The upsurge, witnessed during the couple of years after 1905, however, did not last long. First and foremost, the split in the Indian National Congress caused by the struggle between the moderates and the extremists (the Surat session, 1906) weakened the campaign. Secondly, the repressive measures resorted to by the colonial administration against the mass movement had an adverse effect on its progress. The long prison terms inflicted upon the torchbearers of the campaign left the movement without leaders. In addition to these, the movement had its own weaknesses. Its focus, during this phase, was restricted to a few urban towns across the country with the direct involvement of the peasantry not as pronounced. Those who led the *swadeshi* campaign came from the professional class such as the lawyers, journalists and teachers. The movement did not get support from the masses.

The campaign, however, was the first attempt to confront the colonial dispensation on the streets. Similarly, the slogan of *swaraj*, as it evolved in the context of the campaign, could internalise the concept of rights of the Indian people in its course. The *swadeshi* phase is significant not merely as a chapter in the history of India's struggle for freedom. Instead, it was the period when the spirit of *swadeshi* was consolidated into an ideological framework on which the Indian nation was built.

Gandhi's Emergence: Champaran, Kheda and Ahmedabad

For almost a decade after 1908, the nationalist fervour persisted in a different form and found expression in the attacks, often violent, against individual officers of the dispensation. This indeed was inevitable in the aftermath of the crude repressive measures adopted by the colonial administration to contain the mass involvement in the campaign. It will be un-historical to call these acts as terrorist violence. It will also be improper to suggest that such acts by a band of patriots were witnessed only during the decade after 1908. Instances of violent attacks against the colonial administrators and the institutions identified with the colonial system persisted throughout the struggle for freedom. It is, however, a fact that such acts started around the same time as the *swadeshi* campaign was crushed by the colonial rulers.

It is equally important to refrain from identifying the strategy of violence with any sectarian approaches. A majority of the youth, who participated in those acts, drew their inspiration from images or notions that belonged to the cultural sphere. The *kali* cult (and its variants outside Bengal), for instance, was familiar among the patriotic youth. They were also driven by the images of resistance inherited from the past such as Shivaji in Maharashtra or the Devi in northern India. They also drew inspiration from the tradition of the sepoy mutiny. This, however, does not mean that their ideology was drawn from these images that belonged to the remote and not so remote past. Their moorings, in the ideological sense, were primarily located in the spirit of the *swadeshi* campaign and hence modernist in all senses of the term.

This trajectory was broken by 1917. The break was indeed decisive because the struggle for freedom, from then on, was to mature into a mass movement involving all sections of the Indian people. It began as a set of experiments conducted by Gandhi, a few years after his return from South Africa, in three different parts of the country. Champaran (in Bihar), Ahmedabad and Kheda (in Gujarat) were instances when Gandhi tried to experiment, on Indian soil, what he had tested earlier in South Africa. It was based on the principle of collective defiance of authority. Gandhi insisted that such defiance was the inherent right of the Indian people because the colonial regime lacked any moral authority to lord over them. He called this mode of defiance civil disobedience.

The Champaran story was about the peasants across the district having been forced by British planters to cultivate indigo in at least 3/20th of their land. This was known as the *tinkathia* system and was put in place when the textile industry in Manchester needed the indigo to dye the cloth manufactured there. The advent of chemical dyes (from Germany) rendered use of Indigo redundant. But then, the planters and the British revenue administrators sought to make the best of the situation by insisting that the tenants pay higher rents and some other taxes for releasing the land from mandatory cultivation of Indigo. This led to unrest and the peasantry was faced with the threat of eviction and imminent starvation. This condition was brought to Gandhi's attention by a native peasant, Raj Kumar Shukla. Gandhi landed in Champaran and began studying the situation himself, visiting village after village, in the district. After ascertaining the reality, Gandhi called upon the peasants in the district to refuse paying the additional rent as demanded. The campaign also took up the demand for abolition of the *tinkathia* system; an instance of asserting the rights of the peasant to decide on what he shall cultivate.

Another significant aspect of the Champaran story was the way Gandhi responded to the administration's order externing him from the district. Unlike the leaders of the past, Gandhi refused to stay away from Champaran and he was willing to face the consequences. The first of the many instances when Gandhi put into practice, on Indian soil, the weapon he had devised in South Africa. Interestingly, the administration refrained from arresting Gandhi at that time in Champaran.

Soon after Champaran, Gandhi's attention was drawn to the plight of the workers in the textile industry in Ahmedabad. The mill owners there had decided to dispense with the 'plague bonus' after the epidemic had passed. This was unacceptable to the workers as they realised that it would bring down their real wages substantially. Since there was a steep price rise after the World War I, the scrapping of 'plague bonus', without adequate raise in wages, was bound to erode the real wages. Despite the fact that his close friend and mill owner, Ambalal Sarabhai (who had saved the Sabarmati Ashram from a huge financial difficulty just then) was on the other side, Gandhi insisted that the mill owners agree for a 35 per cent wage increase to help the workers tide over the crisis. The owners refused and even declared a lockout. Gandhi called for a strike by the mill workers and as the strike went on, pushing the workers to starvation, he embarked upon a fast. This brought him closer to the workers and the mill owners relented to the setting up of a tribunal to adjudicate. The tribunal awarded a 35 per cent wage increase.

Just as the dispute in Ahmedabad was on, Gandhi learnt of the difficulties faced by the peasants in the Kheda district. A severe drought condition that year had left the peasants pauperised and a section among them (the poor and the marginal peasants in particular) were unable to pay the revenue demanded of them. The administration resorted to repressive measures, including attachment of the household property and cattle in lieu of revenue dues. They were seeking remission and after a tour, in the course of which such local leaders like Vallabhai Patel and Indulal Yagnik joined him, Gandhi asked the peasants to refuse payment of dues. Gandhi could also convince the rich peasants in the district to refuse paying dues as long as their poor brethren were able to pay. After the campaign grew in strength, the administration issued secret instructions that revenue shall be recovered only from those peasants who could pay.

Champaran, Ahmedabad and Kheda were indeed dress rehearsals of the long battle that was waiting to be waged under Gandhi's leadership. The Gandhian era had begun and the three decades after Champaran witnessed the widening of the scope for a struggle based on the interplay of concepts such as principles of law, justice and morality apart from the idea of rights. It is necessary to stress here that the public discourse in the three decades after 1917 was dominated and determined by the interplay of these notions that were rooted firmly in the socio-economic changes achieved in Europe after the destruction of feudalism there. The Indian nation-state, in fact, was the outcome of this interplay that culminated in the framing of the republican constitution. Let us now discuss the processes and the various stages through which this culmination was reached.

The Nationalist Upsurge: Jallianwala Bagh to Non-cooperation

The experience in Champaran, Ahmedabad and Kheda was significant. This was the context in which the colonial administration came up with the Rowlatt Act. The proposals, when implemented, would deny the Indian people even the right to assemble, leave alone protest against the regime. The motive behind this proposed act was to contain the acts of violence against the British officers. Gandhi soon gave a call, involving the organisation of the Home Rule League, to organise peaceful meetings all over the country to register the Indian people's protest against the proposals. A nationwide programme for *satyagraha* was planned for 6 April 1919. Several towns witnessed massive demonstrations.

Industrial hubs like Bombay even witnessed a general strike and a *hartal*. There were instances of violence too in several towns. Gandhi's plan to visit Punjab (the home of the glorious *Ghadr* tradition), where the response to his call for *satyagraha* was widespread, was foiled by the British administration by an order externing him to Bombay.

The two important leaders of the mass movement in Punjab, Dr Saifuddin Kitchlew and Satyapal, were arrested in Amritsar on 10 April 1919 after a protest march turned violent and the protestors attacked the police station and other government establishments. A meeting was organised to protest the arrests on 13 April 1919 within the precincts of a public park in Amritsar. The British General, Reginald Dyer, who was handed over the charge to restore order in the city, marched there with armoured vehicles. The indiscriminate firing on the unarmed crowd killed 379 people and injured several more. The Jallianwala Bagh massacre sent shock waves and triggered an angry reaction against the regime across the country.

It was in this atmosphere of widespread anger that the idea of *Khilafat* came up before Gandhi. The treatment meted out to the caliph of Turkey by Great Britain after the cessation of World War I had been agitating the members of the Muslim community in India. They felt betrayed by the British who had obtained cooperation of the community in the war efforts. Meanwhile, even the moderate nationalist opinion had lost all faith in the just nature of the British rule in India after they sensed the public support to General Dyer in England. The House of Lords had voted endorsing his action in Jallianwala Bagh. There was a conjuncture of events once again and this time it was in the overall context of a perception among a cross-section of Indians about colonialism and its implication to India's economic development.

The temporary boom witnessed in the industrial arena, triggered essentially by the war-time conditions, were beginning to recede. Its effect on the living condition, especially in industrial and other urban centres, was leading to local unrest. Industrial workers began to organise themselves into unions in this context and agitate against retrenchment and other onslaughts on their rights. The All India Trade Union Congress (AITUC) that emerged into a prominent outfit in later years was set up around this time. The founding of the AITUC in 1920, with Lala Lajpat Rai as its president, was only the culmination of a process that began in the massive general strike in Bombay in protest against the arrest of Bal Gangadhar Tilak in 1905.

Around the same time, Gandhi prevailed upon the Ali brothers—Mohammed Ali and Shaukat Ali—that the Khilafat Committee adopt a programme of non-violent non-cooperation. The Khilafat Committee, in turn, accepted this and wanted Gandhi to lead the movement. This was in February 1920. The Indian National Congress too was veering around to the idea of non-cooperation. Thus, on 1 August 1920, the Indian National Congress formally launched the non-cooperation movement. Tilak passed away that day early in the morning and Bombay observed a *hartal* the same day. The annual session of the Indian National Congress at Nagpur in December 1920 was significant. It was there that the constitution of the Indian National Congress underwent substantial changes. From 'attainment of self-government by constitutional and legal means', the goal of the Congress was redefined to 'attainment of *swaraj* by peaceful and legitimate means'.

While the initial stress in the Congress programme on 'legal means' had meant that the struggle would be restricted to mere prayers and petitioning, the concept of 'legitimate means' internalised the principles of morality and ethics into the demand for freedom. In other words, the Indian National Movement, while internalising the principles of the rule of the law, went on to reject the moral authority of the colonial masters to carry on with administering India. Out of this emerged the concept of civil disobedience and its legitimacy as a form of struggle.

Any attempt to narrate the course of events during the non-cooperation movement and its withdrawal in the aftermath of the incidence of violence in Chauri Chaura will be digressing too much from the scope of this book. However, it is necessary to note here that the non-cooperation movement was perhaps the first of the campaigns whose scope extended into the whole of the Indian nation in the geographical, social and economic sense of the term. The core principle of economic self assertion—*swadeshi*—remained central to the campaign. The campaign against foreign goods, clothes in particular, spread to all parts of the country with added vigour after the advent of Gandhi. In addition, with the launch of the non-cooperation movement, the Congress volunteers were also involved in picketing stores selling foreign clothes. The effect, according to economic historians, was a sharp fall in the quantity of goods imported from Manchester. From Rs 102 crore in 1920–21, the value of clothes imported into India fell to Rs 57 crore in 1921–22.

Another significant development during this phase was the radical changes that were effected in the organisation of the Indian National Congress. A programme for mass enrollment of members, popularising the *charkha* and collection of funds, was launched at the All India Congress Committee (AICC) session in Vijayawada in March 1921. This change took place at a stage when several parts of rural India were witnessing mobilisation of the peasantry. The conjuncture, again, had its lasting impact on the dynamics of the Congress, as a platform, and on the freedom struggle as it emerged. The peasants were being mobilised on the slogan of no-rent campaign, which was one of the important aspects of the non-cooperation movement. Thus, the non-cooperation movement was the context in which the struggle against the colonial set-up struck roots in the countryside. This was not the case with the *swadeshi* movement of 1905–08. The membership of the Indian National Congress reached 50 lakh by this time.

Gandhi's announcement, on 12 February 1922, to withdraw the non-cooperation movement did have a dampening effect on the spirit of the nationalists. But, the quest for freedom was no longer confined to a minuscule section. Indian nationalism had already matured into a mass movement by then. *Swadeshi* and *swaraj* were integral to the life of the masses by this time. The *kisan sabhas,* which had come up in the aftermath of the Champaran and Kheda *satyagraha,* became vibrant organisations in the course of the no-rent campaigns. Similarly, trade unions too were coming of age in all the industrial towns in the presidencies. Thus, even after the movement was withdrawn, the anti-colonial campaign continued. The campaign for boycott of foreign goods provided the space for the incipient bourgeoisie to establish itself in the consumer goods sector apart from pioneering ventures in steel manufacture and hydro-power generation by the house of Tatas.

Of importance to the scope of this book is the expansion of Indian enterprise in the consumer goods sector in general and textiles in particular. Import of textile machinery into India went up substantially in the years after World War I. This would happen because the consumption of cotton piece goods in India continued to expand after World War I. Of immense significance from the concerns of this chapter is the fact that the share of Indian cotton mills in the total domestic production and consumption registered substantial increase in the post-War period. In all these, we find the transformation of the Indian National Congress from a platform consisting of the professionals and other sections of the intelligentsia into an organisation with reach across the length and breadth of India. This transformation, achieved on the initiative by Gandhi, would trigger a dynamic of its own. The following factors marked this context:

- The growth and expansion of Indian industrial enterprise, particularly in the post–World War I period and the emergence of the bourgeoisie committed to the nationalist cause;
- The emergence of workers in these industrial units as active players in the nationalist mobilization;
- The emergence of organisations and collectives representing the interests of the peasantry and their involvement in the non-cooperation movement;
- The no-rent campaign, as part of the non-cooperation movement, bringing large sections of the landed gentry too into the Congress fold.

The developments during the 25 years, after the non-cooperation movement was formally withdrawn (in February 1922), were guided entirely by the dynamics triggered by the constant interplay between the commonality of interests among these socio-economic groups and the areas of conflict between them. The second half of the 1920s witnessed a steady spurt in strikes by industrial workers across the country. The strike wave, in fact, peaked by 1928, leading to the enactment of the Trade Disputes Act in 1928. There were also several instances when striking workers were fired at and other repressive measures let loose. In March that year, the colonial government detained almost all the important leaders of the trade union movement for trial in what came to be known as the Meerut conspiracy case. Those arrested also constituted the core of the Communist Party of India, founded in 1924.

The turn of events, in this context, would also bring to the fore the conflict of interests between the nationalist bourgeoisie and the industrial working class. This was also the period when the countryside was witnessing radical mobilisation behind the *kisan sabhas*. It also led to conflicts between them and the landed gentry in some parts of the country. Thus, despite the withdrawal of the non-cooperation movement and the suspension of civil disobedience, various sections of the Indian people were involved in challenging the colonial authority in their own way.

The Indian National Congress: From Lahore to Karachi

The spirit of *swadeshi,* the civil disobedience and the organisational network built in the context of the non-cooperation movement, did not fade away. This was evident in the protests against the Simon Commission's visit in February 1928. The call, by the Indian National Congress for a boycott of the Commission ignited a cross-section of the people to protest. These were marked by *hartals* and general strikes in Bombay, Calcutta, Lucknow, Lahore, Vijayawada and all other cities visited by the commission. Thus, the stage was set for another round of formal mobilisation on the lines of the non-cooperation movement. The Lahore session of the Indian National Congress, in December 1929, came out with the call for *purna swaraj*. Jawaharlal Nehru, elected as Congress president for the year ahead, declared in his presidential address: 'We have now an open conspiracy to free this country from foreign rule and you, comrades, and all our countrymen and countrywomen are invited to join it.' The session concluded, at midnight of 31 December 1929, when the tricolour was unfurled on the banks of the Ravi River. The Lahore session, thus, marked a culmination of the process set in motion at the Nagpur session in December 1920 when the Congress' goal was redefined from self-rule to *swaraj*.

In Lahore, *swaraj* was further redefined to include the demands and aspirations of almost all sections of the Indian people in the social, economic and above all political sense. This was reflected in the independence pledge that was read out before the large gatherings all over the country on 26 January 1930. The Lahore session of the Indian National Congress had authorised the working committee to decide on the schedule to launch a programme of civil disobedience and also specified that such a programme will include a collective refusal to pay taxes. The working committee, in its turn, left the decision to Gandhi who was by now back in the Sabarmati Ashram. Gandhi's ultimatum of 31 January 1930, to the Viceroy, Lord Irwin, for a charter of demands containing 11 points had expired and civil disobedience was the only way out.

This was when Gandhi began to talk of salt. He wrote: 'There is no article like salt outside water by taxing which the State can reach even the starving millions, the sick, the maimed and the utterly helpless. The tax constitutes, therefore, the most inhuman poll tax the ingenuity of man can devise.' And on 2 March 1930, Gandhi informed the viceroy of his plans to march out of the Sabarmati Ashram with his followers to the Dandi coast and make salt. Civil disobedience again! The march was slated for 11 March 1930 and with *Bapu* marching along the villages, across the 240 miles from Ahmedabad to Dandi, people responded with fervour. Defiance of the salt law was now added to the other acts of civil disobedience such as boycott of foreign clothes, courts, schools and picketing of shops vending foreign goods. The response was overwhelming. The struggle for freedom had come of age. And repressive measures were not going to contain them. The spirit of *swaraj* had reached such levels that the sepoys of the Garhwal regiment refused to fire on the demonstrators in Peshawar. While defiance of the salt law was central to the 1930 movement, in places that were landlocked, the movement took to a no-tax campaign and other forms of collective defiance. This was also the time when Bhagat Singh, Sukhdev and Rajguru had challenged the colonial order in their own way. The Gandhi–Irwin pact followed and the civil disobedience movement was suspended.

The significant turn, insofar as the scope of this study is concerned, was the Congress session held in Karachi in March 1931. It was then that the goal of *purna swaraj* was further expanded and defined on the basis of such concepts as Fundamental Rights in addition to a resolution on the National Economic Programme. By this, the Indian National Congress would define what *swaraj* meant for the masses. 'In order to end the exploitation of the masses,' the resolution said, 'political freedom must include real economic freedom of the starving millions'.

And on the political plane, the Karachi resolution committed the Congress to guarantee the basic civil rights of free speech, free press, free assembly, and freedom of association. The resolution also held out a commitment to put in place a judicial system based on equality before the law irrespective of caste, creed or gender. It was resolved by the Indian National Congress in Karachi that the future government would ensure that the state remained neutral insofar as religious affairs were concerned. It also expressed a commitment to elections based on universal adult suffrage. The Karachi resolution, indeed, was the charter on which the constituent assembly would work to draft the republican constitution.

The resolution, in fact, was the culmination of the process that began when a generation of the intelligentsia—Dadabhai Naoroji, M. G. Ranade and R. C. Dutt—began unravelling the object and the effect of the British rule in India. This led to the *swadeshi* campaign and through the Gandhian era it consolidated into an ideological position. Indian nationalism, hence, was certainly a product of the dynamics unleashed by the colonial enterprise.

III

Indian Capitalists and the Freedom Struggle

> We can no more separate our politics from our economics. Indian commerce and industry are intimately associated with and are indeed an integral part of the national movement—growing with its growth and strengthening with its strength.
>
> — Sir Purshottamdas Thakurdas, in his presidential address to the second annual session of the Federation of Indian Chambers of Commerce and Industry [FICCI], 1928

The national struggle for independence cannot be reduced, in any way, to merely an expression of the self-serving agenda of the Indian capitalist class. Similarly, the Indian National Congress (INC) was not an organisation that represented only the interests of the national bourgeoisie. As we have seen in Chapter II, the national struggle for independence evolved, over a period of time, into a movement that involved all sections of the Indian people. Hence, the dynamics of the movement were guided by the conflicts among the various socio-economic groups. The INC, as a body, was the forum where these conflicts took place. In the course of handling these conflicts, the Congress as a platform, and Gandhi in particular, could negotiate between the groups and among them at the same time. On most occasions, if not all, the Congress turned to be a fair arbitrator. This was how it could represent the Indian people as a whole. Most of the credit for this achievement should go to Gandhi.

This scenario, however, began to change after 1937, when the Congress assumed office in the provinces after the elections based on the Government of India Act, 1935. A number of those who became ministers in different provinces were known for their sectarian views. This was the case not only on issues involving the religious minorities and their position in independent India, but also in the case of their attitude towards workers. This was also the stage when Gandhi's ability to influence the priorities of the INC was beginning to whittle down. It had a lasting impact also on the course of the national struggle for independence. While a detailed discussion on the shift in the attitude of the Congress towards the religious minorities (the Muslim community in particular) will be appropriate at a later stage (Chapter IV), it is pertinent to state here that the Muslim League's resolution (in August 1940) demanding Pakistan will have to be seen in the context of the developments in the INC during this period. Of relevance to the concerns of this chapter is the experience involving the Congress leaders who held positions in the provincial ministries with regard to their attitude towards the demands and aspirations of the peasantry and the industrial workers.

The Congress ministries were on the side of the employer in almost all instances when there was a conflict of interest between the worker and the employer. Those who headed the Congress ministries in the provinces—C. Rajagopalachari in Madras, B. G. Kher in Bombay and G. B. Pant in the United Provinces—did not conceal their predilections on this. This was true even when the conflicts arose out of demands by the workers for better wages and working conditions. An illustration of this was a legislation passed by the Bombay Legislative Assembly (in 1938) imposing severe restrictions on trade union organisations. The Bombay Act formed the basis for a similar legislation in the Madras presidency. It was not enacted in Madras only because the Congress provincial governments resigned in September 1939.

There was no change in the attitude of the Congress leaders even after the resignation of the ministries in September 1939. They persisted with this sectarian agenda, reducing the INC to a platform that invariably sided with the Indian capitalists whenever there was a conflict of interest between labour and capital. This shift, in the overall strategy of the INC, was further established in the context of the post–World War II nationalist upsurge. The Congress leaders in the provinces did not hesitate to order repressive measures to put down the various agitations involving the industrial workers and the peasantry across the country. Instances of police firing at striking workers were commonplace in all provinces in the post–World War II period. The trade union movement, invariably, was being led by the communists. All these reveal a story that will establish the extent to which the Indian capitalist class had emerged into a powerful group to influence the course of the INC.

The incipient capitalist class in India was clear in its perception that liberation from the colonial yoke was the only way to build a capitalist set-up in India. It saw import substitution as the basis for further growth and expansion. The unravelling of the Indian economic reality from the beginning of the twentieth century provided the objective conditions to the maturing of this understanding too. Clarity on these lines and the impact of the *swadeshi* slogan across the country led the national bourgeoisie away from becoming a comprador class. A large number of textile mills had come up in and around Bombay by 1896. While the *swadeshi* campaign helped expansion of the market for Indian goods, World War I led to a situation when sea routes to India were closed for merchant vessels. This aided the Indian enterprise in a big way. The market that the colonial enterprise had created over the years was available, on a platter, for the Indian manufacturer. The Indian enterprise could also enter several areas other than the cotton textile industry that had existed even before the outbreak of war.

The cessation of hostilities in 1918 and the larger crisis of global capitalism that ultimately manifested in the great crash (1929) had its impact in India too. This added to the crisis that was building in the Indian industrial scenario, even otherwise, due to the war-time boom receding and forcing large-scale retrenchment of industrial labour. The workers, radicalised by the shared experience of life within and outside the factories, were responding to the crisis by organising strikes. The rising strike wave peaked in 1928. These issues were becoming a subject matter for concern for the INC too. The widening of the Congress base after the entry of Gandhi and the changes in its constitution in 1920 had brought into its fold a large number of industrial workers. These were factors that led the Congress to define freedom in a radical fashion at the Karachi session. It is important to take note of the distinct and pronounced tendencies in this context. Gandhi, for instance, had developed the slogan of *swadeshi* to form the core of the national struggle for independence. In the same period, we witness the enmeshing of radical ideas, brought into the political discourse by Jawaharlal Nehru. Inspired by the 1917 revolution in Russia, Nehru contributed immensely to the radicalisation of the INC.

This larger context was leading the important members of the Indian capitalist class also to define their own position vis-à-vis the national struggle for freedom. The foundation of the FICCI, in 1927, took place in this context. This was the same time when the trade union movement had established itself into a force. Rather than restricting their concerns to wages and bargaining, the trade unions in India, mostly organised under the banner of the All India Trade Union Congress (AITUC), were explicit about their political agenda too. The industrial working class had, after all, associated itself with the nationalist cause as early as 1905. Recall the general strike in Bombay in protest against the arrest and detention of Bal Gangadhar Tilak. The national bourgeoisie too began to evolve its position vis-à-vis the INC in this context. The statement at the second annual session of the FICCI (in 1928) by its president, Sir Purshottamdas Thakurdas, that the economic advancement of the Indian capitalist class was so closely tied to the national struggle for independence, marked the beginning of a battle for the Congress. Ambalal Sarabhai was more explicit in November 1929 when he stressed the need for the FICCI to ensure an organic link with the INC.

It is clear that the leading lights of the Indian capitalist class were convinced about the need to convert the leadership of the INC into a representative of its own interests. They did this in a calibrated manner rather than in an ad hoc fashion. G. D. Birla's pronouncement in 1930, on 'the need to strengthen the hands of those fighting for freedom', seemed to clarify to those within the FICCI who wondered as to how the rising tide of popular protests could be dealt with. The debate within the FICCI in this regard persisted. Lalji Naranji, for instance, wondered about the adverse impact that could result from a popular movement whose basis was disregard for authority. They were concerned over the adverse effect the idea of civil disobedience could have on the future government, particularly so in the light of the moral high ground that this movement had achieved, thanks to

Gandhi's leading role in it. Lalji Naranji's concern was that such a movement was bound to lead to a tendency that could culminate in organised challenges against private property and political authority even after independence was achieved. Such apprehensions notwithstanding, the Indian capitalist class was clear on the point that it was not in their interest to oppose the INC. The agenda was to ensure a critical role for themselves and influence the Congress' agenda as much possible.

The debate within the Congress on whether to enter office or not during 1935–37 turned out to be an occasion for the national bourgeoisie to play a role and push the INC to enter office. It was G. D. Birla who worked hard towards this end. Once the Congress decided to form its governments, it did so with an explicit statement that the objective was to wreck the constitution rather than working it. Birla then conveyed to Viceroy Lord Halifax that it was imperative for the colonial rulers to ensure that the constitution (of 1935) worked. 'Otherwise', he stressed, 'India would be compelled to take direct action'. He was representing to the colonial rulers the need to ensure that conditions were not created for another round of civil disobedience.

In spite of their reservations against the Congress' strategy of popular mobilisation and the consequent radicalisation of the movement, the national bourgeoisie did not condemn or distance itself from the Congress at this stage. Birla's note to Purshottamdas in the midst of the civil disobedience movement established this clearly. In January 1931, Birla wrote: 'If we are to achieve what we desire, the present movement should not be allowed to slacken.'

This unequivocal stand was evident even in the midst of Gandhi's individual *satyagraha* programme against the colonial government's unilateral decision to involve India in the war efforts. The individual *satyagraha* began in November 1940. Describing the situation as one where the Congress was left with no option but to launch non-cooperation movement, Purshottamdas clearly stood by the national struggle for freedom. This position matured into a categorical statement on 5 August 1942, just four days before the Quit India resolution was moved at the All India Congress Committee session at the Gowalia tank grounds in Bombay. In a joint letter to the viceroy, the leading lights of the FICCI, Purshottamdas Thakurdas, J. R. D. Tata and G. D. Birla made it known that they stood by the Congress' demand for independence as a necessary condition for cooperation in the war effort.

Thus, it is clear that the capitalist class, as it emerged in India, was determined to stand by the national struggle for freedom rather than turn into a comprador class. The story, however, does not end here. Similar developments were noticed around the same time as the Quit India movement was assuming the form of a popular movement and even taking the shape of violent protests against all forms of authority. All this had far reaching implications for the political discourse after 15 August 1947. The period between 1943 and 1947 was the phase when the influence of the nationalist bourgeoisie on the INC was pronounced. In other words, this was the period when the Congress began drifting away from the fundamentals laid out in the Karachi session. It also meant a decisive break by the Congress with the Gandhian tradition, in at least one important area; the premise on which India's post-independence economic policy was formulated.

The Bombay Plan and Nehruvian Socialism

Assured as it was of independence even while the World War II was still on, the FICCI, in 1944, came out with what was known at that time as the Bombay Plan. The Indian capitalist class, by this time had grown into a powerful group. The share of indigenous enterprise in the domestic market was over 70 per cent. Similarly, over 80 per cent of the deposits in the organised banking sector came from the Indian capitalist class. Their future prospects, however, depended on a lot more than mere patronage of the kind they received from the Congress ministries during 1937 and 1939. They realised the need for an economic order that went beyond the rhetoric of free enterprise and they were in search of a leader who was willing to go along with them.

The turning point, in this regard, was the convergence of sorts between the objective of the national bourgeoisie and Jawaharlal Nehru's approach to independent India's economic development. This led to an alliance between the two. Nehru's fascination to emulate the principles of centralised planning and large-scale production of goods, as carried out in the Soviet Union, laid the basis for this alliance. The aspirations of the national bourgeoisie had a lot in common with Nehru's vision of modernity than with the Gandhian paradigm. The Gandhian model, based on small-scale production units and celebrating the artisan, went against the interests of the national capitalist class. This was particularly so when they had appropriated, to themselves, most of the domestic market for goods.

Realising the need to set the agenda, the FICCI set up a committee to draft an economic policy resolution to be presented before the future government of India. Around the same time, G. L. Mehta, in his presidential address to the FICCI's annual session in 1943, stressed the need for a consistent programme of reforms that could act as the most effective remedy against social upheavals. This indeed seemed to have been the framework within which the Post–War Economic Development Committee, set up by the FICCI in 1942, drafted its report. This report came to be known as the Bombay Plan. The Bombay Plan was an attempt that incorporated features inherent to the socialist framework to the extent that it did not dilute the core interests of the capitalist class in India.

Recognising the need for state intervention in economic activity, the Bombay Plan laid thrust on state investment in the infrastructure sector, particularly in areas involving huge capital investments and a long gestation period, apart from social overheads. Other salient aspects of the plan were the poverty-alleviation measures by the state, deficit financing and state investments in those sectors that gave return only in long term. The Bombay plan emphasised that the state must involve itself in economic activity to the extent that it helped in employment generation and, by extension, enlarge the size of the home market. However, another prescription of the Bombay Plan was to erect protective barriers against competition from imports. Radical land reforms and freeing the agrarian sector of its feudal vestiges would have served the same purpose, i.e., enlarging the home market for consumer goods. But then, such a strategy also carried with it the potential of a revolutionary upsurge, which could have, in the final count, spelt the end of their dream. The Nehruvian era (1951–64) witnessed implementation of several important features of the Bombay Plan in the name of socialism. This laid the foundation for the political dynamics during the decade after independence.

IV

Independence and the Emergence of Nehru

> Long years ago we made a tryst with destiny and now the time comes when we shall redeem our pledge, not wholly or in full measure, but very substantially. At the stroke of the midnight hour, when the world sleeps, India will awake to life and freedom.
>
> — Jawaharlal Nehru, addressing the Constituent Assembly and the nation on 15 August 1947

The context in which the colonial rule ended, the alignment of social groups and classes vis-à-vis the Indian National Congress, the colonial regime and the Muslim League influenced the political discourse not only in the immediate context but also the long-term dynamics of the political trajectory of independent India. This chapter will deal with these aspects as they emerged in the few years after the World War II and the dawn of independence; and how these influenced the course of politics in the immediate future as well as in the couple of decades after independence.

A brief foray into some of the developments in the immediate aftermath of the World War II is necessary to see things in perspective. The context that marked the defeat of the axis powers (Hitler's Germany, Mussolini's Italy and Tojo's Japan) paved the way to a new world order. Of significance from the point of view of this chapter is that it knocked the bottom off the idea of empire. The nations whose rulers had considered it their right to set up and retain colonies across Africa and Asia were forced to vacate from there. This larger transition and the post-War nationalist upsurge in India, as it was manifest in the massive show of solidarity across the country with the soldiers of the Indian National Army (INA), the revolt by the ratings of the Royal Indian Navy (popularly described as the RIN mutiny), the spate of industrial general strikes in Bombay, Calcutta and Madras brought home the point that the British could no longer continue with the colonial project.

The Interim Government and the Emergence of Nehru

The changed global scenario in the post–World War II context led to the setting up of the Cabinet Mission. The mission landed in India in March 1946 and began work on its brief: to set up a national government before the final transfer of power. After several rounds of discussions, the mission proposed to constitute a 'representative' body by way of elections across the provinces and the princely states (eligibility conditions to qualify as voters in this case restricted the electorate to a small proportion of the population who held property) and entrust this body with the task of making a constitution for free India. The idea of partition did not figure at this stage. Instead, the mission's proposal was for a loose-knit confederation in which the Muslim League could dominate the administration in the North-East and North-West provinces while the Congress would administer the rest of the provinces. Jinnah did not reject the idea altogether. The Congress, meanwhile, perceived the Cabinet Mission's plan as a clear sanction for the setting up of a Constituent Assembly. Jawaharlal Nehru conveyed through his speech at the AICC that the INC accepted the proposal. This was in July 1946. Jinnah reacted to this and announced on 29 July 1946 that the League stood opposed to the plan.

This development took place at a time when Viceroy Lord Wavell was still mulling over the Muslim League's condition to participate in the interim government. The League had laid out that the INC shall not nominate anyone from the Muslim community to the council. It demanded that the INC accept the Muslim League to be the sole representative of the community and this demand of the League consequently led to the negation of the idea of Indian nationalism as one that transcended denominational factors. It will be useful to recall the events pertaining to the interim government at this stage.

After elaborate consultations, the viceroy issued invitations to 14 men to join the interim government. This happened on 15 June 1946. The invitees were: Jawaharlal Nehru, Vallabhbhai Patel, Rajendra Prasad, C. Rajagopalachari and Hari Krishna Mahtab (on behalf of the INC); Mohammed Ali Jinnah, Liaquat Ali Khan, Mohammed Ismail Khan, Khwaja Sir Nazimuddin and Abdul Rab Nishtar (from the Muslim League) and Sardar Baldev Singh (on behalf of the Sikh community), Sir N. P. Engineer (to represent the Parsis), Jagjivan Ram (representing the scheduled castes) and John Mathai (as representative of the Indian Christians).

Meanwhile, the INC proposed the name of Zakir Hussain among its quota of five nominees in the interim council. The Muslim League objected to this and, on 29 July 1946, Jinnah announced that the League will not participate in the process to form the Constituent Assembly. This position of the League offended the INC as well as the British administration. On 12 August 1946, the viceroy announced that he was inviting Jawaharlal Nehru to form the provisional government. After consultation with Nehru, names of 12 members of the National Interim Government were announced on 25 August 1946. Apart from Nehru, the other members were: Vallabhbhai Patel, Dr Rajendra Prasad, Asaf Ali, C. Rajagopalachari, Sarat Chandra Bose, John Mathai, Sardar Baldev Singh, Sir Shafaat Ahmed Khan, Jagjivan Ram, Syed Ali Zaheer and Cooverji Hormusji Bhabha. It was stated that two more Muslims will be nominated in due course.

Five Hindus, three Muslims and one representative each from the scheduled castes, Indian Christians, Sikhs and Parsis formed the basis of this list. In case of the Hindu nominees, the only change in this list from that of the one that was put forward on 15 June 1946 was the replacement of Hare Krishna Mahtab by Sarat Chandra Bose. The Parsi nominee, N. P. Engineer, was replaced by Cooverji Hormusji Bhabha. In place of the League's nominees, the Congress put in the names of three of its own men: Asaf Ali, Shafaat Ahmed Khan and Syed Ali Zaheer.

The Communal Rift Widens

The League, meanwhile, had given the call for 'Direct Action' on 14 August 1946. There was bloodshed in Calcutta and several other places, including in Delhi. Members of the Muslim community were hounded out in many instances. This was when Gandhi set out on his own course to arrive in Calcutta and decided to stay on at a deserted house in Beliaghatta, a locality that was worst affected. He was accompanied by a handful of followers only. The INC had, by then, transformed itself into the Congress party. All its leaders, including Jawaharlal Nehru, were hardly concerned about the tragedy.

Muslims who were hounded out of their homes in Delhi were held in transit camps (in Purana Quila and other places) without even the basic civic amenities. In one camp with 60,000 Muslims, there was only one water tap and no latrines at all. It was only after Gandhi arrived there (on 9 September 1946) and conveyed that the Muslims were Indian nationals and hence must be protected by the Indian state (Nehru by then was the head of the interim government) that the Delhi authorities began organising rations and building latrines. The attitude until then was that the camps were meant only as transit arrangements before the Muslims went off to Pakistan, and that it was no longer the business of the Indian state to provide for their upkeep.

This was the context when the Congress agreed to the constitution of the interim government. Nehru, with 11 others, had assumed office on 2 September 1946. The constitution of this team, in a sense, also conveyed that Nehru had prevailed against any further efforts to take the Muslim League along the path. This provoked another round of communal violence across the country and more prominently in Bombay and Ahmedabad. Lord Wavell set out on another round of discussion and after sounding out Nehru, the viceroy proposed, once again, to Jinnah that the League participated in the interim government. The Muslim League accepted the proposal but Jinnah refused to join the cabinet, as he considered himself far too senior to work as Nehru's subordinate in the cabinet.

The interim cabinet was reconstituted on 15 October 1946. Those who joined on behalf of the League were Liaquat Ali Khan, I. I. Chundrigar, A. R. Nishtar, Ghazanfar Ali Khan and Jogendra Nath Mandal. It may be noted here that the League played its own game in this instance by nominating a scheduled caste member (Mandal) from out of its quota of five. In the proper course, Sarat Chandra Bose, Sir Shafaat Ahmed Khan and Syed Ali Zaheer submitted their resignations.

The Congress, however, refused to hand over the Home portfolio to the League and after negotiations, the League agreed, with reservations, to one of its nominees holding the Finance portfolio. Liaqat Ali Khan, thus, became the finance minister under Nehru. But there was no let up in the animosity between the Congress and the League and this was reflected in the functioning (rather non-functioning) of the interim council of ministers. The League, meanwhile, was determined against cooperating in the making of the constituent assembly.

At another level, the nation was in the grip of communal violence of scales that were unprecedented. Naokhali in East Bengal was ravaged by communal violence around this time. The Congress session at Meerut, in November 1946, was held with J. B. Kripalani as the president. Although it was Jawaharlal Nehru who was to head the Congress (he was made president after Maulana Azad in July 1946), the turn of events during the few months after July 1946, most important among them being Nehru's emergence as head of the interim cabinet, caused the Congress to elect Acharya Kripalani as president in the Meerut session. Abul Kalam Azad's term as Congress president had witnessed all the tumultuous events, the most prominent among them being the transition of the INC from the platform that guided and conducted the freedom struggle into a party now poised to rule India. This marked the transformation of the Congress from a movement to a political party.

The Meerut session and its relevance could be placed in perspective by way of the following observation by Pattabhi Sitaramayya, whose work remains the official history of the INC. Interestingly, Sitaramayya's work stops with his account on the Meerut session. In Meerut, Sitaramayya writes, the Congress merely confirmed what the AICC had already done in September 1946 and ratified the acceptance of seats on the interim government even while declaring, in categorical terms, that the grouping of provinces on lines prescribed by the Cabinet Mission was not acceptable to the INC. The official historian then adds: 'But the resolution on the Constituent Assembly was a real achievement, for it declared that the Congress stands for an *Independent Sovereign Republic* so that India's future may now be taken as lying wholly outside the British Empire.'

The official history of the Congress, however, does not say anything on the fallout of the Congress–League animosity that was haunting the interim government. The denial of the Home portfolio to the Muslim League and the fact that the Finance portfolio was thrust on the Muslim League, and several other factors (that evolved over a period of time) were held as valid reasons by Jinnah to push the demand for Pakistan further. The members of the League who were part of the interim government refused to participate in the 'informal' consultations that Nehru held before the formal meeting of the cabinet in the viceroy's presence. Similarly, the League ministers never let go an opportunity to register their objections to Nehru's proposals in the cabinet meetings. The ministers from the Muslim League, it seemed, were determined to wreck the interim government from within.

The Constituent Assembly Comes into Being

Even as the relationship between the Congress and the Muslim League was turning from bad to worse and Jinnah began sounding more and more firm on the idea of partition, the Constituent Assembly, elected in July–August 1946, held its first meeting on 9 December 1946. On December 11, the Assembly elected Dr Rajendra Prasad as president. The Constituent Assembly was to have a total strength of 389 members: 296 from the provinces and 93 from the various princely states. The elections were held on the basis of reservation of seats on the basis of religious identities. On this basis, 78 seats out of the 296 were reserved for the Muslim candidates and 4 for the Sikhs.

It may be noted here that the elections were restricted to the provinces directly under the British rule and the electorate consisted essentially of the propertied classes. Only 26 per cent of the adult population was qualified to vote in that election. Universal adult suffrage was still an aspiration and the representative nature of the Constituent Assembly was one of the issues that were raised by the leaders of the Congress Socialist Party. Jayaprakash Narayan (JP) being one of the prominent leaders of this group aired his differences with Gandhi on this count. This was one of the aspects that caused the Congress socialists to set out on an independent course soon after.

While the Congress scored impressive victories in the July–August 1946 elections and secured 199 from out of the 210 general seats, the Muslim League did equally well in seats reserved for the Muslims. The League's tally was 76. All but one of the 76 seats came from the Muslim-reserved constituencies. The League, however, decided against participating in the Assembly. Hence, attendance on the first session of the Constituent Assembly, on 9 December 1946 was only 207 members. Jawaharlal Nehru moved a resolution in the Assembly that set the objectives for the house on 13 December 1946, and after debating on it until 19 December, it was decided to adjourn the Assembly session. The intention was to wait for the members of the League to attend and deliberate as well as to ensure that the people in the princely states were represented in the House.

The Assembly session was convened between 20 and 22 January 1947, exactly a month after the first session was adjourned and the Objectives Resolution was passed without the Muslim League taking part in the proceedings.

Liaquat Ali Khan's Budget Proposals

Meanwhile, the functioning of the interim government was far from smooth with animosity between the Congress and the League growing by the day. The 'informal' meetings of the cabinet intended to settle differences before any proposal was taken to the formal meetings that Viceroy Lord Wavell presided over, could not be held from the very beginning. This situation only worsened after the Constituent Assembly was set up and the Objectives Resolution was passed without waiting for the League to change its stand. By February 1946, a stage had come that Nehru demanded the resignation of the members of the League. Soon after that, Vallabhbhai Patel went to the extent of suggesting that the Congress pull out of the interim government if the League members did not quit forthwith.

The proverbial last straw was the budget proposals presented by Liaquat Ali Khan in March 1947. The finance minister proposed a variety of taxes on industry and trade and proposed a commission to go into the affairs of about 150 big business houses and inquire into the allegations of tax evasion against them. Khan called this a 'socialistic budget'. Interestingly, charges of tax evasion were made against Indian industrialists by Jawaharlal Nehru and Maulana Abul Kalam Azad (who was then the Congress president) in the course of the elections to the Constituent Assembly in July–August 1946. Similarly, the Congress in its election manifesto of 1946 had committed itself to setting up a socialistic pattern of society and for the removal of economic inequities. Liaquat Ali Khan simply pretended to implement the stated positions of important Congress leaders. This put the Congress and Nehru in a dilemma. The interim government was on the verge of collapsing. Liaquat Ali Khan's budget was indeed a calculated bid to hit the Indian industrialists who had, by this time, emerged as the most powerful supporters of the Congress. As for the Muslim League, the fact is that they had joined the interim government to wreck any possibility of united India. The intention was clear: To hasten the partition and prove that there was no way that the League and the Congress could work together towards independence.

The situation, however, was saved, thanks to the developments at another level. The sequence of events that followed Prime Minister Atlee's statement in London that the British were firm on their intention to leave India by June 1948 saved the provisional government from falling apart. The arrival of Lord Mountbatten, in place of Lord Wavell, hastened the pace of India's independence. The Congress too agreed to partition. The only other option, as it appeared then, was to consider Gandhi's proposal: That Jinnah be asked to form his cabinet. This, however, was not acceptable to anyone in the Congress other than Gandhi. While Gandhi, on his arrival in Delhi (towards the end of March 1947), went about persuading Lord Mountbatten to dismiss the interim cabinet and summon Jinnah to constitute the government, Nehru made a public declaration on 20 April 1947 that the League could have Pakistan as long as it committed itself to an agreement that those parts of India that did not wish to join Pakistan will be left free to decide on their own accord.

Within a week from then, on 28 April 1947, Rajendra Prasad, in his capacity as the president of the Constituent Assembly read out a statement that clarified the Congress' stand on this. The statement was a commitment that the Constitution will not be thrust upon any part of the country that did not accept it. The concluding portion of the statement was so categorical that it deserves to be quoted here. It said: 'This may mean not only a division of India but a division of some provinces. For this, we must be prepared, and the Assembly may have to draw up a constitution based on such division.' In other words, Gandhi's position was indeed a cry in wilderness.

The Congress Working Committee, on 1 May 1947, conveyed its acceptance of the idea of partition to Mountbatten. The viceroy left for London soon after and on his return, on 2 June 1947, disclosed the blueprint for partition and, more importantly, the desire to advance the date of British withdrawal from India to 15 August 1947. There were only 11 weeks left between then and the eventual day of independence. The Congress leaders convened a meet of the AICC on 15 June 1947. It was here that the resolution by Govind Ballabh Pant, accepting partition, was moved and approved. It required the persuasive powers of Nehru and Patel as well as the moral might of Gandhi to finally get the majority in the AICC in favour of the resolution. The votes were: 157 for and 29 against the resolution. The opposition to the resolution came predominantly from the Congress socialists. Jayaprakash Narayan was one of those. That Gandhi too supported the resolution at the AICC (where he was present as a special invitee) shocked JP and many others.

The period between March 1946 and 15 August 1947 saw many tumultuous events such as (i) the setting up of the Cabinet Mission, (ii) the formation of the interim government, (iii) the birth of the Constituent Assembly and (iv) the widening of rift between the Congress and the Muslim League leading to the partition and finally the dawn of independence. However, the period is also significant in another sense. This was when the INC was transformed into the Congress party. The most pronounced feature of this transition, however, was the emergence of Jawaharlal Nehru as the supreme leader of the Congress as distinct from the earlier three decades when Gandhi was its supreme commander.

Nehru Emerges as the Leader

While Sardar Patel was not a pushover, the Mahatma did play an important role in having Nehru at the helm. This happened at the time of the constitution of the interim cabinet itself. The most important setting to this was that the invitation by Viceroy Lord Wavell, on 12 August 1946, was extended to the president of the INC to form the interim government. After a long spell as Congress president (1939–1946) Maulana Abul Kalam Azad proposed Nehru's name as his successor. Azad's term turned out to be such a long one not by design. It happened because after his election in the Ramgarh session in March 1940, the Congress got involved in the individual *satyagraha* and was subsequently banned after the August 1942 Quit India resolution at Bombay. The organisational elections, hence, had to wait for the World War II to cease.

Azad, in his biography, recalls that he proposed Nehru's name as president because he was averse to the idea of Sardar Patel as head of the Congress in the specific context that prevailed in March 1946. Thus, when the invitation to form the interim government was sent out, Jawaharlal Nehru happened to be there to 'accept' the 'responsibility'. Jawaharlal Nehru took over as Congress president on 6 July 1946. At the time he took over, it was certain that he would be called upon by the viceroy to form the interim government. One of Nehru's important statements on the day he took over the Congress leadership was to affirm that the Congress remained non-committal on everything proposed by the Cabinet Mission except that of going into the Constituent Assembly. Jinnah's reaction to this was on expected lines. He described Nehru's 6 July 1946 statement as a complete repudiation of the basic form upon which the long-term scheme rested. Within three weeks of that speech, the Muslim League Council met in Bombay where Jinnah prevailed upon his party to withdraw from their earlier acceptance of the Cabinet Mission plan completely and called for observing 16 August 1946 as Direct Action Day.

Meanwhile, there are accounts of the times that suggest that most members of the Congress Working Committee were not happy with the choice of Nehru as head of the interim government. The preference for Sardar Patel, according to many chroniclers of the times, was based on the perception that Patel alone was capable of dealing 'firmly' with Jinnah and the League. Patel, at that time, was the chairman of the Congress Parliamentary Board and the provincial Congress committees had expressed their preference for him as the Congress president. But then, the clincher, so to say, came from Gandhi. The Mahatma reasoned it out as follows: 'Jawahar will not take second place. He is better known abroad than Sardar and will make India play a role in international affairs. Sardar will look after the country's affairs. They will be like two oxen yoked to the governmental cart. One will need the other and both will pull together'. After Gandhi intervened in Nehru's favour, Patel as well as the others in the Congress simply accepted that as the mandate.

Thus, after the partition, the Constituent Assembly was also to play the role of the Central Legislative Assembly and Nehru's council of ministers was accountable to this. The first government after independence, with Lord Mountbatten as the Governor General, was constituted by a 16-member cabinet:

Jawaharlal Nehru (Prime Minister), Sardar Patel (Home), Maulana Abul Kalam Azad (Education), Rafi Ahmed Kidwai (Posts and Telegraphs), Jagjivan Ram (Labour), Rajkumari Amrit Kaur, Dr John Mathai, Sardar Baldev Singh (Defence), Sir R. K. Shanmukam Chetty (Finance), Jairamdas Daulatram, Shyama Prasad Mukherjee, K. C. Neogy, Dr B. R. Ambedkar, N. V. Gadgil, Gopal Swami Ayyangar and Mohanlal Saxena.

Of significance is that this arrangement, with Nehru and Patel like two oxen yoked to the governmental cart, persisted after 15 August 1947 and Rajendra Prasad, another important leader of the Congress then, was accommodated as the president of the Constituent Assembly. The relationship between Pandit Nehru and Sardar Patel strained after a while and this had begun to bother Gandhi. On 30 January 1948, Gandhi's prayer meeting was delayed because he was held up with Patel. The Sardar, that evening had asked for Gandhi's sanction to quit Nehru's cabinet. The assassination of the Mahatma, a few minutes after that meeting, changed things. The Sardar, after that, plunged himself into the nation-building project in the literal sense of the term. The accession of the princely states into the Indian Union, which included the police action in Hyderabad, was indeed his achievement. Nehru too left this task to his deputy in the cabinet.

That the Sardar had reconciled himself to being Nehru's deputy was evident in the context of the Nehru–Liaquat pact in April 1950. The pact was entered into by the prime ministers of India and Pakistan in the aftermath of anti-Hindu violence in East Pakistan (now Bangladesh) and the retaliation against the Muslims in West Bengal. The Nehru–Liaquat pact was primarily a commitment by both nations to protect the life and property of the religious minorities on both sides. There was opposition to this move by Nehru at various levels, including from within the cabinet. Shyama Prasad Mukherjee and K. C. Neogy, the two representatives of the Hindu Mahasabha, quit the cabinet in protest while N. V. Gadgil registered his objections to the pact. Meanwhile, John Mathai too quit the cabinet protesting against what he called Nehru's 'autocratic' way of functioning. Nehru, at this stage, had even contemplated resigning as prime minister; the Congress party organisation, at that time, was behind Patel. It was then that Patel left for Calcutta and campaigned for implementing the Nehru–Liaquat pact from there. It is pertinent to note, in this context, that Patel had stood up against Shyama Prasad Mukherjee, the founder of the Bharatiya Jana Sangh.

There were, however, instances when Patel refused to settle his differences with Nehru. One of them was the question whether Rajendra Prasad should continue as president after 26 January 1950 or whether C. Rajagopalachari should be chosen for the job. According to the chroniclers of the period, Nehru was in favour of Rajaji. Patel, thanks to his hold on the Congress organisation, ensured that Prasad was chosen. Similarly, Nehru and Patel were drawn into a dispute on the issue of electing the Congress president at the Nashik session in August 1950.

While Nehru backed J. B. Kripalani for the position, Purushottam Das Tandon had the backing of Patel. In the elections, Tandon trounced Kripalani and in what was like a repeat of the drama played out in the Congress in 1939 (when Gandhi refused to cooperate with Subhas Bose), Nehru refused to be in the Congress Working Committee. Tandon, meanwhile, refrained from forcing a showdown and offered to step down.

All this came to an end with the passing away of Sardar Patel on 15 December 1950. With Patel dead and Rajendra Prasad as the president of the Republic, there was no challenge at all to Nehru from within and outside the Congress. Thus, at the time of the first general elections in 1951–52, Jawaharlal Nehru was the undisputed leader of the Congress party. He had taken upon himself the leadership of the Congress ahead of the first general elections and after the tussle with Tandon in Nashik. In the Delhi session of the Congress in 1952, he was formally elected as the president of the party. Nehru was re-elected twice after that: at Hyderabad in 1953 and at Kalyani in 1954. An unwritten rule—*one-man-one-post*—that had been followed in the Congress, and because of which the mantle of the Congress presidentship fell on Acharya J. B. Kripalani at the Meerut session in September 1946 (Nehru, who was the initial choice was to head the interim cabinet), was given up until U. N. Dhebar was elected president in the Avadi session in 1955. Nehru's hold over the polity and the Congress had become undisputed by now.

V

The Era of Nehruvian Socialism

> The Congress has made history in India in the past; I have no doubt that it has still to fulfil a historic mission. It has to consolidate our freedom; it has to work for the social and economic advancement of all our millions; it has to help to maintain that broad-minded tolerance and even temper, which was the pride of our people in olden days; it has to keep clear the vision of the future and not allow itself to be deflected by the passion or prejudice of the moment. These are tasks that I do not know who else can perform in the India of the present day.
>
> — Jawaharlal Nehru to Balwantrai Mehta, on the eve of the Congress session in Delhi. Nehru became Congress president in this session on 12 December 1952

The most important development in the few years before the first general elections (the entire process took five months, between 25 October 1951 and 21 February 1952) was the emergence of Jawaharlal Nehru. We have noted this and the fact that one of the key factors that led to Nehru's emergence was the backing he received from Gandhi. Sardar Patel, Gandhi's lieutenant during the Kheda *satyagraha* and someone who could have challenged Nehru from within the Congress, was no more at the time of the first general elections. Patel had passed away on 15 December 1950. Rajendra Prasad, the Mahatma's lieutenant at Champaran, was elevated by then to the post of the president of the republic on 26 January 1950, the day on which the Constitution was adopted. Those who constituted the Congress Socialist Party, a ginger group that had stood by Nehru since the Lahore session of the Indian National Congress (INC) in 1929, had left the fold in 1948 to form the Socialist Party at a conference in Nasik. The prominent leaders of this group were Jayaprakash Narayan, Acharya Narendra Deva and Dr Ram Manohar Lohia; all of them had been members of the Congress Working Committee (CWC) at some stage or the other. Shyama Prasad Mukherjee, another important member of the interim cabinet, after independence had quit the cabinet to found the Bharatiya Jan Sangh in 1951.

As the president of the Congress and the prime minister of the country, Nehru could ensure that the Congress party organisation was reduced to an organ that merely endorsed the government and its policies. The most pronounced outcome of this arrangement was that Nehru could effortlessly obtain acceptance of his own idea of socialism from the Congress party. It is another matter that a substantive lot of the provincial leaders of the Congress were not disciples of Nehru whether it was with regard to the idea of building a secular polity or about the socialist project. While this was most pronounced in Uttar Pradesh and Bihar, the cradle of the Vedic civilisation, the leadership in the other provinces too was not completely wedded to Nehru's ideas. So much so, the socialist project and the secular idea, after being endorsed in the AICC sessions, were either abandoned or implemented piecemeal. All this culminated in the decline of the Congress in due course.

In this chapter, we shall look into: (i) the factors that helped the Congress to emerge as the obvious choice in the first general election, (ii) the genesis of the Nehruvian socialist project in the Bombay Plan and its evolution in the Avadi (1955) and the Nagpur (1959) sessions of the Congress, and (iii) the infirmities in this socialist project that caused the decline of the Congress during the 1960s.

Meanwhile, it is necessary at this stage to qualify that the use of socialism in this chapter will refer to the socialist project as undertaken by Nehru. This was different from the socialism envisaged by the Socialist Party as well as that of the Communist Party of India (CPI). The Nehruvian socialist project was essentially on the lines of the prescriptions laid out in the Bombay Plan, discussed earlier in this book. Hence, it will be appropriate to state that the Nehruvian era witnessed the implementation of the Bombay Plan. Thus, a substantially interventionist state and an economy with a sizeable public sector, governed in the political sphere by a Constitution that provided for a multi-party parliamentary democracy, was put in place.

The Congress Era

The Congress party, under Nehru, could entrench itself in the national psyche in the immediate aftermath of independence for a variety of reasons. And, the credit for forging the Congress into the obvious choice of the Indian people in the 1951–52 general elections should go to Nehru. It was ordained by the Congress-controlled administration that Nehru, being the prime minister, was entitled to use the government aircraft during electioneering. While it was decided that he shall pay for his own passage, the burden was far less than the services availed because the basis for calculation was the notional fare for a person in a regular flight. This, and the fact that the Congress continued, at that time, to be the only party with an organisational set-up in even the remotest of villages gave the party an advantage in the elections.

There were the regional satraps too. Pandit Ravi Shankar Shukla in Central India, Govind Ballabh Pant in the United Provinces and B. G. Kher in Bombay. Similarly, the fact that Babu Rajendra Prasad was associated with the Congress (notwithstanding his differences with Nehru and the fact that he, as president of the republic, was not available for campaigning) held the Congress in good stead in Bihar. Baldev Singh, the defence minister in Nehru's cabinet, was an important leader in Punjab. Similarly, C. Rajagopalachari, despite having quit the Congress in 1942—he left the Congress after his demand that the Congress return to the provincial governments in 1942 was rejected and, hence, he stayed away from the Quit India movement too—bounced back and headed the Congress government in Madras after the first general elections. All this enabled the party to lay claims as the sole legatee of the freedom struggle.

It is true that several other leaders, who belonged to other platforms such as the Socialist Party and the CPI, could legitimately claim to belong to the same legacy. Their role in the struggle for freedom and in building the trade unions and the *kisan sabhas,* and in this sense for the cause of freedom, was no less significant. Jayaprakash Narayan's daring escape from the Hazaribagh jail and his role in organising militant resistance to the British rule in the context of the Quit India movement had made him a national hero. Incidentally, JP led the Socialist Party's campaign in the first elections along with others like Acharya Narendra Deva, Ram Manohar Lohia, Asoka Mehta, Yusuf Meherally and Asaf Ali. They were all known for their role in the freedom struggle and as staunch disciples of Gandhi. But then, they were not in command of a party organisation as strong and extensive as the Congress. The Socialist Party's rise and its failure to occupy the political space in India will be taken up separately.

As for the leaders of the Communist Party, most of them were in prison even after 15 August 1947. The Telengana struggle and the other campaigns they had led—such as the Tebhaga movement in Bengal, the Punnapra-Vayalar armed struggle against the ruler in Travancore (now south Kerala), the industrial general strike and demonstrations in Bombay and other industrial hubs in solidarity with the 'mutiny' by the Royal Indian Navy ratings and against the trial of the Indian National Army (INA) soldiers—were all glorious chapters in the history of the communists in India. The leaders, however, were unable to consolidate these on a nationwide scale. The communist influence was, hence, restricted to a few pockets.

The fact that power was transferred to the Congress party on 2 September 1946 (with Nehru at the helm) also helped the party to get itself entrenched in the power structures in independent India. The party got complete control over the instruments of power across the country and the landlords and other sections of the social elite found the Congress as a platform committed to their vested interests. This aspect was pronounced in the Gangetic belt and it guided the political discourse in Bihar and Uttar Pradesh. In the three-tier caste structure that constituted the society in most parts of the Indian countryside, the Congress party could entrench itself in the top and the bottom rungs. This is where the regional satraps of the Congress played a role. Although they were not pleased with Nehru's socialist project, and Nehru was aware of that, both sides agreed to coexist and build the Congress in their own different ways. For instance, leaders like G. B. Pant, Ravi Shankar Shukla, Rajendra Prasad, Sri Krishna Sinha and many others like them were clearly in favour of preserving the status quo in the social and economic sense. They clearly empathised with the rural elite and were keen on preserving the socio-economic relationship that prevailed. This, in turn, laid the basis for a large chunk of the upper castes—the Brahmins, the Bhoomihars and the Rajputs—who owned large tracts of land in the countryside, turn to the Congress party as their obvious choice.

It is useful to recall, in this context, an important aspect of the strategy that the INC under Gandhi had adopted vis-à-vis its campaign in the countryside. It had consistently refused to resort to a no-rent campaign even while launching, time and again, a no-tax campaign. This had its logic in the context of the freedom struggle. The dominant role that the landed gentry played in the social and economic life of the countryside rendered its cooperation and active support necessary for the success of the *satyagraha* campaigns. The *satyagraha* campaign necessarily meant long terms in jails for those who participated in them. Thus, when the poorer sections were drawn into the campaign, it was necessary that the minimum needs of the kith and kin of the *satyagrahis* were taken care of. This meant the *satyagraha* campaigns needed the active support of the landed gentry, who had the surplus grain to feed the landless. A no-rent campaign along with the no-tax campaign would have meant a battle against the landed gentry and the colonial state at the same time.

This, however, led to instances of confrontation within the INC. The Bihar Pradesh Kisan Sabha (BPKS), under the leadership of Swami Sahajanand Saraswati, launched a no-rent campaign. The BPKS lost its affiliation to the All India Kisan Sabha, under the INC at that time. There were similar conflicts in parts of the United Provinces, the Madras presidency and the Bengal Provincial Congress Committee. However, the INC and its strategy were guided by the long-term dynamics of the struggle for freedom. This also meant that the rural elite could entrench themselves in the organisational set-up of the platform in a big way. As the INC transformed itself into the Congress party, this feature was clearly pronounced.

The decade after 1947, however, witnessed the Congress party emerging into the natural choice of a cross-section of people and not the landed gentry alone. The fact is that the first elections were held on the basis of universal adult suffrage and the Congress won emphatically in that. Hence, the party's victory cannot be explained on the basis of its popularity among the social and economic elite in the countryside. There were other factors that helped the Congress win such a massive mandate as it did in the first general elections.

The scars left by the communal violence and the assassination of the Mahatma, soon after independence, affected the political discourse substantially. Despite the alienation of Gandhi from the affairs of the Congress, the party leaders succeeded in claiming to inherit the Mahatma's legacy, particularly after his assassination.

This was possible due to a combination of reasons. The Mahatma's disciples, particularly those who were committed to the principles of Gandhian socialism, had failed to organise themselves into a political platform until a few years before the first general elections. The Socialist Party was founded only in 1948 and Acharya J. B. Kripalani, another disciple of Gandhi, set out on his course to found the Kisan Mazdoor Praja Party (KMPP) in June 1951. While all of them were leaders with a committed following in their own way, their efforts did not mature into a political party with a nationwide organisation at the time of the first general elections.

Another important factor that helped the Congress party emerge as the natural heir of the Mahatma's legacy can be traced to the formation of the Bharatiya Jan Sangh (rechristened as the Bharatiya Janata Party in 1980) just before the first general elections. The Jan Sangh was founded in 1951, drawing its cadre, predominantly and systematically, from the Rashtriya Swayamsevak Sangh (RSS). A section of the Hindu Mahasabha's ranks too flocked to the Jan Sangh soon after its formation. It is relevant to state here that the Jan Sangh had fielded candidates in 94 constituencies and secured just 3.1 per cent of the votes polled. Three of its candidates were elected in the first general elections. As for the Hindu Mahasabha, the platform secured four seats in the first Lok Sabha; two from Madhya Bharat (consisting of parts of Madhya Pradesh and Maharashtra and Nagpur was its capital) and one each from Uttar Pradesh and West Bengal.

The ideological context that led to the formation of the Jan Sangh, its political programme and its transition into the BJP will be dealt with later in this book (Chapter XII). Of significance here is that the formation of the Jan Sangh, explicitly associated with the RSS and the Hindu Mahasabha, helped the Congress party retain its hold among the Muslims and the Dalits. The Jan Sangh was perceived as the inheritor of the sectarian opposition to Gandhi. Notwithstanding the acquittal of V. D. Savarkar and some of his associates from the Hindu Mahasabha stables of charges in the assassination of the Mahatma, the perception across the country was to the contrary. This helped the Congress strike firm roots with the Muslim community nationwide.

Similarly, the RSS worldview, in the social sense, was rooted firmly in the Vedic prescriptions. It was one that celebrated the *varnashrama dharma* and the caste structure perpetuated on that basis. This also meant that the Jan Sangh was perceived as a political project committed to preserve the unequal socio-economic order. This led the Dalits to rally behind the Congress. This happened despite efforts by B. R. Ambedkar to carve out an exclusive platform for the Dalits in independent India. Yet another factor that helped the Congress to obtain for itself a substantial support base among the Dalits was the presence of Jagjivan Ram, in its fold. One of the founders of the All India Depressed Classes League in 1935, he was associated with the INC in Bihar from 1931 onwards. He was chosen to be a part of the first interim council and given charge of the Labour portfolio. He remained the labour minister in all the councils since 2 September 1946 and was also given additional charge of Health.

The popular support for the Congress as a party was evident in the results of the first general elections. Of the 489 Lok Sabha constituencies, the Congress party fielded its candidates in 479 and won 364 seats. The party secured 45 per cent of the votes polled. The Socialist Party secured 10.6 per cent of the votes polled and won only 12 seats out of the 227 it contested. However, the socialists were next only to the Congress in terms of the votes secured. The KMPP, founded by J. B. Kripalani, essentially due to differences he developed with Nehru just before the elections, won nine Lok Sabha seats, polling 5.8 per cent of the votes. The CPI (undivided) secured 16 seats and thus emerged the largest among the opposition even though the party's share of votes was just 3.3 per cent.

The Socialistic Pattern and Planned Economy

With the emergence of the Congress to power and Jawaharlal Nehru as its leader, socialism became the guiding principle of independent India's economic policy. It is another matter that the fundamentals of this economic policy doctrine were drawn from the Bombay Plan document. It is also significant that the regime could afford to skirt some critical parts of the Bombay Plan. The prescription that the state shall take concerted steps to reduce incidence of poverty, for instance, was among them.

The Nehruvian dispensation did not find the pressing need for this for two reasons. Firstly, the political factors, as discussed above, assured the Congress party of a large support base. This presumption was indeed fine. Another factor that led the Nehruvian dispensation to ignore the prescriptions for poverty alleviation was the presumption that growth, along a wide front, will translate into poverty reduction. This presumption too was not without basis. India, after independence, was not obliged to export grains to finance its budgetary transfer to Britain, a system that contributed to the drain until 15 August 1947. This enhanced the availability of food grain for domestic consumption. A substantial sterling balance, accumulated during the war years, meant that there was no compulsion to export food grain in order to shore up sterling reserves. All this meant an increase in the per capita availability of food grain. Even a calibrated growth in the manufacturing sector, as envisaged in the Bombay Plan, and the employment opportunities that would arise out of such a growth was perceived by Nehru and his associates as adequate means to enhance the purchasing power in the domestic market.

Alongside, the Indian capitalist class that had emerged in the context of the national movement had evolved into a prominent player waiting for its own growth in the aftermath of freedom. So much so, in 1947, the national bourgeoisie had wrested to itself 75 per cent of the market for industrial produce in India. In the banking and insurance sector too, there was a substantial presence of Indian enterprise. There was, however, one area in which the presence of domestic capital was not as pronounced. That was the capital goods sector. The Bombay Plan, 1944, had indeed, referred to this. It had stated this in as many words:

> We consider it essential that this lack of capital goods industries should be remedied in as short time as possible. Apart from its importance as a means of quickening the pace of industrial development in India, it would have the effect of ultimately reducing our dependence on foreign countries for the plant and machinery required by us and, consequently, of reducing our requirement of external finance.

These prescriptions were integral to the first three five-year plans (1951 to 1965). Meanwhile, even before the transfer of power was formally effected (on 15 August 1947), Nehru presided over the Economic Programme Committee of the AICC. It laid down the need for ensuring that such areas as defence, key industries and public utilities were retained in the public sector; the committee also stated that the process of transfer of private undertakings to the public sector should commence after a period of five years. It may be noted here that after his release from prison in 1945, Nehru thundered in a public meeting: 'Blackmarketeers and profiteers have flourished at the cost of the nation. All such persons will be hanged from the nearest lamp post when the Congress comes to power and the country becomes independent'. This, indeed, was what Liaquat Ali Khan proposed in his budget in February 1947.

However, all this was given a quiet burial soon after independence. The Industrial Policy Resolution of Nehru's government in 1948, for instance, specified that the question of nationalisation of private sector undertakings shall be taken up after 10 years. The Congress party followed this up in its Avadi session (March 1955). But nothing was done for over a decade in any of these areas. The nationalisation of banks took place in 1969 and some private sector units, rendered sick and waiting to be shut down, were nationalised in 1976. It was evident that Nehru's commitment to building a socialistic pattern of society was turning into rhetoric in his own times.

The socialist rhetoric, however, helped the Congress party to enlist support from the CPI. Important leaders from within the CPI found in Nehru a determined fighter against sections within and outside the Congress party advocating free enterprise. Although it took more than a decade after independence before an organised opposition to the socialistic pattern to emerge (the Swatantra Party, founded in 1959) there were leaders within the Congress fold who were committed to the idea of free market economy. C. Rajagopalachari, one of the architects of the Swatantra Party, was a known advocate of the free market philosophy. He was made the chief minister of the Madras state by Nehru after the first general elections. There were several others in the Congress stables who joined the free market bandwagon later; Morarji Desai in Bombay, Nijalingappa in Mysore, Neelam Sanjiva Reddy and Brahmananda Reddy in Andhra to name a few prominent leaders in the provinces. They all constituted the core of what came to be known as the syndicate within the Congress party in the context of the 1969 split. Similarly, Lal Bahadur Shastri too belonged to this category; it was during his brief stint as prime minister (between 1964 and 1966) that some of Nehru's premises were questioned. But then, all those leaders were on the margins of the Congress party in the 1950s. They had to wait for at least a couple of decades before baring their opposition to Jawaharlal Nehru's socialistic pattern of society.

From Avadi to Nagpur

It will not be an exaggeration to state that socialistic principles, enunciated from different and sometimes distinct premises, had become the dominant ideology of the era. This was reflected in the composition of the first Lok Sabha. The votaries of free enterprise were indeed a hopeless minority. There were, however, sharp differences within the mainstream about what constituted socialism. The most substantive of these was the debate between those committed to socialism, as espoused by Nehru, and those who stood by Gandhian methods in economic policy.

The Avadi session of the Congress in January 1955 assumed significance for two reasons. First, and in many ways of minor importance, was that Nehru stepped down as Congress president at Avadi. U. N. Dhebar was elected president at the session. Dhebar was, in fact, Nehru's nominee. He continued to preside over the party until Indira Gandhi was elected president at the Nagpur session in February 1959. The second significant aspect of the Avadi session was in the realm of the reassertion made by the Congress party of its commitment to building a socialistic pattern of the society. The immediate context was that it was time, by then, to set the direction for the second five-year plan. At Avadi, the Congress session laid out that the objective for the plan shall be the creation of a society where the means of production are brought under social ownership and the national wealth is distributed equitably.

The second five-year plan laid ample stress on the need to build heavy and capital goods industries and this, in turn, led to a spurt in the setting up of Public Sector Undertakings. P. C. Mahalanobis, an economist of repute, was brought in by Nehru to guide the drafting process of the second plan. While it is true that the second plan expanded the scope of the public sector, the fact is that neither the Industrial Policy Resolution of 1956 nor the plan as such made a mention about nationalising units in the private sector. The focus, by this time, turned to building of a 'mixed economy'. The premise was that the private and the public sectors coexist and compliment each other. It was further laid out that private enterprise shall be encouraged to grow with as much freedom as was possible within the framework of the second plan. And, when the Congress held its session in Indore in January 1957, a resolution was moved and passed to amend the party's constitution. The party's objective changed from building a 'socialistic pattern of society' to making India into 'a socialist co-operative commonwealth.'

These were the evidences of the shifting priorities of the party and in many ways the dilution of the socialist goals. The brave posture by Nehru in 1945 of hanging the corrupt among the businessmen from the nearest lamp post was beginning to sound like a joke: instances of a nexus between the corrupt and the ministers were beginning to surface. Of significance in this context were scandalous deals in the insurance sector and the Mundhra scam. These scandals were brought out, much to Nehru's embarrassment, by the Congress MP from Rae Bareili and the prime minister's son-in-law, Feroze Gandhi. A brief narrative of these will not only present the picture clearly but might also help, by way of a distraction from a narrative of events.

The first of the exposes was about the misuse of funds at its disposal by private insurance firms. The insurance industry, at that time, was under private players. This happened in 1955. Feroze, who was known to be a backbencher in the treasury, presented documents of such misuse by the Bharat Insurance Company run by Ramakrishna Dalmia. His exposé in the Parliament led to two things: One, an inquiry commission was set up to look into the charges, which found the accusations substantive and Dalmia was convicted. Secondly, and more importantly, this led to the nationalisation of the insurance industry.

Later, in February 1958, Feroze made a more stunning exposé and this involved the Congress party's affairs: the Mundhra scandal as it came to be known. Haridas Mundhra, a businessman and a generous contributor to the Congress party's funds, ran into difficulties. This happened in the aftermath of the 1957 elections; Mundhra had contributed substantially to the party's election funds. When in difficulty, he managed help by way of the Life Insurance Corporation (LIC)—now a nationalised concern, thanks to Feroze's exposé in 1955—buying up his company's share. This was done by the LIC on instructions received from Finance Minister T. T. Krishnamachari (known as TTK) and conveyed through the Finance Secretary H. M. Patel. Soon after the shares were purchased by the LIC, it was revealed that the prices of the shares were inflated. Since Mundhra's business was sinking, the shares crashed further. The gross loss for LIC was estimated to be over Rs. 150 lakh. Feroze's exposé embarrassed both the Congress party and Nehru. TTK, held as Nehru's own man, was asked to resign by Nehru. That was when Morarji Desai became finance minister.

The Avadi session, however, had its impact on the political discourse by way of sending the Socialist Party (by this time rechristened as the Praja Socialist Party [PSP]) and the CPI into a state of confusion. While a detailed discussion on the developments within the Socialist Party will be done later in this book (Chapter VII), it is useful to discuss some of the debates within the PSP in the aftermath of the Avadi session. A large group, within the PSP, saw the Avadi resolution reflecting whatever they stood for in their days as members of the Congress Socialist Party and argued in favour of the PSP's merger with the Congress party. Prominent among them was Asoka Mehta. In less than a decade after the Avadi session, Mehta was to join the Congress party and serve as a minister in the union cabinet. In the immediate wake of the Avadi resolution, the PSP landed in a state of disarray. Also of significance here is that the party had split, by then, with one of its leading lights, Ram Manohar Lohia walking out to re-establish the Socialist Party. Another pillar of the socialist edifice, Jayaprakash Narayan, too had found substance in Nehru's socialist rhetoric by this time and turned to the *bhoodan* idea.

Similar confusions were evident in the communist movement too. Important leaders in the CPI were beginning to express in favour of cooperating with Nehru and the Congress. An immediate fallout of this was the rout of the CPI in the first elections to the newly-created Andhra Pradesh state assembly in 1957. The CPI, whose strength in the Madras state assembly in 1952 was substantial (large tracts of Andhra Pradesh were part of the Madras state then), lost heavily after Andhra was formed into a separate state. Incidentally, the ideological debate in the CPI, leading to the split in 1964 (with the formation of the CPI [M]), were rooted in the context of the Avadi session of the Congress and the Andhra Pradesh unit was where this debate was the fiercest. This explains the fact that after the split, both the CPI and the CPI (M) were to elect C. Rajeswara Rao and P. Sundarayya as general secretaries.

Meanwhile, the few years between the Avadi session and the 1957 elections witnessed the passing away of two important leaders. Acharya Narendra Deva, considered the tallest of the socialist leaders (and elected chairman of the party when it was founded in 1948), died on 19 February 1956. His death had indeed left a void insofar as the Socialist movement was concerned. Dr B. R. Ambedkar, with whom Lohia had begun to discuss the prospects of forging a political platform uniting the scheduled castes and the other backward castes, too passed away on 6 December 1956.

The outcome of the second general elections reflected all these. The polls were held between 24 February 1957 and 9 June 1957 for 494 Lok Sabha constituencies (as against 489 in 1951–52). The Congress party, under Nehru, fielded candidates in 490 seats and won 371 seats, securing 47.8 per cent of the votes. This was seven seats more than its tally in the first Lok Sabha—the party's votes went up by almost three percentage points. The CPI too registered an increase in the number of seats and vote percentage. The party secured 27 seats and accounted for 8.9 per cent of the votes against 16 seats and a mere 3.3 per cent votes. The loser, in a sense, was the Socialist Party. A post-poll merger of the Socialist Party and the KMPP had taken the combined strength in the first Lok Sabha to 21 and together the vote share of the two parties was over 16 per cent. The PSP, in 1957, polled just 5.9 per cent of the votes and won 19 seats.

The Congress did well in the state assemblies too. The party, however, lost power in Kerala. Formed out of the Malabar district from Madras and the princely states—Travancore and Cochin—Kerala turned out to be the first state where the Congress lost power. The communists won there and E. M. S. Namboodiripad assumed office as chief minister. It was, in a sense, history because this was the first time ever that the communists came to power through elections. The Kerala development had its impact on Nehru and the Congress party. The party joined forces, whose opposition to the communists was based on a variety of issues and most of all the idea of egalitarianism, to orchestrate the dismissal of the government. The history of the abuse of Article 356, a provision that was retained in the Constitution after everyone agreed that it will remain a dead letter of the law, began with this. Nehru was the prime minister and Indira Gandhi the Congress president when this happened in 1959.

The next landmark event in the Nehruvian era was the Nagpur session of the Congress in 1959. Like it happened in Avadi, the Congress elected a new president in Nagpur. Indira Gandhi, inducted to the CWC in 1955, was now made the Congress president. The other important aspect of the Nagpur session was the economic policy resolution there. Even at the time of the Avadi session, it was evident that the commitment of Congress to socialism was mere rhetoric and the provincial leaders of the party were successful in taking the party and the government on a different path. Nehru, at different points of time, vented his own desire to quit and take a vacation. It is another matter that he did not do that. Meanwhile, the second five-year plan did not progress and all talk of land reforms were becoming empty rhetoric: the legislations on this front remained a dead letter of the law. The Congress party's satraps were beginning to assert despite Nehru's reminders. The *bhoodan* movement was sounding to be a big joke. Most of the land that was distributed to the landless was fallow and in many cases the records of ownership were never transferred. The Nagpur session was held in this context. The Congress party resolved to seek enforcement of land ceilings and for entrusting surplus lands to the panchayats who, in turn, were to conduct farming on those lands through cooperatives of landless labourers.

This resolution was hardly followed up by action on the ground. Neither was the high command worked up on that nor were the regional satraps of the Congress serious about putting the words into practice. But then, if the Avadi Congress resolution had sent the various other socialist platforms into a tailspin and helped the Congress capture support from sections among them, the effect of the Nagpur resolution was to the contrary. The direct fallout of the Nagpur session was the coming together of a whole lot of former Congressmen and sections from outside the Congress fold to organise opposition to the idea of socialism. The initiative came from the All India Agriculturists Federation, whose members had obvious reasons to oppose any talk of land reforms. N. G. Ranga (a former Congressman from Andhra Pradesh), Minoo R Masani (who had travelled from the Congress Socialist Party to be an advocate of high capitalism) and C. Rajagopalachari, joined the league and met in June 1959. Nehru had anointed C. Rajagopalachari as the chief minister of Madras in 1952 but he was removed from that position a couple of years before the Nagpur session. The June 1959 meeting resulted in the formation of the Swatantra Party. In the short history of independent India, it was perhaps the first time ever that a party was born which openly stood for free market principles.

The performance of the Swatantra Party in the 1962 general elections was indeed commendable. The Swatantra Party won 18 Lok Sabha seats and polled nearly 8 per cent of the votes. It also won as many as 107 assembly seats across the country. More than this, the emergence of the Swatantra Party and its electoral gains would embolden, in the following years, those Congressmen who were not pleased with Nehru's socialism but were unwilling to record their opposition within the party. The 1962 elections marked the Congress party's strength in the Lok Sabha drop from 371 in the second Lok Sabha to 361. The party's vote share fell by 3 percentage points: from 47.8 per cent in 1957 to 44.7 per cent in 1962. Similarly, the Bharatiya Jan Sangh increased its strength from a mere four in the second Lok Sabha to 14 in 1962.

The Congress under Jawaharlal Nehru adopted the course of centralised planning and presumed that industrial enterprise alone would break the feudal shackles. This idea was not very distinct from the agenda of the early nationalists to whom national liberation and freedom meant the necessary condition to build India into a modern industrial nation on the same lines as Europe emerged into modernity. It was presumed that industries, as they grow, will ensure that the primordial identities that prevailed even at the time of independence such as the caste system and the religious divide will melt down. The presumption was based on the notion that industries by their very nature will herald modernity as it happened in Europe.

Notwithstanding the quest for modernity and the antagonism that guided Nehru's attitude towards the inequalities inherent in the social structure in rural India, the Congress party did not carry out a concerted campaign against discrimination based on caste. Nehru's own perception was that industrial growth was bound to break the stranglehold of this feudal remnant. This, however, did not happen in India. Most of the leaders of the Congress party in the provinces remained committed to perpetrating the old social order and the economic inequity it perpetuated. This, after all, was the basis of the Congress party's muscle in most parts of the country and pronounced so sharply in Uttar Pradesh and Bihar, where the Vedic or the Gangetic civilisation flourished.

While it may be true that the Congress party under Nehru emerged the natural choice across the country, the factors that led to its decline were set in motion during the same period. The contempt with which Nehru himself dismissed caste as a category and hence refused to pay heed to the demand for affirmative action and positive discrimination in government jobs for the other backward classes alienated the Congress party further from the intermediate caste groups in the three-tier caste structure. This was how the recommendations of the first Backward Classes Commission, also known as the Kaka Kalelkar Commission, got shelved. The details of this and the logic of caste-based reservations will be dealt with later in this book (Chapters XI and XIV). What is significant now is that Nehru's antagonism to the idea of social justice was guided by his notion that the caste-based inequities would vanish with industrial development and the modernity it was bound to usher in. This, however, was not true of many others in the Congress party and more so with the regional satraps. They were unabashed about letting the feudal vestiges persist and the Congress party's political support base was built on this premise. The Congress began losing out its support in stages and suffered serious reverses in 1967. The party lost power in nine states that year.

VI

The End of the Nehru Era, the Shastri Interlude and the Emergence of Indira

> The Indian National Congress had never been a homogeneous or closely knit political unit ... certain new trends and forces emerged in the party soon after the death of Nehru. The most important of these trends ... dominated by Morarji Desai and Indira Gandhi ... a group of state party bosses who ... formed a formidable group ... were in a position to influence the party politics.
>
> — M. M. Rehman, *The Congress Crisis*

The decade after independence can be described as the Congress party's period of glory. This was possible because the opposition to Jawaharlal Nehru and his party had not crystallised into a political force. There was, indeed, no alternative to the Congress.

The results of the first general elections came as a rude shock to the socialists. Rather than prepare themselves for a long haul, the socialist movement began to splinter even while a section of its leaders attempted to consolidate the electoral support it got in the first general elections by way of effecting a merger with the Kisan Mazdoor Praja Party (KMPP), constituted by Acharya Kripalani, just on the eve of the 1951 polls. The post-election merger, even while it helped shore up the combined strength of the socialists (now christened the Praja Socialist Party, or PSP) in the Lok Sabha, did not sustain for long. Sharp differences on ideological and strategic issues caused the splintering of the platform in no time. And, even before the second general elections, held in 1957, Ram Manohar Lohia walked out of the PSP with a substantial portion of the organisation with him to revive the Socialist Party.

The Socialist Party's organisation, however, was built up predominantly by the lower-middle classes. The echelons of its leadership, at all levels, hardly consisted of members from the working class or the peasantry. They were, thus, guilty of treating the vast majority of the Indian people as objects in history rather than as those who could move the wheels of history. The socialist movement, hence, failed to emerge as an integral part of the collective consciousness of the Indian people. So much so, Gandhian socialism remained just an ideal. It did not evolve into a movement of any significance. Another important factor that caused the socialist platform to fail (particularly in the interim between the first and the second general elections) was the exit of Jayaprakash Narayan from its mainstream activities. While JP was moving farther from the socialist platform, another important pillar of the movement, Acharya Narendra Deva, passed away in February 1956.

As for the other party in the political arena, the Bharatiya Jan Sangh, it could hardly achieve a breakthrough in the first couple of elections. In fact, after the death of Shyama Prasad Mukherjee in June 1953 (while in incarceration in Kashmir), the Jan Sangh was unable to pose any serious challenge to the Congress under charismatic Nehru. The Jan Sangh's strength in the second Lok Sabha went up by just one seat: from three to four.

The CPI, meanwhile, was emerging into a force in Parliament. The party's strength went up to 27 in the second Lok Sabha. This was a significant increase from the 16 it had in the first Lok Sabha. In terms of percentage of votes too, the CPI share increased from 3.3 per cent in the 1951–52 elections to 8.9 in 1957. But then, this was also the time when the leaders of the party were engaged in a serious debate over the party's economic philosophy and there were many who disputed the relevance of Nehru's socialism. This debate sharpened and the CPI was caught in a crisis, particularly after the Avadi session of the Congress, laying the seeds for the split in the party in 1964 and the birth of the CPI (M).

All these factors aided the Congress party hold out the idea of Nehruvian socialism to galvanise a cross-section of people. Nehru's socialism did capture the imagination of different classes in both the social and the economic sense of the term. A nation that was born out of a movement, rooted in a modernist vision, saw in Nehru and his socialist principles the path to realise the making of a modern nation. Consequently, all opposition to Nehru was seen as representing a backward-looking ideology. Gandhi's prescriptions against large-scale industrialisation and the idea of small-scale production and the concept of self-sufficient villages were presented by the votaries of the Nehruvian idea as either backward-looking or status quoist. Similarly, although Nehru's socialism had its roots in the prescriptions handed out by the Indian capitalist class (in the Bombay Plan), the Congress party succeeded in presenting it as an evidence of its commitment to an egalitarian socio-economic order. There were, indeed, a large number of leaders within the Congress party who were, in their own way, committed to the free-market principles even at that time. They were the ones who effected the split in the Congress in 1969. But, none of them had the clout to defy Nehru. They waited until Nehru's death to embark upon their project.

In this chapter, we shall briefly discuss (i) the contours of the Nehruvian Socialist project and its impact on the first, second and the third five-year plans, (ii) the objective basis that weakened the Congress, in due course, reflected in the incremental gains made by the opposition parties, beginning with the impressive performance of the Swatantra Party in 1962 and soon after the election of three important leaders of the anti-Congress genre—Ram Manohar Lohia, Minoo Masani and J. B. Kripalani in by-elections in May 1963, and thereafter (iii) the serious reverses suffered by the Congress in the 1967 general elections. These events will be discussed in the context of the crisis within the Congress between the Avadi and Nagpur sessions, when the Nehruvian consensus began to fall apart. The final blow to this came in the aftermath of the Sino-Indian conflict. This will be followed by a brief narrative on the Shastri interlude and then the sequence of events from Indira Gandhi's appointment to the Congress Parliamentary Board (in 1955), her brief stint as Congress president (after the Nagpur session), the Kamaraj Plan and finally her anointment as the prime minister in 1966.

The Five-Year Plans and the Congress Fortunes

A look at the broad contours of the first three five-year plans (1951 to 1965) will reveal the basic thrust of the Nehruvian socialist project. It was based on the assumption that growth in the industrial sector would translate into income poverty reduction. Alongside this thrust, the Nehruvian regime also lent itself to building big dams and promoting irrigation projects with a view to enhance agricultural productivity. This period is perceived as one marked by the green revolution. It was presumed by the Nehru regime that there was no need to lay a specific focus on poverty alleviation. The assumption did not go wrong completely in the specific context. India did not have to export its agricultural produce to finance its budgetary transfer to Britain (a system that contributed to enormous drain of wealth until 15 August 1947). This ensured an increase in the availability of food grain and by extension enabled larger amount of food grain absorption per head of the population. With a substantial sterling balance, accumulated during the war years, there was no compulsion to export food grain in order to shore up foreign exchange reserves too.

This strategy, however, had its own inherent weakness. It depended on regular monsoons and normal harvests. This weakness was revealed in the very first bad harvest after independence in 1964–65, the last year of the third plan. The 1964–65 food crisis was partly because the year witnessed a much faster expansion of mass demand than before (the growth registered by this time in the manufacturing and the service sector leading to higher demands in food grain) and compounded further by a bad harvest for two years in succession: 1964–65 and 1965–66. For the first time after independence, parts of northern India, Bihar in particular, witnessed famine conditions. As much as 20 million tonnes of grain had to be imported to tide over the crisis.

The five-year plans were truncated and annual plans were resorted to until 1970. The thrust now was on promoting the use of fertilisers and building more irrigation projects. A new regime of grain procurement, subsidised supply of fertilisers and the Food Corporation of India (FCI) were put in place along with the public distribution system. All these, however, did not prevent in any significant manner the continuing, and a more rapid rise, in food prices (which rose faster than the prices of other commodities) causing substantial erosion in the real wages of large sections in the rural as well as urban India. This crisis began to manifest itself around the same time as the passing away of Pandit Nehru. Lal Bahadur Shastri, during his brief tenure as the prime minister, did express himself as a votary of pragmatism rather than a hard core stickler for Nehruvian socialism. While it is outside the scope of this book to go into the details of what this pragmatism meant, the point is that Shastri did reveal that he was uncomfortable with the Nehruvian prescriptions. In other words, after the 1965 war with Pakistan, and just before he left for Tashkent, Shastri ensured the resignation of his finance minister, T. T. Krishnamachari. This happened because Krishnamachari was opposed to any suggestion of devaluing the Indian rupee at that stage. But then, this decision to devalue the rupee and some other measures on the same lines, including the impounding of part of the wages of government employees, were carried out by Indira Gandhi soon after. Shastri did not live long after that. He died in Tashkent on 11 January 1966. Meanwhile, it was during his tenure that the tensions within the Congress began to show up in the form of a struggle for control over the party. This was the context in which Indira Gandhi began to position herself as the contender within the Congress. She had joined the Shastri cabinet and held the Information and Broadcasting portfolio. At that time, Indira was beginning to assert herself against Shastri and the high point of this assertion came in the immediate context of the 1965 Indo-Pak war when she landed at the border posts much to Shastri's discomfort. We shall deal with the emergence of Indira, a feature witnessed at least a decade before 1965, now.

From Nehru to Indira

We noticed in the previous chapter that the demise of Sardar Patel and Rajendra Prasad's election as president of the republic had meant that the Congress party was firmly under Nehru's control. It was also a fact that despite the presence of an array of illustrious leaders heading the state governments across the country and many men of eminence holding important portfolios in the union cabinet, Nehru did not have any difficulty in getting the Congress party to endorse his own wishes as the party's policy. It is another matter that Nehru faced hurdles in his path on certain issues, the most significant among them being the choice of the president after Prasad's first term came to an end in May 1957. There were instances (during Prasad's first term) of conflict between the prime minister and the president. One of them was the decision of the president's to go over to Somnath for the consecration of the temple there. Nehru had dissented but Prasad persisted with his decision to go. Prasad had, in fact, set out to write his memoirs of this period after his presidential years came to an end in May 1962 but could not do that due to his death soon after. Prasad passed away on 28 February 1963. While there are several accounts by contemporary chroniclers and observers of the period and all of them suggest bitterness in the Nehru–Prasad relationship, it will be outside the scope of this book to go into the details. However, it will be appropriate to note here that the two leaders were at loggerheads and the bitterness was evident in Nehru's opposition to nominate Prasad for a second term.

Despite Nehru's opposition, there were important members in the Congress party's leadership who argued for a second term for Prasad, and Nehru had to wait until May 1962 to elect S. Radhakrishnan as the president. Sarvapalli Radhakrishnan, after serving as the vice-president for two terms (1952 to 1962) was elected president in May 1962. Nehru had wanted him nominated for presidentship in 1957 itself. The developments in the Congress party in the context of the choice of presidential candidate in 1957, indeed, revealed two things: One that Nehru's writ over the party was not complete and, two, that Nehru, notwithstanding his strong views on men and matters, was someone who was willing to accommodate dissent. This, incidentally, is something that was found wanting in case of Indira Gandhi as it was revealed in the events leading up to the election of V. V. Giri as the president in 1969 and also when the Congress party split a few months later. All this will be discussed in the next chapter.

After the first general elections, Nehru began to come under the influence of his secretary, M. O. Mathai. Chroniclers of the period, without exception, mention him as the most prominent man in the prime minister's establishment and they also note that Mathai was turning into the man whom Congress MPs and timeservers were eager to please. Mathai lived and worked from out of the prime minister's official residence, the imposing building across the Rashtrapati Bhawan in which the British commander-in-chief resided during the days of the Raj (and now the Nehru Memorial Museum or Teen Murti Bhawan). Mathai, however, landed in trouble after it was revealed that he had managed to purchase large tracts of tea estates and that his wealth was disproportionate to his known sources of income. This led to Mathai's physical exit from the prime minister's residence and also from Nehru's grace. The vacuum came to be filled by Nehru's daughter, Indira Nehru Gandhi. While all the tales about Indira and Feroze need not be included, a couple of stories from that aspect will be in order here. One was that ever since Nehru took over as prime minister, Indira was living with him while Feroze worked with *The National Herald* (a paper founded by Nehru), living in Lucknow. There are tales that the marriage was not working and the fact is that even after Feroze moved to Delhi (after his election to Parliament from Rae Bareili in 1952 and also in 1957), Indira continued to live in the prime minister's residence rather than in her husband's official residence. And, after Mathai's exit from there, she landed in his place as the most sought after person for Congressmen.

It was in this context that U. N. Dhebhar, to whom Nehru had handed over the Congress president's post at the Avadi session of the Congress in 1955, mooted the idea of having Indira in the CWC. But, rather than joining the CWC as a nominated member, Indira preferred to join the forum as an elected member. The Congress party constitution prescribed that 10 out of the 21 CWC members were elected while 10 others were nominated by the party president. The logic behind this was to ensure representation of the scheduled castes, tribes, women and marginalised sections were brought into the party's leadership and this was possible only by way of nominations. In addition to the 20, the party president too was a member of the CWC. In less than a couple of years after that and ahead of the 1957 general elections to the second Lok Sabha and the state assemblies, Indira Nehru Gandhi was also made a member of the powerful Congress Parliamentary Board. The board, at that time, was the all-important body vested with powers to finalise the list of party candidates. Indira, thus, was nominated to this supreme forum of the party and remained there until Dhebhar remitted office as party president in 1959. After Dhebhar expressed his intention to step down, the choice in the first instance fell on S. Nijalingappa, at that time chief minister of Mysore. In the Nagpur session, where the Congress party resolved to commit itself to cooperative farming and furthering the socialist project, the delegates also elected a new president. On Dhebhar's suggestion and after active lobbying by Govind Ballabh Pant, who had by that time become the Union Home Minister, 41-year-old Indira Nehru Gandhi was appointed the Congress president. In a hurriedly convened meeting of the CWC, soon after the Nagpur session, Indira's name was proposed by Lal Bahadur Shastri and all the leaders present there accepted her as the new Congress president. Nehru did nothing to prevent this: he could have scotched the idea. Instead, he let the will of Dhebhar prevail.

Though Indira was elected as president for a two-year term, she left that position within a year after her election. The short stint, however, witnessed the Congress party pushing the Union government to endorse two critical recommendations of the party. One of them was the bifurcation of the Bombay state into Maharashtra and Gujarat. This was done on 1 May 1960. While the demand for bifurcation of the Bombay state was a long-standing one and was overlooked by Nehru and others even after the linguistic reorganisation of the states on the basis of the recommendations of the States Reorganisation Committee (in 1956), Indira, as president of the Congress party, pushed the union government to go ahead with the idea. The second, and more important, among Indira's projects was the orchestration of a campaign against the democratically elected state government headed by the CPI in Kerala and its dismissal in 1959.

In the first-ever elections to the state assembly of Kerala in 1957, the CPI won a majority. The state was formed after taking away the Malabar region from the erstwhile Madras state and the merger of Travancore and Cochin, the two former princely states. All this was the result of a persistent campaign among the people of these regions to constitute a separate state for the Malayalam-speaking people. The region, interestingly, had a history of radical and left movements taking strong roots even in the course of the freedom struggle. The Lok Sabha constituencies from these parts had elected communist and socialist party candidates as early as in the 1951–52 general elections and the Travancore-Cochin state came under a PSP government even then. All this was the impact of the popular mobilisation in that region by the communists and Congress socialist leaders since the 1930s which culminated in the historic Punnapra-Vayalar struggle. This brief background and the fact that the communists were in the forefront of the campaign for a separate Kerala state were behind the electoral victory secured by the communists in the first elections to the state assembly. E. M. S. Namboodiripad was elected the chief minister of the state.

Apart from legislative changes to effect radical land reforms, the CPI government in Kerala also came up with a bill in the state assembly aimed at ensuring control over the educational institutions across the state. Prof. Joseph Mundaserri, the state education minister, presented a bill that sought to ensure that schools set up and run by private managements but sustained by grants from the government shall submit to the government's control and the terms for appointment of teachers. The objective of the legislation was to put a leash on the private managements and liberate the mass of teachers from the whims and fancies of the managements. These two measures, for obvious reasons, provoked resistance from vested interests and Indira Nehru Gandhi, as Congress president, ordained the Congress party to lead a violent campaign against the democratically elected state government. Soon, on the pretext that the law and order machinery in the state had broken down, Nehru's cabinet recommended to the president that Article 356 of the Constitution be invoked. This turned out to be the beginning of a long history of wanton misuse of an emergency provision in the Constitution for partisan political gains. Prime Minister Jawaharlal Nehru went ahead with this despite his trusted aide in the Congress party and the union cabinet, V. K. Krishna Menon, and several others raising objections. The Kerala adventure also took Indira's relationship with Feroze to a point of no return. Feroze was to die a lonely man in September 1960. Indira too gave up her post as the Congress president soon after and Neelam Sanjeeva Reddy was elected in her place in 1960.

These two decisions apart, Indira's term as the Congress president was bereft of any serious attempt towards party building. As for the socialistic pattern of society and the idea of cooperative farming, the Congress party hardly showed any concern. But for the setting up of a party training school in Madras (by Indira Gandhi) to educate and train the party men on how they could go about effecting the resolution of the Nagpur session, the Congress party and Nehru did nothing to implement the Nagpur resolution. The Nagpur session, however, provoked a reaction from outside the party fold and culminated in the formation of the Swatantra Party. Incidentally, and also interestingly, the inspiration behind the foundation of the Swatantra Party came from C. Rajagopalachari who was Nehru's choice as the first chief minister of Madras state. Rajaji, however, was replaced by Kamaraj as the chief minister in 1954 and ever since he was waiting to take revenge. The Nagpur session seemed to hand him with an occasion. Meanwhile, it is to be recorded at this stage that while Rajaji was simply explicit about his anti-Nehruvian socialist project, most of the Congress chieftains too belonged to the same mould. The only difference was that they refrained from leaving the Congress party like Rajaji did. The end result was that the spirit of Avadi and Nagpur did not rub on the Congress chieftains at any stage.

These were reflected in the results of the 1962 elections. Although the Congress party's strength in the Lok Sabha fell only marginally (from 371 to 361), the party lost 3 percentage points in terms of its vote share. From 45 per cent in 1951–52, the Congress party's votes had gone up to 47.8 per cent in 1957. In 1962, it came down to 44.7 per cent. Meanwhile, the Bharatiya Jan Sangh's vote share went up only marginally from 5.9 per cent in 1957 to 6.4 per cent in the 1962 elections; the party secured as many as 14 seats in the Lok Sabha against its previous strength of only four. The fledgling Swatantra Party, founded only a couple of years before the third general elections, secured 7.9 per cent of the votes and 18 of the 173 candidates the party fielded were elected to the Lok Sabha. Similarly, the socialists, despite the series of splits and the internecine squabbles among their leaders, managed to retain their number of seats. The PSP won 12 seats and Lohia's Socialist Party secured six seats. Altogether, the 1962 elections brought out the fragmentation of the political space and more so the message that the Congress base was shrinking. It suggested that Nehru's appeal and the Congress party's position as the obvious choice was no longer the case. There were a large number of MPs in the opposition benches by then. At least 80 MPs were there in the opposition benches in the third Lok Sabha. H. V. Kamath and Nath Pai from the PSP and Kishen Pattnaik from the Samyukta Socialist Party (SSP) were prominent among them; they were known for their debating skills and were capable of putting Nehru and his cabinet ministers on the mat very often.

The Sino-Indian Conflict, the Kamaraj Plan and Nehru's Darkest Hour

This was the context in which a crisis was developing along India's borders with China. When Chinese forces marched into Indian territory in October 1962 and the fact that the Indian Army, whose weapons were at best suited to curb internal disturbances, failed to stall the onslaught, prime minister Nehru and his Congress party found themselves in a situation that they did not bargain for. Krishna Menon had to be eased out from the cabinet and like it happened after

Mathai's exit, it left a vacuum in the prime minister's residence. Indira's role expanded further. Meanwhile, vacancies arose for three Lok Sabha seats by early 1963 and to fill these by-elections were held in May 1963. The constituencies were Farukhabad and Amroha in Uttar Pradesh and Rajkot in Gujarat. More than the fact that the Congress party lost in all these by-elections, the significance was that those elected in them were veterans who would give Nehru and his cabinet a torrid time. Lohia, who had fought against Nehru unsuccessfully from Phulpur in 1962, won the by-elections from Farukhabad; J. B. Kripalani, whose conflict with Nehru led him to form the KMPP ahead of the 1951–52 general elections, won from Amroha; and Minoo R Masani, known for his sharp wits and intellect, was voted to Parliament from Rajkot on behalf of the Swatantra Party. When all these men entered the Lok Sabha, the Congress party was already in a quandary after the debacle in the war with China. It was in this context that an attempt was made to gather the entire opposition to the Congress and against Nehru on a single issue. Lohia proposed a motion of no-confidence in the Lok Sabha and suggested the possibility of a combined opposition to the Congress and Nehru. The seeds for an anti-Congress unity were laid now by Lohia.

Another significant feature of the 1962 general elections was the emergence of a distinct political platform into prominence in the Madras state. The Dravida Munnetra Kazhagam (DMK), founded out of the Dravidar Kazhagam in 1949, won seven Lok Sabha seats from Tamil Nadu and all these were at the cost of the Congress party. The party also increased its strength in the state assembly from 25 seats in 1957 to 50 in the 1962 elections. The immediate fallout of this was the election of C. N. Annadurai, the intellectual force behind the platform, to the Rajya Sabha in 1962. Incidentally, it was after Annadurai's forceful argument in the Rajya Sabha that the state was rechristened as Tamil Nadu. It was called the Madras state until then.

The DMK's growth in Tamil Nadu had indeed unnerved the Congress party and the Tamil Nadu chief minister, K. Kamaraj, sought Nehru's sanction to step down from the post and concentrate on refurbishing the Congress party in the state. Biju Pattnaik, who had by that time emerged as the Congress chieftain in Orissa, too mooted a similar proposal. Orissa, incidentally, was from where the Swatantra Party had registered impressive gains in 1962. Nehru, according to contemporary accounts, wondered as to whether this remedial measure could be adopted across the country rather than only in Tamil Nadu. Thus, a conclave of Congress seniors in Tirupati gave shape to a proposal by which all union ministers and chief ministers placed themselves at Nehru's disposal and offered themselves to the task of refurbishing the party. This came to be known as the Kamaraj Plan. The idea received a sense of urgency in the aftermath of the May 1963 by-elections and in August 1963, the ministers in the states and in the union cabinet tendered their resignation. But Nehru chose to accept the offer only from six chief ministers and an equal number of his cabinet colleagues. The chief ministers who were relieved from their posts were Kamaraj (Tamil Nadu), Biju Pattnaik (Orissa), Jivraj N. Mehta (Gujarat), Bhagwati Rai Mandloi (Madhya Pradesh), Chandra Bhanu Gupta (Uttar Pradesh) and Bakshi Ghulam Mohammed (Jammu and Kashmir).

The more significant aspect of the Kamaraj Plan was with regard to the cabinet ministers who were allowed to leave the government by Nehru. Lal Bahadur Shastri, who held the home portfolio, Morarji Desai who held finance, Jagjivan Ram, Minister for Transport and Communication, S. K. Patil, Minister for Food and Agriculture, apart from B. Gopala Reddy and K. L. Shrimali, were sent out of the government ostensibly to refurbish the party. Interestingly, the purpose behind the Kamaraj Plan was to draft senior party leaders, saddled with ministerial work, into party work. This was not pursued. Barring the fact that Kamaraj himself was elected as president of the Congress party, none of those stalwarts whose resignations were accepted were handed with specific charge in the party. At the Congress session at Bhubaneswar in January 1964 (where Kamaraj was elected president of the party), Nehru suffered a stroke and he had to be wheeled out of the venue. This provided an occasion for Shastri's return to the union cabinet as Minister without Portfolio. And, when Nehru passed away on 27 May 1964, Gulzari Lal Nanda, who had taken over as home minister after Shastri's resignation (under the Kamaraj Plan) was made caretaker prime minister.

The Shastri Interlude

The stage was set for Shastri as Nehru's successor even before Nehru's death. In fact, with the benefit of hindsight, it is possible to conclude that the Kamaraj Plan was executed by Nehru with this in mind and the intention clearly was to ensure that Morarji Desai was out of the scene. It is, however, a different matter that neither Nehru nor the regional chieftains of the Congress party, who were behind the scenes at the time, would have foreseen, in August 1963 (when Nehru executed the Kamaraj Plan), the demise of the prime minister a few months later. But then, there are several pointers from the events that preceded and followed the Kamaraj Plan to suggest that the most important objective behind the Kamaraj Plan was to ease out Morarji from the mainstream. One of them was the fact that barring Kamaraj, none of those who were relieved from the government in August 1963 were deputed for party work after that. Secondly, Nehru jumped at the first opportunity that came his way after August 1963 to get Shastri back in his cabinet. Shastri returned to the union cabinet as minister without portfolio on 24 January 1964: within days after Nehru suffered a stroke while the Congress annual session was on in Bhubaneswar. Since then, the prime minister depended more than anytime in the past on two of his cabinet colleagues—Shastri and T. T. Krishnamachari—as well as his daughter.

Shastri, in a sense, was chosen the successor by Nehru himself. But after Nehru died, the Congress chieftains could have altered the course if they wanted. The party high command after Nehru was constituted by a collective of leaders and they were known to be functioning in tandem even during Nehru's time. Apart from Kamaraj, the collective was constituted by Atulya Ghosh (from West Bengal), S. Nijalingappa (from Karnataka), Neelam Sanjiva Reddy (from Andhra Pradesh) and S. K. Patil (from Bombay). Among them, Patil had carved out a special place for himself, thanks to the fact that he commanded the party organisation in Bombay, the financial hub of the nation. This lot, soon came to be known as the syndicate, was emerging into a power block in the party even during Nehru's last days. They, however, took care to refrain from challenging Nehru's authority and were clever enough to let all his socialist rhetoric endorsed in the party. It is another matter that they were hardly concerned with implementing them. And, all of them looked at Morarji Desai with a certain disdain; he was known to be inflexible, intolerant and a stickler to value-based politics. Hence, even while Desai saw himself as Nehru's successor, the party high command was determined against choosing him as prime minister. Shastri, meanwhile, was considered amenable by the high command and his election as prime minister on 9 June 1964 was a smooth affair. Desai refrained from showing any signs of resistance even while resenting the move because he believed that the job was his. Shastri carried on with Nehru's cabinet and the only change he effected was to include Indira Nehru Gandhi as minister for Information and Broadcasting. Morarji Desai, despite his long stint in government and having been Nehru's finance minister (until he was relieved under the Kamaraj Plan), was not included in the cabinet by Shastri.

When Shastri took over, the situation across the country was not the same as they were when Nehru became the prime minister. The Congress party was no longer blessed with the strong organisational network and the Nehruvian socialist project too was beginning to be questioned. As we saw in the beginning of this chapter, the monsoons had failed and parts of the country were reeling under food shortage. Multilateral agencies such as the World Bank and the International Monetary Fund (IMF) were beginning to lay conditions before sanctioning aid. One of them was the devaluation of the Indian rupee and Shastri's finance minister, T. T. Krishnamachari, opposed the idea vehemently. Agitation was also building up in Punjab with the Akali Dal leaders seeking a separate Punjabi-speaking state. Punjab, at that stage, included present-day Haryana and most parts of Himachal Pradesh. Shastri constituted a cabinet sub-committee, headed by Indira Gandhi, to go into these.

Even while Shastri was trying to grapple with these, a different crisis was brewing in Tamil Nadu. It may be noted here that the Congress party had suffered serious reverses in the state even in Nehru's time. The constitutional position was such that by 1965, Hindi was to be adopted as the official language across the country. The DMK resolved to agitate against this and soon after there was unrest in colleges and universities across Tamil Nadu. An act of self-immolation near Tiruchi and the ripples it sent across the state rendered a mass character to the campaign and the agitation. Even as these happened, Prime Minister Shastri and the Congress President Kamaraj stayed put in Delhi hoping that the agitation will peter out. They did not even bother to clarify or reiterate Nehru's assurance that Hindi shall not be imposed on any state's people and that English will continue to be retained as another official language till the people wanted. The agitation was sustained by the DMK and this eventually led to the Congress being voted out in Tamil Nadu and Kamaraj himself was defeated in an assembly constituency in 1967.

The situation, on the whole, was marked by indecision and Shastri looked like an effete leader. All this, however, changed soon with machinations from Pakistan. General Ayub Khan seemed to be waiting for the moment. While the Sino-Indian conflict had taken the morale of the armed forces to a low, the bad rains and the consequent shortage of grain was leading the nation into a crisis. The FCI, an institutional mechanism that was set up in January 1965 to ensure procurement of food grain from grain surplus regions and send them across to the grain deficit states, was yet to grow in size to achieve the objective. And, an ineffective political leadership was the last thing the nation could afford. It was at this stage that General Ayub Khan, having acquired new weapons from the United States, sent his forces to occupy parts of the Rann of Kutch. This part of the land was still not demarcated. The Indian response to this was not effective, particularly due to the difficult terrain of the region. But Britain intervened soon after and both sides were pushed into referring the dispute for arbitration. However in August 1965, regulars from the Pakistan army were pushed into the Kashmir valley.

Shastri ordered the Indian army to launch an offensive and this was not just restricted to the Kashmir valley. The Indian army was also sent on hot pursuit of the enemy in the Chaamb sector and towards Lahore and Sialkot. The offensive was indeed successful but on the United Nations' intervention, both sides agreed to a ceasefire on 23 September 1965. While the implications of the war and the ceasefire on India's relation with Pakistan will not be discussed in detail here, the impact of all this on the domestic political discourse was significant. Shastri became a national hero by the time the war ended. He was credited, in popular perception, for having foiled Pakistan's designs in Kashmir. This was when the prime minister began to assert himself. This change was beginning to appear even earlier. Shastri's first pronounced departure from the Nehruvian tradition was by way of setting up the Prime Minister's Secretariat (PMS). The PMS, with L. K. Jha as the prime minister's principal private secretary at the helm, came into existence before the Indo-Pak war. But after the ceasefire, Shastri began depending more on this new set-up rather than his cabinet colleagues. Indira Nehru Gandhi, for once, was no longer the most important aide of the prime minister, a role that she had assiduously built up ever since her father became the prime minister of independent India.

Prime Minister Shastri's first major act of such self-assertion was on 31 December 1965. Finance Minister T. T. Krishnamachari, who saw himself as Nehru's legatee and for that reason one of the pillars of the government, was asked by Shastri to resign on that day. This happened following a serious debate between the two on the issue of devaluation of the rupee. Krishnamachari was vehemently opposed to the idea. According to chroniclers of the period, Indira did expect that she would be the next person to be asked to leave the cabinet. Accounts are that Shastri was indeed contemplating to send her off to London as India's High Commissioner. However, this did not happen. Shastri, who left for Tashkent soon after and signed the 4 January 1966 declaration jointly with Ayub Khan (by which both the armies had to return to their pre-August 1965 positions), breathed his last on 10 January 1966 in Tashkent itself.

Indira Gandhi as Prime Minister

The brief interlude under Shastri did not affect, in any big way, the clout of the syndicate in the Congress party. It is a different matter that Shastri had, indeed, begun to assert himself and this could have eroded the syndicate's influence over the party if Shastri had lived for long after the Indo-Pak war. But the fact is that Shastri died on 10 January 1966 and hence a vacancy was created for the post of the prime minister. The Congress party had to choose its leader. Morarji Desai, who had refrained from openly staking claim to the post in June 1964, decided otherwise this time. He made his claim to the job explicit. The party bosses, however, continued to perceive him in the same way as they did in June 1964. Morarji, meanwhile, declared that the job of electing the new prime minister must be left to the Congress Parliamentary Party and that the party high command should desist from playing any role in that. In other words, Morarji demanded that the syndicate, which managed to anoint Shastri as prime minister 19 months ago, stay away from the process of electing the prime minister this time. This indeed was seen by the party bosses as an indication of things to come if they let Morarji to take up the top job. To preserve themselves, they decided to stand up for the other serious claimant to the post at that time: Indira Nehru Gandhi. She was turning restless with Shastri and the prime minister too had made up his mind to put her in place. Her visits to the army posts when the Indo-Pak war was raging had convinced Shastri that Nehru's daughter was trying to carve a space for herself. But in the post-war situation, Shastri had become a hero and Indira seemed to have lost the game.

It is part of the political folklore that Kamaraj, the Congress president, persuaded others in the high command (Atulya Ghosh, Nijalingappa, Sanjeeva Reddy and S. K. Patil) on the virtues of backing her against Morarji Desai. In fact, one factor that led them on this course was that their own clout could be sustained with Indira as prime minister. There was also another consideration. They were aware of the fact that the Congress party was no longer the obvious choice of the masses and were conscious that none from among themselves had the charisma to swing votes in the party's favour. They had realised the enormity of the task given the fact that the Congress began losing votes even while Nehru was alive: The by-elections in May 1963 established this. With only 13 months to go before the next general elections (due by February 1967) they had very little time to prepare. Indira, whose enthusiasm to campaign was established even while she was Information and Broadcasting Minister in Shastri's cabinet and aware of the crowds that gathered in her public meetings during that time, turned out to be their choice for the prime minister's post in January 1966. Indira, meanwhile, maintained that she will be guided by the wishes of the Congress party and its president, Kamaraj.

Even while all these events were taking place behind the scenes, Desai stuck to his position that it was the business of the Congress Parliamentary Party (party members of the Lok Sabha and the Rajya Sabha) to elect the next prime minister. The issue, however, got a further twist when the chief minister of Madhya Pradesh, Dwarka Prasad Mishra, led a group of nine Congress chief ministers to issue a joint statement seeking the election of Indira Nehru Gandhi as prime minister. The Congress was in power in all the states at that time, and Mishra would become an important leader in the Congress party for sometime after that. He was, after all, the first Congress leader of any standing to come out in favour of Indira for the prime minister's job. Indira, as we will see later, ensured that all those who stood by her in the Congress party were promoted. Fakhruddin Ali Ahmed, Jagjivan Ram, S. D. Sharma, C. Subramaniam, C. K. Jaffer Sharief and many others who stood up for her in the intra-party conflicts were all to become big in the due course.

The initiative by D. P. Mishra was soon followed by the party bosses and they all declared support to Indira Gandhi as prime minister. Desai, however, was unrelenting. On 19 January 1966, the Congress Parliamentary Party assembled in the central hall of the Parliament. The votes were cast by secret ballot. Indira Nehru Gandhi won by an impressive majority. She secured 355 votes against the 169 votes that Morarji Desai polled. The margin, no doubt, was huge. But the fact is that Desai had managed 169 votes even when the entire high command of the Congress party and the chief ministers from states had campaigned against him. That at least one-third of the Congress party's combined strength in the Lok Sabha and the Rajya Sabha had voted against Indira Gandhi was indeed a significant pointer to the state of the party at that time. In just a few years after having worked to defeat Desai, the party bosses would rally behind him and turn against Indira.

Meanwhile, Indira would emerge as the supreme leader of the party and also the high command after the Congress party split in 1969. This will be taken up in the next chapter.

VII

The Decline of the Congress and Indira's Rise

> I have the privilege of belonging to the Congress even when I was not a member … So it is certainly not my intention ever to do anything that would weaken this great organization. But with all my love and my pride in the Congress organisation, I must say that there is something which is bigger than the Congress and that is our country and that is our people … And the day we forget that … that day will see the weakening of the party.
>
> —Indira Gandhi, at the AICC meet in Bangalore on 12 July 1969

We have seen in the previous chapter that Indira Gandhi's election as the prime minister was made possible by two factors. One was the initiative taken by the then Madhya Pradesh Chief Minister Dwarka Prasad Mishra to orchestrate the demand that Nehru's daughter should be elected. Following that, the party bosses, now familiar in political circles as the syndicate, expressed their choice in favour of Indira and against Morarji Desai. We have also noted that despite all this, Morarji secured the votes of at least one-third of the total strength of the Congress Parliamentary Party. The members of the syndicate had, in fact, assumed that Indira Gandhi lacked a strong personality and, hence, would dance to their tunes. The syndicate, no doubt, was in absolute control of the party at that time in every sense of the term.

It makes sense to recall at this stage a publication as early as in 1963 by Welles Hangen, a Delhi-based American journalist. Hangen's book *After Nehru, Who*? dealt with the names of all those who could be seen as Nehru's successors. It talked about Morarji Desai, Lal Bahadur Shastri and Indira Gandhi—in that order—apart from S. K. Patil and V. K. Krishna Menon. Although Indira had not even contested an election at that time, she was indeed an important player in the Congress party's affairs. Brought into the Congress Working Committee (CWC) as early as in 1955 and the Congress Parliamentary Board a year later, Indira had also been the president of the Congress party after the Nagpur session in 1959. Her clout, it may be recalled, was established after she could prevail upon Nehru in the same year to bifurcate the Bombay state and, more significantly, to misuse Article 356 to dismiss the democratically elected state government in Kerala. In short, Indira was a prominent figure even a decade before 19 January 1966, the day she was sworn in as the prime minister. Incidentally, when she took the oath of office and secrecy, Indira Gandhi opted to solemnly affirm on her conscience (rather than 'in the name of God'), her allegiance to the Constitution.

Indira continued with all those who were in Shastri's cabinet and inducted a few new faces: Asoka Mehta, one of the founders of the Socialist Party who had drifted away from the creed; he was inducted into Indira's cabinet as Minister for Planning. Fakhruddin Ali Ahmed from Assam was made the minister for irrigation and power. He stood by Indira in all her struggles within the party and rose, a decade later, to become the president of the republic and promulgated the Emergency on 25 June 1975 on Indira's instructions. Jagjivan Ram—who had been a part of all the governments since the interim council that Nehru was called to set up on 2 September 1946 until he was eased out under the Kamaraj Plan in August 1963—was re-inducted by Indira as minister for labour. Morarji Desai was not invited to join the cabinet.

In this chapter, we shall deal with the objective conditions that determined Indira's first stint as the prime minister (between January 1966 and March 1967) such as the crisis thrown by the bad monsoons and the consequent fall in grain production, the condition that forced India to resort to devaluation of the rupee in order to get aid from the multilateral lending agencies and the impact of these on the Congress party's electoral reverses in 1967. This will be followed by a section on Indira's tryst with the socialist rhetoric. The third section will deal with the struggle within the Congress leading finally to the split in 1969.

Indira's Initial Challenges

Unlike her father, Indira inherited the mantle when the country was passing through a crisis. While Nehru's authority over his party was unfettered when he became the prime minister in 1952 (he was also the Congress president), his daughter Indira had to deal with a strong group of party bosses. As if this was not enough, she also had to act on the demand for creation of an exclusively Punjabi-speaking state by splitting up the bilingual Punjab. The agitation for a separate Punjabi-speaking state by the Akali Dal had reached its peak during Shastri's period and Indira was deputed by Shastri to deal with that. She was nominally the head of a cabinet panel to study the issue and recommend measures. Shastri, however, did not care to meet her even once and brief her on the issue. Indira did resent this but while all this was happening, Shastri had become a national hero (after the August-September Indo-Pak war) and had begun to assert himself. Meanwhile, the Akali agitators had agreed to wait for a solution until the Indo-Pak hostility came to an end.

Thus, when Indira Gandhi took over as the prime minister, there was a sense of immediacy before her to deal with the demand. The government soon agreed for partition of Punjab and set up a Punjabi-speaking state (consisting of 52 per cent of the people who spoke Punjabi) and the two smaller states of Haryana and Himachal Pradesh. However, the dispute over Chandigarh, as capital, remained unresolved: both Punjab and Haryana claimed Chandigarh as theirs. The two states temporarily shared Chandigarh as the capital. Similarly, the disputes over the sharing of river waters—Ravi and Beas—and several other issues that formed the basis of the Anandpur Sahib Resolution were unresolved. It may be noted, in this context, that some of these issues continue to linger and remain unresolved even today. We shall discuss this in detail in Chapter XII. The more critical challenge before Indira Gandhi as soon as she took over as the prime minister pertained to a set of crises in the economy triggered by the bad rains in two successive years.

The American establishment, meanwhile, looked at the crises as an occasion for settling scores with India: The thrust on heavy industry, the quest for self-reliance and the initiatives during the Nehruvian era on the foreign policy front, the spirit of the Bandung Conference of non-alignment in particular, was not to the liking of the American establishment. Also, Shastri did not waver a bit in condemning America's Vietnam adventure. All this was happening and the Indo-Pak war served as an immediate provocation to America to suspend all aid to the two countries. The most telling impact of this was felt on the US export of food grain to India under Public Law 480 (PL 480). Availability of food grain depended on the arrival of shiploads from the US and, thus, on the whims and fancies of the US administration, which was under Lyndon Johnson at that time.

The American administration as well as the International Monetary Fund (IMF) and the World Bank began imposing a condition that the Indian rupee be devalued. This talk had begun before Indira's arrival as the prime minister. Shastri, in fact, had decided in principle for devaluation. In September 1964, the World Bank had deputed a mission headed by Bernard Bell to India. The mission prescribed three things that were necessary, in its view, to correct the distortions in India's economic policy: high priority to agriculture (against heavy industries), relaxing curbs on import and devaluation of the rupee. Shastri was not averse to this. But there was opposition to this from Finance Minister T. T. Krishnamachari and Shastri had ensured his resignation on 31 December 1965, just before he left for Tashkent. Thus, it was left to Indira to execute what Shastri had agreed to do in principle. She went by the advice tendered by Shastri's man in the Prime Minister's Secretariat (PMS), L. K. Jha, who continued to head the PMS in the first few months of Indira's era too. In addition to Jha, Indira depended on C. Subramaniam, Fakhruddin Ali Ahmed and Dinesh Singh. All of them were in favour of devaluation, unlike TTK, who considered the step as an affront to India's pride.

Similarly, Asoka Mehta, the socialist of the 1950s and the one among those who joined Indira's inner circle, was the deputy chairman of the Planning Commission at that time. He too saw devaluation as a necessary step. Indira's confidantes in the cabinet convinced her that such a step will help boost exports and, thus, enlarge the scope for industrial growth in India. It will be pertinent at this stage to note that currency devaluation is a means that nations resort to with a view to enhance exports and thereby ensure economic growth. In simple terms, where the value of the rupee vis-à-vis the dollar is brought low, it serves as an incentive to the exporters of goods. For, it will ensure that their earnings in terms of rupee go up. This simple logic, however, can work only when all parameters are favourable. In other words, devaluation will work to a country's advantage in ideal conditions. The situation in India in 1966 was anything but ideal.

Within a month after she became the prime minister, Indira had to face the AICC session in February 1966 at Jaipur. The issue before her was a demand for scrapping the ban on movement of food grain across the food zones. Since independence, the country had been divided into six food zones, and in a manner that each zone consisted of at least one grain-surplus state. The purpose behind such a division was to ensure that grain could be moved within such zones and to ensure that grain-deficit states did not suffer from food shortage. In this arrangement, movement of food grain between two zones was banned while free movement was allowed within the zones. This synthetic division, however, was resented by the big landlords and, as a consequence, by the chief ministers of the grain-surplus states. In the decade after independence, the provincial leaders of the Congress party had come under the influence of the landed gentry and the rich peasantry in their states. Yet, they refrained from challenging Nehru's authority and his socialist ideas openly. After Shastri became the prime minister, the regional leaders of the Congress party began to assert themselves and they were emboldened further on Indira's arrival. In the context of the food shortage, they wanted to make the best of the opportunity. The landed gentry and the rich peasants did not want to let go of the opportunity to trade their grain with the highest bidder and the ban on inter-zonal movement of grain was a huge hurdle in their path. They wanted the ban scrapped and were powerful enough to get this demand articulated at the AICC session held in Jaipur in February 1966.

A resolution was moved, urging the central government to lift the ban in inter-zonal movement of grain and when it was put to vote, an overwhelming majority seemed to favour the step. Such a step could only have worsened the food situation in the country, as the limited quantity of grain (in a year of bad harvest) would be bought by people who could afford and the poor would be left to starve. That was when Indira was forced to deal with the crisis: She barely managed to wriggle the party and her government out of the crisis by assuring the AICC delegates that the entire policy would be reviewed, and pleaded that the resolution be withdrawn. The session had to be brought to an abrupt end soon after her assurance. Indira literally stormed out of the session. Worse things were to follow.

Soon after the Jaipur meet, she had to face parliament. It was then that her inability to speak before the public and in parliament became evident. While it was possible for her to avoid parliament as the minister for information and broadcasting, things were different now. She was the prime minister and had to face such veterans as Ram Manohar Lohia, the acerbic socialist, Minoo Masani, who would set new standards in parliament with his wits and sharp debating skills and J. B. Kripalani who had shown the courage to challenge Nehru in the latter's hour of glory. It may be recalled that all of them had entered parliament in the May 1963 by-elections and their arrival, in a sense, had unnerved even Nehru. Indira's inexperience and her problems with public speaking gave these men a handle to taunt her. This was the time when Lohia called her the *goongi gudiya* (dumb doll), an attribute she managed to shed very soon.

The currency devaluation was turning out to be Indira's nightmare. She undertook a visit to the US in March 1966 and the purpose of that (though unstated) was to enlist support—from Lyndon Johnson's administration—for India to tide over the food crisis as well as the foreign exchange crunch. The Indo-Pak war, it may be recalled, was cited as an excuse for the US administration suspending food aid under PL 480. Once there, Indira also amended India's categorical contempt for the US aggression in Vietnam (Shastri was unqualified in his condemnation) by saying that she understood the US anxieties in Vietnam. It appeared that Johnson was satisfied by all these and agreed to revive grain supplies under PL 480 and also to set up an educational foundation in India from out of the money generated in India from the grain supplies. The foundation was to be called Indo-American Educational Foundation (that exists even now as USEFI). On her way back, Indira also visited Moscow and conveyed to the Soviet rulers that her statement on Vietnam was guided by the consideration that the US could not be expected to withdraw from there without a face-saving formula. All this brought her under attack and now there were many within her party doing that. Nehru's confidante and Indira's mentor during her days in London, V. K. Krishna Menon, was among them. Indira, however, described all this as pragmatism.

She invoked the idea of the nation being bigger than anything else in this context. 'If it is necessary to deviate from past policies,' she declared, 'I would not hesitate to do so. I must pursue policies which are in the best interests of the country as a whole'. In what was clearly a challenge to her critics in the party, she added: 'If you do not like these policies, you have every right to remove me and have your own leader... *The Congress is big, but India is bigger.*' This, indeed, was to become her gospel and guided her actions whenever she was challenged in the days to come. Her penchant for placing the nation, and what she perceived as good to the nation, above all institutions was evident when she split the Congress party in 1969 or when she suspended democracy in June 1975 by imposing Emergency.

On 5 June 1966, barely six months after she became the prime minister, Indira Gandhi set out on her independent course and announced devaluation of rupee by a whopping 57.5 per cent. She did this without taking many important men, including the Congress president, K. Kamaraj, into confidence and despite her complete lack of knowledge on matters relating to money and economics; in the press conference she held after the decision was taken, Indira had identified inflation and rising prices as the two problems facing the country. The decision to devalue rupee was Indira's blunder and the opposition to her decision came not only from outside the Congress party but also from her party colleagues. Of significance here is the fact that the CWC condemned the measure. It is another matter that the party and the leaders did not push the matter further into a showdown. They were in no position, at least at that stage, to remove Indira. Elections were due within a year and they could not afford a change of guard. Indira, meanwhile, did not want to look back. On 12 June, she addressed the nation on the All India Radio in which she stressed that devaluation was indeed a strong medicine and it was inevitable to resort to that in order to restore the nation to economic health.

While everything about the decision was clearly guided by the IMF, World Bank and the US establishment, and the decision was intended to ensure American aid and grain supply under PL 480, this did not materialise as expected. The situation remained the same and parts of the country continued to wait for shiploads of wheat from the US. Indira's response was guided by pragmatism once again. On 1 July 1966, she deplored the US bombing of Hanoi and Haiphong and soon after landed in the Soviet Union where she signed a joint declaration with Alexei Kosygin that termed the US presence in Vietnam as an act of 'imperialist aggression'. While an enraged Lyndon Johnson stopped even the handful of ships that carried PL 480 wheat to India, Indira began turning Left. Apart from the former socialist, Asoka Mehta, she was surrounded, by this time, by a new group of Left-leaning men: Inder Kumar Gujral, who would become the prime minister of India in March 1997 (and hold that position only for a few months) was among them.

The devaluation of the rupee took place in June 1966. Meanwhile, Indira was led to depend on a bunch of close aides and some ministers. There were also men like Chandra Shekhar (who became India's prime minister in 1990 and stayed in that post for a mere four months) and Mohan Dharia, both of whom came to be addressed as the 'Young Turks' in the Congress. The 'Young Turks' were determined to reinvent the Congress party as a socialist platform and were ranged against the syndicate. Chandra Shekhar, incidentally, had entered the political sphere through the Praja Socialist Party (PSP). He was elected to the Rajya Sabha as PSP nominee in 1962. He moved into the Congress party, in due course, after Asoka Mehta. They all turned out to be Indira's allies in her battle against the syndicate only to be eased out by Indira and put in jail during the Emergency.

If the decision to devalue the Indian rupee was an adventurist course that Indira resorted to without calculating the perils involved, the moves by the party leaders to distance themselves from this decision of hers pushed Indira to depend on her own chosen men. She embarked upon the leftward course since then. It is another matter that the leftward tilt did not help the party in the 1967 elections; for devaluation simply compounded the crisis. Prices continued to rise and the fiscal scene turned from bad to worse. An inevitable consequence of this was the decision to impound part of the dearness allowance given to the government employees (to hold back the increased wages and treat that as savings in government bonds). This turned the middle classes against the Congress party. We shall discuss this action of the government and its impact in the general election in the following section. Indira, however, was determined to assert herself by this time.

In November 1966, a demonstration of saffron-clad *sadhus* on New Delhi's Parliament Street, demanding a ban on cow slaughter, turned violent. As the Delhi Police tried to stop them from reaching the Parliament House, some of the men were seriously injured and six others were killed in police firing. Indira turned this into an opportunity to get rid of Gulzarilal Nanda, who was the home minister. Nanda, it may be recalled, was the caretaker prime minister on two occasions and was indeed becoming her detractor. Indira asked for Nanda's resignation on grounds that he had failed to handle the agitation in the way it should have been. Nanda had to bow out. Indira, however, was not successful in easing out two others—Finance Minister Sachin Chaudhuri and Foreign Trade Minister Manubhai Shah—from the cabinet. She was reminded by the party bosses that she was subservient to the party. The Central Parliamentary Board of the Congress, meanwhile, began the exercise of selecting the party's candidates for the general election due in March 1967. To her dismay, Indira found her father's confidant Krishna Menon being denied the Congress ticket from North Bombay (which he represented in the Lok Sabha all the while after independence) and also some others meeting the same fate.

That was when, on 25 December 1966 to be precise, Indira spoke out once again. In a statement to the press, Indira said: 'Here is a question of whom the party wants and whom the people want. My position among the people is uncontested'. While she was unable to set things the way she wanted and ensure Congress tickets to her confidants, including Menon, (Krishna Menon left the party to contest as an independent and lost), Indira herself was nominated to contest from Rae Bareli, the constituency from where her late husband Feroze Gandhi had won in 1952 and 1957. Indira did not contest the election in 1962 and after Nehru's death in May 1964, Phulpur near Allahabad was left to her aunt, Vijayalakshmi Pandit. When she joined Shastri's cabinet as minister for information and broadcasting, Indira was, in fact, a member of the Rajya Sabha, elected from Uttar Pradesh. She remained a member of the upper house even after she became the prime minister in January 1966 and until her election to the lower house from Rae Bareli in March 1967.

A Reversal of Fortunes

The Congress party suffered reverses in the general election of 1967. Incidentally, that was the last time when elections to the Lok Sabha and the state assemblies were held simultaneously. For the first time ever, the Congress party's claim to power came under serious threat. The Congress was thrown out of power in nine states: The party was reduced to minority in the state assemblies of Bihar, Haryana, Kerala, Madhya Pradesh, Orissa, Punjab, Rajastan, Tamil Nadu, and West Bengal. While the CPI (M), in alliance with a few regional parties, wrested power—for the second time—in Kerala, in the neighbouring Tamil Nadu, the Dravida Munnetra Kazhagam (DMK) won a majority to form its government. It may be noted, in this context, that the Congress has not been able to revive its fortunes in Tamil Nadu since its defeat in 1967. In Punjab, the Akali Dal secured a majority and formed the government. The Congress was also voted out in West Bengal, where the CPI (M) along with the Bangla Congress (led by a former Congressman, Ajoy Mukherjee) won a majority to form a coalition government.

In Bihar, Madhya Pradesh and Haryana, a combination of forces that were put together by Ram Manohar Lohia on the simple slogan that it was time for all parties to get together and send the Congress party out (came to be known as blind anti-Congressism) pushed the Congress into a minority in the state assemblies. In Rajasthan and Orissa, a combination of forces led by the Swatantra Party won a majority. In short, the Congress lost power in nine states. In Uttar Pradesh, although the Congress managed to form its government immediately after the election—with Chandra Bhanu Gupta as the chief minister—the ministry fell within a month. Charan Singh, a Congress MLA until then, would become the chief minister, as head of an anti-Congress coalition.

Equally significant was the fact that the Congress party's strength in the Lok Sabha came down substantially. The Congress could win in only 283 out of the 516 Lok Sabha constituencies; the majority of Congress was narrow. The party's strength in the third Lok Sabha (1962–67) was 361 out of a total strength of 488. The vote share of the Congress party fell from 44.7 per cent in 1962 to 40.8 per cent in 1967. The downslide was pronounced in such states as Uttar Pradesh, Bihar and Orissa where the Congress party's losses were the gains registered by the socialists. Although the socialist platform had split by this time into the PSP and the Samyukta Socialist Party, both the parties recorded impressive gains; together the two parties had 36 MPs in the fourth Lok Sabha. This was their highest ever tally since Independence. Among them were Lohia (who won from Kannauj in Uttar Pradesh), George Fernandes (from Bombay South), veteran trade union leader, S. M .Joshi (from Poona in Maharashtra) and Bindeshwari Prasad Mandal, who was to become chairman of the second Backward Classes Commission that formulated the basis for reservation in central government jobs (from Madhepura in Bihar). They were among the 23 MPs elected on behalf of the Samyukta Socialist Party. Similarly, the 13 PSP members included Nath Pai (elected from Rajapur in Maharashtra) and S. N. Dwivedy (from Kendrapara in Orissa).

The 1967 elections were significant for the Bharatiya Jan Sangh too. The party's strength in the Lok Sabha went up to 35. In terms of the votes polled, it went up from 6.4 per cent in 1962 to 9.4 per cent in 1967. Atal Behari Vajpayee, who was to become the prime minister twice (in 1998 and in 1999), was one of the Jan Sangh's MPs in the fourth Lok Sabha. He was first elected in 1957 from Balrampur in Uttar Pradesh, lost from there in 1962 and won the same seat in 1967. Of the 35 seats won by the Jan Sangh in the fourth Lok Sabha, 12 were from Uttar Pradesh and nine from Madhya Pradesh. While this will explain the steady rise of the Jan Sangh and later on the BJP in these two states, the other significant pointer in this context was that the Jan Sangh secured six out of the seven Lok Sabha constituencies from Delhi. Among them was M. L. Sondhi, an academic who would become chairman of the Indian Council for Social Science Research (ICSSR) after the BJP came to power in 1998 and soon turn against the party. The lone Congress MP from Delhi in 1967 was Brahm Prakash Choudhury from Outer Delhi, the constituency that is literally and otherwise in Delhi's fringes. Chaudhury would leave the Congress after the Emergency and retain the seat on behalf of the Bharatiya Lok Dal. The Congress party wrested this constituency in 1980 when Sajjan Kumar won the election. Kumar turned infamous for his role in the anti-Sikh riots in 1984.

Equally significant was the performance of the two communist parties. The undivided CPI had secured 29 Lok Sabha seats in the 1962 elections. The party underwent a split in 1964 and the organisational machinery was indeed divided across the country. Yet, in March 1967, the CPI won in 23 Lok Sabha constituencies, including five seats each from Bihar and Uttar Pradesh. Indrajit Gupta, who would become the union home minister in 1996, and the legendary communist and parliamentarian, Hiren Mukherjee, were among those elected. The CPI (M), in the first-ever elections after it was founded in 1964, secured 19 seats in the Lok Sabha. Nine out of the 19 came from Kerala (where the party also won a majority in the state assembly), four from Tamil Nadu and five from West Bengal. Among those elected was Jyotirmoy Bosu (not to be confused with Jyoti Basu) from the Diamond Harbour constituency. Bosu, a tea taster by profession, would carve out a niche for himself as one who used parliament and the privileges granted by the Constitution to MPs, to unravel scandals against Indira and her close aides. He remained MP until his death in March 1982 and during the 15 years as MP, Bosu took the floor to expose such scandals as the Maruti car project of Sanjay Gandhi, the Nagarwala scam and the nexus that Congress minister, A. B. A. Ghani Khan Chaudhury had built with the mafia in the coal mines of Jharkhand. Ghani Khan was the minister for railways at that time.

A brief account of the Nagarwala scandal will be in order at this stage. On 24 May 1971, Ved Prakash Malhotra, the chief cashier at the State Bank of India's Parliament Street branch, hardly a stone's throw away from Parliament House in New Delhi, received a call instructing him to hand over Rs 60 lakh to a man waiting at a specified place and who would identify himself as *Bangladesh ka Babu*.

The caller identified 'herself' as Indira Gandhi. The man waiting turned out to be Rustom Sohrab Nagarwala, a former army officer; he had also worked for the Intelligence Bureau. Malhotra, to his dismay, was told that there was no such instruction given when he reached the Prime Minister's Secretariat (later rechristened as the PMO) to obtain a receipt for the money he had handed over to Nagarwala. The tale turned more curious as Nagarwala was arrested the same day. There was uproar in the parliament but Indira refused to answer as to whether the prime minister had such an arrangement with Malhotra; in other words, how could Malhotra have acted in such manner and particularly where it involved such huge sums of money if it was an incident that was the first of its kind. Nagarwala was tried, in one of independent India's speediest trials and sentenced to four years of rigourous imprisonment. The trial took just three days. The scandal persisted and Nagarwala, who confessed his crime in the immediate aftermath of the scandal, demanded a retrial. While his petition for a retrial was pending, he died in jail in March 1972 and the mystery behind all the events and one in which Indira's involvement was suspected, for good enough reasons, was hushed up. The police officer who investigated the Nagarwala case too died in a car accident six months later.

To get back to the concerns of this chapter, the Congress reverses in West Bengal were substantial in 1967. The CPI (M) emerged as a substantive force in the West Bengal assembly too. It formed a United Front government with the Bangla Congress leader, Ajoy Mukherjee, as the chief minister and Jyoti Basu as the home minister. The Bangla Congress, a breakaway from the Congress party, had won five Lok Sabha seats from West Bengal in 1967 and Humayun Kabir, who was the education minister in Nehru's Cabinet, was among them.

Another state where the Congress party's reverses were stunning was Tamil Nadu. Apart from losing the state government, the Congress won only three out of the 39 Lok Sabha seats from Tamil Nadu. The gains were that of the DMK. The party won 25 Lok Sabha seats from the state, securing over 35 per cent of the votes. C. Subramaniam, one of Indira's aides and among those who advised her to devalue the rupee, lost from Gobichettipalayam; and Congress president, Kamaraj, lost from Virudhunagar, his assembly constituency. The Swatantra Party, whose formation was decided in a public meeting in Madras (after the Nagpur session of the Congress party in 1959) with C. Rajagopalachari (Rajaji) as one of its main leaders, gathered six Lok Sabha seats from Tamil Nadu. The Swatantra Party was an ally of the DMK in that election. Ironically, it was Rajaji's decision as the chief minister of Madras (between 1937 and September 1939) to make Hindi a compulsory subject in schools that laid the basis for the Self-Respect Movement under Periyar E. V. Ramasami's leadership to mobilise a mass movement against the imposition of Hindi. It remained the core issue for the DMK (after its formation in 1949) and even helped the party establish itself as a major force in the context of the anti-Hindi agitation in 1965. In 1967, however, Rajaji—to whom Nehru had entrusted the Congress party in Tamil Nadu soon after the 1951–52 general election to cobble a majority in the state assembly (and Rajaji managed it too)—joined hands with C. N. Annadurai to defeat the Congress party. Rajaji had been removed as the chief minister of Madras in 1954 and since then, he was waiting to avenge.

The Swatantra Party's gains were significant elsewhere too. The party, no doubt had stunned the Congress bosses even in Nehru's time by winning 18 seats and close to 8 per cent of the votes in 1962. In 1967, the party won 44 Lok Sabha seats. It bagged 12 out of the 24 seats from Gujarat (half the seats from the state) and the stage was set for the Congress party's decline in the state in 1967. This fact of history is indeed important to understand the course of politics in Gujarat since then. The other states where the Swatantra Party secured seats were Orissa (eight out of 20) and Rajasthan (eight out of 23). Among them were the legendary Minoo R. Masani, a member of the Nasik group, who set out to form the Congress Socialist Party in 1934 and the one who sailed across the spectrum to the Swatantra Party standing up for unfettered capitalism and a parliamentarian of repute. The Swatantra contingent also consisted of Piloo H. Mody, whose sharp wits and irrepressible sense of humour, would cause discomfort to even Nehru who wallowed in the parliament.

All this meant that Indira Gandhi, in her second term as the prime minister, had to confront challenges from several quarters. Apart from the fact that her party's strength had reduced considerably and that the party bosses were determined to reduce her into their subordinate, she also had to face an array of political veterans like Ram Manohar Lohia, George Fernandes, A. K. Gopalan, Nath Pai and Minoo Masani as well as men known for their humour and sharp-tongue like Piloo Mody, Atal Behari Vajpayee and N. C. Chatterjee, whose son Somnath became the Lok Sabha Speaker in May 2004.

We have seen, in the last chapter, the emergence of Indira Gandhi as the leader of the Congress party in the parliament against Morarji's claim; and also the fact that it happened because her election was ensured by Kamaraj's intervention and the party bosses, some of them even ardent advocates of the free-market principle (as opposed to Nehruvian socialism), rallied behind her. In the true sense, they were opposed to Morarji and hence backed Indira; they thought she was weak and hence will depend on them. The story would repeat itself. After the 1967 general election, Morarji, who had won from Sabarkanta (in Gujarat) with as much ease as Indira did from Rae Bareli, was determined to force a contest. However, Kamaraj intervened again (in his capacity as the president of the Congress party) to ensure a consensus and prevailed upon Morarji to withdraw his nomination. In return, Morarji was accommodated by Indira as number two in her cabinet. Morarji was sworn in as the deputy prime minister and also made the finance minister the same day as Indira was sworn in as the prime minister on 13 March 1967. The compromise was struck on 10 March 1967 after much behind-the-scenes activity. The overwhelming concern of those who worked for a compromise was that the Congress party was considerably weakened; an intra-party struggle was the last thing that they were prepared for. At another level, in March 1967, the party high command, or the syndicate as they were called, was a vanquished lot. Indira, meanwhile, was the favourite of a different set of party bosses from the states; D. P. Mishra, who played a major role in ensuring Indira's ascendancy in January 1966, was joined this time by another important leader, Chandra Bhanu Gupta from Uttar Pradesh.

The settlement or the consensus that ensured Indira as the prime minister and Morarji as her deputy was based on expediency rather than on faith. However, the party bosses, including Kamaraj, found it increasingly difficult to reconcile with the arrangement. This would be revealed when Indira constituted her cabinet. She left out Neelam Sanjiva Reddy from her team. Reddy was the only leader from among the syndicate to win the 1967 elections. He was left out while Indira promoted Dinesh Singh as minister of commerce with cabinet rank. Jagjivan Ram was given the important portfolio of food and agriculture. His qualification was that he was one of Desai's antagonists. Y. B. Chavan, who had become the home minister after Gulzarilal Nanda was asked to quit (in November 1966), stayed on in that position. He was considered Indira's loyalist. Congress President Kamaraj, whose intervention in Indira's favour made all the difference, was not even consulted in the course of cabinet formation.

It is also important to record here that Kamaraj in 1967 was not the same powerful leader he was in May 1964 (at the time of Shastri's election) and in January 1966 when he led the party organisation to elect Indira as the Congress Parliamentary Party leader. He had lost elections from his own assembly constituency. Another important member of the syndicate, S. K. Patil, the resourceful leader from Maharashtra and a member of the Union Cabinet from April 1957 to September 1963 (when he was eased out under the Kamaraj Plan by Nehru), had bounced back soon after Shastri re-inducted him into the Cabinet in June 1964. He remained powerful and was the minister for railways until March 1967. He too lost the election from Bombay South, considered his pocket burrow, in March 1967. Patil's defeat at the hands of the young trade unionist and Socialist Party candidate, George Fernandes, sent waves across the country and in the immediate context the syndicate was rendered weak. George Fernandes came to be known as the 'giant killer' Similarly, Atulya Ghosh lost from Bankura in West Bengal.

The Socialist Shift

Indira sought to make use of the crisis thrown up by the reverses suffered by the Congress party. She began to interpret them as a mandate against the measures initiated during the brief tenure of Lal Bahadur Shastri. The Shastri era was marked by an attempt to move away from the Nehruvian trajectory. She could show the impressive gains secured by the Swatantra Party since 1962 (when the party bagged 18 Lok Sabha seats and emerged as the largest opposition in four states) and now in 1967 when Swatantra Party candidates won from 44 Lok Sabha seats as indication of the enormity of the challenge to Nehru's socialist ideas and her own commitment to that project. But then, during her first year and half as the prime minister, Indira depended on the goodwill of the party bosses, including Kamaraj. In the post-1967 phase, she was at liberty to chart her own course. She chose to identify the core element of her strategy in this battle to be a struggle to reiterate the Congress party's commitment to the Nehruvian path in economic policy. She decided to push ahead and expand the scope of the Nehruvian socialist paradigm. In this sense, the ascendency of Indira in the Congress brought an end to the attempts, initiated in mild doses during the Shastri regime, to shift from Nehru's socialist trajectory.

However, it is important to note at this stage that Indira's recourse to socialism was more of a tactical move on her part to take on the party bosses than borne out of a serious conviction to the idea. In fact, the chief architect of this strategy was not Indira herself but one of her associates during her days in London: P. N. Haksar. A leftist by commitment, Haksar was appointed in the Prime Minister's Secretariat by Indira in May 1967. L. K. Jha, who was brought there by Shastri and stayed on in that position through Indira's first and tumultuous stint as the prime minister, was asked to make way for Haksar. The office of the Prime Minister's Secretariat grew into an institution with unfettered powers, during Haksar's time, and into the most important power centre before which the Cabinet was reduced to a pygmy in due course.

In the party, Indira began to associate more openly with the lot of left-leaning Congressmen; the most prominent among them was Chandra Shekhar. The first signs of these were seen at the AICC meeting in Delhi soon after Indira's election as the prime minister in March 1967. The Young Turks raised the demand to nationalise banks; banking industry was an exclusive preserve of the private sector and demands for nationalisation of this sector were voiced even during Nehru's time. These voices were not bold enough then. At the AICC session in Delhi, the Young Turks raised the issue once again and it was clear, even at that stage, that the concerns were more directed at the inner party struggle. Indira's cheerleaders were aware of the fact that Finance Minister Morarji Desai was opposed to the idea in every sense of the term and, hence, the demand at the Delhi AICC had different connotations. Indira, however, sprang a surprise and instead pitched in for what was called 'social control' over banking. The idea was to appoint ombudsmen to monitor and recommend measures in the area of lending and other such functions of the private sector banks. The Young Turks also raised the demand for abolition of privy purses; the privy purses pertained to allowances to the princes, granted in perpetuity, to their descendents from the Government of India's funds. The descendants of the old rulers were also allowed to hoist their own flags and retain such privileges as their own number plates on their cars.

The fact that a large number of the descendents of the erstwhile rulers had joined the Swatantra Party and were elected to Parliament in 1967 had irritated Indira and her cheerleaders. It is another matter that some such men had entrenched themselves in the Congress party and this included one of Indira's confidante, Dinesh Singh, the Raja of Kalakankar. Dinesh Singh's daughter, Rajkumari Ratna Singh, continued to be the Congress party's 'natural' leader and after her father's demise, she represented Pratapgarh (adjacent to Rae Bareli) in the Lok Sabha for several years. It is also a fact that the Congress party would accommodate a number of such 'Rajas' and 'Maharanis' in due course of time: V. P. Singh, the Raja of Manda, Arjun Singh from Rewa, K. P. Singh Deo from Dhenkanal in Orissa, Amarinder Singh from Patiala and Madhavrao Scindia from Gwalior. Scindia, interestingly, entered Parliament in 1971 on behalf of the Jan Sangh along with his mother, Rajmata Vijayraje Scindia, negotiated peace with Indira's regime during the Emergency (thus, saved himself from arrest and internment) and shifted to the Congress party right in time for the 1977 general election. Indira and her cheerleaders, however, were keen on clipping the wings of the princes in 1967. The Swatantra Party could not have won as many as 44 seats in the Lok Sabha without having fielded many such former rulers. Even in the present times, parties across the spectrum, barring the communists, continue to field such former rulers and are assured, in most instances, of victory. Such is the intense hold they have on the ordinary people. This is a clear evidence of the feudal vestiges that continue to haunt large tracts of rural India even now.

Even while the Young Turks were pushing for nationalisation of banks and placed a resolution at the Delhi AICC to that effect, Indira took the microphone and appealed for social control of banks. A compromise formula was worked out there in the form of a 10-point charter. This, apart from calling for social control over the banks, included such well-meaning programmes as land reforms, poverty-eradication measures and also measures to withdraw the privileges to the princes. The 10-point charter, however, did not talk about abolition of the privy purses. Also, all of it was adopted by the AICC in the same manner as the party's gathering adopted socialistic pattern of society at its Avadi session in 1955 and cooperative farming at its Nagpur session in 1959. Later in the evening, after Indira, Kamaraj, Morarji and many leaders had left the session the Young Turks moved a resolution seeking that the privy purses be abolished. It was a tactical move and the resolution was adopted. The resolution was put to vote before the delegates present and was carried with 17 members voting for it and four against it. The leaders on both sides did not miss the irony of the situation and the fact that it was moved and voted when most delegates had left the venue. But then, there was no way they could question its legitimacy. The Delhi session had committed the Congress party to abolish privy purses.

While the Young Turks persisted with their loud campaign for implementing the 'radical' ideas expressed in the 10-point charter and also the party's commitment to abolish the privy purses, there were others in the party, identified with the party bosses standing up and now rallying behind Morarji Desai. The battle shifted to the Congress Parliamentary Party, and Tarakeswari Sinha, a young lady from Bihar, who had won from Barh Lok Sabha constituency in 1957, 1962 and in 1967, was prominent among Indira's detractors in the Parliamentary Party. She would end up in the doghouse after Indira emerged as the undisputed leader of the Congress party.

The issues that dominated the May 1967 AICC session in Delhi continued to dominate the AICC meet in Jabalpur in October 1967. In addition, the Jabalpur session also decided on a new president for the party. Kamaraj had been there for four years and the Jabalpur AICC decided on S. Nijalingappa as the Congress president. It may be recalled that Nijalingappa's name had come up for the post at the Nagpur session in 1959 but Indira was chosen for the job then. In 1967, he was chosen jointly by Indira and Kamaraj. Although Nijalingappa had all along been a part of the syndicate and, thus, a part of the attempts to contain Indira, his actions as Congress president did not betray this, at least in the initial stages. The CWC, in fact, was constituted in a manner giving equal representation to both the syndicate and Indira loyalists.

This, however, was not the case insofar as the executive of the Congress Parliamentary Board (CPB) was concerned. Out of the eight members who constituted the CPB executive, Indira's camp was outnumbered; apart from herself, only Jagjivan Ram and Fakhruddin Ali Ahmed could be counted as her own men. The other side consisted of Nijalingappa, Morarji Desai, Kamaraj and S. K. Patil. The home minister, Y. B. Chavan was the eighth person in the CPB executive. The composition of the CPB executive would assume significance in the context of the choosing the Congress party's candidate for the presidential elections in July 1969. We shall discuss this in the following section.

The Congress Split

As it happened in the by-elections in 1963, when the Congress lost a few constituencies, provoking concern in Nehru's mind on the future of the party, a similar trend emerged in the by-elections in 1967 too. N. G. Ranga and J. B. Kripalani entered Parliament in April–May 1967 on behalf of the Swatantra Party. In November that year, Murasoli Maran won the Madras South Lok Sabha constituency as the DMK nominee. In 1968, S. M. Krishna won from Mysore as the PSP candidate; Krishna was to join the Congress later on and become the chief minister of Karnataka and much later the governor of Maharashtra (in 2004) after the Congress returned to power in the centre. More than these, the outcome of the by-elections during 1969 was significant. Out of the seven Lok Sabha constituencies where by-elections were held in that year, the Congress party won only two. They were Kamaraj's victory from Nagercoil (Tamil Nadu) in January 1969 and S. K. Patil's from Banaskantha (Gujarat) in May that year. Phulpur, represented by Jawaharlal Nehru until his death and by his sister, Vijayalakshmi Pandit after that, was wrested by the Samyukta Socialist Party nominee, Janeshwar Mishra. Pandit had won Phulpur in a by-election in 1964 and also in the 1967 general election as Congress nominee. She resigned from the Lok Sabha to register her protest against Indira's ways.

It was clear that the Congress party was losing its hold over the people even in 1967 and the pattern persisted in the following years too. The return of Kamaraj and Patil happened around the same time as the Congress president, an integral part of the syndicate, S. Nijalingappa was coming around to the view that Indira's wings had to be clipped. He was encouraged in this by the pattern that emerged in the results of the by-elections in 1969.

Nijalingappa had embarked upon this course a few weeks before S. K. Patil's election victory. In April 1969, at the Congress annual session in Faridabad, the Congress president lambasted the prime minister's priorities in the economic policy front. There was chaos and the Congress president's address was followed by an equally vitriolic address by Indira Gandhi. In the process, the battle that was essentially between personalities was given an ideological coating. For the first time in the few years after Indira's ascendancy, the war seemed to be between those who wanted the Congress party (and the government) to continue with the Nehruvian socialist course and those who stood for free-market principles. Indira became the leader of the socialists and Morarji Desai, backed by the syndicate, advocated the free-market principles. The central issue in these was nationalisation of banks. The Faridabad session, however, came to an abrupt end. The *shamiana* (tent) caught fire soon after Indira concluded her speech. No efforts were made to continue with the show and the fire was let to the tent.

The man who organised the event was Bansi Lal who had become the chief minister of Haryana in May 1967. After the 1967 elections, Rao Birendra Singh, a socialist, had gathered a majority around the Vishal Haryana Party and become the chief minister. This, however, did not last beyond a couple of months and MLAs began shifting parties by the day; that was when political commentators described the situation in the state as one determined by *Aya Rams and Gaya Rams*. Much of this was the achievement of Bansi Lal. He was one of the palanquin-bearers of Gulzarilal Nanda and was anointed the chief minister because everyone, including Nanda, considered him to be one without a base of his own. Bansi Lal, however, proved his mentor wrong and climbed his way up to become one of the confidants of Indira. He managed this by ensuring that Indira's son, Sanjay, got large tracts of land (for a pittance) to further his project. The Maruti car factory in Gurgaon was Bansi Lal's means to endear himself to Indira as much as his role during the Emergency. Another player who got close to Indira by doing his bit to obtain land for Sanjay was a wily man from North Bihar, Lalit Narain Mishra, who would get killed in a bomb blast in Samastipur in Bihar. We shall discuss these in detail in the next chapter.

Meanwhile, President Zakir Hussain died on 3 May 1969. And, in the context where the ruling Congress was caught in a battle within and among its leaders, the task of choosing the next president would also turn out to be a battleground. The party bosses were determined against letting Indira decide the course on this issue while Indira wanted to assert herself. This was the context in which the AICC was scheduled to meet in Bangalore on 10 July 1967. The choice of Bangalore as the venue was not insignificant. Nijalingappa, after his election as Congress president in May 1968, had appointed Veerendra Patil as the Karnataka chief minister in his place. Patil was among those who stayed loyal to the syndicate and had emerged as the combined opposition's candidate against Indira Gandhi in the Chickmagalur by-election in November 1978. Indira, too, was aware of this and also of the fact that she was hopelessly outnumbered in the executive of the CPB, the appropriate forum to finalise the Congress party's presidential candidate.

Once again, acting on the advice of her Principal Secretary P. N. Haksar, Indira was determined to focus on the differences on economic policy issues and to pick up from where she had left at the Faridabad session. She, however, did not arrive at Bangalore on 10 July 1969 and claimed to be indisposed. Instead, she sent across a note, which she described as '*just some stray thoughts rather hurriedly dictated*' to the CWC. It was Fakhruddin Ali Ahmed, one of her staunch loyalists in the Cabinet as well as a member of the CPB, who carried this note from Delhi to Bangalore. Apart from all the good things that were said by the Congress party at Avadi and Nagpur, Indira's note talked about the idea of nationalisation of banks as a definite option. It said:

> There is a great feeling in the country regarding the nationalization of private commercial banks. We had taken a decision at an earlier AICC but perhaps we may review it. *Either we can consider the nationalization of the top five or six banks or issue directions that the resources of banks should be reserved to a larger extent for public purposes.* (emphasis added)

The note underscored the need for banks to set aside specified amounts as government securities. It mentioned that Rs 200 crore had to be made available for the public sector investments in this context. Much to the surprise of everyone, the CWC, including the party bosses, and more particularly Finance Minister Morarji Desai, agreed to incorporate all these 'stray thoughts' into a proper resolution by the CWC on 11 July and had it endorsed by the AICC on 12 July 1969. One factor that led the syndicate, despite their opposition to such socialistic shift, to adopt this course was that the CWC was divided on the issue and even such members as Kamaraj and Y. B. Chavan, who were opposed to Indira, were in favour of the shift. It was Desai who moved the resolution at the AICC and in the presence of Indira Gandhi there. She had arrived in Bangalore on 11 July 1969. The more important task before the Congress leaders at Bangalore on that day was to decide on the presidential candidate. And, this had to be done by the eight members of the CPB executive. The syndicate had already agreed on nominating one of its lot to occupy the Rashtrapati Bhawan. The Lok Sabha Speaker Neelam Sanjiva Reddy was the syndicate's choice. It was determined not to get distracted: So much so, the syndicate had agreed with all that Indira wanted in her 'stray thoughts'.

In the Parliamentary Board executive meeting on 12 July 1969, Indira proposed Jagjivan Ram, and even suggested that this would ensure someone from among the scheduled castes as the President of the Republic and that too in 1969, the centenary of Mahatma Gandhi's birth. There was voting at the CPB. In the eight-member forum, five voted in favour of Sanjiva Reddy while Indira herself and Fakhruddin Ali Ahmed voted for Jagjivan Ram. Those who voted for Reddy as the presidential candidate were: Nijalingappa, Morarji Desai, Kamaraj, S. K. Patil and Y. B. Chavan. Jagjivan Ram, himself a candidate, abstained from voting. Indira had not expected Chavan, her home minister, to side with the syndicate. However, she refrained from showing her anger against Chavan openly. She told the press a day later—13 July 1969—that the party bosses must be prepared for the consequences. She also conveyed that she would have preferred V. V. Giri, then the vice-president and the acting president after Zakir Hussain's death, instead of Reddy as the Congress candidate. She left Bangalore soon after.

Within moments, the acting President V. V. Giri announced his intention to contest the presidential election as an independent candidate. On 13 July 1969, he issued a statement in which he pointed out the decision to field Reddy—who also happened to be the Lok Sabha speaker—smacked of constitutional impropriety. The speaker's office, according to Giri, was above party politics and he faulted the decision to field him as Congress candidate for the post of president. Giri, incidentally, was also a Congress party member. Indira did not react to this.

Instead, she struck elsewhere. On 16 July 1969, exactly three days after she left Bangalore for Delhi, she stripped Morarji Desai of the finance portfolio. In fact, the acting President V. V. Giri would relieve Desai of the finance portfolio within minutes after the prime minister's recommendation to that effect reached him. Indira explained to Desai that she did not want to burden him, the finance minister, with a decision on nationalisation of banks given the fact that he was opposed to the idea from the outset. She, however, appealed to him to stay on as her deputy prime minister. Desai, after placing on record that he had learnt of his removal as the finance minister from the PTI news ticker in his office (at 2.44 p.m.

on 16 July 1969), resented the manner in which he was relieved. He also pointed out that the bank nationalisation issue was never brought before the Cabinet. In a letter to Indira on 17 July 1969, Desai wrote: 'May I ask whether it was fair that you should have taken a unilateral decision and issued a notification with President's consent without even the courtesy of having a word with me?'. On 19 July 1969, Desai resigned from the post of the deputy prime minister too.

Indira, meanwhile, had scripted her play in all its details. On 19 July 1969, just two days before the monsoon session of Parliament, Indira recommended to the president to promulgate an ordinance nationalising 14 private-sector banks. The ordinance and the Act that replaced it was struck down by the Supreme Court on substantive and procedural grounds. However, the measure came to be celebrated on the streets across the country. Indira's cheerleaders, too, played their role by organising crowds to assemble in the vicinity of her official residence—1 Safdarjung Road—in support of bank nationalisation. This, indeed, unnerved those in the syndicate. The strategy was once again devised by P. N. Haksar: That Indira should take her battle with the party bosses to an ideological plane and the socialist hobby horse seemed to work wonders. The only prominent leader from the syndicate camp who gave vent to his anger on the issue was S. K. Patil.

Meanwhile, Indira shifted the battle back to the presidential elections. Here again, her behaviour was baffling. She had signed the nomination papers of Sanjiva Reddy without giving any signs of what she would do in a few days. The Swatantra Party and the Jan Sangh, meanwhile, fielded an elder statesman of that time, C. D. Deshmukh and the other opposition parties such as the Bharatiya Kranti Dal, the SSP and the PSP adopted him as their candidate. Thus, in 1969, there were three contenders in the field for the office of president: Sanjiva Reddy on behalf of the Congress party, Deshmukh backed by the Swatantra-Socialist-Jan Sangh combine and V. V. Giri as independent. In the usual course, Nijalingappa set out campaigning for his party nominee, met with the leaders of the Jan Sangh and the Swatantra Party, seeking their votes. He also got assurance that their MPs and MLAs would cast their second preference votes for Reddy. This, indeed, turned the table against the Congress president. On the face of it, there was no need for the Congress to seek votes from the opposition. The party's strength in Parliament and the various state assemblies was enough to see Reddy through. However, the syndicate had reasons to gather that extra bit, given the context in which Giri had filed his nomination and the manner in which Indira had reacted at the Bangalore meet.

Meanwhile, Nijalingappa's meeting with the Jan Sangh leaders served Indira with a handle. On 11 August 1969, her two confidants, Jagjivan Ram and Fakhruddin Ali Ahmed, demanded that the Congress president explain his action. The letter they wrote was promptly sent across to newspaper offices. On 13 August 1969, the duo wrote another missive to Nijalingappa (and sent copies to the press too); they demanded that the Congress MPs and MLAs be allowed to vote as per their conscience and not be bound by a whip. This they did after Nijalingappa's letter to Indira (in her capacity as leader of the Congress Parliamentary Party) to issue a whip to all party MPs to vote for Reddy. The Congress president's letter was written on 12 August 1969. It may be noted here that the whip, according to the constitutional provisions, will have to be issued by the party leader in Parliament/ Legislatures and there is nothing that the party president can do about it.

On the same day (13 August 1969) on which Ahmed and Jagjivan Ram had written, seeking sanction for conscience vote, Indira wrote to her party president and conveyed that she would not issue a whip to vote in favour of the party's official candidate, Sanjiva Reddy. She conveyed to Nijalingappa that she agreed with her two senior Cabinet colleagues that there was a conspiracy to subvert the Congress party and its commitment to 'socialist policies and secular democracy'. Her letter to the Congress president concluded with the following words:

> Elections are a medium to fight for our values and voting is a process of association with these (socialism and secular democracy) values. I cannot think of winning elections by clouding principles. I do not, therefore, think that in these circumstances and for constitutional reasons, it would be right for me to have a whip issued.

In fact, all this came about because Indira, by now, was convinced that the party bosses would have her removed as the prime minister by the president and that Reddy, having been a part of the syndicate for long, would oblige them.

The Congress president knew Indira's intentions now: that she wanted to vote for Giri. He conveyed this to her in a letter on 16 August 1969.

> Your demand for a free vote is in fact a demand for the right to vote for V. V. Giri, the candidate nominated by the communists and the communalists. History does not record of an instance where a prime minister, after proposing her party's candidate, not only works against him, but proclaims her support for the candidate of the opposition. If the tragic effect was not staring at us, I would have thought of it to be a tale from *Alice in Wonderland*.

All these letters were discussed in the newspapers and the battle within the party was actually fought in the public.

When the ballots were counted on 20 August 1969, the Congress candidate, N. Sanjiva Reddy lost to V. V. Giri, the independent candidate. Giri was formally supported by the two communist parties, the DMK and the Muslim League apart from some other smaller political groups in the states. Giri's victory margin was no doubt narrow. On closer scrutiny, it emerged that only two-thirds of the Congress party MPs and three-fourths of the party MLAs in various states had voted for the official party candidate. Indira's candidate, Giri, could win the elections because he could muster support from a section of the Congress MPs and MLAs in addition to those from parties that sponsored his campaign.

V. V. Giri secured 50.2 per cent of the votes against his nearest rival, Sanjiva Reddy who polled 48.5 per cent of the votes. And, C. D. Deshmukh, fielded on behalf of the Swatantra Party and the Jan Sangh, secured a mere 1.3 per cent of the votes. Giri remained the president for a full five-year term and was replaced by Fakhruddin Ali Ahmed on 17 August 1974. Sanjiva Reddy would live to become the president, for five years, after he was elected unopposed to the office on 6 August 1977 a few months after Indira and her Congress party were routed—in the general election in March 1977—by the Janata Party.

The days after Reddy's defeat were marked by innocuous attempts at reconciliation between the two sides. Chavan, whose association with the syndicate had infuriated Indira, was now back in her fold. The CWC meet on 25 August 1969 was vitiated by Nijalingappa's decision to debar one of Indira's men from the meet. C. Subramaniam was served with a notice that he was not invited to the CWC meet on grounds that the Tamil Nadu Congress Committee had initiated action against him. Indira struck once again and this time with a memorandum with signatures requesting an AICC meet to discuss the election of a new Congress president. Nijalingappa, meanwhile, showed that some signatures were forged in the memo and thus ruled the request to be out of order. Indira's response to this was to seek resignation of M. S. Gurupadaswamy, who was a syndicate loyalist and a member of her Cabinet from Karnataka. He resigned forthwith. The battle continued and Nijalingappa removed Fakhruddin Ali Ahmed from the CWC on 31 October 1969; this was a day before the CWC meeting on 1 November 1969.

The removal of Subramaniam and Ahmed were intended to ensure a majority for the syndicate in the CWC. On 1 November 1969, two different meetings of the CWC were held. One of them at the Congress party's headquarters on Jantar Mantar Road (which also remained the headquarters of the Congress (O) for a while, the Janata Party after 1977, the Janata Dal after 1988 and the Janata Dal (United) since 1999). The property belonged to a trust and this was where the Indian National Congress functioned ever since its headquarter shifted from Allahabad in 1944. Meanwhile, going back to the concerns of this chapter, another meeting of the CWC was held at the official residence of the prime minister, Indira Gandhi at 1 Safdarjung Road.

There were 10 CWC members on both sides and K. C. Abraham, the only member of the CWC who remained non-committal, attended both the meets briefly. Those who turned up for the meeting at the Congress headquarters at Jantar Mantar Road were manhandled by crowds (Indira's supporters) while the Delhi Police personnel looked on. The two sides passed resolutions placing their own positions on record. Indira used this to get rid of Ram Subhag Singh from her Cabinet. An MP from Buxar in Bihar, he was also a close associate of Feroze Gandhi and was the first one to raise the Mundra scandal in Parliament. The CWC at Indira's residence also called for a meeting of the AICC to be held on 22 and 23 November in

New Delhi and authorised Fakhruddin Ali Ahmed, C. Subramaniam (both of them were dropped from the committee by the Congress president) to organise the AICC. Indira also deputed Shankar Dayal Sharma for this job. Sharma would become the vice-president in September 1987 and president of the republic in September 1992. Nijalingappa, meanwhile, issued a show cause notice to Indira. On 12 November 1969, the CWC passed a resolution to remove Indira Gandhi from the primary membership of the Congress party and directed the Congress Parliamentary Party (CPP) to elect a new leader. All this, however, was only a side show.

Indira had charted her own course even earlier and soon after the CWC resolution was made public, Indira convened a cabinet meet in which all the important members reposed faith in her leadership. Those who did not were asked to quit. The following day, it became clear that Indira could enlist the support of a majority in the CPP. All those who voted for Reddy and refused to go with Indira in August 1969 during the presidential elections did not persist that way in November that year. Of the 429 Congress members (from both the houses of Parliament), 310 stayed with Indira. This included 220 members of the Lok Sabha; the total strength of the house was 530. Indira was left with 90 members of the Rajya Sabha out of 250. Meanwhile, 68 MPs of the Lok Sabha and 51 out of the 141 Congress members of the Rajya Sabha went with the Congress (O). Morarji Desai was elected the chairman of the Congress (O) Parliamentary Party.

Indira's Congress party held the AICC meet in Delhi on 22 November 1969 and of the 705 members of the AICC, 446 attended the meet. This established her majority in the organisation too. The AICC removed Nijalingappa from the party president's post and elected Jagjivan Ram as head of Indira's Congress party. She was now in absolute control of the Congress party as well as the government.

The immediate impact of the split, however, was that Indira Gandhi's government was rendered into a minority. The party strength came down to 220 in a house of 530. Indira, however, found support coming from the two communist parties, the DMK and the Muslim League apart from some independents. The communist leaders interpreted the crisis within the Congress as part of a conspiracy against Indira's socialist project. Hence, the minority government had to be saved from falling, according to them. Indira Gandhi, meanwhile, intensified her socialist rhetoric. While, on the one hand, she could reinvent the Congress party's political constituency by this step, the two communist parties could rationalise their support to the Congress government too, on the other. Indira, however, was not the one to let such an arrangement persist. Soon, she decided to advance the general election. This was the context in which the slogan, *garibi hatao,* emerged.

The story of the origin of this battle cry is rather interesting. Disparaging the unity among the forces opposed to her, Indira began describing the opposition to her as bereft of ideology. It was her refrain, from the public forum, that they were united only in their opposition to her and that they lacked any sense of commitment to the country and its people. In fact, just when she decided to go for snap polls, she said: 'They all want to banish Indira Gandhi from the scene (*Indira hatao*); whereas, Indira's agenda is to banish poverty (*garibi hatao*).' That was how *garibi hatao* was made a battle cry by Indira Gandhi. It served the purpose. Of the 65 MPs, who left the Congress to form the Congress (O) in the fourth Lok Sabha (1967–70), only 11 could get themselves elected to the fifth Lok Sabha. This will be dealt with in the next chapter.

Meanwhile, the unity of the opposition parties, scripted by Ram Manohar Lohia, that led to the reverses suffered by the Congress in the 1967 elections (in the northern states) was beginning to show signs of falling apart within months after March 1967. The architect of this unity, Lohia, died on 17 October 1967. He was admitted to the Wellington Hospital for treatment of a swollen prostrate gland and treated with a minor surgery. He did not live after the surgery. Lohia was only 57 years old when he died. The opposition-led governments were faltering and falling by the day in Uttar Pradesh, Madhya Pradesh and Bihar due to the internecine quarrels among the constituents. The opposition, however, persisted with the unity and agreed to fight against Indira's Congress as a combined force—a grand alliance comprising the Congress (O), the Socialists and the Bharatiya Jan Sangh came into place before the elections.

VIII

The Congress Party's Shift to the Command Mode

> The split at the Bangalore session of the AICC, which caused Indira Gandhi to denigrate Morarji Desai, was the outcome of the suspicion that the Old Guard was out to dislodge her and also the result of her political intuition that if she struck a radical posture, she would carry the country and the Congress with her.
>
> — Durga Das, *India: From Curzon to Nehru and After*

In the previous chapter, we saw the context in which the Congress party underwent a split and Indira Gandhi emerged as the supreme leader of the party. The split, even while rendering the prime minister's party a minority in both the houses of Parliament, did not help the opposition to unseat Indira from the post of prime minister. The ruling party's strength in the Lok Sabha was not as much as in the past. And the split had reduced it to a minority. Even before the split, the party had just 19 members more than the simple majority needed in the house. After the split, when as many as 68 Congress party members of the Lok Sabha went with the Congress (O), Indira's Congress, now named Congress (R), the 'R' standing for Requisitionist, had only 220 supporters in the Lok Sabha. However, a no-confidence motion moved by the Congress (O) soon after the split exposed their weakness. The support that Indira had mustered in favour of V. V. Giri against the Congress party's official nominee, N. Sanjiva Reddy, in the presidential polls, was not a one-time affair. The opposition motion was summarily defeated despite the substantive reduction in the ruling party's strength in Parliament.

Indira's government received support from the CPI with 23 MPs, the CPI (M) with 19 MPs, the DMK with 25 MPs, some smaller groups such as the Forward Bloc and the Revolutionary Socialist Party and a few independent MPs. The PSP too had suffered erosion of its strength, with a number of its MPs, following Asoka Mehta, joining hands with Indira. Meanwhile, the Swatantra Party, the Samyukta Socialist Party and the Bharatiya Jan Sangh with 44, 23 and 35 MPs respectively teamed up as a combined opposition. The 68 MPs who constituted the Congress (O) in Parliament teamed up with the opposition at this stage. The situation in the Rajya Sabha, however, was different. While the alignment of parties in the Upper House, had assured the ruling party a majority, in the same way as it happened in the lower house, the margin was not as much as in the case of the Lok Sabha. This was to reflect in the voting on the bill to abolish the privy purses in due course. Indira suffered a blow when the bill, after being passed in the lower house, was rejected by the Rajya Sabha by a single vote. We shall discuss this at a later stage in this chapter. After the split, 51 out of the

141 Congress members of the Rajya Sabha went with the Congress (O). Indira's Congress was reduced to a 90-member strong party in the house of 250.

In this chapter, we shall discuss: (i) the measures undertaken by Indira in the couple of years after the split both in the administrative sphere and in the party, (ii) a brief narrative of the developments in the states, particularly those where the Congress lost power in 1967, and thereafter (iii) the emergence of Indira's son, Sanjay Gandhi, on the scene with his proposal for a car-manufacturing factory.

Dumb Doll to a Ruthless Leader

We saw in the last chapter that the manner in which Indira went about asserting her own position against the party bosses showed that she was anything but a dumb doll. Her strategy, in that context, was devised by her aide in the Prime Minister's Secretariat, P. N. Haksar. A new set of men constituted her 'kitchen cabinet' by this time. Inder Kumar Gujral, who at some point in his early life was associated with the Communist Party, and Chandra Shekhar, who began as a member of the PSP, were prominent among her aides. Indira had also cultivated Romesh and Raj Thapar, who too held similar thoughts as Haksar, as part of her inner circle. This was also the time when a number of prominent leaders of the CPI, led by S. A. Dange (one of the founders of the communist movement in India), began to see in Indira a committed socialist and hence the imperative for them to stand up in her support within and outside Parliament. In a decade after this, Dange would be expelled from the CPI and Mohit Sen, one of his followers, would continue to drum up support to the Congress until his death in 2004. Dange and his followers in the CPI were not perturbed by the fact that Indira had worked overtime to dismiss the CPI-led government in Kerala in 1959.

Indira, on her part, was keen on proving her commitment to the socialistic pattern. As part of this, the managing agency system—that was in vogue in the business scene since the advent of the British East India Company—was abolished. Far more socialistic among Indira's moves, immediately after the split, was the Monopolies and Restrictive Trade Practices Act (MRTP Act) in 1969. While most of its provisions have been annulled by Parliament over a period of time, the act as it came about in 1969, imposed severe curbs on the expansion of private capital. It was intended to ensure that the operation of the economic system did not result in the concentration of economic power to the common detriment and, hence, ensured control over monopolies in trade and manufacture. The Swatantra Party, whose ideology was pronouncedly in favour of free enterprise, opposed the bill; the Congress (O) too joined the stable and this gave Indira another opportunity to position herself as a socialist. The act provided for the setting up of an MRTP Commission to ensure that a single company was not allowed to monopolise trade or manufacture a particular kind of good. The passage of this legislation helped Indira shore up her credentials as someone committed to the socialistic pattern. The propaganda, around this time, by the members of the syndicate that Indira was a communist conspirator only helped her build such an image for herself.

The next major step by Indira was to display her authority over her own party. Yashwantrao Chavan, her aide (and the home minister ever since Gulzarilal Nanda was eased out of that position), was dealt with by Indira now. Chavan had acted against her wishes at the Bangalore meet by voting in favour of N. Sanjiva Reddy in the Parliamentary Board executive. Incidentally, he stayed with Indira while others who supported Reddy (against Jagjivan Ram) went to form the Congress (O) in December 1969. Chavan was moved out of the home ministry and made the finance minister in June 1970. Indira Gandhi assumed the charge of the home ministry. The Intelligence Bureau (IB) controlled the internal security wing as well as the external intelligence gathering or counter espionage until then. But this was bifurcated, and while the IB was left with the task of domestic affairs, a new wing, christened the Research and Analysis Wing (RAW), was set up to deal with counter espionage. Indira also effected changes in the ambit of powers of the finance ministry and took away the Directorate of Revenue Enforcement from its control. As a matter of fact, IB, RAW and the Directorate of Revenue Enforcement were brought directly under the prime minister. This prevails even now. Apart from Chavan, another powerful minister in the union cabinet, Dinesh Singh, with substantive clout until then, was moved out of the foreign office in the reshuffle. Singh was soon dropped from the Cabinet and even suspended from the party soon on the charges that he was hobnobbing with the opposition parties. Indira would persist with this practice—to keep all her Cabinet colleagues on tenterhooks—in future too and this was her way of conveying, time and again, that the Congress party was under her command. The command mode, in other words, began to work in the case of Congress chief ministers too and contribute immensely to the eventual emasculation of the party organisation in several states.

This was the context in which the Prime Minister's Secretariat emerged into a power centre. Indira's response to this charge, however, was that the Prime Minister's Secretariat was not her creation and that it was invented by Lal Bahadur Shastri after he became the prime minister. Apart from P. N. Haksar and in due course P. N. Dhar, there were others who emerged powerful around this time. Bansi Lal, from Haryana, was one of them. Lalit Narain Mishra from Bihar was another. D. P. Mishra, who gathered several chief ministers in January 1966 to ensure that Indira was elected the prime minister, was very much there in her inner circle at this stage. There were also such others as I. K. Gujral, Chandra Shekhar and Nandini Satpathy who began her political life as a member of the CPI in Orissa.

Meanwhile, Indira's party had also suffered erosion of its strength in some of the states. The Congress (O) had the strength in such state assemblies as in Bihar, Gujarat, Karnataka and Uttar Pradesh to wrest control over the governments in those states. Indira Gandhi set out her men to do everything to destabilise the regimes in those states and also in the other states where the Congress had lost to the opposition in 1967. It is also important, to note here, that the unity among the opposition parties in 1967 was not based on any ideological or programmatic considerations. Similarly, the Socialist Party that acted as the harbinger of this unity was constituted by a bunch of leaders with a penchant for internecine squabbles. Also, Ram Manohar Lohia, the architect of this strategy was no longer there. His death in October 1967 had left a vacuum and the Socialist Party was left without a leader who could command the cadre. While this aspect will be discussed in greater detail in the next chapter, here we will see how the lack of a coherent programme behind the anti-Congress unity led to its collapse within months after the 1967 polls, thus, making Indira's attempt to reinvent her own Congress party easier.

Another significant development during this period involved the realignment of forces in Kerala. In 1967, the Congress had lost power to the CPI (M)-led Left Front and that led to E. M. S. Namboodiripad becoming the chief minister of the state for the second time. The CPI (M), like the CPI and several other left-of-centre parties, supported the Indira-led central government in Parliament after the 1969 split. There was, however, a distinction in the attitude of CPI (M) from that of the CPI in that the former's support was qualified. The differences between the two parties widened in due course after the split and a short while after the split, the CPI withdrew support to the EMS ministry. It led to elections to the state assembly in September 1970 in which the CPI joined Indira's Congress as an ally. The results turned the tables. Although the Congress party's strength improved from nine seats to 30 in the new assembly and its newfound ally, the Indian Union Muslim League, romped home with 11 seats and the Kerala Congress, also an ally of Indira, increased its strength to 12 (from the five it won in 1967), the Congress let the government be formed under C. Achuta Menon of the CPI. The CPI's strength in the assembly was only 16 then. Indira would extend this alliance with the CPI to other parts of the country too. In those cases, however, the CPI played second fiddle and the relationship continued until 1977. The CPI, it may be recorded at this stage, was a partner in the Samyukta Vidhayak Dal ministry in Bihar in 1967.

Similar efforts in West Bengal did not yield the same results. The United Front government, headed by Ajoy Mukherjee of the Bangla Congress in which the CPI (M) was a major player, was brought down in November 1967 and P. C. Ghosh was installed the chief minister. The arrangement was unstable and it collapsed soon. In the fresh elections to the assembly in 1969, Indira's Congress was decimated: it won only 55 seats in the 280-member assembly—far less than the 127 it had won in 1967. The United Front emerged winner again and this time the strength of the CPI (M) went up from 43 in 1967 to 80. Although the CPI (M) emerged the single largest party and its strength was more than that of the Bangla Congress, the party decided to continue with Ajoy Mukherjee as the chief minister.

The Bangla Congress leader continued as the chief minister until March 1970. The state went through another election to the assembly in March 1971 and the results threw up a hung assembly. Elections were held again in March 1972 and this time the Congress managed a victory and Indira's trusted aide, Siddhartha Shankar Ray, was made the chief minister. The state assembly elections in March 1972, held as they were in the aftermath of the Bangladesh War, belonged to a different league and we shall discuss this later in this chapter.

In nutshell, in less than a year after she split the Congress party, Indira managed to emasculate the Congress (O), dismantle the united opposition in several states and establish herself as the supreme leader of the Congress party within and outside the Parliament. She also ensured, in this period, that the party's leaders from the states were reduced to vassals whose survival depended on her. Earlier the Congress party's chief ministers and the party bosses would determine who would become the prime minister, as it happened in May 1964 when Shastri was anointed after Nehru, in January 1966 when Indira was chosen against Morarji Desai and once again in March 1967 before the split. But now, the Congress party was firmly under Indira's control. The story of Indira, turning the Congress party into one where loyalty to her own self and nothing else was the thumb rule, will not be complete without recalling an episode involving Jagjivan Ram.

We have noted, at various stages hitherto, the persona of Jagjivan Ram: a member of all the cabinets since Nehru's interim council in 1946 barring the couple of years between the execution of the Kamaraj Plan in September 1963 and Indira Gandhi's arrival as the prime minister in January 1966. He had played the role of being Indira's errand boy (along with Fakhruddin Ali Ahmed) in her battle against the syndicate and had raised the demand for a conscience vote in the 1969 presidential elections. He got rewarded for all this by Indira Gandhi. Jagjivan Ram, who was the minister for food and agriculture, by all means an important portfolio in those times, was promoted by Indira in 1970 and made the minister for defence. In addition, he was also the president of the Congress party; this post had come to him at the party session held in Bombay soon after the split. Jagjivan Ram was the first president of Indira's Congress, known as Congress (R) then.

There were tales, in those times, that Ram had amassed wealth abusing his ministerial position and that Morarji Desai, when he was the finance minister (between March 1967 and July 1969), was indeed aware of this. The Income Tax Department, directly under the Finance Minister, was also aware that Jagjivan Ram had not been filing his income tax returns for at least a decade. In the context of the Congress split and the pro-Indira role that Ram had played, this fact came into the open in the form of a scandal. Indira's response was that her Cabinet colleague was indeed a busy man and hence could not be held guilty of a crime. She defended Ram by stating that it was only a case of forgetfulness and nothing more. It did sound incredible. But then, those were the times when amorality was beginning to be seen as a virtue as long as the person involved in such activity was Indira's supporter. The fact is that Indira made Jagjivan Ram her party's president and entrusted the defence ministry to him much after the scandal broke out. Loyalty to Indira was becoming the creed of the Congress party and this would come to play in another quarter at that time; where it involved her own son, Sanjay.

The Maruti Story

On 13 November 1968, more or less a year before the 'great split', the then Minister of State for Industrial Development, Lalit Narain Mishra, informed the Lok Sabha that a 22-year-old-lad had applied for a licence to set up a car-manufacturing plant and that the proposal was to manufacture a small car that would cost only Rs 6,000 and would run 90 km per litre of petrol at a maximum speed of 85 kmph. This idea of a 'people's car' was indeed on the government's agenda for some time until it was decided that such a venture should go to the private sector. The existing cars—the large Ambassador manufactured by the Birlas and the Fiat with its Premier Padmini version—were the brands available then in the private sector. In this sense, there was nothing unusual about permitting another car manufacturer in the private sector. As a consequence, at least a dozen applications were submitted for grant of licence to set up a plant; among them were such automobile giants like Renault, Citreon, Toyota, Mazda and Morris. All the giants, however, could not offer as low a price that the 22-year old-lad had promised. The most important factor was that this young man, Sanjay Gandhi, also happened to be the son of Prime Minister Indira Gandhi.

Sanjay Gandhi, after having been a difficult child to his mother as well as those who taught him at the Doon School, was sent to London to do an apprenticeship at the Rolls-Royce. The prime minister's son had failed in all his examinations at the school. Before his stint with the London car manufacturer, he was known to have enjoyed stealing cars only to enjoy a ride and abandon them in some other part of Delhi. One of Indira's friends and her biographers, Pupul Jayakar, has this to say: 'Sanjay was rebellious, destructive, uninterested in all school activities, rude to his teachers and altogether unmanageable. He grew up a wild, wayward youth, often in scrapes, fiddling with cars, attracting questionable friends.' Among his friends was Adil Sharyar, whose father Mohammed Yunus was a family friend of the Nehrus. Yunus, during the Emergency would become the chairman of the Trade Fair Authority and after Indira's defeat from Rae Bareli in March 1977, would lend a portion of his official residence in Lutyens Delhi to Indira. She lived in that portion for the while between the time she was voted out as an MP (and hence had to move out of 1 Safdarjung Road) and her return to Parliament through the by-election from Chickmagalur in November 1978. Even in London, Sanjay was held for driving without a licence in December 1966. He was booked before that for rash and reckless driving on many occasions. Sanjay, however, decided to return home after the December 1966 experience in London without completing his apprenticeship at the Rolls-Royce. By early 1967, Sanjay was determined to manufacture cars in India.

Another of his friends was Arjan Das, whose reputation at that time was that of being a small-time gangster in Delhi. With him, Sanjay set up a car workshop in Gulabi Bagh, then an area outside the main city. Vinod Mehta, now a senior journalist, described Sanjay's venture as: 'Surrounded by garbage dumps and overflowing sewers and crowded with bits and pieces of twisted metal and rusting parts.' This was where Sanjay Gandhi began to believe that he could manufacture a car and the Maruti car project was perhaps conceived there. In November 1970, a meeting of the Union Cabinet, presided over by Prime Minister Indira Gandhi, approved the car manufacture unit proposed by Sanjay Gandhi. The Minister for Industries, Dinesh Singh issued the letter of intent to Sanjay Gandhi. The licence was granted to manufacture 50,000 cars every year. The characteristic feature of this small car was not only that it was going to be priced low and, hence, be affordable for a large number of people but also that every bit of the car was to be made in India—the indigenous car and the first of its kind. The land for the proposed factory was not hard to find.

Bansi Lal had risen from being an errand boy at Devi Lal's house to a protege of Gulzarilal Nanda and a Congress MLA. This was the Haryana patriarch's way of dispensing favours. It happened when Devi Lal was in the Congress party. Bansi Lal, however, was not made of stuff to remain an eternal loyalist of his mentor. His 'finest hour' came when the Congress party lost majority in the Haryana state assembly in the 1967 elections. The Rao Birendra Singh government, formed in March 1967 with the support from several independent MLAs, the Jan Sangh and a section of the Congress, was toppled in just a couple of months. In May 1967, Bansi Lal replaced him as the chief minister. He was chosen to the post by Nanda. He would grow in stature soon and become Indira's defence minister and a part of the prime minister's hatchet men during the Emergency years.

The opportunity that Bansi Lal made full use of to find his way into Indira's inner circle came when Sanjay was looking for some land to set up his factory. The Haryana chief minister used his powers to acquire large tracts of agricultural land in Gurgaon (adjacent to Delhi), evicting a large number of small- and medium-scale farmers and handed over 300 acres of land to the 'people's car' project. Even a regulation that prohibited plant construction within 1,000 metres of a defence installation was given a go by in this instance. In fact, the land was sold to the Maruti car factory at prices lower than the existing market value. However, this was not enough for the factory to come up.

Sanjay's project was also short on finances. The nationalised banks and several rich men were pressured into subscribing to the paid-up capital. The then finance minister, C. Subramaniam, expressed reservations against this and also over the appointment of K. R. Puri as the governor of the Reserve Bank of India (RBI). Subramaniam was forced to climb down and soon after, the finance minister was stripped of his powers considerably. The departments of banking, income tax, customs, Industrial Development Bank and credit policy, crucial in the running of the financial affairs of the nation, were removed from his superintendence and handed over to Pranab Mukherjee, a young man from West Bengal who was inducted as the deputy minister for industries and development in February 1973. Mukherjee was elevated to the position of minister of state for finance and made the in-charge of Revenue and Banking on 21 December 1975; he remained in that position until 24 March 1977. This made him the political boss of the RBI. Pranab Mukherjee would rise to occupy important positions in the Congress party and the union cabinet in the years to come. The Maruti enterprise, thus, was a scandal from day one and it raised many more scandals in the following years. Sanjay Gandhi, along with Lalit Narain Mishra, was found to have raised large sums through appointing dealers across the country for a huge fee. In 1973, for instance, Sanjay appointed as many as 75 dealers across the country and collected Rs 5 lakh from each one of them as deposits. He had promised to deliver cars for sale within six months. In addition, the Central Bank of India and the Punjab National Bank (both of them were nationalised by Indira's socialist zeal) granted unsecured loans to the tune of Rs 75 lakh to Sanjay's Maruti project.

When all this happened, the enterprise in Gurgaon, that was granted a licence in November 1970 to manufacture and roll out 50,000 cars a year, had not even managed to test drive its first car. Sanjay had displayed his car at the Asia Trade Fair held in Delhi in 1972. It was, however, unfit for road trials and when it was tried, it revealed problems of all kinds. The steering wheel would not hold, the suspension was faulty and the engine heated up within minutes of running. Uma Vasudev, a journalist who was also working on a biography of Indira then, happened to have the fortune of accompanying Sanjay on a test drive of his car on 5 May 1973. According to her, the car overheated and leaked oil and its doors did not shut properly. Sanjay's car project was a disaster and raised scandals one after the other. But Indira refused to speak against it even once. On the contrary, when an array of opposition leaders raised the issue in Parliament, she held that Sanjay could not have been discouraged from such an enterprise simply because he was her son. The truth was that Sanjay could indulge in such adventure and loot of resources only because he happened to be her son. The Maruti story continued for a few more years. Not a single car rolled out of the factory for at least a decade after it was set up in 1970 by the prime minister's son who secured the licence—even when automobile giants from across the world had applied—and managed to collect money from anywhere and everywhere he could.

The country had to wait for Maruti to be made into a public sector enterprise in 1980, with the government nationalising the unit and also taking over the huge liability that had been accumulated by Sanjay Gandhi. Thereafter, it entered into a joint venture deal with Suzuki Motors from Japan before the small car became a reality. We shall discuss the details of this nationalisation later. In fact, when this would happen, the car would cost several times more than Rs 6,000 (the price that Sanjay had promised) and the car that rolled out, in the initial years, was made of parts imported from Japan; everything except the air in the tubes were imported! Well, the Maruti car would run at a speed higher than 90 kmph but its mileage was less than 85 km per litre of petrol that Sanjay had promised. These are developments that happened long after Sanjay was out of the enterprise. The Maruti story will not be complete without mentioning that it also caused P. N. Haksar's fall from grace.

We have noted, in the earlier chapters and in this one, the enormous clout that Haksar had over Indira in his capacity as Principal Private Secretary in the Prime Minister's Secretariat. And, also the fact that he was the one who guided her, and so efficiently, in effecting the great split and making the whole episode appear to be an ideological battle against the syndicate. Haksar had tried to intervene against the Maruti enterprise from the outset, and had even raised queries with Bansi Lal on the land acquisition for Maruti. In early 1973, when the scandal refused to die, Haksar spoke about that directly with Indira and wondered that it would be advisable if she agreed to send her younger son to some place far away from Delhi and from the political scene. Indira's response to this came later in the year. In September 1973, when Haksar's term as Principal Private Secretary came to an end, she let the same lapse and 'permitted' her old 'Man Friday' to retire from the job. P. N. Dhar took his place and remained there until the Emergency was lifted and Morarji Desai 'let him go'. Haksar's exit and fall from grace was an indication of Indira's intolerance and also the rise of her son, Sanjay, in the political scene.

The Privy Purses and Snap Polls

The lack of majority in Parliament and the dependence on the Left parties and others for survival in Parliament was certainly not a situation that Indira relished. She had to get over this, sooner than later, given her style of functioning. The Supreme Court had found fault with her Bank Nationalisation Act, 1969, on grounds that the compensation paid to the private bankers was inadequate. The apex court had also pointed to procedural infirmities. The ordinance and the subsequent law passed by the Parliament replacing the ordinance were struck down on these grounds. Indira Gandhi managed to overcome the hurdle by first ensuring that the government took over the management of these banks and then getting through the legislation, in due course, and taking her own time to nationalise the banks. This was also followed by measures to widen the scope of banking operations and setting up branches across the country and in the rural areas. This measure was to help Indira's popularity across the countryside and more so among the poor and marginal farmers. She could also present that the syndicate and the others in the opposition were a hindrance to these measures.

Persisting on the same track, Indira Gandhi pushed ahead with a bill to amend the Constitution and scrap the provisions for the privy purses. The Constitution, as it stood, granted some special privileges to the former rajas and their descendants and apart from letting them drive cars with their own number plates and enjoy the comforts of the palaces, they were paid a regular tax-free pension from out of the consolidated funds of India. The pension amounts depended on the size of the kingdoms that they 'ruled' prior to independence. A demand for abolishing these privileges and the point that such things were inimical to democracy and socialism were raised, time and again, within the Congress party. There was the instance when the Young Turks, led by Chandra Shekhar, had managed to get a resolution passed at the AICC session in Delhi in March 1967 that the government scrap all these special privileges given to the former princes. Indira pushed for an amendment to the law and a bill was moved and passed in the Lok Sabha on 2 September 1970. It was supported by 339 MPs while 154 opposed the amendment. In the Rajya Sabha, however, the bill fell short by 1 vote and could not get the two-third majority that was required, on 5 September 1970. Indira's response to that was to advise President V. V. Giri to issue an order abolishing the privy purses. The order, issued the same evening, derecognised the princes and abolished all their special privileges. This, however, was declared null and void by the Supreme Court on 15 December 1970.

Nehru's daughter and her aides were angry with the judges. Those in her inner circle, including P. N. Haksar, began thinking aloud on the need for a committed judiciary. But then, Indira did not restrict herself to mere loud thinking. On 27 December 1970, she spoke to the nation. In her address, through the All India Radio, she announced that the cabinet had recommended dissolution of the Lok Sabha and that the general election would be held in February 1971. This was the first time ever when the term of the Lok Sabha was cut short and polls advanced by a year. A small portion of Indira's address to the nation on 27 December 1970 is worth quoting here. She said: 'Time will not wait for us. The millions who wait for food, shelter and jobs are pressing for action. Power in a democracy resides with the people. That is why we have decided to go to our people and seek a fresh mandate from them.' Indira's statement revealed the fact that she had, by now, matured into a demagogue beyond all others and this attribute of Nehru's daughter would unfold very soon and in a drastic fashion.

The Elections of 1971

Unlike the case in 1967, all the departments of Indira's Congress in March 1971 were under her absolute control, and she was clear about this. In an interview she gave to the *Newsweek*, Indira was asked as to what were the issues before the electorate. Her reply was: 'I am the issue.' The grand alliance that had come about after the great split and frustrated her within Parliament during the 12 months until November 1970 was to persist in the political arena outside Parliament too. The Congress (O) leaders along with the Bharatiya Jan Sangh, the Bharatiya Lok Dal and the Samyukta Socialist Party managed to enter into a seat-sharing agreement in most states. This unity was based on the single issue: to remove Indira Gandhi. But Indira went to the people and sought a mandate for eradicating poverty. *Garibi hatao*! She also took up cudgels against the judiciary this time and this she could do without any additional effort because the Supreme Court's verdict against the order abolishing privy purses was perceived among the masses as a hurdle, in her attempt, to build India into an egalitarian society. The nationalised banks were there, by this time, as evidence of her socialistic credentials.

The general election of 1971 was held in this larger context. Indira's Congress bagged 342 out of the 518 Lok Sabha seats. A great leap indeed from the 283 it won in 1967. In terms of percentage of votes, Indira's Congress secured 43.7 per cent of the votes; at least 3 percentage points more than in 1967. As for the Congress (O), the 1971 polls were a disaster. The party put up candidates in 238 seats and its tally in the Lok Sabha was a mere 16 seats. In fact, even this was possible only because of its performance in Gujarat—Morarji Desai's home—where the Congress (O) won in 11 out of the 24 Lok Sabha seats. The party's vote share, however, was not all that bad. It secured 10.4 per cent of the votes. While the prominent winners were Morarji Desai and Kamaraj, the losers from the Congress (O) included N. Sanjiva Reddy, Ram Subhag Singh, who was elected leader of the Congress (O) in Parliament after the split, and S. K. Patil, who was considered the most important leader of the syndicate. Tarakeswari Sinha, who earned for herself the distinction of being Morarji's cheerleader (she hated Indira for reasons other than political), was defeated from her Barh constituency in Bihar.

The story of the Swatantra Party, that had won 44 seats in 1967, was equally disastrous. It won only eight seats and its vote share came down from over 8 per cent in 1967 to just 3 per cent in 1971. Orissa and Rajasthan returned three Swatantra MPs each and two more won from Gujarat. Minoo Masani, whose sharp tongue and debating skills had lent a lot of strength to the opposition in Parliament, lost the polls in 1971. The only prominent winner from the Swatantra Party was Piloo Mody. The Jan Sangh, also a part of the grand alliance this time, suffered reversals. From 35 MPs in the previous Lok Sabha, its strength came down to 22. The party's vote share too came down by a couple of percentage points from the 9.4 per cent it secured in 1967. The Samyukta Socialist Party, whose leader, Dr Ram Manohar Lohia had scripted the grand alliance in 1967, was reduced to a mere three-member party in the Lok Sabha now. George Fernandes, whose victory against S. K. Patil had sent shockwaves in the political pool in 1967, was trounced in the Bombay South constituency by Indira's Congress nominee. The PSP, whose ranks had depleted considerably by this time with a number of its leaders migrating to Indira's Congress, was reduced to just two members in the Lok Sabha in 1971.

The DMK, whose members in Parliament voted with Indira on almost all her legislative measures between 1969 and 1970, opposed her in the 1971 election, but managed to retain its strength. The DMK won 23 seats in 1971 and this was only a couple of seats less than its previous strength. The CPI (M), meanwhile, wrested seats from the Congress and finished with 25 seats; of this, 20 were won from West Bengal. The party won six seats more than its 1967 tally and its vote share went up from 4.4 per cent in 1967 to 5.1 per cent in 1971. The CPI retained its existing strength of 23 MPs and was Indira's ally in 1971.

The significance of the 1971 polls, insofar as Indira's Congress was concerned were on two counts. One, Indira Gandhi did not have to depend now on the support from other parties. The second aspect, and more important, was that her party now had a two-thirds majority in the Lok Sabha. This, in the constitutional scheme, provided her with the necessary strength to effect any amendment, she desired, to the Constitution. In the context where the supreme leader believed that there was nothing wrong with dismantling the Constitution itself, if she considered that necessary to further her ends, the landslide victory for Indira's Congress was indeed a significant development. Having established herself as the supreme leader of the Congress party, the executive and Parliament, Indira set herself to ensure that the judiciary committed itself to, what she thought to be, the nation's good. The fact that she announced the snap poll in less than a couple of weeks after the Supreme Court annulled the order to abolish the privy purses was an indication that Indira was not willing to let things go against her wishes. Soon after, the Constitution was amended to scrap the provisions for privy purses and there was no difficulty given the massive majority Indira had in Parliament now.

The 1971 poll verdict was interpreted by her and her supporters as a vote for change and that she had the mandate to remove all hurdles in her way. Her first act, on returning to power, was to nationalise the general insurance sector. The life insurance business was nationalised in 1956 and was done after Feroze Gandhi had exposed the scandalous abuse of funds by the private business houses at that time. Indira decided to complete the process in May 1971. Her close circle of aides had a new member by this time. Mohan Kumaramangalam, a communist from his days as a student in London and a friend of Indira, Feroze and V. K. Krishna Menon had left the CPI to join the Congress in 1966. He was made the minister for steel and mines in 1971. He was behind the nationalisation of the coal mines first and later on bringing the steel industry under the public sector and setting up the Steel Authority of India Limited (SAIL). Kumaramangalam did not live long and died in a plane crash on 31 May 1973.

Kumaramangalam's more important role was in the way he took up the brief, in Parliament, to amend the Constitution in a way that the higher judiciary was clipped of its powers. The 24th and the 25th amendment to the Constitution were based on the following premises: (i) That the Constitution cannot be treated in such sacrosanct fashion to allow it to scuttle changes that catered to the larger aspirations of the people; (ii) the understanding that the Fundamental Rights as superior to the Directive Principles of State Policy is inimical to any effort to render economic justice to the masses and hence it is necessary to reverse the order; and (iii) the judiciary cannot be allowed to ride rough shod over the will of Parliament which in other words reflects the aspirations of the people. All these were indeed lofty principles in themselves and more so in the immediate context where the Supreme Court had ruled setting aside Indira's move to abolish the privy purses and the hurdles it had placed in the way of nationalisation of private banks earlier.

A brief foray into some of the constitutional issues will be in order at this stage. The debate on the balance of powers between the legislature and the judiciary began the day the Constitution was promulgated, 26 January 1950. There were, however, not too many occasions for conflict in the initial years. It was only in 1968, that the Supreme Court, in the Golaknath case, declared that Parliament did not have the power to abridge or abrogate the fundamental rights. By the 24th Amendment, passed by Parliament on 5 November 1971, new clauses were added to Articles 13 and 368 of the Constitution that provided Parliament with the powers to change all parts of the Constitution. In other words, the effect of the Supreme Court's verdict in the Golaknath case was nullified. Indira's Congress government brought about the 25th Amendment of the Constitution in April 1972, inserting Article 31-c, and made Parliament the final authority to fix the quantum of compensation as well as the mode of compensation in the event of land or other immovable private property being taken over by the government for 'public purposes'. By implication, issues arising out of the quantum of compensation and the manner in which such compensation is disbursed were rendered outside the scope of litigation. The stated aim behind these constitutional amendments was to achieve the objectives set by the Directive Principles of State Policy in the Constitution and to ensure that the measures in that regard were not frustrated by resorting to litigations in the higher judiciary on grounds that they infringed upon the citizens' fundamental rights.

The immediate context for these legislative interventions by Indira Gandhi and her Congress party, enjoying a two-third majority in the Parliament, was to overcome the hurdles placed by the judiciary on two of her moves; the abolition of privy purses and the appropriation of estates enjoyed by the former rulers, and the nationalisation of banks.

Both the amendments were challenged in the Supreme Court and referred to a 13-member constitution bench. The verdict of the 13-member bench (this was the total strength of the judges in the apex court at that time), known in popular parlance as the Keshavananda Bharati case, put a seal on the dispute. The bench was vertically divided. While six judges seemed to agree with the amendments in letter and spirit, six others held the opposite view. The 13th member of the bench, Justice H. R. Khanna, constituted the third viewpoint. He was in partial agreement with both the sides. As is the norm when opinion is divided in the higher judiciary, the bench delivered a split judgement. Seven-to-six, the majority judgement was binding.

The verdict, on 24 April 1973, laid out the following principles: Even while upholding the abolition of privy purses and the right of Parliament to amend the Constitution, the majority of judges held that such a right was not absolute. It was held that Parliament's right to amend the Constitution was restricted by the extent that the basic structure of the Constitution was not altered. The bench refrained from specifying what constituted the basic structure. The constitution bench also held that the Right to Property did not constitute the basic structure. Indira Gandhi and her partymen were not pleased. They would wait for a while to settle scores.

Chief Justice S. M. Sikri retired on the day after the verdict was delivered. He was among the six judges whose views were completely opposed to Indira's amendments. Justice J. M. Shelat was the senior-most judge on that day and the established convention, until then, was to appoint the most senior as the chief justice. But Shelat had held similar views as that of Justice Sikri in the Keshavananda Bharati case. Two others, who were the next in line in seniority—Justice K. S. Hegde and Justice A. N. Grover—had constituted the six who held the basic structure doctrine. They had also gone against the government in the privy purses case and the bank nationalisation case. Indira's cabinet decided to settle scores with all of them and recommended to the president to appoint Justice A. N. Ray as the chief justice of India. Ray was the most senior among those judges who had agreed with all the changes that Indira sought to make in the Constitution. The Union Cabinet and the ruling Congress simply brazened it out when Shelat, Hegde and Grover resigned to register their protest. All this did not deter Indira and her men. After all, they had a monstrous majority in the Parliament. In the elections to the state assemblies in February 1972, her Congress party had wrested power everywhere except in Tamil Nadu. In the assembly elections held immediately after the triumphant campaign against Pakistan, the liberation of Bangladesh and the instability that marked the opposition-led governments in the states, Indira's Congress party could reverse the trend that had emerged in 1967. She was now the supreme leader with her followers demanding that the nation needed a committed Parliament, a committed bureaucracy and a committed judiciary.

The infamous Nagarwala episode (discussed in detail in Chapter VII) did not bother her partymen. Similarly, rather than raising questions, Indira's colleagues in the Union Cabinet and several Congress chief ministers were willing to bend or even break rules to promote Sanjay's car factory. This was when M. F. Husain painted Indira as goddess Durga, attributing to her all the glory in the campaign to carve out Bangladesh. This was also the time when the Union Government conducted a dubious exercise of placing select documents in a sealed cylinder and bury that under the ground; the objective was to facilitate historical research decades later. And when the capsule was ripped open after a few years, it was found that the documents placed inside were nothing but propaganda material of the Congress party and the government. They were not objective records that could serve as material for historians.

Meanwhile, Jagjivan Ram was replaced by Shankar Dayal Sharma as the Congress president in 1972. Sharma, too, had played a crucial role in helping Indira Gandhi pre-empt S. Nijalingappa on more than one occasion during the days before the Congress split. He was a secretary in the Congress party headquarters and, thus, privy to some of the moves that Nijalingappa was planning with the others in the syndicate. He kept Indira informed of all that regularly and helped her make her countermove. After V. V. Giri's five-year term as president, Indira had no difficulty in getting her own man, Fakhruddin Ali Ahmed, elected to that post in August 1974. Unlike August 1969, this time, when Ahmed was elected, Indira's Congress constituted more than two-thirds of Parliament and was in power in several states. So much so, he secured as high as 80 per cent of the votes against the combined opposition nominee, Tridib Choudhury of the Revolutionary Socialist Party.

All this notwithstanding, the political scenario was taking a new turn. Opposition to the regime was building across the country and across sections of the people. There was popular discontent in the wake of the rising prices. There was the Nav Nirman movement in Gujarat, involving students and sections of the urban middle classes, the student movement in Bihar, the general strike by railway workers and finally the opposition parties gathering around JP against Indira Gandhi and her Congress. We shall discuss all this in the next chapter.

IX

Indira Under Siege and JP Arrives on the Scene

> Despite Mrs. Gandhi's sweeping victory in the Parliamentary and Assembly elections in 1971–72, the Congress Government could not cope with the mounting economic crisis. Some blamed the Congress leadership for this failure and sought for an alternative party or leadership within the system … Direct action for developing pressure and overthrowing the elected government was given credibility by several intellectuals, politicians and some cross-sections of society.
>
> —GHANSHYAM SHAH, *Direct Action in India: A Study of Gujarat and Bihar Agitations*

The sequence of events in the political scene between March 1971 (when Indira's Congress scored an emphatic victory in the national general election) and June 1975 (when she imposed the Emergency) cannot be dealt with exhaustively in a single chapter. This is because these events were guided and made by a set of complex political factors and an attempt to deal with these cannot steer clear of subjective assessments. The JP movement, for instance, can be seen as the outcome of a conspiracy against *Indira's tryst with socialism* as well as a response to her autocratic tendencies. Similarly, the May 1974 railway general strike can be described as an attempt by the stormy petrel socialist, George Fernandes, to carve out a space for himself in the national political scene or as the consequence of Indira's socialist rhetoric.

All this notwithstanding, the developments of this period left their lasting impact on the larger political discourse in India and in many ways influenced the discourse of the present. Hence, it is necessary to deal with the events of this period in some detail. It is, however, not possible to do this without landing up with assessments or passing judgements. This chapter, however, will be an attempt to narrate the several events without passing a judgement to the extent possible.

A brief narrative of the objective conditions that prevailed immediately after Indira Gandhi's emphatic victory in the 1971 general election, the Indo-Pak war and the liberation of Bangladesh, and the Congress party's victories in most states in February–March 1972 when assembly elections were held will form the backdrop for this chapter. Thereafter, we will deal with the crises that engulfed the economy soon after provoking the popular upsurge against the Congress, and then with the protest in Gujarat demanding the dissolution of the state assembly and the successful achievement thereof. After that, we will discuss the student movement in Bihar, which will be followed by a narration of the May 1974 railway general strike. In the subsequent section, we will attempt to trace the various stages in the emergence of JP as the rallying point for the opposition parties from that of being a mere leader of the student movement in Bihar and the manner in which Indira Gandhi and her Congress party responded to the challenges he posed, and his emergence as a contestant in the political space.

Indira's Finest Hour

Within a couple of months after the March 1971 general election, in which Indira's Congress won a two-third majority in the Lok Sabha, developments in Pakistan began having their impact on the government's priorities. The genesis of this lay in the manner in which Pakistan came into existence as a nation, the two chunks of territory—West and East Pakistan—separated by the large land mass; there were cultural differences too. The Eastern portion, now Bangladesh, suffered discrimination from the rulers located in West Pakistan. In the elections held in December 1970, the Awami League led by Sheikh Mujibur Rahman scored an impressive victory securing 99 per cent of the seats in the region. This gave the Awami League an overall majority in Pakistan's national parliament too. General Yahya Khan, the military dictator in Islamabad, however, refused to hand over power to Mujibur Rahman's Awami League and this provoked a revolt in the eastern parts of the country. Khan responded to this by clamping down on the Awami League workers. India was dragged into the conflict due to the large influx of political refugees. By November 1971, the number of refugees was over 100 lakh.

Indira's Congress government decided to go for a long haul. The Mukti Vahini (Liberation army), the armed wing of the Awami League, was offered military training on Indian soil and Mujibur Rahman was allowed to set up his government in exile from India. On 9 August 1971, Indira signed a 20-year Treaty of Peace, Friendship and Cooperation with the Soviet Union with terms of mutual assistance in the event of either of the countries facing military threat. This was done to ward off the possible intervention by the US–China axis against India. The foreign ministers of India and the Soviet Union made a joint declaration, soon after, stating that they 'considered it necessary that urgent steps be taken in East Pakistan for the achievement of a political solution'.

Meanwhile, the rising surge of popular agitation in East Pakistan against domination from Islamabad and the training facilities on Indian soil for the Mukti Vahini strengthened the resistance across East Pakistan. Yahya Khan, in a statement broadcast on the Columbia Broadcasting System on 11 August 1971, said: 'The two countries are very close to war. Let me warn you, for the defence of my country, I will fight a war.' Another Indo-Pak war was imminent. And, Indira Gandhi embarked upon a tour to Moscow, Brussels, Vienna, London, Washington, Paris and Bonn in that order. In a broadcast to the nation on

23 October 1971, Indira declared her objective behind this tour: 'It seemed important, in the present situation, to meet the leaders of other countries for an exchange of views and put to them the reality of our situation.'

On the night of 21–22 November 1971, the Mukti Vahini forces at Jessore (close to the Indo-Bangladesh border) came under concerted attack from the Pakistan Army—consisting of heavy artillery, infantry and the air force—and three Pakistani fighter planes that strayed into Indian airspace were felled by the Indian army; the pilots who had bailed out were captured alive. Khan declared a national emergency in Pakistan the following day and the reason he gave before his Parliament was: 'A grave emergency exists in which Pakistan is threatened by external aggression.' Indira's regime was indeed preparing its armed forces for a battle and the agenda was to liberate East Pakistan from Yahya Khan.

On 3 December 1971, Pakistan attacked India on the Western front and Pakistan's war-planes hit defence installations in the western and northern India. The Indian army too was preparing for this war and was only waiting for the monsoons to abate. In less than a fortnight, despite the advances of the US Navy's Seventh Fleet from Diego Garcia in the Indian Ocean towards the Bay of Bengal (only to be scuttled by similar moves by the Soviet Union) and some initial setbacks on the Western front, the battle for Bangladesh was decisively won on 16 December 1971. Lieutenant General Niazi, who commanded the Pakistani forces in East Bengal, signed the instrument of surrender in Dacca on that day.

Indira had addressed a large public meeting at Delhi's Ramlila Maidan the day before the surrender at which Lata Mangeshkar rendered songs specially scripted for Indira and her leadership qualities. On 16 December 1971, a little while after the lunch recess, Indira arrived in the Parliament to 'inform' the Lok Sabha of the news she had received from Dacca; that 'Dacca is now the free capital of a free country.' She did not lose time before declaring a unilateral ceasefire on the Western front too. The Indian army had advanced into Pakistani territory and held large chunks of land there at that time.

Atal Behari Vajpayee, who would become the prime minister in February 1998, lauded her as 'the incarnation of the Goddess Durga'. M. F. Husain captured Vajpayee's idea on canvas. More than the liberation of Bangladesh, the 1971 Indo-Pak war had decisively established India's armed might against Pakistan. After the war, Indira and Pakistan's Prime Minister, Zulfikar Ali Bhutto, met at Simla (now Shimla) and signed a pact in June 1972 in which they agreed to acknowledge the 1949 ceasefire line in Jammu and Kashmir as the Line of Actual Control (LoC). This meant that the Indian forces retreated from the territory they had captured—about 5,000 square miles—during the war. And, the Pakistan-occupied Kashmir (PoK) would remain with Pakistan, to be negotiated and settled between the two countries and without resort to force or the threat of force. A far more important clause in this regard was that the UN observers, who had settled down in that region, were left without a brief. This meant that the dispute over Kashmir was reduced to a bilateral issue and no longer a subject matter for international arbitration.

Pakistan was forced into accepting these terms in exchange for the return of about 93,000 personnel of their army now held Prisoners of War (PoWs) on Bangladesh soil. The return of these POWs was to take place only a year later after India managed to prevail upon the Mujib ur Rahman regime to let them go without having to face trial for war crimes.

In this way, December 1971 was distinct from the Indo-Pak war of 1965 and certainly a morale booster for the 'nation' after the debacle with China in 1962. General Sam Manekshaw, the chief of the army staff was made the Field Marshall, the first in independent India. The euphoria of the victory was evident across the country. An evidence of it was that posters of the chiefs of the three forces—Sam Manekshaw, P. C. Lal and S. M. Nanda—would adorn the walls of houses across the country. A few years later and after his superannuation from the Air Force, Nanda set out as an arms' agent and his grandson much later, got implicated in a case of culpable homicide—the infamous BMW hit-and-run case—after his swanky car mowed down a hapless traffic police constable in Delhi.

The opposition parties, whose anti-Congress campaign began yielding fruits after the debacle in the Sino-Indian conflict a decade earlier and evolved into a powerful anti-Indira force in 1967, were even otherwise mauled in the 1971 general election. The liberation of Bangladesh left them without a campaign slogan. This was an opportunity that Indira did not want to let go. Elections were due to several state assemblies; this included some of the states where the Congress had lost power in 1967. The term of many state assemblies, barring those in Uttar Pradesh, Tamil Nadu, Kerala and Orissa, was coming to an end by March 1972.

The record of the opposition unity and their state governments between 1967 and 1971 was dismal and marked by instability. In Bihar, for instance, the Bharatiya Kranti Dal government, headed by Mahamaya Prasad Sinha, came to power in March 1967, but fell in less than a year. He was replaced by Satish Prasad Sinha, heading another instant coalition, called the Shoshit Dal in January 1968. Within a month, the Shoshit Dal elected Bindeshwari Prasad as the chief minister. He too lasted only for a month and in March 1968, Bhola Paswan Shastri formed a Congress government, only to bow out of office in June 1968 and President's Rule was imposed in the state. The mid-term polls to the state assembly, in June 1969, led to the formation of a Congress Ministry under Harihar Prasad Singh, only to be replaced by Bhola Shastri within a fortnight and he too had to go within a month. A six-month spell of President's Rule was followed by a Congress government headed by Daroga Prasad Rai that lasted between February 1970 and December 1970. The Bharatiya Kranti Dal wrested power then and Karpoori Thakur became the chief minister to be replaced by the Congress party's Bhola Shastri again in June 1971.

The situation in Uttar Pradesh was no different. The Congress party government, under Chandra Bhanu Gupta, that assumed power soon after the March 1967 elections in the state lasted only for a month. Charan Singh, a former Congressman who had founded his own political party—Bharatiya Kranti Dal—managed a majority in the state assembly and was sworn in as the chief minister in April 1967. Charan Singh, however, lasted only for a few months. In February 1968, Chandra Bhanu Gupta was there as the chief minister once again. In 1969, elections were held again and even though the Congress tally in the assembly went up from 199 to 211 (in a House of 425) and Chandra Bhanu Gupta formed his ministry again, it did not last long. Charan Singh became the chief minister once again in February 1970. Chandra Bhanu Gupta had stayed on with the Congress (O) when the party split in December 1969 and Indira's Congress then decided to support Charan Singh in February 1970. However, by October 1970, Charan Singh was pulled down and Indira Gandhi posted her own man, Tribuvan Nath Singh, as the chief minister of Uttar Pradesh.

The political drama in Haryana crossed all levels of absurdity during this period. It is another matter that Indira's Congress party had managed stability in the state. The combined opposition, headed by Rao Birendra Singh (of the Vishal Haryana Party), that had assumed power in March 1967 was pulled down and Bansi Lal of Indira's Congress had become the chief minister in May 1967. This was achieved after several ruling party MLAs defected to the Congress party overnight. Bansi Lal, after having managed to emerge the consensus candidate of the warring leaders in the state Congress, moved swiftly and endeared himself to Indira Gandhi through her son, Sanjay. We have discussed this and the Maruti story in the previous chapter. Bansi Lal moved out of Haryana to assume charge as the Minister for Defence Production in Indira's cabinet in December 1975 and earned notoriety for his role during the Emergency.

In Madhya Pradesh, too, where the Congress had lost in 1967, the party managed to wrest power by way of defections from the opposition within a couple of years. The Samyukta Vidayak Dal government, headed by Govind Narayan Singh, was dislodged and Shyama Charan Shukla was sworn in as the chief minister in March 1969.

West Bengal, from where the Congress had lost in 1967 to the Bangla Congress-CPI (M) United Front, witnessed a mid-term election in February 1969. Meanwhile, the Ajoy Mukherjee government was pulled down and the Congress party's P. C. Ghosh was installed as the chief minister in November 1967. Ghosh was at the head of a coalition, christened the Progressive Democratic Front. This ministry, however, did not last long and in the mid-term elections held in February 1969, the Bangla Congress–CPI (M) alliance romped home with a larger majority than it had won in 1967. The Congress party's strength in the West Bengal assembly came down from 127 (it had won in 1967) to 55 in 1969. The total strength of the West Bengal assembly was 280. West Bengal went to polls again in April 1971 and the United Front returned to power. The strength of CPI (M) continued to increase all this while: From 43 seats in 1967 to 80 in 1969 and 114 in 1971. The party carried on with the United Front and Ajoy Mukherjee of the Bangla Congress as the chief minister.

In the larger context of her landslide victory in the March 1971 general election and in the aftermath of the liberation of Bangladesh, Indira and her Congress party managed to turn this tide. Against the larger backdrop of instability in the various states and the fragility that marked the opposition unity, the victory in the military campaign and the consequent wave of national 'pride' resulted in a groundswell of support for Indira Gandhi. One had to be extremely naïve to have missed this popular mood. Indira was certainly not that.

In any case, elections were due in several states in March 1972. Among them were Madhya Pradesh, Maharashtra, Rajasthan, Gujarat and Karnataka. The central government ordered dissolution of the state assemblies in Bihar, Haryana, Punjab and West Bengal too. While in case of Bihar, Punjab and Haryana, the term of the state assembly was until 1973, the West Bengal assembly was constituted only in March 1971. Indira Gandhi decided to hold elections in these states too.

The assembly elections in March 1972, held as they were in the immediate aftermath of the liberation of Bangladesh, gave Indira's Congress party a landslide win. The most impressive gain came from Gujarat. Indira's Congress won 140 out of the 168 assembly seats in Gujarat. This was a reversal of the trend witnessed in the 1971 general election in which the Congress (O) had won 11 out of the 26 constituencies from the state. Another important gain for Indira's Congress was in West Bengal. Defying the trend in all the elections since 1967 (when the party was thrown out of power in West Bengal), Indira's Congress won in 216 assembly constituencies out of the 280 in the state. The Congress had won only 104 seats in the 280-member assembly in the elections held just a year ago, in 1971.

Indira's Congress party also wrested power in Punjab where the Shiromani Akali Dal had won a majority in 1967 as well as in 1969. The Congress party secured 66 MLAs in the House of 104 while the Akali Dal's strength was pushed down from 43 in 1969 to 24 in 1972. In Rajasthan, the Congress secured 145 seats in the 184-strong assembly. The party had won only 89 seats in the state in 1967 when a combined opposition wrested power in the state. In Bihar too, Indira's Congress registered impressive gains. The party's strength in the 318-member assembly was 128 in 1967 and despite the instability that marked the opposition regime, Indira's Congress secured only 118 (a loss of 10 seats) in

1969. In February 1972, however, this trend was reversed and the Congress party won 168 seats in the 318-strong house.

The state assembly elections in 1972, thus, strengthened Indira's position and she was in control of the affairs not only in the centre but in most of the states too. The only state that was outside the Congress control was Tamil Nadu. Here, the DMK had consolidated its position significantly. From 50 seats in 1962, the DMK secured 138 seats and power in the state in 1967. In 1971 (Tamil Nadu too opted for early polls), the DMK increased its strength further to 184. The Congress party's strength meanwhile dwindled from 139 in 1962 to 50 in 1967 and a mere 15 in 1971. While the Congress party's dismal show in 1971 can be attributed to the exit of K. Kamaraj from the fold (he remained in the Congress [O]), there are larger issues and factors that contributed to the fall of the Congress in Tamil Nadu. A discussion on that is beyond the scope of this book.

Meanwhile, the DMK, after storming the political scenario in Tamil Nadu in such a manner in 1967, was reduced to a 48-member party in the 234-member Tamil Nadu assembly in 1977. This happened after the party underwent a split in 1972 and M. G. Ramachandran set up his own party, the Anna Dravida Munnetra Kazhagam (ADMK). The Congress party has been reduced, ever since, to a party in search of an ally to survive in the state.

The other states where the Congress was not in power were Goa (the Maharashtrawadi Gomantak Party had retained power), Meghalaya (the All Party Hill Leaders Conference had won a majority) and Mizoram (there were more independent MLAs in the 30-member assembly than the six Congress MLAs). In Kerala, the Congress had set up a coalition consisting of the CPI, the Indian Union Muslim League and the Kerala Congress to win a majority in 1970 itself. And unlike in the other states, the coalition government in Kerala was headed by the CPI. C. Achuta Menon was the chief minister and K. Karunakaran was the home minister. This coalition and the government survived through the Emergency and even returned to power in 1977.

The point is, after the 1972 round of assembly elections, the Congress was in power across the country. The dismal scenario that greeted Indira Gandhi in 1967—the first general election in which she steered her party's campaign—and the challenges that she faced from within her party (leading to the Congress split in 1969) and consequently her dependence on other parties for the survival of her government were stories of the past in 1972. And by now, she went about setting up her own men as chief ministers in the states, a definite shift from the times, not in the distant past, when the chief ministers and party leaders from the states had played a major role in her election as the prime minister. Here, it is pertinent to recall D. P. Mishra, the then chief minister of Madhya Pradesh, taking the initiative and rallying nine other Congress chief ministers to propose her name as the prime minister in January 1966. Instead, Indira Gandhi was now in a position to decide on the chief ministers.

Thus, after March 1972, while Bansi Lal survived and remained the chief minister of Haryana until December 1975 (when he moved to the Union Cabinet), Indira hand-picked Siddhartha Shankar Ray to head the Congress government in West Bengal. He too remained there until the Congress was voted out in 1977. Similarly, P. V. Narasimha Rao, who would become the prime minister in 1991, was the chief minister of Andhra Pradesh since September 1971, and had emerged the natural choice in March 1972 after the elections. He was, however, sent out soon and J. Vengal Rao was chosen by Indira in his place. In Bihar, Indira anointed Kedar Pande as the chief minister in March 1972; he was replaced by Abdul Ghafoor in July 1973. Ghafoor had earned a name as the most effete chief minister that Bihar had until then and was indeed the cause of the popular mobilisation against the Congress, in a few months after he became the chief minister. He too was replaced by Indira in April 1975 by Jaganath Mishra. In other words, Bihar had three chief ministers in the six years after 1972.

In Gujarat, Ghanshyam Oza was chosen by Indira as the chief minister in March 1972 and removed from the post in July 1973. Chimanbhai Patel, whose regime was marked by widespread corruption and was the cause of the student movement and the Nav Nirman Andolan, was chosen by Indira. He remained the chief minister until he was asked to resign in February 1974 when Indira Gandhi finally bowed down to the demand by the agitators. P. C. Sethi (who never tired himself of speaking up for a presidential form of government to please Indira Gandhi) was made the chief minister of Madhya Pradesh in March 1972 replacing S. C. Shukla. While Sethi was not known to enjoy a support base, Shukla was one with a political base to himself. And, Giani Zail Singh who would state, a few years later, that he would pick up a broom and sweep the floor if Indira Gandhi ordered him to do that, was made the chief minister of Punjab. Nandini Satpathy, whose Left leanings were of immense use to Indira Gandhi, was made the chief minister of Orissa. In Uttar Pradesh, Kamalapati Tripathi, who set new standards of loyalty to the Nehru family, was chosen by Indira as the chief minister even earlier.

Similarly, Devraj Urs had emerged as Indira's point man in Karnataka. But, unlike many others in the Congress stable, he could carve out his own political space in Karnataka through a comprehensive land reforms programme as well as initiatives to free the Congress party from the clutches of the status quoist forces. Urs remained the chief minister of Karnataka until 1977 and was a useful counter against Veerendra Patil as well as S. Nijalingappa in Karnataka.

Another important aspect of the 1971 general election and the round of assembly polls in 1972 was the fate of the Swatantra Party. The party, we have seen, had registered impressive gains in the very first elections it faced in 1962 (after its foundation in 1959). In 1967, its presence increased in Parliament to an impressive 44 MPs (to gain the status of the second largest party in the House after the Congress). In 1971, the Swatantra Party was swept aside. Its strength came down to just 8 MPs: three each from Orissa and Rajasthan and a couple from Gujarat. Piloo Mody, the most vocal among the Swatantra Party MPs, retained his Godhra seat, Minoo Masani lost from Rajkot.

The Congress (O) too met with the same fate. From out of the 68 MPs who stayed in the party at the time of the 1969 split, only 16 managed to win from their constituencies. This included Morarji Desai, K. Kamaraj and Satyendra Narain Sinha. Among the prominent losers were Tarakeswari Sinha (from Barh in Bihar) who had emerged as Morarji's cheerleader in Parliament even before the split , Ram Subhag Singh who was elected the Congress (O) leader in Parliament after the split, Neelam Sanjeeva Reddy (whom the syndicate leaders had chosen as their presidential candidate), Sushila Nayar (who had stayed with Mahatma Gandhi until his end and remained in the Congress party and represented the Jhansi Lok Sabha constituency for three terms from 1957) and Sucheta Kripalani. The Congress (O) failed to win even a single seat from Karnataka, S. Nijalingappa's home state.

The only state where the Congress (O) did exceedingly well was Gujarat. Eleven out of the 16 Congress (O) MPs won from Gujarat. This indeed was an indication that among all those who constituted the Congress (O), Morarji Desai, who had challenged Indira Gandhi right from January 1966, was indeed one who commanded a following not only for himself but had managed to take a good chunk of the party organisation with him after the 1969 split. It was, hence, not incidental that the popular mobilisation against Indira's regime would begin from Gujarat and this had helped Morarji Desai emerge as the natural leader of the opposition combine, the Janata Party, that came into place in March 1977. A brief narrative of the crisis that unfolded in the economic scenario will be in order to place the developments in Gujarat in its context.

The Economy in Crisis

The liberation of Bangladesh and the surge of nationalist euphoria that helped Indira Gandhi decimate the opposition in February–March 1972 did have an adverse impact on the economy. The huge influx of refugees from East Pakistan had to be fed and it left the food grain stock depleted. The war also meant larger spending on defence, particularly on import of arms and ammunitions. The expenditures incurred on this account (and most of this were diverted from out of funds meant for development needs) caused its own problems. The budgetary deficit went up. All this was happening in the aftermath of a poll victory that Indira Gandhi had secured based on her promise of *Garibi Hatao*. The euphoria of the victory against Pakistan was beginning to melt down as the economic crisis began to show. In the middle of all this, in 1972–73, there was a general monsoon failure; both the summer and winter rains failed that year. As a consequence, food grain output came down by 8 per cent in that year alone. This sharp fall in grain output and that too in a situation where a large chunk of the surplus stocks were exhausted, on account of feeding the refugees from East Pakistan, was a bad enough cause for a crisis.

There was another factor that caused the food shortage. At the Congress session in Calcutta (the venue was named Bidhan Nagar) Indira announced that the government alone would deal with wholesale procurement of wheat and paddy. This was in 1973. Although the decision was never implemented, the damage was done. The idea to monopolise grain procurement by the government and that too in a year of bad harvest led to food grain vanishing from the farms. The crisis that was already waiting to unfold, due to the fall in production (because the rains failed), was compounded due to hoarding of food grain by the mill owners.

Alongside these came the bigger shock. The various nations in the Persian Gulf got together to form a cartel. The Organisation of the Petroleum Exporting Countries (OPEC) increased oil prices fourfold overnight in 1973. A billion dollars more were required for India to keep its import of oil at the same level. This, in a situation where the government's finances were already in a precarious state, led to a serious crisis and manifest itself in shortage of food grain and essentials on the one hand and a steep rise in their prices on the other. Prices of essentials rose by 23 per cent in 1973. It went up to 30 per cent in 1974. Kerosene became scarce and food grain turned too expensive even for the middle classes. Urban India and the articulate middle classes, that had celebrated Indira Gandhi and her leadership only a few months ago, was turning restive now. Indira Gandhi resorted to the World Bank and the International Monetary Fund track. The Brettonwoods institutions insisted on economic reforms as condition for aid. An anti-inflationary policy package was handed over by them and Indira Gandhi agreed to all that. Government expenditure had to be contained. The prescription was that fiscal deficit shall remain low.

The government announced impounding of an installment of the Dearness Allowance (DA) and also a freeze on wage hikes and negotiations. The DA as a concept had evolved in the industrial scene in India in the midst of the World War II. In order to prevent disruption of production (in the context of the war) and to protect the industrial workers from the rise in prices of essentials, a formula was put in place to neutralise the impact of rising prices on the life of the industrial workers. This had come into place in India in 1942 and was internalised as a right by the salariat and the organised working class. Indira Gandhi's government ordered that the additional installment of DA, due in 1973, be impounded.

This was resorted to in order to contain the fiscal deficit. The decision to impound the DA installment (by which the additional wage intended to neutralise the effect of price rise to the salariat was diverted to government bonds) affected those who were already reeling under the shortage of essentials and the rise in prices of these commodities. They began detesting the regime.

Meanwhile, this was also the time when tales about corruption and favouritism were reaching the people. We have discussed the Maruti story in the previous chapter as well as the Nagarwala episode in Chapter VI. A similar story of corruption was revealed now involving Tulmohan Ram, a Congress MP from Bihar. The story was about Indira's chief fund-raiser and Union Minister for Foreign Trade, Lalit Narain Mishra, persuading Tulmohan Ram and some other Congress MPs to put their name as sponsors to an application, by shady characters, for licences to set up factories in Pondicherry. This was a case of MPs from the hinterland of Bihar, pushing a case for industrial licences in distant Pondicherry. The issue was raised in Parliament and after days of agitation on the floor of the House (when the House was not allowed to function), a CBI investigation was ordered. Although L. N. Mishra was shifted out of the Ministry for Foreign Trade and made Railway Minister, the findings of the CBI were not disclosed. All this brought Indira Gandhi and her Congress party under a cloud. Mishra himself would die on 2 January 1975. A powerful bomb exploded under the dias, while he was addressing a public meeting, at Samastipur in northern Bihar.

In short, a couple of years after she rode to victory with the promise of *garibi hatao,* prices spiraled and food grain was in short supply. Above all, the prime minister and her party were facing a crisis. This was a crisis of political legitimacy.

The Gujarat Movement (Nav Nirman Andolan)

Ghanshyam Oza, who was hardly a leader of significance, was anointed as the chief minister of Gujarat by Indira Gandhi after the state assembly elections in March 1972. Oza, however, could not last long. Within months after he assumed charge as the chief minister, he faced dissidence and his detractors were led by Chimanbhai Patel. With Indira's blessings, Patel managed to replace Oza in July 1973. Chimanbhai Patel had earned a name for himself in the 'art' of raising funds for the party (and for himself). Indira Gandhi needed him because elections were due in Uttar Pradesh and Orissa in early 1974. These two states had witnessed considerable erosion of support from the Congress since 1967 and the Congress could wrest power in Lucknow and Bhubaneswar only by way of buying up MLAs and retaining them in the fold by similar means. All this was happening when the nation was already passing through a crisis and the middle classes, across the country, were reeling under the impact of food shortage and rising prices. Chimanbhai Patel, in particular, was perceived as having allowed the wholesale dealers of vegetable oil to jack up prices in return for the funds he obtained from them.

On 20 December 1973, students of the L. D. Engineering College in Ahmedabad went on strike in protest against high mess bills. There were similar incidents in the same college on 3 January 1974; but unlike the earlier occasion, on 3 January 1974 the police intervened and there were clashes between the students and the police. In an atmosphere that was already charged with anger against the establishment, the incident at L. D. Engineering College, in which several students were arrested, provoked students across the state to protest. A *bandh* was organised on 10 January 1974. Meanwhile, a cross-section of the organised workers in the several factories across Ahmedabad joined the students in the protest and ration shops (and other outlets of food grain) were targeted by the crowds. A statewide *bandh* call on 25 January witnessed violent clashes between the police and the people in as many as 33 towns across the state.

The demand, by this time, was for Chimanbhai's resignation and the protests came to be guided by the Nav Nirman Yuvak Samiti. College and university teachers, lawyers and other such professionals joined the students to form this *samiti* and the movement came to be called the Nav Nirman Andolan. While the lead in all these instances were taken by the college and university students, the processions and other forms of protests were joined in by a cross-section of the middle classes. The intensity of the protests was such that the army was called to restore peace in Ahmedabad on 28 January 1974. Indira Gandhi reacted to this rising tide of protest by asking Chimanbhai Patel to quit as the chief minister. He did so on 9 February 1974 and the state assembly was kept under suspended animation. Even while the students were returning to their classes, the opposition parties stepped in with the demand for the dissolution of the state assembly. The Congress party had 140 MLAs in the 168-member assembly at that time.

Here was an opportunity for the Congress (O), with only 15 MLAs, to reinvent itself in the state. All the 15 MLAs resigned their membership of the assembly demanding dissolution of the House. This happened on 16 February 1974. The three MLAs of the Jan Sangh followed suit. Soon, Congress MLAs faced the wrath of agitating students and the middle class protestors across the state. They were also pressured to quit the assembly. By early March, as many as 95 out of the 168 MLAs had resigned. Morarji Desai, set out on an indefinite fast from 12 March 1974 forcing Indira Gandhi to order dissolution of the state assembly. The Gujarat Legislative Assembly was dissolved on 16 March 1974, thus, bringing an end to the agitation. In the days, between 20 December 1973 —when the students at the L. D. Engineering College protested against high mess bills—and 16 March 1974, the police resorted to firing at several places.

This left about 100 people dead, 3000 injured and 8000 arrested. The agitation, however, did not end with the dissolution of the assembly.

The Nav Nirman Yuvak Samiti, meanwhile, kept up the demand for fresh elections and the opposition parties joined this campaign. This picked up momentum with Morarji Desai setting out on an indefinite hunger strike, again, from 6 April 1975.

Indira Gandhi had to give in for the second time. Elections to the Gujarat assembly were held on 10 June 1975 and the results were announced on 12 June 1975. The same day on which Justice Jagmohan Lal Sinha of the Allahabad High Court declared Indira Gandhi's election from Rae Bareili (in 1971) as null and void on grounds that she had violated the provisions of the Representation of the People's Act, 1952. We shall discuss this in detail in the next chapter. As for Gujarat, Indira's Congress lost power in the state. The party won only 75 seats. Chimanbhai Patel, by then, had set up his own party, Kisan Mazdoor Lok Paksha and contested elections on his own. The Janata Morcha, a pre-poll combine comprising the Congress (O), the Jan Sangh, the PSP and the Lok Dal, secured 88 seats. The combine enlisted support of a few independents to elect Babubhai Patel of the Congress (O) as the chief minister. This government lasted only for nine months. Several MLAs defected and after a spell of president's rule (imposed in March 1976), Gujarat returned to the Congress (I) in December 1976. Madhav Singh Solanki became the chief minister.

The significance of the Nav Nirman Andolan was that it reflected the intensity of the crisis in the economy and also the anger that prevailed among the middle classes against the Chimanbhai regime in Gujarat. The movement was also a manifestation of the anti-Indira sentiments as well as against the increasing incidence of corruption at that time. Chimanbhai seemed to represent all that was going wrong with Indira's Congress. This indeed was how a localised protest, in a city college against high mess bills, soon grew into a statewide protest with students and a cross-section of the urban intelligentsia willing to brave police repression and agitate for the removal of the regime and fresh elections.

The Gujarat movement did inspire JP. It needs to be clarified at this stage that JP had no role to play in the Gujarat movement. His first visit to the state (after the movement had erupted) was on 11 February 1974; a couple of days after Chimanbhai had resigned and the assembly had been kept under suspended animation. He seemed to have been inspired by the movement and expressed this in his column in *Everyman's,* a journal he had started in July 1973. JP wrote this on 3 August 1974:

> I wasted two years trying to bring about a politics of consensus. It came to nothing … I also spent quite some time with the opposition parties to prevent the splitting of votes. However, I do not know what is wrong with them but opposition parties go on splitting into smaller and smaller groups. I came to

> the conclusion that the people must become their own saviours. But how to bring that about? How to activise the people was the problem. Then I saw the students in Gujarat bring about a big political change with the backing of the people ... and I knew that this was the way out.

This long quote from JP himself is necessary to underscore the point that the Gujarat student movement had nothing to do with JP. Instead, the Nav Nirman Andolan had inspired Jayaprakash Narayan. It was from there that JP would set out to lead the students and other sections of the people in Bihar. He called it Total Revolution. Another important aspect of the Gujarat student movement was that the local leaders of the Akhil Bharatiya Vidyarthi Parishad (ABVP), an organisation of students controlled by the RSS, had found in the agitation an opportunity to position themselves in the various organs of the struggle. Narendra Modi, who would emerge as one of the BJP's important leaders in due course, was one of them.

The Bihar Movement (The Total Revolution)

The university and college campuses across Bihar were witnessing sporadic protests around the same time as the students' revolt in Gujarat. However, these did not go beyond sporadic acts. Unlike in Gujarat, where the student movement was hardly political (barring the involvement of a few ABVP leaders), the student leaders in Bihar belonged to political outfits. The ABVP and the Samajwadi Yuvjan Sabha (SYS), whose members had definite links with the Jan Sangh, the Socialist Party and the Lok Dal, were the two important student organisations that were active in Bihar apart from the CPI-controlled All India Students Federation (AISF). The late 1960s and the early 1970s, however, were a period when the CPI had thrown its weight in support of Indira Gandhi. The CPI's line was taken by the AISF too and it turned into an apologist of the Indira–Abdul Ghafoor regime in Bihar. The CPI (M)-controlled Student's Federation of India (SFI), founded in 1970, did not have much of a base in Bihar. The state, meanwhile, had been the hotbed of the socialist politics for long. In all these ways, Bihar was different from Gujarat where the opposition to Indira's Congress was essentially constituted by the Congress (O). It is important to internalise in this context the fact that the Congress (O) was only a political party unlike the ideologically driven socialists or the Jan Sangh. So much so, the Congress (O) did not care to build a student organisation.

The fact that the student movement in Bihar was dominated by outfits that were aligned with parties and that these parties had discredited themselves by indulging in petty quarrels when they were elected to power in the state (between 1967 and 1969) also had its impact on the nature and the spread of the movement in Bihar. In other words, the Nav Nirman Yuwak Samiti was not burdened with a baggage of the past like the student outfits in Bihar. That made the Gujarat movement simpler, while in Bihar the students were unable to make as much impact on the larger society as they could in Gujarat. This notwithstanding, the fact is that the issues for which they were agitating were almost similar. And they had been approaching JP to guide them and lead the agitation for some time.

JP, meanwhile, had tired himself with efforts to bring about unity among the opposition through 1968 and had given up hopes. He had also begun to withdraw himself from the *Bhoodan* movement, into which he had plunged by 1954 (and alienated himself from fellow socialists during that period), and, thus, gone far away from party politics. He was engaged in persuading the youth, who had joined the Naxalite stream, to give up violence. JP was also persuading dacoits, across the countryside in northern India, to reform. He was also involved in mobilising aid from across the world for Bangladesh after the war. While in the thick of this campaign, JP suffered a series of heart attacks and had returned to his native village, Sitabdiara, in the Saran division of Bihar. On 11 October 1972, he announced his decision to take a year-long vacation from public activity. Meanwhile, his wife and companion, Prabhavati, was diagnosed with cancer; she passed away in April 1973. Her death had shaken JP and it appeared to those who were close to him that he was no longer the same person—looking out for people's causes and the one who had an indomitable will to fight for those causes.

Indira Gandhi, meanwhile, was engaged in her game of 'taming' the judiciary. She recommended to President V. V. Giri to appoint Justice A. N. Ray as the chief justice of the Supreme Court. Giri promptly obliged. Justice Ray had superceded three others—J. M. Shelat, K. S. Hegde and A. N. Grover—and the context for this has been discussed in the previous chapter. JP was angry and wrote to Indira Gandhi expressing dismay over her action. He demanded a Parliamentary Committee to suggest amendments to the Constitution in such a manner that the chief justice was selected after an elaborate process of consultation among the various political parties. Indira Gandhi's reaction to this was hostile. However, JP maintained that without such an amendment to the Constitution, the judiciary was bound to become a creature of the government of the day. This exchange of letters took place in June 1973. But JP would reveal these exchanges between him and Indira Gandhi only in December 1973. In an open letter, that he addressed to all MPs on 15 December 1973, JP wrote:

> The simple fact is that if the appointment of the Chief Justice of India remains entirely in the hands of the Prime Minister of India, as has been the case in the present instance, then the highest judicial institution of this country cannot but become a creature of the Government of the day.

In other words, JP's agenda was anything but a confrontation with Indira Gandhi; instead he had a lot of hope to reform her Congress party.

This was also the time that JP believed that the situation was ripe for revolution as it had been in 1942 and declared that he 'felt an inner urge to give a call to the youth to enter the political scene'. He had, by this time, begun addressing meetings and bouncing off ideas of a movement through his writings in *Everyman's*. JP's analysis of the situation was not without basis. The economic situation was bad and this has been discussed in the earlier part of this chapter. The political scene too did not raise hopes with the Congress tending to become more of Indira's preserve and the opposition parties refusing to unite. Corruption was pervading all spheres of public life. The situation in India, in many ways, was not different from what it was in many parts of the world, during the latter half of the 1960s, provoking movements that were led by the students and the youth.

In France, for instance, the students had shaken the political establishment so much that the movement could be put down only by massive repression and also after the establishment managed to rope in the Church into condemning the movement. Germany too witnessed such tumult. Similarly, students and youth, under the banner of the Janata Vimukti Perumuna (JVP), had captured power and held on to that for a few hours in Sri Lanka. The Americas were shaken by the new wave of protest and the university students leading demonstrations, day after day, against the US invasion of Vietnam. The significant aspect of all this was that the protests were carried out by students and were outside the hold of established political parties. JP too was talking about a similar movement in India.

Coming back to Bihar, there was a wave of student agitations against rise in mess charges in college and university hostels during December 1973; on the same lines and time as it happened in Gujarat. Close on its heels, the opposition parties held a statewide *bandh* on 21 January 1974. Meanwhile, the Patna University Students Union organised a convention of student leaders from across Bihar and a Bihar Chatra Sangarsh Samiti (BCSS) was formed on 18 February 1974. Laloo Prasad Yadav, a student at the Patna University at that time, was elected to preside over this body. The BCSS widened the scope of its demands to include measures to contain the prices of food grain and other essential commodities, lowering of tuition fees and prices of textbooks, better amenities in hostels, role for elected students in the various decision-making bodies of the colleges and universities apart from action against hoarders and blackmarketeers. The stamp of JP was already there though he was not involved, in any manner, in drafting these demands.

The BCSS called for a *gherao* at the Bihar Legislative Assembly on 18 March 1974, the opening day of the budget session. Scores of students rallied behind their leaders to block all the roads that led to the assembly. The day was marked by pitched battles between the students and the police in several parts of Patna. The violence led to large-scale destruction of government property and several buildings, including the official residence of Ramanand Singh, a former education minister, were set on fire. That the violence was orchestrated by the state and that the students were not guilty in all the incidents was revealed when the offices of two leading newspapers—*Searchlight* and *Pradeep*—were gutted by fire. The two newspapers were known for their anti-government positions and the police did nothing to intervene even as miscreants were ransacking and setting fire to the two buildings in Patna. This brought out that the ruling party men were involved in violence in the garb of protestors. At least three students were killed in the police firing. The 18 March incidents in Patna provoked students across Bihar to protest.

JP was nowhere in the scene that day. He was recouping from a surgery he underwent for swollen prostrate glands. The police action that day, however, made a profound impact on him. Recall the fact that JP had already made up his mind on the need for mobilising students, to rise in revolt, after his visit to Gujarat in February 1974. On 30 March 1974, JP issued a statement condemning the ways of the Bihar government and announced his intention to lead a procession of students and other citizens. 'This will be the beginning and the rest will follow', he said in that statement. And, in his own way, JP added, 'It is not for this that I fought for freedom'.

Indira Gandhi's Congress party responded to this by accusing JP of trying to bring down a legally elected government and, thus, aiding a fascist takeover. In a public meeting, she addressed in Bhubaneswar on 1 April 1974, Indira Gandhi launched a personal attack on JP. 'How can such persons who continue to seek favours from the *moneyed* people and keep in constant touch with them dare to speak of corruption' she said. The stage was set for a confrontation and JP endorsed the demand of BCSS that the Abdul Ghafoor government in Bihar should go, the assembly dissolved and fresh elections held. The inspiration to this had come from the success of the Nav Nirman Andolan in Gujarat. Also, the police firing in Patna on 18 March 1974 and elsewhere in the state in response to the student agitation in the weeks that followed gave the agitation an emotive basis. The police fired at the agitators in Gaya on 12 April 1974 killing eight students.

JP, meanwhile, had set conditions before the BCSS: That the students leave the colleges and universities and go back to the villages to engage themselves in village reconstruction and such activities to prepare the people for the task of preserving and strengthening the democratic institutions; and that the agitation remained non-violent. He was also clear that his activities could not be confined to Bihar in the physical sense and the students alone. After leading a silent procession, across the streets of Patna on 8 April 1974, JP proceeded to Delhi for the first conference of the Citizens for Democracy, an organisation he had founded with his close associates. The conference, held on 13 and 14 April 1974, adopted a charter that included issues concerning electoral reforms, probity in public life, democratic rights of the citizens and social reforms.

Meanwhile, sections within the Congress and the CPI began accusing JP of being party to a conspiracy to destabilise the democratic edifice. At another level, individual leaders in the Congress party resented Indira Gandhi's pro-Soviet Union position and her closeness with the CPI. Fifty-one MPs of Indira's Congress, in a public statement on 9 April 1974, urged reconciliation between Indira Gandhi and Jayaprakash Narayan. They described any attempt to create a stalemate between the two was desired only by those who did not have the nation's interests at heart. The statement, however, stressed that Indira Gandhi was the 'established leader of the country of whom Congressmen were proud'. Chandra Shekhar, who would leave the Congress in less than a year and spend 19 months in jail as a detainee under Maintenance of Internal Security Act (MISA) during the Emergency, said: 'In the past, many a time, Jayaprakash has got rebuffs for offering his services to create healthy conditions in our public life. But now we can miss this opportunity only at our peril'.

It may be recalled that Chandra Shekhar and most of the MPs who had signed the 9 April statement were Indira's cheerleaders during her confrontation with the party bosses who constituted the syndicate. They remained her core supporters in the Congress Parliamentary Party after the split in 1969. They stood for socialism but differed with the pro-Soviet sections in the party. Several months later, on 20 November 1974 to be precise, a tea party was organised at Chandrashekar's residence in New Delhi to which JP was invited. The tea party, in which as many as 45 Congress MPs, including some senior office-bearers of the Congress Parliamentary Party were present, was a landmark event in the context of the JP movement. For, most of them left Indira's Congress to become part of the Janata Party in March 1977. While a few among them, including Chandrashekhar, Mohan Dharia, Kishen Kant and Sushila Nayyar would do so even before the Emergency and end up spending 19 months in jail, some others did that when Indira Gandhi ordered general election in January 1977.

The general refrain of the MPs was that JP should not lend himself to the campaign and the designs of the parties in the opposition—Socialist Party, Jan Sangh and Lok Dal—and not associate himself with the demand for the dismissal of the Abdul Ghafoor government in Bihar. JP, however, responded to this in the following manner:

> What can I advise you? It is for you to resolve the situation. You should have the guts and be prepared for sacrifices. The difficulty is that most of you are office-seekers. It is too late to say all that you have said. I don't think any Congressman who knows what has happened in Patna and Bihar during the last month will have the cheek to say anything of that sort now.

In a couple of days after the tea party, Indira's Congress organised a brainstorming session of the party's leaders in Narora, a resort in Rajasthan, where a 13-page document, meant only for internal circulation among the party's leaders, was placed.

A brief narrative on the events in Bihar in November 1974 will be in order before discussing the Narora document. After travelling across the country and setting up units of the Citizens for Democracy as well as Chatra Sangarsh Samitis across Bihar in which leaders of both ABVP and SYS were represented, JP gave a call for *gherao* of the Bihar legislative assembly on 4 November 1974. The movement, by now, had also enlisted the support of a cross-section of the people of Bihar and was not just confined to students. This day, 4 November 1974, turned out to be an eventful day. In the words of Minoo Masani, one of those who had founded the Congress Socialist Party along with JP in 1934, left the fold later to join the Swatantra Party in 1959 but remained JP's friend throughout his life, 'November 4, 1974, may well prove to be a major turning point in independent India's history.' Minoo Masani proved to be right.

After conferring the title *Lok Nayak* (leader of the people) at a rally in Patna on 5 June 1974 (that was when JP described the movement as *Total Revolution*), the struggle committee organised *satyagraha* everyday on the state assembly premises. Around 1,600 picketers were arrested and detained for this by 1 July 1974. At least 65 student leaders were in detention under the provisions of MISA. This was a provision that would be used to hold hundreds of opposition leaders and several thousands of political activists as well as Gandhian workers in jail during the Emergency. Detention under MISA meant long jail terms without being charged of any offence. The movement gave a call for a three-day statewide *bandh* beginning 3 October 1974. While addressing a massive public meeting in Patna on 6 October, JP declared that the response to the *bandh* had signaled the end of the 'Indira wave' in Bihar. He announced the next phase of the agitation from there.

A *gherao* of the residences of ministers and MLAs, with a view to forcing their resignation, was to begin on 4 November 1974. In fact, 42 out of the 318 MLAs, including 33 from the opposition parties, had resigned even before that day. While JP had planned a no-holds-barred struggle from 4 November 1974, the Bihar government too decided to pull all the stops. Patna bore the sight of a fortress under siege and police barricades had come up all over the city. Trains from various parts of Bihar to Patna were cancelled a couple of days before 4 November and buses and other vehicles carrying the agitators were stopped long before they reached the state capital. Steamers that ferried people to Patna down the Ganges too were held back. At least one lakh people were stopped from reaching Patna by 4 November 1974. Even the opposition MPs and leaders, who flew down to Patna, were prevented from leaving the airport. Several companies of central forces and most of the personnel from the Bihar Police were deployed in Patna and choppers flew across Bihar villages dropping leaflets warning the people against heeding to JP's call.

Yet, a procession of several thousands, with JP on an open jeep, began moving towards the Gandhi Maidan and then towards the state assembly on

4 November 1974. Letting JP's jeep pass, the police stopped the followers and began reigning *lathi* blows on them. Many braved the police and crossed over the barricade to join JP who began moving towards the homes of the ministers. Teargas shells were lobbed and JP, still in the jeep, was singled out for attack by a posse of policemen. Nanaji Deshmukh, who headed the Jan Sangh then and would play an important role in the Janata Party after 1977, was among those who took most of the *lathi* blows. JP too suffered a fractured rib and fainted.

Chief Minister Abdul Ghafoor, however, maintained that the police had exercised utmost restraint and Union Home Minister Brahmananda Reddy, when confronted by opposition MPs, informed Parliament that there was no *lathi* charge at all and that JP had only suffered a 'slight finger injury' in the melee. All these were proven to be lies by Raghu Rai, a staff photographer for *The Statesman*, who had captured images of policemen raining *lathi* blows on JP and others in the jeep. But Indira Gandhi and her Congress did not care. They were determined to put down the movement with force. This indeed was what JP had referred to in his reply to the Congress party MPs who gathered at the tea party at Chandra Shekhar's residence in New Delhi, a fortnight later, on 20 November 1974.

Indeed 4 November 1974 was the day when the student movement had peaked in Bihar. The various opposition parties had joined the movement and with that the movement too was caught up in sectarian divisions. There were parallel Chhatra Sangarsh Samitis formed at all levels and unlike Gujarat, the movement in Bihar suffered from internal squabbles. This weakness was further revealed when JP called upon the students to dedicate themselves to the cause of Total Revolution by way of giving up their studies for a whole year and fanning out to the villages and involve themselves in rural reconstruction work. Of the 13,000 students in Patna University, only 300 agreed to this. Many more opted to give one day a week to the movement while going back to the classes on other days.

Meanwhile, JP addressed a rally at the Gandhi Maidan in Patna on 18 November. By all accounts, that was the biggest ever gathering in the city. This was a sequel to a public show of strength by the CPI on 11 November and by the Congress on 16 November 1974. It was on 18 November 1974, addressing the massive gathering at the Gandhi Maidan, when JP first spoke of joining the electoral battle against the Congress. He responded to a challenge that Indira Gandhi had thrown at him from a public meeting she addressed at the Ramlila grounds in Delhi on 1 November 1974. Indira had declared that she would rather resign as prime minister than agreeing to dissolve the Bihar assembly; and that if the people were dissatisfied with her government, they shall wait until the next election to remove her and her party from power. Indira had addressed the Ramlila rally after a meeting with JP that morning. We shall discuss this in detail at a later stage in this chapter.

JP responded to the challenge on 18 November. He said: 'I have accepted the challenge. Neither I nor my boys are in a hurry. We shall wait till the next elections for the people's verdict. Since the Prime Minister has dragged the conflict into the election arena, I shall take my position in the battlefield, not as a candidate, but as a leader'. It was from here that JP formulated the rules of the battle and his approach towards the opposition parties underwent a sea change from then on. He declared: 'In the electoral exercise forced on us, there would only be two contestants; the people, the students and the opposition parties with the movement on the one side and their opponents, namely the Congress and the CPI on the other'. In other words, JP laid out his own terms before the opposition parties too. In this sense, it will be incorrect to describe the movement as one that was aimed at a *partyless democracy* in the way some of JP's critics do. Instead, JP had, by 18 November 1974, realised the importance of fighting the battle from well within the party-based democratic system rather than persisting with his animosity towards the opposition parties. In this sense, we may conclude that the foundation for the Janata Party was laid on 18 November 1974 at the Gandhi Maidan in Patna.

Meanwhile, the movement had taken the shape of a *satyagraha* everyday on the state assembly premises from 4 December 1974. From that day, when the assembly convened for the winter session, several hundred volunteers joined the *satyagraha* everyday and courted arrest. Even while Abdul Ghafoor carried on as the chief minister because Indira Gandhi was determined against repeating what she and her aides considered a folly by giving in to the agitators' demand of dismissing the state government and dissolving the assembly in Gujarat, JP began travelling to Uttar Pradesh, Madhya Pradesh, West Bengal and Haryana. Even though there was hardly any movement of significance in these states, his public meetings were massive. The resentment against the Indira Gandhi regime was visible across the country.

We shall get back to discuss JP and his evolution as a leader on the political stage as well as the Congress party's response to this later. But before that a brief foray into the May 1974 railway general strike will be in order.

The Railway General Strike

With over 17 lakh permanent workers and at least 3 lakh who were employed as casual workers, the railways system was the largest employer in India. Unlike in the case of workers in the Public Sector Undertakings (PSUs), where a system of periodical wage revision based on bipartite negotiations existed, the wages of those employed in the railways were determined by the Pay Commissions appointed by the government from time to time. There was no space in this arrangement for bipartite negotiations. This was because the railways were nationalised before independence and hence considered a government arm, unlike PSUs that came into existence after independence and were managed as companies or corporations, and wages and other terms of employment there were determined by way of periodic agreements between the individual managements and the workers. As a consequence, despite falling in the same category of workers who were engaged in manufacturing goods and services, the railway workers were treated in the same way as employees in the government departments. Similarly, the railway administration had institutionalised the trade union set-up in the railways. Apart from the All India Railwaymen's Federation (AIRF), a conglomerate of unions across the zonal railways that were born in the course of several struggles against the Railway Companies (as they existed before independence) and also the British rule, the Railway Board also accorded recognition to the National Federation of Indian Railwaymen (NFIR), an affiliate of the Indian National Trade Union Congress (INTUC). The INTUC, it may be mentioned here, was founded in 1948 and from its inception this central trade union as well as its affiliates functioned more as apologists of the Congress party and its government rather than being a trade union in any sense of the term.

The existence of the NFIR was facilitated by the fact that successive Congress governments ensured that it was accorded recognition by the Railway Board; and by virtue of this, its leaders were invited and entertained as representatives of the railway workers. The AIRF, for all practical purposes remained the representative union of the railway workers. This too had begun to change in the couple of decades after independence and years of being a recognised federation meant that the AIRF too had become a means for patronage by the railway administration. Its leadership was increasingly losing its fighting edge. The central leaders of both the AIRF and the NFIR were provided with facilities such as free rail travel, invites for talks and their offices were located in free space provided by the administration within the railway premises. All these were also extended to the leaders of the affiliates of these two federations at all levels; zonal, divisional and the branches. In other words, the AIRF had been co-opted into the system and there was hardly any difference between this federation, with a long and glorious history of militant trade unionism, and the NFIR. The AIRF, however, pretended to be militant unlike the NFIR.

It was in this context that sections in the railways such as the engine drivers, the firemen (a category that existed in the days of the steam locomotive and vanished along with them after the advent of diesel and electric locomotives), the guards, the station masters and those in the signal and telecommunication department began setting up unions of their own. These were sections that were drawn from among the middle classes and in many ways compared themselves with the workers in the PSUs. They also belonged to categories that were directly involved in running the trains. One of the issues that began to bother them was the long and irregular working hours. The engine drivers, the firemen and the guards, for instance, worked a lot more than the stipulated eight hours for factory workers. The demand for regulation of working hours was put forward by the Loco Running Staff Association (LRSA), which came into existence in the mid-1960s. The leadership of both the AIRF and the NFIR was insensitive to this. There was a series of strikes, across the zonal railways since 1965, and through these the LRSA matured into an all India organisation and also emerged as the militant face of the railway trade union movement. This also encouraged other categories, in the operations department of the railways, to set up similar unions and carve out a space, independent of the federations. The Railway Board, however, refused to recognise these unions and the AIRF as well as the NFIR, would not let the board recognise or even talk with these category unions, as they were called. The AILRSA, meanwhile, was gathering strength and by 1972, after several strikes across the railways, the association could get the railway administration to reduce the working hours from 14 to 12 hours at a stretch.

Then there was a nationwide strike led by the AILRSA beginning 26 May 1973 and despite large-scale arrests and detention of the leaders under the Defence of India Rules (DIR) and other such provisions, as many as 42,000 drivers across the country participated in the strike. The total number of drivers at that time was 70,000. This forced Railway Minister L. N. Mishra to invite the AILRSA leaders for talks. He did not care about the opposition to this from the two recognised federations. The issues remained unresolved and the engine drivers and firemen went on strike, once again, from 2 August 1973. The immediate provocation this time was an order effecting a break in service for all those who were detained during the May 1973 strike. The strike this time was total. After the repressive measures failed (some 400 leaders of the LRSA were arrested and sent to jail), L. N. Mishra invited the leaders for talks again on 10 August 1973. The talks, interestingly, were held even while the strike was on and it was called off only after the government agreed to withdraw all the cases against the strikers and agreed not to take disciplinary action against the strikers; and most importantly, after the railway minister agreed to the introduction of a 10-hour working day. The LRSA leaders refused to concede any role to the AIRF and the NFIR in the course of this negotiation and this they did despite the Railway Board insisting on that.

Thus, the situation in August 1973 was one where the two recognised federations in the Indian Railways were pushed out of the centre stage and the category unions, through militant actions, had captured the imagination of a cross-section of the railway workers.

The picture will be complete if seen in the larger context of the crisis in the economy, discussed in the earlier part of this chapter. Insofar as the railway workers were concerned, the resentment would grow further after the government thrust the recommendations of the third Pay Commission. The recommendations were for a meagerly increase in wages at a time when prices were rising fast. The Basic Pay was raised from Rs 170 per month to Rs 196 per month for the class IV workers.

The prices of essential commodities had risen by 23 per cent in 1973. The overall crisis in the economy, marked by shortage of grain and domestic fuel, charges of corruption against members of the ruling establishment and the rising tide of militancy in the trade union movement laid the basis for a strike. Moreover, the government decided to impound an installment of Dearness Allowance. These were bad enough reasons and a meagre rise in wages, awarded by the third Pay Commission, turned out to be the immediate provocation for a strike in the railways.

The railway worker, by and large, was comparing himself with those in the PSUs; the minimum wage in the steel industry at that time was Rs 297 per month, while in BHEL, a public sector, it was Rs 294 a month and in the Hindustan Machine Tools, another PSU, it was Rs 350 per month. The PSU workers could engage in periodic wage negotiations while the railway worker was condemned to wait and take whatever the Pay Commission recommended.

Meanwhile, caught in a bind where the category unions were gaining strength, the AIRF decided to go for a course correction. In October 1973, at its convention in Secundrabad (in Andhra Pradesh), George Fernandes replaced Peter Alwares as its president. Fernandes, a stormy petrel trade unionist in and around Bombay and then the chairman of the Socialist Party, was brought into the AIRF by sections that were desperate to reinvent the federation as a fighting organisation. That had become necessary in the context of the emergence of category unions and the consequent erosion of the AIRF's base among the railway workers. The Secundrabad convention also voted in favour of a national general strike in the railways.

According to Fernandes, the decision to strike was forced on him by detractors from his own party as well as sections in the AIRF that were affiliated with the CPI, with an intention to paint him as another effete leader. Despite his opposition for a strike, in the convention itself, the delegates voted in favour of a general strike. This, in a sense, reflected the extent of discontent among the workers, who constituted the ranks of the federation. Having been pushed into that, Fernandes says, he decided to make the best out of a bad bargain and went about addressing workers across the railway zones. He also broke ranks with the others in the AIRF leadership by insisting that the AIRF will prepare for the strike in association with the category unions. The other important leaders of the AIRF, including the general secretary, Priya Gautam, also a member of the unified Socialist Party but belonging to the PSP tradition, was opposed to any such joint action with the category unions in general and the LRSA in particular. Fernandes had his way and on 27 February 1974, a convention of over 100 railwaymen unions, including the LRSA, gave concrete shape to the idea of a general strike and a National Coordination Committee for Railwaymen's Struggle (NCCRS) was formed. A memorandum with demands, including wage increase, statutory bonus for railway workers as it was given to workers in the

PSUs, regularising the services of over 3 lakh casual workers was sent to the Railway Board. The board, however, ignored the memorandum.

On 15 April 1974, the NCCRS representatives were called for a meeting with the Railway Board officials and were told that their demands were unacceptable. The NCCRS met the same day and decided to serve notice for a general strike beginning 8 May 1974. The meeting decided to serve the strike notice on23 April 1974 and that notices be served to the administration at all levels, including the various zones and divisions across the country. A 13-member Action Committee with Fernandes as its chairman and representatives from the AIRF, the LRSA, the AIREC, CITU, AITUC and BMS was formed at the NCCRS convention itself. The NCCRS, in many ways, reflected the unity that was emerging among the unions at that time and also the arrival of Fernandes as the leader. It took a while before the union leaders were called for negotiations. To be precise, talks began only on 27 April 1974 and the government's side was represented by deputy minister for railways, Mohammed Shafi Qureshi, a Congress MP from Anantnag in Jammu and Kashmir. While railway minister L. N. Mishra refused to be a part of the negotiating team, Prime Minister Indira Gandhi set out on a visit to Iran on 28 April 1974. The talks were not leading to any settlement. The only thing that the government was prepared to do was to set up 300 food grain shops spread over the railway colonies. The talks, however, kept dragging and remained where it began even on 30 April 1974. They decided to meet again on 2 May after their return from Lucknow where Fernandes, along with many other leaders of the 13-member Action Committee, was to address a May Day gathering of railway workers.

While they did address the Lucknow rally, the talks did not take place on 2 May. Fernandes was picked up at Lucknow, late in the night on 1 May 1974, put in a BSF plane, flown down to Delhi and then driven to the Tihar jail early in the morning on 2 May 1974. Other members of the Action Committee too were sent to jail. News of the arrest spread immediately and railway workers went on strike in many parts on 2 May itself. The gates at the Victoria Terminus and Central Station in Bombay were bolted and locked by the workers. Suburban trains came to a halt. Railway workers were joined by their family members to sit on railway tracks and stop trains in Patna, Gaya and Ferozepur. In the southern railway, where the LRSA had been most militant and dominated the NCCRS, the strike committee decided to begin the strike from 2 May 1974 rather than wait until 8 May. Thus, the workers in the workshops across the country stopped work on 2 May. A general strike was called in Bombay and the city came to a standstill. Bombay, then, was Fernandes's home and he controlled the transport, hotel and municipal unions in the city. Rail workers in the marshalling yards of Moghulsarai and Delhi stopped work and marched in a procession after news of Fernandes's arrest spread.

In a couple of days after 2 May 1974, train services came to a halt across the country. All the major railway workshops across the country – Jamalpur, Chittaranjan, Varanasi, Perambur, Kharagpur, Golden Rock – were closed down. The Indian railway system came to a halt for two weeks after 2 May 1974. A united strike, by over 17 lakh workers in the railways, was something that the government could not have ignored. Fernandes himself impressed upon the workers of this. Addressing a public meeting at Madras on 29 March 1974 (even before the strike notice was served and after the NCCRS was formed), Fernandes is reported to have said:

> Realise the strength which you possess. Seven days' strike of the Indian Railways, every thermal station in the country would close down. A ten days' strike of the Indian Railways, every steel mill in India would close down and the industries in the country would come to a halt for the next twelve months. If once the steel mill furnace is switched off, it takes nine months to re-fire. A fifteen days' strike in the Indian Railways, the country will starve.

The government, too, knew that and Indira Gandhi had decided against giving in to the railwaymen's demands. The official thinking was that agreeing to the demands would cost an additional Rs 450 crore for the government and also trigger similar demands and strike threats from other industries. Thus, the railway administration ordered cancellation of as many as 98 mail and express trains from 25 April 1974 itself. The zonal railway administrations were given powers to order further cancellations. The idea was to restrict the movement of passenger trains and use the locomotives to haul goods trains and build buffer stocks of coal and other requirements to the industries. This was how the administration sought to reduce the impact of the strike and these measures were initiated even before the negotiations began. The thermal generation units were kept going and steel plants could be kept running despite the disruption of train movements due to the strike. In other words, the government had done the needful to neutralise whatever Fernandes had spoken about the power of the railwaymen. It took adequate measures.

This was not enough to break the strike. In the three weeks between 2 May 1974 and 27 May 1974, when the strike was formally called of, as many as 50,000 railway workers were arrested. Of those, 10,000 were put in jail by the evening of 2 May 1974. Most of those arrested were detained under the Defence of India Rules (DIR) and MISA, both of which were in vogue, thanks to the Emergency declared at the time of the Indo-Pak war in December 1971 and was not withdrawn. At least 30,000 families were evicted from the railway quarters all over the country. The threat of eviction from the quarters was one of the means used by the administration to force striking workers return to work. The railway colonies in Moghulsarai, Jamalpur, Jhansi and in many other important railway towns were turned into hunting grounds for the police and paramilitary forces.

The government had decided to crush the strike and pulled all stops. It was clear, right from the manner in which the Action Committee leaders were arrested late in the night on 1 May 1974 and the indiscriminate use of force against the workers and their family members, that the government was determined to treat the strike as a battle for its survival rather than as an industrial dispute.

All that was summed up by Umraomal Purohit, a senior leader of the AIRF: 'The unions, after all, did not prepare for a civil war.' The intensity of the repression and the determination shown by Indira's government to crush the strike and also to crush the union movement itself was evident from the following facts: Even after the strike was called off unconditionally, the railway administration ordered the dismissal of as many as 50,000 workers, all of them being active leaders of the strike. At least 10 lakh workers who persisted with the strike until it was called off on 27 May 1974 (rather than apologising for their action) were taken back to work as fresh recruits; all their past service was not to be accounted for and they lost such of their benefits as pension, provident fund and accumulated leave. Even workers with service of over 25 years were treated as fresh recruits.

Both these decisions were reversed. But not before Indira Gandhi's Congress was voted out in the March 1977 general election and Madhu Dandavate, a close associate of George Fernandes in the Socialist movement, became the railway minister and ordered reinstatement of all the worker leaders who were dismissed for their role in the strike and restored the services of the 10 lakh workers and also annulled the earlier decision to treat many others as fresh recruits.

The railway workers may not have achieved anything in terms of their demands through the general strike of 1974. In a way, the repressive measures that were resorted to by the government destroyed the union movement. The leaders, including George Fernandes, were released from jail on 28 May 1974 and were made to face the workers to own up the defeat. Fernandes, in the very first press conference after the strike, made it clear that he would not want the railwaymens' struggle end up as an orphan. He said this after quoting John F. Kennedy's observation after the Bay of Pigs disaster: 'Victory has a thousand fathers; defeat is an orphan.' A large number of the workers, who struck work until the strike was formally called off, returned to work in processions and to the beating of drums in many places. They were convinced that a point had been made. The railway general strike of 1974 was an event in post-independence history where the working class took on the might of the state and forced the state to resort to all the repressive measures in its command. There is no disputing the fact that the repression let loose against the striking workers was unprecedented and it was a dress rehearsal for what would happen during the 19 months of the Emergency.

Having said this, it is also important to discuss the attitude of the opposition parties to the strike. The CPI, despite its own trade union wing—the AITUC—being a part of the AIRF and other unions that led the strike, indulged in double speak. The state government in Kerala, headed by C. Achuta Menon, went about arresting and detaining strike leaders. S. A. Dange, one of the party's important leaders, was even guilty of asking the workers to return to work midway through the strike. His argument was that the workers had proved a point and that was enough. The Socialist Party, of which Fernandes was the chairman, remained faction ridden. Priya Gautam, who was the general secretary of the AIRF, did not cover himself with glory before the strike and also through the strike. The CPI (M) was perhaps the only political party whose cadre and associates in the union movement involved themselves completely in the strike. The NCCRS, in many divisions was controlled by them and they led the strike from the front. But they could do that only in those areas/zones where they were strong. It is important to mention, in this context, an incident in Madurai (in Tamil Nadu). Ramasamy, a textile mill worker and an activist of the CITU, was crushed under the wheels of a train which the unionists and strike supporters had decided to stop from rolling. This was part of the solidarity action by the trade unions outside the railways. Meanwhile, efforts to mobilise the Posts and Telegraph workers, on a solidarity strike did not materialise.

As for the Lok Dal, Jan Sangh and Congress (O), its leaders were, by and large, unconcerned about the strike. Apart from making some noise in Parliament and outside, the political leaders did nothing to sustain or to mobilise solidarity actions even in places where they were strong. The fact is that there was hardly any procession in the colleges or in the universities across the country. This, indeed, is also a comment on the student movement in Gujarat and Bihar. Recall the fact that the students in Gujarat had succeeded in getting the Gujarat assembly dissolved in March 1974, a couple of months before the strike. And, the Bihar movement was already gaining strength by that time. Yet, there was no evidence of any expression of solidarity with the railway workers struggle. Similarly, there is hardly any evidence of Morarji Desai, who had gone on a fast unto death in Gujarat in support of the students and their demand for dissolution of the assembly, raising his voice in support of the railway strike. This is true of JP too. JP, incidentally, was the president of AIRF in 1948 and also of many trade unions at that time. However, despite his splendid silence in the context of the strike, we find him emerging as the rallying point of the anti-Indira forces within a few months after the strike. We shall deal with this in the following section.

JP Arrives on the Political Scene

Jayaprakash Narayan was held in the Nasik jail after his arrest during the Civil Disobedience Movement with such others as Yusuf Mehrally, Asoka Mehta,

Achyut Patwardhan, Ram Manohar Lohia, Minoo Masani and N. G. Goray. Together they formed the Congress Socialist Party (CSP) in 1934, which was to remain a ginger group within the Indian National Congress and push the INC into taking the socialist path. Acharya Narendra Deva was another important member of this platform, though he was not part of the group in the Nasik jail. Morarji Desai too was at the Nasik jail then but he did not join the CSP at any stage. The CSP declared socialism as its objective and was explicit that Marxism alone could guide the anti-imperialist forces to their destiny. They were also convinced about the need to democratise the organisational structure of the Indian National Congress. JP had returned from the US, where he had been to pursue his higher studies, exposed to Marxian thoughts and the idea of socialism as it was emerging in the Soviet Union.

Thereafter, JP became the general secretary of the CSP and remained a bitter critique of Mahatma Gandhi inside the Congress party for long. He is known to have been a disciple of Jawaharlal Nehru in those years and described Gandhi's thoughts as 'a compound of timid economic analysis, good intentions and ineffective moralizing'. JP had also called it 'dangerous' and his view, at that time, was that 'it hushes up the real issues and sets out to remove the real evils of society by pious wishes'. JP had stood up against Gandhi in the AICC when the Mahatma supported the idea of accepting the constituent assembly at its Meerut session in September 1946. JP was also among those who opposed the idea of partition till the end. He was one of the 29 AICC members who voted against the resolution accepting partition in its Delhi session on 5 June 1947. JP, at that time, was already a national hero. His escape from the Hazaribagh jail and his role in organising the underground resistance as part of the Quit India Movement had become legends by then. This was also the time when JP was beginning to turn against Jawaharlal Nehru after having been one of those who literally worshipped Nehru in the earlier days. He was moving closer to Gandhi by this time.

In April 1948, the CSP held its conference in Nasik (from where the party was conceived) and decided to break out of the Indian National Congress. In a statement there, JP said: 'In order to make democracy a success in our country, an opposition party is essential and we feel that the Socialist Party is the only party which can function as a healthy opposition'. Moving away from the Marxist notions that constituted the core principles of the CSP when it was founded in 1934, JP's opening address at the Socialist Party's foundation conference (in 1950) reflected the idea of Gandhian Socialism. He said; 'If the state is looked upon as the sole agent of reconstruction of society, we get nothing but a regimented society... and the individual is made a cog in a vast inhuman machine... Democracy requires that the people should depend as little as possible upon the state'.

This transition and the shift to Gandhi's ideas, marked the core of JP's thought ever since, and this indeed was at the centre of his campaign in the context of Bihar as well as in the campaign against Indira Gandhi's regime. In other words, JP's idea of Total Revolution emanated from this very conceptual framework.

JP led the Socialist Party's campaign from the front in the 1951–52 general election, though he refused being a candidate. But soon after that he moved away from the party and plunged himself into the *Bhoodan* movement to become Acharya Vinoba Bhave's foot soldier. The *Bhoodan* movement was based on the idea to end inequality in society by bringing about a change of heart among the large land owners so that they agreed to distribute their surplus land to the tiller. JP's association with the *Bhoodan* movement alienated him from the Nasik group and the Socialist Party. JP had detached himself from the party soon after the 1951–52 general election. So much so, Ram Manohar Lohia, his close associate in the days when the Socialist Party was founded and with whom he had spent several months in jail before independence, had turned his bitter critic. Lohia accused JP of reducing Gandhi's ideas to a 'curiously anaemic doctrine'. In his presidential address to the foundation conference of the Socialist Party in December 1955, Lohia said: 'A sterile Gandhism has come into existence which concentrates almost exclusively on changing the heart of the well-placed to the utter neglect of change of the poor-man's heart.'

Although Lohia did not overtly attribute this to JP, it was indeed clear that his angst was against JP. The point is that JP had completely withdrawn from the affairs and activities of the Socialist Party in particular and from party politics in general, after the first general election. In many ways, JP's withdrawal had weakened the Socialist Party considerably. He was, indeed, the only leader in the party who had a nationwide appeal at that time and could have emerged as an effective alternative to Nehru and placed the Socialist Party as the rallying point against the Congress. Acharya Narendra Deva did not live long and Asoka Mehta, finding socialistic virtues in Nehru, had joined the Congress at that time. Achyut Patwardhan, meanwhile, quit party politics and Lohia was left alone to carry on with the party during the 1950s. When the Congress began losing its hold among the masses in the early 1960s, the contours of opposition politics had changed substantially and the Socialist Party was reduced to being yet another player in the opposition along with the Lok Dal, the Jan Sangh and the Swatantra Party in 1967 and the Congress (O) in 1971.

JP, all along this crucial period, was not merely staying away from the thick of electoral politics but was actually expressing contempt over the parties and their moves. This contempt continued to guide him in the initial days of his association with the student movement in Bihar too. He had, time and again, insisted that the opposition parties be kept out of the struggle. In February 1973, for instance, Biju Pattnaik, then the president of the Utkal

Congress approached JP with a proposal that he lead an anti-Congress front. Biju Pattnaik was one of Nehru's cheerleaders and was the one who moved the Socialistic pattern resolution at Avadi in 1955; he was also the one who pushed the idea of building the Congress organisation in 1963 (after the by-election defeats) and insisted on quitting as the chief minister towards this end. He was one of those who promoted the idea of ministers opting for party work and, thus, laid the basis for what came to be known as the Kamaraj Plan. Pattnaik was among the six chief ministers who resigned as part of the Kamaraj Plan in September 1963. He, however, walked out of the Congress after Indira Gandhi took over the party and his differences were more out of his own personal pride being hurt by Indira (for, he considered himself a confidant of Nehru and was hurt when Indira did not treat him with due respect) rather than anything to do with ideology. JP spurned the offer. At a press conference, the day after Biju Pattnaik met him (at Calcutta on 11 February 1973), JP reported that he had told Pattnaik that 'while he was interested for the sake of the country in the promotion of a viable opposition, he would neither take the initiative nor be part of it'.

Meanwhile, he laid out the contours for this 'effective' opposition and placed the following as prescription. That an effective opposition must necessarily represent forces of radical change and at the same time stay committed to peaceful and democratic means; that the consolidation must be based on principles and not opportunistic. Recalling the past experience in this regard, JP made a pointed reference to the spectacle of coalition governments in the various states that came into place after 1967. Last but not the least, that the exercise shall not be guided by the negative slogan of *Indira hatao* but be made out of a positive programme before the people.

However, even while he offered to counsel the opposition parties, JP persisted with the idea of putting the Congress party back on the track and was full of hope that Indira Gandhi would agree to do that. This was his conviction until a few days before 4 November 1974. For instance, JP agreed for a meeting with Indira Gandhi in Delhi on 1 November 1974. This meeting was arranged by P. N. Dhar, Indira's Special Secretary in the Prime Minister's Office, along with Swagata Das Gupta, who was at that time the chairman of the Gandhi Institute in Varanasi. JP was in Delhi on that day after addressing a massive public rally in Ludhiana on 31 October 1974. He placed a nine-point charter before Prime Minister Indira Gandhi, which included the resignation of the Bihar ministry, dissolution of the state assembly and fresh elections there apart from asking for the setting up of committees for education reforms and electoral reforms. In short, he was still hopeful of a settlement with Indira Gandhi and that the Congress party would change its course. Indira Gandhi simply heard out all these and declared from a public meeting she addressed the same evening at the Ramlila grounds (in Delhi) that she would rather resign from the prime minister's post than agree to dismiss the Bihar government. She added that if everything about her and her government was so bad, the people could wait until the next election to defeat her and her party.

This indeed would place the events on 4 November 1974 in proper context and also JP's declaration thereafter, on 18 November 1974, from the Gandhi Maidan in Patna, that he was willing to take up the challenge and lead the battle in the electoral front too. He did not have to wait for long to put this in practice. A by-election was due for the Jabalpur Lok Sabha constituency in Madhya Pradesh on 21 January 1975. JP could ensure that all the opposition parties agreed to rally behind a candidate of his choice. Sharad Yadav, who would emerge on the national scene during the 1980s, was then a student leader at the Government Engineering College in Jabalpur. He was chosen by JP, put up as the 'People's Candidate' and Sharad Yadav trounced the Congress candidate securing as high as 65 per cent of the votes polled.

Meanwhile, the Congress party too was determined against letting JP carry on with his campaign. A national camp of the AICC at Narora (in Rajasthan) that began on 22 November 1974 came out with a 13-page document analysing the JP movement and it was circulated among the members there. It will be appropriate to quote excerpts from the document in this context. It said:

> Behind the façade of a partyless democracy lurk dark forces of Indian fascism, well organized and well poised to destroy the democratic institutions and impose a reign of terror. The Jan Sangh, the RSS and the Anand Marg are the driving forces behind the assault on the citadel of democracy.
>
> When it falls, they will move quickly to occupy positions of vantage. The result can be predicted. A naked dictatorship of the propertied classes will come into existence. It will appeal to the most retrogressive tendencies in our social and political life. Communalism, regional chauvinism and fanaticism of all kinds and a narrow, life-denying cultural revivalism will thrive.
>
> It is not accidental that these forces should strive to challenge democracy at a time of grave economic difficulties … they should seek to confuse the public mind by employing a variety of ruses, such as the call to end corruption, the raising of the issue of electoral reforms … [and] that the parties which have joined the campaign against democracy are simultaneously opposing our whole concept of planning and the Congress policy of cooperation with the Soviet Union and other countries.

A few facts here will help place the Narora document in perspective. One that the Narora meet was held about the same time as sections within the Congress, particularly Indira Gandhi's cheerleaders at the time of the Congress split in 1969, such as Chandra Shekhar and Mohan Dharia, were pressing hard that the Congress supremo talk to JP and listen to him. That this was a pretty large group was evident from the attendance at the tea party at Chandra Shekhar's residence on 20 November 1974. It is another matter that many from that group were apologetic about having been there when they assembled at Narora a couple of days later. This section was indeed unhappy with Indira Gandhi's dependence on the CPI. Indira, by this time, had found a new confidant in Mohan Kumaramangalam; we have dealt with this in the previous chapter.

Secondly, the stress on the socialist project and the method of presenting any opposition to Indira Gandhi as being part of an anti-socialist conspiracy (that was pronounced in the Narora document) was not new in any way. This was how Indira Gandhi took on her detractors in the party after 1967 and until the split in 1969. In 1974, however, the core aspects of the Narora document seemed to come from the CPI. The CPI general secretary, C. Rajeswara Rao, described the JP movement 'as part of a conspiracy of the forces of right reaction to exploit the legitimate discontent and anger of the people against the present regime for building up a reactionary offensive to seize power'. A CPI rally in Patna on 11 November 1974, was full of such slogans that branded JP as an agent of the American establishment.

And lastly, the Narora document reflected the thinking within the Congress party in general and of Indira Gandhi's inner circle in particular, to present all opposition to the regime as part of a conspiracy against the national interests and a tendency to raise the *spectre* of the *foreign hand*. This theme would repeat, time and again, to justify the Emergency and the annulment of the fundamental rights of the citizens. This was also the time when the Congress president, Dev Kant Baruah, came out with a slogan that exposed the ridiculous extent to which sycophancy could be taken to: '*Indira is India, India is Indira.*'

Meanwhile, Indira Gandhi decided to go ahead with a nuclear test in Pokhran (from where the BJP-led NDA would carry out more tests and announce India's nuclear weapons programme 24 years later) on 18 May 1974, to whip up a brand of nationalism. Around the same time, she also found President V. V. Giri showing signs of assertion. Giri had raised some questions on the issue of the appointment of Justice A. N. Ray as the Supreme Court Chief Justice earlier. And when his term came to an end in August 1974, Indira denied him the pleasure of a second term. Fakhruddin Ali Ahmed, who had carried out her orders inside the party against the syndicate in 1969 was chosen, by her, as the party's presidential candidate. With the Congress party now in total command in Parliament and most state assemblies, Ali Ahmed was elected as President of the Republic with ease.

The only dissenting voice against her came from Mohan Dharia, a 'Young Turk' and also Minister of State for Works and Housing in her cabinet. He came out with a statement, on 2 March 1975, condemning the police actions against the agitators and that Indira Gandhi should negotiate with JP. He was asked to quit the cabinet within hours after he made the statement. But the crisis in the economy and the incidence of corruption in high places, involving several Congress chief ministers and her own inner circle (including her son, Sanjay Gandhi) were providing the basis for a popular revolt against the regime. The Gujarat movement, the railway general strike and the reception for JP in many parts of the country were clear reflections of a popular resentment against her.

It was this larger context, marked by intolerance and repression against all agitations and more particularly on the students in Patna on 4 November 1974 that turned JP, too, against the Congress party and convinced him to rally the opposition parties, whom he had detested for long, against the regime. He attended a meeting held by all the opposition parties in Delhi in February 1975. It was decided at that meeting to hold a rally in Delhi on 6 March 1975 and present a charter of demands to the speaker of the Lok Sabha. Realising the potentials that existed for an authoritarian take over as long as the state of Emergency, proclaimed in the wake of the Indo-Pak war in December 1971, was allowed to continue, the opposition parties also decided to launch a national campaign against its continuation and fixed 6 April 1975 for demonstrations in all the state capitals and district headquarters. This Emergency, declared on the basis of Article 352 of the Constitution (where the president is convinced that the security of India or any part of the country is threatened by external aggression or war), provided for arrests and detention under such preventive detention laws as DIR and MISA. These were used by the Indira Gandhi regime against the agitators in Gujarat, the striking railway workers and against leaders in Bihar.

All this was leading to a situation where the opposition parties, that were swept aside in the 1971 elections, were gathering strength at one level and JP agreeing to lead them in the struggle against Indira's Congress. The rally on 6 March 1975 in Delhi was huge by all standards and JP's address clearly revealed that the 72-year-old Gandhian was now determined to carry on with the fight and take it to its logical end. The opposition parties too were willing to declare him the leader. The CPI (M), whose leadership had reservations against the inclusion of the Jan Sangh in the fold, had stayed out of the Delhi show. The party, however, was not averse to the campaign. Indira's Congress was left only with the CPI by this time. Soon after this, Morarji Desai began his second hunger strike on 2 April 1975 demanding elections be held without any further delay in Gujarat. Indira's regime, after dissolving the state assembly in March 1974, had clamped central rule in the state and proposed assembly elections only by September 1975. The prime minister had to give in again and elections were scheduled for 10 June 1975.

On 12 June 1975, Indira Gandhi and her Congress party were woken up by the news of an opposition victory in Gujarat. A combination of forces comprising Congress (O), Socialist Party, Swatantra Party, Jan Sangh and Lok Dal called the Janata Morcha, secured 86 seats in the 181-member Gujarat assembly. Indira Gandhi had led the poll campaign from the front and Chimanbhai Patel, against whom the students had risen in revolt, had by then formed his own party in the state. Indira's Congress secured only 75 seats. The opposition combine, of which Morarji's Congress (O) was the leading partner, formed a government in Gujarat with the support coming from some of the 15 independents who had won the polls. Babubhai Patel was elected as the chief minister of this combine's government. The fragile nature of the opposition alliance would reveal soon and a few independent MLAs withdrew support to the Janata Morcha government in March 1976 (when the Emergency regime was at its height and the opposition parties were targeted by Indira and her government) and cause the fall of this government. After a brief spell of central rule, Indira's Congress managed a majority and Madhav Sinh Solanki became the chief minister in December 1976.

The other bad news came from Allahabad. On 12 June 1975, Justice Jagmohan Lal Sinha delivered his verdict on an election petition by Raj Narain, an acerbic member of the Socialist Party, who had lost to Indira Gandhi from Rae Bareli in March 1971. Sinha pronounced Indira Gandhi's election null and void on grounds that she had violated the provisions of the Representation of the Peoples Act, 1951. The details of this case can wait for the next chapter. For now, the Allahabad High Court verdict pushed the Congress party into a huddle and the opposition, buoyed by the victory in Gujarat and the popular response among the people to JP's campaign, did not waste time and demanded Indira Gandhi's resignation as the prime minister.

The opposition's campaign peaked at the rally in Delhi, at the Ramlila Maidan, on 25 June 1975. Indira Gandhi had gone on appeal before the vacation judge of the Supreme Court, Justice V. R. Krishna Iyer, against the Allahabad High Court verdict. Justice Iyer, contrary to the expectations of the Congress leaders, refused to grant an absolute stay on the High Court verdict. On 24 June 1975, Justice Iyer held that the subject matter—whether Indira's election in 1971 was valid or not—would be decided later. He, however, went on to explain that Indira Gandhi could continue as the prime minister even if she was not an MP. Justice Iyer simply extrapolated on Article 75 (5) of the Constitution that a minister shall remain in that position until only six consecutive months without being a member of either house of Parliament and held that Indira Gandhi may continue to hold the office of Prime Minister but shall not vote on any motion. In other words, Justice Iyer ordered that Indira Gandhi shall not have the right to vote in Parliament but may continue as the prime minister.

The Supreme Court's conditional stay had upset Indira Gandhi and had lent a sense of legitimacy to the opposition campaign demanding Indira's resignation.

Indira, meanwhile, suspected a conspiracy even from within her own ranks. She was, hence, dissuaded, by her younger son and a section of her party leaders against stepping down as the prime minister and nominating another person from the party in her place until she obtained an absolute stay from the Supreme Court on the Allahabad High Court verdict. The opposition, meanwhile, was not prepared to let go the situation. On 25 June 1975, JP called the regime an illegitimate one and expressed that it was not necessary for the armed forces and the police to obey orders of a government that was illegitimate. It may be stressed here that JP, on that day, simply resorted to an argument that Mahatma Gandhi had raised against the British rule. That the regime was based on illegitimacy and that it was the moral duty, as much as a right, for the citizens in that situation to disobey orders from such a regime. In other words, JP invoked the spirit of civil disobedience. The opposition leaders announced a programme of civil disobedience that could go as far as refusal to pay taxes and other such actions. A *satyagraha* campaign was announced from the rally and that was to begin from 29 June 1975.

Indira, meanwhile, had other plans. She got President Fakhruddin Ali Ahmed to proclaim internal Emergency, invoking Article 352 of the Constitution. All the opposition leaders, including JP and those in her own party who had been urging her to talk with JP, were arrested during the intervening night of 25–26 June 1975.

X

The Emergency

> The emergency that was declared in the early hours of June 26, 1975, was a severe setback in the political evolution of India ... Citizens were deprived of their fundamental rights; freedom of the press was curbed ... political dissent was suppressed ... and officialdom assumed arbitrary powers ... In sum, these events changed the basic relationship between the citizen and the state and indeed threatened to change the character of the Indian state itself.
>
> —P. N. Dhar, *Indira Gandhi, the Emergency and Indian Democracy*

The emergency, which lasted for 19 months between June 1975 and March 1977, has been the subject of many books. Most of them are accounts by persons who, in their own way, resisted the undemocratic ways that marked the 19 months. There are also accounts explaining the conditions that led to the declaration of the emergency and the events of that period. The point being that the Emergency marked an important watershed in the evolution of democratic practice in India, most of the published works are either in the nature of holding a brief for Indira Gandhi or accounts that present her as an autocrat personified. There may be truth in all this. In this chapter, we shall present the developments as they happened and in their context.

The Emergency, nevertheless, was a development that the democratic polity in India could have done without. It was also an experience where it was revealed that the Republican Constitution itself provided the scope for an undemocratic shift. The Emergency was as much a constitutional response by Indira Gandhi to the constitutional means as the opposition parties had adopted, to unseat her. In other words, the emergency was an experience that brought out, with ample clarity, that the Constitution contained provisions in it that could both enhance the democratic rights of the people and be used to deny even the fundamental rights to its people.

The very fact that Article 352 of the Constitution, which enabled Indira Gandhi to deny the citizens some of the fundamental rights guaranteed by the same Constitution, continues to be there in the statute should convey that a similar resort is possible even in future. It is another matter that the Article was amended by the Janata Party Government, adding an explicit clause that a recommendation to impose internal emergency will have to be made by the Union Cabinet to the President of the Republic in writing. One of the provisions of the Constitution's 44th Amendment is that an internal emergency can be declared only after the Union Cabinet approves a resolution and the entire process in the cabinet is recorded in writing and sent to the President. Indira Gandhi could get the President to promulgate an internal emergency without such formalities late in the night on 25 June 1975. The nation can no longer be pushed into an undemocratic mode with such secrecy and speed at which Indira Gandhi managed it on that fateful night. Similarly, the Constitution now stands amended by which the phrase 'internal disturbance' has been replaced by 'armed rebellion'.

The other important aspect that needs to be underscored is that the Emergency was the fallout of a whole lot of causes; some of them were longstanding and others immediate. The long-term dynamics that led to the emergency can be traced to the various developments involving the Congress party, such as the erosion of its support base over the years after independence, and its manifestation in the 1967 general elections, the Congress revival of sorts under Indira Gandhi in the 1971 polls, the agitations against the Indira regime such as the Gujarat movement, the Bihar movement and the railway strike in May 1974. These have been discussed in the past few chapters. The immediate cause for the emergency came with the Allahabad High Court judgement, setting aside Indira Gandhi's election to the Lok Sabha from Rae Bareli in Uttar Pradesh, on 12 June 1975.

On that day, Justice Jagmohan Lal Sinha of the Allahabad High Court pronounced that Indira Gandhi had resorted to corrupt electoral practices, as defined in the Representation of the People's Act, 1951, and, hence, her election was null and void. He also allowed three weeks' time for Indira Gandhi to prefer an appeal in the Supreme Court. This meant that the verdict would take effect only if an appeal was not filed or not sustained in the Supreme Court. Indira Gandhi did prefer an appeal. But to her dismay, Justice V. R. Krishna Iyer, the vacation judge of the Supreme Court, refused an absolute stay. This turned out to be the immediate cause for the emergency.

After a narrative on the events that took place immediately after the Presidential promulgation on the night of 25 June 1975, such as the indiscriminate arrests and the imposition of press censorship, we will deal with the institutional changes effected by the Emergency regime including the 42nd Constitution Amendment; thereafter, a narrative on what is described, by a section of political commentators, as the excesses and this will include the ways and means of Sanjay Gandhi; the next section will narrate the various kinds of resistance to the emergency. While an attempt will be made to cover the various acts of resistance, let it be stated that this will not be a complete account of those. A complete account on the resistance to the Emergency will perhaps have to wait for another book.

The Midnight Proclamation and the Clampdown

The significance of 12 June 1975 was that it was on that day that Indira Gandhi received two bad messages. One was the news from Ahmedabad. The Congress party lost to the Janata Morcha, a pre-poll combination of the Congress (O), the Jan Sangh, the Bharatiya Lok Dal and the Socialist Party. Polling was held on 10 June 1975 for the 182 assembly constituencies and the final tally was 87 for the Janata Morcha (of which Morarji was the supreme leader) and 75 for Indira's Congress party. As many as 20 independents were elected and a majority of them were known supporters of the Janata Morcha. It was a bad news, given the long history behind the mid-term elections in Gujarat (discussed in the previous chapter), and also because Indira herself had led the campaign for her Congress in the state. The second and more important (rather decisive) event on that day was the judgement delivered by Justice Sinha. Even if it was on an innocuous election petition, filed by Raj Narain who had lost to Indira Gandhi in March 1971 from Rae Bareli, the judgement had far-reaching implications.

It was innocuous because election petitions are not unusual and Raj Narain, a member of the Socialist Party, was a compulsive litigant. Indira Gandhi's victory margin in Rae Bareli was mighty. She had secured 1,83,309 votes while her nearest rival Raj Narain of the Samyukta Socialist Party (SSP) managed only 71,499 votes. Indira Gandhi's victory margin was 1,11,810. The Congress party was opposed by a four-party opposition front and the SSP was part of it. Indira's Congress had registered an emphatic victory in the 1971 elections from all over India. It may be recalled that the 1971 polls gave Indira Gandhi's Congress party a landslide win against the combined opposition. In Uttar Pradesh alone, the Congress party's strength went up from 47 in 1967 to 73 in 1971. In a sense, there was no way Raj Narain could have hoped to win against Indira Gandhi from Rae Bareli in 1971. Indira had won this constituency in 1967 (her first ever electoral battle) securing 55 per cent of the votes polled and in 1971, she had secured more than 66 per cent of the votes polled. But then, Raj Narain's contention, before the Allahabad High Court, was not based on any irregularities at the time of counting. He had challenged Indira Gandhi's election from Rae Bareli on the ground that by employing Yashpal Kapoor as her election agent she had violated the provisions of the Representation of the People's Act, 1951.

Kapoor was the prime minister's private secretary and was drawing his salary from the Consolidated Funds of the Government of India and hence qualified to be a government servant. The Representation of the People's Act, 1951, laid out that government servants shall not be involved in electioneering. And in the event any candidate did that, it was held as corrupt electoral practice. In this instance, Kapoor had accepted to be Indira Gandhi's election agent in Rae Bareli on 7 January 1971. However, he submitted his letter of resignation from Government service only on 13 January 1971. In other words, he had remained in service for a week after he accepted the appointment as Indira Gandhi's election agent. Moreover, in the eyes of the Allahabad High Court, Kapoor had to be treated as having done Indira Gandhi's election related work from 29 December

1970, the day on which she announced early elections to the Lok Sabha and her candidature.

Apart from this, there was a time lag between the submission of his letter of resignation and the order relieving him of his duties which was issued on 25 January 1971. Kapoor did not find it necessary to wait until his formal separation from the government service before taking over as the election agent. This clearly meant that he continued to be a government officer even while performing the duties as Indira Gandhi's election agent. This was not all. Raj Narain had also submitted evidence that the rostrum on which Indira Gandhi had addressed her election rallies, across Uttar Pradesh, were built by the Public Works Department of the Uttar Pradesh government. This again was a corrupt electoral practice, in the eyes of the law.

All these were innocuous factors. None of them could have influenced the poll outcome and particularly so when Indira's margin of victory was huge. Moreover, the landslide win registered by the Congress party too (in comparison with the 1967 elections) could not have been achieved because Kapoor happened to be her election agent in Rae Bareli or because she addressed an election rally from a rostrum that was a few inches higher than the prescribed limits. The judiciary, however, was not expected to go beyond the letter of the law. Justice Jagmohan Lal Sinha could not have gone into all these. His business was to stick to the law as such and Indira Gandhi was clearly guilty of violations. Sinha said so on 12 June 1975 and declared Indira Gandhi's election from Rae Bareli invalid. The Prime Minister was held guilty of violating the law during the election campaign and hence her membership in the Lok Sabha was now declared illegal. Sinha's judgement was based on Section 123, Clause 7 of the Representation of the People's Act, 1951. The law also prescribed that those found guilty of corrupt electoral practices be disqualified and debarred from contesting elections for a period of six years. Justice Sinha's 12 June 1975 judgement debarred Indira Gandhi from contesting another election for a period of six years. This meant that the Rae Bareli Lok Sabha seat would fall vacant, but Indira Gandhi could not have contested the by-elections there.

Indira Gandhi's lawyer, V. N. Khare, flown in to Allahabad from Srinagar, pleaded before Justice Sinha that he put the judgement in abeyance on the ground that some time was necessary before the Congress party addressed the issue and elected another leader. The disqualification, in this case, was that of the prime minister and some time was needed, he argued, to elect another leader and save the nation from landing in a chaos. Justice Sinha did not refuse and held that the judgement will come into effect only after 20 days. In any case, Justice Sinha would have had to grant sufficient time for the defendant to seek an appeal in the Supreme Court, as this is an accepted practice in the judicial scheme of things. The dictum in this regard is clear: While the power to stay is discretionary, the right to appeal is statutory.

The fact is that Indira Gandhi had pleaded for time to save the nation from chaos and it was impressed upon Justice Sinha that the time will be used to elect another prime minister. This was brought up in the Supreme Court by Raj Narain when Indira Gandhi's petition seeking a stay on the Allahabad High Court judgement came up before Justice V. R. Krishna Iyer (the vacation judge) on 24 June 1975. Justice Iyer refused to entertain the plea on grounds that 'the judicial approach is to shy away from political thickets and view problems with institutionalized blinkers on…' While Indira Gandhi's plea before the Supreme Court was taken up by Nani Palkhiwala, Raj Narain was represented by Shanthi Bhushan. The arguments and the interim orders of 24 June 1975, by Justice Krishna Iyer, granting conditional stay of the Allahabad High Court judgement, meant a lot in terms of its impact on the political developments of India. But before that, let us briefly discuss the developments on 12 June 1975 and in the couple of intervening weeks, until 25 June 1975.

Indira Gandhi was informed by N. K. Seshan, an officer in the prime minister's secretariat, that her election to the Lok Sabha was set aside by Justice Sinha of the Allahabad High Court and that she had been debarred from contesting elections for six years. Indira Gandhi went into a huddle with her cabinet colleagues. One option before her was to step down as the prime minister and 'elect' any one of her loyalists. Jagjivan Ram, Swaran Singh and Y. B. Chavan were the probable choices. But then, none of these men were bold enough to suggest this as an option. Nor did others talk about this. Meanwhile, Indira's son, Sanjay Gandhi, was already on the job. Along with the Haryana chief minister, Bansi Lal (who had landed into his inner circle by arranging land for the Maruti project), R. K. Dhawan (who had replaced Yashpal Kapoor as Indira's private secretary) and Om Mehta (Minister of State for Home), Sanjay was working on other plans.

The word was out that all those who sought Indira's resignation, on moral grounds, were acting on behalf of forces that were determined to destabilise India. Indira Gandhi herself had begun to say, even before the Allahabad High Court verdict was pronounced, that she was high on the hit list of the US administration and that she could face the same fate as Salvador Allende of Chile. She was referring to the CIA inspired coup against Allende in 1973 and his assasination!

Sanjay Gandhi worked at two levels. One was to ensure that all those in the Congress party, with a sense of morality or pangs of conscience (there were hardly anyone of significance in any case), kept their mouths shut. He did succeed in this. The second aspect of his strategy was to orchestrate support for Indira Gandhi on the streets. This was ensured by ferrying people from Haryana, Uttar Pradesh and Rajasthan to participate in rallies in New Delhi. Dhawan, who had risen to be a key person in the prime minister's secretariat from his early beginnings as a clerk in the Ministry of Railways, had issued instructions from the prime minister's official residence to the chief ministers to this effect. The chief ministers were men who had done this earlier in July 1969, that is, drum up support for Indira Gandhi against the party bosses. The crowds that poured into Delhi, day after day, between 12 June and 20 June 1975 were managed by blatant abuse of the administrative machinery, and this came to light (with abundant evidence) at the Justice Shah Commission of Enquiry set up by the Janata Party Government after the emergency was lifted.

As many as 1,761 buses, under the Delhi Transport Corporation, were commandeered by the Congress party to ferry its supporters to rally around the prime minister's residence between 12 June 1975 and 25 June 1975. This was in addition to the fleet belonging to the Haryana State Roadways and the number of trains, in which Indira's supporters could travel, from as far away as Gorakhpur and Varanasi (in eastern Uttar Pradesh) to New Delhi, without having to pay for the fare. While crowds landing in Delhi and shouting slogans seeking Indira Gandhi to stay on, unmindful of the Allahabad High Court verdict, had become an everyday affair, the high point of this campaign was a meeting of the Congress Parliamentary Party on 18 June 1975. A resolution was passed affirming Indira Gandhi's indispensability for not just the party but to the nation. Jagjivan Ram moved the motion and 450 members, a substantial majority of the Congress MPs drawn from both Houses, voted in its favour. There were, however, 44 votes against the motion.

After thus asserting, in a categorical manner, that the party was not going to 'elect' another leader (recall that an assurance to this effect was given in the Allahabad High Court on 12 June by Indira's counsel, V. N. Khare), she held a rally at the Boat Club grounds on 20 June 1975. On that day, apart from Sanjay Gandhi, she had Rajiv Gandhi and Sonia Gandhi by her side on the stage. Indira assured the crowd that she was determined to stay on and serve the nation and its people 'till her last breath' because that was the Nehru–Gandhi family's tradition.

All this, in the name of democracy, based on the firm belief that unseating Indira was a conspiracy against the nation and that the nation was doomed without Indira Gandhi at the helm, was taking place when the opposition, now led by JP, was preparing for a fight to the finish. As early as on 6 March 1975, JP addressed a rally at the Boat Club grounds where he called upon the armed forces to defend Democracy and stand up against authoritarian tendencies. 'It is the duty of the army to defend the Constitution of the country from authoritarian threats. If any party government or party leader intends to use the army as a means to further their party and power interests, it is the clear duty, to my mind, of the army not to allow it to be so used,' JP had remarked. And he repeated this, in almost all the rallies he addressed across the country, since then. Similarly, he had trained his guns at Indira Gandhi even before the 12 June 1975 judgement. In an interview to a newsmagazine, in April 1975, JP said: 'Mrs Gandhi is the fountainhead of all authoritarianism of the ruling Congress. She, as a single individual, can put to shame some of the greatest autocrats of history. I can see the threat to democracy personified in her.'

The Allahabad High Court verdict simply gave impetus to the combined opposition campaign, which had taken shape before the 1967 general elections. Although the unity achieved in 1967 did not last long and the various state governments, led by this combine, had collapsed within a couple of years, the 1971 elections brought them together once again in the form of the 'Grand Alliance'. After March 1975, this alliance had consolidated itself under JP's leadership. The Allahabad High Court verdict gave JP and the opposition parties the moral basis as well as an issue to focus upon. They were determined to take the battle to the streets in the same way as Indira Gandhi was doing in the days after 12 June 1975. A grand rally at the Ramlila grounds in Delhi on 25 June 1975, addressed among others by JP and Morarji Desai, was their response to Indira Gandhi. Unlike in the past, when the focus was on the demand for dissolution of the Bihar assembly, JP and his comrades found a new and direct focus this time: Indira Gandhi must go, now that she stood disqualified by the Allahabad High Court. The fact that she stood disqualified and debarred from contesting or holding any elected office for a period of six years was more than what the opposition had asked for.

Indira Gandhi, meanwhile, was working on the third aspect of her strategy, to appeal against the Allahabad High Court verdict and seek an absolute stay on Justice Sinha's judgement. The Supreme Court was to close down for summer vacation in a few days after 12 June and Indira was advised by her aides to make use of the opportunity and approach Justice V. R. Krishna Iyer. An old associate of the CPI, Justice Iyer would be the vacation judge. The fact that the CPI, like the Congress party leaders, had firmly believed that JP's struggle against Indira Gandhi was part of a larger conspiracy to derail her socialistic measures and throw the nation into a chaos, formed the basis for this line of thinking and the optimism that Justice Iyer would grant an absolute stay. To her pleasant surprise, Nani Palkhiwala, a legal luminary who had fought cases such as the privy purses and bank nationalisation against the government, agreed to take up Indira Gandhi's brief in the Supreme Court.

The petition seeking to quash the Allahabad High Court verdict and an absolute stay on it came up before the vacation judge on 24 June 1975. Justice Iyer baffled both sides with his order. The petition for stay was admitted and by extension Justice Sinha's verdict was stayed. But then, he refused an absolute stay. It will be appropriate to reproduce parts of Justice Iyer's order on the petition at this stage.

> Shri Palkhivala has pressed before me the propriety and urgency of the Court taking into consideration the national situation even while exercising its discretionary power. As a counter-weight to this submission, Shri Shanti Bhushan has claimed that no Republic can surrender its democratic destiny to a single soul without being guilty of overpowering the parliamentary process by a personality cult.

> Shri Palkhivala urged that, after all, the petitioner had been held 'technically' guilty of 'corrupt practice' and that the grounds set out by the learned Judge were too flimsy to stand scrutiny at the appellate level. Therefore, the 'justice' of the case demanded continuance of the 'absolute stay' granted by the trial Judge himself. Shri Shanti Bhushan, on the other side, refuted this submission as specious. His argument is this. 'Corrupt practice' could not be dismissed as 'technical' if one had any respect for the law of the land as laid down by Parliament.

The operative portion of the June 24, 1975 order went on to say the following:

> There will be a stay of the operation of the judgement and order of the High Court under appeal. Consequentially, the disqualification imposed upon the appellant (Indira Gandhi) as a statutory sequel under Section 8-A of the Act (Representation of the People's Act, 1951) and as forming part of the judgement and order impugned (the Allahabad High Court order) will also stand suspended. That is to say, the petitioner will remain a Member of the Lok Sabha for all purposes except to the extent restricted by the following conditions: She will be entitled to sign the attendance register and attend the sessions of the Lok Sabha will neither participate in the proceedings in the Lok Sabha nor vote nor draw remuneration in her capacity as Member of the Lok Sabha. Independent of these restrictions, she shall continue to enjoy her rights as Prime Minister or Minister, so long as she fills that office, to speak in and otherwise to take part in the proceedings of either House of Parliament or a joint sitting of the Houses (without right to vote) and to discharge other functions such as are laid down in Articles 74, 75, 78, 88 etc., or under any other law. She is also entitled to draw her salary as Prime Minister.

Justice Krishna Iyer's order made a lot of difference to the situation. While a stay of the High Court order, in the normal course, would have restored the sense of legitimacy to Indira Gandhi to continue in office, a dismissal of the petition would have further strengthened the opposition parties in the moral sense. The 24 June 1975 order did neither of these. Thus, while the opposition decided to convert their rally, they had planned at the Ramlila grounds the following day, into a decisive event in their battle against what they had begun to characterise as an 'illegitimate' government, Indira Gandhi, along with her son and his close aides, went into a huddle once again. The only person with whom Indira Gandhi would now confabulate with was Siddhartha Shankar Ray, the West Bengal chief minister. Ray had counselled her against resignation on 12 June 1975 and was the one who had planned the appeal in the Supreme Court.

On 25 June 1975, Indira Gandhi seemed to have decided her course. According to Ray, she had spoken to him of 'a drastic and emergent action'. Ray, after chaffing through the Constitution and case laws, informed her of the possibility of a presidential proclamation declaring an internal emergency.

The External Emergency, declared in the wake of the Indo-Pakistan war in December 1971, was not repealed. The government had, even otherwise, assumed powers, to order indiscriminate arrests and detention without trial as long as it was convinced that such arrests were warranted in case of persons who were suspected to be enemy agents. This declaration was issued in December 1971, based on Article 352 of the Constitution. The Defence of India Rules (DIR) was already in operation. Incidentally, the opposition parties had demanded withdrawing the proclamation only a few months before the Allahabad High Court verdict. Ray, in this instance, interpreted Article 352 of the Constitution to contain the scope to suspend such provisions of the Constitution including the Right to Assembly Without Arms (Article 19) and the Right to Recourse to Judicial Remedies against Indiscriminate Arrests (Article 22) even in case of an internal disturbance.

Ray's counsel to Indira Gandhi was that the words 'internal disturbance' in Article 352 can be a reason to declare emergency included political actions against the state. And Indira Gandhi had simply looked forward to this from a legal luminary.

The fact that JP had begun appealing to the armed forces to refuse to obey orders from an 'illegitimate' government had provided Indira Gandhi a handle to present the campaign against her as rebellion and even treason. Morarji Desai, meanwhile, spelt out that the opposition parties planned to *gherao* the Prime Minister and lock her up inside her official residence. In an interview to Oriana Fallaci, an Italian journalist, Desai said: 'We will camp there (outside 1, Safdarjung Road) night and day. We intend to overthrow her, to force her to resign. For good. The lady won't survive this movement of ours.' A five member *Lok Sangarsh Samiti* with Morarji Desai as the chairman and Nanaji Deshmukh, an important leader of the Bharatiya Jan Sangh, as the convener was constituted by JP from the rally at the Ramlila grounds on 25 June 1975.

Indira Gandhi and those with her had characterised the JP movement as fascist even otherwise and the prominent role that was accorded to Nanaji Deshmukh, in the scheme of things that unfolded on 25 June 1975, seemed to lend to her campaign a veneer of secularism too. It is another matter that the Jan Sangh was a legal entity and was registered as a political party, and that public protests and demonstrations are an integral part of the democratic edifice and the opposition campaign on the streets was, by all means, a democratic option.

On 25 June 1975, even while JP and his comrades were at the Ramlila grounds addressing a mammoth gathering, calling upon the crowd that gathered there to launch a *satyagraha* campaign across the country beginning 29 June 1975, Indira Gandhi, along with Ray was busy with her own plans. She drove up to the Rashtrapati Bhawan to meet Fakhruddin Ali Ahmed and brief him about the possibilities and the need to invoke Article 352; she conveyed to the president that the JP movement could well be defined as an 'armed rebellion' and hence warranted a presidential proclamation. Ray accompanied her to the Rashtrapati Bhawan. The two of them also convinced President Ahmed that it was important that the proclamation was issued without insisting on a cabinet resolution. Indira Gandhi convinced Ahmed on the need for secrecy and that the presidential order will be endorsed by the Cabinet within reasonable time.

It may be recalled that Fakhruddin Ali Ahmed, along with Jagjivan Ram, had acted as Indira's henchmen at the AICC meet in Bangalore in July 1969, in her battle against the syndicate bosses. He had remained loyal to her and all this helped him become the president in August 1974. The fact is that Ahmed only needed to be told about the plans and there was hardly any need to make a special effort to convince him on the 'need of the hour'. Thus, even before the opposition rally at the Ramlila grounds was concluded, Indira Gandhi was busy clearing the draft proclamation prepared by P. N. Dhar, the principal secretary in the Prime Minister's Secretariat. The draft was taken to the Rashtrapati Bhawan by her private secretary, R. K. Dhawan, late in the night and Ahmed signed the proclamation. A meeting of the Cabinet was scheduled at 6 a.m. the following day and Indira Gandhi also instructed that intimation about the cabinet meeting shall go only an hour before that.

Dhawan, meanwhile got on the job with Sanjay Gandhi. Minister of State for Home, Om Mehta and the Haryana chief minister, Bansi Lal were also huddled at the prime minister's official residence through the evening when Indira Gandhi was planning the details with Ray. None of the senior members of the cabinet such as home minister Brahmananda Reddy, external affairs minister Y. B. Chavan, agriculture and irrigation minister Jagjivan Ram, finance minister C. Subramaniam and defence minister Swaran Singh were present at 1 Safdarjung Road that evening. They were not even informed of the decision until the Cabinet met at 6 a.m. on 26 June 1975. Similarly, Indira Gandhi did not involve her law minister, H. R. Gokhale, a leading lawyer in his own right, while taking the decision. The cabinet meeting the following morning was a brief affair and the defence minister, Swaran Singh, was the only one to wonder as to whether a separate proclamation was needed when the Emergency declared in December 1971 was in vogue even otherwise. Swaran Singh, was dropped from the Union Cabinet on 21 December 1975 and Bansi Lal replaced him as the defence minister. Swaran Singh, however, was made the chairman of a committee to study and recommend changes to the Constitution. The report and the changes in the form of the 42nd Constitution Amendment will be dealt with in the next section.

While Swaran Singh was allowed to remain in the Union Cabinet for at least six months after the emergency was declared, I. K. Gujral, who held independent charge of the Ministry of Information and Broadcasting did not last there for more than a couple of days after 25 June 1975. It had become mandatory for the All India Radio to broadcast news about the 'massive' crowds in Delhi in support of

Indira Gandhi in the news bulletins every day after 12 June 1975. Gujral, who had begun his political life as an elected corporator in the New Delhi Municipal Corporation, was also among the few backbenchers in the Rajya Sabha who gave company to Indira Gandhi when she entered Parliament in 1964. And this way, he qualified to become a junior minister in Indira's cabinet ever since March 1967.

But Gujral did not fit into Sanjay's scheme of things. As the Minister for Information and Broadcasting, Gujral had failed to prevent some adverse reports on Sanjay's Maruti adventure in the press. The prime minister's son was now concerned about the negative role that the press could play at the time of a 'national emergency.' Gujral too was uncomfortable with Sanjay. On 28 June 1975, Indira Gandhi undertook a minor reshuffle and moved Gujral to the Ministry of Planning. He continued in that position until 12 May 1976, before moving to Moscow as India's ambassador. The information and broadcasting portfolio, in Sanjay's view, had to be headed by a leader-with-a-purpose and Vidya Charan Shukla, who was Minister of State for Planning then, was shifted to the I&B. Shukla's deeds in the ministry during the Emergency, in dealing with the press, was one of the important areas that were taken up by the Shah Commission of Enquiry. Some of them will be narrated later in this section. Gujral, meanwhile, moved on without a whimper.

A narrative on the events after the midnight proclamation will not be complete without talking about the indiscriminate arrests and the crude means by which several newspapers were stopped from being printed that night. Indira Gandhi had reasons to suspect the loyalty of Jagjivan Ram and Swaran Singh on the basis of Intelligence Bureau (IB) reports that the two leaders were in touch with the opposition leaders as well as some others inside the Congress party itself. This was true in case of Jagjivan Ram. He was in touch with the leaders of the opposition for some days before 25 June 1975 but did not pursue that after he realised that his own ambition to become the prime minister was unlikely to be achieved in the given situation. The point is that the opposition, as such, did not add up to any significant number in the Lok Sabha and the number of Congress MPs who were willing to back him against Indira Gandhi was less. However, Indira decided to place him under surveillance of the IB sleuths. Jagjivan Ram had dropped all these plans after some of the Congress MPs, including Chandra Shekhar, Kishen Kant, Ram Dhan and Lakshmi Kanthamma, who had been standing up for JP from inside the Congress, were arrested late in the night on 25 June 1975 and held in confinement charged under MISA.

Even as Indira Gandhi was preparing the presidential proclamation on 24 and 25 June 1975, Sanjay Gandhi, along with Dhawan, Om Mehta and Bansi Lal, was busy making the list of people to be arrested. The Lieutenant Governor of Delhi, Kishen Chand was also involved in this job and the quartet was assisted by officials from the Research and Analysis Wing (RAW). The RAW, meant to be functioning directly under the prime minister had dossiers on all prominent individuals in the political arena including many in Indira Gandhi's party. The business of preparing the list was done in utmost secrecy. So much so, the opposition leaders did not even imagine that they will be put in jail.

Morarji Desai, for instance, was asked by Oriana Fallaci, the Italian journalist, on 23 June 1975 as to whether he apprehended arrest: Desai's reply then was: 'She will never do it. She'd commit suicide'. Fallaci had interviewed Desai a day before Justice Krishna Iyer was to pronounce his verdict on Indira's appeal for staying the Allahabad High Court's verdict. This overconfidence in their own mass appeal and their own calculations that Indira Gandhi will come under siege within her own party, had reduced the opposition leaders into sitting ducks. They were unaware of the fact that Sanjay Gandhi, along with Om Mehta and Dhawan, had even obtained signatures from the Deputy Commissioner of the Delhi Police (the appropriate authority) on blank arrest warrants. P. S. Bhinder, a 1957 batch IPS officer, on whom Bansi Lal had immense trust (and who was a recipient of the Police Medal for Meritorious Services on 26 January 1975), was shifted from Haryana to the Special Branch of the Delhi Police. And Bhinder had the 'authority' to fill up the names of leaders whom he wanted arrested. The quartet, consisting of Sanjay, Bansi Lal, Dhawan and Kishen Chand, had also decided on the law under which the arrests had to be carried out. After thinking aloud for a while that such arrests were possible under Section 107 of the Indian Penal Code (to deal with persons instigating or abetting a crime), the quartet hit upon the Maintenance of Internal Security Act (MISA).

MISA, a preventive detention law passed by Parliament, had come into place in 1971. An Ordinance issued in September 1974 expanded its scope further, providing for arrest and detention without charges for a period of two years. The Ordinance specified that the law would be applied against smugglers, hoarders and black marketeers and the context was the food shortage that affected the people. However, when it came to be used in the context of the Emergency, the regime used a clause in that law by which all that was necessary was an apprehension, in the minds of the police, that the nation and its system would be in danger if such persons were allowed freedom to move about! Unlike the Defence of India Rules (DIR) that had been used against political leaders on several occasions in the past, the quartet preferred MISA because there was no provision in that Act for bail at any time. It was a different matter that the government had assured Parliament, at the time of its enactment in 1971 and later in September 1974, that MISA will be used only against smugglers and hoarders and not used against the political opposition.

JP, who had retired for the day at the Gandhi Peace Foundation premises, after the rally at the Ramlila grounds, was woken up after 2.30 a.m., driven to the Parliament House Police station and then to a government bungalow in Sona, very close to Delhi and in Bansi Lal's Haryana. Chandra Shekhar, Ram Dhan and

Kishen Kant, all of them Congress party MPs, rushed to the Gandhi Peace Foundation on hearing of JP's arrest. They all were arrested from there, taken to the Parliament House Police Station and then taken to Haryana and detained under MISA; a law which was meant to put smugglers and hoarders in jail! The police had also picked up Morarji Desai, from his official residence, around the same time and held him at a guest house in Sona, once again in Bansi Lal's land. It was ensured that Morarji and JP were held in solitary confinement in different rooms in the same bungalow and prevented from communicating with each other.

Among others who were picked up during the night were Jyotirmoy Bosu of the CPI (M), who had earned the wrath of Indira's establishment by raising the Maruti scandal, Charan Singh, who headed the Lok Dal and Raj Narain of the Samyukta Socialist Party. Atal Behari Vajpayee and L. K. Advani of the Jan Sangh and Madhu Dandavate of the Praja Socialist Party were in Bangalore on the night of 25 June 1975 and all of them were arrested under MISA and detained in the Central Jail, Bangalore. All of them were MPs and were in Bangalore as part of a parliamentary delegation. Scores of leaders belonging to these parties were also arrested that night in various states and among them were Mulayam Singh Yadav in Uttar Pradesh and Lalu Prasad Yadav in Bihar. The official count was that 677 persons were arrested and detained under MISA between the time when Emergency was declared and the Union Cabinet approved it at 6 a.m. on 26 June 1975. In other words, most members of the Union Cabinet were not informed of all this until the following morning. It is another matter that none of them tried to make an issue of all that when they assembled at 1, Safdarjung Road, the prime minister's official residence, for the cabinet meeting to formally approve of what had happened through the night.

The arrests were carried out in utmost secrecy and the operation was done in a clinical fashion. Sanjay Gandhi had planned all this, at least a few days before 25 June 1975. The Union Home Secretary, Nirmal Mukherjee (whom Sanjay had considered to be a stickler for rules and procedure) was sent out of the home ministry and S. L. Khurana, a bureaucrat from Rajasthan was posted in his place on 23 June 1975. Khurana was anointed by Sanjay Gandhi and Om Mehta while the Union home minister, Brahmananda Reddy was simply informed of the change.

Only a few leaders evaded arrest. George Fernandes happened to be at Gopalpur, in far-away Orissa, on vacation with his wife. Nanaji Deshmukh, whom JP had appointed as the convener of the Lok Sangarsh Samiti, managed to leave his home in Delhi, hours before the midnight strike, after he received information over phone that he would be arrested soon. Subramanian Swamy, a Jan Sangh member of the Rajya Sabha then managed to escape arrest.

A narrative on the events during the intervening night of June 25–26 1975—the arrests and the fact that it was accomplished without even a semblance of protest or resistance—will not be complete without a brief recall of the measures to ensure that all this were kept away from the public realm. This too was managed by the quartet. Kishen Chand, in his capacity as the Lieutenant Governor of Delhi, had instructed the Delhi Municipal Corporation to switch off electricity in the Bahadur Shah Zafar Marg, the part of the capital city where most newspaper offices were located. This ensured that the newspapers were not printed that evening. Thereby, the news of the opposition rally at the Ramlila grounds, the declaration of the Emergency and the large-scale arrests were kept out from the people in the capital. *The Statesman* and *The Hindustan Times* did not meet with a similar fate because they were located in the New Delhi region and came under the New Delhi Municipal Corporation; and the quartet had failed to switch off power supply there, probably by oversight. The Haryana police made sure that copies of *The Tribune* did not reach the people by burning the newspaper bundles that were sent by trains and road from Chandigarh. This, however, did not happen elsewhere and newspapers announced the Emergency and large-scale arrests in the editions from Bombay, Calcutta and Madras. *The Times of India*, Bombay, for instance carried an obituary on 26 June 1975. It ran as follows: 'D. E. M. O'Cracy, beloved husband of T. Ruth, loving father of L. I. Bertie, brother of Faith, Hope, Justice, expired on 26th June.'

The imposition of pre-publication censorship, for which the orders were issued only on 26 June 1975, ensured that anything that had to do with opposition to the Emergency was not published in the newspapers. The purpose of censorship, as stated in the order, was 'to guide and advise the press to guard against publication of unauthorised, irresponsible or demoralising news items, reports, conjectures or rumours'. The detailed guidelines issued along with the order prohibited, among other things, publication of news such as follows:

- Reproduction of any objectionable matter already published;
- News relating to agitations and violent incidents;
- No reference be made to the places of detention and the names of political personalities detained;
- There should be no indication in the published material that it has been censored;
- Nothing should be published which is likely to bring into disaffection, hatred or contempt or to excite disaffection towards the government established by law in India.

A missive from the chief of UNI to all branches of the news agency, referred to oral orders that he had received from the Censor's office, that banned reports on

- Business to be transacted in the Parliament session;
- The Prime Minister's election case in the Supreme Court; and
- Any statement by any representative of banned parties.

This ensured that the arrest and detention of almost all the opposition leaders and several thousand political workers across the country went without being reported in the newspapers. Radio, which was an arm of the government, would carry only the good things about Indira Gandhi, Sanjay Gandhi and the ruling party. While most of the newspapers agreed to play ball with the regime, such media houses as the *Indian Express* and *The Statesman* in English and some newspapers in Indian languages began bringing out their editions with blank spaces. This too had to stop with the censor officers issuing orders against such a practice. It may be recalled that the Ministry of Information and Broadcasting, was now, headed by V. C. Shukla who had replaced Gujral on 28 June 1975.

Meanwhile, Indira Gandhi addressed the nation through the All India Radio in the morning of 26 June 1975. The address was drafted even before the Cabinet met that morning to approve the decision *post facto*. She blamed the opposition parties and its leaders for having been party to a 'deep and wide conspiracy' aimed at frustrating the 'progressive measures of benefit to the common man and woman of India'. Her address dwelt at length into the several issues such as the nationalisation of banks, the railway strike and the campaigns in Gujarat and Bihar. While she did not refer to the Allahabad High Court judgement in her address, her faithful in the Congress party did not desist from doing that and putting Justice Sinha's name in the list of conspirators.

The Emergency also meant banning political and quasi-political organisations. On 4 July 1975, the Union home ministry notified a list of 26 organisations as banned. Among them were the Rashtriya Swayamsevak Sangh (RSS), the Jamaat-e-Islamia-e-Hind, the Communist Party of India (Marxist-Leninist) otherwise called the Naxalites and the Anand Marg, which was more of a cult rather than an organised political outfit. The ban was a means to arrest all those the state wanted. But then, such unlimited power to arrest alone was not sufficient. The Constitution that contained Article 352 also guaranteed to its citizens such fundamental rights as Article 14 (Equality before Law and Equal Protection) Article 21 (that guaranteed against deprivation of life or liberty except by duly established legal procedure) and Article 22 (that none shall be detained without being informed of the grounds for detention and by this the right to legal remedy). All this was done away with by a Presidential Order on 27 June. The order suspended the right of the citizens to move a court for enforcement of any of the Fundamental Rights. In other words, the constitutional provision for writs under Articles 32 and 226 was suspended by the 27 June 1975 order!

An Ordinance on 29 June 1975 amended the MISA. By this amendment, the police was not required to state the grounds before detaining anyone under the Act. By this, another Fundamental Right guaranteed by Article 22 of the Constitution was also suspended. It meant that the police was not even bound to inform the grounds of arrest and detention before sending anyone to jail. As it was, all those arrested and detained under MISA were denied of the right to be informed about the grounds on which they were in jail. There were as many as 35,000 persons detained under this law by this time and at least 13,000 out of them were known leaders and prominent members of the various political parties. In a few months after June 1975, the total number of arrests under MISA and DIR went up to 1,11,000 across the country and this excluded the number of smugglers and petty offenders. The detentions and the annulment of the constitutional rights by Presidential Orders and Ordinances were challenged in the courts and all that revealed another dirty face of the Emergency.

Tampering with the Law

The arrest and detention of the opposition leaders and a few from the Congress party was not enough. Justice Krishna Iyer, after all, had given only an interim order on 24 June 1975 and posted the case involving Indira's election to the Lok Sabha, before a larger bench. Justice Iyer had also thrown sufficient hints on what could be the fallout of the appeal, given the law under which the Allahabad High Court had disqualified her, when he said, 'Draconian laws do not cease to be law in courts but must alert a wakeful and quick-acting legislature.' In other words, Justice Iyer did warn Indira Gandhi of the possibility of the apex court upholding Justice Sinha's judgement, as long as the Representation of the People's Act remained what it was. Indira Gandhi was quick to take the cue. In addition, Palkhiwala, who had taken up her brief before the vacation judge, Justice Krishna Iyer, declined to pursue the case on her behalf after she declared the Emergency and suspended the rights guaranteed by the Constitution. She had to do something drastic once again because the case was posted for hearing before a five-judge Bench comprising Chief Justice A. N. Ray and Justices H. R. Khanna, K. K. Mathew, Y. V. Chandrachud and M. H. Beg, for 11 August 1975.

Convinced over the imperative for changing the law, Indira Gandhi decided to convene a session of Parliament. The Congress Parliamentary Party, now reduced to being her handmaiden and the few critiques from within the party sent to jail (and thus ensuring that others will not speak out against her actions), she was confident of getting any law passed. High on the agenda was to effect the necessary change in the Representation of the Peoples Act, 1951, so that Yashpal Kapoor being her election agent in Rae Bareli in 1971 and also employing government agencies in the erection of rostrums for public meetings during election campaign, were not violations in the eyes of the law. It was also necessary that this amendment be declared retro-effective so that the Supreme Court Bench looked at her appeal in the light of the law. This business of amending a law and making it retro-effective was, in any case, permitted insofar as civil laws are concerned. However, in terms of public morality, this was an unethical step.

The session was convened on 21 July 1975. And in order to ensure that Indira Gandhi was not put to any embarrassment, the government moved a resolution on day one that 'only urgent and important government business' be transacted in the two houses. This meant that such provisions as Calling Attention Motion, Private Members Bills and even the Question Hour were suspended. This was criticised by those opposition members who were present in Parliament (and not in jail) but the Ministry for Information and Broadcasting had ensured, by way of a circular, that the papers did not publish the text of any speech by any member from the opposition. The press, however, was free to report as to whether a particular member voted against a motion. That was all.

In that way, the speeches by such opposition MPs as A. K. Gopalan and Somnath Chaterjee (both CPI[M]), Era Sezhian (DMK), P. G. Mavlankar (Independent), H.M.Patel (Lok Dal) and Mohan Dharia (by then expelled from Indira's Congress), recording their opposition to the Emergency, went unreported in the following day's newspapers. The motion for approval of the Emergency was moved by Jagjivan Ram and the Lok Sabha gave its approval without much of a debate. The motion was moved in the Rajya Sabha the following day and passed within a couple of hours. Samyukta Socialist Party's MP, N. G. Goray then declared that the opposition would boycott the rest of the session.

This was followed by the 38th Constitution Amendment by which the judiciary was barred from any review of the proclamation of the Emergency and the various ordinances that were issued suspending the fundamental rights guaranteed by the Constitution. The amendment was passed by both the houses on 22 July 1975 and received the presidential assent on 1 August 1975.

The formality of obtaining Parliament's approval for the Emergency, a constitutional necessity, and an amendment taking away the judiciary's powers to review the various proclamations was not Indira's core concern. She had to do something to ensure that the Supreme Court quashed the Allahabad High Court verdict. This came in the form of yet another amendment to the Constitution. The 39th Constitution Amendment Bill, introduced in the Lok Sabha on 7 August 1975, just four days before Indira Gandhi's appeal was to come before the Supreme Court, was passed the same day without any substantial debate. The Rajya Sabha approved it the following day. The Congress party-ruled state governments had convened a special sitting of the legislative assemblies on Saturday, 9 August 1975, where the amendment was endorsed without debate. It became the law, after President Fakhruddin Ali Ahmed gave assent on 10 August 1975. The Union Law Minister, H. R. Gokhale piloted the 39th Constitution Amendment, which took away the powers of the higher judiciary to adjudicate on election petitions against the prime minister and the speaker of the Lok Sabha. Article 329A, which was inserted into the Constitution by this amendment, provided that an election petition against an MP would abate were that individual to become the prime minister or the speaker. It also added that disputes over the election of the prime minister, the speaker, the president and the vice president shall be decided by a body appointed by Parliament.

Mohan Dharia, who was sacked by Indira Gandhi from her cabinet for recording his disdain against the assault on JP (in November 1974), stood up in the Lok Sabha on 7 August to place on record that the bill was 'a surrender of parliamentary democracy to the coming dictatorship'. But then, neither this nor any other voice of dissent was printed in the following day's newspapers, thanks to the censorship guidelines. The Indira Gandhi establishment, meanwhile, placed all these legislations and the changes it had effected to the Representation of the Peoples Act, 1951 (that expenditure incurred by 'friends' and 'others' in the course of an election campaign was not to be included while adding up the expenditure incurred by the candidate for the purpose of determining the expenditure and the ceiling as laid down in the law), in the Ninth Schedule of the Constitution and thus immunising them from any disputes in the judiciary.

All that was intended was achieved. The Supreme Court adjourned the hearing on Indira Gandhi's appeal on 11 August, after Raj Narain's counsel asked for a verdict on the 39th Constitution Amendment first and posted the case for 25 August 1975. While Indira Gandhi was represented by Asoke Sen (after Palkhiwala declined to pursue the brief), Shanti Bhushan, on behalf of Raj Narain, put forth the plea that the act of rendering the amendments to the Constitution and the election laws as retro-effective violated the Basic Structure doctrine. This plea, however ethical it was, did not stand the test of the law. And on 7 November 1975, the five-judge Bench upheld the election of Indira Nehru Gandhi from Rae Bareli. There were instances, in the course of the hearing, when three judges—Mathew, Khanna and Chandrachud—agreed with Shanti Bhushan that changing the law in the middle of a case was unfair. But then, the Bench could not have taken their concerns to fairness and were bound by the legal framework. The Bench, however, struck down Clause 4 of Article 329A that provided immunity to the prime minister and the speaker from the election petitions being adjudicated by the court. Even here, Justice Beg dissented from the others and upheld the 39th Constitution Amendment *in toto*, while the others (and the majority that way) struck down the portion that sought to immunise the prime minister and the speaker, from petitions challenging their election in the higher judiciary.

The legal challenge to the Emergency did not stop here. The MISA prisoners in Bangalore, among whom were Madhu Dandavate, A. B. Vajpayee and L. K. Advani, approached the Karnataka High Court on grounds that they were not served with the grounds for detention when they were picked up late in the night on 25 June 1975 and that the Ordinance issued on 27 June 1975, amending MISA to exempt the police from disclosing the grounds for detention, could not be applied in their case because they were arrested a day before the Ordinance was proclaimed. The plea was to be taken up by the Karnataka High Court and it was clear that the arrests will be quashed because criminal law cannot be applied retro-effective. Indira's regime found a way out. They were released, just before the case was to come up before the Karnataka High Court on 17 July 1975, and arrested afresh immediately. This time it was legal to detain them without disclosing the grounds for the detention under the provisions of the 27 June Presidential Order.

In any case, the Karnataka High Court admitted a habeas corpus petition, on their behalf, under Article 226 of the Constitution. Similar petitions were moved in High Courts across the country. All these petitions challenged the constitutional validity of the 27 June 1975 Presidential Order barring the courts from entertaining petitions seeking a writ of habeas corpus. Among them was one in the Jabalpur Bench of the Madhya Pradesh High Court moved by S. K. Shukla. The court admitted the petition and issued a writ of habeas corpus on 1 September 1975. The verdict in this case—Shiv Kant Shukla vs Assistant District Magistrate, Jabalpur—was challenged by the government in the Supreme Court. A five-member Bench consisting of Chief Justice A. N. Ray along with Justices H. R. Khanna, M. H. Beg, Y. V. Chandrachud and P. N. Bhagwati, before whom all the cases of that kind from the various High Courts were bundled together, passed its order on 28 April 1976. In a four-to-one judgement, the majority upheld the 27 June Presidential Order as valid and denied to the political prisoners the right to legal remedy against arbitrary arrests and detention. Justice Khanna, who dissented with the majority, had to pay the price. Despite being the seniormost judge, he was superseded by Justice Beg in January 1977 to become the Chief Justice. Khanna resigned in protest.

Justice Khanna displayed a lot of courage and declared: 'As observed by Chief Justice Huges, Judges are not there simply to decide cases, but to decide them as they think they should be decided, and while it may be regrettable that they cannot always agree, it is better that their independence should be maintained and recognised than that unanimity should be secured through its sacrifice. A dissent in a Court of last resort, to use his words, is an appeal to the brooding spirit of the law, to the intelligence of a future day, when a later decision may possibly correct the error into which the dissenting Judge believes the court to have been betrayed.'

The story will not be complete without quoting what the others stated to justify their verdict. Chief Justice Ray admonished the counsel for the detenues who brought to mind the Nazi gas chambers and said: 'People who have faith in themselves and in their country will not paint pictures of diabolic distortion and mendacious malignment of the governance of the country.' Justice Beg said: 'We understand that the care and concern bestowed by the State authorities upon the welfare of detenues who are well housed, well fed and well treated, is almost maternal.' Justice Chandrachud went a step further to say: 'Counsel after counsel expressed the fear that during the emergency , the executive may whip and strip and starve the detenue and if this be our judgement, even shoot him down. Such misdeeds have not tarnished the record of Free India and I have a diamond-bright, diamond-hard hope that such things will never come to pass.'

While all those who appealed against their detention (despite losing the case) survived to be released in early 1977, there were others like P. Rajan, a student of the Regional Engineering College, Calicut who was killed due to the torture inflicted on him while in police custody. His dead body was never found. Snehlatha Reddy, an eminent film actor from Bangalore was arrested, detained and subjected to torture. Due to the physical pain and the mental agony that was inflicted on her during the detention, she passed away within days after her release. There was also the case of Lawrence Fernandes, picked up from his home in Bangalore during the night, held in illegal custody for a few days, beaten up continuously leading to several fractures all over his body and finally sent to jail as a MISA prisoner. Fernandes was subjected to all this because he was in touch with Leila Kabir and her son. Leila was wife of George Fernandes who managed to escape arrest on 25 June 1975 and was leading a group of people resisting the Emergency. We will discuss his role in detail later on in this chapter. For now, the story is that Lawrence Fernandes lived for long after the Emergency was withdrawn as a mental wreck. Udaya Shankar, a college student from Mangalore, was held in custody without a warrant, beaten very badly until his body turned blue. He was left in that condition without medical attention after that. Rabin Kalitha, a CPI (M) activist in Guwahati was picked up, tortured and was held in handcuffs even when he was hospitalised for treatment. He died in hospital. Chitti Babu and Sattur Balakrishnan, two young detenues in Tamil Nadu were killed due to police torture.

This, probably, was the parental care that Justice Beg talked about. There was also the story of Bhoomiah and Kiste Gowd, two young members of the CPI (ML), who were summarily tried and hanged to death on 1 December 1975 in Andhra Pradesh. There are also tales (and no records for obvious reasons) of young men killed in 'encounters' with the police across S. S. Ray's West Bengal. This, however, preceded the Emergency and the hunt for Naxalites continued through the Emergency too.

The implication of the 28 April 1976 verdict by the Supreme Court was that Rajan's father, Professor Eachara Warrier, could not seek a writ of habeas corpus (even to realise that his son was dead) until Indira's Congress was defeated in the elections and the Emergency was lifted on 21 March 1977. JP, now on parole because his health had deteriorated while being held at Chandigarh and diagnosed to be suffering from renal failure, had this to say about the apex court's verdict: 'The decision has put out the last flickering candle of individual freedom. Mrs Gandhi's dictatorship both in its personalised and institutionalised forms is now almost complete.' But Indira Gandhi herself did not think that way. She had miles to go.

The stamp of approval by the apex court that Articles 14, 21 and 22 of the Constitution did not operate in case of the Emergency prisoners meant that the bold pronouncements by a number of High Court judges, across the country, ordering the release of MISA detenues on bail and quashing the charges against them, were nullified. All those arrests and subsequent detentions without charge were now perfectly legal. But Indira Gandhi's establishment did not stop there. Those behind the Emergency were clear that the regime could be sustained only by a sense of fear stalking everyone and everywhere. Indira Gandhi's cheerleaders in the party such as K. P. Unnikrishnan and A. R. Antulay had begun talking about the need to formulate some principles to check the judiciary and the need to contain its powers to interpret the Constitution, even while the hearing was on in the Supreme Court. The Congress president, D. K. Baruah, had circulated a 'concept paper' among the members of the bar concerning the power of judicial review, the writ jurisdiction and Parliament's power to amend the Constitution in the same period.

With the leaders of the opposition parties behind bars with no scope for judicial remedy, it was time now for the Emergency establishment to deal with the several High Court judges who admitted writ petitions and let the prisoners out on bail. And as many as 16 High Court judges were transferred to far away locations in May and June 1976. While there was nothing in the law against transferring High Court judges, the established convention was that such transfers were ordered only where the concerned judge sought for it. This convention was broken to 'teach a lesson' to those judges who did not dance to the tunes set by the Emergency establishment.

Among them were the two judges in the Karnataka High Court—D. M. Chandrashekhar and Sadanandaswamy—who quashed the detention orders on Madhu Dandavate, Vajpayee and Advani; Justice Rangarajan of the Delhi High Court, who ordered the release of journalist Kuldip Nayar (arrested for holding a meeting of working journalists at the Press Club of India to protest against the pre-publication censorship); Justice A. P. Sen of the Madhya Pradesh High Court, who admitted and issued a writ of habeas corpus in the S. K. Shukla vs ADM, Jabalpur case; and Justice Rajinder Sachar of the Delhi High Court. There was the case of Justice S. H. Sheth being transferred out of the Gujarat High Court. He filed a writ petition seeking for quashing the transfer order. The petition was against the government and the Chief Justice of India. Sheth was represented in this case by eminent constitutional lawyer H. M. Seervai. This case, popularly known as the Judges Transfer case, remains unresolved to this day. Justice P. M. Mukhi, of the Gujarat High Court died due to cardiac arrest that he suffered on receipt of the transfer order. In any case, the number of judges who suffered this 'penal' transfer remained at 16.

All this turned out to be a dress rehearsal to the final onslaught on the Constitution and the Judiciary in the form of the 42nd Constitution Amendment, which was passed in December 1976. Meanwhile, the life of the fifth Lok Sabha, which was only until March 1976, was extended by one more year by a resolution in July 1975 and yet another extension was obtained in November 1976.

The 42nd Constitution Amendment: Restricting the Judiciary

That the Indira Gandhi establishment was irritated with the Basic Structure doctrine in the Kesavananda Bharti verdict has been brought out in the previous chapter. The ghost, insofar as Indira Gandhi was concerned, continued to haunt her and the Supreme Court's decision to strike down Article 329A, inserted by the 39th Constitution Amendment, was seen by the establishment as a threat to Indira's designs to emerge as the absolute leader. The judiciary had to be contained. But then, it was necessary to couch this in a language that would suggest holier objectives than the desire to clip the judiciary to size. Indira, for long, had fancied herself to be a Jeanne d'Arc. Jawaharlal Nehru mentions this bit about his daughter in at least two of his letters to her. On 26 October 1930, he writes: 'Do you remember how fascinated you were when you first read the story of Jeanne d'Arc, and how your ambition was to be something like her?' And once again, on 1 July 1932 he wrote: 'You know something about Jeanne d'Arc, the maid of Orleans. She is a heroine of yours.' Indira herself would state the following sometime later: 'All my games were political games; I was, like Jeanne d'Arc, perpetually being burned at the stake.'

It has been mentioned, in the previous section, that the Congress president, D. K. Baruah, had circulated a paper titled 'A Fresh Look at Our Constitution—Some Suggestions', among a cross section of lawyers and civil society activists. It was prepared by A. R. Antulay, one of Indira's cheerleaders. It argued the merits of a Presidential system against the Parliamentary democracy and also thought aloud on the need to contain the scope for judicial review on a range of issues. The paper was circulated, without anyone owning it up, towards the end of 1975 and around the same time when the Supreme Court was hearing Indira Gandhi's election petition and the validity of the 39th Constitution Amendment. Meanwhile, the law minister, H.R.Gokhale, addressing the National Forum of Lawyers (a Congress party outfit), at Chandigarh, urged them to think over the obstructions placed by the judiciary to the legislative initiatives against poverty and suggested that the Congress party session scheduled at Guwahati in December 1975 consider raising the demand for scrapping the right to property from among the Fundamental Rights. When the party met at Guwahati (the venue was named Kamagata Maru) in December 1975, it passed a resolution to set up a committee to recommend substantive changes in the Constitution.

D. K. Baruah appointed Swaran Singh (sent out of Indira's Cabinet on 21 December 1975) as head of the panel to study the Constitution, the experience with the judiciary and recommend amendments to enable the statute turn more responsive to the task of poverty alleviation and other such measures. The purpose behind this committee was to obtain a set of recommendations that will ensure (i) immunity to Indira from legal challenges such as the Allahabad High Court verdict of 12 June 1975, (ii) that she is rendered immune from any prosecution and (iii) unfettered powers to her actions in the sense that they are not called into question by the higher judiciary. 'Our basic fight is against the entrenched privilege of the few,' she said speaking at the Guwahati session. The Swaran Singh Committee was made up of 12 members and all of them were Indira Gandhi loyalists. Apart from Swaran Singh, A. R. Antulay, S. S. Ray, Rajni Patel, H. R. Gokhale, V. A. Syed Mohammed, V. N. Gadgil, C. M. Stephen, D. P. Singh, Dinesh Goswami, Vasanth Sathe and B. N. Banerjee constituted the committee. They were all known to be advocating unfettered powers to the supreme leader. Margaret Alva, who would rise to become one of Sonia Gandhi's confidantes years later, attended the meetings of the committee on behalf of party president Baruah.

After a few meetings and working under utmost secrecy, the Swaran Singh Committee report was presented to the Congress president Baruah on 3 April 1976. Baruah, after 'consultations' with his party men, commended the report to be presented by Swaran Singh himself at the AICC on 28–29 May 1976. The Swaran Singh Committee had, among several things, included a categorical statement against the Presidential form of government. Interestingly, Indira Gandhi herself had asserted against the Presidential form in her statement at the time of a visit by the French president, Jacques Chirac in February 1976. Similarly, Rajni Patel, who had tremendous influence in the Swaran Singh Committee (and also while drafting the 42nd Constitution Amendment later on), stressed the need for changes that would ensure a system where the prime minister elected by the popular vote was not subjected to the vexatious pulls and pressures. Patel had made this point while addressing a convention organised by the Bombay Regional Committee of the Congress party. The convention on 'Disciplined Democracy', held in February 1976, was inaugurated by Indira Gandhi. In other words, the Swaran Singh Committee had received clear signals on the issue.

Here are some of the substantial changes recommended by the Swaran Singh Committee to the Constitution:

- Under Article 71 and 329-A of the Constitution, election disputes relating to the offices of President, Vice President, Prime Minister and Speaker are to be decided by an authority or body to be created by a law of Parliament. It is felt that the Constitution should provide for another body or authority to determine all questions of disqualification (including the period of such disqualification) of

Members, both of Parliament and of State Legislatures. This body or authority may consist of 9 members, 3 each from the Rajya Sabha and Lok Sabha and 3 to be nominated by the President.

- The constituent power of the Parliament to amend the Constitution as provided in Article 368 should not be open to question or challenge. Though the language of Article 368, as it stands at present, is clear and categoric, it is considered necessary that the matter should be placed beyond doubt. Hence, a new clause may be inserted in Article 368 to the effect that any amendment of the Constitution, passed in accordance with the requirements specified in that Article, shall not be called in question in any court on any ground.
- Article 31-C provides that no law giving effect to the directive principles specified in clause (*b*) or clause (*c*) of Article 39 shall be deemed to be void on the ground that it contravenes Articles 14, 19 or 31. It is proposed that the scope of the present Article 31-C should be widened so as to cover legislation for implementation of all or any of the directive principles enumerated in Part IV of the Constitution, and that such legislation should not be called in question on the ground of infringement of any of the fundamental rights contained in Part III. Provision should, however, be made that no such law shall affect the special safeguards or rights conferred on the minorities, or the Scheduled Castes, the Scheduled Tribes or Other Backward Classes under the Constitution.
- At present, the constitutional validity of a law, whether Central or State, may be challenged in any High Court or in the Supreme Court. The Committee is of the opinion that the Constitution should be suitably amended so as to provide that the constitutional validity of a Central law and any rule, regulation or bye-law made thereunder may be challenged only in the Supreme Court.
- The number of judges of the Supreme Court who are to sit for the purpose of deciding any case involving a question of constitutional validity of a law shall be not less than seven, and the decision of the Court declaring a law invalid must have the support of not less than two-thirds of the number of judges constituting the Bench. The number of judges of a High Court for the same purpose shall be not less than five, and the decision of the Court declaring a law invalid must be supported by not less than two-thirds of the number of judges constituting the Bench. In a High Court where the total number of judges is less than five the full court shall sit, and the decision as to invalidity of a law should have the support of the whole court.

After some discussion in the AICC, the report was also sent to the chief ministers of several states. On 1 September 1976, the law minister, H. R. Gokhale introduced the 42nd Constitution Amendment Bill in the Lok Sabha. The bill contained all that Swaran Singh had recommended and even more. Apart from such changes in the Preamble of the Constitution where the words *Socialist* and *Secular* were inserted, the Amendment rendered the higher judiciary subservient to Parliament. It was ensured that the Basic Structure doctrine, enunciated by the Supreme Court, in the Kesavananda Bharti case, was negated and Parliament assumed absolute powers insofar as amending the Constitution was concerned.

That the Emergency establishment intended to clip the wings of the higher judiciary was clear from the statements made by Indira Gandhi herself and her cheer leaders in the Parliament when the bill was introduced and debated. Antulay, for instance, discovered a 'conspiracy' in which members of the higher judiciary were involved. Speaking in the Rajya Sabha, Antulay said: 'The conspiracy started in 1967; the Chief Justice resigned to contest for the Presidency and it continued through the intervening years in the attempts to thwart Mrs. Gandhi'. He referred to Justice K. Subba Rao who was the combined opposition's candidate against Zakir Hussain. Baruah went on to add: 'It is the political ambition that entered by the portals of the Supreme Court and judicial restraint and discretion escaped by the window when a Chief Justice campaigned for the Presidency'. Indira Gandhi herself took this a step further in the Lok Sabha to describe Justice Rao's decision to contest for the President's post as 'a blatant indication, not only of the political bias of some of the judiciary, but of their intention to be involved in and interfere in politics'.

It was clearly evident from all this that the concerns were not about the Constitution and the well-being of the people but was about what was good for the Congress party and its supreme leader, Indira Gandhi. And when this was taking place in the two houses of Parliament, the opposition was not there even to register its objection. They had announced boycott of the session. There were a few exceptions though. P. G. Mavlankar declared that it was not merely an amendment to the Constitution but an exercise to alter the Constitution. Mavlankar called it 'a dishonest move on the part of the Government.' Similarly, Kishen Kant, who continued to be a member of Indira's Congress party in Parliament put his decision to boycott on hold and attended the session. In a spirited defence of democracy, Kant concluded his speech in the Rajya Sabha saying: 'People's rights have no place when a dictator wants to take up a programme.'

On 11 November 1976, the 42nd Constitution Amendment was passed by the Rajya Sabha with 190 votes in favour of the amendment and no one to vote against. The outcome was the same in the Lok Sabha too. The bill was passed with 366 votes in favour and just four against the motion. The various state governments went about ratifying the amendment soon after and it received the president's assent on 18 December 1976. The 42nd Amendment changed the Constitution in such a manner that the judiciary was rendered subservient to Parliament and the manner in which the amendment was carried out, revealed so categorically that the Union Cabinet and the Congress party in Parliament were willing to dance to Indira Gandhi's tunes. The ruling party also moved a motion in the same session to extend the life of the fifth Lok Sabha by one more year. Elections were now due only in March 1978.

The most striking feature of all this is the fact that the Emergency regime went about nullifying some of the essential features of the Constitution and pulling down the edifice with impunity and was doing all this in the name of defending and saving the Constitution from its enemies.

Meanwhile, the Emergency was not just about changing the Constitution. Nor was it restricted to arrest and detention of the leaders and the cadre of the political parties. It was not merely a period when the press was told not to report anything that was against the interests of the regime. The Emergency was also about the administration acting against the people. Let us look into some of it in the following section.

Some Features of the Emergency Regime

On 1 July 1976, Indira Gandhi came out with a 20-point programme that was to guide the civil administration in the course of the emergency. On the face of it, all the 20 points were simple thoughts with the best of intentions. They were:

1. Scaling down prices of essential commodities and streamlining their production and distribution
2. Economising government expenditure
3. Implementing agricultural land ceilings and speeding up distribution of surplus land and compilation of land records
4. Stepping up house site availability to the landless and weaker sections
5. Declaring bonded labour illegal
6. Planning for liquidation of rural indebtedness and a moratorium on recovery of debts from the landless labourers, the small farmers and the artisans
7. Reviewing laws on minimum agricultural wages
8. Bringing five million additional hectares under irrigation and preparing a national programme for use of underground water
9. Increasing power production
10. Developing the handloom sector and improving quality and supply of people's cloth
11. Effecting 'socialisation' of urban and urbanisable land and having ceiling on ownership and possession of vacant land
12. Having special squads for valuation of conspicuous consumption and prevention of tax evasion and summary trials and deterrent punishment of economic offenders
13. Special legislation for confiscation of smugglers' properties
14. Liberalising investment procedures and taking action against misuse of import licenses
15. New schemes for workers associations in industry
16. National permit scheme for road transport

17. Income-tax relief; exemption limit placed at Rs 8,000 per annum.
18. Essential commodities at controlled prices to students in hostels
19. Books and stationery at controlled prices
20. New apprenticeship scheme to enlarge employment and training, especially for the weaker sections

Recall that Indira had use for the poor Indian and the landless agricultural worker every time she had a fight with her detractors. It was bank nationalisation during her battle to establish in the Congress party in 1969. It was *garibi hatao* in 1971 and the 20-point programme during the Emergency. The Emergency establishment, however, had other uses.

For instance, the first of the 20 points—scaling down prices of essential commodities—led to an order that shops selling goods displayed the prices prominently. In the context of rising prices of commodities that prevailed in the years before the Emergency, this measure seemed radical. But then, the experience of the Emergency was that it came in handy for the regime to serve another purpose. An illustration of this was as follows. P. N. Haksar, who had guided Indira Gandhi for several years and was with her in her battle against her detractors in the Congress party, had an uncle running a store selling furniture, curtain material and such items in New Delhi's Connaught Place. Sanjay Gandhi did not like Haksar and was unhappy with his mother's dependence on him. Haksar was also known to have conveyed his displeasure over Sanjay's activities to Indira Gandhi. On 10 July 1975, merely a fortnight after the Emergency was imposed and several months before the 20-point programme was announced, Pandit Brothers was raided by inspectors from the Commercial Taxes Department of the Delhi Government. The raids did not yield anything. The orders, however, came from Dhawan and hence something had to be done. A second raid on 14 July 1975 ended in the arrest of R. N. Haksar and K. P. Mushran. They were charged, under sections from the Delhi Essential Articles Rules, because some goods there in the shop did not have a price tag. The 80-years-old uncle of P. N. Haksar and his brother-in-law Mushran were held in jail for three days and were released only after Indira intervened. Mrs Gandhi was informed of this by Aruna Asaf Ali, an old socialist and a social worker at that time.

There were many more raids across the country and not all of them were such acts of vendetta. A Voluntary Disclosure Scheme announced by the finance ministry yielded close to Rs 250 crore as Income and Wealth Tax in that one year. At least 2,000 smugglers were sent to jail during the first year of the Emergency and hoarding and black marketing came to an end. This was because everyone who indulged in such activities was scared of the consequences. And the inflation rate, which had reached as high as 30 per cent in the previous year, came down to 10 per cent. Government officers worked and trains ran on time. The raid at Pandit Brothers, meanwhile, conveyed to the small and big shopkeepers in

Delhi that they were all vulnerable. It is also a fact that the shopkeepers ended up paying off the Youth Congress cadre for protection.

The Emergency regime and the rule of law did not extend to some and especially to Sanjay Gandhi. The Maruti story has been told earlier in this book. The Emergency provided Sanjay with scope to further his prospects through Maruti. After having extracted as much as Rs 10 lakh for himself from Maruti through the Maruti Technical Services (of which Sonia Gandhi was the managing director), Sanjay set up another firm in June 1975. Maruti Heavy Vehicles, was registered as a 'small-scale enterprise', and meant to produce road rollers. Like in the case of the small car project, Sanjay had no knowledge about the machines that make a road roller. But then, he could purchase Ford engines from companies that had import licenses, fix them into the old and rusted bodies of road rollers that were junked, paint them as new and sell them to the Public Works Department of the various state governments. The Congress chief ministers bought these, because that helped them get close to the 'prince'. Those industrialists, who had the import licenses, were lending those licenses to facilitate Sanjay get those scrap engines from the Ford as this would help them escape the law and the punitive measures for abusing the import licenses. All this came out in the course of the Shah Commission's hearings but then Indira Gandhi came back to power in 1980 and these findings were not acted upon.

The fact is that all the laws and the enthusiasm by the authorities against smugglers did not have any effect on Sanjay Gandhi's operations. Meanwhile, Sanjay Gandhi was busy with other things. His small car project did not go beyond the drawing board stage even now. Indira's son, after all, was now busy running the Emergency establishment with his mother. And the Prime Minister just let him do what he liked. As if her 20-point programme was not enough to save the nation, Sanjay Gandhi came up with his own five-point programme.

1. Increase adult literacy (and the slogan was 'Each One Teach One')
2. Abolish dowry
3. End the caste system
4. Beautify the environment (slum clearance and tree plantation being the priority), and last but not the least being
5. A radical programme of family planning.

While the first three of the five points did not receive any great attention, the Emergency establishment was indeed enthusiastic with the idea of making the cities beautiful and containing the population. Sanjay Gandhi had concrete ideas on these. The Union Health Minister, Dr Karan Singh, for instance announced a National Population Policy in April 1976. We shall deal with this later. The policy, in any case, simply internalised whatever Sanjay and his band of activists had been carrying out with gusto since June 1975. The idea of making the cities beautiful was one of the most prominent agenda for those around Sanjay Gandhi and the way they went about it showed what the Emergency meant to the man on the streets.

The arrival of Kishen Chand into Sanjay's inner circle has been discussed earlier in this chapter. Sanjay Gandhi had also posted a young IAS officer and his friend, Navin Chawla, as Chand's secretary. Navin Chawla, years later, would end up as an Election Commissioner after the Congress came to power in the Centre in May 2004. During the Emergency, Chawla would command the Delhi Development Authority (DDA) and along with its vice chairman, Jagmohan (who would become a Union Minister in the Atal Behari Vajpayee cabinet between 1998 and 2004), was as enthusiastic as Sanjay Gandhi was, about removing all the slums and the people who 'defaced' parts of Delhi.

The story is that Sanjay Gandhi, accompanied by Jagmohan, in one of their tours of Delhi, happened to stop by at the Turkman Gate in the old Delhi area. And as the 'Prince' surveyed that part of the city from there, he was irritated by a maze of tenements throughout the stretch from the Turkman Gate to the Jama Masjid. Sanjay decreed that the grand old mosque should be seen, without the maze of tenements, from where he stood. It meant demolishing the several hundred ramshackle houses, shacks and shops that existed there over the years. They all belonged to the Muslim inhabitants of that part of the city. Jagmohan swung into action. On 13 April 1976, the DDA team was there, with bulldozers, to clean up the place. As the demolitions continued, on 19 April 1976 the inhabitants there resorted to a demonstration. The police fired and after a few hours of firing, leaving at least 150 dead (the police claimed only six dead but the Shah Commission recorded the death toll to be 150), that part of the city was ready to be beautified. The inhabitants were provided house sites (measuring 25 square metres), building material and ration cards across the Yamuna. Over 70,000 people, thus displaced, were provided free transport to carry themselves and their belongings to their new location!

Similar programmes were undertaken in other cities too. Agra was chosen for similar activities and so was Varanasi. Slums were cleared in Bombay too. The censorship guidelines ensured that none of these acts, gross violations of human rights in every sense of the term, were reported in the newspapers. But then, the people who suffered displacement had a bitter taste of the Emergency. So did those who came to hear the stories about these high-handed measures through word of mouth. If no one reacted to any of these, it was due to fear. The people, by and large, had come to know, even if the newspapers did not report, the indiscriminate arrests since the night of 25 June 1975. In the one year after the proclamation of the Emergency, Amnesty International recorded that, at least 1,10,000 persons were arrested and detained. This included at least 153 journalists from across the country.

The story of high-handedness will not be complete without touching upon, as briefly as possible, the zeal with which the Emergency establishment went about with the sterilisation drive, which was indeed the one that Sanjay Gandhi seemed to fancy most from out of his five-point programme, apart from beautification of towns and cities.

Some improvement in the health-care system, better levels of nutrition (in comparison with the past) and public hygiene in the couple of decades after independence had led to the death rate falling and this was among the causes for a rise in India's population. In the early Seventies, it grew at an annual rate of 120 lakh. Sanjay Gandhi was not happy with this. He was convinced that India's growth into a powerful nation was dependent on containing its population. His thinking or wishes would turn into government policies with the ministers and the bureaucrats wanting to be in his good books. The cheapest way to contain the population growth, they found, was sterilisation. The men were chosen for this more often than the women and vasectomy was the simple way out. The Emergency came as a blessing to those who favoured this but were unable to carry out sterilisation because of the resistance to such drives in ordinary times.

In April 1976, Health Minister Karan Singh announced the New Population Policy that aimed to bring down the annual birth rate from 35 per thousand at that time to 25 per thousand by 1984. It also announced incentives to those who opted for vasectomy. But then, this was not enough and the story of Sanjay Gandhi's 'achievements' in this regard was one of large-scale coercion, abuse of authority and of scores of men sterilised under duress. All that would come to haunt Sanjay Gandhi and the Congress party, just like the displacement of slum dwellers, in the 1977 elections. The Emergency, for a lot of people, meant the vasectomy tents that came up in the cities and particularly near the slum clusters and the mobile clinics that went around villages to conduct sterilisation operations on anyone and everyone found there. Activists of the Youth Congress were given the job of 'Family Planning Motivators'. Among them was Ruksana Sultana, a model and one of Sanjay's many friends, who enjoyed motivating Muslim men and even the maulanas to opt for vasectomy. Ruksana, and many others like her, were even allowed to run sterilisation clinics in cities including Delhi.

Government servants were forced into 'motivating' a specified number of people for sterilisation and the Shah Commission recorded depositions that revealed that the vagabonds, the beggars and the various other sections of the poor were forced into the sterilisation clinics by the police and the Youth Congress workers. School teachers were another category of people who were given the additional task of motivating people for vasectomy operations. After the sterilisation operation was performed on him, the person would be rewarded with Rs 120, a tin of edible oil and, in some places, a transistor radio. Those were the times when the transistors were replacing the old valve-operated radio sets. The average number of sterilisations in Delhi alone rose from 311 to about 6000 a day during this period. Auto-rickshaw drivers, for instance, had to present a sterilisation certificate at the time of getting their licenses renewed. It is a different story that many managed to obtain forged certificates.

The official statistics put the number of sterilisation operations at 3.7 million in just the first five months of the Emergency and the target of 23 million that was set for the three years beginning June 1976 appeared to be an easy one. The fact is that a majority of those who were forced into the sterilisation clinics and were gifted a transistor radio happened to be the poor and the hapless. In social terms, a large majority of them happened to be Muslims and Dalits, the two social groups that constituted the Congress party's support base over the years. This, indeed, was one of the causes, and a major one at that, behind the summary defeat of Indira's Congress party in the March 1977 general elections. The Emergency establishment did things that alienated the people, in whose name the proclamation was made, from the Congress party.

Meanwhile, the high-handedness of the administration and the Emergency establishment may appear, in a way, to be the fallout of Sanjay Gandhi's presence and in that sense not necessarily the result of the Emergency as such. This has led to describing these and the indiscriminate arrests as the 'excesses' during the Emergency and blame Sanjay Gandhi for all that went wrong. This is far from the truth. The fact is that Sanjay Gandhi was not an aberration. His rise and his role had Indira Gandhi's approval at every stage. Indira, in fact, celebrated Sanjay in the following way: 'He's not a thinker, he's a doer.' She had her own slogans eulogising this mindset and one of them that gained a lot of prominence during the Emergency was: 'Work more talk less.' Sanjay Gandhi did his bit to put this slogan into effect by demolishing the Coffee House at New Delhi's Connaught Place. This was a place where people assembled, every day, to discuss books and issues. Jagmohan, who was Sanjay's aide in the Emergency establishment, maintained, even years after the Emergency, that it was the right thing to do by deriding all that was happening at the Coffee House as the 'tyranny of the Kafkaesque world of papers, full of sound and fury signifying nothing'.

The Emergency establishment went about all this with impunity because those at the helm knew that no one would speak out against them. The extent of fear that stalked across the country was such because anyone who dared speak out could be arrested, detained and even done away with. The regime had ensured this by annulling the fundamental rights, reducing the higher judiciary into a bunch of men committed to the cause of the Emergency establishment and penal transfers of those judges who refused to co-operate. All this notwithstanding, there was resistance against the regime and against the Emergency establishment, and this resistance culminated in the birth of the Janata Party and the people voting for that party in March 1977.

The Story of Resistance

The situation that prevailed on the day after the mid-night declaration can be described, in the most appropriate way, by citing C. G. K. Reddy's note. He recalls his experience on 26 June 1975 as follows: 'As I went round both the New and Old Delhi I expected to see crowds of people roused and agitated, angry and determined to bring down a Prime Minister who had obviously taken this action to save herself and her office. I could hardly believe my eyes when I saw not a sign of any protest, not even groups of people gathered in street corners agitated and discussing the calamity that had overtaken the country. Surely, mine was not an isolated reaction. It was like any other day; people were normally going about their business, office goers were, as usual, proceeding to their offices. Business was as usual. All this I put down at first to shock. I told myself that, as the day advanced, at least a few of the lakhs of people, who had gathered, only the previous evening, to hear JP and had determined to bring down a Prime Minister whose election had been set aside, would organise themselves to resist what was virtually a dictatorship. My expectations and hopes were belied, as the day ended.'

Reddy was both right and wrong. He was right because the Emergency was not resisted on the streets and the people seemed to take Indira Gandhi's decision to suspend democracy without a murmur. Indira Gandhi herself ensured that JP, who had gathered an unprecedented number of people just the other day at the Ramlila grounds, was driven around the streets of Delhi to witness the absolute calm and the quite. After his arrest and remand to a guest house in Sona, JP's health began failing and he was taken to the AIIMS in Delhi first. Indira, however, did not want to keep JP in a New Delhi hospital and Bansi Lal assured her of adequate security in the Post Graduate Institute for Medical and Education Research in Chandigarh. JP, it may be recalled, had escaped from the Hazaribagh prisons during the Quit India movement and organised resistance to the British for at least a couple of years after his daring escape. But Bansi Lal was there, this time, to ensure that JP did not escape. It did not matter to them that JP was now far too old to do whatever he did in 1942. In any case, before driving him off to Chandigarh, the Emergency establishment instructed the police to take the old man around Delhi to show him that the people, whom he had aroused until a few days ago, had accepted the Emergency without a murmur. The few hundred cadres of the RSS who had come out on the streets shouting slogans were promptly arrested and thereafter everything had settled down.

This, however, began to change. The Bombay High Court Bar Association passed a resolution describing the regime as authoritarian. Ram Jethmalani, the president of the All India Bar Association came out in the open to say that Indira Gandhi was behaving the same way as Hitler and Mussolini did in Germany and Italy. Almost all the High Court Bar Associations, barring that of West Bengal, passed resolutions demanding repeal of the Emergency. The fact that the lawyers were unwilling to endorse the Emergency was evident from the number of writ petitions that were filed in the High Courts, across the country, against the arrest and detention of leaders of the various political parties.

Similarly, Gujarat and Tamil Nadu, where the state governments were controlled by non-Congress leaders witnessed open activity against the Emergency. Of importance in this context was the All India Civil Liberties Conference in Ahmedabad on 12 October 1975 presided by Justice J. C. Shah, a former Chief Justice of the Supreme Court. The conference was organised by a collective that consisted of members of the various Bar Associations and under the banner of Citizens for Democracy. Addressing the conference, M. C. Chagla, a former Chief Justice of the Bombay High Court and Jawaharlal Nehru's cabinet colleague, held that the protest by the opposition parties demanding Indira's resignation consequent to the Allahabad High Court verdict was justified both in the eyes of the law as much it was in the democratic context. Chagla stressed: 'There was no conspiracy on the part of the opposition leaders. The conspiracy was by the Prime Minister, I repeat, the conspiracy was by the Prime Minister to put the leaders in jail, to have a press censorship and to deprive the people of India of their civil liberties.'

In his address, where he recalled that the effect of censorship is that the people were denied of even such information that almost all the opposition politicians were in jail, Chagla went on to stress the following: 'Now the Prime Minister goes on to say and says almost every day that India is a democracy, all this is democratic. I am reminded of a story, *Alice in Wonderland*. Humpty Dumpty told Alice, if I say that a word has a certain meaning, that word has that meaning, you cannot change it. So, when the Prime Minister says that dictatorship is democracy, you must accept her word. *She is Humpty Dumpty and she thinks all the nations are Alice in Wonderland*.'(emphasis added). Chagla's speech was published, as a pamphlet, from the printing press inside the Sabarmati Ashram, from where Mahatma Gandhi brought out the *Young India*. The public convention and the publication of Chagla's speech were possible because the Babubhai Patel Government in Gujarat did not allow the Emergency establishment's writ run in the State. The Sanjay Gandhi establishment, however, ordered a raid in the premises of the Ashram and seized copies of *Bhoomiputra*, in which Chagla's speech was printed. For reasons best known only to the Indira Gandhi–Sanjay Gandhi establishment, Chagla was not arrested on his return to Bombay after the 12 October conference. A number of lawyers and former judges protested against the Emergency, but for some reason, they were also not arrested.

This does not mean that the Emergency establishment allowed protests. It is also not the case that the resistance to the Emergency was confined to the Bar. Yet another story of resistance came to light on 24 September 1976, when the CBI filed a chargesheet against as many as 25 persons in a Sessions Court in Delhi. They were charged under Sections 121(A) and 120(B) of the Indian Penal Code (for which the punishment could be death sentence) along with various sections of the Indian Explosives Act, 1884. The case came to be known as the Baroda Dynamite Conspiracy and the accused included C. G. K. Reddy, who recorded his lament over the calmness that marked the streets of Delhi on the day after the mid-night proclamation, among others. To cite Reddy again, 'The accused hailed from several States – Bihar, Uttar Pradesh, Delhi, Madhya Pradesh, Gujarat, Maharashtra, Karnataka, Kerala and Andhra Pradesh. They were drawn from all age groups. The youngest, Padmanabha Shetty, was 21 and the oldest, Prabhudas Patwari, 68. They were from different social strata: A mill worker (Motilal Kanojia); newspaper men (Vikram Rao, Kirit Bhatt, Vijai Narain, Kamlesh Shukla); a lawyer (Prabhudas Patwari); Chairman of a leading industrial company (Viren J Shah); and a student (Padmanabha Shetty). They belonged to almost all political parties; some were not members of any party.'

These men, in various ways, played a role in setting of bomb blasts across the country and even tried to smuggle 500 low-power transmitters into the country with which they intended to broadcast anti-Emergency slogans and speeches that would intrude into the AIR's airspace and thus address the people across the country through the radio sets in their homes. The 'conspiracy' did not work as intended because the transmitters could not be smuggled in and 24 out of the 25 men were captured by the Special Police Squad set up by the Emergency establishment. They exploded bombs on railway tracks and bridges in many places in Karnataka and Bihar between 23 October 1975 and 30 December 1975. The 'conspirators' also set off blasts at the railway bridge near Kings Circle railway station in Bombay on 26 June 1976 and also at the Bombay Central railway station, the Express Highway overbridge near Bandra railway station and at the office of the *Blitz* weekly, which was one of Indira's mouthpiece at that time. The critical fact in all this is that the 'conspirators' ensured that the blasts were triggered without causing human casualties and this was something to which the leader of the resistance group, George Fernandes, had committed himself and others in the group. The other aspect is that these acts of resistance were unknown to the people, across the country, because the press did not report any of these, thanks to the censorship.

But then, the underground resistance to the Emergency, led by Fernandes, could ensure publication of the anti-Emergency statements in the newspapers outside India and also mobilise leaders of the Socialist parties across Europe to pressure Indira Gandhi against persisting with the Emergency. The underground had also organized marches in the USA and other European countries and demonstrations before the Indian missions there. All this enraged the Emergency establishment to the extent that when George Fernandes was finally arrested on 10 June 1976, from a house attached to the St. Paul's Cathedral in Calcutta, he along with his associates were sent up to trial for treason. Lawrence Fernandes, Snehlatha Reddy and Dr Girija Hugoul, a physician in one of the government hospitals in Delhi, were subjected to torture because they were associated with George Fernandes. All the 25 accused in the Baroda Dynamite Conspiracy case would have landed with life terms and even capital punishment. But, then, this did not happen.

While all these activities of the underground were not known to the people of the country, the government ensured publication of the charges against Fernandes and others in the newspapers on 25 September 1976. This was all. The defence statements of the accused and the proceedings of the trial were not allowed to be published in the newspapers in India. A gag order was issued against the publication of a picture of George Fernandes and C. G. K. Reddy, both tied in chains when they were brought to the magistrate in the Tis Hazari courts in Delhi. But then, the accused had their contacts elsewhere in the world and among them were leading members of the Socialist International in Europe. As they were led into the court premises, held in chains, the place was swarming with journalists from the *BBC, The Times, London, Frankfurter Allegemeine, Le Monde, the New York Times, The Voice of America* and many other publications and radio organisations. The accused had copies of a long statement ready with them. C. G. K. Reddy quickly passed the bunch of papers to Werner Adams of the *Frankfurter Allegemeine* and all the foreign correspondents had copies of the statement even before its contents were read out before the magistrate. It was their defence statement and there was this passage in that: '*The chains that we bear are symbols of the entire nation which has been chained and fettered.*' The national press, the day after, did not publish this. The exceptions, however, were *The Statesman* and *The Indian Express*. These two papers carried the quotes in the weekend edition. The Sunday editions of these two newspapers had a column called '*On the Record*', where reports from the foreign publications were reproduced with due credits. Both these papers carried these words attributing them to *Newsweek*.

The trial also brought together a battery of lawyers and the battle against the Emergency, that appeared to be lacking a sense of definite purpose in the several months before September 1976, received a new impetus by now. A defence committee was formed, with Acharya Kripalani as chairman and JP issued an appeal for funds to support the cost of the defence. In C. G. K. Reddy's words, the appeal for funds was only a means to publicise the issue and the accused in the case had found, by that time, an array of lawyers and firms that were willing to underwrite all the expenses. The array of lawyers who took the brief were led by V. M. Tarkunde, a retired judge of the Bombay High Court and among the founders of the People's Union for Democratic Rights (PUDR), Dharmadikari, a former Advocate General of Madhya Pradesh, K. L. Sharma, the president of the Delhi Bar Association. Govind Swaminathan, a former Advocate General of the Madras Government, too joined the defence team and he did so after insisting that he will not take any fee for his services. Assisting the defence was Ravi Nair, a young activist from Madras and an associate of

George Fernandes in his trade union activities in the railways. Ravi Nair would join the Amnesty International, several years later, and he continues to be a prominent fighter against all kinds of human rights violations across the country even now.

As for the other accused in the Baroda Dynamite conspiracy, George Fernandes would become the Minister for Industry in the Janata Party Government (March 1977 to July 1979), railway minister in the Janata Dal Government (December 1989 to September 1990) and the defence minister in the BJP-led NDA Government (March 1998 and May 2004). Viren Shah, after being in the Rajya Sabha representing the BJP, was appointed Governor of West Bengal. Prabhudas Patwari, the elderly Gandhian would become Governor of Tamil Nadu soon after the Emergency was lifted. Kirit Bhatt, the journalist would continue with his fight for democracy and when the BJP Government in Gujarat decided to honour him on the 25th anniversary of the Emergency, on 25 June 2000, Bhatt refused to accept it on grounds that the BJP too represented an autocratic tendency in politics that he had decided to resist on 25 June 1975. Vikram Rao emerged as an important leader of the trade union movement among the journalists. In other words, they came together because they were committed to the idea of democracy and were prepared to fight against any attack on the constitution.

Unlike the other leaders of the opposition parties and the several thousands who were detained under MISA, the accused in the Baroda Dynamite Case remained in jail for longer. Fernandes, for instance, was in jail even at the time of the March 1977 general elections. He was fielded as a candidate from Muzafarpur in Bihar by the Janata Party. A photograph of Fernandes in chains, taken at the Tis Hazari court premises where he was brought for the trial in September 1976, was blown up and put up as his campaign poster across Muzafarpur in that election. He won the 1977 election from there by a margin of 3,34,217 votes. The margin of victory was indeed huge in his case as well as the other stalwarts.

On 22 March 1977, a day after the election results were out and Indira Gandhi's Congress party was routed, Fernandes and the other accused were released on bail. And on 26 March 1977, the prosecution moved for withdrawal of the case and the magistrate allowed that. The Janata Party government was keen on this because the prime minister, Morarji Desai, had decided to induct Fernandes into the Cabinet and it would have been incongruous to induct someone facing a charge of criminal conspiracy as a Union Cabinet Minister. This move, in a sense, reflected the values that prevailed at that time. Political India was still far away from the situation when leaders would hesitate to step down as ministers even after being convicted by the courts. At another level, we did notice, in this chapter that Indira Gandhi had to resort to the Emergency and send at least a lakh of its citizens to jail to stay on as prime minister after the Allahabad High Court held her guilty of corrupt electoral practice!

The story of the resistance to the Emergency will not be complete without recalling the actions, from underground, by the Naxalites in Kerala. For most parts, the Naxalites consisted of young boys, still in their teens and students in some of the best colleges, willing to put their life in line to defend democracy. Of significance here is the resistance in Kerala where the state government was headed by C. Achuta Menon of the Communist Party of India (CPI). The Emergency provided an opportunity to K. Karunakaran, the home minister in the CPI-led ministry, to prove that he was as good as Bansi Lal and V. C. Shukla when it came to handling any resistance. In February 1976, even as it appeared that the Emergency was accepted by a cross section of the people, 13 men, led by K. Venu, by then an important leader of the CPI(ML), got together to attack a police station near Calicut. Their intention was to dispel the notion that the Emergency establishment was invincible. In their perception, fear was the basis on which the establishment survived; hence, it was important that this notion is dispelled. That was why they decided to attack a police station. Apart from Venu, all others who were part of the squad that invaded the police station on the night of 27 February 1976 were students drawn from the Regional Engineering College (REC) and the Medical College in Calicut and the Government Arts College, Madapalli.

The attack on the police station provoked a massive reign of terror. The Kerala police set up special camps in remote areas where hundreds of young men, mostly college students and manual workers, were taken into illegal custody and inhuman torture was inflicted on them before they were sent to jail as MISA detenues. Among them was P. Rajan, who was picked up from his hostel room in the REC Calicut, early in the morning on 1 March 1976 and was killed by the policemen at a temporary camp set up at a place called Ḳakkayam. There were several others who were held there in the camp and tortured. The irony was that the police could do all this without having to inform anyone about the grounds of arrest or detention. As for Rajan, his father had to wait until March 1977, even to file a petition of habeas corpus in the Kerala High Court. The state government, headed by a CPI leader, maintained that Rajan was not in their custody at all. It was only after Abraham Benhur, a young member of the Socialist Party and a research scholar at the University of Calicut, made a public statement that he had seen Rajan at the Kakkayam torture camp, that the government admitted that Rajan was arrested and held in the camp. The government also declared that Rajan was not traceable. Karunakaran had become the chief minister by now. There was a furore and the Congress high command ordered Karunakaran to step down. Benhur too was taken to the torture camp, and like it happened with hundreds of young men who were held there for a couple of weeks, tortured severely. The Crime Branch police had established four such camps across Kerala during the Emergency and several hundred men were subjected to severe torture there because they were associated with small groups that fought for democracy.

The story of resistance is indeed a long one and it is beyond the scope of this chapter or even this book to record them in detail. But then, the most important aspect of the resistance was witnessed across the country in March, 1977. The sixth General Elections to the Lok Sabha, held between March 16 and 20, 1977, was when the people of the country, the ordinary citizens, a majority of them being illiterates and had also been voting the Congress party to power since the days of Indira Gandhi's father, decided to vote against that party. They resisted the Emergency and did that in their own way. Indira Gandhi, who had won the Rae Bareili Lok Sabha seat by a margin on over one lakh votes was summarily defeated there this time. And so was Sanjay Gandhi; his ambitions to enter the Lok Sabha from Amethi was frustrated by the people there.

The victors in the 1977 elections belonged to the Janata Party. The party came into being after the merger of Morarji Desai's Congress (O), Charan Singh's Bharatiya Lok Dal, the Bharatiya Jan Sangh and the Socialist Party. This merger had taken place on 30 January 1977. We will discuss all this in the next chapter. Similarly, the other significant development in this period was the exit of Jagjivan Ram from the Congress party along with H. N. Bahuguna and Nandini Satpathy. This, indeed, was the decisive factor that led to Indira's Congress being wiped out of Uttar Pradesh and Bihar. On 2 February 1977, Jagjivan Ram shocked everyone at a press conference, from his ministerial bungalow in New Delhi, by announcing his resignation from the Union Cabinet and the Congress party. He was flanked by H. N. Bahuguna, who had earned Sanjay Gandhi's wrath for some reason and hence asked to step down as the chief minister of Uttar Pradesh in January 1976 (and was replaced by N. D. Tiwari) and Nandini Satpathy, who was also ordered by Indira Gandhi to resign as the chief minister of Orissa in December 1976 (and was replaced by Vinayak Acharya) on either sides. The trio announced the formation of the Congress for Democracy and added that they were prepared for an alliance with the Janata Party. All this contributed to the first ever non-Congress Government in New Delhi.

XI

The Janata Party

> A mixed sense of relief and apprehension marked the Indian political scene in early 1977 when the … Congress rule was broken by a stunning electoral verdict. It was a unity of resentment, obviously stronger in intensity and wider in extension in Northern India, which transformed disparate opposition parties into a working coalition eager to offer an alternative to the Emergency regime of the preceding two years.
>
> —Jyotirendra Das Gupta, *The Janata Phase: Reorganisation and Redirection in Indian Politics,* Asian Survey, Volume 19, No. 4, April 1979

Late in the night on 20 March 1977, listeners to the All India Radio (AIR) were in for a surprise. The television had not arrived across the country then. They got to hear Kishore Kumar's melodies between the bulletins of the results of the general election. AIR had stopped broadcasting Kishore's songs after he refused to perform at one of Sanjay Gandhi's Family Planning programmes. The perceptive listener to the radio, then, could make out that Indira Gandhi and her Congress party had lost the mandate. After several hours, early in the morning on 21 March, AIR finally announced that Indira Gandhi had lost to Raj Narain from Rae Bareli. Her counting agent, M. L. Fotedar, had sought delaying the process as much as he could and demanded a recount; this he did even when Raj Narain's margin of victory was substantive. Indira Gandhi had lost from Rae Bareli by a margin of 55,202 votes. Sanjay Gandhi, who tried his luck from neighbouring Amethi too was humbled by Ravindra P. Singh, a political novice. The margin of victory in Amethi was 75,844 votes.

The Congress party was swept aside everywhere in the North. All of Indira Gandhi's men were defeated. V. C. Shukla, who shot to fame by emasculating the press, lost from Raipur, Madhya Pradesh; Bansi Lal, the infamous defence minister and executor of all that Sanjay Gandhi wanted, lost from Bhiwani, Haryana; H. R. Gokhale, who lent his legal acumen to aid the Emergency establishment, lost to Ram Jethmalani in Bombay North-West; Sardar Swaran Singh, who lent himself to the making of the 42nd Constitution Amendment, lost from Jalandhar, Punjab; P. C. Sethi, who floated the idea of a presidential form of government during the Emergency, lost from Indore; and G. S. Dhillon, who danced to Indira's tunes as Lok Sabha Speaker during the Emergency, lost from Tarn Taran; Mohammad Yusuf, yet another Sanjay loyalist, lost from Siwan; Asoke Sen, who took up Indira Gandhi's brief in the Supreme Court (after Palkhiwala returned it), lost from Calcutta North-West; V. P. Singh, who had come to be known as Sanjay Gandhi's man, lost from Allahabad. The CPI too was punished by the people. Hiren Mukherjee, who had represented Calcutta North-East continuously from 1952, lost from there in 1977.

A few other players of the Emergency regime, however, did not face the same fate. Among them were Dev Kant Baruah, Y. B. Chavan, Brahmananda Reddy, Karan Singh and C. Subramaniam. They won the 1977 polls only because their constituencies happened to be in states where such aspects of the Emergency, as the compulsory sterilisation, demolition drives and indiscriminate arrests, were less pronounced than in Uttar Pradesh, Madhya Pradesh, Bihar, Haryana and Delhi. These were the states where the parties that came together to form the Janata on 23 January 1977, such as the Bharatiya Lok Dal, Congress (O), Samyukta Socialist Party and the Bharatiya Jan Sangh, did not have a significant presence.

Indira Gandhi's Congress party drew a blank from Bihar (with 54 Lok Sabha seats), Himachal Pradesh (with four seats), Punjab (with 13 seats), Uttar Pradesh (with 85 seats) and Delhi (with seven seats). The party won, a seat each, in Haryana (out of the 10), Madhya Pradesh (out of 40) and Rajasthan (out of 25). In West Bengal, the Congress won just three out of the 42 Lok Sabha constituencies, four out of the 21 seats from Orissa, 10 out of the 25 from Gujarat and 20 out of the 48 from Maharashtra. In all, the Congress strength in the Lok Sabha stood at 154 (in the house of 542), the lowest ever in the party's history. Interestingly, this is higher than the Congress party's strength after May 2004!

Curiously, a large chunk of the 154 Congress MPs came from the four southern states. Indira's Congress won 41 out of the 42 seats from Andhra Pradesh, 26 out of the 28 seats from Karnataka, 11 out of the 20 seats from Kerala (the Congress party's allies including CPI, the Muslim League, the Kerala Congress and the RSP won the rest). In Tamil Nadu, the Congress won 14 out of the 39 seats while ADMK, its ally, won 18 seats and the CPI secured all the three seats it contested. The Congress did well in Assam too winning 10 out of the 14 seats. In other words, 92 of the 154 Congress MPs were from the four southern states.

The winners from the opposition included a whole lot of veterans: Madhu Limaye, Karpoori Thakur and Madhu Dandavate from the Socialist Party; Nanaji Deshmukh and Atal Behari Vajpayee from the Bharatiya Jan Sangh; H. M. Patel from the Swatantra Party; Morarji Desai, Asoka Mehta, and Neelam Sanjiva Reddy from the Congress (O); Charan Singh and Biju Pattnaik from the Bharatiya Lok Dal; Chandra Shekhar, Kishen Kant, Mohan Dharia and Ram Dhan, all of whom were Congress party MPs when the Emergency was declared but landed in jail the same night because they stood up against Indira Gandhi. The winners also included Jagjivan Ram and H. N. Bahuguna, who walked out of the Congress party as late as on 2 February 1977, to float the Congress for Democracy (CFD). The opposition camp also consisted of Justice

K. S. Hegde, who had resigned from the higher judiciary, in protest against the elevation of Justice A. N. Ray as Chief Justice of the Supreme Court and Ram Jethmalani who had stood up against the Emergency in his capacity as the president of the Bar Council. All of them contested on the Bharatiya Lok Dal's symbol, *Chakra Haldhar*, a farmer with a ploughshare enclosed in a circle.

After all the results were announced, Indira Gandhi convened a meeting of her cabinet, late in the night on 21 March 1977, where it was resolved to recommend withdrawal of the Emergency proclaimed on 25 June 1975. This was conveyed to the acting President, B. D. Jatti the same day. President Fakhruddin Ali Ahmed had died, on 11 February 1977, just about the time the campaign had begun for the general elections. The Emergency was, thus, withdrawn and Indira Gandhi submitted her resignation on 22 March 1977. Morarji Desai was anointed the leader of the Janata by JP and Acharya Kripalani on 24 March 1977. After his formal election as Janata Parliamentary Party leader, he was sworn in as the prime minister the same afternoon. Desai who lost the race thrice earlier—in May 1964 to Lal Bahadur Shastri and in January 1966 and March 1967 to Indira Gandhi—was sworn in, as the prime minister, on 24 May 1977. The Janata Party was formally constituted only on 1 May 1977 with Chandra Shekhar as its president. We shall look at the story of the Janata Party from its various dimensions, its travails and finally the collapse of the first ever non-Congress government in July 1979, in this chapter.

After a brief discussion of the context in which the elections were held in March 1977 and the probable reasons why Indira Gandhi chose to go to polls, we will deal with the various stages in the formation of the Janata Party, beginning with the foundation of the Bharatiya Lok Dal on 29 August 1974, the notes that were exchanged between the opposition leaders from within and outside the various jails during the Emergency and finally the constitution of a 27-member National Committee on 23 January 1977 to lead the Party during the elections and its landslide win in March 1977. Thereafter, we will narrate the context in which Morarji Desai was elected prime minister, the travails of cabinet formation and the issues that came up in that regard followed by a discussion on the legislative changes that were brought about in the course of the Janata Government including the 44th Constitution Amendment. Thereafter, a narrative of the various stages, when the fissures in the Janata Party came to the fore, leading to the fall of the Morarji Government on 16 July 1979 and then, the rise and the fall of Charan Singh and eventually the return of Indira Gandhi.

Why Did Indira Decide to Hold Elections?

18 January 1977, the day on which Indira Gandhi announced her intention to hold elections, incidentally, happened to be the eleventh anniversary of

her tenure as the prime minister; she was sworn in as the prime minister, on this day in 1966. This may or may not have had been the reason behind her announcement that day. However, it did come as a shock to everyone. Indira Gandhi had obtained the parliamentary sanction to extend the life of the Fifth Lok Sabha, until March 1978, by way of a resolution moved in the house in November 1976. However, in just a couple of months after that, she decided to hold elections in March 1977. While her apologists hold that the announcement on 18 January 1977 revealed the democratic core in Indira Gandhi and that she was uncomfortable, all the while, with the Emergency and the role that Sanjay Gandhi and his band were playing, there are some others who consider that her intention was to legitimise Sanjay Gandhi's position in the dispensation, and the best way to do that was to ensure that he held a formal position. The actual story would be somewhere between the two. It is a fact that Sanjay Gandhi's abrasive behaviour and his contempt for some of Indira's confidants such as Siddharth Shankar Ray, Devraj Urs and the former communists in the Congress as well as towards the CPI had caused some discomfort in Indira's mind. This, however, was not all that pervasive. That Indira Gandhi was pleased with Sanjay's emergence was evident at the Guwahati session of the Congress. She did everything to promote her son in the same way as her father did to promote her. Similarly, if a formal role for Sanjay was all that she intended, she could have ensured a by-election from anywhere in the country for Sanjay to contest and enter the Lok Sabha.

The point is that Indira Gandhi was impressed, time and again, by her son and his aides that there was absolutely no resistance to the Emergency. She was also convinced by her aides, including P. N. Dhar, her secretary in the PMS, that the Emergency measures had ensured a fall in prices and restored the people's confidence in the dispensation (that was lost in the couple of years before the midnight declaration on 25 June 1975) and that it was ideal, in the moral and the practical sense, to hold elections soon. More than all these, Indira Gandhi had made her own assessment of the opposition leaders. She was aware of the confabulations among those who were released on parole (on health grounds) and the irritants, that were thrown up, every time they discussed unity among them. In other words, Indira Gandhi had the information to suggest that the opposition continued to be in disarray and that the semblance of unity they had established, during the couple of weeks between 12 June 1975 and 25 June 1975, had given way to mutual distrust. She was also aware that a section of the opposition, particularly Charan Singh and Asoka Mehta besides many others, was even willing to surrender.

This was evident in a letter that DMK leader M. Karunanidhi (who had opposed the Emergency in June 1975 and had suffered dismissal of his state government in Tamil Nadu in January 1976) to all opposition party leaders calling them for a meeting, on 15 December 1976, to 'discuss and find a way to normalise the situation in the country by dialogue'. Similarly, H. M. Patel, who was heading the Janata group in Parliament and was an important member of Charan Singh's BLD, wrote to Indira Gandhi (on 26 November 1976), seeking a meeting with her to 'help in ensuring mutual understanding and confidence' between the government and the opposition parties. And finally, there was a letter from Biju Patnaik (once again a Charan Singh aide) to Om Mehta, Minister of State for Home, and Sanjay Gandhi's aide in the Emergency establishment, on 1 January 1977. The burden of this letter too was to seek a series of meetings between Mehta and the opposition leaders 'so that large areas of agreement that exists between the Government and the opposition can be strengthened and the outstanding points resolved'. Indira Gandhi was also aware that these efforts by Karunanidhi, Patel and Biju Patnaik were treated with contempt by JP (out on parole) as well as the other leaders who were still in jail. JP made it clear, in a letter to Asoka Mehta (dated 29 December 1976), where he referred to the idea of a dialogue with the government, that 'the dialogue to be meaningful should begin only after all political prisoners have been released unconditionally, and civil liberties and press freedom have been fully restored so as to facilitate normal political work'.

The fact is that Indira Gandhi had reasons to believe that the opposition was splintered and that elections will only accentuate the divide among them. She hoped that by winning the elections she could legitimise the Emergency and all that happened as part of it before the international community and could also formalise Sanjay Gandhi's position. That, perhaps, was the reason behind her announcement to dissolve the Lok Sabha on 18 January 1977. She, in fact, did that unilaterally, in the same way as she went about the Emergency proclamation. Her cabinet colleagues were shocked and surprised this time too. They were not consulted. In any case, Indira's calculations did not work. The opposition leaders were convinced on the imperative for merger. The experience during the Emergency seemed to have forced them think that way. And the merger was effected within days after Morarji Desai was let out of his solitary confinement, in the Sona Dak Bunglow, on 18 January 1977. Thereafter, on 2 February 1977 Jagjivan Ram and H. N. Bahuguna floated the CFD and announced that the new party would fight the ensuing elections in alliance with the Janata Party. In other words, things did not happen the way Indira Gandhi wanted.

The Formation of the Janata

The genesis of the Janata Party lay in the anti-Congress unity achieved ahead of the 1967 general elections. All the constituents of the 1967 experiment were there to form the Janata in 1977 and they continued to constitute its core. But then, there were new players too. The Congress (O), formed in December 1969, lent itself to the Janata formation and it brought Morarji Desai into the fold. There were such leaders as Chandra Shekhar, Ram Dhan, Mohan Dharia and Kishen Kant who were with Indira Gandhi, but parted ways with her immediately after the declaration of the Emergency, spent several months in jail and lent themselves to the formation of the Janata Party. The Janata Party also consisted of Jagjivan Ram, H. N. Bahuguna and Nandini Satpathy who were with Indira Gandhi until 1 February 1977. Jagjivan Ram, incidentally, was the one who moved the motion seeking parliamentary approval to the Emergency in July 1975!

The Janata Party was different from the 1967 experiment in another way. In 1977, all the constituents merged into one entity and committed themselves to stay that way for good. This had not happened in 1967. They were mere coalitions then. And more important than all this was the fact that the Janata Party in 1977 had accepted a patron in JP. It is a different matter, that all this notwithstanding, the Janata too collapsed in less than a couple of years and in many ways it happened in somewhat a similar fashion as it did after 1967. While Ram Manohar Lohia, in many ways the architect of the 1967 formation did not live to see its collapse, JP, the force behind the making of the Janata Party, witnessed the beginning of the Janata's disintegration before his death on 8 October 1979. JP lived to see the fall of the Morarji Desai Government (on 16 July 1979) as well as the exit of Charan Singh, in humiliating fashion, without facing Parliament even once as prime minister. An explanation as to what went wrong with the Janata Party can be found in the issues that were raised by different leaders at various stages before the party was formed and in the fact that they did not even attempt to resolve them.

While the crisis that engulfed the nation in 1973–74 caused the various opposition parties to join hands with the different sections of the people and the leaders of these parties began associating themselves with the agitating students in Gujarat and later on in Bihar (discussed in detail in Chapter IX), efforts at unity in the political sense began much later. The earliest initiative, in this regard, was taken by Charan Singh in April 1974. His effort led to the formation of the Bharatiya Lok Dal (BLD) on 29 August 1974. The leaders and their parties that came together to form the BLD were: Charan Singh (Bharatiya Kranti Dal), Piloo Mody (Swatantra Party), Biju Patnaik (Utkal Congress), Balraj Madok (Rashtriya Loktantrik Dal), Chand Ram (Kisan Mazdoor Party), Raj Narain (Samyukta Socialist Party) and Baba Mahendra Singh (Punjab Khetibari Zamindar Union). The formation of the BLD was essentially Charan Singh's project and it was in response to the Congress victory in the elections to the Uttar Pradesh Assembly in February–March 1974.

Charan Singh, who began his political life as a Congress MLA, left the party in 1967 to realise his dream and become the chief minister of Uttar Pradesh. He was elected leader of the Samyukta Vidhayak Dal (SVD) and became the chief minister of a coalition government in April 1967. The government, however, lasted only until February 1968. He became the chief minister of another coalition government in February 1970, once again for a brief spell until October 1970. He had emerged a strong force in Uttar Pradesh from then and his Bharatiya Kranti Dal secured 106 seats in the 1974 elections to the State Assembly. But unlike in 1967, a unity of the opposition was not taking place and the Congress formed its government. The man who managed the Congress revival in Uttar Pradesh at that time was H. N. Bahuguna. It was in this context that Charan Singh initiated the unity and merger of smaller parties into his Kranti Dal to form the BLD in August 1974. It may be noted here that the Bharatiya Jan Sangh was not associated with this project in spite of the fact that the party was the second largest opposition group in the UP Assembly with 61 seats. Similarly, the Congress (O) was not involved in the August 1974 exercise. Charan Singh had his own reasons for this. The Congress (O) was represented in Uttar Pradesh by Chandra Bhanu Gupta. He was the one who managed defections from the SVD and ensured Charan Singh's fall in February 1968. It is another story that Gupta and Bahuguna would join the Janata Party in 1977.

A couple of months from then, on 25–26 November 1974 to be specific, the non-communist opposition parties held a detailed discussion in Delhi to formulate some sort of a unity in action. The singular objective behind this was to widen the scope of the Gujarat–Bihar struggle into an all-India movement. A National Coordination Committee consisting of leaders of the various parties was constituted with JP as its chairman. The committee included Nanaji Deshmukh and Atal Behari Vajpayee (Bharatiya Jan Sangh), Asoka Mehta and S. N. Mishra (Congress [O]), Piloo Mody and Raj Narain (BLD), George Fernandes and Surendra Mohan (Socialist Party) Prakash Singh Badal (Akali Dal) and several representatives from the Sarvodaya Mandal. The rally at the Delhi Boat Club on 6 March 1975 (dealt with in Chapter IX) was organised by this committee. The unity was sustained until 25 June 1975 in the opposition rally at the Ramlila grounds where a five-member *Lok Sangarsh Samiti* with Morarji Desai as chairman and Nanaji Deshmukh as its convener came into place. On 25 June 1975, Morarji Desai had emerged the leader of the opposition combine.

The midnight arrests and the detention thereafter of all those opposition leaders (barring just George Fernandes and Nanaji Deshmukh) brought all this to a halt. The Emergency regime began releasing leaders on parole, on health grounds, in stages. This was done in an arbitrary manner and Morarji Desai and some others, were held in jail, until 18 January 1977. JP, for instance, was released on parole on 12 November 1975, after his health deteriorated and doctors at the Post Graduate Institute for Medical Sciences, Chandigarh (where he was held under MISA), recommended that he be taken elsewhere for better medical help. JP was shifted to the Jaslok Hospital in Bombay, diagnosed as suffering from renal failure, and was put on dialysis for the rest of his life. JP did involve himself in political activity since then, but not as actively as he had done before 25 June that year. He was meeting other leaders on parole and communicating with some others, still in jail, from his home in Patna. JP was no longer the pivot around whom opposition political activities moved. By mid-1976, the opposition activities were conducted by the leaders of the Congress (O) and the BLD, who were now out of jail, on parole. This included Asoka Mehta, the president of the Congress (O) and Charan Singh, the chairman of the BLD apart from Surendra Mohan of the Socialist Party and O. P. Tyagi of the Jan Sangh. Interestingly and for reasons best known to the Indira–Sanjay establishment, Asoka Mehta was released even while Morarji Desai was in detention. Similarly, Tyagi was allowed to conduct the affairs of the Jan Sangh while Vajpayee and Advani were still in jail. Surendra Mohan and N. G. Goray were out to run the Socialist Party even while Madhu Limaye and Madhu Dandavate were held in jail. It is striking that almost all the BLD leaders—Charan Singh, Biju Patnaik, Piloo Mody and Raj Narain—were released in less than a year after their arrest on 25 June 1975.

This meant that all the talks about opposition unity and the idea of forming a single opposition party were held at two levels. One of it was inside the various prisons between leaders of the various groups, and this did not lead anywhere in the formal sense. For long after their arrests, the various leaders did not even know where the others from their party were. Those were the days when cellular phones had not arrived. This meant that formal efforts at unity had to wait for the release of some of the leaders and this began in March 1976.

A meeting, on 21 March 1976, attended by representatives from the Congress (O), BLD, Socialist Party and the Jan Sangh set up a steering committee that would set out the broad contours of a single democratic national alternative. Based on the committee's report, the leaders met for two days on 22 and 23 May 1976 and decided to request JP launch a new party. The objectives of that new party contained everything noble and radical: restoration of civil liberties, establishment of a genuine egalitarian social order, independence and the dignity of the judiciary and many such things. JP did concede to the request, as he had been holding on for sometime, that the need was for a single opposition party against the Congress. JP had insisted on that as early as in January 1975 at the Jabapur by-elections and had Sharad Yadav elected to the Lok Sabha. However, the task this time was not as simple as it was in 1975. The stakes, now, were larger than a mere by-election. JP did not seem to realise this when he stated in a press conference, on 25 May 1976, to the effect that all the four parties—the BLD, Jan Sangh, Congress (O) and the Socialist Party—had agreed to dissolve their identities, after the new party had been formally launched, and even set the date for the launch for sometime in the last week of June 1976. But then, JP's focus, at that time, was to reinvent the resistance to the Emergency. He was adamant that the *satyagraha*, that was still on against the Emergency (and people were courting arrest even if the numbers were far and few), shall continue and demanded a commitment to that effect from the opposition parties. Charan Singh, now outside jail, had a different agenda.

A meeting of the National Executive of the BLD, held in Delhi on 30–31 May 1976, set a different tone. On 1 June 1976, Charan Singh wrote a long letter to JP making it clear that JP's press statement on 25 May 1976 amounted to putting the cart before the horse. 'We persistently implored friends of these three parties (read Congress [O], Socialist Party and Jan Sangh), right from April 1974 to April 1975, to join hands with us and strengthen the national alternative which we propose to build or actually built…', the letter stated. Charan Singh did not mince words when it came to blaming JP himself. His letter said: 'We had appealed to you also from October 1974 onwards to bring about the merger of the parties that supported you, but again in vain. Had you alone thrown your weight with us, things in India would have been far different today. Not only that you refused to heed to our prayer; your movement harmed the very cause which you seek, rather deem fit, to sponsor today. Many a public men who would have joined BLD, refrained from doing so because of your movement. I had told you that a motley crowd consisting of widely differing, even conflicting political elements, will hardly add up to an organisation which could carry an agitation through to a successful end or win an election.' Charan Singh insisted that the *satyagraha* be halted and the opposition parties embark upon a programme of constructive work.

In a meeting of the four parties, which Charan Singh attended on behalf of the BLD (the Congress [O], the Jan Sangh and the Socialist Party being the others), he raised objections to letting members of the RSS join the new party. 'It is a question of dual membership which should not be allowed and there should be no scope in the new party for surreptitious work,' he insisted. This issue, incidentally, would come up again in July 1979 and Charan Singh had Madhu Limaye to raise it for him; and it led to the Janata Party splitting into two and the fall of Morarji Desai's government. In the same meeting, Charan Singh ruled out the scope for joint action of any kind. Maintaining that the BLD stood for a united single party, all the 24 hours of the day and 30 days of the month, Charan Singh urged that the national executives of all the four parties resolve forthwith to this idea. This was not possible insofar as the Socialist Party and the Jan Sangh were concerned because most of their senior leaders were still in jail. On 14 July 1976, Charan Singh responded to Asoka Mehta's appeal for unity where he stated: 'BLD is now fed up; even its motives have been doubted. So it has decided to go it alone, free from thought of any duty in this regard—except one, viz., if and when the three parties dissolve or decide to dissolve themselves in order to form one organisation based, by and large, on the programmes broadly indicated by the Father of the Nation, BLD will make haste to join it.'

It was clear that Charan Singh had very little use for JP at that time. He was looking for a negotiated settlement with Indira Gandhi and the Emergency establishment, and through that he could occupy the opposition space completely. The other leaders, now out of jail, such as the Congress (O) president Asoka Mehta did not qualify to don the mantle of a popular leader. There was a further exchange of letters between Asoka Mehta and Charan Singh discussing the name of the 'new' party and its objectives. Charan Singh agreed that the new party could be called the Indian (or National) Democratic Congress and urged that the party commit itself to 'the establishment of an egalitarian society, consistent with individual freedom' in place of the Congress (O) proposal of 'establishment of a socialist state.' The BLD leader, however, made it clear that the 'new' party's flag cannot, in any way, resemble that of the Congress (O). The reason stated was that the Congress (O) flag resembled that of the Congress (R) and that will create confusion at the time of the elections. While the Congress (O) president, Asoka Mehta was indulging Charan Singh and his BLD in this fashion, the Socialist Party and the Jan Sangh were hardly involved in this exchange in any meaningful manner. The senior leaders of these two parties were still in jail.

This was probably the reason why Charan Singh persisted with the talks with Asoka Mehta. He saw, in the unity, a distinct possibility of becoming the leader of the new party. This was clearly revealed when he snapped ties with Asoka Mehta when the Congress (O) working committee decided that the president of the new party could be decided only after Morarji Desai too was released from prison. On 13 October 1976, Charan Singh, in a letter to Mehta, wrote as follows: 'You propose to await the presence of Morarjibhai amongst you before finalising the matter (read unity and formation of a single party). On our part, we consider the present round of talks with all its commitments, which began on September 16, closed.' It was indeed clear from this that Charan Singh's concern for unity and the formation of a single party was to position himself as the leader of the new party.

His sense of urgency or the haste he displayed to settle the leadership issue was caused by the impression that prevailed, at that time, that Indira Gandhi will go for the general elections shortly. The Lok Sabha's extended term was to expire in March 1977 and Indira's game plan to further extend the life of the house by another year (which she did in November 1976 immediately after the 42nd Constitution Amendment was passed) was not anticipated either by Charan Singh or by Asoka Mehta. It was expected that Morarji Desai and the others who were still in jail would be released soon. While Mehta saw in that an opportunity to deny Charan Singh the chance of becoming the leader of the new party, the BLD leader too was unwilling to wait for that eventuality and let go of an opportunity. All that changed after Parliament endorsed the resolution extending the life of the Lok Sabha by one more year; that meant that elections need not be held until March 1978.

This, in turn, led the BLD to negotiate a settlement with the Emergency establishment. The series of correspondence that its leaders H. M. Patel and Biju Pattnaik had with Indira Gandhi and Om Mehta revealed this desperation. It showed the willingness of this section of the opposition to somehow normalise their own status as an opposition party vis-à-vis the Emergency establishment. The fact is that the BLD as well as such leaders as Asoka Mehta were prepared to cringe before the establishment; and this was known to JP and Indira Gandhi. While JP did nothing to intervene in this game and, thus, let the task of forming the new united party go into a limbo, Indira Gandhi found in all this the opportune moment to go for polls. The 18 January 1977 announcement and the release of Morarji Desai the same day came as surprises. The surprise element was not merely with regard to the decision but with the fallout too.

A meeting of the opposition leaders was held at Morarji Desai's official residence, on Dupleix Road, the same evening. And the leaders agreed to meet the following day. On 19 January 1977, the issue of leadership seemed to have been settled. The four parties—Congress (O), BLD, Jan Sangh and Socialist Party—and also the individuals who had revolted against Indira Gandhi and suffered arrest and detention (Chandra Shekhar, Mohan Dharia, Kishen Kant and Ram Dhan), agreed to come together instantly. They had before them a note from JP: Unite as one party or perish. And that he will have nothing to do if they do not form into a single party. This curt message from JP, Morarji's presence and the fact that elections were now round the corner, pushed the leaders into a different mode. By the evening of 19 January 1977, they had agreed to constitute a single party with Morarji Desai as the chairman and Charan Singh as the vice chairman. A 27-member national committee was set up on 23 January 1977, with L. K. Advani (Jan Sangh), Surendra Mohan (Socialist Party) and Ram Dhan (Congress-rebel) as general secretaries. The committee included Asoka Mehta, N. Sanjiva Reddy, P. Ramachandran, Chandra Bhanu Gupta, P. C. Sen and S. N. Mishra, all of Congress (O), H. M. Patel and Karpoori Thakur of the BLD.

The Janata Party, with that name, was launched on 30 January 1977. On that day, the various leaders addressed huge rallies in different cities: Morarji Desai and Atal Behari Vajpayee in the Delhi Ramlila grounds; JP at the Gandhi Maidan in Patna; Charan Singh in Kanpur; Chandra Shekhar in Jaipur; and N. G. Goray in Bombay. The CPI (M), the Akali Dal and the DMK did not agree for a merger but committed themselves for poll alliance with the Janata Party. In order to avoid any further complications, the Janata decided to opt for the *Chakra Haldhar*, the BLD's election symbol. The formalities of dissolving the old parties and drafting the constitution and the programme of the new party was put off for another day.

The Congress party, meanwhile, had announced its list of candidates from Haryana and Maharashtra. Then came the 2 February 1977 announcement by Jagjivan Ram, H. N. Bahuguna and Nandini Satpathy; the Janata Party did not hesitate to make use of the situation and let them into their fold, despite the fact that these leaders had been part of the Emergency regime until its end. Bahuguna had been the chief minister of Uttar Pradesh until January 1976 and did preside over the administration, until he was unceremoniously removed from that post. Satpathy too belonged to the same league and her role as the Orissa chief minister was as bad as that of many others in the Emergency establishment. And Jagjivan Ram had stuck to his post as the defence minister until a few minutes before he made the announcement. The opposition leaders knew what these leaders were capable of, given their social clout, and its impact on the elections. This was particularly true of Jagjivan Ram and Bahuguna. The CFD was taken as an ally by the Janata Party and contested the election under the BLD symbol.

Thus, the polarisation was complete. The Congress party fielded its candidates in 492 Lok Sabha seats, leaving 50 seats to its allies: the CPI (30) and the ADMK (20). The Janata Party contested in 391 constituencies and its various allies contested in the rest of the 147 constituencies: CFD (28), CPI (M) (53), the Akali Dal (8) and the DMK (19). The results were shocking. The Janata won 295 seats in the Lok Sabha and secured an absolute majority. As for its allies, the CPI (M) won 22 seats (of which 17 came from West Bengal) and the Akali Dal won all the nine seats it contested from Punjab. The DMK, the Janata's ally in Tamil Nadu, however, fell by the wayside. It won only one out of the 19 seats it contested. The Congress' strength, as we saw earlier, came down to 154 and the CPI too suffered reverses. Its strength came down from 23 in the previous house to seven this time. And even these were made up of victories from Tamil Nadu and Kerala where it won four and three seats respectively. The ADMK, formed in 1972 by M. G. Ramachandran after he broke away from the DMK, did well in Tamil Nadu. The party won 19 out of the 21 seats it contested in Tamil Nadu and Pondicherry and also won a majority in the Tamil Nadu assembly to wrest power from the DMK.

The Janata Party was now confronted with the task of electing the prime minister of the country, a task that the leaders had postponed in January, when they founded the new party, had to be addressed now and within the shortest possible time. This, indeed, turned out to be the party's nemesis. The crises that guided the short life of the Janata Party Government had its genesis in this very aspect and we shall discuss this now.

Morarji Desai's Election as Prime Minister

The landslide for the Janata Party was not expected by the leaders themselves when Indira Gandhi announced the elections on 18 January 1977. The unity achieved within a week from then was, by all means, a factor that contributed to the Janata Party's victory. This, however, was only one aspect of the Janata story. The other and more significant aspect was that the Janata was made up of of three distinct components or formations. One was such parties as the Jan Sangh, the BLD and the Socialist Party; they had an organisation as well as a social base. The second component of the Janata Party consisted of the Congress (O) and those who left Indira Gandhi's Congress before the Emergency was declared; this component did not rest on an organisation or a social base and were individual leaders with their own constituencies.

The third component of the Janata Party was constituted by the CFD group. While the group did not command an organisation in any sense of the term, both Jagjivan Ram and H. N. Bahuguna commanded a social base. While Ram happened to be the Congress party's poster boy among the Scheduled Castes ever since independence, Bahuguna was considered their leader by the Brahmin community, substantial in terms of its numbers and strong in terms of their social clout, especially, in many parts of Uttar Pradesh. Bahuguna had also cultivated himself as a leader of significance among the Muslim community in the state while he was the chief minister. The contribution of these two leaders to the Janata Party's victory was substantial in this sense.

It is also possible to argue that the clean sweep by the Janata in Uttar Pradesh and Bihar was made possible by the presence of these two leaders in the pantheon as much as that of Charan Singh's BLD, the Socialists and the Jan Sangh. Indira Gandhi's Congress lost both the Brahmin and the Scheduled Caste bases to the Janata in 1977 and this made the verdict decisive.

This aspect was reflected in the composition of the elected MPs too. Although all the newly elected MPs had contested on one common symbol, their loyalties to their respective parties were not dissolved in the complete sense. Out of the 297 Janata Party MPs, only 20, including Morarji Desai, belonged to the Congress (O) and six of them were from Gujarat. The CFD, even if it had not merged into the Janata Party, had also contested under the BLD symbol.

The CFD had put up candidates in 28 seats, most of them from Bihar and Uttar Pradesh and won all that. This included Jagjivan Ram and H. N. Bahuguna. Charan Singh's BLD too had done well. Of the 85 newly elected Janata Party MPs from Uttar Pradesh, at least 20 were Charan Singh loyalists. Of the 54 from Bihar, 13 belonged to Charan Singh's party. Apart from them, a BLD faction in the Janata Party came from Orissa and Gujarat because the Swatantra Party and the Utkal Congress were party to the formation of the BLD in August 1974. The senior leaders of this lot were Charan Singh, Raj Narain, Karpoori Thakur, H. M. Patel and Biju Pattnaik. The Socialists too were a force. At least 16 Janata MPs belonged to the Socialist Party and most of them were senior leaders: B. P. Mandal, Madhu Limaye, George Fernandes from Bihar and Madhu Dandavate from Maharashtra. The erstwhile Jan Sangh added up to over 90 MPs in the Janata Parliamentary Party and they dominated the contingents from Madhya Pradesh, Rajasthan and Himachal Pradesh. At least eight out of the 54 from Bihar and 16 out of the 85 from Uttar Pradesh belonged to the Jan Sangh. The prominent winners included Nanaji Deshmukh and Atal Behari Vajpayee.

This being the case, there were more than one claimant for the Janata victory in 1977 and in that sense electing the leader was not an easy affair. The Janata Party's majority in Parliament now made it far more complicated. The stakes now were higher. The prime minister of India had to be identified. By the time the last result was out, in the morning on 21 March 1977, there were three claimants to the post: Morarji Desai, Charan Singh and Jagjivan Ram. The democratic option before the Janata Parliamentary Party was to hold elections, by secret ballot, among the elected MPs. This, however, would have eliminated Morarji Desai from the field because his own Congress (O) was not a strong force in the Janata Parliamentary Party. Both Charan Singh and Jagjivan Ram would have fought it out and the victor would have been decided by the MPs who belonged to the Jan Sangh and the Socialist Party blocks in the Janata Party. Jagjivan Ram, while addressing a press conference on 22 March, was asked a pointed question: 'Are you ready to assume Prime Ministership if invited to do so?' And his answer was: 'I have never shirked any responsibility in my life which the country wanted me to shoulder.' The CFD leader also announced that his party may prefer to stay as a separate entity than merge into the Janata. The thinking behind this was that the CFD could end up attracting MPs from Indira's Congress and in that event, Jagjivan Ram's strength would go up! A meeting of the CFD executive in the morning, on 23 March 1977, authorised Jagjivan Ram to decide on whether to merge into the Janata Party or remain a separate block.

Amidst this, JP announced his arrival in Delhi on 23 March 1977 as the arbitrator. The interesting side to all this was that the leaders were also working hard to prevent one another from being chosen for the top job. The first to throw the spanner in this regard was Charan Singh. Convalescing after a bout of fever caused by urinary-tract infection, in a farm-house in Bhondsi (in Haryana), Charan Singh sent a message to JP through Raj Narain, that he favoured Morarji Desai as the prime minister. The BLD leader had his own scores to settle with Bahuguna and Chandra Bhanu Gupta, both of whom were now mobilising support for Jagjivan Ram. We have seen the old rivalry between Gupta and Charan Singh earlier. They had scores to settle. Bahuguna, similarly, had emerged the leader of Indira's Congress and was made the chief minister of Uttar Pradesh in November 1973. He had revived the Congress fortunes, consolidating the party's hold among the Brahmins and the Muslims, and thus carved a niche for himself in Uttar Pradesh against Charan Singh. This was the reason behind the Congress revival in Uttar Pradesh and Charan Singh's concerted efforts to defeat the Congress in the March 1974 elections to the state assembly did not yield the desired results. Thus, Charan Singh had developed a sense of animosity against Bahuguna too. Charan Singh's desperation to prevent Jagjivan Ram from becoming the prime minister was caused by another factor. The Jats, who constituted Charan Singh's political constituency, were inimical to the idea of a member of the Scheduled Caste becoming the supreme leader.

Charan Singh's message reached JP a while before he had asked all the Janata MPs to assemble at the Rajghat in the morning on 24 March 1977. A meeting between JP and Jagjivan Ram was scheduled for that morning but did not take place. JP had conveyed to the CFD leader that they could meet in Parliament House where the Janata MPs were scheduled to meet after they affirmed loyalty to the party, at the Rajghat, that morning. At the Rajghat all the newly elected MPs took an oath and affirmed their undivided loyalty to the new party and their complete divorce from the political formations they had belonged to until 23 January 1977. JP had in mind the experience of the coalitions in 1967–68 and hoped that the leaders will be held back from indulging in internecine battles this time. When the MPs returned to the Gandhi Peace Foundation, not very far from the Rajghat, it was clear that Morarji Desai was the chosen one. JP had roped in J. B. Kripalani, an old associate of the Congress and one of those who had left the Congress fold even before the first general elections, to found the KMPP, to announce his decision. Kripalani said to the Janata MPs, now gathered at the Central Hall of Parliament: 'Our considered opinion is that under the circumstances prevailing and examining all conditions, our decision is that you chose Morarji Desai.'

Jagjivan Ram, Bahuguna and several CFD MPs stayed away from that meeting. George Fernandes registered his dissent. Fernandes objected to the 'undemocratic' method of Morarji's election and even wondered whether the new party was following the path set by Indira Gandhi's Congress. 'Plighted words should not be broken and democratic processes should not be sacrificed in an effort to create what is called consensus but what amounts to the point of view of a group,' said Fernandes. Ram Dhan, one of the three general secretaries of the party, announced his resignation in protest against the manner in which Jagjivan Ram was eliminated from the race. The Janata Party could not become another Congress because the party could not and would not settle down with one supreme leader.

Jagjivan Ram, meanwhile, stayed out of the meeting that day along with Bahuguna and as many CFD MPs he could influence. His refrain was that the meeting was that of the Janata Parliamentary Party and that his CFD was not yet a part of the Janata Party. The actual reason, however, was that he felt betrayed. Ram's point was that his exit from the Congress contributed immensely to Indira's party being decimated in the elections and hence he deserved to become the leader. In addition to this, Ram had been the defence minister in Indira Gandhi's cabinet and in that sense the virtual number two. He felt that he deserved the top post in the new dispensation. But all that were not JP's concern for reasons best known to JP himself. All the important leaders of the Janata Party and JP himself were conscious of Jagjivan Ram's importance. Hence they all went to meet him and persuade him to be part of the Janata project.

Desai, meanwhile, did not wait longer. He was sworn in as prime minister the same day, on 24 March 1977. It took two more days for him to announce his cabinet. The nation was under just one man, Morarji Desai, between 24 and 26 March 1977. The dogged negotiations, during the 48 hours after Morarji was sworn in, threw all hints of the shape of things in the Janata Party. The fact is that the Lok Nayak's moral authority was dented within a couple of days after his Janata Party won a majority in the elections.

The Janata Party steering committee decided, late in the night on 25 March 1977, that the cabinet would consist of 13 members, including the prime minister. The leaders had agreed on two representatives each, from the parties that constituted the Janata, two from the CFD and a couple of ministers from among those who were described, by now, as Congress Rebels (who joined the party soon after the declaration of the Emergency). The committee had also decided against reviving the post of Deputy Prime Minister. It may be recalled that Morarji Desai was the deputy prime minister under Indira Gandhi in March 1967 and until his resignation in July 1969 when Indira Gandhi stripped him off his finance ministership. The steering committee had also decided that Charan Singh will be the number two in the cabinet and thát Jagjivan Ram will be the leader of the house. This agreement was breached overnight. Desai added at least half a dozen names, on his own and submitted a list of 19 to be sworn in as ministers to the acting president, B. D. Jatti. All the 19 members were to be sworn in on 26 March 1977. Desai's list had five from the Congress (O) (against the two that was agreed), four from the BLD (instead of two) and three each from the Socialist Party and the Jan Sangh (one more than that was agreed). In addition to this, Prakash Singh Badal from the Akali Dal was added to the list and that was how it became 19. The CFD felt cheated, once again, because there was no parity between the constituents in the cabinet.

The list of ministers to be sworn in on 26 March 1977 was as follows: Charan Singh, Raj Narain, Biju Pattnaik and H. M. Patel (all BLD); Sikhandar Bhakt, P. Ramachandran, P. C. Chunder, Ravindra Verma and Shanti Bhushan (all Congress [O]); L. K. Advani, A. B. Vajpayee and Nanaji Deshmukh (BJS); Madhu Dandavate, George Fernandes and Purushottam Kaushik (Socialist Party); Jagjivan Ram and H. N. Bahuguna (CFD); Mohan Dharia (Congress-Rebel) and Prakash Singh Badal (Akali Dal).

Five out of the 19 did not turn up for the swearing in ceremony on 26 March 1977. They were Jagjivan Ram, Bahuguna, Nanaji Deshmukh, George Fernandes and Raj Narain. They had different reasons: Ram and Bahuguna felt that Desai had reneged on the mandate to keep the cabinet size at 13; Raj Narain was busy negotiating with the CFD and also his own complaints about the portfolio he was to be assigned; Fernandes explained that he would be a misfit in the cabinet after having fought against the establishment throughout his life; and Deshmukh decided to stay out of the cabinet because his name was included by Desai without any consultation and hence resented it. Moreover, he was keen to remain an organisation man. The Jan Sangh nominated Brijlal Verma in his place.

It took a lot of persuasion by JP and also spontaneous demonstrations in Delhi and elsewhere, before Jagjivan Ram, Bahuguna, Raj Narain, Fernandes and Brijlal Verma agreed to be sworn in as ministers on 28 March 1977. Ram agreed to remain the defence minister (which he was when he left Indira Gandhi's party on 2 February 1977) and Bahuguna became Minister for Petroleum, Chemicals and Fertilizers; Fernandes became Minister for Communications (before he was shifted to the industry ministry on 6 July 1977 and from where he ordered that Coca Cola and IBM move out of India) and Raj Narain became Minister for Health. Other cabinet ministers and their portfolios were as follows: Charan Singh (Home), H. M. Patel (Finance), A. B. Vajpayee (External Affairs), L. K. Advani (Information and Broadcasting), Sikhander Bhakt (Housing), Shanti Bhushan (Law, Justice and Company Affairs) P. C. Chunder (Education), Biju Pattnaik (Steel and Mines), P. Ramachandran (Energy), Ravindra Verma (Parliamentary Affairs and Labour), Madhu Dandavate (Railways), Purushottam Kaushik (Civil Aviation), P. S. Badal (Communication) and Mohan Dharia (Commerce). The cabinet was expanded in due course with junior ministers and this was also done after consultations to ensure representation of all the parties that came to constitute the Janata Party.

A brief recount of the political life of the three important leaders of the Janata Party— Morarji Desai, Charan Singh and Jagjivan Ram—will be in order at this stage before we move on to the next section. All of them had aspired to be the prime minister and both Charan Singh and Ram continued to believe that the post was snatched away from them and held that it was their duty to do everything to replace Morarji Desai from that position. This was the cause of the Janata's collapse.

Morarji began as the Minister for Revenue, Agriculture, Forest and Co-operatives in the ministry headed by B. G. Kher in the then Bombay Province in 1937 and remained in that position until September 1939, when the Congress Provincial Governments resigned. After the elections to the state assemblies in 1946, he became the Minister for Home and Revenue in Bombay. In 1952, despite losing the elections, he became the chief minister of Bombay. This happened because Kher, his mentor, had sought retirement from public life. Desai was opposed to the creation of a separate Gujarat State. But that happened in November 1960. Desai, meanwhile joined the Union Cabinet as Minister for Commerce and Industry (on 14 November 1956) and was elevated as the finance minister on 22 March 1958. In 1963, he was eased out of the Union Cabinet under the Kamaraj Plan. He did hope to succeed Nehru as the prime minister in May 1964. That, however, did not happen. He contested against Indira Gandhi and lost the election in the Congress Parliamentary Party in January 1966. In March 1967, Desai joined Indira Gandhi's cabinet as the deputy prime minister and Minister in-charge of Finance. This was a compromise he agreed to after insisting that he was in the race for the prime minister's post. In July 1969, Indira Gandhi took away the finance portfolio from him. While Desai conceded that it was the prime minister's prerogative to change the portfolios of colleagues, he felt that his self-respect had been hurt and hence resigned as the deputy prime minister.

Desai had a son, Kanti Desai. He was a businessman, involved in a whole lot of deals, some of them scandalous, since the early Sixties. Kantibhai was a permanent fixture in his official residence when Morarji was the finance minister, and was present in the Prime Minister's entourage whenever Morarji travelled within the country and outside. This aspect of Morarji's life became relevant and even turned out to be a weapon in Charan Singh's hands against Desai and eventually ended up as a cause of the fall of the Janata Government in July 1979. We shall deal with it later.

Charan Singh continued to be a member of the Congress party until 1967. His association with the Congress had begun even before independence. He had registered his opposition to the resolution on cooperative farming at the Nagpur session (where Indira Gandhi was elected the party president) but remained in the party despite his opposition. He was a minister in the Uttar Pradesh cabinet under Sampoornanand at that time. He soon joined the dissidents, led at that time by Chandra Bhanu Gupta and was among the nine ministers who quit the cabinet forcing a regime change in the state. Gupta replaced Sampoornanand as the chief minister. The story is that Gupta double crossed Charan Singh at that time and this sense of hurt in the latter did not heal. In the elections to the state assembly in March 1967, the Congress party won just 199 seats in the 425-member Uttar Pradesh assembly. Both Gupta and Charan Singh were contenders for the chief minister's job and both of them tried collecting support from within the CLP as well as from the 18 independent legislators. Gupta managed to win in that instance and was sworn in as the chief minister. But then, Charan Singh would not let it pass. On 1 April 1967, he and 16 Congress MLAs voted against the government. The C. B. Gupta government was just 18 days old then. Charan Singh then negotiated with the opposition—the Socialist Party, the Jan Sangh, the Swatantra Party, the CPI—and managed to build a majority in the state assembly to become the chief minister heading the Samyukta Vidhayak Dal (SVD). Charan Singh was hailed by Lohia for this! Charan Singh founded the Bharatiya Kranti Dal (BKD) now. All this lasted for less than a year.

In January 1968, the Samyukta Socialist Party (SSP), a constituent of the SVD with 45 MLAs, launched a campaign against Indira Gandhi's visit to Varanasi to address a session of the Indian Science Congress. Their plan was to *gherao* her and conduct a public trial against her in the city. Charan Singh, as the chief minister, ordered the arrest of the leaders of the SSP including Raj Narain. This enraged the SSP leadership and it was clear that his SVD government would fall. Charan Singh stepped down as the chief minister on 17 February 1968, a day before the state assembly session was to begin. That led the Congress to form its government, once again, in the state and Charan Singh's bête noire, C. B. Gupta returned as the chief minister. Incidentally, Charan Singh recalled all this in his letter to Indira Gandhi on 8 January 1977 and pleaded before her to remember all that he had done to her. This was just 10 days before Indira announced her intentions to hold elections and Charan Singh landed as the key player in the formation of the Janata Party.

Going back to the Uttar Pradesh story, Charan Singh did not have to wait for long to hit back at Gupta. Gupta stayed on with the Congress (O) when the party split on 11 December 1969. By January 1970, his government was faced with a crisis when 16 of his cabinet colleagues resigned. They were Indira loyalists. Gupta's ministry soon lost the majority support in the state assembly. Indira's Congress, led by Kamalapati Tripathi at that time, was also far too short of a majority then. This was when Charan Singh displayed his willingness to simultaneously negotiate with players on either end of the spectrum. Even after announcing that he would form a SVD government, and this time, including Gupta's Congress (O), the Jan Sangh, the SSP and his own BKD, Charan Singh was negotiating with Kamalapati Tripathi for a BKD–Congress (R) coalition. The talks went on, for at least a couple of weeks, before he struck the deal with Indira Gandhi's emissary, D. P. Mishra. Charan Singh returned as the

Uttar Pradesh chief minister, this time with support from Indira Gandhi. The ministry fell soon and through defections, Indira Gandhi managed to install a Congress (R) government in Uttar Pradesh headed by Thribhuvan Narain Singh, by October 1970. Charan Singh's ambition to wrest power in the state in the assembly elections in March 1974 was frustrated once again. The man who revived the Congress fortunes in the State in 1974 was H. N. Bahuguna, who too was now a key player in the Janata Party. C. B. Gupta remained with the Congress (O) and was an important player in the Janata Party in its early days in March 1977. This explains his active lobbying against Charan Singh (along with Bahuguna) before JP decided on who would head the Janata Government on 24 March 1977. Charan Singh too saw Gupta lobbying for Jagjivan Ram and hence decided to favour Morarji Desai.

Charan Singh's wife Gayatri Devi was also one of his advisors. Her name would crop up, every now and then, in stories involving property deals. His son, Ajit Singh, was far away from the political scene at that time. Ajit Singh would step into his father's business only after his demise on 29 May 1987. The Lok Dal had undergone several splits by that time and would splinter into smaller factions after Ajit Singh decided to inherit the legacy. In his own time, Charan Singh had carved a large space in the political stage across Uttar Pradesh, Haryana and Bihar and commanded the loyalty of such leaders as Ram Naresh Yadav, Mulayam Singh Yadav, Raj Narain, Devi Lal and Karpoori Thakur. He could put this to use when he decided to pull down Morarji's Government in July 1979.

Jagjivan Ram, unlike the two others, was an important member of the Congress party and also Indira Gandhi's hatchet man against Morarji Desai. After his induction into the Interim Cabinet by Nehru as the Minister for Labour on 15 August 1947, Jagjivan Ram had been a part of all the cabinets until 31 August 1963. He quit as the Minister for Transport and Communication under the Kamaraj Plan. Ram was on the margins for a while. He returned to the cabinet on 24 January 1966, when Indira Gandhi succeeded Shastri and then remained part of her cabinet and would carry out all her orders until 2 February 1977 when he announced his decision to quit the Congress party and set up his own CFD. It may be recalled that Indira Gandhi wanted him to be the Congress party's nominee for the presidential polls in 1969; she had explained her preference on grounds that a Scheduled Caste as the president would be the most appropriate tribute to Mahatma Gandhi in his birth centenary year.

Jagjivan Ram, along with Fakhruddin Ali Ahmed, had raised the demand that Congress MPs and MLAs be allowed to vote according to their conscience in the presidential elections and this, as we had seen earlier (in Chapter VIII), was a decisive step leading to the victory of V. V. Giri against the Congress party's official candidate, N. Sanjiva Reddy. Ram's record, insofar as corruption was concerned, was cause for Indira Gandhi's embarrassment on several occasions.

He was found to have defaulted in filing his Income Tax returns and this was used by Morarji Desai's supporters to embarrass Indira Gandhi. Indira stood up for him and explained it as merely a small lapse. Jagjivan Ram had tried getting in touch with MPs, who were unhappy with Indira Gandhi, after the 12 June verdict by the Allahabad High Court. But he did not go far in this, once he realised that the numbers were not adding up to much. He moved the resolution seeking the parliament's approval to the Emergency and revolted against Indira Gandhi and the Emergency a couple of weeks after she announced elections. Sanjay had an intense dislike for Ram and it was likely that this old associate of Indira and the Congress party's poster boy (to show its commitment to the cause of the Scheduled Castes) may not have found a place in the party's list of candidates from Bihar in February–March 1977.

Jagjivan Ram too had a son. Suresh Ram was involved in the affairs of the CFD and and also used his fathers's office for his personal ends. Suresh was a source of embarrassment to his father and the Janata Party when *Surya*, a magazine run by Maneka Gandhi, published pictures and a report of his escapades in October 1978. The sex scandal, as it came to be known, came in handy for Charan Singh in his tirade against Jagjivan Ram. Suresh Ram would divorce his wife, Kamaljit, to marry Sushma Choudhury (with whom he was found in a compromising state in the photographs published by *Surya* magazine) before his death in July 1985. Jagjivan Ram's daughter, Meira Kumar would join the Congress party become MP and a Union minister in May 2004 and Lok Sabha Speaker in 2009.

We will discuss these further and in the context of the fall of the Janata Government. There was more to the Janata interregnum than intrigues among the leaders. One of that was the restoration of the Constitution and undoing the changes that were made during the Emergency and some more legislative interventions and administrative measures by the Janata Party government.

Restoring the Constitution

Among the many things that the Janata party's manifesto promised was the repeal of MISA and such other laws and undoing the amendments to the Constitution during the Emergency. The manifesto also promised to punish Indira Gandhi, Sanjay Gandhi and all the others guilty of destroying the democratic edifice. The acting president, B. D. Jatti's address to the joint sitting of the two houses of Parliament, on 28 March 1977, contained a categorical statement that MISA will be scrapped from the statute book. This, however, took longer than anyone expected. This preventive detention law, under which most members of the Janata Cabinet including the incumbent prime minister, Morarji Desai and the Janata Party's patron saint JP, were held in detention without any charge or trial, was removed from the statute books only on 19 July 1978, almost 16 months after the

Janata Party captured power on 21 March 1977. The government, meanwhile, toyed with the idea of changing the Code of Criminal Procedure (CrPC) so as to include similar provisions as were in the MISA. On 23 December 1977, the law minister, Shanti Bhushan, introduced a bill to amend the CrPC to include clauses providing for detention without trial. This came in for severe criticism from even inside the Janata Party with Madhu Limaye, one of its general secretaries, describing the idea as MISA through the backdoor. The point was while MISA was still an emergency provision and its life was bound by a specific time, the amendment that was proposed would have ensured preventive detention as part of the normal law of the land. Thanks to the criticism and the resistance from inside, the proposal was abandoned and the government moved a resolution, repealing MISA on 19 July 1978. The motion was passed without opposition and thus the draconian MISA, brought into force in 1971, was scrapped from the statute book at long last.

It is a different matter that similar laws, in different names, were introduced at different points of time in future too. For instance, the Congress government brought in TADA in the late 1980s and the BJP-led coalition enacted a similar draconian law called POTA in the late 1990s.

Meanwhile, the Janata government got on with the business of undoing some of the other facets of the Emergency. On 27 March 1977, the cabinet recommended an ordinance repealing the External Emergency proclaimed in December 1971, in the wake of the war against Pakistan. Along with that, the notorious Defence of India Rules (DIR) was made inapplicable. On 29 March 1977, the information and broadcasting minister, L. K. Advani, moved a resolution to repeal the Publication of Objectionable Matter Act. This law was used to carry out pre-censorship under the Emergency regime. Advani also moved a resolution to restore the operation of Parliamentary Proceedings (Protection) Act, which was also suspended during the Emergency. By this, the Protection of Publication Act, 1956, otherwise known as the Feroze Gandhi Act, was restored. Feroze Gandhi was the moving spirit behind this legislation that protected journalists from penal action when they reported proceedings of the two houses of Parliament as long as the reports were faithful reproduction of the happenings on the floor and done without malice. The provocation for that, at that time, came from the disclosures in Parliament about the scandalous siphoning of insurance funds by private players in the field and the exposé of that scam led to the nationalisation of the insurance industry.

The following day, Madhu Dandavate, now the Minister for Railways in the Janata government, set aside established conventions while presenting the railway budget for the year 1977–78. The convention was that no other business is transacted in the house except the presentation of the budget. Dandavate rose to seek the Speaker, K. S. Hegde's, sanction to make an announcement. He ordered reinstatement of all those railway workers who were removed from service for their participation in the May 1974 railway strike.

The Janata government was faced with yet another challenge. Justice M. H. Beg, whom Indira Gandhi had made the Chief Justice of the Supreme Court on 28 January 1977 (ten days after elections were announced) superceding Justice H. R. Khanna, was due to retire on 28 February 1978. It may be recalled that Beg was one of the 'committed' judges while Khanna spoke against the Emergency regime in the Habeas Corpus case. There was pressure from within the Janata Party, soon after it came to power, to ensure Beg's exit and appoint Khanna as the Chief Justice. Khanna himself was opposed to this idea and he agreed to take over as the chairman of the Law Commission. In February 1978, the government was faced with another dilemma. Justice Y. V. Chandrachud and Justice P. N. Bhagwati, both of whom had concurred with Justice A. N. Ray and Justice Beg in the Habeas Corpus case, qualified (in that order) to be elevated as the Chief Justice. JP himself had urged that these two be superceded on grounds that it was morally right to do so. But the bar associations across the country felt otherwise and the Janata Cabinet cleared Chandrachud's name as top judge of the apex court after Justice Beg retired on 22 February 1978.

As Chief Justice, Chandrachud would lead a bench of trailblazing judges to espouse the cause of justice to the poor and the marginalised along with such others as Bhagwati, Krishna Iyer, O. Chinnappa Reddy and R. S. Pathak. They all brought out the possibilities of ensuring justice by way of the writ jurisdiction and the genre of law that came to be known, in due course, as Public Interest Litigation (PIL). One such case involved the detention, for years, of the undertrials in jails across the country. The Supreme Court ordered several thousands to be freed and set out the imperative for speedy trial. The principle involved here was that detention shall not exceed the maximum period of sentence, prescribed by law, for the offence under which the accused is charged. This led to justice for several thousands of undertrial prisoners across the country. The Janata cabinet also resolved to rescind the penal transfer of the High Court judges (carried out by the Emergency establishment in the context of the Habeas Corpus case) and the law minister, Shanti Bhushan told the Lok Sabha on 5 April 1977 (within a couple of weeks after the Janata Government came to power), that all those judges who were moved out in May 1976 were free to move back to their old High Courts and that they may do that only if they wished to.

Another important landmark in the Janata era was the Shah Commission of Enquiry. On 28 May 1977, the Janata government issued a notification constituting a Commission of Enquiry to go into the various aspects of the Emergency. The Commission was set up under Section 3 of the Commission of Enquiries Act, 1952 and Justice J. C. Shah, retired Chief Justice of the Supreme Court, was appointed its chairman. Justice Shah, it may be recalled, had presided over a convention at Ahmedabad on 12 October 1975 convened by the Citizens for Democracy in which Justice M. C. Chagla had made a scathing attack on the Emergency.

The terms of reference for the Commission were wide ranging and included (a) the subversion of lawful processes and established conventions, administrative procedures and practices, abuse of authority, misuse of powers during the period when the Emergency was in force or in the days immediately preceding the proclamation, (b) the misuse of powers of arrests or issue of detention orders, (c) the specific instances of maltreatment, atrocities during the Emergency, (d) the specific instances of compulsion and use of force in the implementation of the family planning programme, (e) the indiscriminate high-handedness or unauthorised demolition of houses, huts, shops, buildings in the name of slum clearance or enforcement of town planning or land use schemes during the Emergency. The terms also included that the Commission recommend measures to prevent the recurrence of such abuse of authority, misuse of powers, excesses and malpractices.

The Commission was free to present interim reports and 31 December 1977, was set as the date for submission of the final report. This was extended, subsequently to 30 June 1978. The Commission fixed 31 July 1977 as the date before which complaints were to be filed and began hearing oral evidence of witnesses from 29 September 1977. The Commission's hearings were a public affair and the media, now free from all censorship regulations, reported the proceedings day after day. Those who deposed before the Commission included the victims, officials and most importantly some members of Indira Gandhi's cabinet such as H. R. Gokhale (Law), C. Subramaniam (Finance), T. A. Pai (Industry), Raj Bahadur (Civil Aviation) and S. S. Ray (Chief Minister, West Bengal and her confidant during the days before the 25 June 1975 proclamation). All of them pleaded that they were kept in the dark and held Sanjay Gandhi and his gang of four responsible for most of the abuses.

Their deposition before the Commission, in the first few days of the sitting, exposed the extra-constitutional authority that Sanjay Gandhi had wielded during the Emergency. These leaders, incidentally, were in Indira's Congress party even when they deposed before the Commission. They went with Y. B. Chavan after the split on 2 January 1978. Indira Gandhi, meanwhile, sought to frustrate the Enquiry by all means. Initially, she took the plea that she will not depose before the Commission on grounds that her actions, as the prime minister, were bound by the Oath of Secrecy. When this strategy failed, she demanded that she be allowed to cross-examine the others who deposed. This was also disallowed and finally, Indira would refuse to say anything before the Commission except making a long speech that went on for over 30 minutes. All this notwithstanding, the Shah Commission went ahead with its enquiry and collated oral evidences whose transcripts ran into several hundred pages, before submitting two interim reports and a final report.

The first interim report, submitted on 11 March 1978, dealt with the circumstances leading to the declaration of the Emergency and also on how the press was gagged. About the circumstances leading to the 25 June 1975 proclamation, the report said: 'There was no threat to the well being of the nation from sources external or internal. The conclusion appears, in the absence of any evidence given by Indira Gandhi or anyone else, that the one and only motivating force for tendering the extraordinary advice to the President to declare Internal Emergency was the intense political activity generated in the ruling party and the opposition, by the decision of the Allahabad High Court declaring the election of the Prime Minister of the day invalid, on the ground of corrupt electoral practices… Smt. Gandhi in her anxiety to continue in power, brought about a situation, which directly contributed to her continuance in power and also generated forces which sacrificed the interests of many to serve the ambitions of a few…the inference is inevitable that a political decision was taken by an interested Prime Minister in desperate endeavour to save herself from the legitimate compulsion of a judicial verdict against her.'

On the issue of the Emergency regime's treatment of the media, the Commisison said: 'The reasons for the measures taken against the media in general and the Press in particular was to keep the public in ignorance and instill fear in them thereby suppressing dissent in every form, individual, political, parliamentary and judicial and that it was used as an instrument of the news management aimed at thought control.'

The second interim report, in which the police actions and other atrocities at the Turkman Gate and the role of Sanjay Gandhi was dealt with among other things, said: 'From the evidence on record, it is absolutely clear that Shri Sanjay Gandhi did intervene on behalf of Shri Bhinder and pressurised the District Magistrate and his colleagues and the junior Magistrate to sign and pre-date the firing order. It was a highly improper and unwarranted interference on the part of Shri Sanjay Gandhi to have called the Magistrates to his residence and ordered them to do a wholly improper and illegal act.'

The third and the final report of the Commission was out on 6 August 1978 and this dealt with the individual complaints of torture and the condition in prisons as well as on the atrocities committed in the name of family planning programme. Apart from recommending penal action against those found guilty and this included specific charges against Indira Gandhi, Sanjay Gandhi, V. C. Shukla, Bansi Lal, Kishen Chand, Navin Chawla and P. S. Bhinder among others, the report made the following observation: 'What happened during the Emergency was the subversion of a system of administration.' All this meant that the Janata Government was left with the task of launching prosecution proceedings against those found guilty by the Shah Commission. This was a task easier said than done. Those in the government were aware of the long delays that are part of any legal process.

It was held, by important leaders of the Janata Party (Ram Jethmalani, who defeated H. R. Gokhale was among them) and also many in the cabinet, that the government issue an ordinance to set up Special Courts to ensure speedy trial. This demand began to be made in May 1978, after the first and the second interim reports of the Shah Commission were submitted. Morarji Desai, however, was not in favour of this measure. It was only on 8 May 1979 that Parliament passed an act, providing for the setting up of Special Courts to ensure speedy trial of the cases relating to the Emergency. And two Special Courts, headed by Justice M. S. Joshi and Justice M. L. Jain (both of the Delhi High Court) were set up, at long last, on 31 May 1979. It was too late by then. The government fell on 16 July 1979 and all the hard work done by the Shah Commission and its findings would soon be reduced to a joke by Indira Gandhi and her son, Sanjay Gandhi. After her return to power in January 1980, the Delhi High Court declared the constitution of the Special Courts as illegal and that was how Indira, Sanjay and all those who were found guilty by the Shah Commission were saved from facing trial.

The more lasting impression left by the Janata Party was in the area of restoring the Constitution to its pre-Emergency status by undoing what was done to the Constitution through the 42nd amendment. The leaders had promised to do so in their manifesto and they had campaigned against the amendment and even declared it an illegitimate amendment brought about by an illegitimate parliament. The most vocal sections in the Janata Party were keen on a one-line motion to delete all the insertions and changes in the Constitution brought in through the 42nd Amendment. This, however, was easier said than done. The Janata Party's majority was restricted to the Lok Sabha only and a constitutional Amendment of this nature required a two-thirds majority in both houses as well as a majority in at least 13 state assemblies.

Such a one-line amendment could have been passed with ease in the Lok Sabha: The Janata Party had 298 members and the amendment would have been supported by the 22 CPI (M) MPs, the nine Akali Dal MPs and some others. In other words, it would have been possible, with some effort, to gather 362 MPs (two-thirds of the strength) to vote for such an amendment in the Lok Sabha. But then, the situation was the opposite in the Rajya Sabha. The party position in the 244-member upper house, as in May 1977, was as follows: The Congress (R) had 154 members against the Janata Party's strength of 27. The ruling party could bank on the three CPI (M) MPs and two from the DMK and that was all. The fact was that any amendment restoring the Constitution to the pre-42nd amendment status would require the support of Indira's Congress party MPs in the Rajya Sabha. The same was true of the states too. The Congress was in power in all the states and the ADMK, its ally in Tamil Nadu. It would take long before the party position was altered in the upper house.

This could be achieved, in part, by invoking Article 356 of the Constitution, to dismiss Congress governments in at least eight states, dissolving the state assemblies and ensuring fresh elections there. Invoking Article 356 was both moral and immoral at that time. It was immoral because there was no definite sign, in any of the states, of a breakdown of the constitutional scheme. But then, it was also moral because most of those assemblies were on extended terms after the Emergency regime had obtained the parliamentary sanction to extend the terms beyond the five years in the same way as it was done in the case of the Lok Sabha. In other words, the normal five year term of the state assemblies of West Bengal, Himachal Pradesh, Madhya Pradesh, Bihar, Haryana, Punjab, Rajasthan and Orissa were over in March 1977 but were extended until March 1978 by the Emergency regime.

The Janata Party leaders were convinced over the political correctness of dissolving these assemblies and also of its inevitability. It was considered inevitable because the composition of these state legislatures had to be changed in order to increase their presence in the Rajya Sabha (in biennial elections scheduled for April–May 1978) and also to ensure the election of their own candidate as the next president. The presidential elections were due before mid-August 1977. There was a firm basis in their hopes to achieve all that, given the mandate they received in the March 1977 general elections. Moreover, the Janata's patron saint, JP, had demanded dissolution of these assemblies even during the campaign for the general elections and repeated that after the Janata won the mandate. Morarji, however, did not appear keen on that in the beginning. He rode the high moral position that it would be ideal if the state governments recommended their own dissolution. This was his view at a press conference, on 24 March 1977, soon after he assumed the office of Prime Minister. The majority in the cabinet, however, did not think that way.

When the cabinet began discussing the issue and resolved in favour of forcing the resignation of the state governments and dissolution of the legislatures, it added Uttar Pradesh to the list of states. The elections to the Uttar Pradesh Assembly were last held in March 1974 and its life would go until March 1979. The Janata, however, held that the Congress had lost its mandate to rule and that this was evident from the fact that the party lost all the 85 Lok Sabha seats there. On 18 April 1977, the home minister, Charan Singh wrote to the chief ministers of the nine states, in which he said that it will be appropriate for them to recommend to the respective governors to dissolve the legislatures and call for fresh elections. Charan Singh's letter made it clear that this was the considered view of the Union Cabinet, arrived at after consulting the constitutional experts and that the cabinet was concerned with the 'unprecedented situation caused by the national elections and the resultant climate of uncertainty and diffidence at various levels of the administration' and added that this could lead to a serious threat to the law and order in those states.

This letter was taken by some of the states to the Supreme Court with a plea that the apex court declare it unconstitutional. On 29 April 1977, a seven-judge bench, headed by Chief Justice Beg, dismissed the plea on grounds that the core issue involved was political and not legal. Beg even went to say that the use of Article 356 cannot be excluded if the central government thought the state governments must seek a fresh mandate to prevent a bad law and order situation. Interestingly, Beg had travelled a long way from his earlier times. It could have also been an instance of being on the right side of the political establishment of the day. The state governments, however, did not listen to the home minister's advice. The Union Cabinet, now armed with this endorsement by the apex court, met on the same day to recommend dismissal of the state governments and dissolution of the legislatures invoking Article 356 of the Constitution. The cabinet did not have a report from the governors of these states on the failure of the constitutional scheme of governance. This was not a serious problem because Article 356 also provided for such action by the president even 'otherwise'. The recommendation was thus sent to the acting president, Jatti, the same evening. Jatti, however, dragged his feet and refused to issue the proclamation. Provoked by this, Desai conveyed to Jatti that the cabinet would resign, recommend dissolution of the Lok Sabha and seek fresh elections on that ground. Jatti relented and dissolved the legislative assemblies in the nine States.

The dispute was taken to the Supreme Court once again and the apex court held that the actions of the president, in regard to invoking Article 356, was not justiceable and dismissed the case. It would take about 15 more years, before the Supreme Court held such actions as subject to judicial scrutiny and also setting out clear-cut guidelines and procedures to be followed by the Union Government before invoking Article 356. That happened in the S. R. Bommai and others vs Union of India (1993) and the judgement would render use of the Article impossible, leave alone its abuse. We shall deal with this later (in Chapter XIV).

The Janata Party's contention that the Congress had lost the mandate of the people in these states was borne out by the results of the elections held in June 1977. The Congress lost in all the states. The Janata swept the polls in Uttar Pradesh, Bihar, Haryana, Orissa, Madhya Pradesh, Rajasthan and Himachal Pradesh, the CPI(M) in West Bengal and the Akali Dal in Punjab. In Bihar, the Janata won 214 seats against the 57 by the Congress; in Haryana, it was 75 for the Janata against just three for the Congress; in Madhya Pradesh, it was 230 for the Janata and 84 for the Congress; in Orissa, the Janata won 110 against the 26 by the Congress; in Rajasthan, it was 151 for the Janata and 41 for the Congress and in Uttar Pradesh, the Janata won 352 seats against the Congress party's 47. In Punjab, the Akali Dal and the Janata contested the elections as allies and won 58 and 25 seats respectively against the 17 seats secured by the Congress. In West Bengal, the CPI (M) won 178 seats to constitute a simple majority in the assembly and the Congress was reduced to just 20 seats; the Janata contested the polls on its own and secured only 29 seats.

The Janata's victory in these states exposed the party to new strains. The MLAs, though elected on Janata ticket, continued to constitute blocks based on their affiliation to one or another constituent of the Janata and this would emerge as a flash point in the crisis that rocked the Janata boat in the next couple of years. We shall discuss some of these in the next section. For the moment, the Janata victory in all these states would ensure more Janata members in the Rajya Sabha by April 1978. After the biennial elections to the Rajya Sabha in April 1978, the Janata Party's strength went up to 42; and to 70 in April 1979.

All this also meant that the Janata Party could ensure the election of its own nominee as President of the Republic. N. Sanjiva Reddy, who as the official Congress candidate had lost the elections in 1969, was now elected as president and sworn in to that office on 8 August 1977. Interestingly, the Janata leaders managed to have Reddy elected unanimously this time. Incidentally, they could negotiate this with Y. B. Chavan, now the leader of the Congress party in Parliament, to arrive at this consensus. Chavan, it may be recalled was one of the four members who voted for Reddy in the Congress Parliamentary Board executive in July 1969 against Indira's wishes. It is another matter that he switched over to the Indira camp soon after the July meet of the AICC and was among those who voted against Reddy in the elections then. This time, he would assert himself and committed the Congress party to support Reddy.

All this notwithstanding, it was not possible for the Janata government to restore the Constitution to its pre-Emergency status without support from Indira's Congress. And this did not change even after Indira split the Congress party on 2 January 1978. We shall discuss the details of this split in the next chapter. For now, it suffices to say that the Congress, headed by Y. B. Chavan had 131 MPs (67 Lok Sabha and 64 in the Rajya Sabha) while Indira Gandhi's Congress (I), I now standing for Indira, was reduced to 148 MPs (76 in the Lok Sabha and 72 in the Rajya Sabha).

It was possible for the Janata Government to manage the Chavan Congress to support a one-line amendment to the Constitution. The context of the split in the Congress and the fact that several of those in Chavan's Congress party, including such senior leaders like C. Subramaniam, T. A. Pai and H. R. Gokhale among others, had blamed Indira and her son Sanjay Gandhi for all that went wrong during the Emergency meant that the Janata government could bank on them to reverse the effects of the 42nd Constitution Amendment. But then, the combined strength of the Janata, the Congress, the CPI (M), the Akali Dal and the CPI (which was now coming out of its past) did not add up to two-thirds of the Rajya Sabha's strength, which was 162. Meanwhile, with Indira Gandhi now under siege (with the media publicising the proceedings before the Shah Commission as well as stories of corruption and misdeeds day after day), the Congress (I) came forward to support a Constitution amendment; the party, however, was against a one-line amendment and categorical that the Right to Property shall not be restored as a Fundamental Right.

The Janata Government responded to the situation by introducing the 43rd Constitution Amendment Bill in the Lok Sabha on 16 December 1977. It was a truncated version of what the Janata leaders wished. Apart from deleting Article 31-D (an insertion through the 42nd amendment and a saving clause insofar as Fundamental Rights were concerned for those who were suspected to be engaged in anti-national activities), the bill also scrapped the provision requiring a two-thirds majority in the bench for judicial reviews (this insertion through the 42nd amendment had meant that three judges could frustrate the will of four in a bench of seven) and also restoring to the High Courts the power (under Article 226) to judge on the constitutional validity of a central law. The bill was passed by the Lok Sabha on 20 December 1977. The voting figures were interesting: 318 for the amendment and one against it. All the Congressmen in the Lok Sabha, including Vasant Sathe, Seyid Mohammad and C. M. Stephen, all of whom were members of the Swaran Singh Committee, supported the amendment! Things were not different in the Rajya Sabha too. The house took up the bill for consideration on 23 December 1977 and passed it the same day without a single vote against the amendment. There were two members of the Swaran Singh Committee in the upper house too: V. N. Gadgil and B. N. Banerjee. Swaran Singh himself was not in Parliament as he was defeated in March 1977 from Jalandhar.

After ratification by the state assemblies, the 43rd Constitution Amendment received President's assent on 13 April 1978. The Janata's agenda was not over. There were several other insertions made during the Emergency in the Constitution. And this was taken up for discussion within the Cabinet as well as between the government and all political parties, and the law minister, Shanti Bhushan, introduced the Constitution 44th Amendment Bill in the Lok Sabha on 15 May 1978.

It will be pertinent to cite excerpts from the Statement of Objects and Reasons of the amendment bill in this context. It said: 'A Proclamation of Emergency under Article 352 has virtually the effect of amending the Constitution by converting it for the duration into that of a Unitary State and enabling the rights of the citizen to move the courts for the enforcement of fundamental rights – including the right to life and liberty – to be suspended. Adequate safeguards are, therefore, necessary to ensure that this power is properly exercised and is not abused. It is, therefore, proposed that a proclamation of emergency can be issued only when the security of India or any part of its territory is threatened by war or external aggression or by armed rebellion. Internal disturbance not amounting to armed rebellion would not be a ground for the issue of a proclamation.' The house took it up for discussion on 7 August 1978 in the Monsoon session. It proposed deletion of Article 257-A (power to the Centre to send its forces to a State), scrapping Article 328-A (thus restoring to the Supreme Court the power to decide on election disputes) and that the Right to Property be excluded from the Fundamental Rights and retained only as a constitutional right. It proposed deleting Article 31-C, which had been a cause for dispute involving the conflict between Fundamental Rights and Directive Principles of State Policy and leading to a battle between the judiciary and legislature in the extend of rights to amend the Constitution. This seemed to have been settled by the verdict in the Keshavananda Bharati case but the issue was revived by the 42nd Amendment Act.

The bill also proposed replacing the words 'internal disturbance' with 'armed rebellion' in Article 352, Clause 1, of the Constitution. It also clarified that the president shall act (invoke the powers under Article 352) only on the basis of a written resolution from the Union Cabinet. It may be recalled that the 25 June 1975 proclamation was made on an interpretation that the agitation by the opposition parties constituted an 'internal disturbance' and was done without the Cabinet resolution.

The Lok Sabha voted the amendment bill by 355 votes for and none against on 28 August 1978. It was, however, a different story in the Rajya Sabha. The Congress MPs voted against the amendment and it was sent back to the Lok Sabha. They opposed Clause 8 of the Amendment Bill (that proposed deletion of Article 31-C). Article 31-C ensured that laws enacted to realise any of the Directive Principles of State Policy shall not be subject to judicial scrutiny and struck down on grounds that they violated any of the Fundamental Rights guaranteed by Articles 14 and 19. The Janata had two options: To let the amendment die and give up its agenda to restore the Constitution to its pre-Emergency status or to compromise and let Article 31-C remain in the Constitution. The Janata leaders agreed to compromise rather than let the bill die. And on 7 December 1978, Lok Sabha passed the bill, as amended by the Rajya Sabha. All the mischief that was done to the Constitution by way of the 42nd Constitution Amendment was undone by the 44th Constitution Amendment. On 7 December 1978, when the bill was voted into an act in the Lok Sabha, those favouring it included Indira Gandhi. She had entered the house, by now, winning a by-election from Chickmagalur in Karnataka.

As for the fears that loomed large over the retention of Article 31-C and the apprehension that this had meant taking the clock back to the pre-

Keshavananda Bharati days vesting Parliament with unrestricted powers to amend the Constitution, the Supreme Court settled the issue once again in the Minerva Mills case in 1980. It was held that Parliament's power to amend the Constitution was subject to judicial scrutiny and that constitutional amendments are consistent with the basic structure of the Constitution; as it was decided in the Keshavananda Bharati case.

The story of the Janata regime's achievements will be incomplete without a mention of the setting up of the Second Backward Classes Commission with Bindeswari Prasad Mandal as its chairman. Implementation of the Mandal Commission recommendations, in August 1990, would shake the political edifice and alter the political discourse in a big way. While we will discuss the dynamics of caste and the political implications of Mandal later in this book, it will be appropriate to merely mention some basic facts at this stage.

With the Socialists and the Lok Dal playing a major role in the making of the Janata Party in January 1977, its manifesto, released on 30 January 1977, contained a promise to set up a Second Backward Classes Commission and to rectify the failings of the First Backward Classes Commission, otherwise known as the Kaka Kalelkar Commission. It is important to note here that this was not merely an issue involving partisan politics. It was, instead, a constitutional imperative and this can be found in Article 340 of the Constitution. It reads:

1. The President *may* by order appoint a Commission consisting of such persons as he thinks fit to investigate the conditions of *socially and educationally backward classes* within the territory of India and the difficulties under which they labour and to make recommendations as to the steps that should be taken by the Union or any State to remove such difficulties and to improve their condition and as to the grants that should be made, and the order appointing such a Commission shall define the procedure to be followed by the Commission.
2. A Commission so appointed shall investigate the matters referred to them and present to the President a report setting out the facts as found by them and making such recommendations as they think proper.
3. The President shall cause a copy of the report so presented together with a memorandum explaining the action taken thereon to be laid before each House of Parliament.

It is also relevant at this stage to recall, in brief, the experience with the First Backward Classes Commission. Constituted on 29 January 1953 with Kaka Kalelkar, an eminent Gandhian, as chairman, the commission looked into the various issues and submitted its report on 30 March 1955. The commission report identified as many as 2,399 castes as Backward Classes for the entire country and 837 among them were categorised Most Backward. This was done on the basis of their low social positions in the traditional caste hierarchy of Hindu society, the lack of general educational advancement among the major section of a caste or community, inadequate or no representation in government service and inadequate representation in the field of trade, commerce and industry

The data for this was drawn on the basis of a projection of the castes in the population with aid from the Registrar General and the Census Commissioner, because caste census had been given up in 1931. The report also recommended undertaking caste-wise enumeration in the 1961 census. The First Backward Classes Commission also recommended reservation of 70 per cent of seats in all technical and professional institutions for qualified students of backward classes and reservation of vacancies in all government services and local bodies for OBCs on the following scale: 25 per cent for Class I posts, 33.33 per cent for Class II posts and 40 per cent for Class III and Class IV posts.

But then, Kalelkar had also presented a note, with his recommendation, expressing his discomfort with the use of caste as a category for determining backwardness; and his discomfort was based on his Gandhian convictions that caste as a category had to be abolished once and for all. The Kaka Kalelkar Report along with the Action Taken Report was placed in Parliament on 3 September 1956. The government, under Jawaharlal Nehru, rejected the idea of linking caste with backwardness and set out to find out an alternative basis. The Deputy Registrar General (Census) was asked to undertake a survey to see if backwardness could be linked to occupational groups instead of caste. This, however, did not lead anywhere.

On 14 August 1961, the Union Home Ministry issued a circular to the states that the state governments have the discretion to chose their own criteria for defining backwardness and that in the view of the Union Government, it would be better to go by economic criteria than by caste. This paved the way for several state governments setting out on this course and the appointment of various commissions. Among them were the Manohar Prashad Commission (Andhra Pradesh), Mungeri Lal (Bihar) A. R. Bakshi (Gujarat), Gajendragadkar and A. N. Wazir (Jammu and Kashmir), Naganna Gowda and Havanur (Karnataka), V. K. Viswanathan, G. Kumara Pillai and M. P. Damodaran (Kerala), B. D. Deshmukh (Maharashtra), Brish Bhan (Punjab) and A. N. Sattanathan (Tamil Nadu). While these enquiry commissions recommended that caste cannot be wished away in measuring and determining backwardness, this idea was challenged in the courts in almost all the instances. A decisive case in this regard was the judgement in the Balaji vs State of Mysore (1963). It was held that it is social *and* educational backwardness and not social *or* educational backwardness. The court also held that speaking generally and in a broad way, a special provision should be less than 50 per cent. How much less than 50 per cent would depend on the prevailing circumstances in each case, the apex court held.

This was followed by the judgement in the P. Rajendran vs State of Madras (1968). It stressed that it must not be forgotten that a caste is also a class of citizens and if the caste as a whole is socially and educationally backward, reservation can be made in favour of such a caste on the ground that it is socially and educationally backward class of citizens within the meaning of Article 15 (4) of the Constitution.

This was the point that the leaders of the Socialist Party were making over the years. The various state governments of which they were a part in 1967 and 1969 had also gone about setting out reservation for the other backward classes in state government jobs. And in 1977, the Socialists and the BLD leaders ensured that the Janata Party committed itself to this idea. On 20 December 1978, the Union Government appointed a commission with B. P. Mandal as its chairman. At that time, Mandal was a Janata Party MP representing Madhepura in Bihar. He had represented the same constituency on behalf of the Samyukta Socialist Party between 1967 and 1971. His report was submitted to the government on 31 December 1980, almost a year after Indira Gandhi had returned as prime minister. B. P. Mandal, unlike Kaka Kalelkar, was categorical that the substitution of caste by economic tests will amount to ignoring the genesis of social backwardness in the Indian society.

Based on an elaborate process of field survey and academic debates, the Mandal Commission settled to measure backwardness on the basis of 11 indicators that were grouped under three broad heads: social, educational and economic.

Social indicators were: Castes/classes considered as socially backward by others; castes/classes which mainly depend on manual labour for their livelihood; castes/classes where at least 25 per cent females and 10 per cent males above the state average get married at an age below 17 years in rural areas and at least 10 per cent females and 5 per cent males do so in urban areas; and castes/classes where participation of females in work is at least 25 per cent above the state average.

Educational indicators were: Castes/classes where the number of children in the age group of 5–15 years who never attended school is at least 25 per cent above the state average; castes/classes where the rate of student dropout in the age group of 5–15 years is at least 25 per cent above the state average; and castes/classes amongst whom the proportion of matriculates is at least 25 per cent below the state average.

Economic indicators were: Castes/classes where the average value of family assets is at least 25 per cent below the state average; castes/classes where the number of families living in kuccha houses is at least 25 per cent above the state average; castes/classes where the source of drinking water is beyond half a kilometre for more than 50 per cent of the households; and castes/classes where the number of households having taken consumption loans is at least 25 per cent above the state average.

The data thus collated was then graded with three points for each of the social indicators, two points for each of the educational indicators and one point for each of the economic indicators. Economic indicators were considered relevant because economic backwardness directly flowed from social and educational backwardness.

While all those castes/classes that were part of the survey were subjected to tests under all the 11 criteria, those that crossed the 11 points benchmark (50 per cent) were listed as OBCs. The Mandal Commission's report was shelved by Indira Gandhi and Rajiv Gandhi until it was pulled out for action and implementation by V. P. Singh on 7 August 1990. And this changed the course of the nation's politics. While all this will be discussed in detail at a later stage (chapter XIV) in this book, the fact is that the appointment of the Mandal Commission was one of the major decisions of the Janata Party.

The Janata's Disintegration

The causes for the disintegration of the Janata Party could be located in the manner in which the party was founded in January 1977. Its organisation was constituted by separate blocks belonging to the Jan Sangh, the Socialists and the BLD. Neither Morarji Desai nor Jagjivan Ram could claim to have such an organisation. But then, Desai was backed by JP in the race for the prime minister's job against Jagjivan Ram. And Charan Singh dropped out of the race only in order to eliminate the possibility of Jagjivan Ram making it to the post. When it appeared to Charan Singh that Desai was there to stay, he began working towards achieving his goal: To become the prime minister of India. He did achieve that on 28 July 1979. But then, he also ended up decimating the Janata Party. He was prime minister for only 24 days (28 July 1979 to 20 August 1979) because Indira decided to withdraw support within that time. The collapse of the Janata Party was not merely due to Charan Singh's ambitions but this clearly was the single largest cause. In this section, we shall go through a narrative of the events that ended in the Janata Party's split, the fall of the Morarji Desai Government, Charan Singh's travails as prime minister and his resignation on 20 August 1979.

After the settlement reached among the leaders on Cabinet formation (with Jagjivan Ram, Bahuguna, Fernandes, Raj Narain and Brijlal Verma sworn in as ministers on 28 March 1977), the Janata Party seemed to have arrived on the political scene as a single united party. In April and May 1977, the leaders worked together to set up several Commissions of Enquiry (including the Shah Commission on 18 May 1977 and the Justice Jagan Mohan Reddy Commission to enquire into the Nagarwala scam on 6 June 1977) and also the dismissal of nine Congress state governments and the dissolution of those assemblies. A party workers convention was held in Delhi, on 1 May 1977, in which delegates from all the constituents that came to found the party participated and Chandra Shekhar was elected president. A parliamentary board with Chandra Shekhar, Morarji Desai, Charan Singh, Jagjivan Ram, Atal Behari Vajpayee, George Fernandes, Ramakrishna Hegde, Nanaji Deshmukh, B. S. Nahar and Rabi Ray was also constituted. Chandra Shekhar, in due course, also appointed his office bearers, picking up men from across the spectrum that made the Janata.

Even as it appeared that the Janata Party had settled down with business, trouble began to brew. Although they contested the elections to the nine state assemblies (in June 1977) under one party and one symbol, the newly elected MLAs continued to be wedded to their old parties and this meant that the Janata Legislature Parties in the various states came to be constituted by several factions. This led to contests and feuds among leaders in the states as well as their bosses in the Union Cabinet turning into partisans. Those who belonged to the Bharatiya Jan Sangh constituted a clear majority in the Janata Legislature Party in Madhya Pradesh, Rajasthan and Himachal Pradesh as well as in the Union Territory of Delhi. The election of chief ministers in these states was over without any wrangling.

Kailash Chandra Joshi, an associate of the RSS for long and a Jan Sangh leader until the formation of the Janata Party, was elected chief minister of Madhya Pradesh. In Rajasthan, Bhairon Singh Shekawat, once again an RSS–Jan Sangh veteran, became the chief minister. In Himachal Pradesh, Shanta Kumar, an old RSS–Jan Sangh leader, was elected as chief minister and Kedarnath Sahni, an old RSS hand became chief minister of Delhi.

Nilamani Routray, a Charan Singh loyalist, was elected as chief minister of Orissa without a contest. In Haryana too, where the Janata had made a clean sweep in the elections, Devi Lal, a Charan Singh loyalist was elected leader unanimously. In Punjab, the Akali Dal chose Prakash Singh Badal, now Minister in the Morarji Cabinet to head the government. Badal was replaced by Surjit Singh Barnala in the Union Cabinet. There was, however, trouble in electing the Janata Legislature Party leader in Bihar and Uttar Pradesh.

In Bihar, the 214-member strong Janata Legislature Party was divided into three factions. At least 84 MLAs were loyal to the Congress (O) leader, Satyendra Narain Singh; the Lok Dal leader, Karpoori Thakur commanded the loyalty of an equal number of MLAs (and this included the Socialist Party loyalists) and the rest belonged to the Jan Sangh. There was no way that the MLAs would agree for a consensus and the chief minister had to be chosen through election. Nanaji Deshmukh was sent as Central Observer and Karpoori Thakur was elected leader of the Janata Legislature Party on 21 June 1977. He secured 144 votes to defeat Congress (O)'s Satyendra Narain Singh who managed only 84 votes. It was clear that Karpoori won with the Jan Sangh supporting him. And

Singh charged Deshmukh of facilitating that by ordering the Jan Sangh MLAs to vote for him.

In Uttar Pradesh, the Janata Legislature Party was made of three distinct factions. Ram Naresh Yadav, a Charan Singh loyalist headed the BLD faction and he could count on the support of at least 150 MLAs; his claims for the chief minister's post was contested by Ram Dhan, who had been in the Congress until 25 June 1975 and was arrested with Chandra Shekhar and others that night. Dhan had teamed up with Chandra Bhanu Gupta, the Congress (O) leader and an old adversary of Charan Singh. Like it happened in Bihar, there was election to decide on the chief minister on 22 June 1977. The Jan Sangh, with at least 100 MLAs, voted for Yadav. The votes were: 260 for Yadav and 120 for Dhan. Like in Bihar, the loser accused the Janata high command of influencing the decision and went a step ahead to say: 'The emergence of caste based politics is a potential threat to the Janata Party which might ultimately result in its break-up.' Ram Dhan, it may be pointed out, belonged to the Dalit community and had raised his voice, in a similar manner, when Jagjivan Ram was eliminated from the race for the prime minister's post on 24 March 1977. The fact is that the Janata Party let go an opportunity to elect a Dalit to the top job in Uttar Pradesh and this, as well as similar experiences later on, laid the path for the emergence of a party with a Dalit exclusivist agenda (the BSP) a decade later and culminating in Mayawati, leader of the BSP, steering her party to win 206 seats in the 401 strong assembly and become chief minister on her own in May 2007.

It was clear, by now, that Charan Singh and not Morarji Desai was the most powerful leader in the Janata Party. At least four Janata Chief Ministers—Ram Naresh Yadav, Karpoori Thakur, Devi Lal and Nilamani Rautray—were loyal to him. The Jan Sangh too had consolidated its position. Apart from having its men as chief ministers in four States (Madhya Pradesh, Rajasthan, Himachal Pradesh and Delhi), the chief ministers in Uttar Pradesh and Bihar depended on the party's support to survive. This faction ridden state of the Janata Legislature Parties in two of the most populous States—Bihar and Uttar Pradesh—would play a role in the party's disintegration.

Charan Singh, with the new-found confidence, now geared up to accomplish his wish: To arrest and detain Indira Gandhi in the Tihar jail and in the same cell and conditions in which Rajmata Vijayaraje Scindia was kept during the Emergency! He was stuck on this even while Desai had gone on record that the Janata government will not resort to vindictive action. Charan Singh, as home minister, now had the Central Bureau of Investigation (CBI) under him and this was an arrangement that was part of the deal to get him to agree to be number two in the Cabinet. The CBI, until then, was under the prime minister. In August 1977, Charan had the CBI register a First Information Report (FIR) against

Indira Gandhi, R. K. Dhawan, Yashpal Kapoor and eight others for financial embezzlement and ordered her arrest. The decision was taken in absolute secrecy and Desai ordered it to be stopped at the eleventh hour to Charan Singh's dismay. The home minister would strike again on 3 October 1977, and this time after informing the Cabinet of his plans. The timing of the arrest was also appropriate. Beginning 29 September 1977, T. A. Pai, H. R. Gokhale, Raj Bahadur, D. P. Chattopadyaya and C. Subramaniam, all former ministers, had deposed before the Shah Commission and made statements damning Indira and Sanjay.

At 5 in the evening, on 3 October, the CBI with a posse of Delhi Police personnel arrived at 12 Willington Crescent, New Delhi. After her defeat in March 1977, Indira was left homeless and her old friend, Mohammed Yunus vacated his own premises, 12 Willingdon Crescent, for Indira Gandhi. The Janata Government agreed to allot this bungalow in Lutyens' Delhi to Indira on condition that she paid 'market rent' for the premises. That was how 12 Willington Crescent became Indira Gandhi's official residence. The CBI went there on Charan Singh's instruction to arrest her. Indira, meanwhile, took her own time before showing herself at the door and demanded that she be hand-cuffed. Meanwhile, Sanjay and his aides used all the time to collect a posse of media personnel as well as crowds to shout slogans against her arrest. Indira relented to walk into a police van waiting to take her but not before a scene had been created, before the media and her supporters. And when she was finally driven out of the premises, Sanjay had ensured a fleet of vehicles, with party workers in them and shouting slogans, to follow the police convoy. The drama did not end there.

The CBI personnel wanted to take her to neighbouring Haryana. But Indira's lawyer, Frank Antony (who would be nominated to the Lok Sabha later as representative of the Anglo-Indian community) pointed out that the CBI did not have the authority to take Indira outside Delhi. Indira, meanwhile, got out of the van and sat on a culvert on the roadside. The CBI had to relent and Indira Gandhi was lodged, for that night, at the Police Lines premises in Old Delhi to be produced before a Magistrate's Court the following morning. The drama continued with clashes between her supporters and the Janata's around the court premises and the police bursting tear-gas shells. The CBI had also arrested K. D. Malavya, P. C. Sethi, H. R. Gokhale and D. P. Chattopadhyaya, all of them her former cabinet colleagues; B. B. Vohra (former secretary in the Ministry of Petroleum) and S. M. Aggarwal (former secretary in the Ministry of Communications); R. P. Goenka, M. V. Arunachalam and Jit Paul (heads of business houses).

The CBI had registered four separate FIRs and they dealt with:

1. Acquisition of over 100 jeeps for use in Rae Bareli, costing Rs 40 lakh, which were paid for by the accused industrialists and not by the AICC;

2. Award of a contract to a French firm for oil drilling in the Bombay High at an excess payment of Rs 11 crore;
3. Collection of funds for the Congress from large business houses in the form of advertisements or souvenirs to be published by the AICC before the last elections; and
4. Showing illegal favour to a Japanese firm for supply of some telephone equipment.

Additional Chief Metropolitan Magistrate, Delhi, R. Dayal, before whom Indira Gandhi was presented on 4 October 1977, however, found the CBI's arrest unwarranted on grounds that the CBI had not sought her arrest for interrogation and, hence, ordered her release immediately. Indira Gandhi left the same evening for Bombay, as per her earlier plans, and her three-day tour into Gujarat was turned into an opportunity to lash out at the government. Charan Singh, meanwhile, was blamed by his colleagues for acting in haste. His response was: 'The wrongs committed by her warranted a trial on the Nuremburg model, but the Government rested content with a trial for prima facie offences under the ordinary law of the land.' The Nuremburg trials, it may be recalled, was to prosecute the Nazi's for war crimes after the World War II and held under special laws. The government, meanwhile, filed an appeal against the magistrate's order in the Delhi High Court. The High Court dismissed the appeal on 5 October 1977 on grounds that adequate stamp fees were not paid and hence the appeal could not be entertained.

Indira, meanwhile, had her own troubles. Her isolation in the party was growing and several senior leaders demanded Sanjay's head as well as the expulsion of Bansi Lal and V. C. Shukla. She refused to allow any of this. And on 2 January 1978, 13 of the 21 members of the Congress Working Committee met, to elect Brahmananda Reddy as Congress president. The others who went against Indira Gandhi were: Y. B. Chavan, C. Subramaniam, K. C. Pant, Chandrajit Yadav and Ram Subhag Singh. They were joined by D. K. Baruah, Hitendra Desai, Karan Singh, Manubhai Shah and B. Bhagwati, all special invitees to the CWC.

The Congress Parliamentary Party too split with 131 MPs (67 Lok Sabha and 64 in the Rajya Sabha) deciding to stay with Reddy's Congress. Indira Gandhi's Congress (I) and the I now standing for Indira, was left with 148 MPs (76 in the Lok Sabha and 72 in the Rajya Sabha).

The first and the second Interim Report of the Shah Commission, submitted on 13 March 1978, coming as they did in the context of Indira's isolation in her own party, gave the Janata the much-needed impetus to act and called for cohesion. On 31 May, charge sheets were filed against R. K. Dhawan (Indira's private secretary), Pranab Mukherjee (former minister), D. Sen (former director of the CBI) and P. S. Bhinder (former DIG, Delhi Police) under various sections of the IPC. The charges involved counterfeiting, causing grievous hurt to persons and wrongful confinement of persons. There was talk, in the open, of setting up special courts to try Indira Gandhi, Sanjay Gandhi and others. Prime Minister Desai, meanwhile, left on a tour to European countries and the US on 5 June 1978, without bothering to attend to the idea of setting up special courts.

On 4 June 1977, JP, under dialysis thrice a week and leading a secluded life in his Sadaquat Ashram in Patna, issued a statement that the people were losing hope in the Janata and that it was time now to begin the second phase of Total Revolution. And the Janata Party president, Chandra Shekhar, went ahead with a camp at Narora (in Rajasthan from where Indira's Congress conducted a brainstorm session and launched its attack on JP and the movement in 1974) to train workers for the second phase of the Total Revolution. The Janata Party president called upon the volunteers, to look beyond personalities, in his lecture.

The rift in the national leadership of the party had begun to have its impact in Uttar Pradesh by this time. Satya Prakash Malavya, a minister in the Uttar Pradesh Cabinet was sacked by Chief Minister Ram Naresh Yadav. Malavya was a CFD man and Yadav a Charan Singh follower. This led to dissidence in the legislature party forcing the chief minister to seek a confidence vote in the assembly on 4 June 1978. Yadav won the vote but only because the old Jan Sangh block voted for him. This agreement, between the BLD block and the Jan Sangh block, did not last long. Health minister Raj Narain, now a hard-core Charan Singh loyalist, launched an attack on party president Chandra Shekhar and also against the Jan Sangh. He led a demonstration in Shimla, defying prohibitory orders, putting the Himachal Pradesh chief minister, Shanta Kumar in a fix. As things drifted this way, Charan Singh announced his resignation from the Janata Parliamentary Board on 16 June 1978. Prime Minister Desai was expected in Delhi the following day after his foreign tour.

On arrival, he made a categorical statement that his government did not intend setting up special courts to try Indira and Sanjay. On 19 June, Morarji charged Raj Narain of committing a breach of party discipline (for speaking against party president Chandra Shekhar) and Janata general secretary, Nanaji Deshmukh wrote to Narain seeking an explanation. Attempts by several leaders, including JP, to reconcile the two leaders did not yield any results and the Janata Parliamentary Board, met on 22 June 1977 (without Charan Singh) and show-cause notices were served against Raj Narain, Devi Lal (Haryana chief minister), Jabbar Singh (minister in the Madhya Pradesh Cabinet), Ram Dhan and Sibhan Lal Saxena (both MPs). Barring Ram Dhan, the others were Charan Singh loyalists. It was clear that Charan Singh had now launched his battle against Morarji Desai through his followers and Desai too had decided to join the battle. JP's letter to all the senior leaders was of no use.

Charan Singh struck on 28 June 1977. In a long statement from Surajkund (the BLD leader would go to this Haryana township very often and spend long hours in a guest house there), Charan Singh said:

> Many Emergency victims have come to me repeatedly and implored me that not only should Mrs. Gandhi be arrested immediately but that she should be kept in Chandigarh, in the same circumstances in which Lok Nayak Jayaprakash Narayan was kept, or in the Tihar Jail in the same circumstances in which Maharani Gayatri Devi and Maharani Vijayaraje Scindia were confined. I have no doubt that, if we in the government could only persuade ourselves to accept and implement this suggestion, there would be hundreds of mothers of Emergency victims who could celebrate the occasion as befittingly as another Diwali. Of course, in any other country, she would now be facing a trial on the lines of the historic Nuremburg trial.
>
> I realize that this suggestion may appear to some of my friends as being extremely vindictive but those who know the mood of the country and of the people and still remember the grave misdeeds she had perpetrated would find it very difficult to disagree with the suggestion.
>
> People think that we in the Government are a pack of impotent people who cannot govern the country. In fact, there is even a section of our people, especially among those who suffered grievously under her regime during the Emergency who want that Mrs. Gandhi detained under MISA which is still on the statute book.

This rendered all efforts at rapprochement meaningless and the Union Cabinet, meeting on 29 June 1978, demanded both Charan Singh and Raj Narain to leave the Cabinet. Morarji made a written statement: 'They cannot continue in the Cabinet while persisting with such gross indiscretion contrary to all established traditions of collective responsibility and standards of ministerial conduct.' The Cabinet meeting was attended by 15 out of the 20 ministers and this included Biju Patnaik and H. M. Patel; both belonged to the BLD block just like Charan Singh and Raj Narain. Charan Singh stayed on in Surajkund and Raj Narain was away in Patna, meeting with JP on that day.

Charan Singh and Raj Narain submitted their resignation letters on 30 June 1978 and they were joined in that act by four Ministers of State (Janeshwar Mishra, Narsingh Yadav, Ram Kinker and Jagbir Singh), all Charan Singh followers. President N. Sanjiva Reddy was in Calcutta that evening and Desai hastened to send his recommendation, through a special messenger, that the resignations be accepted with immediate effect. Morarji's faction persisted further to ask Devi Lal to quit as chief minister of Haryana; and in an indication of the intra-party alignment, those from the Jan Sangh block in the Haryana Cabinet quit their posts and announced withdrawal of support to the ministry.

The issue was settled, in a few days time, and Devi Lal could continue as chief minister until June 1979 before being replaced by Bhajan Lal. But then, it was clear by now that the Jan Sangh was in no mood to keep Charan Singh's company.

Charan Singh struck again on 5 July 1978. He told the press that he was asked to leave the Cabinet only because he had sought an enquiry into the affairs of Kantilal Desai, the prime minister's son. Kanti was a permanent fixture at the prime minister's official residence as well as during his foreign tours. Kanti had been friends with a number of people, including one Balasubramiam, known to be a smuggler apart from several dubious business activities. There were records of Balasubramaniam visiting Kanti at 1, Safdarjung Road, the prime minister's official residence. Charges involving Kanti and abuse by him of his father's position had been raised in the Lok Sabha even earlier. In 1968, when Morarji was Indira's deputy prime minister, the Socialist leader Madhu Limaye had moved a motion seeking enquiry into Kanti's business activities, carried out from his father's residence. Indira, however, had dismissed those charges at that time and even argued, as she did in the case of her own son, Sanjay Gandhi, that young men cannot be discriminated against because they were sons of a minister! Kanti continued to live and carry on with his business from his father's residence. Kanti was there, by Morarji's side, when the prime minister addressed the first press conference on 24 March 1977 and this led P. N. Dhar, the secretary in the prime minister's secretariat until that day, to wonder if he found shades of Sanjay there!

These were stories of the past. The one that Charan Singh was concerned now was that Kanti accompanied Morarji during his trip to the USSR and the official aircraft was forced to make an unscheduled detour and halt at Teheran, for Kanti to get off, before Morarji and others flew back to India. Morarji's explanation was that his son got off at Teheran to travel into Europe. This explanation did not convince anyone. The popular perception was that Kanti had been in league with a business house run by non-resident Indians, living in London, who had also benefited out of their proximity with the Shah of Iran. Incidentally, the members of that business house were there at Teheran to receive Kanti when he broke journey. The only plausible explanation for that detour and Kanti cutting short his tour was that some money was to be transferred in connection with the deal between the Shah and the Government of India involving transfer of shares in a deal involving Manganese Ore extraction at Kudremukh in Northern Karnataka (the deal was struck in September 1977) between the players.

Charan Singh had written at least three letters to the Prime Minister in March 1978, on these and other stories about Kanti, urging Desai to set up an enquiry on the issue. Morarji, meanwhile, maintained that he was prepared for an enquiry by a committee of three eminent citizens and not for an official enquiry. The issue was raised in Parliament by Congress Rajya Sabha member, N. K. P. Salve and Desai's refrain, all along was: 'My knowledge of my son's activities has never been of a detailed nature. I have always taken a very detached view and sought to ensure that he does not come, anywhere near the discharge of my official responsibilities'.

Kanti, incidentally was not a good student in school and had failed in his intermediate examinations. He was, however, drafted in as partner by several business firms, including some from outside India, when Desai held the finance portfolio in Nehru's Cabinet. After Desai's exit (under the Kamaraj Plan), Kanti's involvement in business too became rather limited. In 1967, for instance, Kanti's business had reduced to being a director in one private limited company and another proprietary firm that had ceased to do any business. This was stated by Indira Gandhi, in defence of her deputy prime minister, when Madhu Limaye raised the issue in Parliament in 1967. Salve, now, had leveled specific charges that Kanti had exerted pressure on the officers of the Income Tax Department to issue the necessary certificates and put the Kudremukh deal in order. Kanti was also accused of earning huge sums as insurance commission through *benami* agents and his wife, Padma Desai, was charged of tax evasion. The charge was made against Kanti that he ensured that the Income Tax officers reported files involving his return details as missing whenever they were sought for investigation.

Amidst all this came Charan Singh's statement, on the floor of the Lok Sabha, that he had to leave the Cabinet after demanding an enquiry into the affairs of Kantilal Desai. That the Kanti affair was not just an imagination of Charan Singh was evident when President Sanjiva Reddy wrote to Desai about this and many other things on 14 January 1979. Reddy's letter said: 'I had repeatedly drawn your attention to the adverse inferences that were being drawn about your son, Shri Kanti Desai, getting off at Teheran during an unscheduled stop of the plane on your way back from the Soviet Union. If he was disembarking at Teheran to proceed to Europe, as was stated at the time, he could have proceeded from Moscow itself, instead of taking a devious route. The natural inference was that he had preferred to go there for some particular purpose. A few years ago, you made a disclosure in public, that your son had no business interests abroad. When I asked you about his stop-over in Teheran, you told me that he had got off to go to London to wind up his business interests there. I am at a loss to comprehend what is the exact position...'

President Reddy's letter added: 'The implications and consequences of his associations with businessmen who seem to maintain close contact with him both at your official residence and when he accompanies you on your official tours in India and abroad, are matters for your conscience. As far as I am concerned, I have exercised my constitutional responsibility of cautioning you in time, and often enough, about it.' The President had also referred to an incident where

Kanti, accompanying the Prime Minister on a tour abroad, had been to a Casino and lost a large sum in foreign exchange and the letter also referred to Morarji's assurance that he was aware of the incident and that he would enquire about it with his son.

All this and the correspondence between Charan Singh and Morarji Desai on the Kanti affair in March 1978 (they remain classified documents at the time of writing and hence 'secret' and 'confidential') came to haunt the Janata Government for several months after June 1978. The Congress members stalled the proceedings of the Rajya Sabha demanding that those papers be tabled in the house. Morarji refused to concede and this even led to L. K. Advani resigning from the position of the Leader of the Rajya Sabha. The fact is that Kantilal Desai's affairs were not above board and Justice Vaidyalingam (a sitting judge of the Supreme Court) who was appointed to look into the issue conducted a perfunctory enquiry and closed the file. The judge did not conduct elaborate hearings and nobody came to submit evidences before him. All this happened when Morarji Desai was the prime minister. And the Janata's patron saint, JP, did not consider the scandal involving Kanti Desai as important enough to demand a probe or seek Desai's resignation.

The conflict between the Janata leaders was taking place, mostly through the media and maturing into a crisis that was corroding the confidence of the people in the Janata Party. In February 1978, Indira's Congress retained power in Karnataka and Andhra Pradesh while it formed a coalition Government, with Y. B. Chavan's Congress, in Maharashtra. The Janata wave that swept the northern states seemed to recede. Mohsina Kidwai of the Congress (I) won the by-election to the Azamgarh Lok Sabha constituency in Uttar Pradesh in May 1978. Ram Naresh Yadav had won the seat for the Janata Party in March 1977 and the by-election was held because he resigned as MP after becoming the chief minister of Uttar Pradesh.

Thereafter Indira Gandhi was elected to the Lok Sabha from Chickmagalur in Karnataka in November 1978. The Congress MP, D. B. Chandre Gowda (who had won the constituency in March 1977), resigned to facilitate Indira Gandhi's entry into the Lok Sabha. The man who managed this as well as Indira's campaign in the by-election was Karnataka Chief Minister, Devraj Urs. In the Chickmagalur by-election, it was Urs for Indira and George Fernandes for Veerendra Patil. The Janata nominee for the by-election was Congress chief minister of Karnataka in 1968 and would return to the Congress (I) soon after the by-election and become the Karnataka chief minister once again in December 1989. Patil's path to chief ministership, in 1989, was laid by the controversial dismissal of the S. R. Bommai led Janata Dal government in April 1989. The dismissal and the role of the Governor would come up for judicial scrutiny and the Supreme Court laying down the conditions and restrictions for use of Article 356 of the Constitution. In Chickmagalur, Indira won the by-election securing 55.7 per cent of the votes against Patil's 38.4 per cent.

However, Indira could not continue as MP for long. A privilege motion, moved by Madhu Limaye, in the Lok Sabha on 5 July 1978 (at least six months before she won from Chickmagalur), was found to be in order by the Privileges Committee in December 1978. The issue raised by Limaye was that Indira Gandhi, during her tenure as prime minister, had prevented officials of the industrial development ministry from collecting information that was needed to prepare a reply to a question in the Lok Sabha on the affairs of Maruti Limited. The House Committee, after due process and hearing Indira on more than one occasion, held her guilty. On 19 December 1978, Indira Gandhi was expelled from the Lok Sabha and also sentenced to imprisonment until the house was prorogued after the session. The session lasted for a week after that and Indira was held in the Tihar jail for that period. Rather than helping the Janata, this sentence and her expulsion, coming as they did when intra-personal squabbles in the Janata Party was becoming endemic, helped Indira reinvent herself.

Indira Gandhi's first opportunity to bounce back had come much earlier and in May 1977, only a couple of months after the Janata Party came to power. A sleepy little village in Sasaram in Western Bihar called Belchi hit the national news headlines when 11 members of the Scheduled Caste were burnt to death and several thatched homes of the people there were burnt down. The attack, on 16 May 1977, was the handiwork of members of the Kurmi caste, among the intermediate groups that had perceived the Janata Party's electoral victory as also an opportunity to assert its own social clout. Indira arrived at Belchi, within a couple of days, perching on an elephant (she could not travel to the place by jeep because the roads were cut off by incessant rains), and the national and international media in tow. This helped her Congress party reinvent itself among the Scheduled Caste people, who had voted against her party, for the first time in 1977.

Indira Gandhi, however, was in the middle of another crisis in May–June 1978. On 5 May1978, even as she was unwinding at a guest house in Mercara (in the Coorg), she received news that the Supreme Court had ordered that her son Sanjay Gandhi be detained in the Tihar jail for a month. This detention order was in a case pertaining to the destruction of all the copies of a commercial film, *Kissa Kursi Ka*. Produced by a Congress MP, Amrit Nahata, in May 1975, the film was essentially a commercial venture with satirical comments or scenes of political personalities. It was waiting for clearance from the Censor Board in Pune. The information and broadcasting minister, V. C. Shukla, ordered that the reels be sent to Delhi. It was revealed, in the course of the hearings, that the reels were carted to the Maruti factory in Gurgaon and burnt off. Nahata left the Congress, joined the Janata ahead of the March 1977 elections and became Janata MP. The trial court and the Supreme Court found Sanjay guilty of tampering with evidence in the case and hence cancelled the bail he was granted earlier. The Supreme Court ordered that he be held in Tihar, for a month from 5 May 1978.

Justice Y. V. Chandrachud delivered the order in which he stated: 'There was satisfactory proof that the respondent (read Sanjay) has abused his liberty by attempting to suborn the prosecution witnesses. He has, therefore, forfeited his right to be free.' The fact was that some of the key prosecution witnesses, including the two drivers who were employed to transport the film reels to the Maruti factory (they were employees of Sanjay's Maruti Enterprises), turned hostile in the trial court. And Jethmalani, the prosecution lawyer, observed in the court that 'the accused are banking on a change in the political climate'. This was indeed true. Indira Gandhi flew down to Delhi, went straight to the Tihar jail and told her son: 'Don't lose heart. This is going to be your political rebirth.' Sanjay's stay in the Tihar jail lasted longer than the one month he was initially remanded. He was in jail even when Indira stood for elections in Chickmagalur. But then, it was clear that the mother was determined to bank on her son and she did not let him be criticised by anyone including Devraj Urs, who charted her entry into the Lok Sabha.

Urs stood by Indira in her hour of crisis, when she was deserted by several of her former cabinet colleagues, in January 1978. Urs too would fall out with Indira Gandhi soon. At an AICC meeting in April 1979, Urs raised the issue of Sanjay Gandhi's continued dominance in the party. Indira Gandhi made it clear that she did not like that and walked out of the meeting in a huff. The Karnataka strongman, who helped Indira reinvent herself, was soon issued a show-cause notice and expelled from the Congress (I) for six years. Urs would join the Congress (S) and the party would then disintegrate to become the Congress (U). This will be discussed in the next chapter.

Meanwhile, Charan Singh, now out of the Union Cabinet, set out on his own agenda and he could rally Ram Naresh Yadav, Karpoori Thakur and Devi Lal, the chief ministers of Uttar Pradesh, Bihar and Haryana respectively and also Raj Narain behind him. The important leaders in the Janata, meanwhile, were desperate to get Charan Singh back into the Cabinet. They knew the BLD leader was indispensable for the Janata Party to survive. Morarji, however, was unwilling for a settlement without Charan Singh repenting for his remarks against the party president and the government. The Prime Minister, meanwhile, retained the home portfolio himself. The talks went on for six months and all those who mattered in the Janata, barring Jagjivan Ram and H. N. Bahuguna, were engaged in the negotiations with Charan Singh.

On 24 January 1979, after several rounds of negotiations, Charan Singh agreed to return to the Union Cabinet. While Morarji could succeed in ensuring that the BLD leader did not get the home portfolio, he had to concede deputy prime ministership to Charan Singh and to Jagjivan Ram. The Janata thus came to have two deputy prime ministers: Jagjivan Ram was deputy PM and also defence minister, Charan Singh would become deputy PM and finance minister. H. M. Patel, finance minister until then, was shifted to the home ministry on 24 January 1979.

Raj Narain, who held the banner of revolt on Charan Singh's behalf and was asked to quit along with his leader in June 1978, was now left in the lurch. But then, this was a mistake that the Janata establishment would repent for later. Though it appeared that Charan Singh did not care to rehabilitate his follower, the events that unfolded in July 1979 established that Raj Narain continued to work for Charan Singh. The former health minister, whose election petition in the Allahabad High Court turned out to be the immediate cause for the Emergency and in a logical way to the formation of the Janata Party and its victory in 1977, would establish contact with Indira Gandhi's son, Sanjay Gandhi by March–April 1979 and finally ensure the fall of Morarji Desai's government on 16 July 1979.

The crisis was now manifest outside the party too. Anti-Muslim violence broke out in Uttar Pradesh and Bihar. Aligarh, Moradabad, Bihar Sharief and many towns with a large Muslim population began to witness rioting and arson; and this was beginning to have its repercussions in the affairs of the Janata Party. H. N. Bahuguna, the Union Petroleum Minister, began traveling to the towns affected by the violent incidents and laid the blame on the RSS as well as the Jan Sangh ministers in the Uttar Pradesh Cabinet for the incidents. Bahuguna was reprimanded by Prime Minister Desai for meddling with the affairs of the state government. Bahuguna, meanwhile, was also encouraging the Imam of the Jama Masjid in Delhi, to demand that the Janata government resort to a proactive role in containing the anti-Muslim violence. All this were intended to irritate the Jan Sangh elements and this was happening.

A clear realignment of forces was taking place within the Janata Party and the Jan Sangh elements in the Janata were now becoming Morarji's core supporters. This led Charan Singh, to train his guns, against the Jan Sangh. He got Ram Naresh Yadav to sack some of the Jan Sangh ministers in the Uttar Pradesh Cabinet. This cost Yadav his chief ministership. In February 1979, Yadav had to go and Banarsi Das became the Uttar Pradesh chief minister. Bihar chief minister, Karpoori Thakur too had to go, for similar reasons; he was replaced by Ram Sundar Das in April 1979; and Devi Lal was replaced by Bhajan Lal as chief minister of Haryana in June 1979.

While Morarji was now backed by the Jan Sangh and party president Chandra Shekhar, Jagjivan Ram too remained in the same camp because he could not find common cause with Charan Singh. Moreover, the Other Backward Castes such as the Ahirs and Kurmis as well as the Jats, empowered by the Janata's victory, were involved in several incidents of violent and repressive acts, across Uttar Pradesh,

Bihar and Haryana, against the Scheduled Castes. Jagjivan Ram, hence, could not but find common cause with Morarji Desai. Meanwhile, Charan Singh was now prepared to reach an agreement with Bahuguna, his arch rival in Uttar Pradesh. This was the context in which Madhu Limaye began raising the issue of dual membership. Even after the dissolution of the Jan Sangh and its merger into the Janata Party, Vajpayee, Advani and several others continued their association with the RSS and this was against the grain of the Janata's programme and policies. Madhu Limaye's job was to put an ideological coating to Charan Singh's quest for the prime minister's post. There was, however, a long term strategy for Madhu Limaye to raise the issue, i.e., to ensure the support of the Muslim community to the Janata platform and this certainly happened after a decade.

The socialist ideologue was convinced of two things: One, that the Janata Party, as it existed, was losing ground. And two, that unless the party, representing the aspirations of the intermediate castes, managed to ensure the support of the Muslim community too, there was no way it could emerge as a political alternative to the Congress. The unfolding of the political reality, particularly in Uttar Pradesh and Bihar since the late 1980s, brought out the fact that a combination of the OBCs and the Muslims would ensure power to those who belonged to the Charan Singh block in the Janata Party between 1977 and 1979. Lalu Prasad Yadav and Mulayam Singh Yadav belonged to this lineage of the Janata Party and the two of them would emerge strong, in Bihar and Uttar Pradesh respectively, in the post-Mandal political discourse. In other words, the Rashtriya Janata Dal and the Samajwadi Party are products of the long term dynamics of the strategy evolved by Madhu Limaye in 1979.

The rising tide of anti-Muslim violence, the fall of Ram Naresh Yadav, Karpoori Thakur and Devi Lal (all BLD men) from the chief minister's post in Uttar Pradesh, Bihar and Haryana respectively, and top leaders of the Janata Party engaging themselves in a spat, in regular intervals, marked the political discourse between January and June 1979. Raj Narain was now bent upon avenging his exit from the Cabinet and by July 1979, things began to move, in a fast pace, leaving the Janata Party and its leaders gasping for breath in the literal as well as figurative sense of the term. All this was happening at a time when Indira Gandhi was left with Sanjay alone for company. On 5 July 1979, Devraj Urs and Swaran Singh decided to hold a convention of Congress leaders and party workers and announced that Indira Gandhi will be kept away from that event scheduled for 9 August 1979.

Coming back to the Janata affairs, on 2 July 1979, Charan Singh made a public statement that he was parting ways with Raj Narain. On 7 and 8 July 1979, George Fernandes held a convention of the former socialists. It was attended by over 300 delegates from across the country and addressed, among others, by Fernandes and Madhu Limaye; the socialists now resolved to render themselves into a pressure group within the Janata Party. The high point of the two-day convention was a scathing attack by speaker after speaker, including Fernandes and Limaye, against the Jan Sangh block in the Janata Party. Fernandes felt that the Janata Party was losing its credibility and criticised the fact that O. P. Tyagi, a Janata MP belonging to the Jan Sangh block, was allowed to move a Private Members Bill seeking to curtail the citizens' freedom to choose their religion. Limaye, meanwhile explained the reasons behind his opposition to holding organisational elections in the Janata Party; describing the Jan Sangh as a 'party within the party' Limaye said that their intention was to 'capture the organisation.' While other sections in the Janata were disunited, the Jan Sangh had been able to stay united because of its RSS connections, he stressed.

Limaye went on to serve Morarji Desai with an ultimatum to ensure that Vajpayee and Advani dissociated themselves from the RSS or leave the Union Cabinet. Desai would not listen to this. Janata president Chandra Shekhar too refused to entertain this demand. This was the situation on the day before Parliament was to meet for the monsoon session.

On 9 July 1979, the opening day of the Monsoon session of Parliament, nine Janata Party MPs announced their decision to quit the party and sit as a separate group in the opposition. They were led by Raj Narain. Others who left the Janata Party that day were: Mani Ram Bagri, B. B. Tiwari, Ramdhari Sastri, Chandrashekar Singh, Hari Ram, Manohar Lal Saini, M. S. Lather, Hargovind Verma and Sushil Dhara. All the nine MPs belonged to the BLD and were Charan Singh loyalists. This meant that Charan Singh's statement on 2 July that he was parting ways with Raj Narain was just a façade. On the same day, 11 MPs of the Congress (I) announced their decision to leave the party and join Chavan's Congress. This made Chavan the leader of the opposition and the Congress (I) was reduced into the third-largest party in the Lok Sabha.

The resignation of nine of its MPs did not affect the Janata's status in the Lok Sabha. The day after, on 10 July 1979, Raj Narain continued his efforts and his strength increased to 27 in the Lok Sabha. Those who left the party on 10 July were: Hari Ram Choudhry, Anant Ram Jaiswal, R. N. Kushwaha, Kalyan Jain, Ram Vilas Paswan, Lalu Prasad Yadav, Ajit Mehta, Lalu Urao, Hukumdeo Narain Yadav, Mahendra Narain, Ram Avadesh Singh, Vinayak Prasad Yadav, Ram Jeevan Singh, Ram Lal Kureel, Raghuvir Singh and Fakhir Ali. The Janata Party did have a majority of five in the Lok Sabha even after this. The 27 MPs, now with Raj Narain, were all Charan Singh loyalists from Uttar Pradesh and Karpoori Thakur's men from Bihar. They made it public that their return to the party was conditional upon the expulsion of the RSS associates from the Janata. The Janata Party, they declared remained a communal party until then.

The Lok Sabha was slated to take up a no-confidence motion the following day, submitted by Y. B. Chavan, the then leader of the opposition. Chavan had sought to move the motion even before the Janata MPs began deserting and it was intended to be a routine exercise when it was submitted. It was scheduled to be taken up on 11 July 1979. Chavan's Congress had 75 MPs in the Lok Sabha and Indira used to taunt her former colleagues and partymen as the Janata's 'B' team. But then, the pace of events since 9 July, the day the session began, and 11 July, when the motion was taken up, rendered a different complexion to it and also the future of Morarji's government. Raj Narain met with President Sanjiva Reddy in the morning on 11 July 1979 and informed him of the decision by as many as 44 Janata MPs to withdraw support to the government. Seventeen more Janata MPs had joined his ranks by this time. Desai was now facing revolt within the Cabinet too. Charan Singh, Biju Patnaik and Rabi Ray (BLD men) and H. N. Bahuguna, demanded Desai's resignation. Rabi Ray, from Orissa had joined the Cabinet as health minister on 24 January 1979 when Charan Singh had returned to the Cabinet as deputy prime minister. Ray had dissented against the Janata Parliamentary Board's decision to sack Charan Singh and Raj Narain from the Cabinet on 29 June 1978.

Those who left the Janata Party to join Raj Narain's block on 11 July were: Rasheed Masood, Liakhat Hussain, Chandrapal Singh, Manohar Lal, Chandan Singh, Syed Mustafa, Ghulam Mohammed, S. B. Shah, Raghunath Singh, Balbir Singh, Ram Gopal Singh, Chandrawati, Shanti Devi, K. L. Mahla, Tan Singh, D. D. Sara, Gananath Pradhan, Mohamed Rashid, Raghavendra Singh and Dharam Vir Vashist. They were closest to Charan Singh. The Janata Party's strength in the Lok Sabha was reduced to 258 and the government could survive the no-confidence motion only if the Akali Dal and the CPI (M) voted against the motion. Madhu Limaye, meanwhile, began negotiating an alternate government consisting the BLD, the Socialists, a section of the CFD with support from Chavan's Congress, the CPI (M) and the CPI. And Morarji Desai, despite pressure from his cabinet colleagues to relent and step down declared: 'I will remain unruffled even if the Skylab falls.' The Prime Minister was referring to a scare, across the nation, caused in that week with the imminent fall of a man-made satellite, Skylab on earth. The satellite had lived its life and its burning pieces were likely to fall on the earth.

Even as the Lok Sabha continued discussion on Chavan's motion, Raj Narain's ranks were swelling by the day. On 12 July 1979, he had 53 MPs with him. And this included the health minister, Rabi Ray, who had quit the Cabinet that day. Janeshwar Mishra and Jagbir Singh who had resigned expressing solidarity with Charan Singh on 30 June 1978, too joined him that day. All this would take a new turn when C. M. Stephen, leader of the Congress (I) in the Lok Sabha, announced the party's support to Charan Singh as prime minister in the event the

BLD leader formed a government without the Jan Sangh block of the Janata Party. Indira Gandhi was behind this. She sent this feeler after an informal meeting of the Congress (I) Parliamentary Party in the afternoon on 12 July 1979. This indeed was the outcome of parleys between Raj Narain and Sanjay Gandhi, since March 1979, and held frequently since the crisis began to show on 7 July 1979.

On 13 July 1979, Bahuguna left Morarji's Cabinet along with four ministers of state, and Biju Patnaik and Dhanik Lal Mandal resigned from the Cabinet on 14 July 1979. As many as 80 Janata Party MPs had left to join Raj Narain's ranks by then and the CPI (M) announced that its MPs will vote in favour of Chavan's no-confidence motion in the Lok Sabha. Desai refused to quit even then and held on to the post. This, he did, despite the government having lost its majority. Charan Singh, the finance minister in the Cabinet, refused to speak in defence of the government during the debate on the motion. The high point of the debate was George Fernandes defending the government on 14 July 1979 and leaving the Cabinet the same night. At long last, on 15 July 1979, Morarji put in his papers without waiting to be voted out on the floor of the Lok Sabha. Chavan's motion was to be taken up for voting that day. Charan Singh too quit the Janata Party on 16 July 1979 and was elected the leader of the Janata (Secular) Parliamentary Party, the same day. The Janata (Secular), consisting of all those who had joined Raj Narain and some others, had 91 MPs now. It was clear that it was impossible for Charan Singh to form his own government without support from the others. The Janata Party, now left with the Jan Sangh block, Jagjivan Ram's CFD block and the Congress (O) block, still remained the single largest party and again, Morarji insisted that he be allowed to try form an alternative government. After losing this last-ditch attempt to become prime minister again, Morarji Desai convened the Janata Parliamentary Party meeting on 27 July 1979 to announce his decision to relinquish the post of the leader and atone for his lapses. Desai refrained from contesting elections after that. Jagjivan Ram was elected leader of the Janata Parliamentary Party (JPP) that day and he continued in that position until the Lok Sabha was dissolved on 25 August 1979. Ram would remain in the Janata Party, get elected to the Lok Sabha in 1980 from Sasaram, set up his own party called the Congress (J) to win the 1984 elections to the Lok Sabha, once again from Sasaram, before his death on 6 July 1986.

The Charan Singh Interlude

On 16 July 1979, soon after he quit the Cabinet and the Janata Party, Charan Singh went to the president with a list of 300 MPs who, he claimed, supported him as the prime minister. Apart from his own party men, the list contained names of Chavan's Congress MPs; Morarji's Janata too submitted a list of its supporters and there were several names common in both the lists. The final blow to Morarji's efforts came a week later. On 23 July, the Congress (I), with 72 MPs offered to support Charan Singh as prime minister. The Congress (I) declared that it supported a Janata (S)–Congress(U) coalition and qualified its decision saying that it was in order to keep the Jan Sangh out of power.

On 25 July 1979, the Janata Party continued to enjoy the support of 205 MPs and thus remained the single largest party in the Lok Sabha. Charan Singh, meanwhile, had 77 MPs in his Janata (S) and was committed of support from the Congress (75), Congress (I) (72), CPI (M) (22) and ADMK (18) making it to 264 in the house of 539. A majority of the 29 independent MPs, of whom 14 were old members of the Janata Party, extended support to Charan Singh, taking it to 278. On 26 July 1979, President, N. Sanjiva Reddy was reasonably satisfied that an alternative government was possible under Charan Singh and invited him to form the government. The BLD leader, now heading the Janata (Secular)–Congress(U) coalition, was sworn in as prime ninister on 28 July 1979 along with eight others. They were: Y. B. Chavan (deputy prime minister and home minister), H. N. Bahuguna (finance), Biju Patnaik (steel and mines), Purushottam Kaushik (information and broadcasting), Rabi Ray (health), S. N. Mishra (external affairs) and Zulfiquarulla. Raj Narain, the architect of all this decided to stay out of the Cabinet and take care of organisational affairs. Similarly, George Fernandes and Madhu Limaye too decided to stay out of the Cabinet but support Charan Singh.

Incidentally, Chavan was the only Congressman among those sworn in on 28 July 1979. Six others from the Congress(U)were left out at the last minute. They were: C. Subramaniam, Brahmananda Reddy, Hitendra Desai, T. A. Pai, Karan Singh and K. C. Pant. The reason for the last-minute omission was objection to their names from the Congress (I). They were all ministers in Indira's Cabinet during the Emergency and deposed against her and Sanjay before the Shah Commission. And Indira Gandhi would not let Charan Singh induct them into his Cabinet and continue to enjoy her party's support, which was critical for the government's survival. The leaders continued with negotiations and on 30 July 1979, the Cabinet was expanded. Those sworn in that day were: C. Subramaniam (defence), Brahmananda Reddy (industry), Hitendra Desai (commerce), H. R. Khanna (law, justice and company affairs), T. A. Pai (petroleum, chemicals and railways), K. C. Pant (energy), M. S. Qureshi (labour), Karan Singh (education) and Brahm Prakash.

The Congress (I), meanwhile, began flexing its muscles. The two special courts constituted on 31 May 1979 with Justice M. S. Joshi and Justice M. L. Jain (both judges of the Delhi High Court), had begun their hearings against Indira Gandhi, Sanjay Gandhi and many others. The bill to set up these special courts was passed in the Rajya Sabha (where the Janata did not have a majority) only after Chavan's Congress voted in its favour on 8 May 1979. And Chavan's Congress did that only in order to convey its displeasure with Indira Gandhi, who was calling for unity of Congressmen but scuttling all the possibilities for a unity based on honourable terms. Chavan and his colleagues were clearly demanding Sanjay Gandhi's exclusion from the Congress party and Indira would not approve of any such thing. Now with a government depending on the Congress (I) for survival, Indira Gandhi was determined to extract all that she wanted from Charan Singh; scrapping the special courts was on top of her list of demands. It is a different matter that neither Indira nor Sanjay would state this demand in the open. And Charan Singh was not willing to give in to this.

On 18 August 1979, the Congress (I) Working Committee raised a host of issues but not that about the special courts. However, it was clear that the party had decided to oppose the Motion of Confidence that Charan Singh was scheduled to move in the Lok Sabha on 20 August 1979. The government was going to fall. And yet, Charan Singh expanded his Cabinet on 19 August 1979, inducting Bala Pazhanoor and Sathyavani Muthu, both ADMK MPs. Even before these two ministers would take charge, Charan Singh met the president, Sanjiva Reddy, on 20 August 1979 to submit his resignation. Singh was prime minister of the country for 24 days without facing Parliament even for a day. His resignation was followed by renewed efforts by Jagjivan Ram to form another government. But President Reddy would not have anymore of it and dissolved the Lok Sabha and ordered fresh elections. Charan Singh was asked to continue as the caretaker prime minister.

Meanwhile the Janata Party's alienation from JP had taken place even before his death. On the afternoon of 23 March 1979, there was an interruption in the All India Radio's broadcast. That was to announce the death of JP. The announcement was preceded by Lok Sabha Speaker K.S.Hegde informing the house that JP was dead and adjourned the house after a customary two-minute silence. Hegde's announcement was based on information he received from the prime minister, Morarji Desai. But then, JP lived longer. And the Janata Party president, Chandra Shekhar, perhaps the only leader by JP's side at the Jaslok Hospital at Bombay on that day, announced through the loudspeaker to the crowds that had assembled there that the Lok Nayak was alive but critical. JP did overcome the critical state of his illness and lived to watch the edifice he had built crumble down. He died in his sleep on the morning of 8 October 1979. In his death, he was given the honour of a state funeral and almost all those who played a role in the collapse of the Janata edifice paid homage to JP.

Elections were held to the Lok Sabha between 3 and 6 January 1980 and the Congress (I) won 353 seats against a mere 31 by the Janata Party. Charan Singh's

Janata (S) did a shade better winning 41 seats and the Congress (U), contesting the polls in alliance with the Janata (S), won just 13 seats.

As for the special courts, Justice M. L. Jain, who had been conducting the trials since June 1979, realised (after Indira Gandhi's return as Prime Minister on 14 January 1980) that the establishment of that court (Special Court Number 2) was unconstitutional and that the cases before it be returned to the Chief Metropolitan Magistrate, Delhi. Justice M. S. Joshi (constituting Special Court Number 1) followed suit soon after. The grounds cited by Justice Jain was that the law ministry and the home ministry had assigned prosecutions to the special court even before these two ministries were assigned the responsibility for these courts by the Transaction of Business Rules. P. Shiv Shankar, the law minister in Indira's Cabinet, informed Parliament on 30 January 1980, that the special courts were a device that the previous government had hit upon to harass their political opponents. Subsequently, the law ministry wrote to the registrar of the special courts to wind them up before 31 March 1980. The cases that were pending there, as well as those before the different magistrates across the country, involving illegal acts committed during the Emergency were dropped.

Indira Gandhi's return in January 1980 also meant a host of other things. These will be dealt with in the next chapter. The Janata Party, meanwhile, survived in that same name for several years and continues to be a registered political party in the records of the Election Commission. It was reduced into this state after the Jan Sangh block decided to set up the Bharatiya Janata Party in December 1980. Raj Narain would leave the Janata (S) soon and Charan Singh revived his Lok Dal. After his death, on 29 May 1987, Charan Singh's son, Ajit Singh led one faction of the Lok Dal. Jagjivan Ram went away with his Congress (J). While Brahmananda Reddy left the Congress (U) to join the Congress (I) ahead of the 1980 elections, Y. B. Chavan, Karan Singh and K. C. Pant, all of them ministers in Charan Singh's cabinet, returned to the Congress (I) within months after Indira Gandhi's return as prime minister. Devraj Urs ran the party for a few more months, handed it over to 41-years-old Sharad Pawar in September 1981.Pawar renamed the party as Congress (S), the S standing for socialism and secularism. He had with him such others like Ambika Soni, P. R. Das Munshi and A. K. Antony. All the three would emerge as key aides of Sonia Gandhi when the Congress party got to head a ruling coalition at the Centre in May 2004. They had all returned to the Congress (I) after Rajiv Gandhi became its leader and the Congress (S) continued as an opposition party, headed by K. P. Unnikrishnan, who was one of Indira Gandhi's cheer leaders during the Emergency. He too returned to the Congress (I) in 1996 dissolving the Congress (S) finally.

It will be incorrect, however, to say that the Janata Party died with the fall of the Morarji Desai government. The edifice that collapsed in July 1979, would

XII

The Turbulent Years: 1980–84

> Matters of national unity and integrity and the character of Centre-State relations dominated the country's political affairs between 1980 and 1985 ... Rebellious groups threatened national integrity in the border states of Jammu and Kashmir and the Punjab. In Assam and more broadly in the Northeast, too, violence continued to be the rule rather than the exception...
>
> —GRANVILLE AUSTIN, *Working a Democratic Constitution: The Indian Experience*

When the last of the election results were out, late in the evening on 6 January 1980, there was no doubt that Indira's assessment of Sanjay Gandhi was perfect. Those who had urged that she 'liberate' herself from her son, and had set out on their own course to form the Congress (U) on 9 August 1979, realised this fact. Of the 75 MPs, who constituted the Congress (U) in the sixth Lok Sabha, only 13 won the elections in January 1980. Worse than that was the fact that of the seven Congress (U) ministers in Charan Singh's cabinet only two, Y. B. Chavan and Karan Singh, managed to retain their Lok Sabha seats in 1980. Brahmananda Reddy, one of the key movers of the revolt against Indira Gandhi in January 1978 and the industry minister in Charan Singh's cabinet, joined the Congress (I) ahead of the January 1980 elections and retained his seat from Andhra Pradesh. H. N. Bahuguna, whose departure from the Congress in February 1977, along with Jagjivan Ram, had contributed immensely to the Congress party's defeat in 1977, had also returned to Indira's fold and won from Garhwal in Uttar Pradesh as a Congress (I) nominee. Veerendra Patil, the Janata Party nominee against Indira Gandhi in the Chikmagalur by-elections, won from Bagalkot (in Karnataka) as the Congress (I) candidate this time.

Charan Singh's Janata (S) secured 41 seats in the seventh Lok Sabha (1980–84) and as many as 29 of them won from Uttar Pradesh, five from Bihar and four from Haryana. Apart from Charan Singh, the other prominent Janata (S) winners were George Fernandes, Ram Vilas Paswan, Devi Lal and Biju Patnaik. Among those who lost from the Janata (S) included Raj Narain, who had shifted from Rae Bareli to Varanasi and had lost to Kamalapati Tripathi, S. N. Mishra, Rabi Ray, Purushottam Kaushik, Ram Kinkar and Zulfiquarullah, all ministers in Charan Singh's cabinet. Madhu Limaye, a prominent player in organising the fall of the Morarji Desai government and also in constructing the Janata (S), too lost from Banka in Bihar.

The Janata Party too suffered this time. Of the 432 candidates fielded by the party, only 31 managed to win. Among them were Jagjivan Ram, Atal Behari Vajpayee, Chandra Shekhar, Ram Jethmalani and Madhu Dandavate. Morarji Desai did not contest the 1980 elections and Asoka Mehta, Janata Party candidate from Surat (Desai's old Constituency), lost. Desai had won from Surat in all elections since 1957. The other prominent losers from the Janata fold were H. M. Patel, Piloo Mody, Brijlal Verma, Murli Manohar Joshi, Ram Dhan, Vijayaraje Scindia and Sikander Bakht. The Janata Party suffered yet another split, within months after the elections, with the former Jan Sangh elements leaving the party to set up the Bharatiya Janata Party (BJP). Of the 31 Janata Party MPs, 16 belonged to the Jan Sangh and they all joined the BJP when it was founded. We shall discuss this in detail later in this chapter. The 1980 general election brought bad news for the Akali Dal too. The party lost all but one seat from Punjab and Surjit Singh Barnala, a minister in Morarji Desai's cabinet, was among the losers.

It was an emphatic victory for Indira Gandhi and her Congress (I). Her slogan this time was: 'Elect a government that works'. The party won 353 seats of the 529 for which elections were held. Elections were not held for 12 constituencies in Assam and one in Meghalaya. The party had almost swept the polls in Andhra Pradesh, Karnataka, Gujarat, Punjab and Orissa. Along with the DMK, its ally now, the party won all but two of the 39 seats from Tamil Nadu. The only state where the performance of Congress in 1980 was as bad as it was in 1977 was West Bengal; the Congress (I) won only four out of 41 seats there. In Uttar Pradesh, its 1980 tally—51out of 85—was far better than what it was in 1977 when it lost all the 85 seats. In Bihar too, the Congress tally was 30 out of the 54 seats.

In this chapter, we shall discuss the developments in the various factions of the Janata Party in general and the birth of the BJP in particular; the beginnings of aggressive Hinduism as a political programme; the emergence of Sanjay Gandhi, his enhanced clout in the Congress (I), his death and his legacy; the arrival of Rajiv Gandhi on the political scene; the emergence of the regional parties and the consequent resonance in the thrust on federal principles in the political discourse; the Assam crisis in some detail; and the Punjab crisis culminating in Operation Bluestar and Indira Gandhi's assassination.

The Disintegration of the Janata and the Birth of the BJP

It is necessary to elaborate the socio-political aspect of the non-Congress formation in Uttar Pradesh and Bihar in this context. The consolidation of the other backward classes (OBCs), constituting predominantly the Jats and the Yadavs (intermediate castes in the three-tier caste structure that marks the social mosaic in this region) that was first visible in 1967 and later in 1977 was complete in 1980. This platform was represented by Charan Singh along with Devi Lal and Karpoori Thakur in the 1980 elections. It also managed to enlist the support of a section of the minority community in 1980 and this trend was pronounced in the decade after 1980. The basis for this achievement lay in the issues that Madhu Limaye raised in the Janata Party and the ideological veneer it gave to the Janata split in July 1979. We have seen, in the previous chapter, that Limaye raised the issue of dual membership in the Janata Party, seeking the dismissal of the Jan Sangh leaders (Vajpayee and Advani) from Morarji Desai's cabinet as a necessary condition for reconciliation. Charan Singh made this issue integral to his own battle for leadership.

The consequence of all this was that a social alliance, constituting the OBCs and the Muslims, would mature into a political consolidation, particularly in the states like Uttar Pradesh and Bihar. While we shall discuss this in detail at a later stage, it will have to be borne in mind that this trajectory did not unfurl in isolation. It would unfurl, after 1990, to consolidate into a political force, only after the decimation of the Congress (I) in these two states, that is, after the demolition of the Babri Masjid in Ayodhya on 6 December 1992. The interim period was marked by the birth of the BJP, in December 1980, out of the Janata Party, and in tune with the considered decision of the RSS in its quest for power.

It is also important to note here that the BJP was neither a new party that emerged out of thin air nor was its influence restricted to Uttar Pradesh and Bihar. The party would emerge into a strong force in such states as Gujarat and also consolidate in its traditional bases such as Madhya Pradesh and Rajasthan. It may be recalled that the Jan Sangh had dominated the Janata Party organisation in Madhya Pradesh and Rajasthan (apart from Himachal Pradesh) in 1977 and the Janata governments in these states were headed by Jan Sangh men. In Uttar Pradesh too, the Jan Sangh was not a marginal force. The Jan Sangh had won 12 Lok Sabha seats from Uttar Pradesh and 98 seats in the state assembly in 1967. In 1977, out of the 295 Janata MPs, 93 belonged to the Jan Sangh. The Jan Sangh was also in a position to determine the survival of the Janata Party government in Uttar Pradesh, Bihar and Haryana. This background is indeed important before we discuss the birth of the BJP in 1980. In other words, the BJP represented a continuity with the Jan Sangh as well as with the issues that were raised within the Janata Party at the time of its split in July 1979.

The period between 1975 and 1980 was also the one when the RSS expanded significantly. The number of shakhas went up from 8,500 in 1975 to 11,000 in 1977 and to 13,000 in 1978. The Bharatiya Mazdoor Sangh, a trade union centre controlled by the RSS, too increased its membership from 12 lakh in 1977 to 18 lakh in 1980. This increase by 6 lakh was indeed a phenomenal growth. The Akhil Bharatiya Vidyarthi Parishad (ABVP), the student wing of the RSS, expanded too, with its membership increasing from 1,70,000 in 1977 to over 2 lakh in 1980. Of significance here is the fact that unlike in the case of the Jan Sangh, the RSS ensured that the trade union centre and the student organisation that it controlled did not merge into those set up by the Janata Party. The ABVP, for instance, was not merged into the Janata Party's youth wing.

It will be in order to record here the various stages in which the RSS and the Jan Sangh could break out of their isolation and the shell into which they were caught in the decade after Independence. The anti-Congress consolidation in 1967 marked the beginning of this process and the Janata Party, constructed on the basis of the unity against Indira Gandhi's Emergency, marked its culmination. The Janata regime also provided the RSS with an opportunity to avail of the state and its instruments to further its ends. The resources of the various state governments, as well as that of the Union government, having been under the control of the Jan Sangh leaders, helped the RSS in some way. But the Janata label also caused damage to the Jan Sangh and that was indeed evident in the outcome of the 1980 polls. Of the 31 Janata Party MPs who won in January 1980, 16 belonged to the Jan Sangh. This was a steep fall from 93 Jan Sangh men who were Janata MPs in the previous house. The RSS brass realised the perils of associating with the Janata Party. On 5–6 April 1980, the Jan Sangh men in the Janata Party announced the creation of the Bharatiya Janata Party at a convention held in New Delhi. Thereafter, the party was formally launched at its first plenary held in Bombay on 28–30 December 1980. Among those who addressed the convention was Justice M. C. Chagla. Addressing the session, Chagla said:

> I am not a member of the party and I am not addressing you as a delegate. Still I assure you that when I am talking to you I do not feel like an outsider. I honestly and sincerely feel that I am one of you. The BJP is a national party. I admire your discipline, your honesty, and your dedication. This huge gathering is Bombay's answer to Indira. This is the only party that can replace Indira.

It may be recalled that Justice Chagla was among the few who had spoken against Indira Gandhi and the Emergency. Nanaji Deshmukh, an important associate of the Jan Sangh, an architect of the Janata Party and one of its general secretaries, was conspicuous by his absence at the convention. He refused to join the BJP and stayed away from party politics for the rest of his life.

Of the 51 national executive members of the BJP, 31 belonged to the RSS. Out of the 14 special invitees to the executive, 12 belonged to the RSS. Ram Jethmalani and Sikander Bakht were the exceptions. Yet, A. B. Vajpayee, the founder president of the BJP, maintained: 'Our party was born in 1980, the Jan Sangh in 1951, the RSS in 1925. These are separate events. No one can be the other'. As a matter of fact, the objective behind the formation of the BJP was anything but a break with the Jan Sangh. This too was made clear by Vajpayee:

'The task before us,' he said, 'is to retain the old base and win new ground.' To accomplish this, the BJP adopted a two-pronged strategy. The idea of cultural nationalism based on M. S. Golwalkar's definition of nation and nationhood, which had remained central to the Jan Sangh's political programme, was now couched in a different language. The BJP listed nationalism, national integration, democracy, positive secularism and value-based politics as its five core principles. As for the economic policy, the BJP bodily lifted it from the Janata Party's election manifesto of March 1977. It said: 'What the small sector can make, the medium sector shall not attempt; what the medium sector can produce, the large sector shall not make; what goods the large sector can deliver, the multi-national corporations shall not be allowed to produce'. This essentially was a rephrasing of the Gandhian socialist economic programme that the Jan Sangh had adopted, under Deen Dayal Upadhyaya in 1965.

The objective reality of the time provided space for the BJP to emerge as an alternative to the Congress (I). The disintegration of the Janata Party and the fact that the various leaders of the party had failed to build a credible nationwide organisation against the Congress (I) left a vacant space for the BJP to fill and the necessary support for this came from the RSS cadre. The RSS, we saw, had expanded itself in this period and the RSS chief, Balasaheb Deoras was unwilling to let go the opportunity. While the five core political principles were intended to establish a disconnect between the BJP and the Janata Party, even while retaining the core of the Jan Sangh's political philosophy of cultural nationalism, the adoption of Gandhian socialism as its economic policy was meant to widen the party's appeal among groups other than the urban middle classes.

Political expediency demanded the appropriation of Gandhi, and the RSS was not averse to the BJP doing that. That the BJP would give up all that with ease was evident when the party supported the Economic Policy Resolution moved by Manmohan Singh in July 1991 and more so after it captured power in 1998. This will be discussed later. Insofar as its core agenda of aggressive Hindu nationalism was concerned, the RSS could push it into mainstream political discourse with much ease through its various other arms as the Vishva Hindu Parishad (VHP), the Vanavasi Kalyan Ashram (VKA) and the Vidya Bharati. All this would come into play very soon.

On 19 February 1981, only a few months after the BJP was formally launched at a convention in Bombay, as many as 4,000 members of the scheduled castes in Meenakshipuram, a remote village in southern Tamil Nadu, converted to Islam at a public function. It was not for the first time that members of the scheduled castes had resorted to conversion as a symbol of protest. Embracing Buddhism, as an act of protest against the caste system and untouchability, was initiated by B. R. Ambedkar. On 14 October 1956, Ambedkar led a few lakh Dalits, to embrace Buddhism at a public function. This act, before his death on 6 December 1956, and his book The *Buddha and His Dhamma* were unambiguous statements against Hindu orthodoxy. Embracing Buddhism was also Ambedkar's way of conveying that reforms within the Hindu fold and the abolition of untouchability was impossible. This did not provoke the RSS or the Jan Sangh. The Meenakshipuram event, however, led the RSS to express concern. One of the reasons was that the Dalits, this time, embraced Islam and not Buddhism. The RSS demanded a law banning conversions and unleashed the VHP, founded in 1964, with a specific brief of propagating the virtues of Hindu religion and to check the advance of Islamic and Christian missionaries among the tribal population. It may be noted that the VHP had restricted itself to the tribal pockets all this while.

The VHP, promptly, raised the spectre of Hinduism-in-danger and took this slogan to the urban areas. In September 1981, the VHP floated the Virat Hindu Samaj and organised a convention in Delhi where the issue of Meenakshipuram conversions was raised in particular and a law banning conversion was demanded.

As a matter of fact, such a law is very much a part of the Constitution. Article 25 of the Constitution, while protecting the fundamental rights of a citizen to profess, practise and propagate any religion of his choice, also lays down reasonable restrictions in that regard. Conversion on the basis of inducements is a punishable offence under the law. In other words, while the right to convert is a fundamental right, such conversions by way of inducements, financial or otherwise, is forbidden by the law. The VHP's demand, in that sense, was clearly superfluous. This, however, did not matter to the RSS to whom Meenakshipuram was a means to rake up passion and this could be achieved with a measure of success as things unraveled in due course. The VHP's stridency fitted into a larger context where Indira Gandhi had begun spotting 'war clouds on the western frontier', an unambiguous reference to Pakistan, after her return to power in January 1980.

The spectre of 'Hinduism-in-danger' and the location of Pakistan as the other, and the flow of wealth from the Gulf nations into India through thousands of manual and other workers who had made it to those countries in the wake of the oil boom in West Asia, provided the context for a new brand of nationalism at this stage. It may be stated here that this brand of nationalism was quite evident even in the past and was articulated by the RSS as well as a section of the nationalist leadership. This, however, had remained on the fringes of the national sentiment but began to entrench itself in the mainstream in the 1980s. It is important to note that while the RSS took it up as its core agenda and articulated it through the VHP, Indira Gandhi's Congress (I) too was involved in a similar effort. The incidence of anti-Muslim violence across several northern Indian towns—Meerut, Moradabad, Aligarh and Bihar Sharief—and the regular visits by Indira Gandhi herself to Hindu shrines as well as to godmen across the country were reflective of this new trajectory that the Congress (I) was adopting.

It will be in order to note, at this stage, the arrival of Dhirendra Brahmachari, a self-professed yoga practitioner in Indira Gandhi's court.

He had arrived in the household while Nehru was alive and had managed to obtain land in the Himalayan region to set up an *ashram* when Shastri was the prime minister. Brahmachari's proximity to Indira Gandhi increased with Sanjay's rise. In fact, the ill-fated Pitts S-2 Aircraft that Sanjay was flying, and crashed on 23 June 1980, belonged to Brahmachari. The yoga teacher claimed to have received it—along with expensive cars and lots of money—from his disciples abroad as a gift and was, thus, allowed to import it without paying customs duty and other taxes. Brahmachari remained an influential person in the prime minister's household for long and after Indira Gandhi's return to power in 1980 he also emerged as a poster boy, speaking on the television regularly. He enjoyed the right to walk in and out of the offices of the ministers without being checked or stopped. Brahmachari also played a role in projecting Indira Gandhi as a Hindu. This backdrop will help see the rise of aggressive Hindu politics in the early 1980s.

Coming back to the Meenakshipuram conversions and the VHP, the Hindu Unity Conference (that was how the VHP's September 1981 meet in Delhi was described), was presided over by Karan Singh. It was at this convention that the *Virat Hindu Samaj* was floated and Karan Singh was elected its president. Singh was a health minister in Indira Gandhi's cabinet during the Emergency and the man who lent himself—and the services of the ministry he headed—to further Sanjay Gandhi's agenda of forced sterilisation and all the atrocities committed in its name. But then he had joined the revolt against the Indira–Sanjay leadership in the Congress party along with Swaran Singh, Brahmananda Reddy and Y. B. Chavan in 1978. He was elected to the Lok Sabha as a Congress (U) candidate from Udhampur in January 1980, but he began mending fences with Indira Gandhi soon after. Karan Singh belonged to the royal family of Jammu and in that sense remained an icon of the Hindu community in Jammu and elsewhere. His father, Maharaja Hari Singh, was forced to accede to India by the people of the valley who rallied behind Sheikh Abdullah. Karan Singh's iconic status was useful to the RSS and he was also willing to play the politics of aggressive Hinduism.

Karan Singh, incidentally, was the only one of the four office bearers of the *Virat Hindu Samaj*, now registered as a society, from a non-RSS background. Lala Hansraj Gupta (working president), P. C. Gupta (secretary) and Ashok Singhal (organising secretary) were all RSS associates for several years. A *Virat Hindu Sammelan*, organised by the VHP on 18 October 1981, turned out to be a massive affair in terms of the mobilisation. It was attended by 8 lakh people. The conference adopted a five-point programme: (i) unite Hindus, (ii) abolish untouchability, (iii) ban conversions, (iv) ban foreign money for conversions and (v) bring people back to their ancestral faith. The slogans that rent the air at the conference venue were also significant. Apart from attacking Islam and seeking a common civil code, the slogans called for an end to untouchability and this clearly reflected the concerns of the RSS leadership over the events in Meenakshipuram. It made clear that the Dalits would have to be rallied behind to attain its quest for political power. The BJP leaders, interestingly, were not seen around at any of these public events.

Thereafter, the VHP organised a mass mobilisation programme billed as the *Ekatmata Yatra* in November 1983. Three public rallies were launched simultaneously from Haridwar in Uttar Pradesh (now in Uttarakhand) to Rameswaram in Tamil Nadu, from Pashupatinath in Nepal to Kanyakumari in Tamil Nadu and from Ganganagar in West Bengal to Somnath in Gujarat. These rallies, held between 15 November and 15 December 1983, were intended to forge unity among the Hindus across the country. Though conducted by the VHP, the RSS managed to enlist participation of the Arya Samaj, the Jain Society and even the Rotary and Lions clubs in many parts of the country. The dominant themes of the slogans, billboards and the speeches delivered in the course of these *yatras* were anti-Muslim and such ones that raised the spectre of the Hindu faith being in danger. Local functionaries of the Congress (I) participated and even organised public receptions to these rallies in many parts of the country. The *raths* (improvised chariot-like motor vehicles fitted with portraits of Mother India) carrying pots of water from the Holy Ganges—as a symbol of unity of the Hindus and cultural nationalism—traversed as much as 85,000 km across the country and it was ensured that they touched base in as many towns with Hindu shrines and centres of Hindu pilgrimage as possible.

The attendance at the 18 October 1981 convention held by the VHP in Delhi and the association of a cross-section of the people, in the social and the economic sense of the term, in the public campaigns and the *Ekatmata Yatra* in November–December 1983 clearly revealed that aggressive Hinduism had become the dominant political discourse in many parts of the country. The anti-Muslim violence in many towns in northern India as well as places in South such as Hyderabad was merely the manifestation of this. It is not correct to blame only the RSS and its arms for this shift in the national political discourse. Aggressive Hinduism had, by this time, become a core element in Indira Gandhi's scheme too. The religio-political dimension of the crises in Punjab and Kashmir (we will discuss these separately in this chapter) or the fact that a section of the Muslim community had stuck with the Janata (Secular) in the 1980 elections or that the Sikhs were predominantly with the Akali Dal seemed to lead Indira Gandhi to try and appropriate the Jan Sangh's base. That she did by conjuring up images of an imminent aggression by Pakistan. Her frequent reference to 'war clouds on the western frontier' was clearly a part of this new political strategy. All this made the RSS happy.

So much so, the Congress (I) registered huge victories in the elections to the New Delhi Municipal Corporation (NDMC), the Municipal Corporation of Delhi (MCD) and in the Jammu region in the elections to the Jammu and

Kashmir state assembly in January 1983. All these had been the citadels of the Jan Sangh for a long time. The BJP won only 19 of the 56 seats in the MCD and 37 out of the 100 seats in the NDMC. In the Jammu region, the BJP lost all the 27 constituencies it contested and its candidates forfeited their security deposits in 20 out of the 27. In other words, the BJP was supplanted by the Congress (I) in the Jammu region. The RSS was happy with all this because the results clearly confirmed that there was more space for a political campaign based on aggressive Hinduism. The BJP's rout in Delhi provoked Atal Behari Vajpayee to announce his resignation as party president. It is another matter that the resignation was not accepted and Vajpayee continued, for some more time, before being replaced by L. K. Advani in 1986.

The idea of the *Ekatmata Yatras*, in November–December 1983, was based on RSS's assessment that a campaign based on aggressive Hinduism would pave the way for its quest for power. Thereafter, in April 1984, the VHP announced its intentions to 'liberate' the Ram Janmabhoomi in Ayodhya and followed this up with a series of *yatras* across the country. The campaign was marked by the use of visuals depicting Lord Ram behind bars. The issue was that of the Babri Masjid, a sixteenth-century mosque, which according to the VHP was built on the ruins of a temple, by the Mughal Emperor Babur. The VHP roped in saffron-clad saints from across the country, constituted a *Dharam Sansad* (Parliament of Faith) and ensured that the campaign was both religious and political. The Babri Masjid premises had been sealed, thanks to a court order dating back to January 1950.

The first instance of a dispute involving the civil administration and the Babri Masjid was in November 1857. At that time, a complaint was made by Maulvi Muhammad Asghar of the Masjid to the district magistrate of Faizabad against the construction of a *chabutra* close to the mosque. In 1859, the British government erected a fence to separate the places of worship of the Hindus and the Muslims and provide different entries to the two. In 1885, the *mahant* of Hanumangarhi filed a suit seeking legal title over the land on which the *Chabutra* stood and for construction of a temple on that. The judicial commissioner dismissed the petition for a legal title over the land and also disallowed construction of a temple there. The case was then taken to the higher court in the United Province but was dismissed and closed on 1 November 1886.

There was no mention of the site being the Ram Janmabhoomi in any of the litigations till then. On the night of 22–23 December 1949, an idol of Lord Ram was installed inside the mosque and the government declared the premises as disputed and locked up the gates. Uttar Pradesh, at that time, was under Govind Ballabh Pant. Despite Home Minister Vallabhbhai Patel writing to him that the idols installed in a surreptitious manner will have to be removed at any cost (these were the words Patel used in his correspondence), Pant did precious little in that regard. The issue was taken to courts once again. On 16 January 1950, one Gopal Singh Visharad approached the district civil judge, Faizabad, pleading for a declaration that he was entitled to worship at the Ram Janmabhoomi. The case remained unresolved even after the Faizabad district collector, J. N. Ugra, filed a statement that the property had been used as a mosque and not as a temple. For some reasons, the courts, including the High Court, refused to settle the dispute and the premises remained locked till 1 February 1986.

On 1 February 1986, K. M. Pandey, district judge, Faizabad, ordered opening of the lock so that the Hindus could worship. The judge also declared that the Muslims were not to be let inside the premises or offer prayers. We shall discuss this and its consequences, culminating in the demolition of the mosque on 6 December 1992, in the next two chapters.

Now, as we had referred to earlier in this section, the VHP raised the slogan of liberating the Ram Janmabhoomi in April 1984. This was done at the *Dharam Sansad* in which it had mobilised saffron-clad *sants* from across the country. The convention or the session was held at Vigyan Bhawan, a state-of-the-art auditorium, erected and maintained by the Union government, in Lutyens' Delhi, to hold national and international conferences. The VHP was allowed to hold its *Dharam Sansad* at Vigyan Bhawan on 7–8 April 1984. It may be noted here that the VHP had already shown its true colours during the *Ekatmata Yatras* and a spate of anti-Muslim violence were witnessed in towns across the country during the campaign. All this clearly lends credence to the view that the Congress (I) government was not in a mood to challenge and halt the increasing spread of aggressive Hinduism in the political realm.

The *Dharam Sansad* was followed by another *yatra* by the VHP: Starting from Bihar on 25 September 1984 to reach Ayodhya on 6 October 1984. There was a lull in the VHP's activities after this and the reasons were: the assassination of Indira Gandhi on 31 October 1984, the chaos soon after that and the elections to the Lok Sabha in December that year. The opening of the locks in February 1986, the context in which that happened and its consequence, will be discussed in the next chapter. It would take several years before the BJP jumped the bandwagon; it happened in June 1989 at the party's national executive at Palampur in Himachal Pradesh.

Sanjay Gandhi's Rise and Fall

The most striking feature about the composition of the Congress (I) Parliamentary Party in January 1980 was the prominence, in terms of numbers and otherwise, of the Sanjay Gandhi loyalists in it. Sanjay himself had won from Amethi and with a huge margin. Indira Gandhi won from Rae Bareli (defeating Vijayaraje Scindia) and Medak (defeating Jaipal Reddy). Bansi Lal, V. C. Shukla, Mohammed Yunus, N. D. Tiwari and V. P. Singh; all those who were Sanjay Gandhi's executors during the Emergency were back in the reckoning and were Congress (I) MPs. This lot, along with such first-time MPs as, Jagdish Tytler, Sajjan Kumar, Charanjit Singh, Dharam Dass Shastri, K. C. Pandey, Rajest Pilot, Jaganath Pahadia, J. B. Patnaik, Ghulam Nabi Azad, K. K. Tiwari, Santosh Mohan Deb and Kamalnath—all of them hand-picked by Sanjay as Congress (I) nominees in 1980—constituted the Sanjay Gandhi brigade in the Lok Sabha. According to political commentators of the time, at least 150 of the 353 Congress (I) MPs were Sanjay Gandhi loyalists. They ensured that the Opposition's voice was drowned in a din within Parliament. The media described them as the 'shouting brigade'.

It will be appropriate, in this context, to recall the criminal charge against Sanjay and V. C. Shukla in the *Kissa Kursi Ka* case. Sanjay's bail in this case was cancelled and he was held in the Tihar jail after the trial judge found him guilty of destroying evidence and intimidating witnesses. This was in April 1978. The two of them were convicted and were sentenced to two years' imprisonment by the trial court. Sanjay and Shukla had gone on appeal before the Supreme Court against the trial court verdict. The appeal was pending before the Supreme Court in January 1980. But then, after Indira's return, Ram Jethmalani, who had prosecuted the two in the trial court and had appeared on the government's behalf in the Supreme Court, was removed from that position. Such changes are normal and the government lawyers are political appointees. In the very next hearing, the government lawyer changed the course of the arguments and the Supreme Court too hastened to quash the trial court verdict. Far more comical was the fact that Amrit Nahata, who had made the film when he was Congress MP and later complained that the copies of his film were destroyed in the Maruti factory when he was a Janata MP, now swore on oath and submitted an affidavit in the trial court that he was guided by a sense of vengeance when he made the complaint and that his conscience was now troubling him and that he preferred to withdraw the complaint. That was the end of the film and the case.

Indira Gandhi could have inducted her son, Sanjay Gandhi, into the Cabinet. She did not do that. But many of Sanjay's men were inducted as ministers. Pranab Mukherjee, indicted severely by the Shah Commission for abuse of power as Minister of State for Revenue and Banking during the Emergency, became Cabinet Minister for Commerce. Other Sanjay loyalists in the cabinet were: J. B. Patnaik, Minister for Tourism and Civil Aviation, Jaganath Pahadia, Minister of State for Finance and Yogendra Makhwana, Minister of State for Home.

Similarly, with most of the old guard now out of the fold, Indira Gandhi's Cabinet was constituted by a whole lot of new faces. Kamalapati Tripathi was the only Cabinet minister who was also a member of her Cabinet before the Congress lost power in 1977. Tripathi, incidentally, was the railway minister between 1975 and 1977 and he was given the same portfolio on 14 January 1980. All the others in the Cabinet were fresh faces. Zail Singh (home), R. Venkatraman (finance),

P. V. Narasimha Rao (external affairs), Shiv Shankar (law and justice), A. P. Sharma (shipping and transport), B. Shanakaranand (education), Abdul Ghani Khan Chaudhary (irrigation), Vasant Sathe (information and broadcasting), P. C. Sethi (works and housing) and Bhishma Narain Singh (parliamentary affairs). C. K. Jaffar Sharief, a trusted aide of S. Nijalingappa until July 1969, had helped Indira Gandhi gather information on the syndicate's moves before the 1969 split; he was now inducted as the minister of state for railways. In other words, while personal loyalty to Indira Gandhi was a necessary condition for all of them to become ministers, it was also important that Sanjay did not object to them becoming ministers.

The 'test' of loyalty was taken to another level when Zail Singh was chosen by Indira Gandhi as the Congress (I)'s candidate for president of the Republic in July 1982. With the massive majority that the Congress (I) had in Parliament as well as in the various state assemblies, Zail Singh's election was just a matter of formality. Justice H. R. Khanna simply fought a symbolic battle on behalf of the opposition parties. The high point of the 1982 presidential polls was a public statement by Zail Singh: That he would pick up a broom and sweep if he was asked to by Indira Gandhi. Zail Singh's role as Punjab chief minister before becoming the president of India will also be discussed in this chapter.

A little over a month after returning to power, Indira Gandhi set herself to do what the Janata government did to state governments. On 17 February 1980, the Union Cabinet resolved to recommend dissolution of nine state assemblies and Home Minister Zail Singh carried the resolution to President N. Sanjiva Reddy. The term of the state assemblies was until June 1982. The state assemblies that were to be dissolved were that of Uttar Pradesh, Madhya Pradesh, Bihar, Rajasthan, Punjab, Gujarat, Maharashtra, Orissa and Tamil Nadu. The fact was that the Janata ministries in most of the states were unstable by this time, thanks to the internecine fights among the leaders of the party. However, in Maharashtra, the Congress (U)–Janata alliance was in power with Sharad Pawar as the chief minister; there was no instability. The Akali Dal–Janata government in Punjab, similarly, was stable and so was the ADMK government headed by M. G. Ramachandran in Tamil Nadu. But Indira Gandhi decided to dissolve all these state assemblies too. The Congress–ADMK alliance in Tamil Nadu had broken and the Congress (I) struck an alliance with the DMK for the 1980 elections. It may be recalled that the Karunanidhi-led DMK government was dismissed on charges of corruption on 31 January 1976 and a whole lot of DMK leaders were sent to jail under MISA and other laws during the Emergency. All that were allowed to pass and both Karunanidhi and Indira Gandhi decided to get together in 1980.

All this was not necessary in Haryana. Within days after Indira Gandhi returned to power, Bhajan Lal, the Janata Party chief minister of Haryana since June 1979, left the Janata to join the Congress (I). He took 40 Janata MLAs with him to join the Congress and, thus, power shifted from the Janata to the Congress (I) in Haryana without having to go through the motion of fresh elections. Bhajan Lal would remain the chief minister of Haryana until the term of that assembly ended in 1982. In 1982, the Congress was short of a majority in the assembly but then Bhajan Lal was resourceful to organise splits across the opposition parties and continue as the chief minister again until 1986, to be replaced by Bansi Lal.

Elections to the nine state assemblies were held between 28 and 31 May 1980 and the Congress (I) wrested power everywhere except in Tamil Nadu. The Congress (I)–DMK alliance was trounced by the AIADMK in Tamil Nadu. The Congress (I) victories in the other states were emphatic. The party won 309 of the 425 seats in Uttar Pradesh, 246 out of 320 in Madhya Pradesh, 169 out of 324 in Bihar, 118 out of the 147 in Orissa, 133 out of 200 in Rajasthan, 141 out of 182 in Gujarat, 186 out of 288 in Maharashtra and 63 out of 117 in Punjab. The outcome of the dissolution of the assembly and the defeat of the Akali Dal in the polls in Punjab sparked off a series of issues. This will be discussed in detail later in this chapter.

Insofar as the other states were concerned, the victory of Congress (I) in the assembly elections meant a larger role for Sanjay Gandhi. A resolution was passed by the Uttar Pradesh Congress (I) Legislature Party electing Sanjay Gandhi its leader. Neither did Indira approve of it nor did Sanjay want to reduce himself to a chief minister, even if it was of India's most populous state. He was, however, determined to have his way in the choice of the chief ministers. Indira Gandhi too let that happen. V. P. Singh, now a member of the Lok Sabha, was picked by Sanjay Gandhi to become the chief minister of Uttar Pradesh. Jaganath Pahadia, now a minister in the Union Cabinet and a Sanjay Gandhi loyalist, was sent as the chief minister of Rajasthan. A. R. Antulay, a hardcore Sanjay loyalist, was made the chief minister of Maharashtra; the only non-Maratha, perhaps the first time, in that position. In Bihar, Dr Jaganath Mishra was made the chief minister; his brother, L. N. Mishra who died in a bomb blast, was one of the Sanjay loyalists and had risen in Indira's court by endearing himself to Sanjay in the same way as Bansi Lal did. Another Union minister, J. B. Patnaik, loyal to Sanjay, was made the chief minister of Orissa. Arjun Singh became the chief minister of Madhya Pradesh because he could muster support from Kamalnath, Sanjay's pointman in the state; and Madhav Singh Solanki became the chief minister of Gujarat because he could gather support from Yogendra Makwana, also a Sanjay loyalist from Gujarat.

Sanjay Gandhi rose to become the most important leader in the government even though he did not hold a ministerial position. On 13 June 1980, Sanjay Gandhi rode in a procession, accompanied by Indira—from his residence to the AICC office—to be installed as one of the party's general secretaries. Sanjay

Gandhi had also ensured that P. S. Bhinder, the police officer who carried out all the arrests in Delhi on 25 June 1975 and indicted by the Shah Commission for that and many other illegal acts (on Sanjay's bidding), was resurrected and made the Delhi Police Commissioner, overriding the seniority of at least 150 IPS officers, within days after Indira Gandhi's return as prime minister on 14 January 1980. Sanjay Gandhi was allowed by Indira Gandhi to do all that he wanted. Similarly, Navin Chawla, indicted by the Shah commission, would rise in the officialdom and end up as Election Commissioner—a constitutional position—after the Congress (I)-led United Progressive Alliance formed its government at the Centre in May 2004 and the Chief Election Commissioner in April 2009.

But the fateful Monday morning of 23 June 1980 brought a different turn. The Pitts S-2 aircraft—that Sanjay flew for pleasure—crashed into the shrubs barely 500 yards from 12, Wellingdon Crescent, Sanjay's official residence, causing his instant death. Captain Subhash Saxena, flying instructor from the Safdarjung Flying Club, who was flying with him that day, too died in the mishap. This happened at 7.58 a.m. A distraught Indira Gandhi rushed to the site of the crash twice in the course of the day. Sanjay's funeral procession, the following afternoon, was turned into a public event by his followers and the Congress party. Sanjay was cremated a few yards away from where his grandfather Jawaharlal Nehru's mortal remains were consigned to flames in May 1964. Indira Gandhi was devastated. Her hopes and her dreams of anointing her son as her political heir were shattered now. A political commentator had this to say at that time: 'No one will ask where the son would have been without the mother. They would rather ask where the mother will be without her son'.

There was some basis for this perception and Indira Gandhi was pushed into confronting a set of challenges involving the Sanjay legacy in addition to the problems that her government was facing in Assam, Punjab, and Jammu and Kashmir. Before we look at what these problems were, it will be in order, to narrate some of the issues that came up before her at home. Her elder son, Rajiv Gandhi, was unwilling to step into Sanjay's shoes and fill the void. Sanjay's wife Maneka, meanwhile, was emerging into an icon for a section of the Sanjay loyalists, causing a difficult situation for Indira Gandhi to deal with.

There was the Maruti factory where nothing had moved in the 12 years after its inception despite all the money that flowed into it from the nationalised banks and the prospective dealers who were forced into shelling out huge sums in anticipation of the small car. In the couple of years when the Janata Party was in power, Maruti was starved of the flow of funds (contrary to the flow till the Emergency was in force) and the company had drifted into liquidation. Sagar Suri, whose brother Lalit Suri was a hotelier and a close friend of Sanjay Gandhi, had set up an automobile firm called Delhi Automobiles and entered into a collaboration agreement with French automobile giant, Renault. He had presented plans to take over Maruti and set it up to manufacture heavy-duty trucks, buses, tractors and modern medium-sized cars. The takeover proposal, submitted before the official liquidator, involved purchase of shares at par, repay unsecured credit, including share application money and raising Rs 10 crore from family and friends. But Suri had a competitor —Charanjit Singh. Singh owned a soft drink company, Pure Drinks Private Limited, and was Congress (I) MP from South Delhi. He was a Sanjay Gandhi protégé too and had an eye on the Maruti plant on the outskirts of Delhi and the large tracts of land in its possession.

The Punjab and Haryana High Court was ceased of this matter and the case was to come up for hearing on 17 October 1980. Meanwhile, on 13 October 1980, the government issued an ordinance taking over the company. This decision to nationalise Maruti was taken without any consultation, although it involved expenditure to the tune of Rs 500 crore. Law Minister P. Shiv Shankar defended the decision in Parliament, saying: 'We had to take the decision early in order to stall the proceedings in the Punjab and Haryana High Court because this man (Sagar Suri) wanted to grab the entire property for nothing'. Madhu Dandavate, one of the few articulate MPs in the opposition at that time, said: 'When we want more money for power generation and railways, we are giving priorities for [sic] the auto industry'. J. P. Mathur, who would become an important leader of the BJP later, said: 'Maruti was born in sin, ran in sin, died in sin and resurrected in sin'.

It is a different matter that the Maruti car became a reality in a few years after the government took over the company, spending as much as Rs 500 crore, in 1980. The tussle between Sanjay Suri and Charanjit Singh for this property was also reflective of the nature of followers that Sanjay Gandhi had gathered around him. More of this would tumble out into the public domain soon.

In less than a year, the nation came to know of scandals involving other Sanjay protégés: A. R. Antulay in Maharashtra, Gundu Rao in Karnataka and Jaganath Mishra in Bihar. There were scandals involving Sanjay Gandhi protégés in the Union Cabinet too. The Kuo Oil Deal involving Kamalnath and the HDW Submarine deal were prominent among them. Then came the Bofors scandal involving Rajiv Gandhi. While we shall discuss the Bofors in the next chapter, it will be in order to narrate the other scams that were unraveled by the media during this period.

The Kuo Oil Deal was about the officers in the ministry of petroleum being forced into entering a contract with a Singapore-based oil trading firm to import a large quantity of petroleum products. This had happened within weeks after Indira Gandhi returned to power, but came to light almost a year later. The problem with the deal was that the company insisted that the price be fixed at the outset rather than agree to negotiate prices over a period. This was done when the price of petrol was registering a steady decline and it would have made ample sense to negotiate prices at various points of time when the imports were actually made. The scandal came to light when the ministry for petroleum refused to part with the relevant files (and declared that they were missing) to the Parliamentary Committee on public undertakings. It transpired, later, that the files were stacked in the prime minister's office. The Parliamentary Committee could not unravel the scandal as such; the file went missing and was found in the PMO. The file notings, however, became public, thanks to Arun Shourie and *The Indian Express*. The needle of suspicion, in this deal, pointed at Kamalnath, a Sanjay Gandhi protégé and Congress (I) MP from Chindwara in Madhya Pradesh. Kamalnath would get caught in yet another scandal involving transaction of *hawala* funds years later (in 1995) but bounce back into the political mainstream soon and become Cabinet minister for commerce in May 2004.

The HDW deal was about an agreement—entered into in 1982—for purchase of four submarines from Germany. The scandal had two aspects. The first aspect was that the German manufacturer had deposited as much as Rs 70 crore into secret accounts in Swiss Banks. The second aspect was that the HDW had violated the terms of the contract and supplied the sketches of the submarine to the apartheid regime in South Africa. HDW had also agreed to a contract with South Africa to supply submarines that were an improvised version of those that were sold to India. The issue was that the sketches should not have been shared and that the consent of the Government of India should have been obtained before the company entered into a deal where it involved supply of an improvised version of the product to another country. The scandalous part of the issue was that the Government of India refused to protest against HDW sharing the sketch with South Africa and thereafter against the supply of submarines to that country because the HDW had paid Rs 70 crore as kickback. While the first part of the scandal pertained to Indira Gandhi's period, its second part pertained to the Rajiv Gandhi regime.

The man who was behind pushing the HDW deal was Arun Nehru, drafted into the government's affairs by Indira Gandhi, within weeks after her return to power. Indira had vacated Rae Bareli (retaining Medak) and Arun Nehru was elected to Lok Sabha from Rae Bareli in February 1980. By the beginning of 1981, Arun Nehru was already involved in the business of raising funds for the Congress party, which is normally the job of the party's treasurer. Sitaram Kesari continued to hold that position in the party but Arun Nehru was the treasurer *de facto*. The HDW deal came into public discussion much later. We shall discuss all this in detail in the next chapter. The fact is that the Indira Gandhi regime came to be seen as involved in corruption and this was prevalent even in deals involving defence purchases. Indira Gandhi reacted to this by declaring that corruption was a 'global phenomenon'.

The first major exposé of corruption in this era was carried out by Arun Shourie in *The Indian Express* in September 1981. That involved the Maharashtra chief minister, A. R. Antulay. Between October 1980 and March 1981, Antulay had set up as many as seven trusts and together these controlled a corpus of Rs 30 crore.

Among them was the Indira Pratishthan whose objective was to recognise and encourage talent in the fields of literature and fine arts, by way of grants and awards. Of the Rs 5.2 crore that constituted the corpus of this trust, Rs 2 crore came as grant from the state government and the rest was collected as donations. The first part of the scandal was that orders were issued by the government that the sugar cooperatives across the state collect Rs 2.50 for every tonne of sugar from the factories and pass it on to the trust. The orders were issued in such manner that an impression was created that the trusts were under the government whereas they were not. The second part of the scandal was that the trust deeds were drafted in such a way that Antulay would be able to take the money with him whenever he decided to wind up the trusts. The third part of the scandal came to light in October 1981. The Bombay High Court admitted a case against Antulay; he had abused his office as chief minister to allot large quantities of cement, scarcely available at that time, to select buyers. Among the beneficiaries of this were the Rahejas; they managed to get 700 tonnes of cement in return for a donation of Rs 5.6 lakh to the Indira Pratishthan. In other words, they had paid Rs 40 to Antulay for each bag of cement they got out of turn.

Antulay was allowed to stay on as the chief minister despite all this. This led to a feeling that Indira Gandhi was aware of the scandalous ways and she did not find anything wrong with all that her son's protégé was guilty of. He remained the chief minister until January 1982, when Justice B. Lentin of the Bombay High Court, pronounced him guilty in the cement scandal. Indira replaced him with Babasaheb Bhonsle. Antulay, incidentally, was caught carrying contraband when his official car was checked at an inter-state check post (Wadhkhal Naaka) in 1963. He was a junior minister in Maharashtra at that time.

Bihar chief minister, Jaganath Mishra, yet another Sanjay Gandhi protégé, was turning the state into a lawless land. In September 1980, the media reported that as many as 31 undertrial prisoners in the Bhagalpur Central Jail were blinded by the prison authorities and police officers, including those in the rank of Superintendent of Police, by pouring acid into their eyes. It was revealed in the course of the case in the Supreme Court (the case was taken up by a public-spirited lawyer, Hingorani) that such incidents were happening in the jail during June–July 1980. Attempts by the affected prisoners to complain before the higher authorities were in vain. This brutal act by the police, brought before the nation by a sensitive media, shook the conscience of the people. But Indira Gandhi did nothing to hold Mishra responsible. The return of the Congress in Bihar was also marked by escalation of violence against the Dalits. While the killing of Dalits in Belchi, discussed in the previous chapter, was turned into a national issue by Indira Gandhi, similar violence in Pipra, once again in Bihar in February 1980, did not agitate Indira Gandhi. In February 1982, Parliament was informed that as many as 960 members of the scheduled castes were killed in various instances of violence across the country during the past two years. In other words, there was an escalation of atrocities against the members of the scheduled castes after Indira Gandhi's return to power in January 1980. A large part of this and the number of deaths happened in Bihar.

The point here is not that the Congress (I) was involved in these acts. The increasing violence had to do, in a way, with the clout that the members of the intermediate castes found in the ascendancy of the Lok Dal and such platforms in the past few years. But then, the state governments did nothing to stop this and protect the lives of the poorest of the poor in the countryside. It was a sign that Indira's promise to provide a 'government that works' was indeed a far cry. As for Jaganath Mishra, he remained the chief minister for long after Bhagalpur and Pipra; he even introduced a bill, in the state legislative assembly, providing for arrest and imprisonment of the journalists whom he felt were indulging in 'scurrilous' writings. It provoked protests across the country and Indira Gandhi did not ask Mishra to change course. Since it warranted changes in the provisions of the IPC, it was necessary that the president assented to it. For some reason and certainly not because of the nationwide protests, Jaganath Mishra announced withdrawal of the bill on 21 July 1983. In any case, faction feuds in the Congress (I) Legislature Party in Bihar had reached its peak by this time; and Mishra was asked to go and Chandra Shekhar Singh was made the chief minister in August 1983.

In the South, there was Gundu Rao, Karnataka chief minister and also a Sanjay Gandhi protégé. In March 1982, Rao was found to have abused his office to divert as much as 4000 tonnes of cement to builders whom he favoured. Cement, as we found in the context of Antulay's case in Maharashtra, was a scarce commodity at that time and such diversion to builders was indeed a major act of corruption. The scandal involving Gundu Rao was brought to light by the Public Accounts Committee of the state legislative assembly. Indira did not bother to ask Rao to explain his misdeed. He was allowed to remain the chief minister of Karnataka until January 1983. In the elections to the state assembly in January 1983, the Congress lost power to the Janata Party. The Congress lost elections for the first time ever in the history of Karnataka.

Another Sanjay protégé, Uttar Pradesh chief minister, V. P. Singh, was not found guilty of corruption. But his term as the chief minister was marked by the failure of the state machinery to protect the lives of the people. While the central cause for this had to do with the caste-guided social structure and its relation to the institutions of political, economic and administrative power, the failure of the police to contain violent incidents leading out of this came to be pronounced after the 1980 elections. Uttar Pradesh, thus, turned into a cauldron of caste as well as communal conflicts.

On 13 August 1980, just a couple of months after the Congress (I) returned to power in Uttar Pradesh, Moradabad, a small town in the state and closer to

New Delhi than Lucknow, witnessed violence against the Muslim community. Such instances of communal violence where the Muslim community was targeted had been happening in Uttar Pradesh even earlier. We did refer to this in the previous chapter and its impact on the Janata Party's affairs. The Moradabad carnage was different in a sense that the perpetrators of the violence happened to be policemen. Personnel from the Provincial Armed Constabulary (PAC), a wing of the Uttar Pradesh police, were found to have carried out the violence that left at least 100 people dead. There was similar violence reported from Meerut and in this case, the role of the PAC was recorded and established by the media.

On 14 February 1981, 20 members of the Rajput caste, predominantly a land-owning caste and known to draw their superior position in the society from the feudal context, were done to death in a village called Behmai near the industrial town of Kanpur. The killer, in this case, was a woman called Phoolan Devi. Belonging to the Mallah community, classified as most backward caste, Phoolan Devi was pushed into lawless ways by the oppressive socio-economic order. The Behmai killings were an act of revenge. Phoolan Devi would surrender before the police a few years later, serve 11 years in jail and after her release, contest elections to the Lok Sabha and become MP in 1996 and again in 1998 from Mirzapur in eastern Uttar Pradesh. She also died a violent death, gunned down in Lutyens' Delhi in broad daylight. The killer escaped. But that is another story. In the context of this chapter, Behmai was not just an isolated incident.

On 18 November 1981, 24 members of the Jatav caste (scheduled castes again) were killed by a gang of armed Rajputs in Dehali, a sleepy village in Mainpuri district in western Uttar Pradesh. These Jatavs were awarded with title deeds by the state government for small portions of land (10 *bighas* each) as early as in 1973. However, these titles were just on the record and were uncultivable land anyway. The upper caste men had ensured that the boundaries of these lands were unmarked and that the Jatavs worked as agricultural labour (at Rs 6 as daily wage) on their own land. V. P. Singh visited Dehali on 23 November 1981 and gave himself a month to restore the law and order situation in the state. He declared that he would quit as the chief minister in the event it did not happen. Singh had made similar announcements on 13 September 1980 (after the Moradabad carnage) and in February 1981 (after Behmai) but never carried out his threat. In this instance too, he remained the chief minister after 23 December 1980 despite the fact that none of the killers of Dehali were apprehended.

But then, the state police was let loose and as many as 299 'dacoits' were killed in encounters with the police across Uttar Pradesh in a month after 23 November 1980. The numbers went up to 325 by 6 January 1982. In most of those incidents, the dead turned out to be innocent young men. These facts were exposed by the media, from time to time, but V. P. Singh stayed on. On 30 December 1981, while Singh was being patted on his back by Indira Gandhi for his efficiency at a function in Lucknow, the upper caste men struck again in Sadhupur. Ten Jatavs, including five women and four children, were killed that day. Singh remained the chief minister and the indiscriminate killings by policemen and the practice of branding those killed as 'dacoits' continued.

In April 1982, Chandra Shekhar Prasad Singh, a judge of the Allahabad High Court, was shot dead in the Bargarh forest (near Allahabad); Singh had been there for hunting. He was Chief Minister V. P. Singh's brother. There was yet another massacre of Dalits in Dastampur (near Kanpur) on 28 June 1982. And, V. P. Singh resigned, at long last, as Uttar Pradesh's chief minister. He was now replaced by Sripath Mishra. It will be in order to note here that these killings, along with other factors, cumulatively contributed to the consolidation of a Dalit exclusivist agenda orchestrated by Kanshi Ram around the same time. The failure of the state to contain acts of lawlessness, happening as they did, in the larger context of the failure of the established political parties (the Janata Party as well as the Congress) to ensure members from the scheduled castes become a chief minister of the state and the perception that Jagjivan Ram was denied prime ministership because he happened to belong to a scheduled caste, added credence to the agenda. This led to the birth of the Bahujan Samaj Party (BSP) and its emergence into a force in Uttar Pradesh, polling 10 per cent of the popular vote in the 1989 elections to the state assembly. In fact, the BSP would grow to win a simple majority in the state assembly in May 2007.

Gujarat was on the boil around the same time. A system of reservation for members of the scheduled castes in educational institutions was followed in Gujarat, as in the other states, since independence. In 1981, an upper caste student lost the race for admission to a super-speciality medical course because that particular seat was reserved that year for a scheduled caste student. The system in vogue was that of a roster where seats were reserved by rotation. The students went on a general strike against what they called 'injustice'.

The strike against the reservation in the medical college grew into violent protests across Gujarat and also provoked counter violence. For four months, 18 out of the 19 districts in Gujarat were engulfed in violence and curfew was imposed there at various points of time, for days on end, during the four months. Chief minister Madhav Singh Solanki stood firm on reservations and normality was restored in due course. Parliament passed a resolution, affirming the nation's commitment, to carry on with reservation for the scheduled castes and tribes in educational institutions and jobs. It will be in order to note here that Solanki was constructing a social alliance consisting of the Kshatriyas, Harijans, Adivasis and Muslims (KHAM) in order to break the monopoly of the Patels in the state's political space until then. In other words, he was attempting a social alliance, different from the traditional base of the Congress, in Gujarat and this was on the lines of an OBC-Dalit-Muslim alliance that the socialists were seeking to construct and would manage to achieve, a decade later, in Uttar Pradesh and Bihar to decimate the Congress party in those two states. This was the factor that saved the Congress party from being decimated in Gujarat. It is important to note here that when all this was happening, the Mandal Commission report, recommending 27.5 per cent reservation for the OBCs in Central government jobs, submitted on 30 December 1980 was gathering dust at the shelves of the Union welfare ministry.

Incidentally, Solanki was among the few Congress chief ministers, elected in 1980, to continue in that post for a considerable length of time until he was asked to resign in January 1985, a few months before the elections were held in the state. The same thing happened in Madhya Pradesh too; Arjun Singh was asked to quit by the high command in January 1985 and was replaced by Motilal Vora a couple of months before the elections. Uttar Pradesh had three chief ministers—V. P. Singh, Sripati Mishra and N. D. Tiwari—between 1980 and 1985. In Maharashtra, Sanjay Gandhi protégé A. R. Antulay was shown the door after he was indicted in the cement scandal by the Bombay High Court in January 1982; he was replaced by Babasaheb Bhosale who remained the chief minister for just about a year; Vasantdada Patil became the chief minister in February 1983 and held that post until the elections in June 1985. In Rajasthan, Jaganath Pahadia remained in that post only for a year and was replaced by S .C. Mathur in July 1981. All these changes, it may be stressed, were the fallout of faction feuds and dissidence in the Congress (I) legislature parties and encouraged by the high command. A similar story was witnessed in Andhra Pradesh too and there was trouble in Assam and Punjab as well during this period. It will be appropriate to discuss these separately. A brief narrative on the ascendancy of Rajiv Gandhi on the scene will be in order at this stage.

Rajiv Gandhi's Arrival

Rajiv Gandhi took almost a year, after his brother Sanjay died, to make up his mind and join the political mainstream. He continued with his job in the Indian Airlines, flying the Avro and the Fokker Friendship (both passenger aircrafts) since February 1972 till 5 May 1981. He resigned from service that day, paid a rupee to obtain his membership in the Congress (I) and filed his nomination papers on 11 May 1981 from Amethi, the Lok Sabha constituency that his brother Sanjay represented between 6 January and 23 June 1980. Rajiv had begun associating himself with the party's affairs even earlier. A kisan rally organised by the Congress party on 16 February 1981, for which Rs 200 crore was spent by a conservative estimate, was an occasion where Rajiv Gandhi's skills to supervise events were at display. He was an employee of the Indian Airlines at that time.

He won the Amethi by-election with a victory margin of 2,37,000 votes, took oath as MP on 17 August 1981 and plunged into the affairs of the Congress party soon after. On 2 February 1983, he was appointed the general secretary of the Congress (I). Though there were five other general secretaries, Rajiv Gandhi was certainly the most important of them. Indira, for some reason, refused to make him the Congress (I) president even if it was demanded by her partymen. Kamalapati Tripathi, the grand old man from Varanasi, was made the working president of the party after being dropped from the Union Cabinet in November 1980. But then, Rajiv Gandhi's hoisting was taking place even before he was made the party's general secretary. One such occasion was the national convention of the Youth Congress (I) in Bangalore in January 1982. The city was filled with the party workers, brought in from across the state, a usual practice. The unusual part was the attendance of 18 Cabinet ministers, over 60 Congress ministers from various states and three Congress chief ministers apart from Gundu Rao himself, 200 Congress MPs and 900 Congress MLAs at the convention. All this was to welcome and honour Rajiv Gandhi. Addressing a meeting of Congress (I) workers in Ahmedabad in May, 1981, the then Finance Minister R. Venkatraman (he would succeed Zail Singh as the president of the Republic in September 1987), said: 'Rajiv Gandhi has achieved what his grandfather, Jawaharlal Nehru, could not achieve in his lifetime'.

The only opposition to Rajiv Gandhi's ascendancy in the Congress (I) came from Maneka Gandhi and a few Sanjay loyalists around her. Most of Sanjay's men had switched loyalty to Rajiv and the Youth Congress show at Bangalore was an illustration of that. There were, however, a few who were loyal to Maneka Gandhi. One of them was Akbar Ahmad 'Dumpy', active in eastern Uttar Pradesh. He organised a convention of the Sanjay Vichar Manch in Lucknow on 28 March 1982. Indira Gandhi was then in London at the Festival of India, an event intended to showcase India and its culture to the people in Europe. Maneka Gandhi addressed the convention in Lucknow and on her return to Delhi found Indira Gandhi furious. Maneka was asked to leave the prime minister's residence—1, Safdarjung Road—late in the night on 29 March 1982. While the immediate spark for the showdown was Maneka's attendance at the Lucknow convention, trouble was brewing in the household for sometime and the issue was about filling the space left by Sanjay Gandhi.

Indira clearly preferred her son to her daughter-in-law. Maneka too knew that even before the fateful night of 29 March 1982. Maneka, in fact, had sold off her stakes in Surya, the magazine that was useful to Indira to scandalise the Janata leaders, while she was out of power, to persons who were close associates of the RSS even earlier. In January 1984, the Sanjay Vichar Manch candidate defeated the Congress (I) nominee in a by-election to the Malihabad assembly constituency. Malihabad was part of the Amethi Lok Sabha constituency, represented by Rajiv Gandhi at that time. Maneka herself contested against Rajiv Gandhi from Amethi in the December 1984 elections. But the 1984 general election was held in the immediate aftermath of Indira Gandhi's assassination and Rajiv was then riding a massive sympathy wave that ensured his victory from Amethi as well as 405 seats for his party in the Lok Sabha. Maneka would then join V. P. Singh's Janata Dal—win from Pilibhit in 1989—become a junior minister in the Cabinet, retain the seat for herself in successive elections and also become a minister in the Atal Behari Vajpayee Cabinet between 1998 and May 2004.

That the Union ministers and chief ministers of various states were vying with one another in singing Rajiv's praise (like they did with Sanjay) was evident everywhere. Rajiv was beginning to decide on the party's affairs. An illustration of that was the manner in which T. Anjaiah, an effete but senior leader of the Congress party and then chief minister of Andhra Pradesh, was humiliated by Rajiv Gandhi at the Hyderabad airport in front of officials and party functionaries. In February 1982, Rajiv Gandhi decided to visit Hyderabad and the chief minister, Anjaiah, organised a massive reception for the leader on the same lines as Gundu Rao had done in Bangalore in January 1982. Huge crowds were hired and gathered at the airport and welcome arches were erected all over the place. Anjaiah, however, was in for a rude shock and was reprimanded by the prime minister's son. He did not murmur. After Rajiv Gandhi returned to Delhi, Anjaiah was told by Indira Gandhi to resign as the chief minister. He was told about this on 13 February 1982 and he put in his papers on 20 February 1982. Bhavanam Venkatrama Reddy replaced him as the chief minister and he too was asked to vacate the chair for K. Vijaya Bhaskara Reddy in September 1982. Between March 1978 and January 1983, Andhra Pradesh had four chief ministers: M. Chenna Reddy, T. Anjaiah, B. Venkatrama Reddy and K. Vijaya Bhaskara Reddy, all from the Congress (I).

The public humiliation of Anjaiah and the frequent change of guard in the state and the fact that the chief ministers were left at the mercy of the party high command created ground for the emergence of the Telugu Desam Party (TDP), headed by matinee idol N. T. Rama Rao, in Andhra Pradesh. There was also the aspect of caste. NTR, as he was known, represented the aspirations of the Khammas; the community perceived the Congress (I) as dominated by the Reddys and the TDP came to represent, within a short period of its existence, a combination of forces that were unhappy with the Congress party. In the elections to the state assembly in January 1983, the TDP won 202 of the 294 seats. The Congress lost power in Andhra Pradesh for the first time.

The Rise of Regional Parties

The emergence of TDP and its pre-eminence in the state's political space signaled two things. One, it reflected a strong sense of revulsion among the people against the tendency to centralise powers with the high command and its vulgar manifestation in the manner in which the chief ministers were shuffled. The humiliation of T. Anjaiah by Rajiv Gandhi seemed to spark this sentiment and NTR was there to consolidate on that. Anjaiah also happened to belong to the scheduled castes, the Congress party's traditional support base. Such a development was witnessed in Tamil Nadu almost a couple of decades before 1980. The DMK's emergence as a strong force, as early as in 1957 and the party capturing power in Tamil Nadu in 1967, was a fallout of similar factors as well as a reaction by the non-upper caste majority to the Congress party's Brahmanical leadership. However, the DMK remained the only regional party in power since 1967. This phenomenon began to change after 1983.

This indeed was the second and the more important aspect of the TDP phenomenon. It reflected the beginning of the marginalisation of the national parties. Interestingly, a combination of the non-Congress opposition, consisting of the Lok Dal, the Janata Party, the Bharatiya Janata Party, the Congress (S) and the Republican Party of India, offered to accommodate NTR's TDP in their alliance to contest the Andhra Pradesh assembly elections. The offer they made, in October 1982 (elections were to be held in January 1983), to the TDP was 174 seats out of the 294 seats in the assembly. The TDP leader refused to consider the offer and contested alone and won 202 seats. The BJP won just three seats and the Janata Party only one. In the 1984 general election, the TDP won 30 seats in the Lok Sabha, to emerge as the largest party in the opposition. While the poor showing of the various other parties in 1984 may be attributed to the sympathy wave in favour of the Congress (I) after Indira Gandhi's death, the fact is that the TDP managed to win 30 out of the 42 Lok Sabha constituencies in Andhra Pradesh despite the pro-Congress tide elsewhere in the country. The choice of N. T. Rama Rao as the chairman of the National Front (that came up before the November 1989 elections) had its roots here. This trend was further pronounced in May 1996, when regional parties from across the country, would form a United Front and form the government at the Centre.

January 1983 was bad time for Indira Gandhi's Congress for another reason. The party lost power in Karnataka too. This was unprecedented. The voters of Andhra Pradesh and Karnataka, it may be recalled, had stood by Indira Gandhi even in 1977 and she was even elected to the Lok Sabha, in December 1978, from Chickmagalur in a by-election. Indira Gandhi was representing Medak in Andhra Pradesh in the Lok Sabha now. In the January 1983 elections to the Karnataka assembly (held along with Andhra Pradesh), the Janata Party, reduced to a rump in the Lok Sabha after the formation of the Bharatiya Janata Party, secured 95 seats in the 224 member Karnataka assembly and Ramakrishna Hegde, with 14 independents, formed the government in the state. Hegde had with him the Kranti Ranga, an outfit floated by former Congress leader, S. Bangarappa. The BJP too had made a mark in the Karnataka elections by securing 18 seats in the assembly.

In January 1983, the Congress (I) was left with just one state in southern India—Kerala—where it was in power. In Kerala too, the Congress (I) was heading an unwieldy coalition that was constituted by at least a dozen MLAs who belonged to the Congress (U), the various factions of the Kerala Congress and the Muslim League and the Government survived on the support of a lone independent MLA, Lonappan Nambadan. Moreover, the ministry was precariously placed and its motions could be passed only on the strength of the assembly speaker's right to cast his vote in the event of a tie during a division. The Karunakaran ministry came to be called the casting-vote-ministry. The Congress (I) had, in fact, lost the elections to the Kerala assembly in June 1980. A CPI (M)-led coalition with the CPI, the Congress (U) and the Kerala Congress (Mani) had formed the government in the state at that time. On 16 October 1981, A. K. Antony, leader of the Congress (U) in Kerala withdrew support of his 22 MLAs and Mani of the Kerala Congress followed suit within a week, reducing the CPI (M)-led ruling coalition into a minority. E. K. Nayanar resigned and the state was placed under President's rule. The Congress (U) faction then decided to support K. Karunakaran to form government in December 1981.

After the January 1983 round of assembly elections, the number of states with non-Congress governments increased to five. The CPI (M)-led Left Front that had captured power in West Bengal in 1977 had retained its position in the 1982 elections too. In Jammu and Kashmir, the National Conference had been in power from 1975 and Sheikh Abdullah had transferred the crown to his son, Farooq Abdullah in August 1982. In Tamil Nadu, M. G. Ramachandran's ADMK that captured power (in alliance with the Congress) in 1977, was dismissed in February 1980 (along with the eight other state governments); the ADMK fought the 1980 assembly polls alone and won 128 seats of the 234 seats in the assembly. Now, after January 1983, with the opposition governments in Andhra Pradesh and Karnataka, there were five states ruled by non-Congress parties. When this happened, trouble was already brewing in Assam and in Punjab (both of which will be discussed in the following sections elaborately). This along with the frequent removal of Congress (I) chief ministers in other states and the scenario that reduced the chief ministers to the mercy of the high command, lent credence to a radical thinking that sought strengthening the rights of the states. These state governments, meanwhile, would initiate poverty reduction programmes such as subsidised supply of foodgrain to the poor and this began affecting the financial status of the state governments. The prevailing mood was that the Centre controlled most of the revenue raising measures (in the form of taxes) and reduced the state governments to depend on the Centre for everything.

The initiative in this context came from the Karnataka chief minister, Ramakrishna Hegde. He convened a meet of the southern chief ministers in Bangalore on 20 March 1983. While Kerala chief minister, K. Karunakaran refused to attend, the meet was attended by N. T. Rama Rao, M. G. Ramachandran and

Pondicherry chief minister D. Ramachandran (also of the ADMK). Notwithstanding Hegde's insistence that the meet had nothing to do with partisan politics and that his objective was to raise issues involving the rights of the state governments, the impression and the outcome was different. The Bangalore meet was seen as an opposition conclave. This was followed by a meeting of leaders from 14 opposition parties in Vijayawada on 28 May 1983. Among those present at the Vijayawada meet were Farooq Abdullah, the chief minister of Jammu and Kashmir; Jagjivan Ram, who had by this time walked out of the Janata Party to set up the Congress (J); H. N. Bahuguna, who left the Congress (I) once again to set up his own outfit called the Dalit Mazdoor Kisan Party; L. K. Advani, who was now the general secretary of the BJP; Maneka Gandhi, who was heading her Sanjay Vichar Manch; S. S. Barnala of Akali Dal; Sharad Pawar of Congress (S) and M. Basavapunniah of CPI (M). The leaders resolved to work towards establishing a political brotherhood that was necessary to fight against the undemocratic Congress (I).

Indira Gandhi, meanwhile, reacted to the Bangalore meet, and announced the setting up of a Commission to go into aspects of the Centre-State relations and named Justice R. S. Sarkaria as its chairman. Justice Sarkaria, a former judge of the Supreme Court, had headed a commission of enquiry that went into charges of corruption against M. Karunanidhi in 1976. The report is understood to have found evidence of corruption in Karunanidhi's dealings as the chief minister. It is a different story that the report was shelved and buried deep after the Congress struck an alliance with the DMK before the 1980 general election to the Lok Sabha. Justice Sarkaria could begin his work on the Centre-State relations only several months after the commission was announced and the report, submitted in two volumes in 1988, was rich in content, substantive in analysis and strong insofar as the recommendations were concerned. It made a strong case for decentralisation of powers, both political and fiscal and also pointed to the severe abuse of Article 356 of the Constitution over the years. The Commission recommended several checks against such abuse and most of them were internalised by the Supreme Court bench in the S. R. Bommai and others vs Union of India case. However, the then Congress (I) government, headed by Rajiv Gandhi, did not find anything significant in the Sarkaria Commission's recommendations and copies of the two volumes were left to gather dust in the strong rooms of the various ministries.

The Congress (I), meanwhile, was irritated when Farooq Abdullah attended the Vijayawada conclave of the opposition leaders. Sheikh Abdullah had appointed his son Farooq as chief minister on 23 August 1982. Sheikh passed away soon after this and Farooq Abdullah rode to power, on his own, in September 1983. The September 1983 elections to the Jammu and Kashmir assembly, however, bore ominous signals. While the National Conference swept the polls in the Kashmir valley, the Jammu region voted for the Congress candidates in a big way. Indira Gandhi resorted to the Hindu religious identity card in that election and the victory she secured in the Jammu region, thanks to this, would leave its lasting impact on the politics of the region. The National Conference won 46 seats (all from the Kashmir valley) against the 26 seats won by the Congress, all of that were in the Jammu region.

Fresh from this victory, Farooq Abdullah organised the next conclave of the opposition chief ministers in Srinagar for three days between 5 and 7 October 1983. The agenda was to discuss Centre–State relations. The resolution passed in that conclave identified specific provisions of the Constitution that were to be altered or scrapped. Article 356 was among the provisions where radical changes were demanded and Article 360 was sought to be scrapped. The statement also sought widening of the tax base of the states. Indira Gandhi's response to all this was one of anger rather than conciliation. She had made up her mind to tame Farooq Abdullah.

There was dissidence against Farooq within the National Conference. G. M. Shah, the chief minister's brother-in-law, believed that the throne belonged to him and that Farooq had usurped it. Farooq was a National Conference MP when he was anointed chief minister by his father while Shah was a senior minister in the Sheikh Abdullah cabinet for sometime. Indira Gandhi sought help from her cousin and the governor of Jammu and Kashmir, B. K. Nehru, to teach Farooq a lesson and when he refused to play ball, he was shifted to the Gujarat Raj Bhawan. Jagmohan, the infamous executor of Sanjay Gandhi's agenda in Delhi during the Emergency, was sent as the governor of Jammu and Kashmir in February 1984. On 2 July 1984, Shah met Jagmohan with a list of 12 National Conference MLAs supporting him as the chief minister against Farooq Abdullah. Shah also claimed support from the 26 Congress (I) MLAs. Jagmohan instantly dismissed Farooq Abdullah and installed Shah as the chief minister of Jammu and Kashmir. Farooq Abdullah was denied the opportunity to prove his strength in the assembly as Jagmohan was convinced that Shah commanded the majority.

The Union Cabinet also added a shade of 'national interest' to justify the toppling game; Home Minister P. V. Narasimha Rao told the Rajya Sabha that his ministry had information of 'anti-national and secessionist activities in Kashmir since mid–1983' and justified the toppling game.

The dismissal evoked sharp protests and N. T. Rama Rao sought to raise it in the chief ministers' meet held in Delhi on 12 July 1984. Denied of an opportunity to do this, Rao along with Hegde, Jyoti Basu, M. G. Ramachandran and D. Ramachandran walked out of the chief ministers' meet. The media, across the board, called the dismissal of Farooq Abdullah a brazen display of partisan politics. *The Indian Express* went a step further to describe that Governor Jagmohan was allowed to behave like a viceroy. B. K. Nehru, who was shifted out of the Srinagar Raj Bhawan, made it clear that there was no trace of secessionist activities in the valley and that the dissidence was orchestrated by the Congress (I). Nehru described the events as an intrigue against Farooq Abdulah. All this notwithstanding, Shah continued as the chief minister until March 1986; he was removed then and the state was placed under Central rule. Militancy had raised its head by this time and worse things were to follow. Farooq Abdullah made up with Rajiv Gandhi soon after and the National Conference–Congress (I) alliance 'swept' the assembly elections in 1987. This victory against the Muslim United Front, an amorphous coalition of militant and young political elements, was managed by extensive rigging at both the polling stage and at the time of counting. All this led Kashmir into a problem. We shall discuss this later.

The toppling game was next tried in Andhra Pradesh and exactly a month after N. T. Rama Rao led the charge against the dismissal of Farooq Abdullah at the chief ministers' meet in Delhi. On 16 August 1984, Rama Rao had just returned from the USA and was still convalescing after a heart surgery. That was when he was informed, by the governor, Ram Lal (who was sent as the governor after having been removed as the chief minister of Himachal Pradesh), of his dismissal on grounds that he had lost the majority support in the state assembly. The intrigue was played a couple of days before 16 August and executed by Rama Rao's senior cabinet colleague N. Bhaskara Rao. He was a Congressman for long and had joined the TDP just before the January 1983 elections. Bhaskar Rao had, in fact, gone around collecting signatures from the TDP MLAs on a letter that contained adulatory mentions about Rama Rao and in the course of this, seeking that the party MLAs be involved more in the process of decision making and formulating its policies. While a few of the signatures were there on the same page as the letter was, most of the MLAs signed on sheets appended to the letter. Bhaskar Rao then changed the front page and replaced the letter with another one that stated that the MLAs were withdrawing their support to Rama Rao and instead supporting Bhaskar Rao as leader of the TDP Legislature Party. This letter, along with the sheets bearing the signatures of the MLAs, was handed over to Governor Ram Lal on 15 August 1984 by Bhaskar Rao. The governor hastened to dismiss Rama Rao and Bhaskar Rao was sworn in as the chief minister the day after.

Unlike in the case of Farooq Abdullah, there was no semblance of dissidence in the TDP. Rama Rao's managers, Chandrababu Naidu (his son-in-law and a former leader of the Youth Congress) and P. Upendra (a former officer in the Indian Railways), got into the act on the evening of 16 August 1984 to get 163 TDP MLAs into the Ramakrishna Studios (owned by one of Rama Rao's sons) and ensured that they were kept away from the outside world. Bhaskar Rao was unable to even establish contact with them. They were all taken to New Delhi and the MLAs paraded before President Giani Zail Singh. The dismissal triggered of protests across the country and when it was raised in Parliament, Prime Minister

Indira Gandhi stood up to say that she was unaware of the intrigues and that she came to know of Rama Rao's dismissal only after it was put out by the news agencies. Indira's refrain provoked angry reactions and the CPI leader, Indrajit Gupta, intervened and wondered aloud as to whether the prime minister was speaking the truth. Gupta's refrain was that if what Indira claimed was the truth, then there were doubts as to who ruled the country. The truth, in fact, was that the Andhra Pradesh operations were carried out by Arun Nehru, but with Indira's blessings. The operations, as we saw, were frustrated by the TDP managers and Bhaskara Rao could not enlist defections even after being sworn in as the chief minister and with all the might that came with power. The situation was allowed to continue for at least a month and finally N. T. Rama Rao was reinstated as the chief minister on 18 September 1984.

The Congress (I) and Indira Gandhi could not recover from the shame. The protests against the toppling game were so intense that it brought life to a standstill all over Andhra Pradesh during the month when Bhaskar Rao was the chief minister. The return of Rama Rao also gave a fillip to the opposition parties in their campaign against Indira Gandhi. The TDP leader sought dissolution of the assembly in December 1984 and in the elections to the state assembly, held simultaneously with the Lok Sabha polls, the TDP secured 202 seats in the 294-member assembly and the Congress (I) strength came down to 50 against the 60 in the previous House. The other important development was that the TDP won 30 Lok Sabha seats from Andhra Pradesh and emerged as the largest opposition block in the Lok Sabha. This was achieved by the TDP despite the sympathy wave that Rajiv Gandhi rode in that election held within a couple of months after Indira Gandhi's assassination. The Congress (I) won just six out of the 42 constituencies from Andhra Pradesh in December 1984.

There were other developments too in this period and they impacted the political discourse of independent India in a far more significant manner than all these tumultuous events; the crisis in Assam and in the Punjab.

The Assam Problem

We did see that in Assam, elections were held in only two Lok Sabha constituencies—Karimganj and Silchar—in 1980. Both these constituencies are in the southern part of the state. In the rest of Assam, known as the Brahmaputra valley, elections were not held in 1980. The Election Commission found the law and order situation there as not conducive for polling. The decision to countermand elections was taken after the notification was issued. Candidates were prevented from filing their nominations by masses of the Assamese people picketing the centres where nominations were to be filed and, hence, the Election Commission decided to countermand the elections in 12 out of the 14 Lok Sabha constituencies from the state. The issue involved was the popular perception, among the people, that foreign nationals (Bangladeshis) were registered, in large numbers, as voters in the various constituencies across Assam. While there was enough evidence that Bangladesh nationals were enrolled as voters, the trouble was that the local people had perceived the Bengali-speaking people who had migrated over the years from West Bengal, as Bangladeshis. The truth was that the migrants from West Bengal, thanks to their educational attainment, were better placed to grab employment in the government and the public sector undertakings as well as private enterprises in Assam and the new generation of Assamese found themselves discriminated against in their own land.

The slogan of 'sons-of-the-soil' had begun to capture the imagination of the Assamese-speaking people over the years and evidence of a large number of Bangladeshis figuring in the voter list, found out in the revised electoral rolls in January 1979 in the Mangaldoi Lok Sabha constituency (in the northern part of Assam), sparked off protests. A by-election to the Mangaldoi Lok Sabha constituency was due in June 1979. The by-elections were not held. Assam was, at that time, under Janata Party government, headed by Golap Chand Borbora. The Janata Party had captured power, like in many other states, in March 1978. By June 1979, when the agitation against the 'foreign nationals' was beginning to take a mass proportion, the state government had landed in a limbo as a result of the crisis in the Janata's national leadership. The All Assam Students Union (AASU), an organisation that had existed for several years, gave a call for a statewide *bandh* on 8 June 1979 protesting against the presence of non-Assamese people in the state and their predominance in the various walks of civil and political life. The *bandh* was a success across the Brahmaputra valley. This was the beginning of a long and drawn-out agitation, violent in times, culminating in the Asom Gana Parishad, a political party led by student leaders, forming the state government in December 1985. The course of politics in Assam in the intervening years between 1979 and 1985 was full of tumult and turmoil and causing the death of several hundred people.

Encouraged by the success of the 8 June 1979 Assam *bandh* and the response they got for their call to boycott the Independence Day celebrations on 15 August 1979, the various groups that were campaigning against the domination of Bengali-speaking people in Assam came to constitute the All Assam Gana Sangram Parishad on 27 August 1979. Apart from the AASU, there were eight other organisations that came together under this platform. But the core leadership of the Gana Sangram Parishad remained with the students. There was no space given for leaders from the established political parties in the Gana Sangram Parishad, the only exception being Dinesh Goswami, a former Congressman and a lawyer at that time. Goswami would become a Union minister in the V. P. Singh Cabinet between December 1989 and November 1990.

Meanwhile, the Borbora government collapsed due to internal strife and J. N. Hazarika became the chief minister on 9 September 1979 heading an amorphous coalition of sections in the Janata and various other smaller groups. The Gana Sangram Parishad called for a day-long picketing of the government offices across Assam on 15 September 1979. An effete political leadership led the civil administration to collapse and incidents of violence against the Bengali-speaking people were reported from various parts of Assam on 9 November 1979. This led the chief minister of West Bengal, Jyoti Basu, to react and soon the CPI (M)'s cadres too began to be attacked by the agitators. The CPI (M) had established strong bases in parts of the valley and particularly in the tea estates. The party had won as many as 11 seats, in the 126-member assembly, in the 1978 elections. The agitation, now turning violent and targeting the Bengali-speaking people, was further intensified after the AASU called for boycott of elections to the Lok Sabha as long as the electoral rolls were not cleansed of the 'foreign nationals'. The AASU called for picketing of the roads leading to the centres where nominations were to be filed. On 10 December 1979, Khargeswar Talukdar, a functionary of the AASU in Barpeta, lost his life when the police tried to disperse the picketers who had gathered to prevent Begum Abida Ahmed, a Congress (I) candidate for Barpeta, from filing her nominations. The Hazarika ministry collapsed in a couple of days after that and Assam was brought under Central rule and the assembly kept under suspended animation. That was when the Election Commission decided to countermand polling in all but two constituencies. Violence broke out again, in the form of clashes between the agitators and the immigrants, across the state between 5 and 8 January 1980 and Assam was now declared as 'disturbed'. This meant unbridled powers to the police and the paramilitary forces, now deployed in many parts of the state.

A fortnight after being sworn in as the prime minister, Indira Gandhi got on to address the Assam issue. The AASU leaders were invited for talks and the first round of talks were held on 2 February 1980. Prime Minister Indira Gandhi was taken by surprise when the AASU leaders called for a two-minute silence, just before the talks, in memory of the 'martyrs' of the agitation. There in that meeting, the AASU presented its charter of demands. The charter read:

1. Detection and deportation of foreigners from India;
2. Removal of their names from the electoral rolls and tightening of rules to make it impossible for foreigners to get enlisted as voters in future;
3. Effective protection of international frontiers;
4. Issue of identity cards to all Indian citizens residing in Assam;
5. Constitutional provision for 15 to 20 years to protect the identity of the indigenous people of the Northeast;

6. Rejection of doubtful citizenship certificates granted by the governments of Tripura and West Bengal; and
7. Grant of citizenship certificates only by the Central Government.

The demands were, indeed, quite ordinary. All the issues raised were nothing but principles enshrined in the Constitution. AASU, on the face of it, was only demanding that the government implement all that the Constitution guaranteed. This, however, was not all. The dispute was about the cut-off date to identify immigrants from Bangladesh as illegal. The AASU's demand that 1 January 1966 be set as the cut-off date meant that those who came into India as refugees even before the political crisis there (in 1971), would have to be deported. The government's position was that the cut-off date be fixed as 25 March 1971; from when there was a heavy influx of refugees into India. The other issue was that of Bengali-speaking people in Assam and to send them out of the state would be un-constitutional in all senses of the term. Interestingly, the AASU did not place this demand on its charter but the agitators had been targeting the Bengali-speaking people since June 1979. There was also the issue about terming all the Bengali-speaking Muslims as Bangladeshis and the AASU agitation had led to several attacks on these people, a large number of them being poor and daily wage earners, in Assam.

The first round of talks went on until 8 February 1980 and there were 21 more rounds of talks between the agitation leaders and the Union government (represented by senior ministers and Prime Minister Indira Gandhi, and Rajiv Gandhi after her demise, on some occasions) before a settlement was reached in the small hours of 15 August 1985 in Delhi. During the five years, Assam remained a disturbed area. While blockade of road transport and the oil pipelines to and from the Indian Oil Refineries at Digboi was an integral part of the agitation, it also lent itself to the idea of posting the army and the paramilitary forces across the state during this period. The AASU leaders were arrested at various points of time and released while they were invited for talks in Delhi. As part of the agitation, the AASU called for boycott of Independence Day and Republic Day celebrations; a new form of protest—blackout—when lights would go off in all homes across the state was an innovation of this agitation. The AASU leaders also objected to the national anthem on the ground that it was in the Bengali language. The culmination of this violent agitation was the massacre in Nellie, on 18 February 1983, in which at least 1,000 men, women and children were left dead. All the dead were Bengali-speaking Muslims. The Nellie massacre was the agitators' response to the fact that these poor people voted in the 13 February 1983 elections to the Assam assembly that the AASU had decided to boycott. The story of the 1983 elections in Assam is worth recalling.

On 6 December 1980, the Congress (I) cobbled together a majority in the assembly, that was placed under suspended animation, and foisted Anwara

Taimur as the chief minister. Plagued by dissidence from within the Congress (I) and from the supporting groups, the Taimur ministry failed to have the vote on account passed in the assembly and a constitutional crisis was averted only because the governor adjourned the assembly sine die and the Centre issued an ordinance, enabling the state government's expenditure until 30 June 1981. Taimur finally resigned on 27 June 1981 after it became clear that she did not enjoy a majority. President's rule was imposed and the assembly was once again placed under suspended animation. The violence now took the form of bomb blasts in the government offices and killing senior government functionaries, including the commissioner of Upper Assam Division in Jorhat. Indiscriminate attacks on the Bengali speaking people became an order of the day across Assam by now. The installation of another Congress (I) ministry, headed by K. C. Gogoi, on 13 January 1982, was resented by the AASU as well as the opposition parties and a *bandh* call on 18 January 1982, evoked huge response in the Brahmaputra valley. After a few more rounds of talks, the Gogoi ministry was asked to resign by the Centre and the assembly was dissolved on 19 March 1982.

It became imperative then that the elections were held and a new assembly constituted before 18 March 1983. The Constitution, after the 44th amendment, had set one year as the maximum period for a state to be placed under Central rule. The agitation continued and the talks were leading to nowhere near a solution. The February 1983 elections were notified in this larger context; elections were scheduled for the assembly as well as the 12 Lok Sabha constituencies where they were countermanded in December 1979. The AASU persisted with its call for boycott because they were going to be held according to the electoral rolls of January 1979. The government, however, went ahead holding the polls with the help of the army and the paramilitary forces. The polling was far too low and reports of the security forces forcing the voters to cast their votes came from across the state. The AASU leaders, arrested on 7 January 1983, were held in jails during the elections. They were arrested at the Guwahati airport on their return from Delhi after the 22nd round of talks held on 4 and 5 January 1983.

The candidates were prevented from campaigning in many places across Assam. The bloodiest manifestation of the violence happened on 18 February 1983 at Nellie, one of the dozen villages in the Nowgong district, where a majority were Bengali-speaking Muslims. Nellie is only 45 kilometres away from Guwahati. The carnage that left at least 1,000 dead, their bodies strewn all over the fields, was in reaction to the fact that the people of this village had defied the AASU's call for boycott of elections. They had cast their votes on 14 February 1983 because the army and paramilitary forces had protected them on that day. Pictures of slain bodies, strewn across the fields, including that of a large number of children, stunned the nation. But then, the Congress (I), which had swept the elections, winning 91 out of the 101 seats for which elections were held, installed Hiteshwar Saikia as the chief minister. The AASU stepped up its agitation and enforced boycott of the assembly and the ministers were greeted with *bandhs*, blackouts and blackflag demonstrations everywhere. All that continued and the Saikia ministry, whose members were protected by security men all day and everywhere, finally resigned on 18 August 1985 and recommended dissolution of the assembly.

This was one of the terms of the settlement reached between Rajiv Gandhi and the AASU leaders, during the small hours, on 15 August 1985. The other crucial aspect of the settlement or the accord was to hold 1 January 1966 as the cut-off date for identifying foreign nationals. In other words, all those who came into Assam after 1 January 1966 were to be identified as foreign nationals and deported to Bangladesh. The AASU and a few other outfits founded the Asom Gana Parishad (AGP), contested elections to the state assembly held in December 1985, won 65 seats in the 126-member assembly and Prafulla Kumar Mahanta, a student in the Guwahati University and president of the AASU in the years of the agitation, was sworn in as the chief minister. The AGP would get caught in internal squabbles and split into factions and also face charges of corruption in a few years after it captured power.

Turmoil in Punjab

Indira Gandhi's assassination on 31 October 1984 was the direct fallout of her decision to send the army into the Golden Temple in Amritsar to flush out Jarnail Singh Bhindranwale and his band of armed followers from the premises. While 'Operation Bluestar', as it was called, that lasted for three days and nights between 4 and 6 June 1984, had become necessary and the only way, to restore normality in Punjab, the fact is that the situation was allowed to lead into that by Indira Gandhi herself. A narrative, as brief as it can be, will be in order to understand the crisis that haunted the society in Punjab and the rest of the country for at least four years from 1980. This is not to say that the issue was settled with the Operation Bluestar or that it died out along with Indira Gandhi's death. Operation Bluestar, in a way, drove the terrorists out of the Golden Temple and out of Punjab. The nation continued to pay a heavy price in the form of lives lost in the several bomb blasts in Delhi, for at least a couple of years, after June 1984. The slogan of Khalistan continues to be heard, every now and then. But it certainly does not excite passions among the members of the Sikh community any longer.

While the history of the Sikh religion and the intermingling of the religious and the political go back to the foundation of the religion by Guru Nanak (1469–1539) and the construction of the Akal Takht by Guru Hargobind (the sixth Guru), the more significant date for the purpose of our understanding of the Punjab issue will be 1925 and 1966. The Shiromani Gurudwara Prabandhak Committee (SGPC) Act, 1925, laid the foundations for a Sikh exclusive electoral college to manage the affairs of the Gurudwaras across Punjab and elsewhere in the country. The SGPC leaders are elected by an exclusive electoral college consisting of the Sikh community and this heralded the birth of the Shiromani Akali Dal (SAD), a Sikh exclusive political party. The SAD, thus, came to represent the political aspirations of the Sikhs in the modern sense of the term and after the adoption of the Republican Constitution, in November 1950, the Akali Dal was registered as a political party with claims to represent all the members of the Sikh community. This claim, however, was hollow. Notwithstanding the ideal of a casteless order that was internal to the Sikh religion, the Dalit converts to the religion remained excluded from the affairs of the SGPC and the Akali Dal remained a preserve of the non-Dalit Sikhs. The Jat Sikhs too were held on the fringes of the community. The Congress party filled this space among the Sikh community and the Akali Dal could not emerge as the natural choice of all the Sikhs in Punjab. Moreover, the Sikhs constituted less than half of the population of the Punjab state.

Master Tara Singh, head of the Akali Dal at the dawn of independence, led agitations demanding a Sikh majority Punjabi Suba; while his demand was couched in the demand for linguistic organisation of states, the fact was that religious identity was at the roots of the Akali Dal's demand. Jawaharlal Nehru resisted the demand for a Punjabi-speaking state. In fact, the States Reorganisation Committee too disapproved the idea. The Akali Dal leadership was passed over to Sant Fateh Singh, a Jat Sikh, in the 1960s and he too persisted with the demand. Prime Minister Indira Gandhi conceded the demand in March 1966. This was one of her decisions within months after becoming the prime minister in January 1966. However, even after Haryana and Himachal Pradesh were carved out, taking away the Hindi-speaking districts from Punjab, the demographic composition of Punjab did not change drastically. The Sikhs constituted only 56 per cent of the population of Punjab. And, with the caste factor still prevailing within the religious identity and the Congress continuing to hold on among the Dalit Sikhs, the Akali Dal could not make it to power.

In 1967, when the Congress lost its popular support in several states, it lost power in Punjab too. The Akali Dal won 30 seats in the 108-member assembly. It cobbled a majority with its pre-poll ally, the Bharatiya Jan Sangh, several independents and the Left parties to form its government, headed by Justice Gurnam Singh. The government was caught in dissidence and Lachman Singh Gill replaced Gurnam Singh in November 1967 and by August 1968, the government collapsed leading to imposition of Central rule. The Akali Dal won again in February 1969; Gurnam Singh became the chief minister again only to be replaced by Parkash Singh Badal in March 1970. The Badal regime was stable but Indira Gandhi dismissed the government and dissolved the assembly. The Congress wrested power in Punjab (as in all other states except Tamil Nadu in 1972) and the victory had to do more with Indira Gandhi's 'achievement' in Bangladesh in December 1971. Giani Zail Singh became the chief minister. He began pushing the Akali leaders, even otherwise busy fighting their own battles, into a corner by attempting to appropriate the agenda of Sikh identity politics. This, as well as the defeat in the 1972 assembly elections, led the Akali Dal leaders into a state of desperation. They assembled at the Anandpur Sahib (in Talwandi, an important Gurudwara for the Sikhs where Guru Gobind had constituted the *Dal Khalsa*, or the Army of the Pure), to pass a resolution demanding that the Union Government's role in Punjab shall be restricted to defence, foreign relations, currency and communications. The Anandpur Sahib Resolution, which would become a slogan more than a reference point, in the several rounds of talks between the leaders of the Akali Dal and representatives of the Union Government after 1982, was passed around the same time when Jagjit Singh Chauhan raised the demand for Khalistan from London. Chauhan appointed himself as the 'President' of the 'Republic of Khalistan.'

The Anandpur Sahib Resolution was soon forgotten and the Akali leaders were not heard pursuing the demand during the Emergency. Nor did they raise any of the issues that were settled in 1970, involving the transfer of Chandigarh to Punjab (Chandigarh remained the capital for both Punjab and Haryana), in exchange for Abohar and Fazilka (two districts with fertile agricultural land and constituted predominantly by Hindi-speaking people), with Haryana. They did not bother about the sharing of the waters flowing in the Ravi and Beas between Punjab, Haryana and Rajasthan. The 1970 agreement was about building the Sutlej-Yamuna-Link canal, to reach some of the water to Rajasthan. These issues were not taken up throughout the 1970s when the Congress was in power in both the Centre and in Punjab or when the Akali-Janata combine captured power in Punjab and at the Centre between 1977 and 1979.

The 1977–79 period, however, witnessed the rise of Jarnail Singh Bhindranwale, a small-time preacher of the Sikh religion, transforming into a militant Sikh leader commanding a band of gun-toting young men who would go about killing anyone and everyone who came in their way. The fact is that Bhindranwale was assiduously cultivated by Sanjay Gandhi and Zail Singh during 1977–79 and their intentions were clear: To delegitimise the Akali Dal leaders in Punjab. They were bothered, at that time, with the stability that the Akali Dal had achieved in the political affairs of the Punjab state. The Congress had lost all the Lok Sabha seats from Punjab to the Akali Dal-Janata combine in the 1977 general election and was reduced to having only 17 seats in the assembly in the elections held in June that year. Unlike in the past, the Akali Dal leaders appeared to have settled their own turf wars now: Harchand Singh Longowal was now accepted the supreme leader, Gurcharan Singh Tohra was left to run the SGPC, Parkash Singh Badal found his place in the Union Cabinet and Surjit Singh Barnala as chief minister. The Akali Dal ministry appeared stable now. The Congress was determined against letting this happen. This was behind the idea of propping up Bhindranwale. When the Barnala ministry was dismissed on 17 February 1980, Bhindranwale had emerged into a 'leader' of some importance.

On 13 April 1978, the holy day of Baisakhi, Bhindranwale led his followers into a convention that the Nirankari sect was holding at Amritsar. Bhindranwale called it a march into the 'enemy camp'. The Nirankaris were a sect, within the Sikh tradition, that believed that God was formless (*nirankar*) and that He could be realised only through a living Guru. The fundamentalists of the religion, however, held that Guru Gobind Singh was the last of the Gurus and the *Granth Sahib* (the holy book) represented the continuity. Both the sects existed side by side for long. The 13 April march led by Bhindranwale, however, changed the course and 13 Sikhs were killed in the clashes that ensued in Amritsar that day. Thereafter, clashes between the two sects were reported frequently and Nirankari Baba Gurbachan Singh, head of the sect, was shot dead in April 1980. It was widely perceived that Bhindranwale was behind the killing. He had, by now, collected a band of armed followers and had emerged a challenge to the Akali Dal leaders as well as a votary of Khalistan. The Akali Dal lost the 1980 elections to the assembly and Punjab came under Congress (I) rule in July 1980. The demand for Khalistan was already in the air and the Akali Dal leaders were losing ground to Bhindranwale and his militant politics.

On 9 September 1981, Jagat Narain, a politician who owned a chain of news publications was shot dead. Narain was seen as pro-Nirankaris and also opposed to the idea of Khalistan. It was clear that Bhindranwale was involved in the murder; despite an arrest warrant against his name, he was travelling across Punjab for days after the murder. Zail Singh, who had propped him up, was now the union home minister and Darbara Singh, Congress chief minister of Punjab, could not do anything that Zail Singh did not want. Bhindranwale was taken into custody on 20 September 1980. In fact, it happened only because he decided to 'surrender' and he did that at a place of his choice: the Mehta Chowk gurudwara, near Amritsar. There were violent protests soon after his arrest and all that left 17 dead. An Indian Airlines plane, bound for Srinagar, was hijacked to Lahore within days after the arrest and the hijackers demanded Bhindranwale's release. The 'Sant', as he was described by Sanjay Gandhi and Indira in the early days of his ascendancy, in one of his sermons, said: 'If the Pandey brothers hijack a plane for Mrs. Gandhi, they are rewarded with political positions. If the Sikhs hijack a plane to Lahore, they are dubbed traitors'. The Pandey brothers, Bholanath and Devendra were involved in hijacking an Indian Airlines plane in 1978 when Indira was put in jail. Both of them became Congress (I) MLAs in Uttar Pradesh in 1980.

It was clear, by now, that Bhindranwale was no longer a hatchet man for the Congress (I), as it was intended by Sanjay Gandhi and Zail Singh when they began seeing him in 1977. His concerns were political and associated with the demand for Khalistan. The Akali Dal, meanwhile, found Bhindranwale indispensable. Such was his appeal among the Sikh community. The Akali Dal now submitted a memorandum, listing out their demands, that included the transfer of Chandigarh, the sharing of river waters and such old things. But the first of the demands in that charter was the unconditional and immediate release of Bhindranwale. Indira Gandhi ordered Bhindranwale's release on 14 October 1981 even before the charges were framed against him in the Jagat Narain murder case. Bhindranwale now moved into the Golden Temple complex, accompanied by his band of followers, with arms and ammunitions.

Thereon indiscriminate killings by motorcycle borne terrorists began to happen day after day. While it was clear that Bhindranwale was behind all that, neither did the Akali Dal leaders murmur nor did the Congress (I) governments in the state and the Centre raise their little finger. The victims of the terror strikes were officials, both Hindus and Sikhs, and sometimes low-level cadre of the Congress (I) and all that caused a sense of insecurity across Punjab. The Akali Dal leadership, meanwhile, insisted on the transfer of Chandigarh to Punjab (without letting Abohar and Fazilka to be transferred to Haryana); that the Centre grant the money required to build another capital city for Haryana; and that the construction of the Sutlej-Yamuna-Link canal to ensure flow of some of the Ravi-Beas waters to Rajasthan (which they had agreed to in 1970) be stopped. The Akali Dal also protested against the indiscriminate killings of innocent youth; their allegation that the claims of encounter deaths by the Punjab police, happening day after day, were, in fact false and that the victms in many instances were innocent Sikh youth. This turned out to be true. In other words, the police actions were leading to the alienation of the state from the people and this had contributed, in good measure, to legitimise Bhindranwale among the Sikhs.

All the while, talks were held, intermittently, between the Akali Dal leaders and the Union Government and at every stage, the Centre would insist that any settlement was possible only after the Akali Dal leaders ensured Bhindranwale's concurrence. Indira Gandhi's government did this while Bhindranwale was now entrenched inside the Golden Temple and had accumulated a huge cache of arms and ammunition. His followers were going about killing innocents and political workers across the state. On 6 November 1982, H. S. Longowal, now the supreme leader of the moderate Akalis (Bhindranwale had come to represent the extremists), set out on a march to Delhi and threatened that his men would demonstrate in the capital, where the Asian Games were to be held. The Asiad, incidentally, was Rajiv Gandhi's project and Indira Gandhi ordered that the Akali march be stopped at all costs. All roads to Delhi, from Punjab, passed through Haryana. Bhajan Lal, now a favourite of Indira Gandhi and desperate to out-do Bansi Lal in that business, pulled all the stops. The Akali Dal leaders as well as every Sikh who travelled to Delhi, at that time, were 'handled' by the Haryana police personnel. All this, naturally, lent legitimacy to Bhindranwale and the feeble voices against his militant ways were silenced. Bhindranwale began attacking the Akali leaders and he moved into the Akal Takht, fortified the structure and began killing supporters of the moderate Akali leaders within and outside the Golden Temple. Longowal's message to Indira Gandhi and his plea that Bhindranwale be contained, conveyed over the telephone, did not evoke any response.

On 23 April 1983, A. S. Atwal, Deputy Inspector General of the Punjab Police and a practising Sikh, was shot dead at the main entrance to the Golden Temple. Atwal was just on his way out, after offering prayers, and the bullets that felled him came from inside the complex. The government did nothing to apprehend the killers of the high-ranking police officer from within the precincts of the Golden Temple. On 5 October 1983, a bus to Delhi was stopped in Punjab and five of the passengers, all Hindus, were killed. Darbara Singh, chief minister, was now dismissed, the assembly dissolved and the state placed under Central rule. This was too late and too little. Bhindranwale was now entrenched inside the Golden Temple and the arms he possessed, as it was known after the Operation Bluestar, were huge and a lot more than assault rifles and grenades.

An operation to flush out the militants had become inevitable even by the end of 1983. But then, it took six more months before it was ordered and carried out between 4 and 6 June, 1984. Preparations for the operation began in the last few days of May 1984 with 70,000 army men moving into the various parts of the state and also the reinforcement of paramilitary men in the streets around the Golden Temple. The sand-bag bunkers were reinforced and new ones put up. The forces provoked the militants, now inside the temple, to open fire at various points of time. The idea was to ensure that they exhausted their ammunition stocks. The army and the paramilitary had laid siege to the Golden Temple by then. But on 4 June 1984, they realised that they needed artillery fire; the militants fired rocket-propelled grenades that day. The army then realised the need for battle tanks and Armoured Personnel Vehicles. These were brought and 40 commandos, with a specific brief to rescue the moderate Akalis caught inside, sneaked into the complex on the night of 5 June 1984. The tanks and the Armoured Personnel Vehicles moved into the complex and this ensured that the infantry men, mostly commissioned officers, occuppied the various buildings inside the complex, barring the Akal Takht. All this happened on the night of June 5. At least 100 men from the army were dead by then. Bhindranwale and his men were now entrenched inside the Akal Takht and they remained there through the day on June 6. As dusk fell, the soldiers moved towards the Akal Takht, supported all the while by firing from the tanks, to shoot down Bhindranwale, his lieutenants Shahbag Singh (a former Major General in the Indian Army), Amrik Singh and several others there. At least 1000 extremists and 200 army men were killed inside the complex in the operations.

The Akal Takht was demolished but there was no damage to the Harminder Sahib. There was outrage among the Sikhs. But then, after things were allowed to come to such a pass, the army operation was inevitable. And after Bhindranwale was eliminated from the scene, Longowal began negotiating a settlement of the Punjab dispute with the Centre. This began in April 1985 and an accord was signed, on 24 July 1985, between Prime Minister Rajiv Gandhi and Longowal. Bhindranwale's followers, however, were still around, striking terror across Punjab and in Delhi too. On 20 August 1985, Longowal was gunned down in his own village. Such killings continued. On 10 August 1986, General Vaidya, who had retired from the army, was shot dead in broad daylight in far away Pune in Maharashtra. It would take long before normality returned in Punjab.

Meanwhile, the direct effect of Operation Bluestar was the assassination of Indira Gandhi, by her own security guards on the morning of 31 October 1984. President Zail Singh appointed Rajiv Gandhi as prime minister and he was sworn in the same evening, even before the Congress (I) Parliamentary Party went through the formality of electing Rajiv Gandhi, the leader. The only one to murmur against that was Pranab Mukherjee. That was too faint to be noticed. For three days after that day Sikhs across Delhi and many other towns in northern India were hounded out of their homes and burnt alive on the streets. The pogrom that continued between 1 and 3 November, 1984, in which several local leaders of the Congress (I) were involved, shook the conscience of the nation. But then, Rajiv Gandhi, sworn in as prime minister in the evening on 31 October 1984, maintained that when a big tree falls the whole ground shakes. Rajiv Gandhi said this on 19 November 1984, addressing a public meeting on Indira's birth anniversary at the New Delhi Boat Club. Indira Gandhi's funeral procession was turned into a spectacle and Prime Minister Rajiv Gandhi recommended dissolution of Parliament and asked the Election Commission to hold elections to the Lok Sabha as early as possible. The Lok Sabha's term, in any case, was to end by early January 1985.

Elections were held on 24 December 1984 and the Congress (I), now under Rajiv Gandhi, won a landslide; 415 in the House of 542. The states where the Congress (I) did not sweep the polls were Andhra Pradesh, Assam and Punjab. Even in West Bengal, where the CPI (M)-led Left Front had done well in 1980 (winning 38 out of the 42 Lok Sabha seats), the Congress (I) managed to secure 16 seats in 1984. The Lok Dal (the new name for Charan Singh's Janata-S) won just two seats from Uttar Pradesh in 1984 against the 29 seats it had won in 1980. Most veterans from the opposition parties were defeated by political novices nominated by the Congress (I) in December 1984. Rajiv Gandhi defeated Maneka Gandhi, whom the opposition parties supported, with a huge margin. He was sworn in as prime minister, for the second time in three months, on 31 December 1984.

XIII

The Rajiv Gandhi Era

> On New Year's eve, Rajiv Gandhi was sworn in as Prime Minister by President Zail Singh – for the second time in two months. ... On October 31, a fateful day of shock and grief, he took over as Prime Minister in a depressing atmosphere. ... But now the prize was his – in his own right, earned in a national contest.
>
> — K. K. Katyal, *Frontline*, Volume 1, No. 3

The Congress (I), in October 1984, was indeed a pale shadow of its own self in January 1980. We did see, in the previous chapter, that the party had lost state assembly elections in Andhra Pradesh and Karnataka; the trouble in Punjab and Assam; the opposition parties gathering together and that this time, it was happening with a new set of leaders, representing regional aspirations such as N. T. Rama Rao, Farooq Abdullah, Ramakrishna Hegde and Jyoti Basu. This is not to say that the opposition parties were consolidating once again. The element of disunity among them was worse than it was in 1980. Charan Singh's Janata (Secular) was renamed as Dalit Mazdoor Kisan Party (DMKP); this new party had weakened significantly after the old Socialists left the fold to join the Janata Party and Raj Narain floated his own outfit called the Rashtriya Janata Party. The Janata Party itself was not the same as it was in 1980. The Jan Sangh group had left to form the Bharatiya Janata Party in December 1980. Jagjivan Ram too had left the Janata to float his own Congress (Jagjivan). All this had rendered the character of the opposition into a far too complex mosaic.

Indira Gandhi's 'martyrdom' on 31 October 1984, altered the course once again. The term of the seventh Lok Sabha was to expire in January 1985. Rajiv Gandhi was left with only a couple of months, after he was sworn in as prime minister on 31 October 1984, to face a general election. But then, he did not wait for long. Within a couple of days after the seven-day mourning period, Rajiv Gandhi recommended dissolution of the Lok Sabha and fresh elections. Since Rajiv Gandhi commanded a majority, President Zail Singh did not demur. Elections were held between 24 and 28 December 1984. The Congress (I), for the first time, engaged a professional advertisement company (Rediffusion) to conduct its propaganda and the overwhelming sense of insecurity among the people, caused by the crisis in Punjab, Assam and other parts, was used effectively in its campaign. The party could also play upon the sympathy that Indira Gandhi's assassination evoked across the country. When the results were announced, the Congress party won 401 seats for itself and along with the few allies— the AIADMK in Tamil Nadu, the Muslim League and the Kerala Congress in Kerala—the ruling alliance was constituted of 415 MPs in the Lok Sabha of 542. In comparison with the previous Lok Sabha, where the Congress (I) had won 333 seats, the 1984 election victory was unprecedented insofar as the Congress party was concerned.

The Janata Party won just 10 seats out of the 219 it contested; prominent among them were H. M. Patel, Madhu Dandavate, Biju Patnaik and Jaipal Reddy. The Lok Dal won just three out of the 174 seats it contested; Charan Singh was one of them. The BJP won only two seats out of the 229 it contested. The CPI (M) won 22 seats out of the 66 it contested and the CPI won just six out of the 66 it contested. Those who lost the elections included Atal Behari Vajpayee, Vijayaraje Scindia and Ram Jethmalani (BJP); Chandra Shekhar and George Fernandes (Janata Party); Ram Vilas Paswan, Karpoori Thakur, Devi Lal and H. N. Bahuguna (Lok Dal).

The state of the opposition was pathetic. Against the 492 candidates fielded by the Congress (I), the Janata Party could field only 219 candidates; Charan Singh's DMKP had fielded 174 candidates (contesting on the Lok Dal symbol because the new party was not even recognised) along with the Congress (J); the BJP fielded candidates in only 229 constituencies. In other words, none of the opposition parties could field half the number of the candidates fielded by the Congress (I) nationally.

Rajiv Gandhi, assisted by his old friend Arun Singh and his cousin Arun Nehru, unleashed a new campaign style. Full-page advertisements were placed in all newspapers in which a careful blend of visuals and slogans suggested that the nation would simply collapse and disintegrate if the opposition was allowed to wrest power. The campaign suggested that the Congress (I) was the only force that could save the nation from this danger. The strategy seemed to work in the larger context of violence and disruptions that were witnessed across the country and particularly in Punjab and Assam. The opposition parties were also painted guilty of encouraging the forces of disruption. Memories of the shabby behaviour of the opposition leaders during the 1977–79 Janata rule were also revived in the Congress (I) advertisement campaign with effect. The sympathy evoked by Indira's assassination and the fact that Rajiv Gandhi happened to be young and modern, influenced the poll verdict.

A visible dimension of this was the defeat of a number of veterans from the opposition stable by political novices that the Congress (I) fielded. Vajpayee, for instance, lost Gwalior to Madhavrao Scindia; Bahuguna lost to Amitabh Bachchan in Allahabad. CPI (M) veteran Somnath Chatterjee lost to Mamta Banerjee in Jadavpur and the party's Politburo member, Samar Mukherjee, lost to P. R. Dasmunshi in Howrah. This was certainly the outcome of the sympathy wave that the Congress (I) rode after Indira Gandhi's assassination. Rajiv Gandhi himself secured a comfortable victory against Maneka Gandhi, who contested the elections as an independent candidate, supported by all the opposition parties.

This had implications insofar as the nature of the opposition was concerned in the new Lok Sabha. The only state where the Congress (I) wave did not strike was Andhra Pradesh. N. T. Rama Rao's Telugu Desam Party (TDP) won 30 out of the 42 Lok Sabha seats, leaving only six seats to the Congress (I). The implication of this was the emergence of the TDP, with 30 seats, as the main opposition party in the eighth Lok Sabha (1984–89). The 'national' parties such as the Janata Party, the BJP, the Lok Dal, the CPI (M) and the CPI won less number of seats than the 'regional' TDP.

Another aspect of the 1984 election result was that the BJP, despite winning only two seats in the Lok Sabha (one each from Gujarat and Andhra Pradesh), had secured the number two position in as many as 102 Lok Sabha constituencies. Most of these were in Madhya Pradesh, Rajasthan, Himachal Pradesh and Delhi—all of them being traditional strongholds of the Jan Sangh—and Gujarat where the Jan Sangh had been gaining strength gradually. In Bihar and Uttar Pradesh, the Lok Dal remained the number two party. All this had implications for the nature of the political discourse in these states as well as in the national arena in 1989 and thereafter during the 1990s.

Insofar as 1984 was concerned, Rajiv Gandhi arrived as the prime minister in his own right and commanding a huge majority in the Lok Sabha. On 31 October 1984, it was a truncated Congress (I) Parliamentary Board that 'elected' him the leader of the Congress (I) Parliamentary Party. In the nine-member executive of the Congress (I) Parliamentary Board, four were vacant at that time. And, with Indira Gandhi dead, there were just four members—Kamalapati Tripathi, Maragatham Chandrasekhar, Pranab Mukherjee and P. V. Narasimha Rao—on that fateful evening. Tripathi and Maragatham Chandrasekhar were far from Delhi and, hence, Rajiv Gandhi was chosen by just two members—Mukherjee and Rao—that evening and the choice was endorsed by the Congress (I) Working Committee on 3 November 1984 and thereafter by the Congress (I) Parliamentary Party on 5 November 1984.

All this was a thing of past and Rajiv Gandhi's election, as the 'leader' of the Congress (I) Parliamentary Party, though a foregone conclusion, was carried out after going through the necessary motion this time. He was sworn in on 31 December 1984. There was no doubt about the fact that he was the supreme leader of the party. And he conveyed this, in categorical terms, by excluding Pranab Mukherjee—virtually the number two in the previous Cabinet—from the new team that was sworn in along with him on 31 December 1984. Mukherjee had been the finance minister between 15 January 1982 and 31 December 1984. He accompanied Rajiv Gandhi from Calcutta to New Delhi on 31 October 1984 and was a part of the truncated Parliamentary Board that 'elected' Rajiv Gandhi as the leader on that fateful evening. There were rumours on that day that Mukherjee was keen to push his own case for the prime minister's job. He was, after all, number two in Indira's Cabinet. He denied all that but Rajiv Gandhi certainly seemed to believe the rumours. Mukherjee himself did not let it pass and ended up being expelled from the primary membership of the Congress (I) for six years. This happened in April 1986. It is another story that Pranab Mukherjee would emerge an important player in the Congress (I), and as a close aide of Sonia Gandhi, a couple of decades later.

Rajiv Gandhi's Cabinet, sworn in on 31 December 1984 consisted of the following: S. B. Chavan (Home), P. V. Narsimha Rao (Defence), V. P. Singh (Finance), H. K. L. Bhagat (Parliamentary Affairs), K. C. Pant (Education), Abdul Gafoor (Works and Housing), Bansi Lal (Railways), B. Shankaranand (Irrigation and Power), Buta Singh (Agriculture and Rural Development), Rao Birendra Singh (Food and Civil Supplies), Virendra Patil (Steel, Mines and Coal) and Mohsina Kidwai (Health and Family Welfare). All of them were loyal to Rajiv Gandhi, the Congress (I) and were not known to be ambitious.

The Congress (I), now under Rajiv Gandhi, did well in the round of state assembly elections, held in March 1985, within a couple of months after he was sworn in as the prime minister. Of the 11 states that went to polls in March 1985, the Congress retained power in nine. Andhra Pradesh and Karnataka, however, re-elected the TDP and the Janata Party. The TDP won 202 seats—the same number it won in 1983—in Andhra Pradesh while the Janata Party secured 139 seats in Karnataka to retain power in the state. This clearly showed that the pro-Congress (I) wave that prevailed in Karnataka in December 1984 (the Congress-I won 24 out of the 28 Lok Sabha seats from the state) was not sustained and the Janata Party, under Ramakrishna Hegde, could bounce back within a couple of months.

Rajiv Gandhi, however, had a reason to smile. His party retained power in nine states and that too in an emphatic way. In Bihar, the Congress (I) won 187 seats against a mere 42 by Karpoori Thakur's DMKP and 11 by the Janata Party. In Himachal Pradesh, the Congress (I) won 58 seats in the 68-member house and the BJP, the main opposition party, won only seven seats. In Gujarat, the Congress (I) won 149 seats, the Janata Party 14 and the BJP only 11. The Congress (I) secured 250 seats in Madhya Pradesh against 58 seats won by the BJP. In Maharashtra the Congress (I) secured 162 seats in the 288-member house and the Congress (S), now led by Sharad Pawar, ended up as the main opposition party with only 54 seats. Pawar would merge his party into the Congress (I) a couple of years later. The Congress (I) retained power in Orissa with a huge margin: 117 seats against a measly 20 for the Janata Party in the house of 147. In Rajasthan, the Congress (I) secured 113 seats against 38 by the BJP and 10 by the Janata Party. In Uttar Pradesh, however, the story was somewhat different. Even if the Congress (I) won 266 seats in the 425-strong house and, thus, managed to retain power, this was far less than the party's strength, of 309, in the previous assembly. Charan Singh's DMKP won 84 seats and, thus, increased its numbers from 59 (secured by the Janata-Secular) in 1980. The Congress (I)'s decline in Uttar Pradesh, over the years, followed a pattern that was established in 1985.

The signs of the decline of Congress (I) could be traced to the outcome of the March 1985 round of state assembly elections. Beneath the appearance of resurgence and stability, lay the story of its decline. The Rajiv Gandhi era, in fact, witnessed frequent Cabinet reshuffles—one in every two months. There were 16 occasions when chief ministers of Congress-ruled states were changed. Faction feuds among leaders in various states, endemic to the Congress (I) affairs even earlier, took new dimensions during this period. The Congress (I) lost power in various states beginning with Assam and Punjab (in 1986), Haryana and Kerala (in 1987); the party's hold slackened considerably in Uttar Pradesh by 1988 before it crumbled in 1989. The immediate cause for the decline of Congress (I), this time, in Uttar Pradesh was the expulsion of Union Finance Minister V. P. Singh from the party. He ended up rallying the opposition behind him and formed a non-Congress government at the Centre in November 1989. Rajiv Gandhi's close aides, Arun Nehru and Arun Singh, too left him around this time. All these developments, cumulatively, contributed to the decimation of the Congress (I) as a national party soon. The crisis of this period also led to the emergence of a coalition of regional parties, a process that began in the early 1980s (seen in the previous chapter), culminating in the formation of the National Front. The period also witnessed the rise of the BJP, securing 85 seats in the ninth Lok Sabha.

As we narrate the sequence of events in this period, we will deal with the Punjab and Assam accord; the Congress Centenary session in Bombay in December 1985 and the growing dissidence in the party; the scandals that came to rock the Rajiv Gandhi dispensation; the issues thrown up, following the Supreme Court judgement on the Shah Bano Case; and the beginnings of the Ayodhya controversy and the context in which the opposition parties and forces rallied behind V. P. Singh.

The Punjab and the Assam Accords

The Rajiv Gandhi dispensation got down to address the Punjab crisis within weeks after 31 December 1984. The first step in this direction was the release of various Akali Dal leaders, including the high priest of Akali politics Harchand Singh Longowal, from prison. Longowal, Parkash Singh Badal, Gurcharan Singh Tohra and Surjit Singh Barnala were all sent to jail soon after the June 1984 'Operation

Bluestar'. The Rajiv Gandhi government ordered their release in January 1985 and let them travel across Punjab, addressing public meetings. On 12 March 1985, Arjun Singh was relieved of his charge as the chief minister of Madhya Pradesh and made the governor of Punjab. This step was clearly in accordance with an agenda to restore the political process in Punjab and Arjun Singh acted as Rajiv Gandhi's point man in Punjab. Rajiv Gandhi visited Punjab on 23 March 1985 to lay the foundation stone for a martyrs' memorial in Hussainwala and the prime minister also announced an economic package for the state. By April 1985, Longowal sent out a clear message: Negotiations could be held on the basis of a seven-point charter. This charter was clearly within the framework of the Constitution and Longowal also spoke out against the demand for Khalistan. The Union government, meanwhile, set up an Enquiry Commission under Justice Ranganath Mishra to enquire into the November 1984 anti-Sikh violence in Delhi.

Thereafter began a series of talks, but in utmost secrecy. It was ensured that many of the prominent players in Punjab affairs in the past, including President Zail Singh, Union Minister Buta Singh and former Punjab Chief Minister Darbara Singh, were kept unaware of the talks. On 23 July 1985, Longowal, accompanied by Barnala and Balwant Singh, arrived at Prime Minister Rajiv Gandhi's office inside Parliament House. Longowal was closeted there with Rajiv Gandhi for about an hour and the two sides agreed to draft an agreement. The Cabinet Committee on Political Affairs met the day after and approved the draft. The agreement was then signed by Rajiv Gandhi on behalf of the government and H. S. Longowal, now the supreme leader of the Shiromani Akali Dal, within hours after the Cabinet approval for it, on 24 July 1985. Here is the text of the agreement:

1. *Compensation to innocent persons*: Along with *ex gratia* payment to those innocent killed in agitation or any action after 1.8.82, compensation for property damaged will also be paid.
2. *Army recruitment*: All citizens of the country have the right to enroll in the army and merit will remain the criterion for selection.
3. *Enquiry into November incidents*: The jurisdiction of the Justice Ranganath Commission enquiring into the November riots of Delhi would be extended to cover the disturbances at Bokaro and Kanpur also.
4. *Rehabilitation of those discharged from the Army*: For all those discharged, efforts will be made to rehabilitate and provide gainful employment.
5. *All India Gurdwara Act*: The Government of India agrees to consider the formulation of an All India Gurdwara Bill. Legislation will be brought forward for this purpose in consultation with the Shiromani Akali Dal, others concerned and after fulfilling all relevant constitutional requirements.

6. *Disposal of pending cases*: The notification applying the Armed Forces Special Powers Act to Punjab will be withdrawn. Existing Special Courts will try only cases relating to the following type of offences; (a) waging war, (b) hijacking. All other cases will be transferred to ordinary courts and enabling legislation if needed will be brought forward in this session of Parliament.
7. *Territorial claims*: The Capital Project Area of Chandigarh will go to Punjab. Some adjoining areas which were previously part of the Hindi or Punjabi regions were included in the Union Territory. With the capital region going to Punjab, the areas which were added to the Union Territory from the Punjabi region of the erstwhile State of Punjab will be transferred to Punjab and those from Hindi region to Haryana. The entire Sukhna lake will be kept as part of Chandigarh and will thus go to Punjab. It had always been maintained by Mrs Indira Gandhi that when Chandigarh is to go to Punjab, some Hindi-speaking territories in Punjab will go to Haryana. A commission will be constituted to determine the specific Hindi-speaking areas of Punjab which should go to Haryana in lieu of Chandigarh. The principle of contiguity and linguistic affinity with village as a unit will be the basis of such determination. The commission will be required to give its findings by 31 December 1985 and these will be binding on both sides. The work of the Commission will be limited to this aspect and will be distinct from the general boundary claims which another commission referring to boundary disputes between Punjab and Haryana will deal with. The actual transfer of Chandigarh to Punjab and areas in lieu thereof to Haryana will take place, simultaneously, on 26 January 1986.
8. *Centre-state relations*: Shiromani Akali Dal states that the Anandpur Sahib resolution is entirely within the framework of the Indian Constitution; that it attempts to define the concept of centre-state relations in a manner which may bring out the true federal characteristics of our unitary Constitution; and that the purpose of the resolution is to provide greater autonomy to the State with a view to strengthening the unity and integrity of the country, since unity in diversity forms the cornerstone of our national entity.

   In view of the above, the Anandpur Sahib resolution, insofar as it deals with Centre-State relations, stands referred to the Sarkaria Commission.
9. *Sharing of river waters*: The farmers of Punjab, Haryana and Rajasthan will continue to get water not less than what they are using from the Ravi-Beas system as on 1-7-1985. Waters used for consumptive purposes will also remain unaffected. Quantum of usage claimed shall be verified by a tribunal

to be set up and presided over by a Supreme Court Judge. The decision of the tribunal will be rendered within six months and would be binding on both parties. The construction of the Sutlej-Yamuna-Link (SYL) canal shall continue. The canal shall be completed by August 15, 1986.

10. *Representation of minorities*: Existing instructions regarding protection of interests of minorities will be re-circulated to the State Chief Ministers and the Prime Minister will write to all Chief Ministers.
11. *Promotion of Punjabi Language*: The Central Government may take some steps for the promotion of the Punjabi language.

Signed by Rajiv Gandhi and H. S. Longowal, the accord said: 'This settlement brings to an end a period of confrontation and ushers in an era of amity, goodwill and cooperation, which will promote and strengthen the unity and integrity of India'. Meanwhile, elections to the Punjab assembly were due before 6 October 1985; Rajiv Gandhi held out that there would be no further extension of President's rule in the state (in force from October 1983) and that elections would be held on time.

While the accord was celebrated as a great achievement by both the Congress (I) and the Akali Dal, there were discordant notes heard even then. The 'United Akali Dal' headed by Baba Joginder Singh (Bhindranwale's father), termed it a sellout. This was only expected. Longowal, after all, had agreed to the construction of the SYL canal; recall the fact that he had led a campaign against that in 1982, when militancy had still not intensified. The bigger hurdle came from the Lok Dal in Haryana. Its leader Devi Lal termed the transfer of Chandigarh to Punjab without Haryana getting the Abohar–Fazilka region (predominantly Hindi-speaking regions in the south western Punjab) as injustice and launched an agitation against that aspect of the accord. The agitation caught popular imagination and the transfer of Chandigarh would never take place. The Congress (I), meanwhile, ended up losing elections in Haryana in March 1987.

The crisis in Punjab did not come to an end with this. On 31 July 1985, Lalit Maken, a trade unionist and Congress (I) MP, was shot dead in front of his office in South Delhi. Maken's name had figured among those who played a key role in the anti-Sikh violence in Delhi in November 1984. Then, on 20 August 1985, less than a month after signing the accord, Harchand Singh Longowal was shot dead inside a gurdwara at Sherpur village near Sangrur. Longowal had been traversing Punjab, addressing meetings, explaining the terms of the accord. He was shot dead while doing so at Sherpur on that fateful day. The Akali leader had turned into a sitting duck after the accord and his killing seemed to raise questions about the future of the accord and also about the elections to the state assembly, now on the cards. The Union government, meanwhile, ordered a state funeral for Longowal and also made it clear that elections would be held as scheduled.

The Election Commission had scheduled polling in Punjab on 22 September 1985. Meanwhile, there was yet another killing in Delhi on 4 September 1985. Arjan Das, an old friend of Sanjay Gandhi and a councilor of the New Delhi Municipal Corporation, was shot dead at his office. His name too had figured prominently among those involved in the November riots in Delhi. These killings were not isolated incidents and continued for at least a few more years.

Meanwhile, elections were held to the Punjab assembly on 22 September 1985. When the votes were counted, the Akali Dal secured 73 seats in the 117-member assembly. This was unprecedented. The Akali Dal had won only 58 seats even in the 1977 elections and that was in the context of the anti-Indira wave. Surjit Singh Barnala, who had emerged as the top leader after Longowal's assassination, was sworn in as Punjab chief minister. The Congress (I) won only 32 seats in the assembly.

As for the accord, the transfer of Chandigarh to Punjab remains unaccomplished to this day. The Justice Mathew Commission, set up to determine the Hindi-speaking parts of the Union Territory to be transferred to Haryana, submitted its report in March 1986. The report said that it was not possible to identify villages with a Hindi-speaking majority in the region that were also contiguous with Haryana. Only a couple of months were left for 26 January 1986, the date set in the accord for transfer of Chandigarh to Punjab. Rajiv Gandhi set another deadline for the transfer—21 June 1987—and set up another commission under Justice Venkatramaiah. The commission identified 15,000 acres of territory in the Rajpura *tehshil* of Punjab to be transferred to Haryana to build a new capital city there. Haryana chief minister, Bhajan Lal, accepted that but also presented a list of 483 villages—in Punjab where the population was predominantly Hindi-speaking—for transfer to Haryana. This was in May 1986. Rajiv Gandhi replaced Bhajan Lal with Bansi Lal as Haryana chief minister. The objective was to ensure that there was no resistance to the transfer of Chandigarh to Punjab.

Meanwhile, militancy continued unabated in Punjab and elsewhere in the country. On 26 January 1986, followers of Bhindranwale entered the Golden Temple in Amritsar, hoisted the 'national flag' of Khalistan and opened an office of the Damdami Taksal inside the complex. Damdami Taksal was the name of the 'dera' or the headquarters of Bhindranwale in Chowk Mehta village near Amritsar. The 'dera' in Sikh tradition is the abode of the preacher and the 'taksal', or the mint, meant the physical location from where pure interpretation of the religious scripture emanated. The Shiromani Gurdwara Prabandhak Committee (SGPC), now under the control of the Shiromani Akali Dal and located inside the Golden Temple, retreated without even a semblance of resistance and relocated to the Anandpur Sahib Gurdwara. The militant leaders, this time, attacked the Union government and also Surjit Singh Barnala's state government. The Akali leadership came under fire once again. On 25 July 1986, 15 passengers, all

Hindus, were pulled out of a bus and shot dead in Muktsar. This, in many ways, marked a distinct shift in the nature of militant activities in Punjab. The Muktsar killings were the first instance of the trouble assuming communal dimensions. It happened exactly a year after H. S. Longowal was shot dead on 24 July 1985. On 10 August 1986, General Arun Vaidya was shot dead near his residence in Pune. General Vaidya was the Chief of Army Staff at the time of Operation Bluestar; he had retired from service on 31 January 1986.

The Punjab crisis continued to rattle the national political discourse with motorcycle-borne terrorists killing unarmed people and police officers with impunity. The Akali Dal government in the state, headed by Barnala, was a mute spectator to all this. On 30 November 1986, militants killed 22 bus passengers in Hoshiarpur. The Hoshiarpur killings caused violent reactions in Delhi. But the anti-Sikh violence was contained this time. Bomb blasts in crowded market places became a regular feature in Delhi and all this lent credence to the view that the Akali Dal government in Punjab lacked the political will to contain the pro-Khalistan elements in the state. This, indeed, was an irony since the victims of extremist violence during this period included the rank and the file of the Akali Dal, the Congress (I), the BJP and the Left parties as much as it included the Sikhs and the Hindus. The extremists had entrenched themselves inside the Golden Temple once again. The drift was pronounced and the Barnala government was now a lame duck dispensation. Arjun Singh was replaced, by this time, by Siddhartha Shankar Ray as Punjab governor and Ray's appointment was based on his track record of containing the naxalite movement in West Bengal as the chief minister from 1972 to 1977. Rajiv Gandhi stated this, in so many words, while exchanging notes with Kamalapati Tripathi in April 1986.

On 11 May 1987, Ray recommended dismissal of the Barnala government and imposition of Central rule in Punjab and the Union Cabinet endorsed the recommendation the same day, invoking the provisions of Article 356 of the Constitution. This was the eighth time that Punjab was placed under Central rule after independence. In 1951–52 (the state was called PEPSU then), 1966, 1968–69, 1971–72, 1977, 1980 and 1983–85. Unlike in the past, when the action was seen as abuse of the constitutional provision, the 11 May 1987 proclamation seemed inevitable given the Barnala government's inability to govern. There was, however, an element of partisan political consideration this time too. Election for the Haryana state assembly was scheduled on 17 June 1987 and the Congress (I) was finding it difficult there.

Chandigarh's transfer to Punjab, as part of the Rajiv–Longowal accord, put the Congress (I) in an unenviable position in Haryana. Chief minister Bhajan Lal was seen as a potential source of trouble in this regard by the Rajiv Gandhi establishment even at the time of the accord. It may be recalled that he had left the Janata Party to join the Congress (I), with a large majority of the Janata

MLAs in 1980. The Congress (I) high command, however, was committed to the accord and replaced Bhajan Lal with Bansi Lal as the chief minister of Haryana on 4 June 1986. But then, the transfer of Chandigarh to Punjab had given an emotional issue to Devi Lal, now a prominent leader of the Lok Dal, to whip up passions against the Congress (I) in Haryana and Bhajan Lal's removal simply served Devi Lal's cause. The 11 May 1987 proclamation of central rule in Punjab was just one last attempt by the desperate Congress (I) high command to revive its fortunes in Haryana. This was of no use. The Congress (I) could win only five seats in the 90-member Haryana Assembly. Devi Lal, now the Haryana chieftain of the Lok Dal (Bahuguna), had contested the polls in alliance with the BJP; the results were 58 seats for the Lok Dal (B) and 15 for the BJP. The Lok Dal (Ajit)–Janata Party alliance was swept aside in this election. Devi Lal became the chief minister of Haryana. We shall discuss the impact of Devi Lal's victory, the dynamics of the Lok Dals and the Janata Party and related developments later in this chapter.

Rajiv Gandhi also found himself engaged in settling the crisis in Assam. Unlike in Punjab, the talks towards a settlement of the Assam crisis were on from February 1980 and a draft settlement was ready in August 1985. We have discussed the details of the Assam crisis and the issues involved in the previous chapter. The accord was signed between the AASU leaders and Rajiv Gandhi in the small hours of 15 August 1985. The two important elements of the accord were: 1 January 1966 was to be the cut-off date for determination of foreigners in Assam; all those who came into Assam after that date were to be denied voting rights and other such rights of the citizens. Also that the Congress (I) ministry would resign, the assembly constituted in February 1983 (when all parties barring the Congress-I had boycotted the polls), be dissolved and fresh elections held to the assembly.

Chief minister Hiteshwar Saikia submitted his resignation on 20 August 1985 and recommended dissolution of the assembly. In the elections to the Assam assembly, held on 16 December 1985, the Asom Gana Parishad secured 65 seats in the 126-member assembly. Prafulla Kumar Mahanta, a prominent leader of the AASU, was sworn in as the chief minister in Assam soon after.

The Congress (I), which rode to power with a massive majority on 31 December 1984, was now beginning to lose its hold. Punjab and Assam now had a non-Congress government. Yet, Rajiv Gandhi and his aides called this a victory. The Congress (I) described the election results from Punjab and Assam as a demonstration of the vitality of democracy in India. The rhetoric was that even if the Congress (I) lost power in these two states, the results reflected the party's commitment to democracy.

The significance of the poll outcome in Punjab and Assam was that it provided impetus to the moves that the TDP chief, N. T. Rama Rao, was now engaged in forging a coalition of regional parties against the Congress (I). All this culminated in the emergence of the National Front government in 1989. Even while the Janata Party and the Lok Dal continued to remain a pale shadow of what they were in 1977, the claim of Congress (I) to be the natural choice of the people was now under dispute in more states than it was in January 1985. Assam, Andhra Pradesh, Karnataka, Punjab and West Bengal were under non-Congress rule in December 1985. More states—Kerala and Haryana—would come under this category in a couple of years. All this reverberated at the Congress centenary session held in Bombay where Rajiv Gandhi spoke against the increasing influence of 'power brokers' in his own Congress (I) and called for a revamp.

The Congress Centenary Session

There was an element of incongruity in the Bombay celebrations. Rajiv Gandhi's Congress (I) was certainly not the sole inheritor of the legacy of the Indian National Congress. A number of those who were a part of that legacy were now in the opposition parties and many others had retired from active politics. The Indian National Congress had split even before 1947 with Subhas Chandra Bose forming the Forward Bloc. Those who constituted the Congress Socialist Party, a ginger group inside the INC, had charted a different course to found the Socialist Party, merging into the Janata Party in 1977 and later landing themselves in the various opposition outfits that emerged across the country. The Congress split in 1969 when Indira Gandhi walked out of the parent party was followed by yet another split in 1978 leading to the formation of the Congress (I). All these have been discussed in detail earlier. However, in 1985 the Congress (I) remained the largest party with 415 members in the Lok Sabha. Rajiv Gandhi, now the president of the party, went about organising the three-day centenary celebration of the Indian National Congress in December 1985 in Bombay. But, beneath all this lay a reality; the Congress (I) was beginning to weaken and the claim to that glorious legacy was no longer enough to revive its fortunes.

The crisis was not merely about the Congress (I) losing power in Punjab and Assam. In Gujarat, after winning a majority in the March 1985 assembly elections, chief minister Madhav Singh Solanki could last only for a few months. The immediate provocation was widespread communal violence that rocked the state on 18 March 1985, the day Solanki was sworn in. The army was called in at various places and remained there for four months till 15 July 1985. There was a long-term dimension to the crisis as well. Dissidence against Solanki, who had been the chief minister from June 1980, from within the Congress (I), was pronounced. He was seen pushing the upper caste men from out of positions of importance in the administration and the political leadership. Solanki was the architect of a socio-political alliance consisting of the Kshatriyas, Harijans, Adivasis and Muslims (known as the KHAM factor in Gujarat) and this social alliance was strong enough against the Patel dominance of the state's political discourse.

The dissidents turned desperate after Solanki was allowed to continue as the chief minister after the March 1985 assembly elections. Solanki, meanwhile, charted a course to consolidate his own position and deal with the dissidence. He pushed through an administrative order, on 11 January 1985, to increase reservation for the OBCs in educational institutions from 10 per cent to 28 per cent. On 6 February 1985, students from the Morvi Engineering College in the Saurashtra region went on a strike and the agitation spread to other parts of the state in a fortnight. The agitation was orchestrated by Solanki's detractors in his own party. It is also a fact that the protests fizzled out, but the government decided to postpone school examinations indefinitely.

On 15 April 1985, there was anti-Muslim violence in Ahmedabad and the canker spread to several towns in no time. The army was called in to take positions in Ahmedabad, Surat and Baroda. Anti-Muslim violence was not new to Gujarat. In 1969, a spate of communal violence, provoked by a quarrel over cattle straying into a prayer ground on a Friday afternoon, resulted in massive violence that left 1,500 people dead and over 30,000 members of the Muslim community homeless in Ahmedabad alone. The situation was brought under control after a visit by Prime Minister Indira Gandhi. She was accompanied by Khan Abdul Ghaffar Khan. The state government, under Hitendra Desai, was found wanting on various counts at that time. It may be recalled that this was also the time of the Congress split and Morarji Desai, the only leader among those who challenged Indira Gandhi with a mass base, was from Gujarat. There were several instances of violence after that in Gujarat. Given this long history of hatred and mistrust, the anti-Muslim violence in April 1985 was as much a fallout of communal hatred as it was a conspiracy by political players to settle partisan scores. Gujarat was allowed to burn for several weeks before Solanki was asked to quit as the chief minister, on 15 July 1985. Amar Singh Chaudhury, the home minister in the Solanki Cabinet, replaced him. It was Rajiv Gandhi's decision.

Solanki would wait for a while before venting his anger in a note to Rajiv Gandhi. It said:

> The mass of enthusiasm and euphoria of early 1985 is on a gradual wane … The frequent reshuffle of the Union Cabinet, chief ministers, party executives and bureaucratic slots has generated a sense of instability and the people perceive it as a situation of flux and continuing adhocism in the decision making process at the higest level. As the "replacements" have not often proved better, the very wisdom of the change-mechanism is now being increasingly questioned.

Solanki went on to take a dig at Rajiv Gandhi's close aides. The note said: 'The rejection of untested transplants by the body politic may create serious consequences for the long-term health of the party.' The reference here was to Arun Singh, Arun Nehru and other close friends of Rajiv Gandhi who were now in the thick of running the Congress (I) affairs. On 25 September 1985, Arun Nehru was shifted out of the ministry of energy and made the minister of state for home (with independent charge of internal security); Arun Singh was inducted into the Cabinet as minister of state for defence; P. V. Narasimha Rao was moved out of defence to become minister for human resources development and Rajiv Gandhi took defence himself; N. D. Tiwari, chief minister of Uttar Pradesh, was shifted to the Union Cabinet. Solanki was, in fact, referring to these changes in his note, sent sometime in early 1986. He was not the only dissident against Rajiv Gandhi and his style of functioning. There was the party's working president, Kamalapati Tripathi, Pranab Mukherjee, A. P. Sharma and many others who were bold enough to vent their criticism.

However, the December 1985 Congress centenary session did not indicate any of this. The party resolution, running into 59 paragraphs, simply glossed over these harsh truths by recourse to rhetoric and poetic flourishes and that 'within the first year of Rajiv Gandhi's assumption of office as prime minister, there has been worldwide acclaim for his forward looking approach and vision for the nation's entry into the 21st Century'. That the resolution and the discussion on it refrained from any assessment of the implications of this new vision was a different matter. This, notwithstanding a senior leader Brahmananda Reddy, former president of the Congress, had made critical reference to the newfound thrust for technology and modern management techniques at an AICC session as early as in May 1985.

On the challenge thrown by the regional parties, the resolution did not show any evidence of an attempt to see this as essentially a fallout of the party's inability to internalise the regional aspirations and of the command mode into which the party had moved into from Indira Gandhi's time. The resolution said:

> There is no anti-thesis between a strong centre and strong states. In actual practice, the two mutually support and reinforce each other. The psychology and the language of confrontation, specially developed for transcient political ends, will do immense harm to our national and political fabric.

The high point of the Bombay session was Rajiv Gandhi's address, running into 75 minutes, in which he went about debunking the functioning of almost all the democratic institutions, including his own party machinery, the opposition, the administration, the educational system, the trade unions, industry, the press and the judiciary. Of significance was the way he described the Congress (I) organisation itself. He said:

> Millions of ordinary workers throughout the country are full of enthusiasm for the Congress policies and programmes. But they are handicapped, for on their backs ride the brokers of power and influence who dispense patronage to convert a mass movement into a feudal oligarchy. They are self-perpetuating cliques who thrive by involving the slogans of caste and religion and by enmeshing the living body of the Congress in their net of avarice.

Then the Congress (I) president declared: 'The Congress will be reorganised and revitalised. The war on corruption will go on without let or hindrance'. This reference to the affairs in his own party and the brave declaration that the drift would not be allowed to persist was, however, mere rhetoric as the developments soon after proved. The series of scandals that unfurled in the couple of years after the Bombay session—the Bofors scam in particular—knocked the bottom off the claim that Rajiv Gandhi meant what he said. His 'Mr Clean' image would soon turn around as scandals of corruption would unfold, one after another, in just a couple of years.

Rajiv Gandhi's strategy was to de-legitimise the existing institutional structures and establish himself as the supreme head of the political establishment. He was only following his mother, Indira Gandhi, towards achieving this end. An evidence of this was found in the choice of leaders who sat in the front row of the rostrum at the plenary session at Bombay. P. V. Narasimha Rao from Andhra Pradesh, Gundu Rao from Karnataka, Darbara Singh from Punjab and G. K. Moopanar from Tamil Nadu: They were all from the states where the Congress (I) was voted out of power and in a sense, leaders without a base. There were others whom Rajiv Gandhi promoted. Among them was V. P. Singh, his finance minister and Arif Mohammed Khan, minister of state for home and energy. Both of them had been in the Congress party since the 1970s and belonged to Uttar Pradesh. In many ways, they were seen as the prominent faces of the Congress (I) in the Rajiv Gandhi era and were emerging into powerful leaders of the party from Uttar Pradesh against such old guards as Kamalapati Tripathi, the party's working president. Others who emerged as leaders were P. Chidambaram, Jagdish Tytler, Madhavrao Scindia and Rajesh Pilot. Along with Arun Singh, Arun Nehru and M. L. Fotedar, they began to represent the new face of the Congress (I).

The euphoria that marked the Congress centenary session in December 1985 did not last long. The party began to slip into a crisis mode within a couple of months after the centenary session. Incidentally, the canker of corruption and abuse of office that Rajiv Gandhi referred to, unfurled into public domain in Bombay itself. On 12 March 1986, Justice M. L. Pendse of the Bombay High Court passed severe strictures against Maharashtra chief minister, S. P. Nilangekar. The case involved his daughter's admission to a postgraduate programme in the KEM Medical College. It was found that her answer papers to the entrance examination were doctored to manage her admission. Rajiv Gandhi was left with no other option but to ask Nilangekar to quit. He was replaced by Union Home Minister S. B. Chavan as the chief minister. The home ministry was now put under additional charge of Narasimha Rao and Arun Nehru remained the minister of state for home and his clout increased multi-fold now; that would have terrible consequences for the Congress (I), the government and the nation.

Earlier, in February 1986, Arif Mohammed Khan resigned from the Union Cabinet. The provocation for Khan's resignation was Rajiv Gandhi's decision to push a constitutional amendment to nullify a Supreme Court judgement affirming the right of divorced Muslim women to maintenance. This amendment, in fact, was not an isolated act. It was linked to yet another move by the Rajiv Gandhi government in February 1986 involving the dispute, in a magistrate's court in Faizabad, over the Babri Masjid in Ayodhya. These two would dominate the nation's political discourse, causing the death of several hundred people and culminate in the demolition of the Babri Masjid on 6 December 1992. Arif Mohammed Khan described the sequence of events at that time:

> Rajiv Gandhi announced at Delhi's Siri Fort Auditorium that on the first day of the forthcoming Parliament session the Bill to undo the Supreme Court ruling, as agreed between the Muslim Personal Law Board and the Government, will be introduced. This was 10-15 days before the locks of Ayodhya were opened. But the session was still about a month away. If I remember correctly, Parliament session started either on February 5 or 7, 1986 and the locks were opened on February 1. So, first he made the announcement; then he got the locks opened; and then he introduced the Bill.

Thereafter, on 22 April 1986, Congress (I) working president Kamalapati Tripathi, addressed an 11-page note to the party president, Rajiv Gandhi. The note, in many ways, was a litany of charges and a comment on the failing health of the party. According to reports in the press at that time, the draft of the note was prepared by Pranab Mukherjee; Tripathi then added a few things to it, shared it with Gundu Rao (former chief minister of Karnataka), Sripat Mishra (former chief minister of Uttar Pradesh) and a few Congress (I) MPs before sending it to Rajiv Gandhi on 22 April 1986. It happened to be Mahavir Jayanti and Tripathi chose that day because he considered it auspicious. Excerpts from Tripathi's note will tell the story better.

> Not only the common Congressmen and women are puzzled and bewildered at the rapid disintegration of the party at all levels, but they are shocked at the casual, ad hoc and inept handling of the party matters by you and your so-called operators ... Whom did you mean as power brokers? Did you mean those persons who, simply because of the proximity to you, are enjoying both administrative and organizational power? Did you mean them as power brokers who did nothing in their whole life to strengthen the organisation but today are enjoying the fruits of the struggle of this great organisation?

There was more:

> Frequent changes in party and administrative offices have become a style of your functioning. Since November 12, 1984 to January 19, 1986, you have appointed and removed as many as nine general secretaries. In one key ministry, the incumbents were changed five times during this period. The impression left by the musical chair style is that you are not sure of the capabilities of the persons you select. You are not only making (sic) injustice to them but deliberately you are injecting uncertainties in the whole system.
>
> The impression given by the economic policy-makers since last year's Budget is that this government is primarily concerned with the welfare of the well-to-do sections of society. The pro-poor stance of your mother's policy is the story of the past though the party still theoretically stands committed to socialism. I know that many economic pundits will come forward to challenge this contention and would try to establish that your model of economic growth would lead this country to the 21st Century… but the moot point is whether you would take the whole country to the 21st Century or only a chosen few will enter into the coming century and millions would be left not only in the 20th Century but perhaps in the 19th Century.

The 11-page note made direct reference to the Punjab and the Assam accord. 'The party was not consulted but asked to endorse a fait accompli', it said and added that the approach to these complex issues in an over-simplified manner caused more problems than solving the crisis. It ridiculed that part of the resolution at the Bombay session—that the accords and the elections results in the two states demonstrated the vitality of democracy in India—despite the total rout of the Congress (I) wondering as to whether it was a statement that the Congress (I) did not stand for democracy. In the conclusion, Tripathi aimed at Rajiv Gandhi:

> One expected that you would concentrate your energies in solving these national issues affecting our life, but unfortunately, instead of doing that you are busy in building up your own coterie with the discredited persons who deserted your mother at the most difficult time of her political career.

Tripathi had taken a few names of such men: Siddhartha Shankar Ray, now the governor of Punjab, who had deposed against Indira Gandhi before the Shah Commission; P. R. Dasmunshi, now the West Bengal Pradesh Congress (I) president, who had left Indira's fold to join the Congress (U); and Abdul Ghafoor, now a union minister, who had turned into an Indira detractor after the defeat of the party in 1977.

Rajiv Gandhi's response to the note was strategic. Though the letter was sent on 22 April 1986, it remained under wraps for at least a month. When it hit the public domain, sometime in the end of May 1986, Rajiv Gandhi struck. Pranab Mukherjee, who had prepared the draft of Tripathi's note, was expelled from the party for a period of six years. This is the maximum punishment prescribed in the Congress (I) constitution for anti-party activities. Three others—former chief minister of Uttar Pradesh, Sripat Mishra; former West Bengal governor, A. P. Sharma and Prakash Mehrotra, who had been India's high commisioner in London—were placed under suspension. The three suspended men were involved in preparing the draft along with Mukherjee. A meeting of the Congress (I) Working Committee was held on 2 June 1986. The agenda was to have Mukherjee's expulsion endorsed and also to take up Tripathi's note for discussion.

Tripathi's note was literally torn to shreds in the meeting but the octogenarian leader was treated with due respect by the Congress (I) president. Tripathi's contention that he, as working president of the party, had the right to communicate with the president on the party's affairs was acknowledged for the record. Tripathi too refrained from speaking up for Pranab Mukherjee at the Working Committee. Rajiv Gandhi, certainly, knew the importance of Tripathi for the Congress (I) in Uttar Pradesh; he probably knew the effect of Hemawati Nandan Bahuguna's exit from the party in February 1977. The Congress (I) high command seemed to think that humiliating a senior Brahmin leader of the party from Uttar Pradesh could cause severe damage to itself. On 2 June 1986, it appeared that the rebellion in the Congress (I) had been stemmed. This, however, did not mean that the party's affairs were settled in different states. Dissidence against the incumbent chief ministers was out in the open in Bihar, Uttar Pradesh, Maharashtra, Gujarat, Rajasthan and Madhya Pradesh.

Amidst this drift, Rajiv Gandhi began talking to Farooq Abdullah. It may be recalled that Abdullah's government in Srinagar was toppled after a group of National Conference MLAs teamed up with G. M. Shah and cobbled a majority in the assembly with support from the Congress (I). This was the Congress (I)'s response to Farooq joining the opposition chief ministers and hosting a convention in Srinagar where issues relating to the rights of the states were raised. Shah was installed as the chief minister in July 1985. In less than a year, the Congress (I) began thinking otherwise and withdrew support to Shah and decided to support Farooq again. After a few months of Central rule, Farooq Abdullah was sworn in as the chief minister again on 6 November 1986. The National Conference–Congress (I) alliance, swept the elections to the Jammu and Kashmir state assembly held on 23 March 1987. It won 63 out of the 76 assembly seats in the state. The elections, however, were anything but free and fair. The Muslim United Front, a combination of the Kashmiri youth, polled 49 per cent votes but could win only four seats. The fact is that the counting of the votes was manipulated and all this had implications on the simmering dissent among the youth in the Kashmir region.

The 23 March 1987 round of assembly elections brought bad news to the Congress from West Bengal and Kerala. The party's strength in the 294-strong West Bengal assembly fell from 54 (in the last election) to 40. The CPI (M)-led Left Front retained power in West Bengal and also wrested power in Kerala. The Front secured 76 seats in the 140-member Kerala assembly against the 61 seats that the Congress (I)-led UDF won. Tamil Nadu was the only state where the Congress (I) could claim some presence in the South; the state was ruled by the AIADMK, an ally of the Congress, since 1984.

Meanwhile, Arun Nehru had fallen out with Rajiv Gandhi. The exact cause for this is unknown. On 22 October 1986, Rajiv Gandhi shuffled his Cabinet, for the twenty-sixth time since October 1984 and Arun Nehru, the powerful minister of state for home, was dropped from the Cabinet. He was replaced by P. Chidambaram as minister of state for home. All this, however, did not add up to a major tumult. Then came the rift between Rajiv Gandhi and his Finance Minister V. P. Singh in just a couple of months after the 22 October 1986 cabinet reshuffle. Meanwhile, on 8 December 1986, the Congress (S), now led by Sharad Pawar, announced its merger with the Congress (I), at a convention in Pawar's bastion, Baramati in Maharashtra. The merger, though resisted by a small section within the Congress (S), led by K. P. Unnikrishnan, was good news to Rajiv Gandhi. Even while large parts of Uttar Pradesh, Maharashtra, Gujarat and Hyderabad in Andhra Pradesh witnessed anti-Muslim violence, Rajiv Gandhi set out on a holiday to the Andamans along with his family and close friends.

While the prime minister was frolicking with his wife, children and close friends, on the beaches of the Andaman and Nicobar Islands, Amitabh Bachchan Congress (I) MP from Allahabad, flew to the Islands from Burma. Bachchan did not go there to join his friend on a holiday but with a specific complaint against Finance Minister V. P. Singh. That was about the finance ministry and the Enforcement Directorate pursuing investigations against Ajitabh Bachchan, the brother of the actor-turned-MP, and a businessman in London. V. P. Singh too was in the Andamans at that time. Rajiv Gandhi had called a meeting of high officials there to discuss plans to develop the Islands and the finance minister was asked to be there for that purpose. It was a different matter that the meeting lasted for just about an hour and that was only a pretext.

Singh, along with his secretary Vinod Pande and Enforcement Directorate Chief Bhure Lal, had taken Rajiv Gandhi's call to cleanse the government stable of power brokers a bit too seriously. The finance minister had set up his officers to catch tax evaders and other such offenders without bothering as to who they were. Among those 'affected' in this cleansing drive was Dhirubhai Ambani. Enforcement Directorate raids were becoming the order of the day and the indirect-tax receipts in 1986–87 touched a new high. Customs revenue went up by 20 per cent and excise revenue by 12 per cent, thanks to the drive by Finance Minister V. P. Singh. Rajiv Gandhi, incidentally, was getting close to Dhirubhai Ambani around the same time.

On Saturday, 24 January 1987, a terse communiqué from the Rashtrapati Bhawan announced that V. P. Singh was shifted out of the finance ministry and made the defence minister. V. P. Singh at that time was preparing the budget for 1987–88 to be presented on 28 February 1987. Rajiv Gandhi explained the shift as being necessitated by a threat of war from Pakistan and that the situation warranted a full-time defence minister. Until then the defence portfolio was handled by the prime minister himself, with Arun Singh as minister of state. However, it was only a laboured explanation.

It turned out later that the Enforcement Directorate, under Bhure Lal, was involved in hiring Fairfax, a private investigating agency in the USA run by Michael Hershman, to investigate Ambani's financial dealings and Foreign Exchange Regulation Act (FERA) violations. In order to ensure that the investigations were carried out in utmost secrecy (which was not possible if Hershman's fees had to be paid by the Directorate, given Ambani's reach in the corridors of power at that time), it was agreed that Nusli Wadia of Bombay Dyeing arranged the funds for Hershman. Bhure Lal's decision to engage Fairfax was approved by the finance minister. We shall discuss Fairfax in detail later in this chapter. For now, Rajiv Gandhi's decision to shift V. P. Singh out of the finance ministry was guided by the pressure exerted upon the prime minister by Dhirubhai Ambani. It was certainly not the one that was stated; that the situation on the border warranted a full-time defence minister. Singh also ended up ordering an enquiry into the HDW submarine deal in his capacity as the defence minister.

The HDW submarine deal was between the governments of West Germany and India. Singh, after taking over as the defence minister, sought to know if the price could be brought down and the Indian ambassodor in Bonn, conveyed, through a telex message, quoting a German official saying that a further reduction in the price was not possible because of a huge commission having been paid to an Indian agent. Singh was convinced that the Hindujas were the ones referred to as the 'Indian agents' and he ordered a departmental enquiry and made his decision public, in a press conference, the same evening.

This happened towards the end of March 1987; the Fairfax controversy had reached the public domain by now and a discussion on that was scheduled in Parliament on 31 March 1987. Singh had discussed the HDW deal and the telex message he received from Bonn with Prime Minister Rajiv Gandhi. The discussions were held in the context of the departmental enquiry he had ordered. Rajiv Gandhi was informed by V. P. Singh that about 7 per cent commission was paid by the German government to an Indian agent (the Hindujas), amounting to Rs 30 crore. When this was conveyed to him on 11 April 1987, Rajiv Gandhi's reaction was: 'Why will HDW disclose the names; it pays so many heads of states and governments and if they disclose the names they will be out of business'. V. P. Singh's response to this was terse: 'It is not our job to give the HDW business… what happens to HDW has nothing to do with us'. Singh decided to resign from the Cabinet that day. He, however, held on for one more day because he had committed to preside over a Defence Investiture Ceremony. On 12 April 1987, after the ceremony, Singh asked his son to drive his personal car to the prime minister's official residence to hand over his resignation letter. The resignation was accepted on 24 April 1987.

A number of events between 24 January 1987, when V. P. Singh moved out of the finance ministry, and 12 April 1987, when he resigned as the defence minister, establish beyond doubt that Rajiv Gandhi's call from the centenary session of the Congress, to fight against corruption, was mere rhetoric. V. P. Singh's exit from the Cabinet on 24 April 1987, his subsequent expulsion from the Congress (I) in July 1987 and the news of the Bofors scandal on the Swedish National Radio broadcast on 16 April 1987, knocked the bottom off Rajiv Gandhi's claim to cleanse the stable of corrupt elements. All these would contribute to the defeat of the Congress (I) in the 1989 elections.

Rajiv Gandhi, now, was faced with yet another crisis involving his relationship with President Zail Singh. The relationship between the prime minister and the president was restricted to mere exchange of letters. Rajiv Gandhi had stopped visiting the Rashtrapati Bhawan to brief the president of important developments. On 13 March 1987, *The Indian Express* published the text of Zail Singh's letter to Rajiv Gandhi, dated 9 March 1987. The CBI raided Ramnath Goenka's guest house in New Delhi and found a draft of Zail Singh's letter there. All hell broke loose. There was a clamour for Zail Singh's impeachment and there were allusions that Zail Singh was involved in a conspiracy to dismiss Rajiv Gandhi and install someone else as the prime minister. The raids were conducted on 15 March 1987; the same day S. Gurumurthy, a Chennai-based chartered accountant and a close aide of Ram Nath Goenka, was arrested. Zail Singh's 9 March 1987 letter to Rajiv (which was published in *The Indian Express*) brought up that the prime minister did not brief him about the Assam, Punjab and Mizo accords; that the prime minister did not go through the routine courtesy of briefing the president after his visit to the US and the USSR and added that it was distressing that constitutional provisions regarding furnishing of information to the president were not being followed.

Zail Singh's term as the president was due to end in July 1987 and Rajiv Gandhi was determined against a second term for him. Singh, on his part, upped the ante before he moved out of Rashtrapati Bhawan. The crisis in the Cabinet amidst this, and the fact that such leaders as Arif Mohammed Khan, Arun Nehru, V. C. Shukla, Ram Dhan and V. P. Singh were now coming together had begun to rattle the Congress (I) establishment in a big way; a series of scandals (the HDW deal first and then the Bofors scandal) were now in the public domain and then the confrontation with the president. Rajiv Gandhi waited for the presidential elections scheduled for 13 July 1987. R. Venkatraman, vice-president since August 1984, was nominated as the Congress (I) nominee for the post of president. He defeated Justice V. R. Krishna Iyer, put up by the TDP, CPI, CPI (M), Janata Party and the Lok Dal. The contest was symbolic given the numbers in Parliament and the various state assemblies.

On 15 July 1987, Arun Nehru, V. C. Shukla and Arif Mohammed Khan were expelled from the Congress (I). Like it happened with Pranab Mukherjee earlier, the expulsions were carried out summarily without going through the motions of a show cause notice or an enquiry. V. P. Singh protested against this in a letter to Rajiv Gandhi. At long last, he too was expelled from the Congress (I) on 19 July 1987.

V. P. Singh was not a Pranab Mukherjee. An important difference between the two was that Singh happened to be from Uttar Pradesh and belonged to the Rajput caste. The Rajputs, along with the Brahmins, happened to wield enormous clout in the political discourse in Uttar Pradesh. The political clout of the Congress (I) in Uttar Pradesh (and also in Bihar) depended on the Rajputs to a large extent while the party's mass base was constituted by the scheduled castes and the Muslims. This social chemistry helped the party retain its dominance and also to revive itself in the post-Janata phase because the Janata Party in Uttar Pradesh was represented by the intermediate castes, a base built up by the socialists to begin with and by the Lok Dal after Charan Singh carved out a Jat socio-political constituency behind him. V. P. Singh's expulsion from the Congress (I) had implications for the party in Uttar Pradesh in the sense that it rattled the socio-political chemistry that sustained its political supremacy in the region.

A brief narrative of some developments within the Congress (I) leading to V. P. Singh's resignation as defence minister on 12 April 1984 and his expulsion from the party will be in order at this stage. It did appear, at least in the earlier days of the conflict, that V. P. Singh would have opted for a life in the oblivion after his resignation. Rajiv Gandhi, instead of letting that happen, seemed to encourage his cheerleaders to push V. P. Singh to 'dig in and fight'. In the end, Singh emerged as the rallying point for a desperate and a disparate opposition as well as for the people who were determined to defeat the Congress (I), the party they had elected with such a huge mandate in 1984.

We did see earlier that V. P. Singh's actions as the finance minister against industrialists and particularly against Ambani led Rajiv Gandhi to move him out from finance ministry. The prime minister could not have dropped Singh from the Cabinet because that would have been perceived as punishing someone who worked, so relentlessly, towards cleansing the system. That, probably, was the reason why Singh was made the defence minister. But then, the raids at Gurumurthy's residence and subsequently on Ramnath Goenka's premises, triggered by *The Indian Express* publishing the text of President Zail Singh's correspondence with Prime Minister Rajiv Gandhi, opened a pandora's box. Among the documents seized by the CBI was a letter from Fairfax suggesting that the US agency's services were hired by Gurumurthy to investigate the affairs of Dhirubhai Ambani's Reliance Industries. The CBI found the scope for a case against Gurumurthy because such an engagement must have involved payment in foreign exchange and hence a violation of the FERA. Gurumurthy had written a series of articles, in *The Indian Express*, exposing financial irregularities by Reliance. *The Indian Express* was also carrying out a crusade against Rajiv Gandhi at that time.

The issue, however, took a different dimension after Hershman, of Fairfax, issued a rejoinder that categorically denied any deal between his agency and Gurumurthy and went on to state that he was employed by the Enforcement Directorate of the Union government. The opposition parties jumped in to demand an explanation from the government as to why a foreign agency was employed, raising apprehensions over the implications of such a deal on the security of the country. Hershman, incidentally, was involved, in some way, with the Watergate Scandal that caused the exit of President Nixon from his office. The government, now on the mat, found to its dismay, that the issue on hand was a lot more complicated than it looked like when it set out against Gurumurthy. All this was now before a court to prosecute Gurumurthy and hence it was too late to hush things up.

On 6 February 1987, Bhure Lal, Director of the Enforcement Directorate had put up a note to Revenue Secretary Vinod Pande that he had hired the services of Fairfax during his visit to the US in the first week of January 1987 and that payment to the agency would be made on the basis of the material it supplied. Bhure Lal and Pande, IAS officers belonging to the Uttar Pradesh cadre, were associated with V. P. Singh when he was the chief minister of the state between June 1980 and 1982. They had a reputation of being upright and possessing a relentless zeal to take on wrong-doers. They were brought to the centre by Singh when he joined Rajiv Gandhi's Cabinet as finance minister on 31 December 1984. They played a significant role in the campaign against tax violations by the industrialists. The fact of the matter is that Bhure Lal realised the inherent limitations, placed on the personnel at the directorate, when it came to investigating violations by Indian industrialists in instances where it called for obtaining documents from outside the country. This was particularly pronounced in the case of Dhirubhai Ambani. This, indeed, brought Bhure Lal and Gurumurthy close; and the idea to employ Hershman of Fairfax was borne out of this. It so happened that Nusli Wadia of Bombay Dyeing had an axe to grind against Reliance and was willing to commit to any investigation that would put Ambani in trouble.

While there was no evidence to suggest that money was paid to Fairfax, the fact that Fairfax was engaged by the Enforcement Directorate was reason enough to raise a storm in Parliament and the government had to deal with the issue in the public domain. Minister of State for Finance, Brahm Dutt had come across the 6 February 1987 note by Bhure Lal to Revenue Secretary Vinod Pande and found something strange in it. Hence, he put up queries before officials in the finance ministry. Bhure Lal, himself, was moved out of the Enforcement Directorate a few days after he put up the note. However, the logic of file movements in government departments defy time and space. By the first week of March, even as the files containing Bhure Lal's note were moving around in the finance ministry, V. P. Singh, now defence minister, sent a note to the finance ministry that the Enforcement Directorate had engaged Fairfax on the basis of his 'verbal' authorisation to do so. In other words, Singh stood up for Bhure Lal.

Thus, when the Fairfax issue came up before Parliament on 31 March 1987, the Congress (I) was caught in a bind. There was evidence of an impropriety in the act of engaging a foreign investigating agency with the sanction of the then finance minister. The party, as things unraveled in the days to come, decided to train its gun against V. P. Singh in Parliament. Singh seemed to have prepared his own counter strategy by ordering a departmental enquiry into the HDW deal to establish the identity and the modus operandi of the India agent who was paid Rs 30 crore as commission. That Singh made this decision public was his own way of hitting back at Rajiv Gandhi.

The high point of the debate in Parliament, on 31 March 1987, was the choice of leaders fielded by the Congress (I). Dinesh Singh, a Rajput leader who was once an important member of Indira Gandhi's 'kitchen cabinet', but sent into oblivion for several years now; Rangarajan Kumaramangalam, Baliram Bhagat and Jaganath Kaushal. They were all hand-picked by Rajiv Gandhi and his aides in the party and briefed, that very morning, by a team consisting of Home Minister Buta Singh, Commerce Minister P. Shiv Shankar, Special Secretary in the PMO Gopi Arora and Finance Secretary S. Venkitaramanan. The strategy was to isolate V. P. Singh, still the defence minister.

Dinesh Singh's speech on the floor of the Lok Sabha was marked by a flurry of questions: Did the finance ministry check out the antecedents of Fairfax? Had its competence to handle economic issues been assessed? Was the agency hired through Indian investigative agencies or directly by the finance ministry and if that was the case, the ministry must clarify on certain procedural requirements. All the other Congress (I) MPs also raised doubts, hinting at the involvement of the CIA and such agencies in the affair, given the fact that Fairfax was also involved in the Watergate scandal and alluded that the agency was given a chance to dabble with Indian politics. All these questions could have been raised within the party and in the Cabinet and V. P. Singh could have been asked to clarify. The party high command, however, decided against this and instead washed the dirty linen in public.

Dinesh Singh, in the course of his speech, said that V. P. Singh engaged Fairfax without taking the prime minister, Rajiv Gandhi, into confidence and this forced him to wonder if the finance minister did something of such magnitude behind the prime minister's back with an ulterior motive. It was clear that the Congress (I) high command had decided to get rid of V. P. Singh. Madhu Dandavate, one of the few leaders of the opposition in Parliament at that time, remarked: 'This is an insinuation against the Defence Minister V. P. Singh'.

Meanwhile, Congress (I) MPs and party leaders from Uttar Pradesh took the cue to call V. P. Singh a traitor. The government, on its side, announced the setting up of a judicial commission, under the Commission of Enquiries Act, to probe into the engagement of Fairfax. As soon as the announcement was made, V. P. Singh, present in the House throughout the debate, walked out without waiting for the Speaker to adjourn the House for the day. It was clear that his days in the Cabinet were numbered and that the stage was set for his exit from the Cabinet. It happened on 12 April 1987.

The Judicial Enquiry Commission was constituted on 6 April 1987 with Justice M. P. Thakkar and Justice S. Natarajan, both sitting judges of the Supreme Court. The Thakkar–Natarajan Commision had a clear brief: To indict V. P. Singh, Bhure Lal and Vinod Pande. Its report, tabled in Parliament in December 1987, did exactly that.

V. P. Singh was summoned to depose before the commission weeks after he quit the Cabinet and was asked to explain as to why the defence minister had sought for the file containing Bhure Lal's note and Brahm Dutt's queries. Singh, now attacked by almost everyone in the Congress (I), minced no words: 'I did not want the file itself but did want to go on record to say that I had given oral clearance when the matter was mentioned to me by the Secretary, Revenue'. He went on to justify engaging Fairfax:

> With hardly any network of our own and the expenditure in foreign exchange that would be involved in frequently sending our officers abroad, apart from the loss of work this may entail, it seemed the most cost-effective way of obtaining hard evidence without entailing any financial risk; that is to make payments only after receiving concrete evidence without any obligation of expenditure.

He also pointed out to the Commission that 'paying for information is a practice which is not new to revenue intelligence, and within the country the principle finds expression in the form of rewards to informants'.

The Commission's report, running into 293 pages, turned into a long list of observations, some of them, bordering on absurdity. One of it, for instance, was that the Enforcement Directorate functioned in secrecy when it came to dealing with its informers and recorded its objections to this as follows:

> Particularly distressing is the fact that the department has functioned in a cloak-and-dagger atmosphere of secrecy. Meetings take place in hotels and public parks, oral talks take place of which no written record is made in any file, even subsequently, let alone making a contemporaneous record.

It was strange that the commission expected the intelligence agencies to put in writing their dealings with informers or to have formal agreements signed between the sleuths and anyone from whom they would gather crucial information.

As for the omissions, the Thakkar–Natarajan Commission refrained from even a cursory enquiry into the facts of the case, which was about financial irregularities by Indian business houses on which Fairfax was meant to collect information and pass them on to the Enforcement Directorate. This clearly established that the purpose of the commission was to indict V. P. Singh, Bhure Lal and Vinod Pande. S. Gurumurthy and Nusli Wadia refused to depose before the commission, despite a notice to them, and the commission recorded its lament over this in the report.

The Commission report and the storm it raised in Parliament, when it was tabled in December 1987, ensured that V. P. Singh came out as a knight in shining armour. It also emerged that Rajiv Gandhi's intention was to persecute V. P. Singh rather than those who indulged in corruption. This happened because the Bofors scandal had become a part of the national political discourse by this time. Arun Singh, minister of state for defence, had resigned from the Cabinet on 18 July 1987. It was clear that the Bofors scandal was the reason behind his resignation. Arun Singh would confirm this in a statement in the Rajya Sabha on 11 May 1988. The Bofors scandal was brought to light by the Swedish National Radio in its broadcast on 16 April 1987; the radio revealed that the Swedish Gun Manufacturer paid kickbacks to Indian politicians and officials in the defence ministry to secure the contract to supply 155 mm Howitzer guns to the Indian Army. On 20 April 1987, Prime Minister Rajiv Gandhi told the Lok Sabha that neither was there any middleman in the deal nor were kickbacks paid. This development, within days after V. P. Singh's resignation from the Cabinet, lent a new dimension to the political discourse.

As for V. P. Singh, he refrained from speaking about the Bofors scandal and stuck to defending his actions as finance minister (engaging Fairfax) and as defence minister (ordering a departmental enquiry into the HDW submarine deal). Singh's focus was on the fact that a large amount of money was being stashed away by Indian industrialists in secret accounts in foreign banks. This was evident in the exchange of innuendoes between Rajiv Gandhi and V. P. Singh in May 1987 within a month after the Bofors scandal broke out. On 16 May 1987, Rajiv Gandhi made an oblique reference to him in a public meeting in Delhi; the country's independence, he said, was lost whenever 'traitors' like Mir Jaffar and 'Raja' Jai Chand allied with external forces and cautioned the people against 'those who tried to help foreign powers and sell the country's interests abroad'. The message was not lost; the reference to 'Raja' before Jai Chand was pointed at Raja V. P. Singh and the foreign powers he referred to was Fairfax. V. P. Singh reacted to this the following day: 'The real Mir Jaffars and Jai Chands are those who are siphoning money out of the country, bleeding it of its resources and stashing it in foreign banks and strengthening the economy of other countries at the cost of ours'.

The point is that all these charges and counters were taking place in the public. The Allahabad city unit of the Congress (I) announced suspension of V. P. Singh for six years. This happened even when the Congress (I) constitution laid out that local units had no authority to take action against party MPs and MLAs. The AICC hastened to clarify this soon after and V. P. Singh remained a Congress (I) member, affirming his loyalty to the party and its leader, Rajiv Gandhi. But then, beneath the apparent expression of loyalty by Singh to the party and its leader and the inaction by the high command, both the sides were pulling all the stops to provoke each other to resort to something drastic.

On 3 May 1987, V. P. Singh addressed a gathering in Lucknow where he said that he would make some startling revelations in a month's time and that he would continue his fight against corruption even if he was sent to jail. At the Congress (I) Parliamentary Party meeting on 8 May 1987, the thrust of the speeches by several members was to demand severe action against Singh. On 27 May, V. P. Singh was scheduled to address a rally of the Uttar Pradesh Employees and Teachers Confederation in Lucknow. The state government, now headed by Vir Bahadur Singh, banned rallies and public meetings across the state and leaders of the confederation were arrested. V. P. Singh arrived in Lucknow, to a tumultuous welcome, rode around the city in a jeep and left without even a semblance of resistance against the ban. He did not say anything against the ban or against the state government. This game of hide and seek would continue until Singh's summary expulsion on 19 July 1987.

This was the case with the others who had rebelled against Rajiv Gandhi for their own reasons. Arif Mohammed Khan, Arun Nehru, V. C. Shukla and Ram Dhan were all being tolerated by the party high command for a specific reason; the presidential elections were due on 13 July 1987. The rebels too were only planning to set themselves up as a ginger group within the Congress (I). The first concrete move towards this formation of a collective happened on 26 June 1987. The occasion was V. P. Singh's birthday and a party was organised at Arif Mohammed Khan's residence. Arun Nehru and V. C. Shukla joined the celebrations that day. These leaders decided to present a charter to Rajiv Gandhi. It contained:

- Fullest action against economic offenders and defence agents, for the protection of national interest and for setting at rest the questions in people's minds as regards to capital flight and money in Swiss Banks. Pending other steps, full use of the FERA powers, requiring Indian nationals suspected of having assets abroad to furnish all details and publishing them in the case of a false statement. 'Use of this provision of law will instill fear in the heart of many who have properties or money abroad and will act as an active deterrent'.
- Harmful effects of the businessman-politician-bureacrat nexus, is the natural corollary of the politico-economic system we are running. As a way out of the adverse influence of money power on the working of the political system, elections to be funded through a 'political cess' on luxury items, which will obviate the need for the political parties to turn to donations from big business. Though the money raised would be the same, the political impact will be different because 'donations mean obligations and therefore compromises, whereas, the tax is a matter of right and there is obligation to none'.
- In the days to come, the influence of corporations will be growing as they grow bigger and elections become costlier. As the corporations work under the umbrella of the state, they compulsorily have to build bridges with the political system to safeguard their interests which they do by developing lobbies within the bureaucracy and also the political system. They need policies to protect profits while the political system opens itself to them because of its need for funds to run the party and fight elections. These linkages lead to non-democratic even anti-national influences. In the case of defence it may be jeopardizing the security of the country.
- Other issues: The need for extending labour participation to the management of big business houses, difficulties of the landless, terms of trade between the agricultural and manufacturing sector and non-fulfilment of the quota of the Scheduled Castes and Tribes in services.

This charter, on the face of it, sounded perfectly in tune with Rajiv Gandhi's call to his partymen, in the Congress centenary session, in December 1985. It was presented to Rajiv Gandhi on 14 July 1987. On that day, Rajiv Gandhi had the resignation letter from Mufti Mohammed Sayeed from the Union Cabinet. Mufti had resigned protesting against the Congress (I)–National Conference alliance in Jammu and Kashmir. While the alliance, struck in November 1986, ahead of the March 1987 elections to the state assembly, had ensured a clean sweep for the combine in the assembly (winning 63 of the 76 seats), Mufti saw it as an arrangement that would push the Congress (I) into a position of playing second fiddle to the National Conference in the state. In other words, Mufti saw his own chance of becoming the chief minister of Jammu and Kashmir receding for all times to come. Mufti Mohammed Sayeed too would end up with V. P. Singh in the Janata Dal, become the Union home minister, ensure the resignation of Farooq Abdullah by sending Jagmohan as the governor of the state and contributing, in many ways, to the crisis in Kashmir. We shall discuss this in the next chapter.

Coming back to the charter, Rajiv Gandhi was not naïve. The Congress (I) rebels had scheduled a mass contact programme and V. P. Singh had left for Haridwar in Uttar Pradesh along with Arif Mohammed Khan and V. C. Shukla to address a public meeting there. That was the context in which Arun Nehru, Shukla and Khan were expelled from the Congress (I) on 16 July 1987 followed by V. P. Singh's expulsion on 19 July 1987.

The crisis, insofar as the Congress (I) was concerned, was not merely the revolt inside the party. After the reverses in West Bengal and Kerala, in March 1987, the party lost power in Haryana in June 1987. Meanwhile, dissidence in the party units in Bihar, Uttar Pradesh, Madhya Pradesh and Gujarat was growing. Led by V. P. Singh, the rebels began touring the length and breadth of the country and the crowds that gathered at their public meeting simply proved that the Congress (I), under Rajiv Gandhi, had now lost the credibility that it commanded in December 1984. However, the rebels could not gather more than a handful of supporters from within the Congress (I) Parliamentary Party. The anti-defection law ensured that more MPs did not join V. P. Singh.

Rajiv Gandhi, meanwhile, went about shuffling the Cabinet and also changing chief ministers in the states at regular intervals. In January 1988, Harideo Joshi was replaced by S. C. Mathur as Rajasthan chief minister; in February 1988, Bindeswari Dubey was replaced by Bhagwat Jha Azad as Bihar chief minister and Motilal Vora was replaced by Arjun Singh as Madhya Pradesh chief minister. Dubey and Vora were made Union ministers along with Dinesh Singh and a dozen others. In June 1988, Uttar Pradesh chief minister Vir Bahadur Singh was shifted to the Union Cabinet and N. D. Tiwari sent as chief minister. Madhav Singh Solanki, who had challenged Rajiv Gandhi in February 1986, was accommodated in the Union Cabinet in June 1988. Sharad Pawar was made Maharashtra chief minister and S. B. Chavan returned to the Union Cabinet as finance minister on 25 June 1988. This was the twenty-fifth Cabinet reshuffle by Rajiv Gandhi since he became the prime minister on 31 December 1984.

The desperation was evident in his address to the AICC (I) session at Maraimalainagar, near Madras, on 23–24 April 1988. It so happened that *The Hindu* published reports, with documentary evidence, of payments made by the Bofors into coded accounts in Swiss Banks, on the day the AICC session opened. The reports established that the coded accounts—Moresco and

Pitco—belonged to the Hindujas. And, unlike the introspection that marked the tone of Rajiv Gandhi's address at the Bombay session in December 1985 when he wanted the party to be freed from power brokers, the address at the Maraimalainagar session was marked by a no-holds-barred attack on the opposition parties.

Thereafter, there were by-elections to seven Lok Sabha constituencies across the country on 16 June 1988. The most significant among them was in Allahabad. Having stunned the nation by defeating H. N. Bahuguna in the 1984 general election, Amitabh Bachchan resigned as MP in July 1987 stating that he was disgusted with the allegations against him. His brother, Ajitabh Bachchan, was accused as a recipient in the Bofors payoff to begin with and even after it emerged to be a wild accusation, the actor-turned-politician was hounded by fresh charges. That was the context in which he threw in the towel.

When by-elections were announced to the constituency, the opposition, though caught up in its own internecine battles, decided to support V. P. Singh as its candidate. Singh won the 16 June 1988 elections polling 52 per cent of the votes against Congress (I)'s Sunil Shastri who ended up with just 23 per cent of the votes. Contesting the election as an independent candidate, V. P. Singh gathered almost all the national leaders and an array of regional party chiefs to campaign for him. The other significant aspect of the Allahabad by-elections was the arrival of Kanshi Ram and his Bahujan Samaj Party (BSP). The BSP chief polled close to 18 per cent of the votes in that election. Kanshi Ram's campaign rested on a simple slogan: 'We will not allow your government with our votes'. The 'your' meant the upper castes and the 'our' meant the scheduled castes. The BSP registered a steady growth ever since to emerge as a partner in a coalition (with Mulayam Singh Yadav's Samajwadi Party) that won the state assembly elections in November 1993, form its government with support from the BJP, for short spells in 1996 and 1998, and emerge into the ruling party with absolute majority of its own in May 2007.

V. P. Singh's victory in the Allahabad by-elections and his arrival in the Lok Sabha thereafter lent a new dimension to the composition of the opposition in Parliament, when the House assembled for the Monsoon Session in July 1988. He emerged the leader around whom the opposition gathered inside Parliament. The report of the Joint Parliamentary Committee to enquire into the Bofors deal, set up on 6 August 1987, was tabled in the House on 18 July 1988. It provided another spark for the opposition to attack Rajiv Gandhi and his government. The issue would dominate the proceedings of both the houses of Parliament for days on end and the national political discourse after the Parliament session. In many ways, the Bofors scandal turned out to be the most important and the most immediate cause for the Congress party's woes.

The Bofors Scandal

Sometime during the last few months of the Indira Gandhi regime, the Indian Army began looking for a field gun. This was also the time when the regime in New Delhi was seeing 'war clouds on the western frontier'. Pakistan had then acquired a fleet of F-16 fighters and this justified the Indian Army's demand for a field gun. A committee under the then defence secretary, S. K. Bhatnagar, shortlisted Bofors (from Sweden) and Sofma (from France) guns for the purpose. After he took over as the prime minister, Rajiv Gandhi decided to speed up the process; he also declared that the government will not deal with the agents of arms' manufacturers. This declaration, itself, raised eyebrows. All defence deals by the government, until then, were carried out through agents and a commission upto 3 per cent of the total deal was paid by the seller in all these cases. The new policy of eliminating middlemen fitted in perfectly with the 'Mr Clean' image that Rajiv Gandhi had put on.

This, however, was only a façade. It was part of a new fund-raising scheme, evolved by Rajiv Gandhi and his principal advisors at that time. Arun Nehru was credited with formulating this new means to raise funds. The traditional method of raising party funds—selling licences to industrialists or by way of contributions from businessmen in return for ignoring acts of tax evasion and FERA violations—was creating problems. These sources were now being tapped by the regional chieftains of the Congress (I) as well as those in the opposition and the high command was left with crumbs in many instances. This was the context in which Rajiv Gandhi and his advisors hit upon the idea of making money out of the purchase of equipment and spares from foreign manufacturers by the public sector undertakings. The army's equipment orders, in any case, constituted a huge part of such purchases. It was known, to anyone who cared to know, that hundreds of crores were paid to agents as commissions on defence purchases and the Congress (I) managers hit upon the idea, to ask the sellers to sack their agents and pass on their commissions to the party. The advantage of this was: The commissions would be paid by whoever got the contracts and would not be seen as bribes paid to influence the award of the contract as it would be the case with issuing licences to industrialists and traders.

Even if this new idea seemed to be a fine one, there was a problem with this insofar as the arms manufacturers were concerned. They could not afford to break their contracts with the agents only because one particular deal demanded that. The dealers were an integral part of the armament industry across the world. In other words, Bofors could not have sacked its agents because they were needed for the company elsewhere. Bofors had its agent in India; a company called Anatronics, run by Win N. Chadha. Bofors then reworked the arrangement with him. Anatronics was hired for a fixed amount to function as its consultant in India.

Nobody was sure whether the directive banning agents applied to consultants as well. Chadha continued to function—for all practical purposes—as Bofors' agent in India.

Insofar as the choice of the gun was concerned, the procedures were followed and the army elected Bofors the winner. The Swedish gun would 'shoot-and-scoot' (it could be moved after it had fired) while the French gun, Sofma, would not do that. Negotiations began on 13 December 1985 and concluded on 23 March 1986; the Rajiv Gandhi government took just 24 hours to endorse the recommendation; and the contract to supply 400 of the 155 mm Howitzer guns was finalised. Win Chadha threw a party at Delhi's Maurya hotel on the same day, which went unnoticed. No one wondered as to why Chadha threw a party at that time. Nobody cared to wonder about the efficiency with which the government worked to clinch the deal. The fact is that the deal would have remained in limbo for several months if it was not clinched before 31 March 1986. The rules warrant that budgetary allocations are spent before the end of the fiscal year by all ministries and in the event they fail to do that, the funds lapse.

No one had noticed the deal until 16 April 1987; a Swedish National Radio broadcast revealed that Bofors had paid bribes to secure the contract. At that time political India was already engaged with the Fairfax issue (the Thakkar–Natarajan Commission was already constituted) and also the departmental enquiry into payment of commission to an Indian agent in the HDW submarine deal. The Budget Session of Parliament was on and the opposition parties did not let go the opportunity. On 20 April 1987, Rajiv Gandhi declared in Parliament that the Bofors deal did not involve any middlemen and that there was no kickback paid.

The opposition refused to buy this and continued raising the issue within and outside Parliament. Rajiv Gandhi responded to this by setting up a Joint Parliamentary Committee (JPC) to look into the allegations. This he did only after he was convinced that the ruling party could use the institution of the JPC to further its case rather than unraveling the truth. The numbers in the two houses were such that the opposition representatives would constitute only a minority in the JPC. Parliamentary rules allow representation in a JPC in direct proportion to a party's strength in the house. The opposition was made up of only one-fifth of the strength of the house. Hence, the 30-member strong JPC would have just six opposition representatives. On 6 August 1987, the Lok Sabha speaker announced a JPC and appointed B. Shankaranand, health minister in the Rajiv Gandhi Cabinet, as its chairman. The opposition parties refused to join the committee and announced boycott of its proceedings.

After extensive travel to army bases, evaluating the Bofors gun (on which the MPs hardly had an expertise) and a visit to Sweden to meet with the Bofors officials, the JPC gave a clean chit to the government, the gun manufacturer and the gun itself in its report presented before Parliament on 26 April 1988. There was, however, a dissenting note to the report appended by Aladi Aruna. This was an interesting story. Aruna had joined the JPC in his capacity as an AIADMK MP; the AIADMK was an ally of the Congress (I) then. In due course, thanks to some political churning in Tamil Nadu after M .G. Ramachandran's death, the alliance broke and Aruna decided to place his dissenting note. His 20-page note ended thus: 'The conclusion of the report, no doubt, conceal the facts of the deal and cover up the connivance of our government with Bofors and refuse to identify the recepients who could be none other than Indians or Indian associates or both'. In the debate that followed the presentation of the report in the Lok Sabha, S. Jaipal Reddy, an opposition MP then, said:

> If Bofors kickbacks is the biggest scandal in India's history, the JPC report may well be described as the biggest whitewash in Parliamentary history. After going through the report I am convinced that the uncanny wisdom of the entire opposition to keep off the Bofors committee has been vindicated.

The truth, however, was brought out by the media even while the JPC was carrying out the cover-up job for the government. On 23 April 1988, only three days before the JPC submitted its report, *The Hindu* published documents establishing payments by Bofors into a coded account named Pitco in the Swiss Banks and traced the holders of that account to Sangam Limited and also established that this company was owned by the Hindujas. This was evident from the mailing address for the Pitco cheques. It was 'care of G. P. Hinduja, New Zealand House, Haymarket, London'. The report appeared on the day when Rajiv Gandhi arrived in Madras (now Chennai) to address the AICC meet in Maraimalainagar, a suburb south of Madras. The government responded to this saying that the payments pertained to an earlier contract of 1979 and that these were winding up charges on some other deal. The Hindujas, incidentally, were the ones to whom the German government had paid a 7 per cent commission (Rs 30 crore) for the HDW submarine deal.

This lie too was nailed when *The Hindu* published another set of documents on 25 June 1988. These documents, in the form of computer-generated printouts of official banking information, related to payments into such coded accounts as *Lotus, Tulip* and *Mont Blanc*. These coded accounts that belonged to *Moresco-Moineao* were again traced to the Hindujas and payments were found to be made into these accounts after December 1986, the time when the Bofors negotiations had commenced. The Hinduja connection with Bofors was further established when *The Hindu* reproduced a letter, dated 8 February 1987, from G. P. Hinduja to Martin Ardbo, president of Bofors at the time of the deal, confirming a business association between them.

Thereafter, facsimile prints of Martin Ardbo's entries in his diary were published, once again, in *The Hindu*. Ardbo used codes in his diary, which were not all that complicated. For instance, he referred to his partners in managing the cover-up as 'Hansens' and that they lived in London and India and that one of them, when he was not described as Hansen, was called GPH. It was plain and simple. The Hansens were the Hindujas and that GPH was G. P. Hinduja. There were other entries that clarified this. One entry read: 'GPH's enemies are Serge Paul and Nero'. The battle between the Hindujas on one side and Arun Nehru and Swaraj Paul on the other were far too well known at that time. The implications were obvious. Excerpts that were published from the diary revealed a lot more than was suspected at the time when the scandal broke out.

Ardbo wrote, on one day, that he was meeting with a 'Gandhi trustee lawyer' to finalise details of the cover-up and that he no longer cared about 'the consequences for N' (obviously a reference to Arun Nehru, now out of the Congress party) but 'Q's involvement could be a problem because of closeness to R'. Ardbo's diary was picked up by the Swedish police and presented as evidence in the courts to prosecute the Bofors executive. The prosecution was on in connection with illegal export of arms to Iran and was launched in April 1988. If R was Rajiv, then Q had to be somebody who was close to him. It was clear then that Q was Ottavio Quatrocchi, the Delhi representative of Snamprogetti, the Italian multinational whose friendship with Rajiv had been a subject of controversy even otherwise.

It was then that the opposition leaders managed to connect some innocuous references in the JPC report and put the Bofors story together. The JPC did make some interesting revelations in this context. It revealed that Bofors had two agents in India; Pitco and Svenska. The JPC was told by Bofors that the company had terminated the agreements with Pitco and Svenska (belonging to Win Chadha) after the government asked it to sack its agents. As for the payments made to these agents, who were not to be involved according to the terms of the contract, Bofors explained them as winding-up charges for terminating the contract. This, however, did not explain the existence of a third agent called *AE Services* after it had terminated the arrangements with Pitco and Svenska. AE Services was hired after Pitco and Svenska were sacked. The gun manufacturer had told the JPC that it was an oversight. The company's officers had forgotten that there was no scope for agents in the contract. It was strange that the JPC was convinced by this and put it in its report. The terms with AE Services were specific: It was entitled for a commission only if the contract was signed before 31 March 1986. It so happened that the deal was pushed through just before the deadline expired.

While Pitco belonged to the Hindujas and Svenska to Win Chadha, AE Services remained a mystery. The Bofors explained that it was a British firm headquartered in Guildford, Surrey, owned and promoted by a Major Bob Wilson. The JPC accepted the story. It was discovered, later, that AE Services had no office. The address was of a post box in a solicitor's firm. The total capital of the company was £100 divided into a hundred shares of one pound each.

Major Wilson owned one share. The rest were owned by a shadowy Leichtenstein corporation. There was nothing to establish Quattrocchi's involvement in this and the 'Q' in Ardbo's diary remained a mystery.

The mystery could have been solved easily. The Swedish National Audit Bureau's report had revealed that Bofors had deposited as much as 250 million US Dollars (Rs 64 crore by the exchange rate at that time) into three coded accounts in a Swiss Bank: Svenska, Pitco, and AE Services. Bofors could have been confronted with a demand that it disclose the faces behind these coded accounts. All that the Indian government had to do then was to convey to Bofors that the company had committed a breach of the contract by employing middlemen in the deal; that this provided the ground for India to cancel the deal without having to pay damages. The Government of India could also have conveyed to Bofors that the deal would be cancelled unless the company revealed the names and other details of those to whom the commissions were paid.

This course was suggested to Rajiv Gandhi by none other than his confidant and the minister of state for defence, Arun Singh. On 10 June 1987, soon after the Bofors scandal was reported by the Swedish National Radio broadcast, Arun Singh put up a note to K. C. Pant, then defence minister, to be forwarded to Rajiv Gandhi. It said:

> It is my understanding that the (Swedish) National Audit Bureau has confirmed unequivocally that payments have been made and I stand by my statements in the Rajya Sabha that such payments are grossly violative of all stated policy as communicated to and understood by both Bofors and the Swedish Govt. It must therefore follow that we as GOI must pursue this matter to its logical conclusion.

The note then went on to specifics:

> To inform both the Swedish Govt and the company that unless they give us the information we want, we will have no alternative but to cancel the contract. I am fully cognisant of the fact that this cancellation will have some negative impact on our defence preparedness but you may like to reconfirm with COAS (Chief of Army Staff) whether we can live with that. In my view, we must be prepared to go to the extent of cancellation because our very credibility as a Govt is at stake and what is worse, the credibility of the entire process of defence acquisitions is also at stake.

Thereafter, the Defence Secretary S. K. Bhatnagar put up the file before General K. Sundarji, Chief of Army Staff. On 13 June 1987, the General noted:

> We should go to the extent of threatening to cancel our contracts if they do not part with this information. If the threat does not work, and in the worst case, leads to the cancellation of the contract, I believe that the delay on the procurement of 155mm guns would perhaps be about 18 months to 2 years. I believe that we could live with this delay and take a calculated risk.

It was, thus, clear that pursuing the truth and the identity of those who received the illegal payments was possible without putting the nation's security in jeopardy. Rajiv Gandhi, however, thought otherwise. He seemed to know more about defence preparedness than the Chief of Army Staff. On 15 July 1987, Rajiv Gandhi put his thoughts on the file. His reply to Arun Singh revealed a lot.

> It is unfortunate that MOS/AS (Minister of State/Arun Singh) has put his personal prestige above the security of the nation before even evaluating all aspects. Has he evaluated the actual position vis-a-vis (sic) security? Has he evaluated the financial loss of cancellation? Has he evaluated how GOI prestige will plummet if we unilaterally cancel a contract that has not been violated? To the best of my belief, the Swedish Audit report upholds GOI position and does not contradict it. Knee-jerk reactions and stomach cramps will not serve any purpose.

Arun Singh resigned from the Union council of ministers on 18 July 1987. While participating in a debate on the Bofors scandal in the Rajya Sabha on 11 May 1988, the former minister of state for defence clarified his position. He stressed that the 155 mm Howitzers from Bofors was an excellent gun bought at an advantageous price. He did not stop there and went on to say that Bofors had committed a 'breach of faith' with India by making payments to the tune of 319.4 million SEK (Swedish Kroners), in 1986, to faceless recipients; that these payments cannot be accepted as 'winding-up charges' but must be regarded as 'contract related payments'; that the Government of India must demand a full payback of the 'breach of faith' payments plus damages; and if that did not work, Bofors must be blacklisted.

In other words, Rajiv Gandhi could have got to the truth. He refused to do anything in this regard and instead went on accusing all those who were involved in exposing the scandal as enemies of national interest and of being a part of a conspiracy to destabilise the nation. The scandal, meanwhile, turned into an integral part of the political discourse, played a big role in the making of V. P. Singh into a leader, around whom the opposition parties rallied and Rajiv Gandhi's image of Mr Clean now changed into that of a corrupt prime minister. It is likely that Rajiv Gandhi knew, at some stage, that the mysterious 'Q' in Ardbo's diary was Ottavio Quattrocchi, his family friend. It was then that he took help from the Hindujas (referred to as Gandhi Trustee Lawyer in Ardbo's diary) and all this left a trail that could be traced by the sleuths of the CBI as and when they were ordered by the political establishment to do so.

Meanwhile, on 18 July 1989, the Comptroller and Auditor General (CAG) submitted his report to Parliament. The reports are usually delayed and this one presented in July 1989 was the audited report of the defence ministry for 1985–86. The auditor's report pointed out that the government had incurred a loss because the amount paid as commission, by the gun manufacturer, must have been deducted at the time of payment. The report pointed out that since the contract did not allow middlemen, the commission amount must have been a saving for the government. The opposition, by now, had realised the use of the Bofors scandal in the political sense of the term and elections to the Lok Sabha were due in November 1989. After raising a lot of noise, all the opposition MPs in the Lok Sabha resigned *en masse*. Seventy-three Lok Sabha members, belonging to the opposition parties, submitted their resignation on 24 July 1989. In the elections held in November 1989, the Congress (I) was voted out of power and the V. P. Singh government initiated measures to find out the faces behind the coded accounts. The case was left to the CBI.

With cooperation coming from the Swedish and Swiss authorities, the CBI was getting close to the truth. However, the Congress (I) returned to power and the then external affairs minister, Madhav Singh Solanki, was caught handing over an anonymous note to his Swiss counterpart conveying that the investigation into the Bofors deal be slowed down. The incident caused some embarrassment to the Congress (I) and the then Prime Minister P. V. Narasimha Rao asked Solanki to leave the Cabinet. Solanki, who had accused Rajiv Gandhi of doing harm to the Congress in 1986 (discussed in the previous section), had now become a loyal soldier of the party, refused to identify the source of the note that he carried and claims that he did not know the person who passed on the note to him.

Thereafter, on 23 July 1993, it was revealed by the Swiss Courts that AE Services was a shell company operated by Colbar Investments, incorporated in the Panama Islands and that it was controlled by Ottavio Quattrocchi and his wife Maria Quottrocchi. It was now clear that of the Rs 64 crore paid into the three coded accounts by Bofors, 73 lakh US Dollars (Rs 18.7 crore) went into Quattrocchi's account in the Nordfinanz Bank in Zurich. The deposit was made on 3 September 1986. It was now clear that the 'Q' mentioned in Ardbo's diary was Ottavio Quattrocchi.

Quattrocchi represented Snam Progetti, an Italian firm involved in the setting up of fertiliser plants in India since 1964, and had become an influential player in Delhi after 1984. Bofors engaged him to help swing the gun deal and clinch it before 31 March 1986 and he was paid 73 lakh US dollars for the service he rendered. Most of the funds were transferred to the Union Bank of Switzerland, Geneva into the account of Colbar Invesment and moved out of that account too (within a couple of months) to yet another bank in the British Channel Islands. Quattrocchi remained in India for several years after the scandal broke out in April 1987 and even after V. P. Singh became the prime minister. He was trying to block the release of his bank papers by the Swiss Bank authorities. And, when the Swiss courts confirmed, on 23 July 1993, that Quattrocchi was the man behind AE Services, the Italian national flew off to Malaysia from New Delhi on the night of 29 July 1993. The next small step in the Bofors story was possible only after May 1996; this was after the United Front government, a non-Congress (I)–non-BJP coalition of regional parties, headed by H. D. Deve Gowda of the Janata Dal, came to power in New Delhi.

The CBI enquiry into the case was pursued once again with some seriousness and the agency finally received the relevant documents from the Swiss banks in November 1996. The documents confirmed all that were only presumptions until then. That Win Chadha, the Hinduja brothers and Ottavio Quattrocchi had made a lot of money out of the Bofors deal. The CBI continued to pursue the case and the first chargesheet implicating Quattrocchi (along with others) was filed on 22 October 1999. The chargesheet read:

> M/s Bofors had paid an amount equivalent to SEK 192,156,200 (approximately 270 lakh US dollars) during April 1986 and March 1987 in the name of M/s Svenska Inc, Panama in connection with the said deal with the Government of India. This has been found to have been credited to the personal account of Win Chadha in Swiss Bank Corporation, Geneva.
>
> Similarly, another amount of SEK 540,63,966 (approximately US dollars 73 lakh) was paid by M/s Bofors to M/s A.E. Services Limited, UK. Investigation has disclosed that 97 per cent of this amount was transferred to the account of Colbar Investment Limited, Panama, controlled by Ottavio Quattrocchi in the Union Bank of Switzerland, Geneva. It had been found that Win Chadha and Ottavio Quottrocchi had been transferring the said funds from one account to another account and from one jurisdiction to another to avoid detection.

The chargesheet also contained Rajiv Gandhi's name. He was listed as an accused but not sent for trial—that is the legal procedure insofar as the dead are concerned. Rajiv Gandhi was killed in a bomb blast on 21 May 1991. The CBI also informed the court that efforts were being made to seek deportation/extradition of Quottrocchi, Chadha (who had left for Dubai by now) and Martin Ardbo and that further investigation was also going on, through several Letters Rogatory, sent to Switzerland, Sweden, Panama, Luxembourg, Bahamas, Jordan, Liechtenstien, Austria, etc., to probe the role of several other persons, including G. P. Hinduja, Prakash Hinduja, Srichand Hinduja, Hersh Chadha and Maria Quattrocchi.

The government by this time was headed by Atal Behari Vajpayee of the BJP and the Congress (I) was in no way able to influence its decisions. While the case was pending for trial in the special court, Quattrocchi successfully fought a legal battle against being extradited to India, from Malaysia. The CBI, through the Crown Prosecution Service in London, managed to have Quattrocchi's account in the London branch of the BSI-AG Bank (another Swiss bank) frozen. This action was upheld by a three-member bench of the High Court in London. All this happened in 2003, a year before the Congress returned to power. The CBI was doing its job; but not for long. After the Congress returned to power, the CBI failed to pursue the case against the Hindujas in the same manner; the Delhi High Court dismissed the case on grounds that the papers presented by the investigating agency were not authenticated by the Swiss authorities. The agency could have gone on appeal after rectifying the technical shortcoming. It did not. The Congress (I) was back in power by now. Then, the Union Law Minister H. R. Bhardwaj sent an officer to London where he met with officials of the Crown Prosecution Service and asked them to do everything to let Ottavio Quattrocchi operate his account in the BSI-AG bank. And in April 2009, the Red Corner notice by the Interpol against Quattrocchi, obtained by the CBI earlier, was withdrawn by the Government of India.

Bofors would not be such a scandal were it to happen a decade later. There were scandals, involving sums several times more than Bofors, in India during the 1990s. However, when it happened, Bofors was a scandal that nobody had imagined could happen. In December 1985, some 15 months before the scandal broke, Rajiv was 'Mr Clean'; he had promised to cleanse the political stable, including his own party, of the corrupt elements and the power brokers. By December 1987, his government was seen pulling all the stops to cover up a scandal involving purchases for the army. Among the suspects was Ottavio Quattrocchi, a friend of his family. There was a sense of outrage.

The scandal knocked the bottom of the government's credibility. All this happened when the Congress (I) was confronted by dissidence across its units and the opposition parties rallying behind a former Congress (I) loyalist, V. P. Singh. Moreover, the Rajiv Gandhi era was also marked by a substantial dilution of the commitment of Congress (I) to the idea of secularism. The orchestration by Rajiv Gandhi's government of the Ayodhya controversy, beginning with a Faizabad District Court order on 1 February 1986, and the Muslim Women (Protection of Rights on Divorce) Act, 1986, were the two prominent markers of this dilution.

Ayodhya and Shah Bano

Late in the evening on Saturday, 1 February 1986, Judge Krishna Mohan Pandey of the Faizabad District Court read out an order on a petition by Umesh Pande, a practising lawyer, seeking unrestricted rights for him and others to offer prayers and worship the idol inside the Babri Masjid. The petition before the district court was a sequel to advocate Pande's plea before a Munsiff Court in Faizabad, on 23 January 1986, that the court allow unrestricted worship at the Ram Janmabhoomi whose gates were locked at that time. The Munsiff Court did not pass any order on grounds that the leading suit to this case was still pending before the Allahabad High Court. Advocate Pande then went on appeal before the Faizabad District Court on 31 January 1986 and District Judge K. M. Pande ordered unrestricted rights for the petitioner and others to worship at the Babri Masjid. It is important to stress here that devotees were allowed to enter the compound, and up to an enclosure of grills, even earlier. There were two gates fixed to the grills and one of them, gate 'O', was open for the priests to enter and conduct *puja*. The other gate remained locked since January 1951. The petition before the district judge was that this restriction be removed. Judge Pandey, after examining district magistrate, I. K. Pande and district police chief, Karam Veer Singh, read out his order.

- It is clear that the members of the community, namely Muslims, are not going to be affected, by any stretch of imagination, if the locks of the gates 'O' and 'P' are opened and the idols inside the premises are allowed to be seen and worshipped by the pilgrims and devotees. It is undisputed that the premises is presently in the court's possession and Hindus have an unrestricted right of worship as a result of the court's order of 1950 and 1951.
- If the Hindus are offering prayers and worshiping the idols, though in a restricted way, for the last 35 years, then the heavens are not going to fall if the locks of the gates 'O' and 'P' are removed. The District Magistrate has stated before me today that the members of the Muslim community are not allowed to offer any prayer at the disputed site. They are not allowed to go there. If this is the state of affairs, then there is no occasion for any law and order problem arising as a result of the removal of locks.

The district judge's order will have to be seen in a context and this will require a short recall of the facts of the case between 23–24 December 1949 (when the idols were installed on the premises) and 1 February 1986, the day on which Judge Pandey passed the order. On 19 January 1950, the Faizabad district civil judge had issued an order, restraining the state administration and Muslim individuals, from removing the idols from the disputed site and from interfering with the *puja* that was being carried out since 24 December 1949. This order was confirmed by the Allahabad High Court. There were various other civil suits lying before the various courts across Uttar Pradesh even earlier, apart from the conflict of opinions as to whether the Babri Masjid stood on a site where a temple stood before 1528, the year Babur's officer, Mir Baqi, annexed the region from the former rulers.

As for the 19 January 1950 order, the issue was merely about the status of the idols on the premises and the right of the Hindus to worship there. As the order provoked communal conflicts, the district administration declared the premises as a disputed property and also declared any assembly of men there as unlawful. This declaration was made under Section 145 of the IPC. That brought the situation under control and the premises were locked up by the administration to ensure the safety of the idol inside. The 31 January 1986 plea by advocate Pande before district judge, K. M. Pandey was to have the locks removed and Judge Pandey, with ample cooperation coming from district magistrate I. K. Pande and police chief Karam Veer Singh, ordered that the locks be opened.

City magistrate, Sabhajit Shukla, on whom the order was served, did not wait for a moment. Within a few minutes, Shukla rushed to the premises and hammered open the locks at gate 'P' to let in the flow of devotees. That no one waited to think of an appeal against the district judge's order was significant. This clearly established that all the developments during the 48 hours between 31 January 1986 (when advocate Pande approached the district judge with his plea) and 1 February 1986 (when judge Pandey issued his order) had followed a script. The Congress (I) government in Uttar Pradesh, headed at that time by Vir Bahadur Singh, had instructed the concerned civil servants (district magistrate I. K. Pande and police chief Karam Veer Singh), to convince district judge, K. M. Pandey, that the locks could be opened. City magistrate Sabhajit Shukla too was under instruction to implement the judge's order without losing time. Vir Bahadur Singh did that because he had the instructions to do so from the Congress (I) high command.

In other words, the developments in the Faizabad District Court and the turn of events in the couple of days were influenced by a new political strategy that the Congress (I) was formulating at that time. We have seen that the Congress (I) had begun to lose power in the southern states beginning with the defeat of the party in Andhra Pradesh and Karnataka in the January 1983 elections to the two state assemblies. The significance of these was not lost on the Congress (I) managers. These two southern states from where the Congress party managed to retain popular support even in 1977 (67 out of the154 Congress MPs in the sixth Lok Sabha were from these two states), were now with the opposition parties. The Congress (I) had been reduced to a marginal player in Tamil Nadu for over a decade now; the party could not wrest power in the state after its defeat in 1967 and could stay relevant, only by way of alliances either with the AIADMK (in 1977 and 1984) or with the DMK (in 1980). In Kerala, the Congress (I) was now dependent on a whole lot of sub-regional groups such as the Kerala Congress and the Muslim League to win elections. In this scenario, the party's managers, consisting of Arun Nehru, M. L. Fotedar and Vishwajit Prithvijit Singh (whose love for the computers was extensively publicised), began working on a new strategy for the Congress (I).

The critical input for this came from a peculiar reading of the experience from Assam. The results of the December 1985 assembly elections from Assam led them to believe that an electoral victory was possible without having the support of the Muslims. The new thinking of the new strategists was based on two considerations. One, that the Congress (I) evolved a strategy to entrench itself in the Hindi-speaking parts of the country; this was based on an understanding that the Congress (I) was in no position to reverse the rising tide of regional parties such as the TDP, the AGP, the Akali Dal, the National Conference, the

DMK or the ADMK. Two, that the old social alliance of the upper castes, the scheduled castes and the Muslims that sustained the party in the Hindi-speaking region was now cracking up; it was necessary to reinvent the party with a different social alliance. The experience from Assam, where the AGP could sweep the polls despite its anti-Muslim stance, seemed to impress Rajiv Gandhi's computer boys. Towards this end, the Rajiv Gandhi dispensation orchestrated the 1 February 1986 order by the district judge, K. M. Pandey.

All this will have to be seen in a larger context of the campaign by the VHP on this issue as has been discussed in the previous chapter. The Virat Hindu Sammelan on 18 October 1981 followed by the *Ekatmata Yatra* between 15 November and 15 December 1983 in which the dominant theme of the slogans, billboards and the speeches delivered were anti-Muslim, clearly revealed that aggressive Hinduism had become the dominant political discourse across the country. The anti-Muslim violence in many towns in northern India as well as such places in the south as Hyderabad was merely the manifestation of this. The VHP was not alone in this. It was guided, no doubt, by the RSS. In fact, aggressive Hinduism had by this time become a core element in Indira Gandhi's scheme too. The religio-political dimension of the crises in Punjab and Kashmir and the fact that a section of the Muslim community had stuck with the Janata (Secular) in the 1980 elections guided her. The idea was to grab the Jan Sangh's social constituency. Her frequent reference to 'war clouds on the western frontier' was clearly a part of this new political strategy. Ayodhya did not figure anywhere in the political discourse until the VHP raised it at a *Dharm Sansad* (Parliament of Faith) at the Vigyan Bhawan on 7–8 April 1984. Similarly the Congress (I) government in Uttar Pradesh, headed by Sripat Mishra, began to develop parks and such projects at the Ramayana sites, which included Rama's route to Lanka, renovation of the *ghats* on the banks of Saryu in Ayodhya, construction of a *parikrama* route around Ayodhya and a Ramayana Study Centre in the town.

After the *Ram-Janaki rath yatras*, starting from Bihar on 25 September 1984 and reaching Ayodhya on 6 October 1984, there was a lull in the VHP's activities. The reason was the assassination of Indira Gandhi on 31 October 1984 and the elections to the Lok Sabha in December that year. The Ayodhya campaign, in fact, seemed to have lost its steam during 1985 barring some localised activities by the Ram Janmabhoomi Mukti Yagna Samiti, a collective of saffron-clad *sants* from various *akharas* in Ayodhya, sponsored by the VHP. Ram Chandra Das, head priest of the *Digambar Akhara* issued a threat to immolate himself if the locks at the Babri Masjid were not unlocked by 9 March 1986. The significance of the date was that it happened to be *Shivaratri*. The demand by the *mahant* was made on the basis of the 'fact' presented by a VHP team consisting of its president S. N. Katju, former chief of the Uttar Pradesh Police, S. C. Dixit and some others, in December 1986, that there was no official order on any of the records to justify the locking up of the premises. The contention was that there was no sanction—judicial or administrative—to keep the premises locked. The Uttar Pradesh Chief Minister Vir Bahadur Singh was aware of this. The events that unfolded on 31 January and 1 February 1986 were a sequel to this 'realisation' by the VHP as well as the Congress (I) governments in Uttar Pradesh and in Delhi.

The developments in the Faizabad District Court on 1 February 1986, hence, could have been anticipated by the political leadership and necessary measures could have been taken. This, however, was not to be. The opening of the locks, late in the evening on 1 February 1986, provoked two things. While the VHP and its associates organised celebrations across Uttar Pradesh, the Muslim community reacted to the events by organising *bandhs* in towns where they were present in significant numbers.

A pan-Muslim body called the Babri Masjid Movement Coordination Committee (BMMCC) was set up and the committee took the issue to the Allahabad High Court seeking a directive that the status quo that prevailed before 1 February 1986 be restored. This was also the time when the Muslim community was being prompted, by the clergy, to agitate against another judgement in another court. That was about the right of a divorced Muslim woman to seek maintenance from her former husband. The case came to be known as the Shah Bano case.

Shah Bano, daughter of a head constable, was married at the age of 16 to her cousin, Muhammad Ahmad Khan. By the time the couple settled in Indore, where Khan established his legal practice, Shah Bano had borne him three children. After 43 years of conjugal life and two more children, Khan threw Shah Bano out of his house and took a second wife. Shah Bano was 70 years old at that time. For two years he paid her Rs 200 per month as maintenance and stopped thereafter though his income at that time was reputed to be in excess of Rs 5,000 per month. In 1978, Shah Bano sought relief in a local court under Section 125 of the Code of Criminal Procedure, 1973. The CrPC, under Section 125, dealt with the legal measures for prevention of vagrancy and destitution and the court was enabled to order a maintenance upto Rs 500 per month. The case was still pending when Khan divorced Shah Bano, in the unilateral fashion available to him under Muslim Personal Law, depositing with the court Rs 3,000 that he owed her as *mehr*. He then claimed that he was no longer obliged to pay her anything. The magistrate, however, ruled that Khan should pay Shah Bano Rs 25 per month; this was enhanced to Rs 179.20 by the Madhya Pradesh High Court where she went on appeal. Khan, however, preferred an appeal before the Supreme Court and here his claim was that the *Shariat* prescribed him to pay Shah Bano her maintenance only during the period designated as *iddat* (three months) and that was already paid by him.

Shah Bano was represented by Daniel Latiffi, an eminent lawyer, in the

Supreme Court. The case was heard by a five-member bench consisting of Chief Justice Y. V. Chandrachud and Justices O. Chinnappa Reddy, E. S. Venkatramaiah, Ranganath Mishra and D. A. Desai. The bench, in a momentous judgement, on 23 April 1985, ruled that regardless of any consideration of the religion of the parties involved, Section 125 of the CrPC required a former husband to provide for his divorced wife if she had no means of supporting herself. The judgement was indeed one that marked a significant step towards social transformation and establishing the rights of the Muslim women. Notwithstanding the specific provisions in the Constitution (included among the fundamental rights) to assure the right to the minority communities of their religious and cultural freedom, the court's verdict, that Section 125 of the CrPC was common to all the citizens, was indeed a step towards abolishing social differentiation and in tune with Article 44 of the Constitution. In other words, it was in tune with the objective to ensure a common civil code that was enshrined as one of the Directive Principles of State Policy. As it is the case, the Supreme Court judgement, had the force of law now.

This was not to be. A storm broke out and barring a small number of committed individuals and organisations, all major Muslim outfits and 'leaders' of the community came out to protest against the ruling. There were protest meetings everywhere and uproar in Parliament where several Muslim MPs demanded that the law is amended to annul the Supreme Court verdict. Rajiv Gandhi, at first, stood by the Supreme Court ruling and Arif Muhammad Khan, an important member of his Cabinet, defended the apex court verdict in the Lok Sabha. The occasion was a debate on a private member's bill moved by the Muslim League MP, G. M. Banatwala to annul the effect of the apex court's judgement on the law. But as the protest became more vociferous, Rajiv Gandhi did a volte-face, and pushed his minister of state for forests and environment, Zia-ur-Rahman Ansari, to speak up for the amendment. The immediate context to this volte-face was evident from the time it happened. The events of 1 February 1986 in Faizabad were indeed the cause for this; the bill was introduced in the Lok Sabha on 23 February 1986 and Arif Mohammad Khan resigned from the Union Cabinet. In May 1986, the government got the Muslim Women (Protection of Rights on Divorce) Bill passed by both the houses of Parliament, to deny Muslim women the right of obtaining relief under Section 125 of CrPC. The apex court's judgement on the Shah Bano case now stood annuled. Arif Mohammed Khan claims to have the evidence that the bill was the fallout of a deal between Rajiv Gandhi and Maulana Ali Mian, a Lucknow-based theologian.

The Muslim Women (Protection of Rights on Divorce) Act, 1986 provided the following remedies to the divorced women:

> A Muslim divorced woman shall be entitled to a reasonable and fair provision and maintenance within the period of *Iddat* by her former husband and in case she maintains the children born to her before or after her divorce, such

> reasonable provision and maintenance would be extended to a period of two years from the dates of birth of the children. She will also be entitled to *Mehr* or *Dower* and all the properties given to her by her relatives, friends, husband and the husband's relatives. If the above benefits are not given to her at the time of divorce, she is entitled to apply to the magistrate for an order directing her former husband to provide for such maintenance, the payment of *Mehr* or *Dower* or the delivery of properties.
>
> Where a Muslim divorced woman is unable to maintain herself after the period of *Iddat*, the magistrate is empowered to make an order for the payment of maintenance by her relatives, who will be entitled to inherit her property on her death ... If anyone of such relatives is unable to pay his or her share on the grounds of his or her not having the means to pay, ... the magistrate would order the State Wakf Board to pay the maintenance ordered by him or the shares of the relatives who are unable to pay.

The fact that Rajiv Gandhi—who had spoken of his commitment to prepare the nation to march into the 21st century—and his computer boys could think that the State Wakf Boards are entrusted with ensuring maintenance to the divorced Muslim women, betrayed their total ignorance of the reality as well as perception of progress. The Wakf Boards were known to be in shambles both financially and otherwise. In any case, the Wakf Boards approximated the community's treasury (*baitul maal*) and the Muslim law placed on them the responsibility to take care of the destitutes. In other words, the boards were obliged by Islamic tenets to ensure maintenance to the destitute women even otherwise. The fact is that the traditional arrangements did not work in the modern context and that was why Shah Bano had to take recourse to remedies under Section 125 of the CrPC. Rajiv Gandhi, however, thought otherwise because he was advised that pandering to the demand by the fundamentalist fringe of the community would help the Congress (I) tide over the crisis triggered by the opening of the locks in Ayodhya.

Rajiv Gandhi's party persisted with its new strategy to reinvent itself as a representative of the Hindu majoritarian agenda. The second important date in the Ayodhya saga is 9 November 1989. The VHP, all the while, was engaged in mobilising the saffron-clad *sadhus* to push for the construction of a temple at the site where the Babri Masjid stood while the BMMCC, now under Syed Shahabuddin, a former Foreign Service officer and a Janata Party MP (he won a by-election from the Kishenganj Lok Sabha constituency in Bihar in December 1985 and emerged as a spokeman for the fundamentalist fringe in the community in the political arena) went about whipping up passions among the Muslims and the campaign to reclaim the structure. The dispute triggered communal violence across Uttar Pradesh and Bihar. It peaked on 18 May 1987 when communal violence marred Meerut. Media reports revealed the active involvement of the Provincial Armed Constabulary in the violence, this time too, against the Muslims in the city and it went on for 10 days. There was violence against the Muslim community in Delhi too around this time.

The VHP campaign, by now, had acquired a great deal of momentum while Rajiv Gandhi's Congress (I) was working on the new strategy. An important element of this was the use of television. Television in India did not go beyond Delhi until the 1970s. Even when it expanded, it remained an exclusive privilege of those with means in the state capitals. It was in 1982 when the ninth Asian Games were held in Delhi, that the government decided to take TV to cities outside Delhi. That was also the year when colour TVs were allowed to be imported. Thereafter, the government invested heavily in setting up transmitters across the country; the number increased from 39 in 1982 to 140 in 1985. This ensured that as much as 70 per cent of the population was now under the coverage area. All this while, Doordarshan enjoyed its monopoly. The government also liberalised import of TV sets and colour-picture tubes and, thus, ensured that Doordarshan reached a large part of the people.

Apart from news, which had turned into a vehicle for propaganda for the Congress (I), Doordarshan depended on serials that helped the broadcaster earn revenues from commercial sponsors. *Hum Log* and *Buniyaad* were two such experiments that left a lasting impression and also served as a business model. Then came the *Ramayana*. Ramanand Sagar's *Ramayana*, based on *Ramcharitmanas* by Tulsidas (and ignoring the traditions of many other *Ramayanas*), ran into 78 episodes. The decision to show this was certainly guided by the Congress (I)'s quest to reinvent itself as the defender of the Hindu majoritarian agenda. The telecast began on 25 January 1987 and lasted till 31 July 1988. Over 60 million people watched it, Sunday after Sunday. Many would bathe before the serial began at 9.30 in the morning and even burn incense sticks in front of their TV sets. *Ramayana* fetched Doordarshan over Rs 9 crore in advertising revenue alone. Thereafter, B. R. Chopra too got into the act and came up with the *Mahabharata* that ran 94 episodes through 1988 and 1990.

The effect of telecasting *Ramayana* on Doordarshan was tremendous. The image of Rama with trident, bow and arrow had become a part of the people's memory and along with it that of a militarist Hindu deity. The perception of Rama, abstract in the minds of a cross-section of people in India, was now concretised in the national psyche. This imagery and the VHP's campaign with the *Ram Janmabhoomi* in the focus, together, ensured Ayodhya becoming a part of the political consciousness. In other words, the VHP's campaign could now be taken to different states and not merely restricted to Uttar Pradesh. This was also the time when the RSS decided to associate itself openly with the campaign and through the celebration of K. B. Hedgewar's centenary.

It is important to note here that the BJP, all this while, was not involved with the campaign in the organisational sense of the term. This notwithstanding, the fact is that the VHP and the Bajrang Dal (another RSS outfit) were engaged, in a concerted manner, to blend Ayodhya into a politico-religious campaign. The high point of this strategy came in January 1989 at the *kumbh mela* in Allahabad. A *Dharm Sansad* there announced that the foundation stone for the Ram Janmabhoomi Temple will be laid in the precincts of the Babri Masjid complex on 9 November 1989. A six-member committee was set up with a specific brief; to advance the date of the *shilanyas* in the event the dates for the general election were advanced. It was clear that the campaign had more to do with the quest for political power than devotion. This was clarified, sufficiently well, in the resolutions from the *sant sammelans* in Haridwar (27–28 May 1989) and Ayodhya (13 July 1989): 'Every political party will have to show deference to Hindu sentiments if they want their electoral support'.

The business of involving the saffron-clad *sadhus* in a political game was not restricted to the VHP–Bajrang Dal combine. A *sant sammelan* was held at Chitrakoot in Madhya Pradesh on 3 June 1989. Presided over by Swami Swaroopanand, Shankaracharya of the Dwarka *math*, all the arrangements for the show were made by the Madhya Pradesh state government. Motilal Vora was the chief minister of the state at that time. A new outfit—Sri Ram Janmabhoomi Uddhar Samiti—sprung up at this time and Madan Mohan Gupta, whose association with the Congress (I) was fairly known, happened to be its convenor. The Chitrakoot convention was facilitated by transport organised by the state government to ferry a whole lot of saffron-clad *sants*. The resolutions passed at the convention bared the intentions. One of it praised Rajiv Gandhi for having taken steps to cleanse the Ganga. Another called for resolution of the dispute either through talks between the Hindus and the Muslims (that were being carried out by the Union Home Minister Buta Singh) or through the judicial process. The convention also demanded that the cow be declared the national animal and learning Sanskrit be made compulsory in schools.

On 21 June 1989, N. D. Tiwari, now chief minister of Uttar Pradesh, announced construction of a *Ram Katha* park in Ayodhya at the cost of Rs 15 crore. Tiwari made this announcement while inaugurating the *Ram-ki-pauri* at Ayodhya, constructed at the cost of Rs 8.5 crore. This was one of the projects initiated by Sripat Mishra when he was the chief minister. The Rajiv Gandhi government was playing up the religious card as early as June 1989; there was ample evidence to the cynical games that the Congress (I) was determined to play. In fact, 9 November 1989 was not too far away and communal violence had now become a regular feature across Uttar Pradesh and also in other parts of the country. The Congress (I) managers remained unfazed.

It was in this context that the BJP too resolved to join the Ram Janmabhoomi campaign. In its national executive session in June 1989 at Palampur (in Himachal Pradesh), the party resolved to join the VHP's campaign to liberate the Ramjanabhoomi. The Palampur resolution read: 'The sentiments of the people must be respected and Ram Janmasthan handed over to the Hindus—if possible through a negotiated settlement, or else by legislation. Litigation certainly is no answer'. The importance of this resolution and the fact that the BJP jumped into the campaign only as late as in June 1989 is not to say that the party was innocent until then. The BJP had taken up an aggressive Hindutva position since its plenary session at Delhi on 9–11May 1986. That was when L. K. Advani replaced Atal Behari Vajpayee as party president. And, unlike in the past, Vajpayee came out forthright, in his address that he was proud to have been in the RSS. He said: 'If the RSS which had been in the forefront of all democratic struggles could be called fascist, then I am proud to be called a fascist'. But then, the fact that there was no mention, whatsoever, of the dispute in Ayodhya in the party's plenary, held only a few months after the Faizabad District court's order on 1 February 1986, was significant. It is a different matter that Ayodhya became BJP's identity in a few years and that the party achieved a lot by that. This will be discussed in the next chapter.

The Ayodhya dispute, meanwhile, was now before the Lucknow Bench of the Allahabad High Court. In July 1989, Deoki Nandan Aggarwal, a former judge of the Allahabad High Court and now the VHP vice-president, filed a petition before the Faizabad District Judge. The petition was filed on behalf of *Ram Lalla*! There were two other title suits pending before the Lucknow Bench of the Allahabad High Court at that time. Mohammed Hashim Ansari had filed a suit before the High Court on 3 February 1989 and another by the Sunni Wakf Board; both the suits pleaded settlement of the dispute over the title to the land where the Babri Masjid stood and the land adjacent to it. These were civil disputes and any resolution had to be on the basis of land records of the revenue department. The Uttar Pradesh government simply ensured that the cases were delayed.

Aggarwal's plea, seeking a perpetual injunction against anyone interfering with or placing objection to the construction of a new temple building after demolishing the existing buildings and structures, was admitted by the Faizabad District Judge. That was when the state government pushed its plea before the High Court that all the suits pending before the various courts be transferred to a Special Bench of the High Court. On 14 August 1989, the High Court ordered transfer of all the pending cases regarding the title to the properties in and around the Babri Masjid. The High Court also ordered that status quo be maintained insofar as the disputed properties were concerned. This interim order of 14 August 1989 was interpreted by the Congress (I) governments in

Delhi and Lucknow to mean that construction activities would be permitted outside the disputed land. They treated this as an order permitting the *shilanyas* (laying the foundation stone), announced by the VHP, on 9 November 1989. The site chosen by the VHP happened to be a six-hectare plot adjacent to the Babri Masjid. This land belonged to one Dharam Das and he had donated it to the *Ram Janmabhoomi* Trust.

The game plan was clear. To let the VHP go ahead with its plans even if that meant a convoluted defiance of a High Court order that status quo be maintained in the land that was under dispute. The VHP, by now, had taken the Ayodhya campaign to remote villages across the country. The strategy towards this end was laid out by the RSS and it involved carrying bricks with '*Sri Ram*' inscribed on them into the remote parts of the country, holding *yagnas* there, and also raising, through individual donations, a sum of Rs 25 crore. The RSS had set out to collect Rs 1.25 from each household as a contribution towards the construction of a temple. The 6000 bricks, made to order, were carried in *raths* to remote villages and the VHP had also printed posters of a grand temple that it planned to construct in Ayodhya.

The *shila yatras* that began on 30 September 1989, in which the bricks were taken around the villages across the country, were to reach Ayodhya before 9 November 1989. And as they traversed across the towns, they left a trail of anti-Muslim violence in Meerut, Moradabad, Aligarh, Bhagalpur, Bhiwandi and Hyderabad.

Meanwhile, the term of the eighth Lok Sabha was to expire on 14 January 1980. The Constitution warranted 37 days between the Election Commission announcing the schedule—seven days of alert and 30 days between the formal notification—and the date of polling. The Rajiv Gandhi Cabinet met on 17 October 1989, resolved to recommend dissolution of the Lok Sabha and ask the Election Commission to announce the poll schedule. President R. Venkatraman took only a few minutes to convey the Cabinet resolution to the Election Commission.

The Commission announced the schedule and polling was to be held between 22 and 26 November 1989. The clinching evidence that the Congress (I) was desperate and determined to use the Hindu majoritarian agenda as its campaign plank was the occasion of the launch of the party's poll campaign. Rajiv Gandhi inaugurated the party's election campaign from a public meeting in Ayodhya on 3 November 1989 and promised that his party, if elected again, will usher in *Ram Rajya*. The context, the venue and the timing betrayed all attempts to present this promise as being the same as Mahatma Gandhi's *Ram Rajya*.

The next important date in the Ayodhya story was 9 November 1989. Rajiv Gandhi allowed the assorted *sants* and *sadhus*, mobilised by the VHP, to perform *shilanyas* for the Ram temple on the disputed land that was dubiously declared, by the Uttar Pradesh government, as undisputed. Union Home

Minister Buta Singh was sent to Ayodhya and the *shilanyas* took place under his 'supervision'. Another round of communal violence followed the *shilanyas* and this clearly vitiated the atmosphere during the general election. The Ayodhya controversy, causing the death of several hundred people and destruction of property and finally the demolition of the Babri Masjid on 6 December 1992 and the political changes in that context were all the outcome of this strategy. It is another matter that this new strategy, intended to reinvent the Congress (I), ensured the fall of the party and its decimation in most parts of the Hindi-speaking region.

Meanwhile, it will be appropriate to quote excerpts from L. K. Advani's deposition before the Justice Liberhan Commission of Enquiry (set up after the Babri Masjid was demolished on 6 December 1992) to place the whole issue in context. Advani said:

- The BJP would not have thought of participating in the movement if the Shah Bano episode had not taken place, if the government had not actively facilitated the *shilanyas* and opening of Ram Janmabhoomi temple gates.
- The BJP joined the movement as it was another occasion for the party for strengthening nationalism in the country.
- From 1950 onwards, no one had ever thought of changing a decision of court through agitation. However, certain Muslim organisations found that the then government succumbed to their agitation against the Supreme Court judgement on the Shah Bano case and we did take into consideration all these things, in 1989, when we adopted a resolution on Ayodhya, urging the Rajiv Gandhi government to adopt a positive approach in respect of Ayodhya.
- It did surprise the BJP that most political parties seemed inclined to support the stand of the Babri Masjid Action Committee in consideration of their vote bank politics… When the ruling party was facilitating the construction of the temple for consideration of votes, we supported the Vishwa Hindu Parishad, *sadhus* and *sants* openly as there was a great resemblance between the Somnath temple movement and the Ayodhya temple movement.

The political scene involving the general election of November1989, however, was constituted by another aspect too. The BJP, no doubt gained significantly both in terms of the percentage of votes and the number of seats in the Lok Sabha and these gains were possible only because of its direct association with the Ayodhya campaign. But then, the victor in that election was the National Front, a pre-poll combine, consisting of several regional parties getting together with the Janata Dal, a party founded on the ruins of the Janata Party of 1977–79.

The National Front and the Janata Dal

We have seen that the Janata Party, the Lok Dal and the Bharatiya Janata Party had suffered severe reverses in the 1984 elections. Among the leading lights of the Janata Cabinet (1977–79), only five leaders managed to win the elections in December 1984. And, they now belonged to different parties: Jagjivan Ram (Congress-J), Charan Singh (Lok Dal), H. M. Patel, Madhu Dandavate and Biju Patnaik (all Janata). There was, however, another side to the story. The Lok Dal, even if it won just three seats, the party candidates had come second in 90 Lok Sabha seats; of these, 58 were from Uttar Pradesh and 16 from Bihar. Similarly, the Janata Party won just 10 seats. But its candidates had come second in 73 constituencies; 18 each from Karnataka and Orissa, 11 from Gujarat, nine from Maharashtra and eight from Bihar. Though the BJP won just two seats, its candidates had come second in 101 constituencies; 36 from Madhya Pradesh, 15 from Rajasthan, 12 from Maharashtra, nine from Gujarat and five from Delhi. This meant that the splinters of the Janata Party, of 1977, were very much there in the political discourse even if their presence in the eighth Lok Sabha was insignificant. They all emerged into significant forces in 1989 and ensured the defeat of the Congress (I) in the general election.

Meanwhile, the TDP with its base restricted to Andhra Pradesh, had emerged as the single largest opposition party in the eighth Lok Sabha. The party, in fact, had captured power in Andhra Pradesh earlier in January 1983. That was also the time when the Congress (I) had lost power to the Janata Party in Karnataka. These non-Congress chief ministers had organised conclaves to raise issues relating to the rights of the state governments vis-à-vis the Centre; these conclaves were also used by them (and in due course various opposition leaders) to discuss political alliances. The first of such meets of opposition chief ministers held in Bangalore on 20 March 1983, was convened by Ramakrishna Hegde. Thereafter, N. T. Rama Rao hosted a meeting of leaders from 14 opposition parties in Vijayawada on 28 May 1983. It is a different matter that the Vijayawada conclave did not lead to any substantial unity among the opposition parties.

After the elections, encouraged by the profile of his party in the national discourse, N. T. Rama Rao converted his party's annual meet (the TDP *Mahanadu*) into a national event. On 4 January 1986, a forum of opposition parties was formed at that meet in Hyderabad. The significance of this event was the profile of the leaders present on the stage. Apart from NTR, those present included Karnataka chief minister and Janata Party leader, Ramakrishna Hegde, Punjab chief minister and Akali Dal leader Surjit Singh Barnala, Dinesh Goswami (representing the AGP, now in power in Assam), Abdul Rashid Kabuli (from the Jammu and Kashmir National Conference), C. T. Dhandapani (from the DMK) and K. P. Unnikrishnan (Congress-S). The seeds were sown for a political platform consisting of the regional parties, now in power or in the reckoning, in various states, against the Congress (I) and the national parties joining the collective.

The objective basis for this was to be found in the state of affairs in the national parties. Even when the Congress (I) was caught in a round of internal battles (culminating in the expulsion of Pranab Mukherjee and the resignation of Arif Mohammed Khan), the national level parties were oblivious to the need for unity within their own parties. Unity between them was still a far cry.

For instance, the Janata Party, led by Chandra Shekhar, remained a divided house with its leaders refusing to shed their penchant to fight among themselves. A number of its senior leaders who left the party to join Charan Singh's Janata (Secular) in July 1979 had returned to the fold after the Jan Sangh elements formed the BJP in 1980. But they were all unrelenting when it came to indulging in internecine squabbles. This was evident at the National Executive of the Janata party in April 1986 at Parandwadi near Pune in Maharashtra. A debate between Pramila Dandavate and Syed Shahabuddin on the Shah Bano judgement and the government's moves to annul that, by way of a legislation, led to a showdown among the delegates. The re-election of Chandra Shekhar as party president was also marred by disputes. Swami Agnivesh, an activist known for his campaigns against child labour and other such issues, insisted on a contest and lost the election. The Janata Party, however, consisted of an array of leaders: Madhu Dandavate, Biju Patnaik, George Fernandes, Ravindra Verma, Jaipal Reddy, Ramakrishna Hegde, Subramanian Swamy, H. D. Deve Gowda and such others.

The Lok Dal was in no better shape. An ailing Charan Singh was now trying hard to install his son, Ajit Singh, as the party chief. Ajit Singh had stayed away from the political arena all his life and had returned from the US, where he was working as a computer engineer. Charan Singh's nomination of his son to the Rajya Sabha, soon after his return to India, was resented by the others in his party. They were also leaders who had carved out bases for themselves. H. N. Bahuguna, a veteran in politics for several years; Karpoori Thakur, an icon in the opposition political arena in Bihar; Devi Lal, a former Congressman and now a cult figure in Haryana; and Mulayam Singh Yadav, who had emerged as a strong leader with a strong socio-political constituency in Uttar Pradesh. All of them had reasons to feel that they were now being short-changed by Charan Singh. The first time the conflict came out in the open was in February 1987. On 9 February 1987, Mulayam Singh Yadav lost his position as the leader of the Opposition in the Uttar Pradesh assembly after 43 of the 83 Lok Dal MLAs turned against him. They were all Ajit Singh loyalists.

When Ajit Singh donned the mantle of party chief after Charan Singh's death on 29 May 1987, the Lok Dal underwent a split. While Ajit Singh headed the Lok Dal (Ajit), the others went ahead to form the Lok Dal (Bahuguna). The Charan Singh legacy was, thus, split between his son (who managed to hold on to the party's network and base in western Uttar Pradesh) and the Lok Dal (Bahuguna). The Lok Dal (B) turned into a confederation of party units run by individual leaders. Devi Lal donned the mantle in Haryana, Karpoori Thakur in Bihar and Mulayam Singh Yadav in the rest of Uttar Pradesh. Bahuguna, now the party's working president, was allowed to remain the leader as long as he did not meddle with the affairs of the different leaders in their own small fiefs. Karpoori Thakur's death, on 17 February 1988, left the Bihar faction of the Lok Dal (B) to be taken over by Lalu Prasad Yadav.

The BJP, meanwhile, was going through an existentialist crisis. The party couldn't decide if it wanted to hang on to the Jan Sangh legacy (as well as its attitude towards the RSS) or follow the programme it set out in 1980 that aimed at capturing the centrist political space. The party's plenary at Delhi between 9–11 May 1986, where L. K. Advani replaced Atal Behari Vajpayee as party president, seemed to suggest that the crisis had been resolved. Vajpayee did not mince words when he recalled his association with the RSS from his early days and that he had learnt his first lessons in patriotism at *shakha pathshalas*. Similarly, the thrust on such concepts like tradition and culture in the resolution on national integration, adopted at the session, conveyed a message. There was also the specific mention in the resolution as to what the party meant by Indian culture: that culture that kept India, as one over the ages, in spite of political squabbles and external invasions.

The BJP had, by now, come out clear on its determination to hold on to Jan Sangh's tradition.

Advani further clarified at the session that the link between the BJP and the RSS was historical if not organisational. All this pointed to a definite strategic shift insofar as the BJP was concerned and particularly so in the context of the events in Faizabad on 1 February 1986 and the developments leading up to the party's national executive meeting in Palampur in June 1989. The Delhi plenary of the BJP, in May 1986, was indeed significant. But then, the party's organisation was not vast enough at that time. Advani himself declared that at the plenary: 'The BJP may not yet have a nationwide political set-up to offer as an alternative to the ruling party, but it certainly has an alternative political culture to offer'.

Jagjivan Ram, another important leader of the Janata Party, was now heading the Congress (J). His political clout had shrunk and he was the only one to be elected from his party to the eighth Lok Sabha. He died on 6 July 1986 and his daughter, Meira Kumar, had joined the Congress (I) a year before his death, to become an MP from Bijnor in Uttar Pradesh. The Congress (J) too died with the leader.

The only opposition to the Congress (I), during 1986, came from the non-Congress (I) chief ministers and this movement was headed and inspired by NTR.

The TDP chief could mobilise the Punjab chief minister Surjit Singh Barnala and the Assam chief minister Prafulla Mahanta in this movement. Ramakrishna Hegde, though belonged to the Janata Party, was relevant in this movement only in his capacity as Karnataka chief minister. This was true of West Bengal chief minister Jyoti Basu too. The concerns at the meetings were the fiscal and the political rights of the state governments.

The round of state assembly elections in 1987—Kerala and West Bengal in February and Haryana in June that year—as well as the trouble inside the Congress involving V. P. Singh and the Bofors disclosures set the stage for a political realignment. The first step in this direction was the formation of the Jan Morcha on 2 October 1987. V. P. Singh, now heading a group of expelled Congress (I) leaders—Arif Mohammed Khan, Arun Nehru, V. C. Shukla, Mufti Mohammed Sayeed, Ram Dhan and Satyapal Malik—decided to keep the Jan Morcha as a front rather than a political party. This was intended to ensure further dissidence from the Congress (I). The anti-defection law, passed in March 1985 (the tenth schedule of the Constitution), would cause disqualification from Parliament or the Legislative Assembly if an elected member left his party and joined another. The only way to evade the provisions was to muster one thirds of the strength of the Parliamentary Party to leave the fold or when the MP/MLA was expelled from the party.

V. P. Singh and his fellow rebels were convinced that such an exodus (at least 130 MPs) from the Congress (I) Parliamentary Party was too much to even dream. The Jan Morcha being a front and not a political party would ensure, in their scheme, that Congress (I) MPs could join them and yet save themselves from being disqualified from Parliament. V. P. Singh was expelled from the Congress (I) on 19 July 1987 and the Jan Morcha was given a formal shape on 2 October 1987. V. P. Singh then undertook a tour across Uttar Pradesh and the response was massive.

This, in turn, gave shape to a larger political alignment. On 9 January 1988, N. T. Rama Rao celebrated the fifth anniversary of the TDP government in the state by organising a public function at Hyderabad. Those who participated in the function were Surjit Singh Barnala (Akali Dal), V. C. Shukla and Arun Nehru (Jan Morcha), Ram Jethmalani and Vijayaraje Scindia (BJP) and H. N. Bahuguna and Devi Lal (Lok Dal [B]). This was followed by a similar celebration at Bangalore. Hegde's Janata Party Government too completed its fifth year in office on 10 January 1988. A rally followed by a public meeting, marking the occasion, was addressed by an array of leaders: V. P. Singh, Maneka Gandhi, H. N. Bahuguna, K. P. Unnikrishnan, Parkash Singh Badal and also the non-Congress (I) chief ministers like Devi Lal, Jyoti Basu, Rama Rao, Prafulla Mahanta and E. K. Nayanar.

The most important message that emerged from the Bangalore show was V. P. Singh's evolution as a rallying point for the opposition. Hegde, an important leader of the Janata Party, as well as Devi Lal, now the man with the largest clout in the Lok Dal (B), were part of this consolidation. This, however, was not to the liking of the Janata Party president, Chandra Shekhar. On 7 March 1988, Chandra Shekhar announced merger of the Janata Party with Ajit Singh's Lok Dal (A). This move by Chandra Shekhar and Ajit Singh was clearly intended to close the possibility of the Lok Dal (B) becoming a part of the united opposition. Ajit Singh was now anointed president of the Janata Party. The proposal for a merger of the opposition parties was mooted first in July 1987 and it was intended, at that time, to gather the two Lok Dals and the Janata under one unified party.

Meanwhile, unity moves were afoot everywhere in the opposition and on 29 May 1988, a conclave of opposition parties in Vijayawada witnessed the whole gamut of opposition leaders present to address a public meeting. There were representatives from 10 parties in the conclave. Ajit Singh, Hegde, Biju Patnaik (Janata Party), Devi Lal (Lok Dal [B]), Atal Behari Vajpayee (BJP), Ram Dhan (Jan Morcha), N. T. Rama Rao (TDP), Sarat Chandra Sinha and K. P. Unnikrishnan (Congress [S]), Brighu Phukan (AGP), Bhim Singh (Panthers Party), Pritish Chandra (SUCI) and J. K. Sharma (Manipur Peoples Party) attended the Vijayawada meet.

The next important event in the course of this was the by-elections to the seven Lok Sabha constituencies, including Allahabad. While almost all the opposition leaders were there campaigning for V. P. Singh (who had filed his nomination as an independent candidate), one of his close aides in the Jan Morcha, Arif Mohammed Khan, was deliberately kept out of the campaign. V. P. Singh himself ensured this in order to avoid ruffling the Muslim voters in Allahabad. Khan's identity remained that of one who left the Congress (I) in protest against the passage of the Muslim Women (Protection of Rights on Divorce) Act, 1986. With the clergy in favour of the act, Singh did not want his prospects to be marred by Khan's presence by his side in Allahabad. The Jan Morcha chief, meanwhile, did not mind having Syed Shahabuddin campaign for him in Allahabad. The Allahabad by-election was an instance that established V. P. Singh's willingness to practise politics as the art of the possible.

The high point of the Allahabad by-election campaign, however, was the foregrounding of the Bofors scandal in the political domain. The issue had by this time got entrenched into the national political discourse, thanks to the exposé in the media and the crude attempts by the Rajiv Gandhi government to cover up the scandal by way of denying the opposition demand for a prominent place in the Joint Parliamentary Committee (JPC). The opposition parties had stayed out of the JPC but were determined to ensure that all the dirty linen was washed in public. Devi Lal's role in the by-election campaign was conspicuous. The Haryana chief minister dispatched a volunteer force of 1,000 men to ensure that the Congress (I) did not rig the elections. The green brigade did make an impact in Allahabad and when the votes were counted, V. P. Singh emerged a clear winner. The Congress (I)'s Sunil Shastri (son of Lal Bahadur Shastri) was defeated decisively.

The monsoon session of Parliament soon after, when the JPC report on Bofors was placed, facilitated a grand unity of the opposition parties. It was now clear that the rallying point in this unity was V. P. Singh. On 26 July 1988, the opposition leaders announced the formation of the Samajwadi Janata Dal in Parliament and it consisted of the Jan Morcha, the Janata Party, the Lok Dal (B) and the Congress (S). A meeting of the front leaders, on 27 July 1988, resolved to set up a National Front. The decision was taken by V. P. Singh, N. T. Rama Rao, Devi Lal, Prafulla Mahanta, H. N. Bahuguna and Ajit Singh. In a sense, even those leaders who refused to see eye to eye, until about a month ago, were now willing to come on a common platform against the Congress (I). And V. P. Singh had become the rallying point for all of them.

This process then culminated in the formal launch of the National Front at a public rally on the Marina beach in Madras, on 17 September 1988. Unlike in the past, the leaders announced a concrete organisational structure of the National Front at the Marina meeting: N. T. Rama Rao as chairman and V. P. Singh as convenor. Among those present at the Marina meeting were V. P. Singh and Arun Nehru (Jan Morcha), Ajit Singh, Biju Patnaik and Subramanian Swamy (Janata), H. N. Bahuguna and Devi Lal (Lok Dal [B]), K. P. Unnikrishnan (Congress [S]), Prafulla Mahanta (AGP), M. Karunanidhi (DMK), N. T. Rama Rao (TDP) S. S. Barnala (Akali Dal) and trade union leader Datta Samant from Bombay. The significance of the exclusion of the BJP from this meet could not be lost. And similarly, the absence of Chandra Shekhar and Ramakrishna Hegde was conspicuous.

While the BJP not being invited to the Madras meet was a fallout of the categorical opposition to any such joint front with the party from the Left as well as sections in the Lok Dal (B), in the wake of the increasingly strident posture that the Ayodhya campaign was assuming in the northern Indian states, the absence of Ramakrishna Hegde, one who inspired the unity moves, had to do with the developments within the Janata Party. Hegde had to quit as Karnataka chief minister on 12 August 1988. The immediate cause for Hegde's exit was a news report that telephone lines of a host of political leaders, including that of H. D. Deve Gowda, were being tapped. That the telephone lines were tapped turned out to be a fact. But Hegde himself insisted that he was not involved in that. The episode turned murkier when it was known that the man who brought the issue up in the media was none other than Subramanian Swamy, an important member of the Janata Party then, against his own party colleague.

Hegde, however, managed to ensure that S. R. Bommai replaced him as chief minister and Deve Gowda, identified as Chandra Shekhar's point man in

Karnataka (and PWD minister in Hegde's Cabinet), was denied a place in the new Cabinet. Gowda would wean away Janata MLAs and bring about the fall of Bommai's government by April 1989. Bommai was dismissed on 21 April 1989 without being given a chance to show his majority support on the assembly floor. He challenged the governor's action in the Supreme Court, and a Constitution Bench, in 1994, declared the dismissal as unconstitutional and ruled the dismissal of chief ministers without giving them the chance to test their strength on the floor of the state assembly *ultra vires* of the Constitution. The S. R. Bommai and others vs Union of India case was a significant development in the constitutional history of India. The roots of that lay in the fall of the Bommai government caused by Deve Gowda's machinations. Gowda would join the Janata Dal in 1994 and even become prime minister in May 1996. Bommai ended up as minister for human resources development in Gowda's Cabinet and Hegde was expelled from the Janata Dal, the day after Gowda became the prime minister.

Coming back to the developments in the Janata Party in August 1988, Subramanian Swamy's battle against Hegde was waged on behalf of Chandra Shekhar. And, Chandra Shekhar's agenda was to prevent Hegde from emerging into a key player in the Janata Party. Hegde had, by this time, begun to endorse V. P. Singh as the rallying point of the united opposition. The 7 March 1988 merger of the Lok Dal (Ajit) into the Janata Party, and the crowning of Ajit Singh as Janata president, was also intended to check V. P. Singh's rise. Chandra Shekhar found this necessary after Devi Lal, now the most important leader of the Lok Dal (B), announced V. P. Singh as the leader of the united opposition and its prime ministerial candidate. Even if all these issues were settled and V. P. Singh ended up as the natural choice to lead the Janata Dal (when the party was founded on 11 October 1988) and as the prime minister on 2 December 1989, Chandra Shekhar waited for his moment to retaliate. In other words, the causes for the disintegration of the Janata Dal in October–November 1990 lay in the clashes that dogged the formation of the Janata Dal in August–October, 1988.

In 1977, the clash between the various opposition leaders was overwhelmed by the experience of the Emergency and this finally led them to unite against Indira's Congress. In 1988–89, the leaders were forced to reconcile their differences and even animosities by the overwhelming mood, across the country, against Rajiv Gandhi's Congress (I). The leaders were convinced that the Congress (I) will be voted out if they united and this immediate context led them to hasten the formation of the Janata Dal on 11 October 1988.

An example of this overwhelming urge to push the differences under the carpet was evident in the turn of events involving the top Janata leaders within days following 17 September 1988 (the day on which the National Front was formed). As many as 46 senior leaders of the Janata Party national executive requisitioned a meeting of the National Council and even specified that it be held in Bangalore. The issue they wanted to resolve was the 7 March 1988 merger of the Lok Dal (Ajit) into the Janata Party. Ajit Singh, now president of the party, refused to see any case in the requisition and instead convened a meeting of the Parliamentary Board on 22 September 1988. The requisitionists objected to this on grounds that the Parliamentary Board was not a duly constituted body. The fact was that Ajit Singh and Chandra Shekhar were in a minority in the National Council and the strategy of the requisitionists (predominantly Hegde loyalists) was to commit the party to a time-bound programme for wider unity, including with the Lok Dal (B) and the Jan Morcha, and thereafter ensure that V. P. Singh led the united party. A split appeared imminent. But both the camps reconciled soon after and on 22 September 1988, the leaders agreed to further unity and more significantly to the formation of a steering committee with V. P. Singh as chairman. They all agreed to hold the foundation conference of the new party on 11 October 1988 in Bangalore. The fact was that Chandra Shekhar was humbled by others in the Janata Party and Ajit Singh too decided to bury the hatchet.

The chosen day, 11 October 1988, happened to be Jayaprakash Narayan's birth anniversary. Between 22 September and 11 October 1988, the leaders moved fast and the turnout at the rally at the Palace Grounds in Bangalore on 11 October 1988 was massive. Hegde was the master of the show while Devi Lal, in his own inimitable style, announced, even before the convention, that all issues were settled and that V. P. Singh was the supreme leader of the Janata Dal. The new party was formed by the merger of the Janata, the Jan Morcha and the Lok Dal (B). The leaders also clarified that the Janata Dal would be a constituent of the National Front, born at the Marina grounds in Madras on 17 September 1988. The formality of electing V. P. Singh as the party's president was completed after Ramakrishna Hegde made a formal proposal at the rally and Devi Lal placed a turban on Singh's head. Ramakrishna Hegde was appointed vice-president of the party and Ajit Singh as secretary general. Apart from Singh, Devi Lal and Hegde, others present at the dias at the Bangalore rally included Chandra Shekhar, Ajit Singh, Madhu Dandavate, George Fernandes, Biju Patnaik, S. R. Bommai (all Janata), Mulayam SinghYadav, Lalu Prasad Yadav (Lok Dal [B]), Maneka Gandhi, Akbar Ahmed Dumpy (Sanjay Vichar Manch), V. C. Shukla, Arun Nehru, Arif Mohammed Khan, Sanjay Singh (Jan Morcha) and a host of others.

The resolution, announcing the birth of the Janata Dal, the statement of policies and programmes, its constitution, symbol and the flag was passed unanimously. The meet also fixed a one-month time table for the completion of the merger formalities in order to go to the Election Commission for recognition. The new party's flag was a slight variation of the Janata Party's flag and the Janata Dal proposed to have the Janata Party's symbol (a *kisan* carrying a plough on his shoulder) as its election symbol. This warranted a resolution by the Janata Party's National Council, endorsing the merger and changing its name as the Janata Dal.

There were some significant absentees too. The Lok Dal (B) president, H. N. Bahuguna was conspicuous by his absence. Bahuguna had his own problems with V. P. Singh (going back to the early 1970s inside the Congress when Singh led the campaign for his ouster at Sanjay Gandhi's behest); he also felt left out of the process when he was excluded from the steering committee (set up on 22 September 1988) that finalised the draft resolutions and details of the merger before the 11 October 1988 meet. Though without a mass base, Bahuguna did command some support in the Lok Dal (B) organisation and also the goodwill among the Muslim community, a constituency he had cultivated over the years. This had implications on the merger process and also on the new party's registration with the Election Commission. But then, Bahuguna died on 17 March 1989 and the Lok Dal (B) too was buried with him.

Likewise, Subramanian Swamy (Janata) did not attend the Bangalore meet. This would have an adverse impact on the Janata Dal's claim to the Janata Party's election symbol. Swamy did manage to ensure that the Dal's claim to the Janata Party's symbol was rejected by the Election Commission and kept the Janata Party alive. He would lend the symbol to the Samajwadi Janata Dal (that Chandra Shekhar, Devi Lal, Mulayam Singh, Deve Gowda and some others floated in November 1990 after they split the Janata Dal) in the 1991 general election. The Janata Party remains a registered-unrecognised party in the Election Commission's records and Swamy continues to remain its president even at the time of writing of this book. Swamy's objection led the Janata Dal to adopt the 'Wheel' as its symbol for the 1989 general election. It remained that way until 1992–93 when the Election Commission ordered freezing of the symbol in the wake of a dispute when two factions (Ajit Singh and S. R. Bommai) staked claim for it. The point is that the causes for several splits and the decimation of the Janata Dal, in less than a decade of its formation, lay in the context in which the united party was founded.

The leaders of the Congress (S), now a marginal force with a thin base in Kerala and Assam (after Sharad Pawar had walked out and joined the Congress [I] in December 1987), were also absent at the Bangalore rally. K. P. Unnikrishnan had offered to merge his party into the new party but decided to pull out of the exercise because he felt slighted at being excluded from the steering committee that finalised the draft resolution for the Bangalore show. This issue, however, was settled effortlessly but the party refused to merge into the Janata Dal and remained a distinct partner in the National Front at the time of the 1989 elections. Unnikrishnan won as an MP in 1989 and was included in the Cabinet by V. P. Singh.

The issue of organisational merger was far more complicated than those behind the trouble before the Bangalore meet. Both the Lok Dal and the Janata Party had their own organisational units at the state, district and village levels and those who ran these units had been involved in fighting against each other, at the local level, even while they were anti-Congress. That the Janata and the Lok Dal were not mere paper organisations was evident from the fact that the candidates of these two parties were placed second in the 1984 elections in a large number of constituencies. There was a direct link between this organisation and some of the national leaders. The working arrangement in these parties, where ideology and policies did not form part of the conscience of its cadre, rested a lot on the networks that each of the leaders had established and nurtured over the years. This was true of the Congress (I) too but there was the overwhelming presence of a supreme leader, who belonged to the Nehru dynasty, whose authority was beyond dispute.

The Janata Dal belonged to another league and there was no place in it for a supreme leader. At the bottom of this system is the party worker at the village level. He would maintain the contacts with the people and help convert them as votes for the party. And every one of these local leaders maintain a contact with different leaders at the district level and through that with one or another important leader of the party at the state level. This network ensured dispensing or receiving favours by way of small contracts or licences when the party wrested political power. In the absence of ideology or policies that bound them together, these networks were based on personal loyalty to the leader and this in turn helped the leaders too to be nominated as party candidates at the time of elections. The strength of this process is that the cadre sailed with the leader for all times. The weakness of this arrangement was that any attempt to integrate these distinct networks threw up problems. V. P. Singh as president of the Janata Dal, thus, had a difficult task ahead.

Similarly, notwithstanding the euphoria and the impression that the Janata Dal was a national alternative to the Congress (I), the fact was that the party was essentially a force in parts of the Hindi-speaking India, namely, Uttar Pradesh, Bihar and Haryana. The only other states where the party was a force were Karnataka and Orissa. In the three northern Indian states, the Janata Dal drew its strength from the fact that the party could now rest on a huge social base. With the merger of the Lok Dal and the Janata and the fact that a whole array of leaders from these two parties now constituting one party, the Janata Dal's social base—Yadav-Jat-Gujjar-Rajput—would ensure a clean sweep for the party. This, in turn, pushed various leaders to position themselves at the helm of the party and thus, ensure for themselves the prime place in a government that was most likely to be theirs. It was important for each one of them to ensure that the state units in Uttar Pradesh and Bihar were led by their loyalists.

V. P. Singh's strategy was to render the party's central leadership into an omnibus collective of almost all the leaders of the constituent parties. He announced a 140-member National Council with almost everyone who led the Lok Dal, Janata Party and the Jan Morcha, before these parties merged to form the Janata Dal. A seven-member Political Affairs Committee (PAC) and a Parliamentary Board were set up alongside the National Council. This was frowned upon by Chandra Shekhar; he was left out of the PAC even while being in the Parliamentary Board. Chandra Shekhar found Ajit Singh, whom he had propped up as Janata Party president in March 1988, now teaming up with V. P. Singh. This led him to team up with Devi Lal, whose animosity towards Ajit Singh was known; the Haryana leader had earlier walked out of the Lok Dal in protest against Ajit Singh's rise in the party.

Chandra Shekhar flexed his muscle and stayed away from a couple of meetings of the Janata Dal Parliamentary Board. The party president tried to make up by co-opting him into the PAC and also setting up a seven-member committee that was meant to look into the organisational issues at all levels, including the constitution of the party's leadership in various states. Of the seven members of this committee, Yashwant Sinha and Chimanbhai Patel were Chandra Shekhar loyalists; Sharad Yadav and O. P. Chautala were Devi Lal loyalists. With Chandra Shekhar and Devi Lal now belonging to the same camp, the seven-member committee turned into a means for the two leaders to hit at others. The three other members of the committee, Arif Mohammed Khan (Jan Morcha), Jaipal Reddy (Hegde loyalist) and Rashid Masood (Ajit Singh loyalist) were pushed to the margins.

The battle for space between the Devi Lal–Chandra Shekhar combine on the one side and the V. P. Singh–Ajit Singh duo (with Hegde loyalists supporting them) was now fought in the terrain of appointing party chiefs in Uttar Pradesh, Bihar, Madhya Pradesh and Rajasthan. Four of the members in the seven-member committee, entrusted with this task, happened to be Devi Lal–Chandra Shekar loyalists. With this, they ensured that Mulayam Singh Yadav was made the Uttar Pradesh Janata Dal chief and Raghunath Jha the Bihar Janata Dal chief. Jha had begun his political life in the Congress (I) and remained close to the Bihar Congress (I) chief Jaganath Mishra even after joining the Janata Dal. But then he was made the state party chief against the claims of Ram Sundar Das, who was supported by the Lok Dal (A), Socialist and Jan Morcha factions in the Bihar party. They all got together, subsequently, to replace Jha with Ram Sundar Das as Bihar Janata Dal chief in May 1989.

Similarly, when Mulayam Singh Yadav was made the party's Uttar Pradesh unit chief, it was resented by Ajit Singh who had wanted Ram Naresh Yadav, Janata Party chief minister in 1977 and a Lok Dal (A) man, as the state party chief. Mulayam Singh was a junior minister in Ram Naresh Yadav's Cabinet in 1977. It may be recalled that Ajit Singh had ensured Mulayam Singh's removal as the leader of the opposition in the UP assembly (in February 1987) and thus, laid the basis for the Lok Dal split in a few months. Similarly, Mulayam Singh and V. P. Singh had shared an antagonistic relationship since the early 1980s. As the leader of the oppostion in the UP assembly, when V. P. Singh was the chief minister, the two leaders had no love lost. If Mulayam Singh defied Bahuguna and attended the Janata Dal foundation rally in Bangalore on 11 October 1988, it was because he knew that his own political fortunes lay in the unified opposition rather than in a truncated Lok Dal (B). With his appointment as the Uttar Pradesh Janata Dal chief, Mulayam Singh teamed up with Sanjay Singh (who had left the Congress [I] after V. P. Singh's exit from the party and constituted the muscle for the Jan Morcha until its merger into the Janata Dal) and managed to establish himself as the supreme leader of the Janata Dal in Uttar Pradesh even while he was seen bending over backwards to make peace with Ajit Singh.

Ajit Singh resented that V. P. Singh did not throw his weight against Mulayam Singh at the Janata Dal Parliamentary Board meet on 19–20 February 1989. But the resentment did not build into an open confrontation. As for V. P. Singh, he was content with the appointment of V. C. Shukla as the Janata Dal chief in Madhya Pradesh. Shukla, it may be recalled, was one of Sanjay Gandhi's close aides during the Emergency and had left the Congress (I) only because he was upset over the rise of Arjun Singh, his old rival in Madhya Pradesh politics, in the Rajiv Gandhi establishment.

All this jostling, in fact, was taking place when the DMK, a constituent of the National Front, wrested power in Tamil Nadu. In the elections held to the state assembly in January 1989, the DMK won 146 seats in the 234-member house. The DMK's return to power in Tamil Nadu, after 12 years (it lost to the ADMK in March 1977) was, in fact, the outcome of a split in the ADMK—after M. G. Ramachandran's death—between MGR's widow Janaki Ramachandran and J. Jayalalitha. The Congress (I) walked out of the alliance it had with the ADMK and in a four-cornered contest, the DMK romped home to form its government. The point is that the DMK victory was more due to a division in the ADMK rather than any indication of the National Front's resurgence in Tamil Nadu. This was confirmed in the general election to the Lok Sabha in November 1989 when the ADMK–Congress (I) combine swept the polls winning all the 39 Lok Sabha seats from the state; and the DMK drew a blank.

The infighting that appeared to suggest that the Janata Dal was going to collapse was, however, disproved. All its leaders were clear, in their minds, that they shall not stretch their disputes to a breaking point. Veterans that they were in understanding the popular pulse, the leaders were aware of the fact that the Janata Dal was made up of a combination of social groups that can inflict a crushing defeat on the Congress (I). Even while they were seen fighting among themselves in the open, the leaders were also negotiating with the BJP behind the scenes while V. P. Singh and a few others were holding talks with the Left parties. The CPI (M) general secretary, E. M. S.Namboodiripad had declared, as early as in May–June 1989, that an understanding between the Janata Dal and the BJP shall not happen.

But then, in early June 1989, Devi Lal facilitated a preliminary discussion between the Janata Dal and the BJP. The talks were held at Surajkund, a tourist resort in Haryana, for two days. Devi Lal (authorised by the party to hold talks with potential allies) was accompanied by the Janata Dal secretary general Ajit Singh while the BJP was represented by Atal Behari Vajpayee and K. L. Sharma. There was some broad agreement at Surajkund on the number of seats that each party would contest from Gujarat and Haryana. As for other states, the leaders agreed to leave it to their state leaders to negotiate. That all this was taking place around the time when the BJP had resolved (in Palampur) to join the Ayodhya campaign, raised some concerns among sections of the intelligentsia that had joined the V. P. Singh bandwagon by now. It may be recalled that the BJP was kept out of the unity moves from the time when the National Front was thought of in July 1988. That was a clear break from the past.

Now, the talks were clearly for seat adjustments at the time of elections. The overwhelming concern for the leaders was to avoid division of the anti-Congress (I) votes. Achieving this was not a major problem in such states as Madhya Pradesh, Rajasthan, Himachal Pradesh and Delhi. These were the traditional strongholds of the Jan Sangh and the BJP had established itself as the pivotal force against the Congress (I) in these states. This was evident in the 1984 elections too. At least 60 of the 101 constituencies where the BJP came second in 1984 happened to be from these four states. None of the Janata Dal's constituents (the Lok Dal or the Janata) could claim any significant presence in these states. The Left parties too did not have any presence here. The Janata Dal leaders agreed to leave these states to the BJP and take whatever was offered to them. The Janata Dal contested 11 seats in Madhya Pradesh while the BJP did in 33 seats. In Rajasthan, the Dal fielded its candidates in 13 constituencies while the BJP did in 17. There were a few constituencies where the two parties contested against each other but these did not come in the way of a joint campaign elsewhere. In Delhi, the arrangement was perfect with the Janata Dal fielding two candidates and the BJP fielding five.

In Gujarat too the story was the same as in Delhi and Madhya Pradesh. In 1984, the Janata had come second in 11 constituencies and the BJP in nine. In 1989, the Janata Dal and the BJP arrived at a perfect understanding. The Dal fielded its candidates for 14 constituencies and the BJP in the remaining 12 Lok Sabha constituencies from the state. Significantly, the BJP won all the 12 seats it contested in 1989 from Gujarat while the Janata Dal won 11 out of the 14 it contested.

Insofar as Uttar Pradesh and Bihar were concerned, the objective basis was different. The Lok Dal was a strong force in these two states and its roots go back to the mid-1960s. The Lok Dal had come second in as many as 58 Lok Sabha constituencies from Uttar Pradesh and 16 constituencies from Bihar in 1984.

The Janata too had a presence here. The Lok Dal's social base, in these two states, was constituted by the Yadavs, the Jats and various other backward castes. The Janata Dal, with V. P. Singh at the helm, could now be rest assured of not only the traditional social groups but also the powerful Rajput community on its side. As for the BJP, it could claim some influence in the Jharkhand region of Bihar and a thin base across Uttar Pradesh. In 1984, the party had come second in just seven constituencies each from Bihar and Uttar Pradesh. The Ayodhya campaign, most intense in these two states, may have given the party some space to grow but there was very little in the air to suggest any surge in its support base in 1989. The two parties agreed to achieve as much as unity as was possible in these two states.

In the 1989 general election, the Janata Dal fielded candidates in 69 out of the 85 constituencies in Uttar Pradesh while the BJP fielded just 31. This arrangement ensured a combined opposition against the Congress (I) in over 75 Lok Sabha constituencies out of the 85 from Uttar Pradesh. In Bihar, the Janata Dal contested in 38 while the BJP fielded candidates in 24 constituencies. The fact is that the Janata Dal and the BJP had ensured against division of the anti-Congress votes in most Lok Sabha constituencies across the northern Indian States. V. P. Singh, the most important campaigner for the opposition, once again displayed his ability to balance conflicting interests and reducing politics to the art of the possible. One example of this was his message to his partymen to ensure that the BJP ranks did not carry their party's flag to elections meetings he addressed. He did this to assuage the Left parties who were categorical that the BJP must not be included in the National Front. But Singh did nothing to scuttle the concerted efforts by his partymen to strike adjustments with the BJP. He also ensured that the Janata Dal did not bargain hard in such states as Madhya Pradesh, Himachal Pradesh and Delhi, which were BJP citadels.

Thus, when elections were held on 22 and 24 September 1989, the National Front and the BJP had arrived at an understanding that ensured that the Congress (I) was confronted by a single opposition candidate in a majority of the constituencies. Coming back to the affairs of the Janata Dal, the fact was that most of the leaders who constituted the party's leadership had faded into the background after they were trounced in their own constituencies in 1984. But each one of them retained the loyalty of functionaries at various levels, and thus, commanded political clout, though not as strong as it used to be in the past. As the political mood began to swing, in the wake of charges of corruption at high levels and Rajiv Gandhi's authority in the Congress (I) beginning to be questioned, these leaders found the prospects to reinvent themselves. Then they began exploring the means through which their separate vote-gathering abilities could be deployed for the greater good of all. The emergence of V. P. Singh as a knight in shining armour (and the media playing a major role in building this up) gave them a sense of purpose and even an urgency to integrate their separate networks under one banner. The Janata Dal was the culmination of this process. And, in the National Front that included the various regional parties from across the country (TDP, DMK, AGP and the Akali Dal), the Dal emerged as the pivot.

Even while the leaders found the arrangement cumbersome and disputes arose over their claims to positions in the new party, the various moves by the Rajiv Gandhi government forced them to bury the hatchet and unite. The JPC report on the Bofors scandal tabled in Parliament in July 1988 (just a month after V. P. Singh's Allahabad by-election victory), ensured the coming together of the opposition parties. The next instance that united the opposition to the Congress (I) was when Rajiv Gandhi, in a show of desperation, introduced the Defamation Bill in August 1988. The law was a desperate attempt, by the regime, to gag the media. Introduced on 29 August 1988, the proposed law provided for summary trial of journalists and also debarred the judges from dispensing with personal appearances throughout the trial against journalists charged for defamation. The law also turned the established principle of criminal jurisprudence by rendering the onus of proving innocent on the accused. It was clear that the law was Rajiv Gandhi's response to the role of the media in exposing the Fairfax muddle, the HDW deal and the Bofors scam.

The media, as a whole, rose up in arms against the bill, already passed by the Lok Sabha where the Congress (I) had a huge majority. It was now before the Rajya Sabha. A rally at the Boat Club grounds on 5 September 1988 saw the opposition parties, the journalist fraternity, including the owners of various newspapers and the intelligentsia, marching together against the government. The media industry went on a day's strike on 6 September 1988; and on 22 September 1988 Rajiv Gandhi beat a hasty retreat to withdraw the bill.

Thereafter, the report of the Justice Thakkar Commission, which enquired into Indira Gandhi's assassination, was tabled in Parliament in March 1989. The opposition parties were united once again to corner Rajiv Gandhi, who had rehabilitated R. K. Dhawan (Indira's secretary at the time of her assassination), against whom the commision had made some incriminating remark. The unity this time was reinforced when all the opposition MPs were suspended from Parliament for a week after they raised a storm on the report.

The dismissal of Karnataka chief minister, S. R. Bommai in April 1989, without giving him the chance to prove his majority in the legislative assembly ended up uniting the leaders inside the Janata Dal and also the others. And then came the CAG report, pertaining to the Bofors deal, in July 1989 provoking the *en masse* resignation of the opposition members from the Lok Sabha.

All these, cumulatively, got the opposition parties to gather into a united entity. Within days after Rajiv Gandhi announced the decision to go to polls, the National Front leaders girded up their loins to put up a united face. On 20 October 1989, the National Front leaders released their manifesto at New

Delhi. All of them were there. V. P. Singh, N. T. Rama Rao, Chandra Shekhar, Ajit Singh, K. P. Unnikrishnan, M. Karunanidhi, Devi Lal, R. K. Hegde, Prafulla Mahanta, Surjit Singh Barnala and a host of others.

That the opposition parties had decided to go for Rajiv Gandhi and hit him where it would hurt most—corruption in high places in general and the Bofors scam in particular—was revealed in the manifesto. It said:

> The National Front vows to track down the money amassed in Bofors and other deals, restore it to the nation and have the guilty punished. It draws the people's attention to the new heights in corruption and inefficiency. The nation is a whirlpool of crises—the crisis of confidence, crisis of character, and crisis of leadership—a fallout of the policies pursued by successive Congress (I) governments in the last five years. Today India witnesses corruption at the highest level in government and administration, an irresponsible Government unable to resolve conflicts and maintain law and order, spiraling prices, man made scarcities, a currency shrinking in value and a mounting lot of foreign debts.

V. P. Singh was 'elected' leader of the Janata Dal Parliamentary Party on 2 December 1989 and soon after by the National Front Parliamentary Party. He was sworn in as prime minister on 2 December 1989. There was intrigue in the way V. P. Singh was elected. Chandra Shekhar was denied the job. This would continue to haunt V. P. Singh's government and it fell on 7 November 1990.

XIV

The V. P. Singh Era

> It is certainly true that reservation for OBCs will cause a lot of heart burning to others. But should the mere fact of this heart burning be allowed to operate as a moral veto against social reforms. A lot of heart burning was caused to the British when they left India. It burns the heart of all whites when the blacks protest against apartheid in South Africa. When the higher castes constituting less than 20 per cent of the country's population subjected the rest to all manner of social injustice, it must have caused a lot of heart burning to the lower castes. But now that the lower castes are asking for a modest share of national cake of power and prestige, a chorus of alarm is being raised on the plea that this will cause heart burning to the ruling elite.
>
> —From the report of the Backward Classes Commission

When the last of the election results were out on 26 November 1989, it was clear that Rajiv Gandhi's Congress (I) had lost the mandate. From 415 MPs in the previous Lok Sabha, the party's strength came down to 197. No matter, this was a better show than that of Indira's Congress party in 1977. The party had won just 154 seats then. Moreover, Rajiv Gandhi had retained his own Lok Sabha seat in 1989. There was, however, a similarity between the poll results in 1977 and 1989: the Congress (I) had done well in the southern states this time too. Of the 197 Congress (I) MPs, 39 came from Andhra Pradesh, 27 from Karnataka, 14 from Kerala and 27 from Tamil Nadu. In addition, the ADMK, an ally of the Congress (I), secured 11 seats from Tamil Nadu. In Kerala, its allies such as the Muslim League won two seats and the Kerala Congress one seat. In other words, more than half the Congress (I) MPs in the Ninth Lok Sabha were elected from the four southern states. The party had won 28 seats from Maharashtra too.

There was another important aspect of the 1989 election results. Despite the fall in its strength, by more than half in comparison with the Eighth Lok Sabha, the Congress(I) remained the single largest party in the Ninth Lok Sabha. Notwithstanding the fact that the opposition parties had achieved a unity of sorts and managed to ensure a one-to-one contest in most constituencies, the Janata Dal and the BJP had insisted on maintaining their separate identities, unlike in 1977. And then, there was the Left Front too. As for the regional parties, which constituted the National Front along with the Janata Dal, they all lost in their strongholds. The Telugu Desam Party (TDP), which had emerged as the largest block in the opposition in the Eighth Lok Sabha with 30 seats, was now reduced to a two-member party. The Shiromani Akali Dal was swept aside from Punjab and so was the DMK from Tamil Nadu.

The factors behind the verdict in November 1989 were multifold. These are significant because all these have implications for the political discourse in the decade after that. For once, the verdict was a manifestation of the several layers of fractures that had set in the polity. And this left a permanent impact on the nature of the political formations across the country. The most substantive impact of that would be felt in the fissures, which would appear and widen in the polity, in the manner of caste, religious and regional identities and all these turning into determinant factors in the political discourse of the country.

The second largest party in the Ninth Lok Sabha was the Janata Dal with 143 MPs. Of that, 54 came from Uttar Pradesh and 32 from Bihar. The party had won 16 MPs from Orissa and 11 each from Rajasthan and Gujarat. While the Janata Dal's sweep in Orissa was steered by the personality of Biju Patnaik, the party's performance from Gujarat and Rajasthan had to do with its alliance with the BJP. Meanwhile, more than half the Janata Dal Parliamentary Party was constituted by MPs from Uttar Pradesh and Bihar. In a sense, the Dal's emergence was firmly rooted, in form and content, in the nature of the opposition in these two states as it evolved in the 1960s—Lohiaite in the ideological sense and the Charan Singh legacy in the political sense.

The consolidation of the other backward classes (OBCs) against the Congress party was achieved as early as in the decade after Independence and with the Jats joining this conglomeration, the consolidation had taken concrete shape after 1967. Charan Singh had emerged as the rallying point of this political formation. Singh himself had worked on this process by enlisting Mulayam Singh Yadav into his fold. Mulayam Singh Yadav belonged, initially, to the Samyukta Socialist Party. He left the fold as early as in 1969 to join Charan Singh's Bharatiya Kranti Dal. In 1977, Charan Singh ensured Yadav's induction as Minister for Cooperatives and Animal Husbandry in the Ram Naresh Yadav ministry. The nexus was of immense use to both. While the BKD leader looked at it as a means to extend his social base and, thus, build a larger social constituency than the exclusive Jat base, Mulayam Singh too managed to build himself as the most important representative of the Yadav community, in Uttar Pradesh, in the process.

This helped Mulayam Singh emerge as the leader with a large social base made up of the numerously large Yadav community at one level and also positioning himself as a strong anti-BJP political force in Uttar Pradesh. It helped him stay afloat as a powerful leader, with a political organisation, after Charan Singh's death. His rivalry with Ajit Singh led him to walk out of the Lok Dal along with Devi Lal and Karpoori Thakur to form the Lok Dal (B). We have seen all this in the previous chapter. Mulayam Singh's powerful position and the organisational machinery at his disposal made it imperative for V. P. Singh, his old rival in the Uttar Pradesh political scene, to bend over backwards to accommodate Yadav. For Yadav too, a prime place in the Janata Dal was better than staying loyal to H. N. Bahuguna. Mulayam Singh Yadav, thus, was made the president of the Janata Dal's Uttar Pradesh unit. That Ajit Singh too had joined the Janata Dal meant that the traditional social alliance, consisting of the Ahirs (Yadavs), the Jats and such other backward castes as the Gujjars, rallied behind the Janata Dal. And with V. P. Singh at the helm of the new party, the Rajputs too rallied behind the party in Uttar Pradesh. A similar process had taken shape in Bihar too. Lalu Prasad Yadav, who inherited Karpoori Thakur's legacy in the state, had emerged an important Lok Dal (B) leader and steered the Janata Dal to victory in the state.

In nutshell, the Janata Dal's show in Uttar Pradesh and Bihar was determined by the AJGAR factor—the *A*hir, *J*at, *G*ujjar *A*nd *R*ajput alliance. A party that could muster the services of men from these castes could control the poll process in the region. This social alliance was more powerful, in terms of its clout, than the old order dominated by the Brahmins and the Bhoomihars, and the Janata Dal benefited from that. It is another matter that this social alliance was also a brittle one; the Rajputs, who rallied behind the Janata Dal, thanks to V. P. Singh, could not remain comfortable with the assertive Ahirs (Yadavs) and the Gujjars. And the Jats had their own sense of discomfort with the Yadavs dominating the scene. All these will have implications to the very survival of the Janata Dal. But then the AJGAR combination was achieved in time for the November 1989 elections.

There was another important development insofar as the November 1989 elections were concerned. And that was the stunning performance of the BJP. The Ayodhya plank and the strident Hindutva campaign that the party joined in June 1989, helped the BJP emerge as the third largest party in the Ninth Lok Sabha with 85 MPs. The fact that the Congress (I), under Rajiv Gandhi, was seen as having orchestrated the Ayodhya controversy (since February 1986) and caving in to the VHP's campaign caused a serious erosion of its vote base among the Muslim community. As it happens in realpolitik, the party could hardly make itself the beneficiary of the resurgent Hindu vote base. This had gone to the BJP. Then there was the Bahujan Samaj Party (BSP), a new entrant on the political scene in Uttar Pradesh, presenting a Dalit exclusivist slogan. The BSP, it may be recalled, had made a mark in the Allahabad by-elections with Kanshi Ram, the party's founder and president, securing as much as 18 per cent of the votes. The BSP won two Lok Sabha seats from Uttar Pradesh in the November 1989 elections. Of additional significance was the fact that the party had polled close to 10 per cent of the votes. This showed the extent to which the Congress (I) had suffered erosion across its social base.

The Congress (I) lost a section of its upper-caste supporters (the Rajputs) to the Janata Dal, the Brahmin votes to the BJP and a substantial part of the Dalits to the BSP. All this meant that the Congress (I), even if it won as many as 15 Lok Sabha seats from Uttar Pradesh, was turning into a sinking ship in the state. Its strength would fall further in successive elections. The Congress (I) also lost power in Uttar Pradesh in November 1989. Elections to the state assembly were held simultaneously with the Lok Sabha polls. The Janata Dal wrested power in Uttar Pradesh too. It is important to note here that the Congress (I) would progressively lose its strength in the Uttar Pradesh assembly in successive elections after 1989 and end up with just 23 seats in the 400-strong assembly in May 2007. The beginning of this downslide could be located in the factors that guided the political discourse in the region in November 1989. A similar story would unfold in Bihar too.

As for the BJP, the 1989 elections were a landmark. Out of the 85 BJP MPs, 27 were elected from Madhya Pradesh, 13 from Rajasthan and 10 from Maharashtra. The party won three out of the four Lok Sabha constituencies from Himachal Pradesh and four out of the seven Lok Sabha seats from Delhi. The November 1989 poll outcome revealed that the party's base in its traditional strongholds from the Jan Sangh days—Madhya Pradesh, Rajasthan and Himachal Pradesh—had remained intact and had even grown. It could now claim to be the strongest anti-Congress (I) formation in these states. The BJP also made substantial gains from Maharashtra (winning 10 seats), Gujarat (winning 12 seats) and the Jharkhand region in Bihar (from where it won five seats) in November 1989. It is not a mere coincidence that these states would emerge as BJP strongholds in the decade after 1990 and some significant improvement in Uttar Pradesh would land the BJP, as head of a ruling combine, in the Centre in 1998. The November 1989 elections and the developments thereafter, hence, had a very significant impact on the course of the national politics as well as that in the various states.

In this chapter, we shall look into the context of V. P. Singh's election as prime minister and the formation of the National Front government; the round of assembly elections in various states that resulted in the Janata Dal and the BJP consolidating their positions in their traditional strongholds; the crisis in the Janata Dal, caused by the decision to implement the Mandal Commission's recommendation, the BJP's decision to rake up the Ayodhya issue once again and the eventual collapse of the government; and the formation and the collapse of the Chandra Shekar government and the context of the general election in May–June 1991 leading to the formation of yet another minority government under P. V. Narasimha Rao.

V. P. Singh's Election as Prime Minister

The Janata Dal had secured 143 seats in the Lok Sabha, the BJP won 85 seats and the Left Front, consisting of the CPI (M), CPI, Forward Bloc and the Revolutionary Socialist Party (RSP) had 52 MPs in all. A non-Congress (I) government was possible only if the Janata Dal, the BJP and the Left Front came together. This task, even if it appeared insurmountable, was achieved with ease. The fact is that the leaders of all these parties were convinced that the mandate was against the Congress (I) and they will have to make the best of the situation. Rajiv Gandhi too was aware of the reality. On 29 November 1989, Rajiv Gandhi, the elected leader of the Congress(I) Parliamentary Party, drove to the Rashtrapati Bhawan to hand over his resignation as prime minister to President R. Venkatraman. This, in fact, foreclosed one of the options that Venkatraman as president could have tried out—to invite the leader of the single largest party to form his government and ask him to prove the majority in Parliament within a reasonable time. Venkatraman would make a virtue of this reality, later on, in his memoirs.

It may be recalled that Morarji Desai had put forth this idea in July 1979 (that he be invited to form another government on grounds that his Janata Party remained the single largest party in the Lok Sabha) only to be rejected by President N. Sanjiva Reddy. And this option would be exercised by Shankar Dayal Sharma, in May 1996, when he invited Atal Behari Vajpayee to form the government. Vajpayee was sworn in as prime minister on the basis that the BJP, even while falling short of a majority, had emerged as the single largest party in the Eleventh Lok Sabha. Sharma was criticised for this and the Vajpayee government fell in thirteen days.

All these did not happen in 1989. And this was ensured by the CPI (M) and the BJP. On 28 November 1989, the leaders of the Left as well as the BJP made it clear that they supported the formation of a non-Congress (I) government and President Venkatraman was informed of this. Rajiv Gandhi's decision, on 29 November 1989, to resign and desist from staking claim was indeed determined by this. There was, however, trouble brewing in the Janata Dal over the choice of the JDPP leader. It was clear, even on 27 November 1989, that the Janata Dal had difficulties in electing its leader. The Janata Dal had emerged the second largest party in the Lok Sabha with 143 seats and V. P. Singh had emerged, even before the elections, as the rallying point of the opposition unity. The post-poll scenario, however, was different. A general body of the Janata Dal Parliamentary Party, scheduled for 3.00 p.m. on 28 November 1989, was cancelled at the last minute and re-scheduled for the day after. It was postponed further to 30 November 1989 and cancelled once again. And it was only on 1 December 1989, that the Janata Dal finally managed to decide, amidst high drama, on V. P. Singh as the leader. All the while, the drama unfolded in different venues in the national capital and theatrics crossed all limits at the JDPP meeting at the Central Hall of Parliament on 1 December 1989. This was the fallout of individual egos and personality clashes that existed, even at the time of the party's formation in October 1988, but pushed under the carpet by the various players all the while. All that came to the fore, on 27 November 1989, when it became clear that the next prime minister will be from the Janata Dal.

A brief narrative of the developments in the four days between 27 November and 1 December 1989 will be in order. On 27 November 1989, Devi Lal visited L. K. Advani to explore the possibilities of his own chances to become the prime minister. Devi Lal, it may be recalled, had been the BJP's best friend in the Janata Dal and had taken the initiative to have seat adjustments between the two parties, as early as in July 1989, even while V. P. Singh was ambiguous on this issue. And that had ensured a perfect pre-poll adjustment between the two parties in Haryana, Rajasthan, Gujarat and Madhya Pradesh ahead of the November 1989 general elections. But then, the Haryana patriarch was told point blank by Advani that the opposition's gains were caused by V. P. Singh and hence the BJP's support was conditional upon Singh becoming the prime minister. Even while Devi Lal relented that evening, his son Om Prakash Chautala, along with Chandra Shekar, persisted with the idea of denying the throne to V. P. Singh. Chandra Shekhar, had realised by now, that his own strength in the JDPP was no match against V. P. Singh's but maintained that he was willing for a contest when a delegation consisting of N. T. Rama Rao, A. B. Vajpayee and Devi Lal called on him on 28 November. He also made it clear that he was willing to step out of the race in favour of Devi Lal. Chautala clung on to this and pushed his agenda throughout the day on 29 November 1989. He orchestrated a public show of support, organising crowds from Haryana, to pressurise Devi Lal; the pressure began to work on the Haryana patriarch.

It was at this stage that V. P. Singh let loose his own men. Arun Nehru, Arif Mohammed Khan and V. C. Shukla, all Jan Morcha men in the Janata Dal, got CPI (M) leader Jyoti Basu and the BJP president L. K. Advani to clarify in the public that their support to a non-Congress (I) government was conditional upon V. P. Singh being elected as prime minister. Devi Lal had snapped his contacts with V. P. Singh by this time and was busy contacting his Lok Dal (B) men such as Lalu Yadav, Sharad Yadav and Mulayam Singh Yadav on 30 November. V. P. Singh stayed in the background, all the while, leaving the operations to his old Jan Morcha men. And on 1 December, when the Left Front leaders and the BJP were losing their patience and the JDPP meeting scheduled for that morning was postponed for the evening that day, Arun Nehru drove up to Devi Lal, now holed up in the Haryana Bhawan. He managed to persuade Devi Lal to strive for unity in the party and take him along to the Orissa Bhawan where V. P. Singh was waiting. V. P. Singh told Devi Lal then that he would himself propose the patriarch's name for prime minister. Arun Nehru interjected then, to obtain an assurance from Devi Lal, that he would decline the post and propose Singh for the job. This 'honourable' settlement satisfied Devi Lal as long as he did not come into contact with his son, Chautala. The Jan Morcha men managed that effectively.

Devi Lal, now in Arun Nehru's company, invited Chandra Shekhar to the Orissa Bhawan and he was informed that V. P. Singh would propose Devi Lal and that he could second the proposal. All this were conducted with just a few minutes left for the JDPP meeting scheduled for 3.15 p.m. on 1 December 1989. The leaders, therafter, drove up to Parliament House to attend the meeting at the appointed hour. Madhu Dandavate was appointed Election Officer and he called for nominations. That was when the drama unfolded, much to the dismay of political observers and Chandra Shekhar. Singh rose to propose Devi Lal and Chandra Shekhar hastened to second the proposal. Wire services put out the flash news of Devi Lal's election as Prime Minister and the crowds outside began celebrating their leader's election. The Haryana patriarch walked up to the podium, thanked V. P. Singh for his support. And within moments added: '*Haryana mein, jahan log mujhe tauji tauji karke pukharte hain, main waha tauji hi banke rahna chahta hoon.*' (I prefer to look after Haryana, where the people regard me as their elder uncle). Thus, declining the nomination, Devi Lal then proposed V. P. Singh's name and Ajit Singh hastened to second the proposal. Dandavate, without waiting for long, declared Singh elected. All this was pre-arranged and Chandra Shekhar was perhaps the only one who was unaware of the script. He did not conceal his shock and anger at being taken for a ride. He walked out of the National Front Parliamentary Party meeting, convened by N. T. Rama Rao, within hours after the JDPP elected V. P. Singh. The backroom manipulations that went into the election as well as the fact that neither the Janata Dal on its own nor the National Front as a combine had a majority of its own in the Ninth Lok Sabha had implications for the stability of the V. P. Singh government.

President R.Venkatraman was left with no other option than inviting V. P. Singh to form the government. He did so late in the evening on 1 December 1989. The Rashtrapati Bhawan communiqué that evening was a commentary on the fractured nature of the mandate:

> Since the Congress (I), elected to the Ninth Lok Sabha with the largest membership, has opted not to stake its claim for forming the Government, the President invited Mr. V. P. Singh, leader of the second largest party/group, namely the Janata Dal/National Front to form the Government and take a vote of confidence in the Lok Sabha within 30 days of his assuming office.

V. P. Singh was sworn in, the following day, on 2 December 1989 as prime minister. And along with him, Devi Lal was sworn in as deputy prime minister. This was the price Singh had to pay for involving the Haryana patriarch in the manipulations the previous day. Within a couple of hours after his becoming the deputy prime minister, Devi Lal quit as Haryana chief minister and anointed his son Chautala in his place. That things would cross all limits, that were set by the developments during the past few days, was revealed when the Haryana governor, Dhanik Lal Mandal, was brought to Delhi and made to swear in Chautala as chief minister from the Haryana Bhawan in Delhi. The various leaders of the Janata Dal were busy jostling for positions in the Cabinet when this happened. Prime Minister

Singh was unable to finalise the list of his cabinet colleagues to be sworn in with him on 2 December. This would take place only on 5 December 1989.

Meanwhile, there was trouble brewing in Lucknow. The Janata Dal had secured 204 seats in the 421-member Uttar Pradesh assembly and emerged as the decisive winner. The legislators, however, were divided in their loyalty between Mulayam Singh Yadav and Ajit Singh. There were smaller groups too. Prominent among them being MLAs loyal to V. P. Singh. While Mulayam Singh, president of the state unit, seemed a natural claimant to the chief minister's post, there were others such as Ajit Singh (whose rivalry with Mulayam went back to the days when the Lok Dal underwent a split after the death of Charan Singh) and Sanjay Singh, whose proximity with V. P. Singh made him important. However, Sanjay Singh's aspirations were dampened due to his own defeat in the elections. On 2 December 1989, Madhu Dandavate was sent to Lucknow (along with Chimanbhai Patel and Mufti Mohammed Sayeed) as central observers to oversee the election of the JDLP leader. The stakes were high and the 2 December meeting was preceded by behind-the-scenes activity in Lucknow as well as in Delhi. This, notwithstanding the fact, that Mulayam Singh supporters outnumbered the other groups. Ajit Singh, meanwhile, rested his hopes on an assurance, he claimed to have obtained, from V. P. Singh in return for his contribution in keeping Chandra Shekhar out of the race for the prime minister's post. The former Lok Dal (A) leader, it may be recalled, was in the loop when the Jan Morcha men were managing the affairs in New Delhi until the previous day. He was the one who seconded V. P. Singh's name for the prime minister's post in the JDPP. Ajit Singh also banked on Sanjay Singh, again a Jan Morcha man, in Lucknow.

The central observers, however, seemed to have had a different brief and after consulting with the 203 MLAs, they announced Mulayam Singh the consensus candidate for the chief minister's post. The legislature party went through the formal motion of electing Yadav, within moments after the observers announced his name; Ajit Singh's supporters, gathered outside the hall where the JDLP meeting was held, went into a rage and insisted that Ajit Singh refuse to join the Union Cabinet. They felt let down by V. P. Singh and Devi Lal. The controversy, however, blew over then and there itself.

Ajit Singh returned to Delhi the following day and was among those who were sworn in as Union Ministers on 5 December 1989. The formation of the Union Council of Ministers was not a smooth affair. Devi Lal demanded his pound of flesh and his nominees had to be included. V. P. Singh himself was obliged to his Jan Morcha colleagues. There were also the veterans in the Janata Dal who belonged to the Janata Party Cabinet. In addition to all these, Singh was committed to keeping the National Front alive; the poor showing by the regional parties in the November 1989 elections notwithstanding, he was determined to include some of their nominees in the Cabinet. That was the only way to ensure representation of the southern states, Punjab and the Northeast, in the Union Cabinet. The Janata Dal, as we saw, was restricted to Bihar, Uttar Pradesh and Orissa. The National Front chairman and TDP leader, N. T. Rama Rao, meanwhile, sought another deputy prime minister's slot for himself but did not persist with it for long. After several rounds of drawing-room negotiations that led to the swearing in ceremony being delayed by six hours from the scheduled hour, Singh arrived at a list of 17 members. It indicated that the prime minister was just the first among the equals with equally powerful leaders as his cabinet colleagues.

The V. P. Singh cabinet was constituted by such veterans from the Janata Cabinet: Madhu Dandavate (finance) and George Fernandes (railways). The Lok Dal (B) group was represented by Sharad Yadav (textiles) apart from the deputy prime minister, Devi Lal (agriculture) while the Lok Dal (A) was represented by Ajit Singh (industries) and Ram Vilas Paswan (labour and welfare). I. K. Gujral (external affairs) earned the berth on his own merit and Neelmani Routray (environment and forests) was Biju Patnaik's nominee. M. S. Gurupadasamy (petroleum and chemicals) was included to represent Karnataka, where the Janata Dal had faired poorly. And K. P. Unnikrishnan (telecommunications), being the sole MP from the Congress (S) turned out to be the natural choice for a cabinet berth. The DMK's Murasoli Maran (urban development), TDP's P. Upendra (information, broadcasting and parliamentary affairs) and AGP's Dinesh Goswami (law and justice) were all inducted into the Cabinet on behalf of the National Front allies. They were all Rajya Sabha members. Manubhai Kotadia (MoS, water resources) was Chimanbhai Patel's nominee and Maneka Gandhi (MoS, environment and forests) was V. P. Singh's nominee. The Shiromani Akali Dal, which drew a blank from Punjab went unrepresented in the Union Cabinet. Singh's list consisted of Yashwant Sinha, a close associate of Chandra Shekhar, as a minister of state. Sinha, however, walked out in a huff, from the swearing-in ceremony, and this clearly confirmed that all was not well between Prime Minister Singh and Chandra Shekhar.

The largest group in the Cabinet came from the Jan Morcha. Apart from V. P. Singh himself (and he retained the defence portfolio), Arun Nehru (commerce and tourism), Arif Mohammed Khan (civil aviation and energy) and Mufti Mohammed Sayeed (home), constituted the Jan Morcha block in the cabinet.

Sayeed, who belonged to Kashmir, had left the Congress (I) in protest against the Rajiv Gandhi–Farooq Abdullah accord in 1987. He joined V. P. Singh's Jan Morcha soon and the Janata Dal right from its inception. In November 1989, Sayeed contested from Muzafarnagar in Uttar Pradesh and his induction into the Union Cabinet as the home minister, was celebrated by the media. It was for the first time that a Muslim was made the Union Home Minister in independent

India. It may be recalled that Jawaharlal Nehru's Congress had rejected such a demand from the Muslim League at the time of the formation of the Interim Government in October 1946. And Sayeed also happened to belong to Kashmir. His appointment, as home minister, at a time when militancy was growing in strength in the valley was seen as a positive message.

The assembly election, in Jammu and Kashmir, in 1987, was indeed a watershed. We have seen that the Congress (I)–National Conference alliance swept the polls. But all that was not achieved by fair means. Insofar as the percentage of votes polled, the Congress(I)–NC combine managed to poll a fraction of a percentage point more than the Muslim United Front (MUF). But then, there was a huge difference in the number of seats and this was achieved only by way of manipulations at the stage of counting of votes. A number of the MUF candidates in the 1987 elections turned into militant leaders in the valley in the following years. The first direct manifestation of the alienation of the youth from the political mainstream was evident in a bomb blast in Srinagar in July 1988 and the Jammu Kashmir Liberation Front (JKLF), founded several years ago but lying dormant, emerged into a platform for militant expression of the aspirations of the youth in the valley. Mufti Sayeed's appointment as Union Home Minister was seen as a positive message in this context too. The celebration, however, did not last long.

On 8 December 1989, just a couple of days after the Mufti became the Union Home Minister, Rubaiya Sayeed, his youngest daughter, then studying in the medical college in Srinagar, was kidnapped by the JKLF. The kidnappers demanded release of five of their men, charged of criminal offences, and detained in the various jails in the state.

Any decision on this had to be taken by the state government and the Union Home Minister's role could at best be restricted to persuasion. The Mufti's relationship with the chief minister, Farooq Abdulla, was guided by antagonism. Abdullah, at that time, was convalescing in the USA after a heart surgery. The Jammu and Kashmir cabinet, however, met in his absence the same day and decided in principle to agree to the demand. The modalities of the release had to be worked out. On his return to Srinagar on 10 December, Chief Minister Abdullah insisted that his government would release just one of the five militants—Hamid Sheikh—in exchange for Rubaiya Sayeed. The militants rejected this and things came to an impasse once again.

The negotiations between the militants and the government were conducted by Justice M. L. Bhatt of the Allahabad High Court. Justice Bhatt had the record of being a strong votary of human rights and had issued orders, to that effect, on several instances involving militants in the valley and had, thus, earned respect and the confidence of the youth. This made him the best person to negotiate at the time of the crisis. And on 13 December 1989, Bhatt concluded the process of a negotiated settlement of the crisis. The political leadership of the National Front had managed, by then, to prevail upon Farooq Abdullah to release all the five detainees. It was done on 13 December and Rubaiya too arrived at her home three hours after the militants were released. Any impression that the Rubaiya kidnap episode would ease the tension between the Mufti and Farooq Abdullah was belied in less than a month.

The Mufti's partisan agenda unfurled in January 1990. He managed to persuade Prime Minister V. P. Singh to appoint Jagmohan as governor of Jammu and Kashmir. In doing so, Mufti's calculations were perfect. He was aware that Chief Minister Farooq Abdullah would resent Jagmohan as governor. He had been sent as governor of the state earlier on 26 April 1984 and he recommended dismissal of Farooq Abdullah on 2 July 1984. That was done at Rajiv Gandhi's behest and G. M. Shah was installed as chief minister. In a couple of years, once again at Rajiv Gandhi's behest, and after the Congress (I) and the National Conference entered into an alliance, Shah was dismissed in March 1986 and after a brief spell of Central rule, Farooq Abdullah became the chief minister. The zeal with which Jagmohan went about addressing the Kashmiri Pundits to leave the valley (to be settled in refugee camps in Jammu) or went ahead with renovating Hindu shrines in the Jammu region had contributed, in a big way, to the alienation of the youth in the valley. He remained governor until 11 July 1989 and was recalled after Farooq demanded that from Rajiv Gandhi. General K. V. Krishna Rao was sent as governor then.

Jagmohan (the leading executioner in the Turkman Gate demolitions during the Emergency when he was chairman of the Delhi Development Authority), was also preferred by the BJP, to be sent as Jammu and Kashmir governor. In the days, immediately after the release of militants in exchange for Rubaiya, the BJP stepped up its pressure on V. P. Singh pushing its own agenda. The party chief, L. K. Advani had, in fact, sought a commitment from the National Front to scrap Article 370 of the Constitution, imposition of a Uniform Civil Code and treating the demand for a Ram temple in Ayodhya as a national aspiration at the time of extending outside support to the government. It is a different matter that Advani did not make that a condition for support.

In one of those instances, where the demands of two sections in the political spectrum seemed to be common, Mufti Sayeed and the BJP agreed on sending Jagmohan as governor to Jammu and Kashmir again. While the BJP's endgame was that he would carry forward its own agenda in the state, the Mufti was convinced that such a move will irritate Farooq Abdullah and provoke him to quit as chief minister. Farooq had made it known that he would resign in the event the Centre imposed Jagmohan as governor. Despite this, Jagmohan was sent as governor of Jammu and Kashmir on 19 January 1990. Farooq Abdullah resigned the same day and Jagmohan recommended dissolution of the state assembly. On 20 January 1990, just a day after Jagmohan took over as governor, over 100 people were killed in an attack by security forces in Gawakadal. It was, indeed, a cold-blooded massacre by the security forces and intended to be a signal to the anti-government protestors. This led to worsening of the crisis in the valley. From the sporadic acts of militant violence the situation changed and mass protests on the streets became the order of the day.

It was in this context and in an attempt to contain the damage that V. P. Singh appointed George Fernandes as Cabinet Minister in-charge of Kashmir Affairs on 11 March 1990. Fernandes held this post in addition to being the Railway Minister and he was chosen for the job given his extensive contacts with a cross section of the militant leaders. The veteran socialist would visit the valley, hold talks with a cross section of the militants and seemed to cover a lot of ground within weeks after his appointment. But all this was taking place even while governor Jagmohan was pushing ahead with his own agenda in collusion with Mufti Sayeed. On 21 May 1990, the Mirwaiz Maulavi Farooq, a respected member of the clergy, was killed, allegedly by pro-Pakistan militants in the valley. The funeral procession at Srinagar, on the same day, was a massive one. The police-fired indiscriminately at the mourners, killing at least 50 people. Jagmohan was held responsible for this provocative action and Prime Minister V. P. Singh was now under pressure to make amends. Jagmohan was asked to resign on 25 May 1990 and G. C. Saxena, a senior officer with the Research and Analysis Wing (RAW), was sent as governor of Jammu and Kashmir on 26 May 1990. The change of governor was only a small measure at that time and the crisis in the Kashmir valley would persist for several years even after that. Jagmohan, meanwhile, was made a member of the Rajya Sabha. He was nominated to the upper house where 12 seats are meant for men of eminence and the V. P. Singh regime used this provision to accommodate him; and through that, the BJP was also mollified.

The Assembly Elections and the Mehem Controversy

Even while the crisis was deepening in the Kashmir valley, the Janata Dal was faced with the challenge of establishing its popular support in several state assemblies. Elections to the state assemblies in Bihar, Orissa, Madhya Pradesh, Maharashtra, Gujarat, Rajasthan, Himachal Pradesh, Arunachal Pradesh and Pondichery were scheduled for 27 February 1990. And along with these, the Election Commission also announced by-elections for the Mehem assembly constituency in Haryana. The by-elections ensued after the incumbent Janata Dal MLA resigned his membership to facilitate election of chief minister Om Prakash Chautala to the assembly. Chautala had been a Rajya Sabha member at the time of being sworn in as chief minister.

Barring Arunachal Pradesh and Pondichery, the Janata Dal and the BJP were prominent players in all the other states where elections were to be held now. It was imperative for the two parties to establish their popularity against the Congress (I) in these elections. As it happened for the Lok Sabha elections in November 1989, the Janata Dal entered into a pre-poll alliance with the BJP in Gujarat, Rajasthan, Madhya Pradesh and Himachal Pradesh and decided against such an adjustment in Bihar and Orissa. In Orissa, Biju Patnaik rode the Janata Dal like a colossus and the BJP did not even exist. In Bihar, the Janata Dal was made up of the legatees of Madhu Limaye, who had set out on the idea of an anti-Jan Sangh–anti-Congress opposition from the time the Janata Party was shaking. The Jan Sangh had a presence in Bihar. It may be recalled that the RSS and the ABVP had emerged as powerful forces even at the time of the JP movement. The decision of the Janata Dal's Bihar unit against an arrangement with the BJP was a manifestation of an arrangement that V. P. Singh, who continued to steer the party in the absence of a formal organisation structure, sought to put in place; to parcel out the business of running the party and let the various leaders in the state units to decide on alliances rather than the high command deciding on their behalf.

The results of the February 1990 round of assembly elections revealed two things. The anti-Congress wave of November 1989 had not subsided. Maharashtra was the only state where the Congress (I) could retain power. Sharad Pawar, who had returned to the party after steering the Congress (S) for a while, led the Congress (I) to win 141 seats in the 288 member assembly in the 27 February 1990 elections. The BJP won only 42 seats and the Janata Dal just 24 seats. These two national parties, in fact, had secured fewer seats than the Shiv Sena. This was the first ever assembly elections that the Shiv Sena had contested and it won 52 seats. The BJP–Shiv Sena alliance in 1995 won a majority in the Maharashtra assembly to form the first non-Congress government in the state.

In Gujarat, the Janata Dal and the BJP managed to reach an agreement for a one-to-one fight against the Congress (I) in 136 out of the 182 assembly constituencies; the two parties were engaged in friendly contests in 46 constituencies. When the results were announced, the Janata Dal had won 70 constituencies and the BJP in 67 constituencies. The Congress (I) won just 33 seats. Chimanbhai Patel, against whom the students had launched a decisive struggle in 1974 and on which the Janata Morcha was built in May–June 1975, was now the Janata Dal's boss in Gujarat. He decided to head a coalition government with the BJP in the state.

In Rajasthan too the BJP and the Janata Dal had reached an agreement for 160 seats. The two parties put up a one-to-one contest against the Congress (I) in 80 seats each and entered into a friendly contest in 40 seats. Out of this, the BJP won 85 and the Janata Dal won 54. The Congress (I) won just 50 seats. Bhairon Singh Shekawat, a Jan Sangh veteran, became the chief minister. Shekawat was

Rajasthan chief minister earlier between 1977 and 1980 when the Janata Party had won elections to the assembly. The Janata Dal joined the Shekawat ministry.

In Madhya Pradesh, the BJP and the Janata Dal had agreed to a one-to-one contest in 291 of the 320 constituencies. And the BJP won 219 seats, the Janata Dal 28 seats and the Congress(I) 56 seats. The BJP's Sundarlal Patwa became the chief minister. It may be recalled that Kailash Joshi and V. K. Saklecha who headed the Janata Party government in Madhya Pradesh between 1977 and 1980 belonged to the Jan Sangh.

In Himachal Pradesh, the BJP and the Janata Dal had entered into a pre-poll understanding for all the 68 seats. The BJP won 44 seats, the Janata Dal 11 and the Congress (I) only 8. Shanta Kumar of the BJP became the chief minister. He was the chief minister of the state between April 1977 and March 1980 when the Janata Party had won the elections.

It was a different story in Orissa where the Janata Dal was the sole opposition to the Congress (I). The party won 123 seats out of the 147 assembly constituencies in the state and the Congress (I) was reduced to just 10 seats and Biju Patnaik became the chief minister. Patnaik was an associate of Jawaharlal Nehru in the fifties and had moved the Socialistic-Pattern-of-Society resolution at the Congress session in Avadi; he was one of the six chief ministers who were drafted for party work as part of the Kamaraj plan in 1963; was Minister for Steel and Mines in the Janata Party government between 1977 and 1979; and now the Janata Dal's supreme commander in Orissa.

Bihar was another story. The Janata Dal and the BJP fought the elections separately. And this had an impact on the poll outcome. It was a hung assembly with the Janata Dal winning 120 seats, the Congress (I), 71 and the BJP, 38. The Jharkhand Mukti Morcha won 19 seats, the CPI, 22 and the CPI (M), 6. Another significant aspect of the Bihar elections was that the Indian People's Front (IPF), an outfit of the CPI (ML), floated ahead of the November 1989 general elections, won nine seats in the assembly. The IPF had won the Arrah Lok Sabha seat in 1989. It was an important development, insofar as the CPI (ML) was concerned, in that the party, for the first time since the 1967–69 Naxalbari uprising had chosen to fight elections. The IPF and the CPI (ML-Liberation) continue to remain a distinct political force in Bihar and influences the discourse in the state in a significant manner; and make an impact in the specific context of the state's socio-political scene dominated by the vestiges of feudalism and the violent means that the lords of the old order resort to. A detailed discussion on that should, in all fairness, be taken up in a separate book.

The relevance of the 27 February 1990 Bihar assembly election results, from the viewpoint of this chapter, was the high drama that marked the government formation and the emergence of Lalu Prasad Yadav as chief minister. Unlike in the other states, where assembly elections were held in this round, there was no clear winner in Bihar. The Janata Dal had emerged as the single largest party with 120 seats in the 324 member assembly. The CPI, the JMM and the CPI (M) informed the governor of their support to the Janata Dal. And this along with a few independents, added up to more than the 163 that was required to form a Janata Dal government in the state. There was, however, trouble in the party when it came to electing the leader.

There were three contenders to the post: Lalu Prasad Yadav (backed by Devi Lal), Ram Sundar Das (backed by V. P. Singh) and Raghunath Jha (backed by Chandra Shekhar). All the three leaders were unrelenting. The struggle, in many ways, was on in the Bihar unit of the Janata Dal even at the time when the Janata Dal was formed in October 1988 and we have discussed the instances of clash of these personalities and the fact that these were mere extensions of the battles between the party's national leaders, in the previous chapter. While the issues were pushed under the carpet at that time, the battle this time was for positions of power and control of the state government. It was natural that the resolution of the conflict in such a situation was more difficult. Efforts by the party's central observers—George Fernandes and Ajit Singh—to evolve a consensus, came to a naught. A contest was the only way out.

Lalu Prasad Yadav, a MP at that time, backed by Devi Lal and Sharad Yadav, defeated Ram Sundar Das (who had replaced Karpoori Thakur as Janata chief minister in April 1979 and V. P. Singh's nominee) and Ragunath Jha (Chandra Shekhar's nominee) to emerge as the Janata Dal Legislature Party leader. He became the chief minister of Bihar. His government depended on support from the CPI, JMM, CPI (M) and few independents. Lalu Yadav, a key player in the JP movement in 1974–75, was first elected to the Lok Sabha from Chapra in 1977. When the Janata Party split in July 1979, he joined Charan Singh's Janata Party (Secular) and went along with him to the Lok Dal. He lost the 1980 elections to the Lok Sabha. Lalu, however, won from Sonepur assembly constituency in the June 1980 assembly elections and remained an MLA from that constituency until November 1989. When the Lok Dal split up after Charan Singh's death in May 1987, Lalu Prasad joined the Lok Dal (B) of which Karpoori Thakur was the boss in Bihar. He became the leader of the opposition in the Bihar assembly after Karpoori's death on 17 February 1988 and thereafter inherited the Lok Dal (B) organisation in Bihar. Like Devi Lal and Mulayam Singh Yadav, he too defied the party's working president, Bahuguna, to merge the Lok Dal (B) into the Janata Dal at the Bangalore convention on 11 October 1988.

Once elected chief minister, Lalu Prasad managed to reduce Ram Sundar Das and Raghunath Jha into insignificant players and build himself as the supreme leader of the Janata Dal in Bihar. He would also carve out a social alliance of the OBCs, the Dalits and the Muslims, in due course, to steer the Janata Dal to winning a huge majority in the assembly in 1995. He remained chief minister until August 1997 and anointed his wife, Rabri Devi as chief minister, when he had to quit after the CBI issued an arrest warrant against him in what came to be known as the fodder scam. Even after that, he continued to decide on the affairs of the government in Bihar until May 2005, when his party lost the assembly election. Thus, by March 1990, the Janata Dal was in power in Uttar Pradesh, Orissa, Bihar and Haryana and also in the ruling coalition with the BJP in Madhya Pradesh, Rajasthan, Gujarat and Himachal Pradesh.

Amidst all this, there was bad news for the party from Mehem in Haryana from where the Janata Dal chief minister, Om Prakash Chautala, was a candidate. Chautala's rise in the party and his eventual anointment as chief minister on 2 December 1989 was resented by his brother, Ranjit Singh, who was a minister in Devi Lal's Cabinet at that time. And Ranjit Singh had organised a crisis for Devi Lal by getting Dr K. R. Punia (industry minister) and seven other MLAs to resign from the Janata Dal a few weeks before the November 1989 general election. Devi Lal simply let things come to a pass and have the rebels expelled from the Janata Dal. Ranjit Singh, however, was persuaded to stay on in the party and after Chautala became chief minister, he was persuaded by his father, now deputy prime minister, to join the new cabinet as agriculture minister. But then, the Ranjit Singh camp was pushed over by Chautala, and Anand Singh Dangi, who was the chairman of the Subordinate Service Selection Board (one such position that was handed out to influential politicos who were not legislators to retain them in the party), resigned from his position to contest against Chautala in Mehem. Dangi, in fact, was the candidate of the Janata Dal rebels and Ranjit Singh had associated with him to spite Chautala contesting from Mehem.

In his own way, Dangi had cultivated a large base to himself by way of appointing thousands of youth in government jobs from the Mehem Chaubisi panchayat. This illegitimate act of Dangi, however, was useful to him in the fight against Devi Lal's steamroller tactics to anoint his son. The Mehem Chaubisi panchayat, a confederation of the dominant Jat clans of the area, resolved to support Dangi in the Mehem by-election against Chautala. Ranjit Singh resigned from the cabinet, soon after, along with power minister Virendra Singh and forest minister Raghuvir Singh Khadian. All of them now associated themselves with the rebels led by Dr Punia to constitute the Jan Hit Morcha. Although Chautala continued to enjoy a majority in the Janata Dal Legislature Party as well as in the assembly, even after all these resignations, it was clear that the number game could turn against him in the event he lost from Mehem.

It was hence, imperative, for him to win from Mehem. And this had become a difficult task after the Mehem Chaubisi panchayat resolved to support Dangi against him. The panchayat had influenced the outcome of elections in Mehem, as well as in many other parts of Haryana, thanks to the clout of its members over the Jat community. Hence, Chautala was determined to pull all the stops to ensure his victory in the by-election and his son, Abhay Singh, was entrusted with the task of ensuring that. On his part, Chief Minister Chautala ensured a strong police force under the command of officers committed to him so that son Abhay Singh had a free run. The Dangi camp too was not innocent of all the machinations; but their own followers, despite their determination to teach Chautala a lesson, were no match to the combined might of the state government and Abhay Singh's private army. Polling on 27 February 1990 appeared to be 'free and fair' except in eight booths. The Election Commission ordered repoll in these eight booths where it found evidence of unfair poll practices. The repoll was to be held on 28 February 1990.

Chautala, however, had glossed over one aspect, that Mehem was so close to Delhi and the significance that the media had assigned to the by-election in the larger context of Chautala's ascendancy. The manipulations on election day by Chautala's administration and Abhay Singh's private army drew national attention to the repoll on 28 February 1990. Abhay Singh, meanwhile, was determined to persist with his task and while he was carrying out the capture of a booth in Bainsi village, Dangi's supporters managed to organise a large crowd and locked up the school gates where the booth was located. Abhay Singh, holed up inside the school, is reported to have fired at the crowd and was helped out of the compound by a huge posse of policemen who fired indiscriminately into the crowd (to rescue the chief minister's son). The police action left 20 men dead in Bainsi. This brought Mehem and the by-election there to the nation's attention and the V. P. Singh government, a little over hundred days in power now, had to take a position on Chautala's moral right to continue as chief minister.

The campaign against Chautala was not merely from Dangi and the people of Bainsi village. The BJP, uncomfortable with Devi Lal's ways and with the anointment of Chautala as Chief Minister, was now quite unhappy. The Janata Dal and the BJP were allies in 1987 (for the assembly elections) and also in November 1989. However, after 28 February, the party's central leaders demanded that Chautala should go. The Left parties too conveyed a similar message to V. P. Singh after Mehem. And Devi Lal's detractors in the Union Cabinet were not in a mood to let go an opportunity. Ajit Singh, who had to remain content with the Jat base in western Uttar Pradesh because Devi Lal took away the Haryana Jats with him after Charan Singh's death, found Mehem an opportunity to hit back. He had Arun Nehru, George Fernandes and Ramakrishna Hegde with him to raise this demand. A meeting of the Janata Dal's Political Affairs Committee (PAC), the decision-making body in the absence of any other formal organisation structure, scheduled for 2 March 1990 was postponed at the last minute on grounds that Prime Minister V. P. Singh had some other task to attend. The real reason was that the deputy prime minister, Devi Lal, was unflinching in his support for son

Chautala's continuance as chief minister. He had ensured that a majority of the party MLAs in the Haryana assembly continued to support Chautala.

The crisis lingered on even while the PAC met in the morning on 3 March 1990 and the meeting turned out to be a venue for a direct clash between Devi Lal and Ajit Singh. The two leaders exchanged abuses against each other even while the others, including Chandra Shekhar, watched. Chandra Shekhar saw in this an occasion to embarrass V. P. Singh and Devi Lal against whom he had issues, even while sending unambiguous signals that he stood by Chautala. The PAC met again the same night with the party chief ministers, who attended as special invitees. It emerged that Mulayam Singh Yadav, Lalu Prasad Yadav and Biju Patnaik were inclined to seek Chautala's exit. Devi Lal was cornered now and even Sharad Yadav, his other supporter, was in no mood to back him in defence of son Chautala. The PAC, even now, refused to take a principled stand and left it to a subcommittee consisting of Ajit Singh, George Fernandes, Sharad Yadav, Arun Nehru and Yashwant Sinha. Even Sinha, a Chandra Shekhar loyalist (who had declined to become a junior minister in Singh's cabinet only three months ago), had by now turned against Chautala's continuance as chief minister. And on 4 March 1990, the committee sought the party to ask the Election Commission to hold a repoll in the whole of Mehem (rather than restrict it to the eight booths where violence marred the polls on February 28) and that Chautala be asked to resign forthwith.

The subcommittee's recommendation for a repoll was a calculated move. A repoll would mean that Chautala would remain locked in the contest against Dangi and in the given situation it was clear that he would be defeated, as and when the repoll is held. The Election Commission, however, met on 7 March and decided to countermand the polls. This meant that Chautala had the choice to walk out of the contest and look for another constituency and ensure his election to the assembly before 2 June 1990, when the six months deadline before which he had to get elected, would end. Ajit Singh, meanwhile, refused to relent and he visited Mehem on 9 March. At a public meeting there, he stated that 'democracy had been murdered in Mehem'. Gayatri Devi, Charan Singh's widow, meanwhile, showed up in a public meeting at Bainsi, along with Dangi. Devi Lal, isolated in the party by now, responded by announcing his resignation as deputy prime minister and walked out of the PAC meeting on 16 March 1990. It is another matter that it remained an announcement and the *tau* did not follow it up with a formal resignation letter. V. P. Singh, meanwhile, made a statement in Parliament that his party took a dim view of rigging whether it took place at Mehem or Amethi. The reference to Amethi was about the violence witnessed in Amethi and the attempt on the life of Sanjay Singh during the general election in November 1989. And alongside, he began to appease Devi Lal. In a letter to the *tau* conveyed through Chimanbhai Patel and Mulayam Singh Yadav, on 18 March 1990, Singh pleaded for his continuation in the Cabinet and the PAC.

Devi Lal, clearly encouraged by this, agreed to remain deputy prime minister and struck at Ajit Singh. As chairman of the Party's Parliamentary Board, he appointed Yashwant Sinha as secretary of the board. The party constitution, however, prescribed that this post be held by the secretary general of the party. Ajit Singh in his capacity as secretary general was de-facto secretary of the Parliamentary Board too. Another crisis was averted when Sinha declined the appointment and made it clear that it was untenable as long as Ajit Singh remained the secretary general. Dangi, meanwhile, had set out on a march to Delhi demanding justice, with 1,000 suporters from Mehem and a huge rally at the Ram Lila grounds on 18 March 1990, indicated the popular resentment against Chautala's continuance as chief minister. Even after the PAC meeting of 9 April 1990 took a vote and all the members decided against Chautala's continuance (Devi Lal had stayed out of that meeting), the party refused to convey the decision to Chautala. The Dal, now, was undergoing another kind of crisis and it involved putting an organisational structure in place.

On 10 April, it resolved, at V. P. Singh's behest, that an electoral college consisting of all the party's MPs and MLAs elect an interim president of the party. The electoral college was widened further, when it was decided to include all those who contested elections to the Lok Sabha and the various assemblies in November 1989 and in February 1990 as voters. Madhu Dandavate was appointed the Election Officer.

Chautala grabbed the opportunity and announced his support to S. R. Bommai for the party president. Bommai had support from Chandra Shekhar too and Devi Lal joined the gang. Other candidates in the fray were S. Jaipal Reddy, propped up by Ramakrishna Hegde, Ajit Singh and some others. Reddy had expected support from V. P. Singh too. Hukumdeo Narayan Yadav, Janata Dal MP from Bihar, also jumped into the fray but he was left to fend for himself. Voting looked imminent; but Reddy decided to withdraw from the contest after he realised that Prime Minister Singh was in no mood to take sides. Hukumdeo Narayan Yadav too was persuaded to withdraw and Bommai was unanimously 'elected' Janata Dal president on 19 May 1990. Chautala had played a role in Bommai's election as party president and it was only natural for him to expect a favour in return and let him remain chief minister of Haryana. The furore over the 27–28 February violence in Mehem seemed to have got muted by now and Chautala had now filed his nomination from Darba Kalan, apart from Mehem. Polling in these two constituencies was scheduled for 26 May 1990.

All these plans were upset on 16 May 1990, when the dead body of Amir Singh, an independent candidate from Mehem was found lying aside the Delhi–Hissar–Fazilka National Highway No. 10. Chautala's police promptly registered a case against Dangi and went to arrest him. Dangi had gone into hiding and the police force went on a shooting spree soon after. The Election Commission, once again, countermanded the poll process in Mehem. Unlike in February, when Mehem turned on a battleground between the various factions in the Janata Dal alone (the Congress [I] was in a state of shock at the loss of power in all states except Maharashtra that went to polls the same day), the 16 May episode was grabbed by Congress (I), as an opportunity, to attack V. P. Singh and his government. Rajiv Gandhi arrived in Mehem, visited Dangi's home and also of those killed and injured in the police firing in the village. The Janata Dal, now, had to address the issue in real earnest.

Another round of drawing-room confabulations followed, for days on end. And Bommai, on the day he was elected Janata Dal president, was presented with the challenge of dealing with Chautala. Late in the night on 19 May 1990, the Union Cabinet, resolved to order a CBI investigation into the murder of Amir Singh and a judicial enquiry by a sitting judge of the Supreme Court into the violence. The PAC directed Bommai to convey to Chautala, on 20 May 1990, the day after he was 'elected' as the Janata Dal's president, that he quit as chief minister. Chautala agreed to resign but set his own terms including the right to choose his replacement. He resigned on 23 May 1990 and a meeting of the Janata Dal legislators held the same day, with the Gujarat chief minister, Chimanbhai Patel, as central observer 'elected' Banarsi Das Gupta as leader. Gupta, deputy chief minister under Chautala since 2 December 1989, was sworn in as chief minister by Governor Dhanik Lal Mandal on 23 May 1990.

There was no doubt that Chautala continued to command the government and this was evident when Devi Lal's other son, Ranjit Singh (who had quit as minister in the wake of Mehem in February), was kept out of Gupta's Cabinet. And Sampat Singh, whose role as home minister in the context of the Mehem violence had come under cloud, was retained as home minister by Gupta too. All those in the Chautala cabinet remained ministers in Gupta's Cabinet with their old portfolios.

Chautala was elected to the assembly from Darba Kalan on 26 May 1990, winning by a huge margin of 55,000 votes. All the eight other candidates against him, including the Congress (I)'s Jagdish Nehra, forfeited their security deposits. His return as chief minister, now looked imminent. The only stumbling block to this was a public statement by V. P. Singh that Chautala will have to get himself elected from Mehem, as and when elections are held there, for him to return as chief minister. The Dal leaders, however, were willing to bend over backwards to appease Devi Lal and his son. A deal was struck to appoint Chautala as one of the Janata Dal's general secretaries and a Rajya Sabha seat for Ranjit Singh to be followed by his induction into the Union Cabinet. It was decided to scrap the post of Parliamentary Board Chairman, a post held by Devi Lal in the earlier set up. Bommai announced the list of general secretaries on 12 July 1990 and Chautala was one of them.

No sooner did Bommai board a plane from Delhi to Bangalore than Haryana chief minister, Banarsi Das Gupta, announced his resignation. Gupta was in Delhi when he announced his resignation and so was Governor Dhanik Lal Mandal. The resignation was accepted promptly. Party MLAs were instructed, by the police wireless (those were days when mobile telephony had not arrived), to reach Delhi before evening. Chautala was in Sirsa at that time and he was ferried to Delhi by a special helicopter. He was 'elected' leader of the legislature party and sworn in as chief minister, at the Haryana Bhawan, within minutes after his 'election'.

Only 50 days ago, the party leadership had forced him to resign and Om Prakash Chautala was Haryana chief minister once again on 12 July 1990. In many ways, Prime Minister V. P. Singh's role in Chautala's reinstallation was suspect. The judicial enquiry that was promised in May was not initiated even in July and the promise that the murder of Amir Singh will be probed by the CBI was not carried out. The Banarsi Das Gupta ministry did not seek a CBI probe. This was imperative for an order to that effect, going by the Constitution. Questions were raised by members of the party, and Singh's cabinet colleagues as well, on the nature of the discussion V. P. Singh had with Devi Lal on 8 July 1990. The prime minister and the deputy prime minister had a one-to-one meeting that day in Delhi and Janata Dal leaders were unwilling to take Singh's statement that he was unaware of the plans to reinstall Chautala in a few days.

The BJP, meanwhile, stepped in with a categorical demand that Chautala be sacked and made it clear (unlike in the past) that it was willing for an alternate arrangement in Haryana in the event Chautala walked away with his loyal MLAs. The BJP had 17 MLAs in the 90-member house and the party was in a position to help another Janata Dal government, consisting of anti-Chautala MLAs, even if Chautala carried out his threat to walk away with a section loyal to him. BJP president L. K. Advani told V. P. Singh to sack Chautala immediately and the CPI (M) Politburo, came out with a similar demand on 13 July 1990. The pressure was now on the prime minister and it came from the parties whose support from outside was critical for the survival of his government.

The Janata Dal, as a party, remained in a limbo throughout the day. Bommai was asked to return to Delhi and explain the situation to the party. Things began moving from the evening on 13 July 1990 and the movement, this time, was triggered when Arun Nehru, Arif Mohammed Khan and Satyapal Malik (all from the Jan Morcha block of the Janata Dal) tendered their letters of resignation to the prime minister. V. P. Singh finally reacted on 14 July 1990 by announcing that he too had decided to quit as prime minister. Rather than handing over the resignation letter to President R.Venkatraman, Singh presented his letter to National Front chairman, N. T. Rama Rao, and Janata Dal president, S. R. Bommai. He urged them to convene a meeting of the Front's Parliamentary Party and elect another leader. Singh clarified that he chose to hand over the letter to his party boss rather than President Venkatraman to prevent the Congress (I) wresting power.

At an extended meeting of the Janata Dal high command, late in the night on 14 July, attended by almost all the party leaders and chief ministers, Devi Lal was clearly isolated. But he chose to train his guns against Arun Nehru. He began spreading the rumour that Arun Nehru had resigned only because his involvement in the Bofors deal had now come to light and that the resignation was to pre-empt himself being sacked from the Cabinet. Bommai was keen on further consultations even now, but more ministers submitted their resignation letters. The number of ministers who resigned added up to 15 on 15 July 1990. However, unlike Arun Nehru, Arif Khan and Satyapal Malik who quit in protest against Chautala's reinstallation, the others who resigned did so to 'strengthen' V. P. Singh's hands.

At another level, the National Front leaders too stepped into the scene after V. P. Singh announced his desire to quit. On 15 July, the National Front presidium met. Among those who attended the meet were Tamil Nadu chief minister M. Karunanidhi and Assam chief minister Prafulla Mahanta. The meeting made it clear to V. P. Singh that he shall remain the prime minister (a point made by the Janata Dal PAC the same day) and that it was now necessary that he acted and removed Chautala. Armed with all this, V. P. Singh finally conveyed to Bommai to take a decision on Chautala's continuance soon. And on 16 July, Chandra Shekhar, Ajit Singh, George Fernandes and Yashwant Sinha were joined by Biju Patnaik, Mulayam Singh Yadav, Lalu Prasad Yadav and Chimanbhai Patel to work on a definite agenda: to ensure Chautala's resignation as chief minister. A series of meetings, in the same way as it happened in November–December 1989 before V. P. Singh was elected JDPP leader, were held in the various Bhawans in Delhi. For a while, they agreed to give in to Devi Lal's formula that Chautala would resign if Arun Nehru, Arif Khan and Satyapal Malik were kept out of the Union Cabinet. Prime Minister, V. P. Singh refused that. He wanted Chautala's resignation to be unconditional and without further delay.

An extended PAC with the party chief ministers and all its senior leaders met on 16 July 1990 and conveyed this to Devi Lal. The *tau* agreed to this finally and Chautala was replaced by another loyalist, Hukam Singh, as Haryana chief minister on 17 July 1990. The truce, however, was only for the time being. On 30 July 1990, Devi Lal released a letter, purportedly written by V. P. Singh (as defence minister in 1987), implicating Arun Nehru in the Bofors scandal. It turned out to be a forged letter and Prime Minister Singh conveyed to Devi Lal that he resign from the Cabinet. Devi Lal refused to heed and on 1 August 1990, President R. Venkatraman issued a communiqué, dismissing Devi Lal from the Union Cabinet, on the basis of a recommendation to that effect, by the

Prime Minister V. P. Singh.

The dismissal of Devi Lal may have been a simple affair insofar as the constitutional aspect was concerned. In parliamentary democracy, it is the prime minister's prerogative to decide the composition of the cabinet and there was no court of appeal against his action in the event of a minister's removal from the cabinet. But then, politics happened to be a game of leaders with their own mass base and in the given situation, Devi Lal commanded the loyalty of the Jats. And ever since Charan Singh's arrival on the scene, the Jats had come to constitute a strong anti-Congress social constituency in Uttar Pradesh, Haryana and Rajasthan. And Devi Lal, without doubt, was now the leader of the Jats in Haryana. The amorality in the anointment of Chautala as Haryana chief minister and the violence that marred the Mehem by-elections were not going to alienate the Jats from Devi Lal. His ouster, in such unceremonious manner, on the contrary, would help the Haryana patriarch consolidate his hold among the community.

V. P. Singh had learnt all this from the bumpy terrain of realpolitik and internalised the socio-political reality into his understanding of the art of politics. He was aware of the impact that Devi Lal's dismissal would have on the Janata Dal. Even if he could assure himself that the Haryana patriarch's ability to unsettle the Janata Dal Parliamentary Party was limited, he knew that Devi Lal's dismissal would dismantle the party's social support base. With the alienation of a section of the Jats now imminent, V. P. Singh was under pressure to reinvent the Janata Dal's social identity. It was another matter that the Janata Dal could depend on Ajit Singh to relate with the Jats; but then, this was limited to western Uttar Pradesh and given the antagonistic relationship between Ajit Singh and Mulayam Singh, such calculations rested on tenuous grounds.

Devi Lal, meanwhile, responded to his dismissal by calling for a *kisan* rally at the Boat Club grounds on 9 August 1990. As things began moving on that front, it became clear that the Haryana patriarch was not alone. Chandra Shekhar, waiting for an opportunity to strike at V. P. Singh, conveyed his decision to attend the 9 August rally. There were such others like H. D. Deve Gowda (who had scores to settle with Ramakrishna Hegde and S. R. Bommai), Akali Dal leader Prakash Singh Badal (who was angry with the Janata Dal's friendly overtures towards the Akali Dal [Mann]), BSP leader Kanshi Ram and farmers' leader Mahendra Singh Tikait (waiting to carve out a space for himself in western Uttar Pradesh), who had announced their decision to join the rally and throw their weight behind Devi Lal.

It was in this context that the Janata Dal decided to remember one of the promises from its Election Manifesto; to implement the recommendations of the Mandal Commission.

Mandal, Mandir and the Fall

Submitted on 31 December 1980 the Report of the Second Backward Classes Commission was gathering dust in the office of the Ministry of Welfare. The Janata Dal had promised implementation of the recommendations and this had figured as the 36th item in the party's manifesto. It may be recalled that the Commission, with Bindeswari Prasad Mandal, a veteran Socialist, as chairman was appointed on 20 December 1978 (when Morarji Desai was the prime minister). When the report was submitted, the Janata Party government had collapsed, the Charan Singh interlude was over and Indira Gandhi had returned as prime minister. Indira, after her return on 14 January 1980, extended the term of the Mandal Commission twice (for six months each) but did not attend to the recommendations. Rajiv Gandhi too did not care to look into the report. The Janata Dal, despite having remembered to include its implementation in its manifesto, seemed to let the five-volume report rest in peace in the initial months. Madhu Limaye, who had played an important role in the formation and the disintegration of the Janata Party, lamented that the government was dilly-dallying on the Mandal Report when the media approached him for a comment on V. P. Singh's performance in the first 100 days as prime minister. That was in March 1990.

The BSP leader Kanshi Ram, meanwhile, was campaigning with fervour demanding the implementation of the Mandal Commission's recommendation. The party's cadre would hold demonstrations in Delhi's Mandi House circle, every day without fail, pressing this demand.

There were expectations that the report and its recommendations will be given life after the National Front government assumed office in December 1989. This was in the context of a constitutional amendment effected in December 1989, extending the scheme to reserve Lok Sabha and state assembly constituencies for the scheduled castes and scheduled tribes. This pertained to Articles 330, 332 and 334 in Part XVI of the Constitution.

The founding fathers of the Constitution had laid out that 22 per cent of the total number of seats in the Lok Sabha and the various state assemblies will be reserved to members from the scheduled castes and scheduled tribes. This reservation was to last for 30 years. This was done in order to ensure the representation of the scheduled castes and the scheduled tribes in the institutions because they were convinced, at the time of drafting the Constitution, that these social groups will not gain representation without such a special provision. The 30-year stipulation (Article 334 of the Constitution) was based on undue optimism that the marginalised groups will mature, in this time, to compete with the advanced sections of the society. In 1980, there was realisation that the optimism was misplaced and hence the parties, across the spectrum, decided to extend the life of the provision by 10 more years. As soon as the National Front government came to power, the consensus was that it warranted yet another extension and the Constitution was amended (62nd Amendment Act) to extend the reservation for 10 more years with effect from 20 December 1989.

This had nothing to do with reservation in jobs for the scheduled castes, which was governed by the Constitution (First Amendment) Act, 1951, by which Articles 15 (Prohibition of discrimination on grounds of religion, race, caste, sex or place of birth) and Article 16 (equality of opportunity in matters of public employment) were amended to include an additional clause (Clause 4 of both the Articles) that laid out that nothing in those articles or any other provision of the Constitution shall prevent the state from making a special provision for the advancement of any of the socially and educationally backward classes of citizens or for the scheduled castes and Tribes (for Article 15) and reservation in jobs for any backward classes of citizens, which in the opinion of the state are not adequately represented in the services of the state (for Article 16). On this basis, the Union as well as the state governments had reserved 22.5 per cent of the posts in government departments for the SCs and STs from the very inception of the Republic.

The passage of the Constitution 62nd Amendment Act in December 1989 and the fact that the Janata Dal's manifesto had promised implementation of the Mandal Commission's recommendation seemed to lead sections of the upper-caste youth to believe that reservation in government jobs for the other backward classes was now imminent. Anti-reservation rallies were organised, particularly in Uttar Pradesh, in January 1990. The protests turned violent in many places and it spread into Bihar, Rajasthan and Gujarat soon after. The Janata governments had initiated OBC reservations in state government jobs in these states in 1977–78 and there were violent reactions to that even then. The agitation, this time, were based on apprehensions that the same will be done with Central government jobs as recommended by the Mandal Commission. These, however, did not last for long and normality was restored within a couple of weeks.

That the AJGAR social alliance, in which the Rajputs (the largest section of the upper castes), remained supporters of the Janata Dal was clear in the results of the 1989 general elections as well as in assembly elections in February–March 1990 in Bihar. Insofar as the other states (Rajasthan, Madhya Pradesh, Himachal Pradesh and Gujarat) were concerned, the Janata Dal was just a junior ally of the BJP and the combine was strong enough to defeat the Congress (I) decisively. Even if AJGAR was relevant mostly to Bihar and Uttar Pradesh only, the fact that the BJP–Janata Dal arrangement swept the polls in the other states was a clear indication that the National Front was in no mood to let go the unity of social forces against the Congress (I) by invoking Mandal. The Janata Dal leaders had allayed fears over the Mandal Commission recommendations (that caused the upper castes to agitate) by February 1990 and it was left to the BSP to agitate for implementation of the report.

Meanwhile, V. P. Singh was aware of the implications of Devi Lal's dismissal for the Janata Dal. The Haryana patriarch had managed to enlist Chandra Shekhar and Kanshi Ram to attend his August 9 rally. The Lok Dal (B) leaders such as Mulayam Singh Yadav, Lalu Prasad Yadav and Sharad Yadav may have stood up against Devi Lal in the context of Chautala and Mehem. But then, there was nothing that suggested that they were happy with his dismissal from the Cabinet. The only section that celebrated the exit of Devi Lal was the Jan Morcha leaders. All this led V. P. Singh to pull out the Mandal Report.

On 7 August 1990, a couple of days before Devi Lal mobilised a few lakh supporters at the Boat Club grounds, Prime Minister V. P. Singh informed the Lok Sabha of the government's decision to implement some parts of the Mandal Commission's recommendations. The statement was welcomed by thumping of desks across the house. The initial reaction was one of universal appreciation from the members present in the house that day and this included the Congress (I) as well as the BJP and the Left parties apart from those in the treasury benches. V. P. Singh, through this move, could enlist the support of such leaders as Mulayam Singh Yadav, Lalu Prasad Yadav and Sharad Yadav; they would stand by him and not go with Devi Lal.

The Boat Club rally on 9 August 1990, was a massive affair with crowds from far away districts of Uttar Pradesh as well as from Haryana and western UP. And Devi Lal declared that he would fight for the cause of the peasantry, even if it meant his expulsion from the Janata Dal. It was clear from the rally that the Haryana patriarch was determined to take on V. P. Singh. But then, he had not envisaged V. P. Singh's masterstroke by way of Mandal.

It took a while before the implications of Mandal would sink in. Prime Minister V. P. Singh's independence day address, was replete with rhetoric and included a declaration that the 1990s will be a farmers' decade. The prime minister's speech, from the ramparts of the Red Fort, did indicate his intentions to prepare for a snap poll. As for the 7 August 1990 declaration implementing 27 per cent reservation in central government jobs for the OBCs, based on the Mandal Commission's recommendations, some feeble notes of protest came from the BJP and the Left parties (whose support from the outside was crucial for the government's survival). Even these were on the ground that the government did not consult them and take them into confidence before making the announcement. Some members of the Union Cabinet too spoke on these lines and that was all. The Union Government notified the decision to reserve 27 per cent of its jobs to OBCs on 13 August 1990. The notification specified that those castes that figured in both the central list (put out by the Mandal Commission in its report) and in the lists of the various state governments were eligible for reservations to begin with. A National Commission for OBCs was also constituted accordingly and this commission was vested with the powers to include or delete castes from the national list, after going through the claims and objections, in due course.

The Congress (I), meanwhile, did not react. Its leaders were busy engaging Devi Lal and Chandra Shekhar and the engagement was more in the way of exploring the possibility of collaborating at some future date. When the Congress (I) Working Committee took up the issue a fortnight later, it spoke of the need to rework the criteria, to ensure that economic backwardness was included rather than resting the entire basis on caste. The BJP and the CPI (M) too spoke in the same breath but none of the parties were prepared to antagonise the OBCs, a substantially large section of the population.

The Congress (I) leadership, meanwhile, also knew that Chandra Shekhar and Devi Lal, together, were in no position to rally as many as 47 Janata Dal MPs, one-third of the party's strength necessary for a split, in the immediate context. The duo was also aware that mustering as many as 70 party MPs against V. P. Singh and thus replace him as JDPP leader was a tall order. Notwithstanding this, there was an attempt to present a charge sheet against V. P. Singh before the JDPP meeting on 30 September 1990 and only 29 MPs (from both Houses) signed the letter demanding Singh's resignation. The rebel leaders were let down by Mulayam Singh Yadav, Biju Patnaik and Chimanbhai Patel (all chief ministers) who, together, commanded the loyalty of 35 MPs.

All these machinations were happening in the midst of a violent agitation against the implementation of the Mandal Commission recommendations. The initial reaction to the 7 August 1990 declaration by V. P. Singh was in the form of demonstrations in Lucknow. In a few days, such protests were organised in other towns in Uttar Pradesh and in Patna, Jaipur and Ahmedabad. The protest took violent forms in Haryana with anti-reservation crowds burning buses and blocking roads. That the Hukam Singh government let all that happen was clear. There were feeble voices against the government in Delhi too with students from the various colleges holding rallies. The agitation, in fact, was showing signs of subsiding in early September 1990. This changed after 19 September 1990, when Rajiv Goswami, a college student in Delhi, set himself on fire at a crossroad junction near the Delhi University. Goswami sustained 50 per cent burns and was taken to the All India Institute for Medical Sciences (AIIMS) for treatment. He seemed to succeed raking up passions against V. P. Singh and the government, putting anti-Mandal on the centre stage. His attempt to commit suicide, in any case, was a crime punishable under the penal code.

In quick succession, suicide attempts were made by others in Delhi, Hissar, Sirsa, Ambala, Meerut, Lucknow and other towns. One of those, Surinder Chauhan, set himself ablaze at the crossroads near the AIIMS, where hundreds of students and anti-reservation protestors had assembled since the time Goswami was admitted to the hospital, and sustained 90 per cent burns. Chauhan died within a few hours provoking violence all over Delhi. The police, in many instances, remained mute witness to the violent mobs vandalising government property. The protests took the form of candle-light processions in middle-class localities. The Anti Mandal Commission Forum (AMCF) was set up and its constitution revealed the conspicuous absence of any representative from any of the political parties. The fact was that the political parties were unwilling to come out against the Mandal-based reservations due to fear of losing the support from the numerically large OBCs. By all estimates, these castes constituted more than half the nation's population.

The local leaders of the various parties, however, were playing an active role in the agitation. And Mahendra Singh Tikait, seeking to build himself as the leader of the Jat peasantry in western Uttar Pradesh, now saw an opportunity in the context of the anti-reservation protests. In the given context, where Ajit Singh stayed on with V. P. Singh (despite Mandal and the fact that the Jats from western UP were not included in the OBC list), Tikait wanted to position himself as the leader of the Jats in western UP. Tikait called for an anti-Mandal rally at the Boat Club on 2 October 1990. He was, however, unaware of the fact that the AMCF in Delhi, though controlled and led by the students, was by this time infiltrated by local Congress (I) leaders. Among them was Sajjan Kumar, known to have played a prominent role in the anti-Sikh violence in November 1984; the CBI had secured an arrest warrant against him by this time.

And on 2 October 1990, the rally at the Boat Club, turned violent, leaving three dead and 20 injured. The AMCF crowd, most of them students from the Delhi University and the Jawaharlal Nehru University, were in for a rude shock when they reached the Boat Club lawns from the AIIMS crossing. The 2 October rally was supposed to illustrate the unity of the peasantry with the students in Delhi against the Mandal report. But then, the lumpen elements, who had joined the crowd in good numbers, ensured that the agitation lost its steam and the AMCF was left in a disarray. The Boat Club rally, in fact, marked the culmination of the criminalisation of the agitation, a process that had begun, in the form of incidents of violence after Chauhan succumbed to the burn injuries at the AIIMS crossing.

The constitutional validity of the 13 August 1990 order, meanwhile, was challenged through a writ petition before a five-member bench of the Supreme Court. The petition was admitted on 11 September 1990; but the apex court refused to issue a stay order. It was brought up again on 25 September 1990 and the petitioners drew the court's attention to the violent reactions to the order, to press for a stay. The court refused to stay the order again. However, on 1 October 1990, the five-judge bench stayed the operation of the 13 August 1990 order and posted the matter to be heard by a nine-member bench. In other words, the concerns of the AMCF were partly attended to by the stay order and this led to the agitation petering off. The violence at the Boat Club rally, the day after, contributed to the campaign losing whatever little steam it had.

The dispute (Indra Sawhney and Others vs Union of India) was brought to an end on 16 November 1992, when the nine-member bench of the Supreme Court, in a 6:3 judgement, held the 13 August 1990 order constitutionally valid. The judgement, in fact, put a stamp of approval on a host of earlier judgements, that caste as a category shall be used to determine social and educational backwardness. The nine-member bench, in fact, upheld the verdict in the M. R. Balaji vs State of Mysore case (1963) that caste is a valid category to determine social and educational backwardness and that job reservations, in all cases, shall not exceed 50 per cent of the total number of posts. The leading judgement was given by Chief Justice M. H. Kania along with Justices B. P. Jeevan Reddy, M. N. Venkatachalaiah, A. M. Ahmadi, S. Rathnavel Pandian and P. B. Sawant. The dissenting minority was constituted by Justices T. K. Thommen, Kuldip Singh and R. M. Sahai.

The bench also added that the elite among the OBCs shall be excluded and ordered the Union Government to identify the creamy layer among the OBCs for that purpose. The Congress (I), in power by now, went about the task and a government order on 8 September 1993, setting out the criteria for identifying the creamy layer, ensured the implementation of 27 per cent reservation in Central government jobs and in the public sector undertakings for the other backward classes. The relevance of Mandal, however, was not restricted to a few thousand Central Government jobs. The impact of it, on the political discourse, made Mandal and the 7 August 1990 declaration by V. P. Singh into a significant event.

The immediate fallout of it was that the social alliance, that gave the Janata Dal its advantage and the winning edge in the November 1989 elections as well as in the state assembly elections in Uttar Pradesh and in Bihar in February 1990, was broken. Even if the Janata Dal could retain a large part of the Jats in western Uttar Pradesh as long as Ajit Singh was held back in the party, the Rajputs were now ranged against the party. The members of this powerful upper caste, with a substantial political muscle that they derived out of the feudal context that determined the election process in Uttar Pradesh and Bihar (from where over one-fifth of the Lok Sabha MPs were elected), had rallied behind the Janata Dal in November 1989. They were supporters of the Congress party over the years but turned against the party after V. P. Singh was meted out with a shabby treatment. In the post Mandal context, this social group saw V. P. Singh as the villain and the decade after Mandal saw them searching for a platform that could defeat the Janata Dal.

The Congress (I) could have been their natural choice. But then, the Congress (I), in this period would also get alienated from the Dalit support base; the arrival of the BSP in Uttar Pradesh and the social alliance that it cobbled with the OBCs, represented by Mulayam Singh Yadav's Samajwadi Party (that won a majority in Uttar Pradesh in November 1993), rendered the Congress (I) a weak alternative to the Janata Dal. Moreover, the Muslims, yet another support base of the Congress (I), were now turning against the party in the wake of its machinations over Ayodhya. This led the Rajputs to flock behind the BJP.

Mandal also led the BJP decide its own course, building itself into an alternative to the Congress(I), a goal that the party had set for itself at the time of its foundation in Bombay in December 1980. Atal Behari Vajpayee, it may be recalled, had outlined this at the foundation of the BJP: 'The task before us is to retain the old base and win new ground.' While the old base that constituted the Jan Sangh was retained, the party had set the basis to win the new ground through its association with the Ayodhya campaign openly after the Palampur National Executive in June 1989. This helped the BJP to emerge as the third largest party in the Lok Sabha winning 85 seats in the November 1989 elections. The BJP leaders, however, were aware of the fact that their march to power will be accomplished only if it gathered further strength in Uttar Pradesh and Bihar, from where more than one-fifth of the Lok Sabha MPs were elected. Of the 139 Lok Sabha seats from these two states, the BJP had won only 16 in 1989. And in the three states where the Jan Sangh was strong—Madhya Pradesh, Rajasthan and Himachal Pradesh—the BJP's performance, in November 1989, had peaked (43 out of 77). In other words, it was imperative for the BJP to break new grounds in Uttar Pradesh and Bihar to capture power in Delhi. In these two states, the Janata Dal had even refused to have a pre-poll alliance with the BJP.

In the post-Mandal era, the Janata Dal's social alliance—the AJGAR—collapsed and it was clear that the party was in no position to repeat its November 1989 performance in Uttar Pradesh and Bihar. Such calculations had become relevant because the events in September, involving its leaders, pointed to the imminent collapse of the V. P. Singh government and elections.

The dismissal of Devi Lal on 1 August 1990, the reaction against the 7 August declaration on Mandal and a calculated move by Rajiv Gandhi, who now declared that the Congress (I) will support another Janata Dal Government as long as it was led by anyone other than V. P. Singh, sent a distinct signal to the Janata Dal MPs that the only way to avoid another election, at that stage, was to show V. P. Singh the door. And even if the stay on the implementation of the Mandal Commission report on 1 October 1990 seemed to have saved the day for V. P. Singh (with the anti-Mandal protests abating), there were several other fronts where the National Front government was found faltering.

The situation in Jammu and Kashmir was on a permanent course of drift and some of it was directly the fallout of Home Minister Mufti Mohammed Sayeed's partisan agenda. The removal of George Fernandes as minister in-charge of Kashmir affairs, on 26 May 1990, had brought to a naught the efforts to gather sections of the militants to negotiation. The Punjab crisis, meanwhile, worsened with incidents of killings becoming a regular feature. The emergence of the Akali Dal (Mann), winning five Lok Sabha seats in November 1989 and the friendly overtures to it from V. P. Singh, had alienated the Akali Dal leaders such as Badal and Barnala. The National Front government displayed its lack of farsightedness when it moved a Constitution amendment, in early October, in a special session to extend the tenure of President's rule in Punjab by another six months. Elections were due, otherwise, before 10 November 1990. There was trouble in Assam too. The AGP, a partner in the National Front and in power in Assam, had failed in all senses and incidents of violence involving the United Liberation Front of Assam (ULFA) were on the rise.

It was in this situation that the BJP set out on its own course and prepared itself for the battle and reinvent its Hindutva base. The party had refrained from making a concerted attempt at this, in November 1989, even while it was conscious of its potential. L. K. Advani, the BJP president, after all, had steered the party into the Ayodhya campaign since Palampur and was aware of the ground swell of support for the party. The BJP had improved its strength in the Lok Sabha that way. A conclave, attended by the BJP leaders along with the top brass of the RSS, at Delhi on 12 September 1990, had drawn up the plans for another *rath yatra*. And the BJP National Executive meet at Bhopal between 14 and 16 September 1990 endorsed this. The *yatra* was to begin at Somnath in Gujarat on 25 September 1990 and reach Ayodhya on 30 October 1990, traversing 10,000 kilometres, through 10 states and touching 200 Lok Sabha constituencies. Advani was going to ride the *rath*.

A lot of thinking had gone into drawing the route of the *yatra*. The *rath*, a light commercial vehicle with an air-conditioned anteroom for Advani to rest in between halts, was scheduled to halt in several towns where the party had planned to organise large public meetings. The towns were Rajkot, Ahmedabad, Vadodara and Surat (Gujarat); Bombay, Thane, Pune, Nagpur and Solapur (Maharashtra); Hyderabad and Adilabad (Andhra Pradesh); Jabalpur, Bhopal, Indore and Mandsaur (Madhya Pradesh); Udaipur and Bayawar (Rajasthan); Khetri and Rohtak (Haryana) to reach Delhi on 13 October 1990. The BJP president would stay back in Delhi until 19 October 1990, while the *rath* would reach Dhanbad in Bihar and wait for him to re-start the *yatra* from there on 20 October 1990. From Dhanbad, the *rath* would halt at Ranchi, Gaya, Samastipur and Muzafarpur (Bihar); Deoria, Varanasi, Allahabad, Kanpur and Lucknow (Uttar Pradesh) before reaching Ayodhya on 30 October 1990. At Ayodhya, Advani was to participate in a *kar seva*, a symbolic beginning, to construct the temple.

Even if the BJP had 'suspended' its formal association with the Ayodhya campaign after the V. P. Singh government had assumed office in December 1989, the VHP had kept the momentum on, since then, by way of organising *sant sammelans* and an attempt was made to lay the foundation stone for the proposed temple in June 1990.

The anti-Mandal agitation, which was at best sporadic, at the time when the BJP executive met at Bhopal had turned into a movement by the time Advani had got on to the *rath* at Somnath on 25 September 1990; the turning point being the self immolation bid by Rajiv Goswami on September 19. Advani had a taste of the intense hatred that the students had towards V. P. Singh and also the fact that the BJP, on whose support the government survived, was held equally responsible for the Mandal decision when he went to the AIIMS to visit Goswami. He was attacked by the agitators and prevented from entering the premises. Hence he attacked the August 7 decision in the course of the *rath yatra*. Advani was setting up the BJP on an anti-Congress–anti-Janata Dal track and his speeches, wherever the *rath* stopped, were a blend of aggressive Hindutva and anti-Mandal. And in the context of the lull in the anti-Mandal agitation after 2 October 1990, Advani provided the upper-caste youth, across the northern states, with a political alternative that they could look up to. The association of the symbol of Ram and Ayodhya with this also helped the BJP forge a Hindu identity that was not restricted to the upper castes and had a lot of space for the OBCs, the Dalits and the Adivasis, among whom the VHP had been active for some years now.

The BJP–VHP nexus was evident as the *rath yatra* began from Somnath. In Gujarat, the organisational aspects of the *yatra* were handled by Shankarsinh Vaghela and Narendra Modi. A prominent feature of the *yatra* in Gujarat was the tridents held by the volunteers who accompanied the *rath* and those who lined up the roads. The organisers took care that the tridents, distributed by the VHP, were all a bit shorter than six inches. This ensured that the police, even if the political leadership had wanted, could not arrest them under the provisions of the Arms Act. Under the Act, possession of a trident longer than six inches was liable for arrest. It was another matter that the Janata Dal government in Gujarat, headed by Chimanbhai Patel, had no intention to stop the *rath* or arrest the VHP men.

As the *rath* traversed across Gujarat, Maharashtra, Karnataka, Andhra Pradesh, Rajasthan and Haryana to reach Delhi on 13 October 1990, it left a trail of anti-Muslim violence in all towns and cities with a large Muslim population. The *rath yatra* was also one of the events where the BJP focused on managing the media. Pramod Mahajan, who would emerge into a powerful leader in the BJP when the party headed the Union Government (1998–2004), was Advani's aide during the *yatra*. He ensured that Advani had regular interfaces with the media during the *yatra*. The *rath yatra* and Advani's utterances, thus, grabbed a lot of space in the newspapers, day after day.

The recurring theme in Advani's speeches, during the *yatra* and also in his interactions with the media, was that Somnath was rebuilt in 1950 with government patronage which is now being denied to the Ram Temple. This, in fact, was the tone of the message from the RSS chief, Balasaheb Deoras, on the day Advani set off on the yatra on September 25: 'It is appropriate especially because it is starting from Somnath. By this, the country can be told that immediately after independence, with Sardar Patel's initiative and the Central Government's support, this temple was rebuilt.'

The V. P. Singh Government, meanwhile, revived its efforts at 'negotiation' between the Babri Masjid Action Committee and the VHP. But the RSS was now determined to push the Ayodhya agenda into a confrontation and paint the government as anti-Hindu. The Sangh, in other words, was now determined to engage in a confrontation with the V. P. Singh government and the BJP too had decided to withdraw support to the government. V. P. Singh, meanwhile, had set out addressing public meetings in the various district headquarters in Uttar Pradesh, along with Chief Minister Mulayam Singh Yadav, and declared in all those meetings that the Union Government will pull all the stops to prevent the *rath* entering Uttar Pradesh. Mulayam Singh went ahead to declare that the state government will not allow even a bird to enter Ayodhya on 30 October, the day Advani's *rath* was set to roll into the town. The stage was set for a confrontation and it was now only a matter of time before the government, supported by the Left and the BJP from outside, collapsed.

This, however, did not prevent the government and the BJP leadership from negotiating. And the efforts reached its peak during the week when Advani took a break in Delhi between 13 and 19 October 1990. V. P. Singh deputed two of his cabinet colleagues—George Fernandes and P. Upendra—to talk with the RSS chief Deoras, who was then, present in Delhi. The two leaders were told, in unambiguous terms, that the RSS will not settle for anything short of a temple at the site where the Babri Masjid stood. A meeting between Prime Minister Singh and Advani on 19 October 1990, ended without any tangible results. And Advani left for Dhanbad, informing the prime minister that his party will withdraw support to the government if the *rath yatra* was stopped.

At another level, late in the night on 19 October 1990, the Union Government announced a three-point formula:

- Takeover of the disputed Babri Masjid and surrounding areas through a Presidential Ordinance,
- Handing over of the undisputed land to the Ram Janmabhoomi Yagna Samiti for the construction of the temple and
- Refer the disputes to the Supreme Court for quick disposal.

It appeared, for the moment, that a settlement had been reached, but then, on 20 October 1990 (the day after the ordinance was issued) the shahi imam of the Jama Masjid, protested against the government takeover of *wakf* lands. The VHP too conveyed its opposition to the formula. And on 21 October 1990, the Union

Government beat a retreat and recommended that the 19 October ordinance, taking over the Babri Masjid and the land around that, be revoked. That the V. P. Singh government was in serious trouble was reflected even on 17 October 1990, when the Congress (I) and the BJP boycotted an all-party meeting called to discuss the crisis.

Meanwhile, Advani had boarded a train to Dhanbad from Delhi on 18 October 1990 to continue his *rath yatra* from there the day after. Prime Minister V. P. Singh was now left with two options: to let the *rath* roll into Ayodhya and ensure his government's survival, or to stop it and provoke the BJP to withdraw support to his government. He was aware, by now, that to let the *rath* roll into Ayodhya would lead to losing the Muslim support base, assiduously drawn away from the Congress during the past decade, now with the Janata Dal. Moreover, the Janata Dal chief ministers in Bihar and Uttar Pradesh—Lalu Prasad Yadav and Mulayam Singh Yadav—were ones who had internalised the strategy that Madhu Limaye had set out in 1978–79 (to build the Janata Party as a secular platform by pushing the Jan Sangh elements out of the fold) and these two leaders had defined the Janata Dal's existence in their states as an anti-Congress–anti-BJP platform even before the November 1989 elections.

This, in fact, meant that both Lalu and Mulayam, on their own would be uneasy with the idea of letting Advani persist with his anti-Muslim agenda. Yet, Prime Minister Singh dissuaded Lalu Yadav from stopping the Rajdhani Express (which Advani had boarded from Delhi to reach Dhanbad) as it entered Bihar and arresting Advani. Thus, the *rath yatra* was resumed from Dhanbad on 20 October 1990 and it reached Patna late in the evening on 22 October 1990 after traversing through Ranchi and Gaya. After addressing a public meeting at the Gandhi Maidan at Patna, Advani arrived at a government guest house in Samastipur late in the night. It was then that it had become clear that Prime Minister Singh, at long last, had decided to stop the *rath* from rolling. Earlier in the day, on 22 October, the prime minister came under concerted pressure at the chief minister's conference in Delhi. The conference was convened with the *rath yatra* and the Ayodhya issue as its agenda. And Uttar Pradesh chief minister, Mulayam Singh Yadav, without mincing words, conveyed his determination to stop the *rath* rolling into his state. West Bengal chief minister Jyoti Basu and Kerala chief minister E. K. Nayanar too conveyed that the Left parties will settle for nothing less than halting the *rath*. And V. P. Singh chose to address the nation, during prime time that evening (on 22 October 1990), on Doordarshan and the AIR; even if he did not speak of an arrest, Singh did convey, that evening, that the *rath yatra* will not be allowed to continue.

Advani was woken up early in the morning and the district magistrate showed him the arrest warrant. The BJP leader, indeed, was waiting for that. He took some time off to write down a letter, addressed to the President R.Venkatraman, informing him of the party's decision to withdraw support to the V. P. Singh-led

National Front government. Advani entrusted the letter with BJP secretary, Kailashpati Mishra, to be handed over to the president. The BJP president was taken to an airstrip first and from there to Dumka by a helicopter that was kept ready for that purpose. Advani, accompanied by Pramod Mahajan, was then driven to a government guest house in Masanjor, in the Bihar–West Bengal border. The arrest and the detention under the National Security Act (NSA), a preventive detention law then under force, meant that there was no need to file a charge sheet.

The BJP, however, refrained from demanding the dismissal of the V. P. Singh government. The BJP Parliamentary Party leader, Atal Behari Vajpayee refused to give a direct answer to querries from journalists as to whether the BJP would support another National Front government in the event V. P. Singh was replaced by another leader. V. P. Singh, meanwhile, met President R.Venkatraman, later in the morning on 23 October 1990 and made it clear that the government's survival will be decided on the floor of the Lok Sabha. There was a sense of irony about this assertion. The government was reduced to a minority without the BJP's support. The Janata Dal's 140 MPs along with the 52 Left party MPs did not add up to a majority in the 544 member Lok Sabha. The Janata Dal, however, seemed to hedge its bets on a thinking that the Congress (I) leadership will now come under pressure from the 'secular' elements in the party, against teaming up with the BJP in the Lok Sabha to pull down the government.

This, however, was wishful thinking. The Congress (I) president Rajiv Gandhi had already set up his emissaries to negotiate with Chandra Shekhar and Devi Lal. The two leaders had set the ball rolling to orchestrate a revolt against V. P. Singh as early as on 30 September 1990. A charge sheet against Prime Minister Singh, though signed by only 10 Lok Sabha MPs, was presented at the JDPP meeting that day. Yashwant Sinha had initiated that move. This, in fact, was a trial balloon floated by Chandra Shekhar. And after the BJP withdrew support, on 23 October 1990, the possibility of a mid-term election loomed large. The rebels' hope to enlist more MPs on their side was not misplaced in this context. V. P. Singh's response that he was not going to run away from the battle pushed the Janata Dal MPs to defect. And within days, the strength of the rebel camp was increasing and moving closer to 46 MPs, which was necessary to save themselves from being disqualified as MPs.

The anti-defection law, as enacted in 1985 when Rajiv Gandhi was prime minister, empowered the speaker to decide on the question of disqualification of a member who defects. Disqualification was prescribed if a MP voluntarily gave up membership of the party or defied a whip while voting in Parliament. The law, however, recognised splits and mergers of parties. For a split, at least one-third of the total membership of the Parliamentary party must defect.

President Venkatraman, meanwhile, had set 7 September 1990 as the date, before which V. P. Singh had to seek a confidence vote in the Lok Sabha. This enhanced the pace of events in the Janata Dal rebel camp. Assured of support from the Congress (I), in the event the Janata Dal replaced V. P. Singh with another leader, the rebels were now able to gather more MPs behind them; this was the only way to avoid a mid-term election. V. P. Singh, now certainly was captain of a sinking ship. And the Janata Dal MPs were concerned about themselves. The Chandra Shekhar–Devi Lal combine was the safety boat. On 3 November 1990, Devi Lal, without mincing words, said: 'I tell all those who come to me that if they want elections they should go to V. P. Singh but if they do not want elections, they should go to Chandra Shekhar.' Three junior ministers had resigned from the Cabinet by then: Minister of State for Forests, Maneka Gandhi; Deputy Minister for Parliamentary Affairs, Jagdeep Dhankar and Deputy Minister for Sports, Bhakta Charan Das. Minister of State for Home, Subodh Kant Sahay resigned on 4 November 1990. Devi Lal, who until now had refrained from stating his demand in specific terms, did that on 4 November; that V. P. Singh resign as prime minister.

A meeting of the Janata Dal Parliamentary Party, convened for 5 November 1990, could have been the appropriate place for the rebels to give a final push to their campaign against V. P. Singh. But then, they realised that they did not command a majority in the JDPP. Instead of attending the meeting, the rebel MPs assembled at Devi Lal's residence. The Haryana patriarch proposed Chandra Shekhar's name as the JDPP leader and a resolution to that effect was passed unanimously. They described the meeting as the JDPP general body and V. P. Singh was expelled from the party. The Janata Dal leadership struck, later in the day, by expelling 30 MPs (25 from the Lok Sabha and 5 Rajya Sabha members), including Chandra Shekhar from the party. Those expelled on 5 November 1990 included Maneka Gandhi, Subodh Kant Sahay, Manubhai Kotadia and Bhakta Charan Das, all junior ministers in V. P. Singh's cabinet. The Rajya Sabha members expelled that day included Yashwant Sinha (who initiated the anti-VP campaign on 30 September) and Sanjay Singh (V. P. Singh's kin and one of his associates from the Jan Morcha days). And keeping up with the tradition of intrigues, Devi Lal, at whose residence the rebels had met and elected Chandra Shekhar, was not among those expelled.

It will be in order to explain the intrigue behind the decision to expel only 25 Lok Sabha MPs even when the rebel camp consisted of many more on that day. The anti-defection law provided that MPs expelled from the party will not be disqualified. Thus, the 25 expelled will remain MPs. The intrigue was that the expulsions brought the JDPP's strength to 115. That meant that the rebel camp will now have to rally at least 39 MPs (one-third of the 115), to avoid disqualification. This was still a tall order for the rebel camp. Chandra Shekhar and his group, meanwhile, challenged the expulsion on grounds that it was done without a show-cause notice, as provided for in the party Constitution and also from the larger principle of natural justice. All this was happening even while it became clear that the Congress (I) Parliamentary Party was united behind Rajiv Gandhi's decision to vote against the government even if that involved voting on the same side as the BJP. In other words, the V. P. Singh government was destined to fall. The situation was aptly described by Hasan Suroor, a perceptive journalist at that time, as follows: 'Like one of those innocent early Hollywood thrillers in which "whodonit" and the "why" were known right from the beginning, the collapse of the V. P. Singh government had become a certainty on October 23, the day the Bharatiya Janata Party (BJP) withdrew support to it following the arrest of L. K. Advani, party president, leading a *rath yatra* to Ayodhya. Given the heavy numerical odds in the Lok Sabha against the National Front Government, even Sherlock Holmes' companion Dr. Watson would for once have found it "elementary" to predict the outcome of the vote of confidence sought by it on November 7.'

Late in the evening, on 7 November 1990, after a marathon seven hour-long debate, the confidence motion was put to vote in the Lok Sabha. The government was voted out decisively. The voting figures were: 356 votes against the motion, 151 for the government and six (all Akali Dal [Mann]) abstentions. Eleven MPs were not present in the house to cast their votes. There were 20 vacancies in the 544 member House on that day. The National Front government, sworn in on 2 December 1989, collapsed in 11 months and 14 days.

The fate of the government was sealed on 23 October, when the BJP withdrew support. But the voting figures revealed something more. As many as 31 Janata Dal MPs, including Devi Lal, had defied the party whip and voted against the confidence motion. This clearly revealed that the decision to restrict the expulsions to 25, on 5 November 1990, was meant to frustrate the rebel camp's moves. It is another matter that the rebellion against V. P. Singh could not be contained. In other words, the rebel camp had grown in size with 56 MPs between 30 September (when hardly 10 MPs put their names demanding V. P. Singh's resignation) and 7 November 1990. It went up further, in a couple of days, to 60.

Soon after the vote, the rebels constituted themselves as the Janata Dal (Socialist) to stake claim. President Venkatraman, however, insisted on going by the book and invited Rajiv Gandhi, in his capacity as leader of the largest party in the Lok Sabha, on 9 November 1990. The Congress (I) leader declined the offer and informed the president of the party's support to Chandra Shekhar. President Venkatraman invited Chandra Shekhar to form the government the same evening and he was sworn in as prime minister on 10 November 1990, along with Devi Lal as deputy prime minister.

Born in Ibrahimpatti village in eastern Uttar Pradesh, Chandra Shekhar had completed his masters in Political Science from the Allahabad University. Inspired by Acharya Narendra Deva, one of the founders of the Socialist Party, Chandra Shekhar joined the Praja Socialist Party in the 1950s. He then moved on to the

Congress party in 1964 and identified himself with Indira Gandhi. He stood by her in the battle against Morarji Desai and others. He was one of the 'Young Turks' who pushed the Congress into bank nationalisation and abolition of privy purses. He was a member of the Rajya Sabha between 1962 and 1967. He, however, fell out with Indira Gandhi, over the manner in which the regime treated JP, and was arrested on the night of 25 June 1975 and detained under MISA until 18 January 1977. He then joined the Janata Party and won the elections to the Lok Sabha from Ballia, a constituency that he continued to represent until his death in May 2007, except between 1984 and 1989. He became the president of the Janata Party on 1 May 1977 and remained in that post, even after it underwent several splits; the Lok Dal (Ajit) merged into the Janata party in March 1988 and Ajit Singh became the president. He was a hesitant participant at Bangalore, on 11 October 1988, when the Janata Party merged into the Janata Dal. He was denied the prime minister's job, which he thought was his own, on 2 December 1989 by V. P. Singh and Devi Lal, at the JDPP meeting. He did not let go an opportunity to become the prime minister, even if that meant depending on the Congress (I) and Rajiv Gandhi for its very survival.

An indication of this shape of things, insofar as the Janata Dal was concerned, was available on 1 November 1990. The Gujarat chief minister, Chimanbhai Patel, set himself free from the Janata Dal, to float his own Janata Dal (Gujarat). The Janata Dal had only 70 MLAs in the 182-strong Gujarat assembly and the ministry depended on the support from the 67 BJP MLAs for survival. Patel was, at that time, heading a Janata Dal–BJP coalition government in Gujarat. The Janata Dal president S. R. Bommai instructed him to drop the BJP ministers from the cabinet, in the situation following 23 October; it was imminent that the government would fall. That was when Patel set out on his course to manage a majority in the assembly by striking a deal with the Congress (I), which had 33 MLAs in the assembly. And he won a confidence vote in the Gujarat assembly on 1 November 1990.

Similarly, Uttar Pradesh chief minister, Mulayam Singh too broke ranks with the Janata Dal after 30 October 1990, the day on which the VHP–Bajrang Dal men stormed into the Babri Masjid premises provoking the police to open fire. Almost all towns in Uttar Pradesh witnessed anti-Muslim violence in the 10 days after 23 October 1990. Mulayam Singh had his own issues with V. P. Singh, some of which went back to the early 1980s when Singh was the chief minister of Uttar Pradesh and Yadav the leader of the opposition in the assembly. There was also a lot of suspicion that Yadav nursed against Singh involving the Union Government's approach towards Advani's *rath yatra*. This had led Mulayam Singh Yadav to instruct Janata Dal MPs, loyal to him, to vote against the government on 7 November 1990, and rally behind Chandra Shekhar. Like Chimanbhai Patel in Gujarat, Mulayam Singh too struck a deal with the Congress (I), which had 94 MLAs in the assembly of 425 members and continued as chief minister even after the Janata Dal Legislature Party split and the V. P. Singh camp and the Ajit Singh camp withdrew support to him.

The Janata Dal's amorphous nature was evident in Rajasthan too. The BJP government, headed by Bhairon Singh Shekawat, depended on support from the Janata Dal, a pre-poll ally, to survive. The BJP had only 85 MLAs in the 200-strong assembly but had the support of the 54 Janata Dal MLAs. After 23 October 1990, it appeared that the Janata Dal could topple the government in the state. This, however, did not happen. Twenty of the party's MLAs, most of them Rajputs, revolted against the high command to form a separate block and declare support to Shekawat.

V. P. Singh, however, had the Bihar chief minister Lalu Prasad Yadav and Orissa chief minister Biju Patnaik and also such others as Ajit Singh, Ramakrishna Hegde, Sharad Yadav, Ram Vilas Paswan and George Fernandes with him. And all of them, one after another, would walk out of the party in a few years after that. Ajit Singh formed the Janata Dal (Ajit) in 1992 taking away 20 MPs and end up as the Congress (I)'s partner soon after. George Fernandes split the Janata Dal in 1994, taking away 14 MPs to form the Samata Party; and the party allied with the BJP in 1996. Hegde was expelled from the Janata Dal in 1996 and he too founded the Lok Shakti Party to join the BJP-led NDA in 1998. Lalu Yadav walked out of the party in 1997, to form the Rashtriya Janata Dal (RJD) and thereby ensure the Janata Dal's decimation in Bihar. After Biju Patnaik's death in 1997, his son, Naveen Patnaik formed his own Biju Janata Dal and joined the BJP-led National Democratic Alliance in 1998. Sharad Yadav set up his own Janata Dal (United) in 1999 and Paswan founded the Lok Jansakthi Party (LJP) in the same year and both of them joined the BJP-led NDA government. In other words, the Janata Dal was split into several splinters and a decade after it was formed in October 1988, to capture the imagination of the people in November 1989, it lay in shambles.

Chandra Shekhar, meanwhile, won the confidence vote on 16 November 1990. With support from the Congress (I) and its allies (the AIADMK, the Muslim League and some smaller outfits), it was a foregone conclusion. In the house of 505, there were 280 MPs voting for the government, 214 against the government and there were 11 abstentions. Chandra Shekhar had scheduled the confidence vote to 19 September 1990. This was advanced to 16 September 1990 because the prime minister was to attend a session of the SAARC in Male, Maldives the same day. The Union Cabinet now consisted of the prime minister and the deputy prime minister. One of the issues before him was that the Janata Dal (Socialist) had only 60 MPs (including those in the Rajya Sabha) and a full-fledged cabinet would have meant inducting all of them as ministers.

On 21 November 1990, President Venkatraman affirmed the oath of office to 15 more Cabinet ministers and a host of ministers of state and deputy ministers. The prime minister retained the home portfolio himself; Deputy Prime Minister Devi Lal was given tourism. Finance went to Yashwant Sinha, who had acted as Chandra Shekhar's executioner in the Janata Dal. Subramanian Swamy, who had sent Ramakrishna Hegde running for cover (the telephone tapping scandal) was rewarded with a cabinet berth and given the commerce, law, justice and company affairs portfolio. V. C. Shukla, one of the powerful men during the emergency and an associate of V. P. Singh in the Jan Morcha and then the Janata Dal, was made Minister for External Affairs. Asoke Sen, who had appeared for Indira Gandhi in the Supreme Court (against the Allahabad High Court verdict disqualifying her as MP), was made Minister for Steel and Mines. Rajmangal Pande, a former Congressman and one of V. P. Singh's pointmen in Uttar Pradesh for long, was made Minister for Human Resources Development. And Sanjay Singh, who had been in the Congress, the Jan Morcha and then in the Janata Dal and also a close relative of V. P. Singh was made Minister for Telecommunication.

Amidst the incongruity about the whole arrangement—a government by a party with just about one-tenth of the strength of the Lok Sabha surviving on the outside support of the Congress (I) with 197 MPs—Prime Minister Chandra Shekhar was also plagued with a host of problems. A ruling by Lok Sabha Speaker, Rabi Ray on 11 January 1991 added to this incongruity. The anti-defection law vested the speaker with quasi-judicial powers to sit on judgement over the status of MPs in the event of defections. And Ray had declared the 25 Janata Dal MPs, including Chandra Shekhar, who were expelled from the party as unattached members on 7 November 1990. He clubbed the others who defied the whip on 7 November 1990, and recognised them as Janata Dal (Socialist) in the Lok Sabha. They added up to 54 MPs. The Speaker, however, had a different attitude towards eight other MPs who remained with V. P. Singh, until the confidence vote that Chandra Shekhar had moved on 16 November 1990, but joined the Janata Dal (Socialist) later on. They were disqualified and among them were V. C. Shukla (Minister for External Affairs), Bhagey Govardhan (Minister of State for Human Resources Development), Sarwar Hussain (Minister for Food and Civil Supplies), Shakilur Rahman (Minister of State for Health) and Basavaraj Patil (Minister of State for Steel). This brought down the strength of the ruling party from 60 to 52.

The BJP, meanwhile had wreaked havoc across the country. The police firing in Ayodhya on 30 October 1990 and the anti-Muslim violence that engulfed almost all towns, with a substantive Muslim population, had shaken the foundations of the democratic polity. Chandra Shekhar's approach to this was to engage the BJP and the VHP in talks for a negotiated settlement. While talks were held in regular intervals, there was no concrete proposal on any issue and in that sense it was unlikely to lead to any settlement of the Ayodhya dispute. The anti-Mandal campaigners too saw Chandra Shekhar as their hero because he had frustrated V. P. Singh. The economy was in a shambles with the foreign exchange reserves touching an all time low. There was also the public perception that the regime was only a stopgap and elections were round the corner. Meanwhile, Chandra Shekhar allowed the US war planes, involved in the war against Iraq, to land in Indian army bases for refuelling and it provoked widespread protests from across the political spectrum.

In December 1990, the foreign exchange situation was causing anxiety and it was decided, at the highest level, involving the prime minister, his economic adviser Manmohan Singh and finance minister Yashwant Sinha, to pledge the gold reserves as collateral for loans. The transaction was carried out in absolute secrecy and in two stages. In the first stage, gold that was confiscated from smugglers and kept with Government of India, was transferred to the State Bank of India and the bank then took a loan from a Swiss bank on a sale and repurchase transaction. The second stage involved the gold stocks with the Reserve Bank of India. The International Monetary Fund (IMF) had imposed the condition that India agree to use its gold reserves as collateral. India's request that the gold that was pledged will be kept in our own territory was rejected by the IMF; the agency insisted that the gold be physically moved out to London and deposited at the Bank of England.

The crisis as such was the fallout of the liberalised import regime that was set in motion since 1981, accentuated after 1986 and had blown into a crisis when oil prices hit a new high after the US–Iraq conflict. The decision to pledge a part of the gold reserves, inevitable in the given context, sent the middle classes into a state of shock and Chandra Shekhar had to carry all the blame for the perceived loss of the nation's prestige. The media reported the transaction, meant to be carried out in secrecy. Chandra Shekhar had consulted Rajiv Gandhi before the decision was taken.

Meanwhile, under pressure from the AIADMK, an ally of the Congress (I), Chandra Shekhar's Cabinet recommended the dismissal of the DMK government in Tamil Nadu, dissolution of the state assembly and imposition of Central rule in the state. President Venkatraman acted on this, within moments, after the Cabinet recommended this to him on 30 January 1991. This was done without a report from the governor; the Constitution provides for invoking Article 356 with or without a report from the governor. Surjit Singh Barnala resigned as governor to register his protest against this.

All the while, the Congress (I) continued to support the government simply because the party was not prepared for an election in the immediate context. Rajiv Gandhi's party also had other compulsions and the most important being the investigations into the Bofors case. The CBI had got on with investigating the Bofors trail in real earnest after V. P. Singh became prime minister and was moving closer to finding the identity of the coded accounts in the Swiss bank.

The Congress (I) was interested in getting the CBI to change track. Chandra Shekhar too was willing to oblige.

Even as things seemed to move on, there was ruckus, in both houses of Parliament on 5 March 1991. The Congress (I) MPs marched into the well of the house shouting slogans against the government. The provocation for this came from reports in the newspapers that two constables from the Haryana Police were hanging around 10 Janpath, the official residence of Rajiv Gandhi in Delhi. It was a fact. The Congress (I) MPs called that surveillance and demanded action against the Janata Dal (Socialist) government in Haryana. Speaker Rabi Ray adjourned the house for the rest of the day. For want of a face-saving formula, to settle a dispute that was raked up without any serious thought gone into it, the Congress (I) announced boycott of Parliament the following day. That Rajiv Gandhi and his party were now looking for a settlement was clear. This was evident from the fact that the Congress (I) MPs were waiting in the Central Hall, adjacent to the Lok Sabha, when the house assembled in the morning on 6 March 1990. The Lok Sabha was slated to take up voting on the Motion of Thanks to the President's Address to the joint sitting, a constitutional imperative, that day.

Chandra Shekhar shocked everyone when he announced that he was going to the President Venkatraman to submit his resignation. He did not wait for a moment, to oblige the Congress (I) MPs, now waiting just outside the Lok Sabha hall to enter the house. The game was up. Chandra Shekhar was at the Rashtrapati Bhawan, hardly a couple of minutes drive from Parliament House, to submit his resignation and recommend dissolution of the Lok Sabha and hold fresh elections. Desperate afforts by the Congress (I), soon after, to salvage the situation included a statement by Rajiv Gandhi that his party continued to support the government and the issue at hand was only a small irritant, did not succeed. Chandra Shekhar had decided to go and he was firm on that.

President Venkatraman, however, succeeded in convincing the Prime Minister to let some urgent legislative business to be transacted. They were:

1. A Vote on Account be taken so that that funds from the consolidated funds be drawn to run the Government between 1 April and 31 July 1991. This was a constitutional imperative.
2. Parliament pass a Vote on Account for Assam, Punjab, Jammu and Kashmir, Tamil Nadu and Pondichery; these states were under Central rule at that time.
3. A Constitution Amendment to extend central rule in Punjab for six months beyond 10 May 1991.

All these were carried out in the Lok Sabha on 7 March 1991, without even a semblance of discussion and President Venkatraman ordered dissolution of the

Tenth Lok Sabha and conveyed to the Election Commission to conduct elections at the earliest. Chandra Shekhar continued as caretaker prime minister. This arrangement would have come to an end, in the normal course, sometime in the third week of May 1991. But it lasted until 21 June 1991.

The Fallout

The Election Commission announced a three-phase poll schedule on 20, 23 and 26 May. The BJP, the Congress (I), the National Front parties led by V. P. Singh's Janata Dal and Chandra Shekhar's Janata Dal (Socialist) got on to the campaign mode even before the schedules were announced. The commission had also announced simultaneous polls to the state assemblies in Tamil Nadu (where the assembly had been dissolved in January 1991), Uttar Pradesh (after Mulayam Singh Yadav recommended dissolution of the assembly on 4 April 1991), West Bengal and Kerala (the CPI [M]-led Left Front had recommended early elections though the assembly terms there were until February 1992) along with the polls to the Eleventh Lok Sabha. Polling was completed in 204 out of the 510 Lok Sabha constituencies (elections were not held in Punjab and Jammu and Kashmir in 1991) on 20 May 1990. This included 17 in Andhra Pradesh, 36 in Bihar, all the 10 in Haryana, 15 in Rajasthan, 28 in Madhya Pradesh, all the four in Himachal Pradesh, 42 in Uttar Pradesh, all the 42 in West Bengal and all the seven in Delhi.

And on 21 May 1991, Rajiv Gandhi, campaigning for the Congress (I)–AIADMK alliance in Sriperumbudur in Tamil Nadu, was assasinated by an LTTE mercenary. This led to the postponement of the second and third phase of polling, scheduled for 23 and 26 May to 12 and 15 June 1991. Incidentally, polling was over on 20 May 1991, in Amethi from where Rajiv Gandhi was a candidate. And the Election Commission had to go through the process of counting the votes on 18 June 1991 and declare him the winner.

The three months long election campaign between mid-March and mid-June 1991, the longest ever after the 1967 elections (the first, second and third general elections were held over a period of few months because of the logistics involved), ended in a split verdict. Like in 1989, the 1991 elections too threw up a hung Lok Sabha. There was, however, a significant difference in that the Congress (I) had secured 224 seats and along with its pre-poll allies such as the AIADMK, the Muslim League the Kerala Congress and the UCPI the combine had 240 MPs in the House. Elections were held in only 511 constituencies; of that, the poll process was countermanded in seven constituencies. In other words, the Congress (I)-led combine was short of a majority by only 13 MPs. This was, indeed, different from the outcome of the November 1989 elections. Another significant aspect of the outcome of the 1991 polls was that a large part of the Congress (I) MPs in the Tenth Lok Sabha were elected from constituencies where the elections were held on 13 and 15 June 1991; in other words, the verdict in their favour was clearly influenced by the context of the discourse after Rajiv Gandhi's assassination. This was so clearly evident in the case of the 39 Lok Sabha constituencies from Tamil Nadu: The Congress(I)–ADMK–UCPI combine won all the seats. And in the elections to the Tamil Nadu assembly too, the AIADMK–Congress (I) combine won 224 out of the 234 seats in the assembly. The DMK was reduced to just two MLAs.

The other big gainer in the 1991 elections was the BJP. The party won 119 seats against the 85 it had won in 1989. It must be noted here that in 1989, the BJP had seat adjustments with the Janata Dal in many states. And in 1991, it won its seats on its own. The only state where the party had an alliance was in Maharashtra with the Shiv Sena; the Sena won four Lok Sabha seats in 1991. This, clearly was the fallout of the aggressive campaign by the BJP on the Ayodhya issue. The fallout of Mandal—the collapse of the AJGAR social alliance—leading the Rajputs to flock behind the BJP was another factor that contributed to its enhanced strength in the Tenth Lok Sabha. This was evident from the fact that 51 out of the 119 BJP MPs were from Uttar Pradesh, where both Mandal and Mandir were the two major election issues. The BJP had won only eight seats from Uttar Pradesh in November 1989. The BJP wrested a number of seats from both the Janata Dal and the Congress (I) in Uttar Pradesh. The Congress (I)'s tally, in Uttar Pradesh, came down from 15 in 1989 to five in 1991. And the Janata Dal won only 22 seats from Uttar Pradesh in 1991 against the 54 it won in 1989. This was indeed the fallout of a vertical split in the OBC base between the Janata Dal and the Janata Dal (Socialist) represented by Mulayam Singh Yadav in the state.

This trend was evident in the outcome of the elections to the Uttar Pradesh assembly held simultaneously. The BJP emerged with 221 seats in the 425 member assembly to form its government in the state. The Janata Dal managed to win 92 MLAs and Mulayam Singh's Janata Dal (Socialist) won only 34 seats in the assembly. The BSP, by now a force in Uttar Pradesh, secured 12 MLAs. The BJP's victory in Uttar Pradesh would have far reaching implications for its Ayodhya campaign. With Kalyan Singh as the chief minister, the BJP could ensure the mobilisation of its ranks, to march to Ayodhya, without being stopped by the police (as it happened on 30 October 1990) and the eventual demolition of the Babri Masjid on 6 December 1992.

The BJP gained substantially in Gujarat too. As against the 12 seats it had won from Gujarat, in alliance with the Janata Dal in 1989, the party won 20 Lok Sabha seats out of the 26 from the state. The Janata Dal, represented by Chimanbhai Patel in 1989, was totally discredited. Patel himself managed to remain the chief minister only by striking a deal with the Congress (I). The Congress (I) won just five Lok Sabha seats from Gujarat in 1991. This outcome of the 1991 general election from

Gujarat laid the basis for the BJP's growth in the state (on the rumbles of the Congress [O] and the Janata Party). And the party won a decisive majority in the assembly—121 seats in the assembly of 182—when elections were held in 1995. The Congress (I) won just 45 seats and the Janata Dal lost everywhere. The BJP retained its hold in the state in 1998 when assembly elections were held again.

The hatred against the Muslim population across the state, built over the years by the partisan games that the Congress had begun playing since 1969 (when Gujarat was rocked by anti-Muslim violence that left over 3,500 people dead), was cultivated by the various arms of the RSS and all this led to the pogrom against the Muslims in February–March 2002. Narendra Modi, who had taken over the BJP by then, led the party to another victory in the state assembly election in September 2002 and again in 2007.

And yet, the BJP's final tally was restricted to 119 in the Tenth Lok Sabha because the party did not do as well in 1991 as it did in 1989 from Madhya Pradesh, the Jan Sangh's traditional bastion. Against the 27 seats it had won from Madhya Pradesh in 1989, it won only 12 in 1991. Elections were held in most of Madhya Pradesh after Rajiv Gandhi's assassination; similarly, the BJP failed to make an impact in the southern states (barring the four seats it won from Karnataka). It also failed to make significant gains from Bihar (its five seats coming from the Jharkhand region of the State) and remained a non-starter in Orissa and West Bengal.

The party managed to address this shortcoming in 1998 by way of striking alliances with the Samata Party in Bihar, the Biju Janata Dal in Orissa, the Trinamool Congress in West Bengal, the AIADMK in Tamil Nadu, to constitute the NDA and form its government at the Centre.

As for the Janata Dal, the outcome of the 1991 polls were not all that bad. The party won 59 seats. Of that, 31 came from Bihar. Lalu Prasad Yadav managed to ensure this for the party by way of forging a social alliance consisting of the OBCs (Yadavs constituting the bulk of them) and the Muslims. The Mandal–Mandir cauldron that dominated the poll campaign helped the Janata Dal consolidate itself in Bihar. The Muslim–Yadav social alliance (it came to be known as the MY factor) helped the Janata Dal hold itself in 1991. Lalu Prasad Yadav, certainly, benefited out of that for several years and even after the decimation of the Janata Dal itself. It may be noted, in this context, that the party could not manage this in Uttar Pradesh because Mulayam Singh was not in the fold there. The Janata Dal did retain some of its hold in Uttar Pradesh and this was Ajit Singh's contribution to the party. More than half the 22 Janata Dal MPs from Uttar Pradesh were Ajit Singh loyalists and this was established when the Jat leader left the party to form his own block of 20 MPs in 1992 to support the Congress (I). Apart from a few from Orissa and Bihar, most of the 20 MPs, who flocked behind Ajit Singh, were elected from Uttar Pradesh.

Chandra Shekhar's Janata Dal (Socialist) contested the 1991 elections on the Janata Party's symbol and ended up winning just five seats from out of the 349 it contested. Chandra Shekhar was the only minister from that Cabinet to win the election in 1991. All the others, including Devi Lal, were defeated in the polls.

As for the constituents of the National Front, a small group even in the Ninth Lok Sabha, the only party to gain in 1991 was the TDP. It won 13 seats against the two it had in 1989. The Congress (S) remained a one-MP party and the Jharkhand Mukti Morcha (JMM), with six MPs, became a part of the combine in 1991. Both the TDP and the JMM contingents were vulnerable for poaching and this enabled the ruling Congress (I) to manage a majority in the Tenth Lok Sabha. All that would happen within months after P. V. Narasimha Rao was sworn in as prime minister on 21 June 1991. Incidentally, Rao was not an elected member of either of the houses when he was chosen as leader of the Congress (I) Parliamentary Party on 20 June 1991. He was among those who were denied a party ticket in April 1991, and ended up becoming the prime minister and also the Congress (I) president within a month. He presided over the Congress (I) as well as the government until May 1996, when the party lost power, once again to a coalition of non-Congress–anti-BJP parties, headed by H. D. Deve Gowda of the Janata Dal.

Epilogue

The National Front government (2 December 1989 to 7 November 1990) was, in fact, just the beginning of a long phase, in independent India's political history, of an era of coalitions. It marked the end of single party rule. The short spell when Chandra Shekhar headed a government (with a ramshackle group of 60 MPs) supported by the 197 Congress (I) MPs fell on 7 March 1991. The elections in May–June 1991 threw a hung Parliament again. Another minority government under P. V. Narasimha Rao (as head of a pre-poll alliance consisting of Congress (I), AIADMK, Indian Union Muslim League and Kerala Congress–Mani added up to 240 MPs) was sworn in on 21 June 1991. A three-tier cabinet, with 58 members, was sworn in that day. Rao was elected leader of the Congress (I) Parliamentary Party on 20 June 1991; Sharad Pawar and Arjun Singh were other aspirants for the position. But Rao was chosen after due process of consultations. He was, in fact, the second choice. The Congress (I) had elected Sonia Gandhi as party chief on 22 May 1991, the day after Rajiv Gandhi's assassination. But she refused to accept that and the mantle fell on Rao.

Despite having only 240 MPs, Rao managed to win the confidence vote in the Lok Sabha. This was achieved because the opposition parties walked out of Parliament at the time of voting. More than the ruling Congress (I), it became the responsibility of the opposition to keep the government in place. The only surprise in the Cabinet was the inclusion of Manmohan Singh, a career bureaucrat, as finance minister. Other prominent members of the cabinet were Arjun Singh, Sharad Pawar, V. C. Shukla, Madhavrao Scindia, P. Chidambaram and Madhav Singh Solanki.

The first ever test for the new government came in the by-elections to 16 Lok Sabha constituencies scheduled for 16 November 1991. This included Amethi (from where Rajiv Gandhi had been declared elected) and Nandyal (in Andhra Pradesh), from where the Congress (I) MP resigned to facilitate Rao's election to Parliament. The Congress (I) went into a tailspin, with hysteric cries from the rank and file that Sonia Gandhi be nominated from Amethi. Narasimha Rao, the Congress (I) president remained non-committal and it was left to Sonia herself to propose Satish Sharma, a family loyalist, as party's candidate from Amethi. The by-elections were held on 16 November 1991 (for only 12 constituencies after violence in the four others led to the poll process being countermanded) and the Congress (I) won eight out of them. This included Amethi and Nandyal.

The election in Nandyal had some dramatic twists. The TDP leader and the National Front chairman, N. T. Rama Rao, declared his party's support to

Narasimha Rao and also insisted that the Janata Dal too did not field a candidate against the prime minister. The decision of TDP to support Rao was on the ground that he represented the Telugu pride as well.

Within a month after being sworn in, the Congress (I) government came up with an economic policy resolution that marked a clear and pronounced departure from the Socialistic pattern that the party was wedded to since 1952 and redefined at different points of time by Jawaharlal Nehru, at Avadi in 1955 and at Nagpur in 1959, and by Indira Gandhi during her struggle against her own party colleagues between 1967 and 1969. Manmohan Singh, who had been Prime Minister Chandra Shekhar's economic adviser at the time when India's gold reserves were pledged in exchange for loans from the IMF and other institutions, was the finance minister. On 21 July 1991 (exactly a month after he was sworn in), Singh obtained Parliament's sanction for his economic policy resolution. It received support from the BJP, now the largest opposition party in the Lok Sabha. The BJP's floor leader, Jaswant Singh, qualified his party's support to the New Economic Policy resolution by pointing out that it reflected the BJP's thinking and that the Congress (I) had appropriated it.

The Left parties and the Janata Dal opposed the resolution but with support coming from BJP, it was approved by the Lok Sabha. It is another matter that a shift in the economic policy framework did not require Parliamentary sanction as such. But the fact that it was approved by an overwhelming majority in the Lok Sabha, and with the ruling combine and the main opposition endorsing it, reflected a consensus among a large section of the political establishment to the change. A debate on the impact of the shift and the nature of the economic growth in the decade and a half since the new policy was put into practice, is beyond the scope of this book. Nevertheless, it had implications on the nation's political life and the most pronounced of them being the retreat of the welfare state. The roots of the reforms programme, as the shift came to be known, could be traced to the conditions that came along with the IMF loans in 1981 and the liberalisation of imports, beginning with the Union Budget for 1986–87 that V. P. Singh presented on 28 February 1986. While enlarging the scope for jobs in specific sectors such as the services and trade, the adverse impact of the new policies are evident in such sectors as agriculture and manufacture. All these are issues that belong to the immediate present and it is too early to record them in a book of this nature.

As for the political mosaic, elections were held to the state assembly and the Lok Sabha constituencies from Punjab on 19 February 1992. It was a farce in many ways. The Union government and the Election Commission were aware that the situation in the state was far from being conducive for a free and fair election. Extremist violence was persisting and killings were reported from the state almost every day. Yet, the poll schedule was announced and keeping in view the violence in the state, the EC reduced the campaign period from 21 days (as it was in the law then) to 14 days. The other development that reduced the exercise to a farce was that almost all the Akali Dal groups had announced their decision to boycott the polls. The Congress (I), the BJP, the Janata Dal, the Left parties and the Akali Dal (Kabul), headed at that time by Captain Amarinder Singh (he would become Congress [I] chief minister of Punjab in 2001), participated in the polls. The percentage of votes polled, across the state, was less than 30 and there were several villages where not a single vote was cast. The outcome was as expected. The Congress (I) won 12 Lok Sabha seats out of the 13 from the state and 87 assembly seats out of the 117 to form its government.

After the November 16 by-elections and that for the Lok Sabha seats from Punjab, the strength of Congress (I) increased from 224 in June 1991 to 244 in March 1992. The ruling combine's strength was now 260 MPs in the Lok Sabha. This too was short of majority in the house whose total strength was 535, including the nominated Anglo Indian member. There were nine vacancies of which six were from Jammu and Kashmir. This was the context in which the Narasimha Rao government faced its first crisis of confidence. Voting on the motion of thanks to the president's address to the joint session of Parliament was scheduled for 9 March 1992. And, the opposition sent signals that it was willing to close ranks against the government.

The Congress (I) had begun looking out for supporters even earlier and the Janata Dal's Ajit Singh was willing to oblige. The Janata Dal was caught, once again, in internecine quarrels and it was between V. P. Singh and Ajit Singh now. Ajit Singh had yet to gather at least 20 MPs behind him to escape disqualification. The pace of events was hastened in the wake of the 9 March vote in the Lok Sabha. The Janata Dal expelled four MPs close to Ajit Singh before the vote. However, this was not enough to put Narasimha Rao in a fix. As many as seven Janata Dal MPs (in addition to the four expelled by the party) were not present in the Lok Sabha when the voting took place. They had defied the party whip. Similarly, nine Telegu Desam Party MPs were absent when the voting took place. The government sailed through the crisis with ease (with at least 55 votes more than it required) and also managed to reveal the pathetic state of affairs in the opposition. The Janata Dal and the Telugu Desam were in a mess. Lok Sabha speaker, Shivraj Patil, recognised a six-member group of TDP as a separate party in the Lok Sabha. The split in the Janata Dal Parliamentary Party was formalised on 12 August, 1992 when 20 MPs, led by Ajit Singh (including the seven who defied the whip on 9 March) met Speaker Shivraj Patil and presented themselves as a separate group in Parliament. The Janata Dal, which began with 59 MPs in June 1991, was now reduced to 39 MPs. It would splinter once again when 13 MPs (one-third of the 39 MPs) led by George Fernandes and Nitish Kumar walked out to form the Samata Party in May 1994.

Meanwhile, the Narasimha Rao-led Congress (I) that came to power on 21 June 1991 as a minority government was turned into a majority government by August 1992. With 280 MPs supporting the government, Narasimha Rao could assure to himself a full five-year term as prime minister. This stability, however, was restricted to the apparent level. The BJP, convinced as it was, that it owed its growth in the Lok Sabha to the Ayodhya campaign, was determined to keep the pot boiling. In October 1991 (within a few months after Kalyan Singh was sworn in as chief minister), the Uttar Pradesh government took over 2.77 acres of vacant land in front of the Babri Masjid to build amenities for the pilgrims and to promote tourism. The VHP, meanwhile, had ensured transfer of most of the land around the Masjid to itself. The land acquisition, however, was challenged in the Allahabad High Court and in the Supreme Court. The apex court ruled that the state government shall not transfer the property during the pendency of the case. The courts also held that no permanent structure was built on the land. This, in a sense, scuttled the VHP's plan to start building activities around the Masjid and present a case for its demolition as a *fait accompli*. The Narasimha Rao government, soon after that, initiated talks with the VHP to reach a negotiated settlement of the dispute.

As things seemed to move, on 30 October 1992, the VHP declared the start of another round of *kar seva* from 6 December 1992. The BJP now decided to jump into the campaign and Advani set out on another campaign trail across the country to reach Ayodhya on 6 December 1992 to join the *kar seva*. The BJP was in power in Uttar Pradesh (and this guaranteed that the *kar sevaks* would not be stopped), and also in Madhya Pradesh, Rajasthan and Himachal Pradesh. Advani's campaign, this time, culminated in the demolition of the Babri Masjid on 6 December 1992. Uttar Pradesh chief minister, Kalyan Singh, was present in Ayodhya along with Advani and all other leaders of the BJP, including Murli Manohar Joshi who had become the party president in February 1991, when the Masjid was pulled down. Kalyan Singh, incidentally, had sworn before the Supreme Court, only a couple of days before 6 December, that his government will do everything to ensure the status quo and that meant protecting the 428 years old Masjid. Within hours after the demolition he announced his resignation as the chief minister.

The demolition on 6 December 1992 could have been prevented. Prime Minister Narasimha Rao was under pressure to invoke Article 356 of the Constitution and dismiss Kalyan Singh during the week before that day. The prime minister refused to act. He assured the National Integration Council, a couple of days before 6 December 1992, that the Union government had prepared a contingency plan in the event the *kar sevaks* turned violent and resorted to destruction of the Masjid. But as things unfolded on Sunday, 6 December 1992, a huge posse of paramilitary forces was made to wait, away from Ayodhya, while the mobs pulled down the structure. The act of demolition took over six hours and the Narasimha Rao government, which claimed to have a contingency plan in place, did nothing to save the Masjid. The cynical games that began on 1 February 1986, when an order by the Faizabad District Court to open the locks of the premises was implemented, ended in the demolition of the Babri Masjid on 6 December 1992.

Babri Masjid is now being addressed to in the popular discourse, quite ironically, as a disputed structure. The day, 6 December 1992, also marked a stage, in the national political discourse, of the abject failure of the democratic institutions to halt the march of revanchist forces. This, in turn, provided grist to Islamic fundamentalist elements to gather support and lay the foundation for the emergence of terrorist groups. The anti-Muslim pogrom in various towns across India—Delhi, Meerut, Moradabad, Bombay, Surat, Ahmedabad and Hyderabad—left several hundred Muslims dead and their property destroyed and led India into an era of communal strife. The violence in Bombay, triggered by the Shiv Sena in particular, during which the Congress (I) government in Maharashtra allowed the killer mobs to carry on with their violence with impunity, would end only in March 1993 after a series of bombs went off killing more people. The March 1993 blasts in Bombay were indeed a reaction to the anti-Muslim violence in the preceding months. Also, the fact that the post-December 6 violence was possible only because the government in the state let that happen was established, with substantive evidence and logical arguments, by Justice B. L. Srikrishna, a sitting judge of the Bombay High Court at that time.

The P. V. Narasimha Rao regime, however, was not shaken by any of these. A no-confidence motion against the regime, in January 1993, moved by the Left parties and the Janata Dal was defeated decisively. The BJP abstained from voting and the Congress (I) managed to sail through the crisis. In the new reality, where the Left parties and the Janata Dal had committed against joining hands with the BJP, the Narasimha Rao regime looked stable again. Sharad Pawar, who had aspired for the top job in June 1991, was now sent as Maharashtra chief minister in place of Sudhakar Rao Naik. Meanwhile, Arjun Singh, minister for human resources development, began looking for a larger role to himself. This game had begun at the AICC plenum at Tirupathi between 14–16 April 1992.

Narasimha Rao, in his own way, was keen to legitimise his position as the supreme leader of the Congress (I). An AICC session at Tirupathi, the first time in the history of independent India without a Nehru family member at the helm, elected Rao as the party president. Rao also pushed the idea of elections to the Congress (I) Working Committee (CWC). The party constitution prescribes that the 21-member CWC is constituted by 10 members elected by the AICC, 10 others to be nominated and the party president himself being the 21st member. In the election at the Tirupathi plenary, Arjun Singh, former chief minister of

Madhya Pradesh, former governor of Punjab and now the minister for human resources development, won with the highest votes. Sharad Pawar too was elected to the CWC.

Narasimha Rao, an old hand in the affairs of the party, knew the significance of this. On 17 April, just a day after the session, five of the CWC members—Jitendra Prasad, Ahmed Patel, K. Vijayabhaskara Reddy, Ghulam Nabi Azad and Balram Jhakhar—resigned from the CWC. They did that at the instance of Narasimha Rao. Five others—Arjun Singh, Sharad Pawar, A. K. Antony, R. K. Dhawan and Rajesh Pilot—refused to play ball. It clearly revealed that Narasimha Rao was yet to emerge as the supreme leader of the party as were Nehru, Indira and Rajiv.

Arjun Singh, in fact, had been working to a definite plan since the Tirupathi meeting and the tragic turn of events in Ayodhya on 6 December 1992 gave him a handle. Singh toured the violence-hit towns and pushed Narasimha Rao to react. The Union HRD Minister joined the Janata Dal-Left parties combine to demand the dismissal of the BJP governments in Madhya Pradesh, Rajasthan and Himachal Pradesh. Rao was forced to accept that in January 1993. The Union Cabinet recommended invoking Article 356 of the Constitution to place the three other BJP-ruled states under Central rule. The Uttar Pradesh government was dismissed within hours after the Babri Masjid was reduced to rubble on 6 December 1992 and around the same time as Kalyan Singh resigned as Chief Minister.

The dismissal was challenged by the Madhya Pradesh chief minister, Sundarlal Patwa, before the High Court and the Indore bench of the Madhya Pradesh High Court declared the dismissal unconstitutional. The Centre went on appeal against the High Court verdict and the Supreme Court bundled it, as well as cases pending in this regard in the Himachal Pradesh and Rajasthan High Courts, with the S. R. Bommai vs Union of India case. On 11 March 1994, a nine-member bench of the Supreme Court upheld the dismissal of these governments. The majority judgements came from Justices P. B. Sawant, Kuldip Singh, B. P. Jeevan Reddy, S. K. Agrawal and Rathnavel Pandian. The judges who dissented were in a minority; Justices A. M. Ahmadi, J. S. Verma, Yogeshwar Dayal and K. Ramaswamy. It held that these state governments failed in their responsibility to uphold the Constitutional scheme of things and elaborated this by stressing that secularism is very much a part of the basic structure of the Constitution.

The bench, however, declared the dismissal of S. R. Bommai as Karnataka chief minister in 1989 as unconstitutional. The judgement would have far-reaching implications—it redefined the scope of Article 356, invoked a hundred times since 1959 (when the Namboodiripad ministry was dismissed)—in such a manner that it became impossible for parties in power, at the centre, to abuse this emergency provision of the Constitution. So much so, the Rabri Devi government in Bihar, despite failing to check atrocities on the poor agricultural workers—who also happened to be Dalits—by the Ranbir Sena, a private army of the land-owning upper castes at regular intervals, could not be dismissed for want of support to such a decision in Parliament. This happened in February 1999, when after a massacre at Miapur, the BJP-led Union government dismissed the government. It was forced to go back on the decision and reinstall Rabri Devi as the chief minister when the Congress (I) refused to endorse it in the Rajya Sabha. The verdict on the Bommai case had also helped the BJP in Uttar Pradesh earlier (in October 1997) when a Congress (I) orchestrated game, to replace Kalyan Singh with its own Jagadambika Pal (aided by a pliant Romesh Bhandari as the governor), was upset after the Allahabad High Court intervened to order a composite floor test (between Kalyan Singh and Jagadambika Pal) in the Assembly. The BJP leader won the test and he was reinstated as the chief minister.

Sonia Gandhi was turning restive. On 21 May 1993, she visited Amethi and launched an attack against the government and charged that it did not do enough to unravel the conspiracy behind Rajiv Gandhi's assassination. The background to this lay in the Bofors story. The Bofors investigation was moving and this was happening despite some concerted attempts by the Narasimha Rao government. On 23 March 1992, *The Indian Express* reported that External Affairs Minister, Madhav Singh Solanki had passed on an anonymous note to his Swiss counterpart (who he met at a trade summit in Davos) wherein it was stated that the Government of India was not enthusiastic about pursuing its request (of January 1990) to have the names behind the coded accounts into which money was deposited by the Swedish gun manufacturer. The news-break raised a din and Rao had to ensure Solanki's resignation. Solanki continues to maintain that he does not remember the face or the identity of the person who handed the note to him to be passed on to the Swiss foreign minister.

And on 23 July 1993, the Swiss Federal Court verdict revealed the men behind the coded accounts. Apart from Win Chadha and the Hinduja brothers, Ottavio Quattrocchi was named as the person behind one of the accounts—AE Services. It was now evident that he was one of the recipients of the payoffs from Bofors. Quattrocchi remained in Delhi for a few more days and left for Malaysia by a late night flight from Delhi on 29 July 1993. Arjun Singh had Sonia Gandhi's backing and it became evident when he circulated a note against Rao and also at the Surajkund session. Among the others who joined the anti-Rao campaign was Sheila Dikshit. When Sonia Gandhi finally agreed to become the Congress (I) president these two were rewarded for their loyalty. Arjun Singh, however, remained in Narasimha Rao's cabinet until he was asked to quit on 24 December 1994.

The defining moment for Narasimha Rao, however, was not in relation to the Bofors investigation. A scam had been reported,involving nationalised banks and other financial institutions aiding irregular dealings in the stock market through a broker, Harshad Mehta, in June 1992. The CBI, to whom the case had been handed over, promptly registered an FIR in which Mehta was named. The issue kept coming up in the public discourse, through the media, without a break since then and the CBI investigation into the case was not showing much progress.

On 16 June 1993, Mehta convened a press conference in Bombay to claim that he had paid off Rs one crore to the prime minister Narasimha Rao. Mehta's claim, in the form of a sworn affidavit, shook the nation. He followed it up with one more press conference on 23 June 1993 where he circulated copies of the transcript of a telephone conversation between him and one Lalit Mittal (who had acted as the intermediary between him and Rao) and that was also in the form of a sworn affidavit. Mehta was assisted in these by Ram Jethmalani.

The Monsoon session of Parliament met in this charged atmosphere and a motion of no-confidence was moved. The Lok Sabha took it up for discussion on 25 July 1993 and voting on the motion was scheduled for 28 July 1993. The division in the opposition benches, after the 6 December 1992 demolition of the Babri Masjid, that had helped the Narasimha Rao government all these months, was now gone. The Left Front–National Front combine in the house was now in a mood to close ranks with the BJP and the government appeared to be on the verge of collapsing until the night before 28 July 1993, the day the motion was to be taken up for voting in the Lok Sabha. Arjun Singh, now an unattached member of the Lok Sabha (after his expulsion from the Congress [I]), was making moves to enlist support from the Congress (I) MPs against Rao. Ajit Singh, who had left the Janata Dal with 20 MPs, was now against the government.

But, Narasimha Rao, with his close aides—Petroleum Minister Satish Sharma and Haryana Chief Minister Bhajan Lal—managed to woo seven MPs from Ajit Singh's group of 20 and also six Jharkhand Mukti Morcha (JMM) MPs and ensure the defeat of the no-confidence motion. Interestingly, these MPs were paid huge sums of money and given other favours, including licences to operate petrol pumps, on the night before the vote. This fact was established. It so happened that the JMM MPs took the money to a nationalised bank in Delhi to put it in fixed deposits. The case went to the Supreme Court and after initial indications that the scandal could lead to a judicial censure of the government, the apex court ruled that there was no case. The basis for this was that the MPs were protected by Article 105 of the Constitution (Parliamentary privileges) and, hence, the way they voted on the floor of the house was outside the judiciary's purview.

As for the stock market scam, here is a brief narrative of what it was and what happened in that regard. The first news in this regard came in April 1992: the State Bank of India asked Harshad Mehta to return Rs 500 crore he had illegally put to work on the stock market. Within a couple of weeks it was revealed that Mehta had managed to have funds from Maruti Udyog Limited, now a Public

Sector Undertaking, diverted into his own accounts and, thus, provoked a 570-point fall in the Sensex. A sustained furore in Parliament led to the formation of a Joint Parliamentary Committee (JPC) in June 1992 to investigate the matter. As the JPC went about its job, the media was agog with reports of misappropriation of funds from banks and public sector units at regular intervals. Harshad Mehta, meanwhile, was sent to jail for custodial interrogation. It was on his release that he claimed to have paid off prime minister Narasimha Rao.

The JPC Report, tabled in Parliament in 1993, provided a comprehensive and coherent picture of both the scale and mechanics of the securities fraud. But the Action Taken Report (ATR), mandatory under the Constitution in the context of Parliamentary Committee Reports, was a whitewash and Prime Minister Rao came under a cloud. The CBI took longer than the JPC to put up a criminal case against the wrongdoers. It was only in October 1997 that a Special Court was set up to hear the securities scandal-related cases. Seventy-two sets of charges relating to criminal offences were filed and the CBI managed to secure convictions in only four. In September 1999, Mehta received a four-year sentence for defrauding Maruti Udyog Limited but he went on appeal. Hiten Dalal, an accomplice of Mehta, was perhaps the only one to be convicted in the case. The Harshad Mehta scam was not very different from that of Haridas Mundhra in 1957 (for which Finance Minister T. T. Krishnamachari had to quit). In 2001, Ketan Mehta, another operator in the stock market, did a similar thing involving the funds with the Unit Trust of India (UTI).

This was followed by reports of a scandal in obtaining import licences for sugar, by Kalpnath Rai, a minister in Rao's cabinet. Prime Minister Rao asked Rai to quit the Cabinet when the opposition raised the issue in Parliament. He was arrested for interrogation subsequently. Irregularities and corruption were detected in the Union Urban Development Ministry when the Supreme Court, in the course of dealing with a case involving out-of-turn allotment of government quarters in New Delhi, found that the minister concerned, P. K. Thungon was guilty of corruption. A decision by the Indian Railways to import 30 locomotives from ABB, a German company, raised a controversy and it emerged in due course that the decision was influenced by kickbacks. Prime Minister Rao now showed the door to C. K. Jaffer Sharief, the railway minister. There were allegations of corruption behind a decision by the ministry of steel and mines to handover some of the richest iron ore mines in Bailadilla (now in Chhattisgarh) to Nippon-Denro, a Japanese steel company. Similar allegations in the decision by the ministry for power, to sanction the setting up of fast track power plants, came up soon after. The most prominent among them was the Enron power project in Dabhol (Maharashtra) and it emerged that the American company was involved in fraudulent deals in the US too and had spent money on illegal gratification towards setting up the Dabhol plant.

Narasimha Rao's commerce minister, P. Chidambaram, had to leave the Cabinet when it was revealed that he had obtained shares (under the promoters' quota) from a business house when he was a minister. This was in violation of the law and Chidambaram was asked to quit the cabinet. It was in this context, when the Narasimha Rao government was rendered vulnerable to much ridicule, that the Jain *Hawala* scandal surfaced. A diary seized from B. R. Jain, a Bhilai-based industrialist (who was being investigated by the CBI in a case that involved money laundering business), revealed details of illegal fund transfers from all parts of the world to a cross-section of leaders in the political parties. The list contained names of a host of political leaders cutting across parties. There were Cabinet ministers, MPs and chief ministers. Among them were: V. C. Shukla, Balram Jhakhar, Madhavrao Scindia, R. K. Dhawan, C. K. Jaffar Sharief, Buta Singh, Kamalnath, Arvind Netam (all members of the Narasimha Rao Cabinet); L. K. Advani, Kailash Joshi, Madan Lal Khurana (all BJP); S. R. Bommai, Arif Mohammad Khan, Sharad Yadav (Janata Dal); Arjun Singh, N. D. Tiwari (Congress [T]); Devi Lal, Yashwant Sinha, Ranjit Singh, Harmohan Dhawan (Janata Dal [S]); Kalpnath Rai, A. K. Sen, Natwar Singh and L. P. Shahi (Congress (I) MPs).

The list revealed two things. That the *hawala* transactions had been taking place over the years and pertained to periods when the recipients were holding positions from where they could influence decisions. The second, and more important, aspect was that this cut across parties, barring the Left. In many ways, this aspect marks the political discourse since the 1990s in a big way. The politician–corruption nexus today cuts across parties. Narasimha Rao's response to the scandal was to ask those of his Cabinet colleagues, whose names appeared in the list, to resign and the CBI filed the charge sheets against them all.

It will be of interest, at this stage, to mention the context in which the entire scam unfolded. In February 1991, two Kashmiri students in Delhi—Shahabuddin Ghauri and Ashfaq Lone—were arrested under the Terrorist and Disruptive Activities Act (TADA). The investigating officers suspected that the two were acting as conduit for passing on *hawala* money to terrorists. The sleuths working on the case were led to the Jain brothers—S. K. Jain, N. K. Jain and B. R. Jain—from whom the diaries were seized and the scam came to light.

The term of the tenth Lok Sabha, meanwhile, was coming to an end by June 1996. Elections were announced for May 1996. The Congress (I), for the first time after independence, now had to face the elections without a member from the Nehru family. In any case, the party's vote base had been on a course of decline since 1989. Its emergence as the single largest party in 1991, in fact, was made possible only in the context of the sympathy wave generated by the 21 May 1991 assassination of Rajiv Gandhi. The party had lost its traditional social base in Uttar Pradesh to the BJP, the Janata Dal and the BSP in 1991. This trend was confirmed in the assembly elections in November 1993 when Mulayam Singh Yadav's Samajwadi

Party, in alliance with the BSP, captured power in the state. The Congress (I) was reduced to a mere 46 MLAs in the 425-member house in that election. Lalu Prasad Yadav, meanwhile, consolidated his hold in Bihar and the Janata Dal swept the assembly elections in 1995. Biju Patnaik's Janata Dal had wrested power in Orissa in February 1994.

Even in the southern states—Andhra Pradesh and Karnataka—the TDP and the JD had wrested power in the assembly elections in 1994. In 1995, the BJP had won the assembly elections in Gujarat and the BJP–Shiv Sena combine had wrested power in Maharashtra. The only major state where the Congress (I) was in power at the time of the 1996 general election was Madhya Pradesh. The forced exit of such leaders as Madhavrao Scindia, V. C. Shukla and Kamalnath from the Cabinet in the wake of Jain *Hawala* scandal—and these leaders charting their own course—rendered the party weak in Madhya Pradesh too. They were all influential leaders of the Congress (I) in the state like Arjun Singh, who too had been sent out of the party earlier.

The Congress (I), under Narasimha Rao, in 1996 was weaker than it was under Rajiv Gandhi in 1991. With a slew of corruption charges against almost all the ministers, including Prime Minister Rao himself, the party's fate was sealed even before the votes were cast. In what turned out to be a blunder, Narasimha Rao decided to persist with the Congress (I)–ADMK alliance in Tamil Nadu. ADMK chief Jayalalitha was also facing a slew of corruption charges and almost all the important leaders of the Congress (I) from Tamil Nadu opposed the alliance. Rao insisted and provoked them to leave the party; they set up the Tamil Maanila Congress and entered into an alliance with the DMK. The DMK was now out of the National Front.

When the final results of the general election were out, the strength of Congress (I) in the Lok Sabha was reduced to 140 seats. This was lower than the number of seats the party won in 1977: despite the Janata wave, Indira Gandhi's party had won 154 seats then. In 1996, the BJP emerged as the single largest party in the eleventh Lok Sabha with 161 seats. The Janata Dal ended with 46 seats: this was 14 less than what it had won in 1991. The Left parties (CPM, CPI, RSP and Forward Block) won 52 seats among themselves. The significant aspect of the 1996 verdict was that the 'national' parties could win only 400 seats among themselves in the 544-member Lok Sabha. The rest went to the regional parties. These were: TDP (16), DMK (17), TMC (20), Samajwadi Party (17), AGP (5), BSP (11), Akali Dal (8), Shiv Sena (15), Samata Party (8) and Haryana Vikas Party (3). This had implications on the formation of the next government.

President Shankar Dayal Sharma, after going through the due process of consultations, invited Atal Behari Vajpayee, leader of the single largest party in the Lok Sabha, to form the government and prove majority support in the house within three weeks. Apart from the 161 BJP MPs, Vajpayee had letters of support from the 15 MPs of Shiv Sena, eight MPs each from the Akali Dal and Samata Party and also three Haryana Vikas Party MPs when he met the President in the evening on 14 May 1996. All these were pre-poll allies of the BJP and the ruling combine added to 201 MPs. This was far too short of the 272 required in the house of 544. However, Vajpayee was sworn in as prime minister on 16 May 1996 along with 12 others as ministers. It was clear that Vajpayee would not survive as prime minister for too long.

The Janata Dal, the Left parties, the TDP and the Samajwadi Party (with 131 MPs between them) were determined against supporting the BJP–led combine. These parties had also managed to enlist the DMK and the TMC on their side and this took the combine's strength to 168 MPs. The stumbling block, however, was that they needed the Congress (I) to refrain from staking claim and offer its support to them. The Congress (I) president Narasimha Rao, even while he was convinced that there was no way the non-BJP opposition would support a Congress (I) government, decided to hedge. Rao delayed the formality of informing the President of the party's support to a non-BJP government even after the Congress (I) had decided to do so. There was also the issue of these parties electing their leader. Their first choice was V. P. Singh. He refused to oblige and even avoided meeting the leaders who went to him. Late in the night on 13 May 1996, they decided to offer the job to West Bengal chief minister, Jyoti Basu. Basu seemed to be interested in the job but his party denied him the chance. The CPI (M) Central Committee met on 14 May 1996 to reiterate its position that the party shall not participate in any government where it did not have the strength to implement its agenda.

It was at this stage that President Shankar Dayal Sharma decided to invite Vajpayee. Ironically, the leaders decided on Karnataka chief minister, H. D. Deve Gowda, as their choice for prime minister around the same time on 14 May 1996. Narasimha Rao woke up from his sleep to inform the President of the party's decision to support Gowda as prime minister. This, indeed, sealed Vajpayee's fate. The parties that constituted the non-BJP opposition were now convinced of forming the government and, hence, stood firm against the BJP-led combine. The unity against the government was evident on 23 May 1996, when P. A. Sangma was elected as Lok Sabha Speaker. A Congress (I) MP from Meghalaya, Sangma, was the common candidate of the Congress (I) and the non-BJP parties, now constituting the United Front.

The BJP, meanwhile, went about pulling all the stops to gather support from the DMK and the TDP in particular. Its efforts failed. On 28 May 1996, after a marathon debate on the confidence motion, when it became clear that there was no way he could manage a majority in the Lok Sabha, Vajpayee informed the house that he was going to the President to submit his resignation. The government was out of office in just 13 days after it was sworn in. Vajpayee continued as caretaker prime minister for three more days.

Gowda waited for the auspicious hour and day. On 1 June 1996, he was sworn in as prime minister. Gowda, it may be recalled, was behind the dismissal of the S. R. Bommai government in Karnataka in February 1989. He had refused to join the Janata Dal and had kept the Janata Party alive. He teamed up with Devi Lal and was among those who participated in the Boat Club rally on 9 August 1990. He then joined Chandra Shekhar and became part of the Janata Dal (Socialist) in 1991 and was among the five Samajwadi Janata Party MPs in the tenth Lok Sabha. He joined the Janata Dal in 1994, a few months ahead of the assembly elections in Karnataka. When the Janata Dal won a majority in that election, Gowda became the chief minister of Karnataka.

The Janata Dal did well in the Lok Sabha elections from Karnataka in April 1996 winning 16 of the 28 seats from the state. But, a larger chunk of the Janata Dal Parliamentary Party came from Bihar; 22 out of the 46 Janata Dal MPs came from Bihar. Lalu Prasad Yadav, the party's Bihar chieftain, too was interested in the prime minister's job. His ambitions, however, were scuttled by other important leaders from Bihar such as Ram Vilas Paswan and Sharad Yadav. Similarly, Lalu was not acceptable to Mulayam Singh Yadav, whose 17 MPs were at his beck and call. Gowda, meanwhile, could command support of the Janata Dal MPs from Karnataka and none of the United Front leaders were opposed to him. The lone voice of dissent came from Ramakrishna Hegde; he was also keen on becoming the prime minister, but there was nobody in his party to even suggest his name.

Gowda's Cabinet reflected the infirmities that marked the arrangement. A government, headed by the leader of a party with just 46 MPs, constituted by five other parties (with 75 MPs among them), depending on outside support from 52 MPs of the Left parties and 140 of the Congress (I). This arrangement was more complicated than the V. P. Singh regime and even the Chandra Shekhar regime in a sense. In fact, it was reflected in the constitution of the Cabinet. The Janata Dal, with just 46 Lok Sabha MPs, bagged 10 Cabinet berths and among them were S. R. Bommai, C. M. Ibrahim (an old associate of Sanjay Gandhi and Gowda's close aide in recent years), I. K. Gujral and Ram Vilas Paswan.

Mulayam Singh Yadav's party, with 17 MPs managed to get four ministers; Yadav himself became the defence minister. The TMC managed just two berths, including the finance minister's job for P. Chidambaram. The DMK too got just two berths with Murasoli Maran becoming the commerce minister. The TDP, whose leader and Andhra Pradesh chief minister Chandrababu Naidu had become the United Front's convenor, got three berths. The CPI, after deciding to join the government (unlike the CPI [M]) on 18 June 1996, got two Cabinet berths; Indrajit Gupta, until then the party's general secretary, became the home minister and Chaturanan Mishra became the minister for agriculture.

Balwant Singh Ramoowalia, who did not belong to any party and was not a MP at that time, was sworn in on 1 June 1996. His name came from the CPI (M) and it helped ensure representation from Punjab in the Union Cabinet. The Akali Dal had stayed with the BJP-led NDA. Such states like West Bengal, Gujarat, Maharashtra, Rajasthan, Madhya Pradesh, Delhi and Haryana went un-represented in the Cabinet.

There were several power centres too. Gowda, as prime minister; Chandrababu Naidu as United Front convenor; the CPI (M); and the Congress (I). All of them had their own reasons to assert. In addition to all this, the Janata Dal, as a party, was caught up with the battles among its leaders. Biju Patnaik, despite having been elected to the Lok Sabha, was denied of a Cabinet berth on grounds that he was facing charges of corruption investigated by the Crime Branch in Orissa and he insisted, for a while, that none from Orissa be included in the Cabinet. It took a lot of persuasion before he agreed to Srikant Jena being made a minister. Similarly, Sharad Yadav, still facing trial in the Jain *Hawala* case, had to be mollified by creating a new post in the party. He was made the Janata Dal's Working President while Lalu Prasad Yadav was the president. However, Bommai was inducted into the Cabinet despite the fact that he too faced charges in the *Hawala* case.

Gowda, meanwhile, won the confidence vote in the Lok Sabha on 12 June 1996. A day later, he struck against Hegde. The prime minister could persuade his party president, Lalu Yadav, to expel Hegde. It was evident on that day that he was in command insofar as the Janata Dal was concerned. There was no one in the Janata Dal to speak for Hegde. Not even J. H. Patel, who had replaced Gowda as Karnataka chief minister and a known Hegde loyalist. Hegde, it may be recalled, was the moving force behind the convention at Bangalore on 11 October 1988 where the Janata Dal was born and Gowda had stayed away, from the event and the party, until 1994.

The Congress (I), meanwhile, was caught in a crisis. Narasimha Rao was now charged in the JMM payoffs case and was facing trial. Then came an allegation by Lakhubhai Pathak, an NRI businessman, that he had paid off several crores to Rao to grab a business contract to import fertiliser into India. The shipment, carrying the cargo, was lost in the high seas and the government had lost several crores that were paid for the cargo. The Congress (I) Working Committee asked Rao to quit as party president and also as Leader of the Parliamentary Party. Sitaram Kesri became the Congress (I) president and also the leader of the Parliamentary Party. At the AICC plenary held in Kolkata in August 1997, which Sonia Gandhi chose to attend, Kesri gave the call that she lead the party. Sonia did not react.

The Gowda government, meanwhile, got moving on the Bofors front. The highest court in Switzerland had pronounced its verdict on India's request for the documents pertaining to the coded accounts. The CBI Director, Joginder Singh went to Berne and returned with the documents on 22 January 1997. This led to charge sheets being filed in the special court. It was imminent that the truth behind the Bofors story would now be out. The CBI's case was that Ottavio Quattrocchi had made money and that he could do it because of his proximity to the Gandhi family. Gowda, with documents in his possession, began threatening the Congress (I). In addition to this, an old case of murder against Congress (I) president Sitaram Kesri was revived and an FIR was registered. It was clearly a game of one-upmanship by Gowda and the Congress (I) president was not in a mood to take it.

On 30 March 1997, Kesri drove up to the Rashtrapati Bhawan to inform President K. R. Narayanan that the Congress (I) withdrew its support to the Deve Gowda government. Gowda's game was up. It was simple arithmetic. But, Gowda insisted that he should be given a chance to prove his majority in the Lok Sabha. He did expect pressure to build on Kesri to rethink his decision. Kesri had taken the decision unilaterally. The threat that the BJP would form the government or general election would be held soon was floated around to work on the Congress (I) MPs. Gowda's calculations were not entirely wrong. Kesri came under pressure. In a few days, the Congress (I) president made it clear that his party was not averse to supporting the United Front as long as Gowda was replaced by another leader as prime minister. Gowda did not bargain for this. He went ahead seeking a confidence vote in the Lok Sabha.

The motion was moved and after a debate, it was voted upon late in the night on 11 April 1997. The numbers were as expected: 388 against the motion and 188 for the motion. The Congress (I) and the BJP voted against the government. Deve Gowda's government lasted just 10 months and 11 days. Even as Gowda was making his speech in the Lok Sabha, swearing that the United Front will teach a lesson to the Congress (I) in the elections that were now inevitable, the United Front convenor Chandrababu Naidu and others from the coalition and the Left parties were meeting at the Andhra Bhawan—only a couple of miles from Parliament House—to identify another leader. The Congress (I) had promised to support anyone but Gowda.

The front-runner this time was Mulayam Singh Yadav. He was backed by the 16 other Samajwadi Party MPs and also by the CPI (M) general secretary, Harkishen Singh Surjeet. Mulayam Singh, in fact, commanded the support from the largest number of MPs at that stage. But, Mulayam Singh's name was opposed by Lalu Yadav. The Bihar chief minister who now knew that he did not stand even an outside chance suggested I. K. Gujral's name. Gujral, after all, had depended on Lalu Yadav to get elected to the Rajya Sabha and he did not resent being treated like a creature by Lalu Prasad Yadav. All the others, barring Mulayam Singh Yadav, agreed on Gujral. Congress (I) president Kesri was duly informed and his consent obtained with ease.

On 21 April 1997, 10 days after Gowda's government was voted out, I. K. Gujral, minister for external affairs in Gowda's Cabinet, was sworn in as prime minister by President K. R. Narayanan. All those who were in Gowda's Cabinet were sworn in as ministers with him the same day. The TMC refused to join the Cabinet initially but was persuaded into it soon. The prime minister retained the external affairs portfolio while the others too continued with their old portfolios.

Gujral began his political life as a student activist of the Communist Party in Lahore. After Partition, his family moved to Jalandhar and then to New Delhi and Gujral himself ended up as a civil contractor. His vocation took him to the Congress party and he became a corporator in the New Delhi Municipal Corporation (NDMC) and eventually the vice-president of the NDMC. He had cultivated himself as a negotiator by now and entered the Rajya Sabha as Congress member in the early 1960s. This was around the same time as Indira Gandhi entered the upper house. He was part of the backbenchers' club in the upper house with Indira Gandhi. Thus, began a relationship that would earn him the job of minister of state for information and broadcasting, when Indira Gandhi became the prime minister in January 1966.

At the time of the Congress split in 1969, Gujral helped Indira in a big way by managing the All India Radio as minister of state for information and broadcasting. He remained in that position until the Emergency was declared on 25 June 1975. But a couple of days later, Sanjay Gandhi—who had a disdain for some of his mother's friends—ensured his shift to the ministry of planning. Gujral did not grudge and remained in that position until he was sent as ambassador to Moscow. That's where Gujral began sporting a French beard. He was retained as Indian ambassador in Moscow by the Janata Party government and on his return to Delhi, Gujral confined himself to academic discussions on foreign affairs at the India International Centre (IIC). In the process, he had cultivated a relationship with V. P. Singh, now out of Congress. In December 1989, Singh chose him as minister for external affairs. Gujral stayed on in the Janata Dal even after the V. P. Singh ministry was voted out of power. He was the Janata Dal's candidate from Patna in the 1991 general election; the polls were countermanded due to violence and Lalu obliged him with a Rajya Sabha seat. He took a small house on rent in Patna, in order to prove himself to be a resident of Bihar (the rules ordained that way) and was happy sitting in Delhi and attending discussions at the IIC. In June 1996, he was the natural choice as minister of external affairs in the Gowda Cabinet. After Gowda's fall, he was chosen to be the prime minister.

Apart from the Bofors case, in which the charge sheets were to be filed, Gujral had to negotiate a crisis involving his own mentor and promoter, Lalu Prasad Yadav, caught by the CBI for siphoning out funds meant for the Animal Husbandry Department in Bihar. The Rs 950 crore fodder scam, indeed, was larger than the

Bofors scandal. Lalu Prasad's attempt to cover it up (by restricting the enquiry by the Bihar Police sleuths) was frustrated when the Patna High Court ordered the CBI to investigate. The court order was in conformity with the law. While a CBI enquiry is normally ordered only when the state government concerned seeks it, the higher judiciary could order a CBI enquiry even where the state government did not ask for it under the writ jurisdiction. The CBI found prima facie evidence of Lalu Prasad Yadav's involvement in the scandal and a charge sheet was filed against him in May 1997. Along with him, Chandradeo Prasad Verma, a minister in Gujral's Cabinet, was also facing charges of corruption. Gujral persuaded Verma to quit the Cabinet, but there was no way he could do that with Lalu Yadav. Pressure was built on Lalu Yadav to resign as party president. The Janata Dal leaders scheduled organisational elections for 3 July 1997.

Lalu Yadav and his followers, including 17 Lok Sabha members of the Janata Dal—among them were three Union ministers: Raghuvansh Prasad Singh, Jainarayan Prasad Nishad and Kanti Singh—boycotted the elections in which Sharad Yadav was elected as Janata Dal president. On 5 July 1997, Lalu Yadav held a convention attended by his followers, including the three Union ministers, at New Delhi to float the Rashtriya Janata Dal (RJD). The Janata Dal's strength in the Lok Sabha now came down to 29 MPs. Of the 22 JD MPs elected from Bihar in 1996, 17 went with Lalu Yadav's Janata Dal. Prominent among those who stayed in the Janata Dal were Sharad Yadav and Ram Vilas Paswan.

The next stage in the drama was an arrest warrant by the CBI against Lalu Yadav on 30 July 1997. Lalu Yadav held on for some time, refusing to quit as chief minister and after some posturing, he resigned, anointed his wife Rabri Devi in that place and offered himself to be arrested the following day. The arrest on 31 July 1997 was converted into a political demonstration with all the ministers in the state cabinet accompanying Lalu Yadav until he entered the jail premises in Patna. For days on end, after 31 July 1997, the Rashtriya Janata Dal cadre would stop trains, block the roads and brought life to a standstill across the state. The Union ministers from Bihar—Raghuvansh Prasad Singh, Jainarayan Nishad and Kanti Singh—organised these agitations. Lalu continued to act as Bihar chief minister from his cell in the central jail in Patna. Prime Minister Gujral did not even murmur. All this was happening when India was gearing up to celebrate the 50th anniversary of its independence.

The RJD as a party was not admitted into the United Front and this led to an incongruous situation with three Union ministers continuing in the Cabinet even while their party was not a part of the ruling front. Gujral let that be until his government was brought down on 28 November 1997 when the Congress (I) president, Sitaram Kesri, announced withdrawal of the party's support to the government. Unlike in March 1997, Kesri's decision, this time, was after due consultation within the party and blessed by Sonia Gandhi.

The Justice Milap Chand Jain Commission of Enquiry, set up in 1991 to investigate the conspiracy behind Rajiv Gandhi's assassination, had presented its interim report to the Home Minister Indrajit Gupta on 28 August 1997. Even before the government had studied it, excerpts from it were published in the media and they pointed fingers at the DMK. Even before ascertaining the veracity of the media report (the commission had not concluded its enquiry at that time), the Congress (I) demanded that Gujral sack the DMK ministers in the Cabinet. The United Front parties, including the TMC—whose leaders were Rajiv loyalists in the first place—stood up for the DMK rather than give in to the Congress (I) demand. Thus, the atmosphere was charged and the fate of the Gujral government hung in balance. Parliament was scheduled to meet on 19 November 1997 and there was hardly any time for the government to study the report and have an Action Taken Report (ATR) ready. An ATR must accompany any enquiry commission report while it is tabled in Parliament.

While negotiations were on between the United Front leaders and those in the Congress (I), Kesri came under pressure from his partymen. On 13 November 1997, Kesri served an ultimatum to the government: that the interim report along with the ATR is tabled in the house on 19 November 1997. The Congress (I) had also conveyed what it meant by 'action' on the report: to sack the DMK ministers from the Cabinet. The United Front was now united behind the DMK and Gujral conveyed this to Kesri, late in the evening, on 27 November 1997. The Congress (I) Working Committee met on 28 November and Kesri drove to the Rashtrapati Bhawan with a letter informing President Narayanan of the decision to withdraw support to the Gujral government. In an hour's time, Gujral handed over a letter to the President. It said: 'My government has lost its majority and does not want to continue in office on moral grounds'. Gujral, for some reason, did not seek dissolution of the Lok Sabha.

This gave hope to the Congress (I). The party had staked its claim to form a government even at the time of handing over the letter, withdrawing support to Gujral. This, however, did not take off. The United Front met soon after and convenor Chandrababu Naidu made it clear that the Front did not support any alternative formation. A delegation of the United Front leaders, led by Naidu and including the Left parties, met the President late in the night to convey that the front did not support either the BJP or the Congress (I). It was evident, by now, that elections were the only way to break the impasse. Yet, the Congress (I) was not keen on that option. It continued to send feelers to the United Front for a compromise. The United Front leaders refused to budge. The BJP too tried breaking the United Front and the Congress (I) to shore up a majority. That too did not happen. President Narayanan then sent a discreet message to Gujral saying that a resolution by the Cabinet, even if it was reduced to that of a caretaker status, recommending dissolution of the Lok Sabha will help. The formal communication was received by the President, late in the evening on 3 December 1997 and by mid-afternoon, on 4 December 1997, the eleventh Lok Sabha was dissolved.

General election was announced and the Congress (I) turned desperate. Kesri was aware of his inability to gather crowds and he had been nudging Sonia Gandhi and her daughter Priyanka Gandhi to take over the party since the AICC plenum at Kolkata in August 1997. The octogenarian leader of the Congress (I) had made a spectacle of himself at the session when he begged Sonia and Priyanka to go to the dais. Sonia responded to the pleas on 29 December 1997, announcing her decision to campaign for the Congress (I) in the elections. Interestingly, Sonia Gandhi did not care to address a press conference or give a television interview or even issue a statement in her own name to announce this. A statement, signed by her secretary V. George, said:

> A large number of Congress workers from all over the country have requested Mrs. Sonia Gandhi to take active interest in the affairs of the Congress Party which is at the moment passing through a very crucial phase. On 17th December 1997, the Congress president conveyed to Mrs. Gandhi, the unanimous request of the extended Congress Working Committee, to campaign for the party at this difficult moment. Mrs. Gandhi has acceded to these requests. Details for putting this decision into practice are being worked out by the AICC.

An excited Kesri decided to announce the momentous news himself rather than leave it to anyone else. The veteran Congress leader from Bihar did not seem to foresee that his days as party president were numbered. This happened on 14 March 1998. The election results had come and the hopes of Congress (I) to form the government were dashed. Kesri came under attack at the party's working committee meeting on 14 March 1998. He had declared his intentions to quit, owning responsibility for the poor show (the party won just 141 seats this time), if the party demanded that from him and walked out of the meeting in a huff. But the others continued with the meeting and passed a resolution. It said: 'To remove the confusion and the state of uncertainty leading to the irreparable and immense harm to the party, the CWC resolves to appoint Mrs. Sonia Gandhi as president of the Indian National Congress with immediate effect'.

Kesri protested in the open. He told newsmen: 'I am still the Congress president. This takeover is illegal. I had said I would respectfully step down at the AICC session and invited Sonia to take over respectfully but not in this way'. This was of no use. The script was prepared even before the drama unfolded. Sonia Gandhi was involved in preparing the script. Within hours after the CWC resolution was passed, Kesri's nameplate was removed from his office at the AICC headquarters and his office was cleaned up of all papers and furniture. Sonia Gandhi presided over the CWC the following day (15 March 1998) and she was also elected the Congress (I) Parliamentary Party chairperson. The irony was that Sonia was not a MP at that time. Her election was regularised at an AICC meeting at Delhi's Siri Fort auditorium on 6 April 1998.

The February–March 1998 elections resulted in the BJP increasing its strength in the Lok Sabha to 182 seats. The Congress (I), with Sonia Gandhi campaigning hard, merely held on to its earlier strength of 141. The United Front went to the polls in 1998, as a pre-poll combine (unlike in 1996 when the parties came together only after the elections), and ended up winning lesser number of seats than in 1996. Its combined strength came down from 120 in 1996 to 46 in 1998. The Samajwadi Party won 20 seats (three more than its 1996 count) while the TDP won 12 seats (four less than in 1996). The DMK won just five seats and the TMC only three; the two parties had won 38 seats from Tamil Nadu in 1996.

The Janata Dal that headed the Front won just six seats. Among the winners were I. K. Gujral (Jalandhar), H. D. Deve Gowda (Hassan), S. Jaipal Reddy (Mehboobnagar) and Ram Vilas Paswan (Hajipur). While the party won just three seats from Karnataka (against the 16 it had won in 1996), in Bihar Paswan was the lone winner from the Janata Dal. Lalu Prasad Yadav's RJD won 17 seats from Bihar and this clearly established that the party in Bihar was constituted by Lalu Yadav. The JD was wiped out of Uttar Pradesh too. The CPI (M) won 32 seats (same number as in 1996); all these came from West Bengal (24), Kerala (6) and Tripura (2), traditional strongholds of the party. The CPI ended with nine seats (against the 12 seats it had won in 1996). Together with the Forward Block and the Revolutionary Socialist Party, the combined strength of the Left in the twelfth Lok Sabha stood at 47. This was 11 less than its strength in the previous house.

One of the significant features of the twelfth Lok Sabha was that as many as 288 MPs were first timers in Parliament. This, in a way, reflected the resentment among the voters. Among those who lost elections in 1998 were Devi Lal, Pramod Mahajan, Ajit Singh, Sharad Yadav, Arjun Singh, K. Karunakaran and a host of ministers in the United Front Cabinet.

Even if the BJP's strength had increased from 161 to 182 and the party's pre-poll allies—Samata Party, Biju Janata Dal, Shiv Sena, Akali Dal, AIADMK, PMK, MDMK, Tamil Nadu Rajiv Congress, Trinamul Congress, Lok Shakti Party and Haryana Vikas Party—added 73 seats, the combine was short of the 272 mark. It was a different matter that the BJP, now heading the National Democratic Alliance (NDA), had gathered at least 13 more MPs in the house from the north eastern states as well as independents like Buta Singh, home minister in Rajiv Gandhi's Cabinet and, thus, managed a majority in the Lok Sabha.

But, the CPI (M) general secretary, Harkishen Singh Surjeet, initiated some desperate moves to keep the BJP out of power. He went about assuring the Congress (I) with 141 seats (and 25 more MPs from its allies including Lalu Yadav's RJD) of support from the Left and the United Front to form a government.

The Congress (I) seemed keen on this idea and so were some others in the United Front. The project, however, did not go too far with the United Front convenor, Chandrababu Naidu, making it clear that his TDP was not willing to play ball with Surjeet. In any case, even if all the United Front partners had agreed to this, there were other imponderables. The combined strength of these parties stood at 266 and it would have had to muster support from the BSP (with five MPs) and some single-member parties to take it to 272. This set the stage for the BJP-led NDA to form the government. The fallout of this move by the CPI (M) leader was the exit of Chandrababu Naidu from the United Front. He declared that the 12 TDP MPs will abstain at the time of the confidence vote.

Atal Behari Vajpayee was sworn in as prime minister on 19 March 1998. The BJP's increased strength—21 more than that it won in 1996—was achieved by way of incremental gains it made in Uttar Pradesh, Gujarat, Bihar and Madhya Pradesh to offset the losses from Rajasthan and Maharashtra. The surge in Karnataka (from six to 13) and in Orissa (winning seven Lok Sabha seats for the first time from there) in addition to the four seats from Andhra Pradesh and three from Tamil Nadu helped it increase its strength in the Lok Sabha. The National Democratic Alliance (NDA) that consisted of BJP, Samata Party and Akali Dal in 1996 was now constituted by more parties and the pre-poll alliance with these parties helped the BJP increase its vote percentage by more than 5 percentage points: from 20.29 per cent in 1996 to 25.59 per cent in 1998.

This was also reflected in the constitution of Vajpayee's Cabinet. Of the 22 ministers, including Prime Minister Vajpayee, 11 belonged to non-BJP parties. Of the 21 ministers of state, seven were from the allies. The AIADMK, headed by Jayalalitha, had delayed Vajpayee's swearing in by a couple of days when she refused to hand over the letter of support to the president and returned to Madras in a huff. She had to be cajoled into doing so by Vajpayee's trouble shooter, Jaswant Singh, sent to Madras for that purpose.

The NDA got a breather when the TDP leader Chandrababu Naidu decided to side with Vajpayee after quitting the United Front. He did so only after the NDA had agreed to have a TDP nominee, G. M. C. Balayogi, as Lok Sabha Speaker. The Congress (I) and the rest of the United Front, however, forced a contest for the speaker's post by fielding P. A. Sangma, speaker of the eleventh Lok Sabha. But Balayogi won the contest by a voice vote on 24 June 1998. When Vajpayee moved the confidence motion on 28 March 1998, the government's majority was established; 274 votes for the motion and 261 against it. The fact that the government had just 13 votes more than the opposition meant that the TDP's support was critical for its survival.

The first major signal that the new government sent was from Pokhran in Rajasthan. At 3.45 p.m. on 11 May 1998, Prime Minister Vajpayee announced that three nuclear devices had been exploded that day in the Pokhran desert. Two more devices were exploded on 13 May 1998. Amidst sanctions by the nuclear haves, the Vajpayee government announced its decision to go ahead with the nuclear weapons programme. Pakistan followed suit on 28 and 30 May 1998 conducting six explosions in Chagai. The political discourse was dominated by celebration, with parties in the opposition making just one qualification: That the decision (to conduct the tests) was taken unilaterally by the ruling side and that it must have been done after consultation with them. The BJP, meanwhile, was riding high despite the crisis of sorts that had caught the regime in April 1998; Telecommunication Minister Buta Singh and Minister for Surface Transport S. Muthaiah had to quit the Cabinet on 20 April 1998 (exactly a month after they were sworn in), following charge sheets against them in corruption cases. It was another matter that Home Minister L. K. Advani was being investigated for his role in the 6 December 1992 demolition of the Babri Masjid by the CBI at that time.

Jayalalitha persisted with putting pressure on Vajpayee at regular intervals demanding, among other things, the dismissal of the DMK government in Tamil Nadu. Subramanian Swamy, who had spent several months between 1991 and 1996 campaigning against her (when the AIADMK ruled Tamil Nadu), listing out corruption charges against her, had become her ally before the 1998 general election and was now her aide. The NDA government was on a permanent state of instability ever since March 1998 and Jayalalitha was the cause. On 14 August 1998, it appeared that Vajpayee will not remain the prime minister to hoist the national flag from the ramparts of the Red Fort. The crisis was tided over after a marathon meeting between Defence Minister George Fernandes and Jayalalitha in Madras until late in the night on 14 August 1998.

The calm, however, did not last for long. Jayalalitha decided to rock the boat in early April 1999. On 6 April 1999, she asked the AIADMK ministers in the Union Cabinet to quit. They obeyed her orders without a murmur. The ADMK then announced its decision to pull out of the ruling coalition's coordination committee. She arrived in Delhi on 12 April 1999 and made it clear that there was no scope for rapprochement. On 14 April 1999, Jayalalitha met President Narayanan and handed over a letter, informing him that the 18 MPs (17 from her party and Subramanian Swamy), withdrew their support to the government.

Parliament was in session and Vajpayee moved a confidence motion on 15 April 1999. Even while the debate on the motion was on for three days, the managers of the ruling coalition were busy, behind the scenes, mustering support from wherever they could. The BSP, with five MPs, was most sought after. The motion was put to vote late in the night on 17 April 1999. The BSP, after hedging all the while, decided to abstain. In the final count, the motion of confidence was lost by one vote. The Congress (I) had got Giridhar Gomango, now chief minister of Orissa, to vote in the Lok Sabha; he was yet to resign his membership of the house and there was nothing illegal about it. He had six months to become a member of the Orissa assembly and could retain his Lok Sabha membership, until he was sworn in as MLA. This was the law and Speaker Balayogi ruled that Gomango could vote. That made the difference. Vajpayee and his partymen called it immoral. But then, almost all the political parties had compromised on moral principles over the years.

Though the BJP raised its pitch for fresh elections and without any delay, there was no way Vajpayee could impose such a decision on the President after having lost majority in the Lok Sabha. Moreover, the Congress (I), now under Sonia Gandhi, had begun working on the possibility of forming another government even before the votes were cast in the Lok Sabha on 17 April 1999. Sonia met President Narayanan on 22 April 1999 and staked her claims to be invited to form the government. President Narayanan, however, was not prepared to hasten the process. He conveyed to Sonia Gandhi that she must convince him that she had a majority in the Lok Sabha. The Congress (I) chief promised to return with the letters of support the following day and announced, through the press, that she had the support of 272 MPs.

Her claims were based on the assumption that the 273 votes against Vajpayee on 18 April would translate into votes for her. This was not the case. Mulayam Singh, with 20 MPs, threw the spanner when he said that the Samajwadi Party did not support her as the prime minister. Yadav also raised the issue of her foreign origins and held this as the prime reason behind his party's objection. The other reason was that the Congress (I) had ruled out a coalition government and, thus, denied a place for the supporting parties in the Cabinet. Mulayam Singh was not happy with that. President Narayanan waited until Sonia Gandhi met him on 26 April 1999 to express her inability to cobble up a majority in the Lok Sabha. The Lok Sabha was dissolved the same evening and the Election Commission was entrusted to conduct fresh elections.

The BJP demanded polls in June. The Election Commission, however, set its own time frame and announced elections (in five phases) for 4, 11, 18, 25 September and 3 October 1999. In the meanwhile, incursions by the Pakistani military personnel were found in Kargil on 8 May 1999. The Indian Army battled against the intrusion between 8 May and 14 July 1999 and the snow-clad mountains were recaptured. The battle was fought when India had a caretaker government. The BJP sought to make use of the victory against Pakistan in the same way as Indira Gandhi had done in the state assembly elections in March 1972 after the December 1971 liberation of Bangladesh. However, 1999 was not 1972.

This was established by the results of the general election held in September 1999. Though the BJP-led NDA returned to power, the BJP's strength in the thirteenth Lok Sabha remained at 182. The Kargil war and the surge of nationalist sentiments did not help the BJP increase its electoral support in any way. The NDA continued to have all the parties that were in the combine in 1998, except in case of

Tamil Nadu; the AIADMK went out of the fold and the DMK, a constituent of the United Front—that existed to keep the BJP out of power—was now a constituent of this BJP-led front. The TDP, similarly, contested the elections as an ally of the BJP. The BJP lost heavily in Uttar Pradesh. From 57 seats in 1998, the party won only 29 from the state in 1999. This happened because the Ayodhya campaign was losing steam and in addition to that, the party's support to Mayawati's BSP government in the state (after the 1996 elections to the state assembly) led a section of the upper castes to desert the party. The losses from Uttar Pradesh, however, were made up from the BJP's gains in Madhya Pradesh and Maharashtra. The party won 29 seats from Madhya Pradesh (as against 10 seats in 1998) and in Maharashtra, it won 13 seats in 1999 (as against four in 1998).

As for the BJP's allies, the Samata Party had attracted such leaders as Sharad Yadav and Ram Vilas Paswan by now to reconstitute itself as the Janata Dal (United). This ensured 21 seats for the party from Bihar in 1999 against 10 seats in 1998. The Shiv Sena won 15 seats in 1999 against six seats in 1998. The TDP too gained substantially. From 12 seats in 1998, its strength went up to 29 in 1999. The BJD, an NDA partner in Orissa, won 10 seats in 1999. In 1998, the BJD had nine MPs. Mamata Banerjee's Trinamool Congress had won seven seats in 1998 and it won eight in 1999. The BJP's allies in Tamil Nadu did well; DMK won 12 seats, the MDMK four and the PMK five and the BJP itself won five seats from Tamil Nadu.

The Congress (I), even after having Sonia Gandhi as its president, ended up with 114 seats; this was 27 seats less than the 141 seats it had won in 1998. Sonia Gandhi was one of the 114 MPs; she won from Amethi with a comfortable margin. The Sonia Gandhi magic, however, did not work in any way in Uttar Pradesh. The party won just 10 out of the 85 Lok Sabha seats from Uttar Pradesh, once a bastion of the Congress. This was less than the number of seats won by the Samajwadi Party (26 seats against 20 in 1998) and the BSP (winning 14 seats against five it won in 1998). Lalu Prasad Yadav's RJD, a Congress (I) ally this time, won only seven seats as against the 17 it won in 1998. In Tamil Nadu, the Congress (I)'s ally, Jayalalitha's AIADMK, ended up with just 10 seats as against 18 seats it won in 1998 as a BJP ally. It was bad news for the Congress (I). But unlike in 1998 (when Kesri was pushed out as party president after the poor showing in the elections), the Congress (I) remained loyal to Sonia Gandhi. Those who objected to Sonia—Sharad Pawar, P. A. Sangma and Tariq Anwar—were out of the fold in any case and the Nationalist Congress Party (NCP), born out of their opposition to a foreign-born as their leader, had won eight seats in the Lok Sabha in the 1999 elections. The NCP would end up as the Congress (I) ally in the United Progressive Alliance (UPA) that formed the government in May 2004.

The Janata Dal of 1989 had splintered into small groups and the leaders of the party were all over the place. One of the groups—the Janata Dal (S) —won just one seat in the Lok Sabha in 1999. As for the Left parties, the strength of CPI (M) in the thirteenth Lok Sabha was 33, one seat more than it had in the previous house. The CPI, however, suffered losses and ended up with only four seats in the twelfth Lok Sabha. The RSP and the Forward Block retained their numbers as in the previous Lok Sabha.

On 13 October 1999, Vajpayee was sworn in as prime minister for the third time. Of the 69 ministers sworn in that day, 40 belonged to the BJP and the 29 belonged to the allies. Among them were George Fernandes and Sharad Yadav (both were members of the V. P. Singh ministry that was brought down because the BJP withdrew support), Ram Vilaș Paswan and Murasoli Maran (who were ministers in V. P. Singh's Cabinet and the United Front Cabinet) and Mamata Banerjee and Ajit Panja (who left the Congress to team up with the BJP). Unlike in 1998, the business of winning the confidence vote was only a formality in 1999. The ruling combine had 298 MPs in the 544-member Lok Sabha. With this comfortable majority in the house, the government lasted its full term.

Among the important watersheds in this period was the scandal involving NDA's Defence Minister George Fernandes (the Tehelka exposé), charges of corruption in the divestment of Public Sector Corporation shares and the privatisation of several state-owned hotels. At the political level, the anti-Muslim violence in Gujarat in February–March 2002, the attack on Christian missionaries in the Dangs region of Gujarat and the brutal killing of Graham Steines, an Australian missionary in Orissa, exposed the un-democratic nature of the democratic experiment.

The DMK, which joined the government, was not like the AIADMK. It remained in the fold until December 2003 (a few weeks after Murasoli Maran, the DMK's Delhi face and union minister for commerce in the Vajpayee Cabinet died) and decided to quit the combine then. Along with the DMK, the others in the combine from Tamil Nadu—the PMK and the MDMK—too left the fold. This, however, did not precipitate a crisis insofar as the life of the Vajpayee government. It is another matter that the collapse of the BJP-centred alliance in Tamil Nadu cost the party heavily in the May 2004 elections. All these parties entered into an alliance with the Congress (I) before the elections and that ensured a sweep for the Congress-led front in the May 2004 general election.

The Congress (I) also consolidated its understanding with Lalu Prasad Yadav's RJD in Bihar and made friends with Sharad Pawar's NCP in Maharashtra. From the position it took at a brainstorming session at Pachmarhi (in 1998) against entering into a coalition with any party at the national level, the Congress (I) swung to the other extreme in May 2004. It managed to gather allies by promising the regional parties their share in the ministry in the event the coalition won a majority. The BJP, meanwhile, had failed to cater to the aspirations of a cross-section of people. This was the case with its allies too. On 13 May 2004, when the votes were counted, the BJP lost seats from everywhere. The party won only 138 seats in the Lok Sabha; a fall by 44 seats from its 1999 tally. It was the case with its allies too. The strength of Janata Dal (United), TDP and Shiv Sena came down and AIADMK its ally in 2004, drew a blank from Tamil Nadu.

The Congress (I), in May 2004, had Rahul Gandhi in addition to Sonia Gandhi campaigning for the party. Both of them were candidates too. In addition to this, it had entered into an alliance with the DMK, PMK and MDMK in Tamil Nadu, the NCP in Maharashtra and the RJD in Bihar. The Congress (I) ended up with 145 seats. Even if this was far too short of a simple majority in the 544-member house, the Congress (I) happened to be the single largest party in May 2004. It had seven MPs more than the BJP. The pre-poll alliance it headed too was short of majority. The deficit, however, was managed when the Left Front, with 60 MPs (the highest number of MPs since 1951–52) declaring support from outside. President A. P. J. Abdul Kalam invited Manmohan Singh to form the government. He was sworn in as the prime minister on 22 May 2004. A 67-member council of ministers (28 with Cabinet rank and 40 ministers of state), drawn from the Congress (I), NCP, RJD, DMK, PMK and other parties was sworn in the same day. The era of coalition, which began in 1989, had by now matured into a political arrangement that could not be dismissed by the Congress party. Manmohan Singh, indeed, was the second choice. The Congress (I) Parliamentary Party had elected Sonia Gandhi and she decided to offer the throne to Manmohan Singh. The process was filled with high drama and a riot of emotions involving the Congress (I) MPs and its leaders.

The coalition of social groups that the Congress had represented at the time of independence and retained with ease for two decades after independence was shaken in 1967. The Congress party lost elections in several states then. The next important stage when this was disturbed was in the context of the Mandal Commission recommendations and its implementation. This time, the impact on the political structure was far reaching and permanent. During the decade and a half after Mandal (1990–2004), the political parties, across the spectrum, could not afford to ignore the complex caste mosaic that the Indian polity is made of and the dynamics of the political discourse in this context. Of significance in this regard is the consolidation of the other backward classes, constituting over one half of the population, behind parties that built themselves on the foundations laid by the Socialist Party (founded in 1948) in various parts of the country. The guiding principle of this dynamic was underscored by Bindeswari Prasad Mandal, chairman of the Second National Backward Classes Commission when he set the terms for its enquiry as against that of the First Backward Classes Commission headed by Kaka Kalelkar.

This consolidation at one level and the reaction to that from the upper castes against the 13 August 1990 notification by the V. P. Singh government—the anti-Mandal agitation in particular—led to a unity between the Dalits and the other backward classes in the immediate context. The synthetic chemistry, however, did not last long for the simple reason that it was not organic. This, in turn, led to the consolidation of the Dalits on an exclusivist agenda (exemplified by Mayawati's BSP in Uttar Pradesh) in which the 'other' came to be constituted by the OBCs. This dynamic laid the basis for a unity of the Dalits and the non-OBCs against the OBC-dominated parties. The trigger to the Dalit exclusivist consolidation came from the manner in which Jagjivan Ram was denied the prime minister's job at various instances (between 1977 and 1980) and this shared experience as well as the realisation among a section of the scheduled castes of their own numerical strength and the impact that such a consolidation could have in the context of elections. This long socio-political history reveals the basis for the fragmentation of the society in the present and its implication for the political discourse, particularly in electoral politics.

At another level, the collapse of a consensus for nation-building among the political platforms based on the foundations laid by the national struggle against British colonial rule (outlined in the early chapters in this book) was pronounced in the early 1970s, exemplified in the Emergency (1975–77), the anti-Muslim and anti-Sikh violence during the 1980s and the pervasive nexus between the corrupt and the political class that raised its head in the 1990s. The effect of all these, in the larger context of the social fragmentation, as well as the retreat of the state from governance, set the stage for violent conflicts in the name of caste, religious and other such identities. It also led to the retreat of ideology from the political discourse and set the stage for political alliances (pre-election and post-election) that are opportunist and unethical on the face of it. The fact that we now have parties, described as regional and even sub-regional (and most often in a pejorative sense), guiding the course of government formation at the centre as well as in the states, is indeed a culmination of the long trajectory that has been discussed in this book. In this scenario, these parties align with the 'national' parties that stand on opposite ideological poles as long as it helps them lay their hands on the instruments of power.

The BJP-led NDA and the Congress (I)-led UPA are strong examples of this process. We have similar experiences in the various states too. The absurd levels to which this could be taken was evident in Karnataka (where Deve Gowda would switch between the Congress and the BJP of and on) or in Jharkhand where an independent MLA became the chief minister with the Congress (I) sustaining the government from outside. It is too early, even now, to pronounce a judgement on the future of democracy. But the tryst with destiny that Jawaharlal Nehru referred to in his midnight address at the Central Hall of Parliament on 14/15 August 1947 is still in the process of being realised insofar as the political realm is concerned.

Bibliography

Abbas, K. A. (1966). *Indira Gandhi: Return of the Red Rose.* Bombay: Popular Prakasan.

_________ (1973). *That Woman.* Delhi: Indian Book Company.

_________ (1985). *Indira Gandhi: The Last Post.* Bombay: Popular Prakasan.

Abdullah, Farooq (1985). *My Dismissal.* New Delhi: Vikas.

Abraham, Itty (1998). *The Making of the Indian Atomic Bomb: Science, Secrecy and the Post Colonial State.* Hyderabad: Orient Longman.

Ali, Tariq (1991). *The Nehrus and the Gandhis: An Indian Dynasty.* London: Picador.

Austin, Granville (1999). *Working a Democratic Constitution: The Indian Experience.* New Delhi: Oxford University Press.

Azad, Maulana Abul Kalam (1988). *India Wins Freedom.* New Delhi: Orient Longman.

Baruah, Sanjib (1999). *India Against Itself: Assam and the Politics of Nationalism.* Philadelphia: University of Pennsylvania Press.

Beteille, Andre (1992). *Society and Politics in India: Essays in a Comparative Perspective.* New Delhi: Oxford University Press.

Bhattacharya, Sabyasachi (1971). *Financial Foundations of the Raj.* Simla: Indian Institute of Advanced Studies.

Bidwai, Praful., Harbans Mukhia, and Achin Vanaik (eds.) (1996). *Religion, Religiosity and Communalism.* Delhi: Manohar.

Bhushan, Shashi (1977). *Feroze Gandhi: A Political Biography.* New Delhi: Progressive People's Sector Publications.

Brass, Paul R. (1994). *The Politics of India Since Independence.* Cambridge: Cambridge University Press.

Butler, David, Ashok Lahiri and Prannoy Roy (1995). *India Decides: Elections 1952–1991,* Delhi: Living Media India Limited.

Chagla, M. C. (2000). *Roses in December: An Autobiography.* Mumbai: Bharathiya Vidya Bhavan.

Chakrabarty, Bidyut (ed.) (2003). *Communal Identity in India: Its Construction and Articulation in the Twentieth Century.* New Delhi: Oxford University Press.

Chandra, Bipan, Mridula Mukerjee, Aditya Mukerjee, K. N. Panikkar and Sucheta Mahajan (1988). *India's Struggle for Independence.* New Delhi: Penguin.

Chandra, Bipan (1999). *Essays on Colonialism.* Hyderabad: Orient Longman.

_________ (2003). *In the Name of Democracy: JP Movement and the Emergency.* New Delhi: Penguin.

Chandra, Bipan, Aditya Mukherjee and Mridula Mukherjee (1999). *India After Independence.* New Delhi: Penguin.

Chatterjee, Bhola (1984). *Conflict in JP's Politics*. New Delhi: Minerva Associates (Publications) Private Limited.

Das, Durga (1969). *India: From Curzon to Nehru and After*. New Delhi: Harper Collins.

Devasahayam, M. G. (2004). *India's second Freedom: An Untold Saga*. New Delhi: Siddharth.

Dhar, P. N. (2000). *Indira Gandhi, the 'Emergency' and Indian Democracy*. Delhi: Oxford University Press.

Dutt, Brahm (1978). *Five-Headed Monster – A Factual Narrative of the Genesis of the Janata Party*, New Delhi: Surge.

Dutt, R. P. (1970). *India Today*. Calcutta: Manisha Grantalaya.

Erdman, Howard (1967). *The Swatantra Party and Indian Conservatism*. Cambridge: Cambridge University Press.

Frank, Katherine (2001). *Indira: The Life of Indira Nehru Gandhi*. London: Harper Collins.

Frankel, Francine R. (1978). *India's Political Economy: 1947–1977*. Delhi: Princeton University Press.

Gandadharan, K. (1978). *The Inquisition: Revelations before the Shah Commission*. New Delhi: Path Publishers.

Gandhi, Arun (1983). *The Morarji Papers: Fall of the Janata Government*. Delhi: Vision Books.

Gandhi, Indira (1971–1986). *Selected Speeches and Writings of Indira Gandhi*. New Delhi: Publications Division, Ministry of Information and Broadcasting. (Volumes 1–5).

Gill, S.S. (1996). *The Dynasty: A Political Biography of the Premier Ruling Family of Modern India*. Delhi: Harper Collins.

Gopal, S. (ed.) (1991). *Anatomy of a Confrontation: The Babri Masjid-Ramjanmabhoomi Issue*. Delhi: Viking.

Graham, B. D. (1990). *Hindu Nationalism and Indian Politics: The Origins and Development of the Jana Sangh*. Cambridge: Cambridge University Press.

Haksar, P. N. (1979). *Premonitions*. Bombay: Bombay Interpress.

Haksar, P. N. (1990). *One More Life*. Delhi: Oxford University Press.

Hasan, Zoya (ed.) (2002). *Parties and Party Politics in India*. Delhi: Oxford University Press.

Jaffrelot, Christophe (1996). *Hindu Nationalist Movement and Indian Politics*. New Delhi: Viking.

Jagmohan (1978). *My Frozen Turbulance in Kashmir*. New Delhi: Allied Publishers.

Jayakar, Pupul (1992). *Indira Gandhi*. New Delhi: Penguin.

Joshi, Ram and R. K. Hebsur (eds) (1987). *Congress in Indian Politics: A Centenary Perspective*. Bombay: Popular Prakasan.

Kanungo, Pralay (2002). *RSS's Tryst with Politics: From Hedgewar to Sudarshan*. Delhi: Manohar.

Kapur, Rajiv (1986). *Sikh Separatism: Politics of Faith*. London: Allen & Unwin.

Kishwar, Madhu (1998). *Religion at the Service of Nationalism and Other Essays*. Delhi: Oxford University Press.

Kochanek, Stanley (1968). *The Congress Party of India: The Dynamics of One-Party Democracy*. Berkeley: University of California Press.

Kohli, Atul (ed.) (1991). *India's Democracy: An Analysis of Changing State-Society Relations*. Delhi: Princeton University Press.

Kosambi, D. D. (1975). *An Introduction to the Study of Indian History*. Bombay: Popular Prakashan.

Kothari, Rajni (1970). *Politics in India*. Delhi: Orient Longman.

_________ (ed.) (1970). *Caste in Indian Politics*. Delhi: Orient Longman.

_________ (1980). *State Against Democracy*. Delhi: Ajanta Publications.

Krishna, B. (1995). *Sardar Vallabhai Patel: India's Iron Man*. New Delhi: Harper Collins.

Kumar, Arun (1997). *The Turning Point: 1996 Poll Story*. New Delhi: Konark.

_________ (1998). *On Coalition Course*. New Delhi: Gyan Publishing House.

Limaye, Madhu (1994). *Janata Party Experiment: An Insider's Account of Opposition Politics, 1975–1977*. Delhi: B.R.Publishing.

_________ (1995). *Manu, Gandhi and Ambedkar and Other Essays*. New Delhi: Gyan Publishing House.

Lohia, Ram Manohar (1963). *Marx Gandhi Socialism*. Hyderabad: Ram Manohar Lohia Samata Vidyalaya Nyasa.

_________ (1964). *The Caste System*. Hyderabad: Navahind Prakasahan.

Ludden, David (ed.) (1996). *Making India Hindu: Religion, Community and the Politics of Democracy in India*. New Delhi: Oxford University Press.

Malhotra, Inder (1989). *Indira Gandhi: A Personal and Political Biography*. London: Hodder and Stoughton Limited.

Malik, Yogendra and V.B. Singh (1994). *Hindu Nationalism in India: The Rise of the Bharathiya Janata Party*. Delhi: Vistaar Publication.

Masani, Minoo (1975). *Is JP the Answer?* Delhi: Macmillan.

Masani, Zareer (1975). *Indira Gandhi*. London: Hamish Hamilton.

Mathai, M. O. (1979). *My Days With Nehru*. New Delhi: Vikas.

Mehta, Vinod (1978). *The Sanjay Story*. Bombay: Jaico Publishing Company.

Merchant, Minhaz (1991). *Rajiv Gandhi: The End of a Dream*. Delhi: Viking/Penguin India.

Mishra, D. P. (1993). *The Post-Nehru Era: Political Memoirs*. New Delhi: Har-Anand Publications.

Mishra, Salil (2001). *A Narrative of Communal Politics: Uttar Pradesh, 1937–39*. New Delhi: Sage Publications.

Mohan, Surendra (ed.) (1997). *Evolution of Socialist Policy in India*. Delhi: Janata Dal.

Mukhopadhyay, Nilanjan (1994). *The Demolition: India at Crossroads*. New Delhi: Harper Collins India.

Mukhopadhyay, Tarun Kumar (1992). *Feroze Gandhi: A Crusader in Parliament*. New Delhi: Allied Publishers.

Mustafa, Seema (1995). *The Lonely Prophet: V.P.Singh A Political Biography*. New Delhi: New AGE International (P) Limited.

Nanda, B. R. (1998). *The Making of a Nation: India's Road to Independence*. New Delhi: Harper Collins.

Narayan, Jayaprakash (1978). *Towards Total Revolution*. Bombay: Popular Prakasan. (Volumes I to IV).

Nargolkar, Vasant (1975). *JP's Crusade For Revolution*. New Delhi: S.Chand & Co. (Private) Limited.

Nayar, Kuldip (1969). *Between the Lines*. Bombay: Allied Publishers.

_________ (1971). *India the Critical Years*. New Delhi: Vikas.

_________ (1973). *Supercesion of Judges*. Delhi: Hind Pocket Books.

_________ (1975). *India After Nehru*. Delhi: Vikas.

_________ (1977). *The Judgment: The Inside Story of the Emergency in India*. Delhi: Vikas.

_________ (1978). *In Jail*. Delhi: Vikas.

Nehru, B. K. (1997). *Nice Guys Finish Second*, Viking Penguin India, Delhi, 1997.

Nehru, Jawaharlal (1997). *The Discovery of India*. Delhi: Oxford University Press.

_________ (1997). *Glimpses of World History*. Delhi: Oxford University Press.

Pandey, Gyanendra (ed.) (1993). *Hindus and Others: The Question of Identity in India Today*. New Delhi: Viking Penguin India.

Patnaik, Prabhat (2003). *The Retreat to Unfreedom: Essays on the Emerging World Order and Other Essays*. New Delhi: Tulika.

Prasad, Rajendra (1957). *Autobiography*. New Delhi: National Book Trust.

Rahman, M. M. (1970). *The Congress Crisis*. New Delhi: Associated Publishing House.

Rajagopal, Arvind (2001). *Politics After Television: Hindu Nationalism and the Reshaping of the Public in India*. Cambridge: Cambridge University Press.

Reddy, C. G. K. (1977). *Baroda Dynamite Conspiracy: The Right to Rebel*. New Delhi: Vision Books.

Roy, Ramashray and Paul Wallace (eds) (1999). *Indian Politics and the 1998 Elections: Regionalism, Hindutwa and State Politics*. New Delhi: Sage.

_________ (2007). *India's 2004 Elections: Grass-roots and National Perspectives*. New Delhi: Sage.

Sarkar, Sumit (1983). *Modern India*. Delhi: Macmillan.

Scarfe, Allan and Wendy (1997). *J.P. His Biography*. Hyderabad: Orient Longman.

Selbourne, David (1977). *An Eye to India: The Unmasking of the Tyranny*. Harmondsworth: Penguin.

Shah, Ghanshyam (ed.) (2002). *Social Movements and the State*. New Delhi: Sage.

Sharda Prasad, H. Y. (ed.) (1976). *The Speeches and Reminiscences of Indira Gandhi: Prime Minister of India*. New Delhi.

Sherlock, Stephen (2001). *The Indian Railways Strike of 1974: A Study of Power and Organised Labour*. New Delhi: Rupa.

Singh, V. B. and Bose, Shankar (1984). *State Elections in India: Data Handbook on Lok Sabha Elections 1952-1980*. Delhi: Sage.

_________ (1994). *State Elections in India: Data Handbook on Lok Sabha Elections 1986-1994*. Delhi: Sage.

Sitaramayya, Pattabhi (1946–47). *The History of the Indian National Congress*. Vol. 1 and 2, Bombay: Padma Publications Limited.

Tarlo, Emma (2003). *Unsettling Memories: Narratives of India's 'Emergency'*. New Delhi: Permanent Black.

Thakur, Janardhan (1977). *All the Prime Minister's Men*. New Delhi: Vikas.

_________ (1978). *All the Janata Men*. New Delhi: Vikas.

_________ (1989). *V.P.Singh: The Quest for Power*. New Delhi: Warbler Books.

Vasudev, Uma (1973). *Indira Gandhi: Revolution in Restraint*. New Delhi: Vikas.

_________ (1977). *Two Faces of Indira Gandhi*. New Delhi: Vikas.

Weiner, Myron (1967). *Party Building in a New Nation: The Indian National Congress*. Chicago: University of Chicago Press.

_________ (1989). *The Indian Paradox: Essays in Indian Politics*. Delhi: Sage.

Party Documents, Government Reports and Supreme Court Judgements Consulted and Used

ADM Jabalpur v. S. K. Shukla, AIR 1976 SC 1207

All India Congress Committee (I), *A Centenary History of the Indian National Congress: 1885–1985* New Delhi: All India Congress Committee, 1985.

Balaji v. State of Mysore, AIR 1963 SC 649

Bharatiya Jana Sangh: Party Documents 1951–1972, (5 Volumes), Bharatiya Jana Sangh, New Delhi, 1973.

Champakam Dorairajan v. State of Madras, AIR 1951 Madras 120

Gandhi, Indira. *India. The Speeches and Reminiscences of Indira Gandhi, Prime Minister of India*. New Delhi: Ministry of Information and Broadcasting

Golaknath, I. C. v. State of Punjab, AIR 1967 SC 1643

Government of India. 1978. *The Shah Commission of Enquiry, Interim Report I.* New Delhi: Ministry of Information and Broadcasting, March 1978.

Government of India. 1978. *The Shah Commission of Enquiry, Interim Report II.* New Delhi: Ministry of Information and Broadcasting, March 1978.

Government of India. 1978. *The Shah Commission of Enquiry, Memorandum of Action Taken on the Interim Reports.* New Delhi: Ministry of Information and Broadcasting, May 1978.

Government of India. 1978. *The Shah Commission of Enquiry, Third and Final Report.* New Delhi: Ministry of Information and Broadcasting, August 1978.

Government of India. 1980. *Report of the Backward Classes Commission,* (Volumes 1-5), New Delhi.

Indira Nehru Gandhi v. Raj Narain AIR 1975 SC 2299

Indra Sawhney v. Union of India, AIR 1993 SC 497

Kesavananda Bharati v. State of Kerala, AIR 1973 SC 1461

Madhavrao v. Union of India, AIR 1971 SC 530

Minerva Mills Limited v. Union of India, AIR 1980 SC 1789

Muhammed Ahmed Khan v. Shah Bano Begum, AIR 1985 SC 945

P. Rajendran v. State of Madras, AIR 1968 SC 1012

R. C. Cooper v. Union of India, AIR 1970 SC 564

Sharma, Dhirendra (1977). *The Janata (People's) Struggle: the finest hour of the Indian people (with underground documents, resistance literature and correspondence relating to the advent of Janata Party)*. New Delhi: Philosophy & Social Action.

State of Rajastan v. Union of India, AIR 1977 SC 1361

S. R. Bommai v. Union of India, AIR 1994 SC 1918

Vineet Narain v. Union of India, AIR 1996 SC 3386

Newspapers and Magazines Consulted and Used

Various issues of the following newspapers and news magazines were consulted and used:

Frontline (1985 to 2000).

India Today (1975 to 2000).

The Hindu, Chennai.

The Indian Express, Delhi.

Index

D

M

Q

R

S

T

U

V

W

Y